Indian Government and Politics

INDIAN GOVERNMENT AND POLITICS

Fourth Edition

PEU GHOSH
Associate Professor and Head
PG Department of Political Science
Hooghly Mohsin College
Chinsurah, Hooghly
West Bengal

PHI Learning Private Limited
Delhi-110092
2026

In fond memory of ***Shri Asoke K. Ghosh*** *(October 1942 – February 2024), Founder Chairman and Managing Director of PHI Learning, whose vision endlessly inspires.*

The Legacy Continues....

Published by Pushpita Ghosh, PHI Learning Private Limited, Rimjhim House, 111, Patparganj Industrial Estate, Delhi-110092 and Printed by Gopsons Printers Pvt. Ltd., A-14, Sector-60, Noida, Gautambudh Nagar, Noida, Uttar Pradesh-201301.

₹950.00

INDIAN GOVERNMENT AND POLITICS, Fourth Edition
Peu Ghosh

ISBN-978-93-5443-889-9 (Print Book)
ISBN-978-93-5443-951-3 (e-Book)

The export rights of the book are vested solely with the publisher.

Contents

Preface

The historical trajectory of the politics of India, a Republic born on 15 August 1947, has been interposed by political events since its birth, which have challenged the functioning of Parliamentary democracy in the country, time and again, the latest being the threats emanating from the civil society movements. Mapping the evolution of politics in India is not an easy task. This book on *Indian Government and Politics* presents not only the institutional aspects of Indian politics by underlying, in details, the provisions of the Constitution, the law of the land, but also brings out the real working of the institutional framework in an ever-changing, socio-politico environment. The Country celebrated the 60th anniversary of the first sitting of the Indian Parliament which was initiated on 13 May, 1952, but the effectiveness of India's Parliamentary democracy after 75 long years is being put to question often. The 23 Chapters of this book, therefore, endeavour to give a deep insight into the various dimensions of politics in India followed by a comprehensive analysis of the same.

The book begins with the history of constitutional development in India (Chapters 1–2) and then throws light on the soul of the Constitution, the Preamble (Chapter 3), then it moves on to a detailed overview of the Fundamental Rights and Directive Principles of State policy (Chapters 4–5) and nature of Indian federation with special emphasis on Union-State relations (Chapter 6). The next couple of Chapters provide an elaborate discussion on the Executive, Legislature and Judiciary at the national and state level (Chapters 7–13). Chapter 14 provides an idea about the procedure of Constitutional amendment in India, along with a detailed list of all the amendments till date. Chapter 15 deals with the Local Self-governments at rural and urban level encompassing the Panchayati Raj Institutions and the Municipal Corporations and Municipal Councils. The party system in India, with elaborate discussions on various national and regional parties, are also covered in this book (Chapters 16–17). Chapters 19, 20 and 21 are focused on State-Society interface and highlight the interaction between the State and the various groups, mass media and social media, social movements in which civil society plays an integral role and other socio-cultural factors which have definite impact on the politics by way of their being politicized in India. Chapters 18 and 22 give an elaborate idea about some important Councils, Committees, Commissions and other functionaries which have an important role in shaping the politics of India. Chapter 23 provides insights into the development in the contemporary administrative structures and new programmes and policies of the Government of India. The new edition is thoroughly updated with till date updates of Indian Politics and a new chapter on current important policies and missions in the Indian political scenario. The Chapter-end exercises are intended to equip the students to enable them to address both short and essay type questions, and also help them in developing analytical skill and critical aptitude.

This book is not only a useful guide for the students and teachers of Political Science for both undergraduate and postgraduate honours and general courses but also for those aspiring for various competitive examinations such as NET, SLET, IAS, IPS and other Central and State services where the knowledge of Indian Government and Politics is a primary requirement. This book is also a useful guide for the students of law.

I am thankful to my colleagues of Lady Brabourne College for being so cooperative.

It is pertinent on my part to take an opportunity to thank the editorial and production team of my publisher, PHI Learning for their careful processing of the manuscript and continuous cooperation. Last but not the least, my most sincere regards go to my parents, Mr. Subhas Kumar Ghosh and Mrs. Krishnasree Ghosh for their rock solid support without which the completion of this book would not have been possible.

Peu Ghosh

1

History of Constitutional Development in India

INTRODUCTION

India became independent in the year 1947. The passage of the Indian Independence Act, 1947, passed by the British Parliament marked the independence of India, followed by the traumatic partition of the country into India and Pakistan. The Constituent Assembly was given the responsibility of drafting the Constitution of India after its election in July 1946, and the first meeting of the Constituent Assembly was held on 13 December 1946. After independence, it became a sovereign body, and functioned as the legislature of India alongside its original function of framing the Constitution of India. Within 35 months of independence, the Constituent Assembly completed its work and the Constitution was finally adopted on 26 November 1950. The final session of the Constituent Assembly was held on 24 January 1950, and Dr. Rajendra Prasad was unanimously elected as the first President of India. On 26 January 1950, the Constitution of India came into force. On this day, India was proclaimed as a full-fledged sovereign, democratic republic with an objective of securing justice, equality and fraternity for all the Indians.

Constitutional development in India has a long history. Several Charters and Acts passed during the British period can be viewed as the sources of Constitutional development in India. A brief review of the series of Acts and Charters passed by the imperial British power from 1773–1947 will provide a glimpse of how each of them was a step forward in the path of Constitutional development.

REGULATING ACT OF 1773

The background which prompted the British Parliament to pass the Regulating Act of 1773 is quite interesting. Queen Elizabeth, by the First Royal Charter of 1600, had given the East India Company the exclusive right to trade with the East Indies. This Charter was later supplemented by several later Charters of 1609, 1661, 1669, 1677, 1683 and 1686. By virtue of these Charters the Company became a semi-sovereign body competent to make civil, criminal and military laws regarding its servants in India, and even the authority to declare war and enter into peace with the native powers.

The Company garnered its position utilizing the authority given by the Charters and the prevailing conditions in India, as a result of the dilution of control and authority of the *Mughal* rule. The Company nurtured the desire to acquire gradual territorial hold over India. In Bengal especially, they were successful, and with the battle of Plassey in 1757, the Company strengthened its stronghold in the region. After the victory of the British in the Battle of Buxar, in 1764 against the *Nawabs* of Oudh and Bengal and the Emperor of India under whose legal authority the war was waged by the *Nawabs*, the complete control over the administration of Bengal was taken over by the Company. In 1765, Lord Clive was called back to India, and it was then when he realized the constraints of maintaining a proper administration in India. During that period he introduced the system of *diwani* or dual government in Bengal. The grant of *diwani* led to the adoption of the system of double government in the region with Mohammed Reza Khan as a puppet *Naib Nawab* whose role was only restricted to collecting the revenue and administering civil and criminal justice. The superintendence of the collection and disposal of the revenue, however, was undertaken by the company without the assumption of any responsibility for the actual administration.

With the assumption of the office by Lord Warren Hastings as the Governor of Bengal, the diarchy or dual government set up under *diwani* was put to an end. But situation was such that there was a need to intervene in the working of the Company in India. From 1767, the Company was required to pay an annual amount of £400,000 as a tribute to the British exchequer for retaining their territorial acquisitions and revenues derive from them. But in 1773, the Company was not in a position to pay this annuity. The British Parliament sought this opportunity to intervene in the working of the Company in India. In 1772, a secret committee was appointed to present a Report regarding the administration of the Company. On the basis of the adverse Report of the committee against the working of the Company, the Regulating Act 1773 was passed.

Main Provisions

1. The Regulating Act gave the right of vote to the shareholders holding the stock to elect the Directors of the Company.

2. Provision was made for a Governor-General of Bengal and Council of four members. They were vested with "the whole civil and military Government of the said Presidency, and also the ordering management and Government of territorial acquisitions and revenues in the kingdoms of Bihar, Bengal and Orissa." Warren Hastings was appointed the first Governor-General of Bengal. The Governor-General was also given the power of superintending and controlling the Presidencies of Madras and Bombay except in times of emergency and direct orders from the directors in London.
3. Governor-General-in-Council was given the power to make ordinances and regulations for the good order and civil government of Company's territories in India.
4. The Regulating Act provided for a Supreme Court with a Chief Justice and three Puisne judges with wide jurisdiction.
5. The Act prohibited the receiving of presents and bribes by the servants of the Company.
6. No British subject was to charge interest at a rate higher than 12%.

The Act was flawed in many ways, as jurisdiction of the Governor-General-in-Council and the judges of the Supreme Court, and the position of the Governor-General vis-à-vis his Council remained unclear. Also, there existed vagueness as far as the asserting of sovereignty of the Crown or Company was concerned. It was often rebuked as a medley of inconsistencies. Nevertheless, it marked the beginning of a system of written regulation by the British Parliament. The political functions of the Company were recognized without the British Crown directly assuming the responsibility. The Parliament reserved the power to impose whatever Constitution or whatever form of government within the Company's territory.

PITT'S INDIA ACT, 1784

The defects of the Regulating Act were tried to be removed by another Act of 1781, and then by the Dundas' Bill, 1783 and the Fox India Bill, 1883. However, George III rejected the Fox India Bill in the House of Lords, and dismissed the coalition ministry in December 1783. He appointed Pitt to form the new ministry, who introduced his own Bill which came to be known as Pitt's India Bill, and sought to do away with the defects of the Regulating Act. The main provisions of the Act were:

1. It established a system of dual government with the creation of Board of Directors and Court of Directors. Board of Control comprised six Privy Councillors, the Chancellor of the Exchequer, and the Secretary of the State. The President of Board of Control was vested with real power.

2. The Board of Control was given comprehensive power of supervision and control over Indian administration.
3. The Directors were to retain the right of making appointments to different offices in India.
4. The Court of Proprietors was deprived of its right of overriding the decisions of the Court of Directors.
5. The Governor-General-in-Council was given the power and authority to superintend, control and direct the several Presidencies which enhanced the control of the Bengal government over the other Presidencies.
6. A Committee of Secrecy, of not more than three members, was appointed out of 24 directors.
7. The Regulating Act provided that the Council of the Governor-General should consist of four members, but under the Pitt's India Act the Councils of the Governor-General and the Governors were to consist of three members.
8. The Governor-General-in-Council was not authorized to declare war or make peace without the permission of the Court of Directors. The Presidencies could declare war only with the approval of the Governor-General-in-Council.
9. The Governor-General was to be appointed by the Directors with the approval of the Crown and the Crown could recall the Governor-General.

The long title of the Act ran as **An Act for the better Regulation and Management of the Affairs of the East India Company and of the British possessions in India, and for establishing a Court of Judicature for the more speedy and effectual Trial of Persons accused of Offences committed in the East Indies.** It is quite evident from the title itself that for the first time the East India Company's territory in India was referred as "British possessions in India." It also introduced a dual system of control from England. Although much vagueness prevailed over the relation between the Board of Control and the Court of Directors and resulted in conflict between the two on many occasions, but it cannot be denied that the Act helped in the unification of India by making the Governor-General supreme over the Governors of the Presidencies. The system of dual control, though modified many times, remained in force till 1858.

THE CHARTER ACT OF 1813

Important Acts subsequent to the Regulating Act were passed after every 20 years to renew the privileges of the Company for another 20 years. Therefore, subsequently in 1793 an Act was passed to renew Company's privileges for another 20 years. The Charter Act of 1793 was supposed to be renewed in

1813, but a lot of dissatisfaction arose during the time of renewal. As the principle of *laissez faire* became prevalent during this time, the English people demanded the abolition of the monopoly of the Company and opening of the Indian trade to all. The main provisions of the Charter of 1813 thus were:

1. This Act renewed the Charter of the East India Company for 20 years, but the Company was deprived of its monopoly of trade in India except in China. To tackle the huge inflow of British traders to India, the system of issuing of license by the directors to those who applied for permission to trade in India was introduced.
2. The powers of superintendence and direction of the Board of Control were not only defined, but also enlarged to a great extent.
3. The Governor-General and Commanders-in-Chief were to be appointed by the Court of Directors "subject to the approbation of his majesty to be signified in writing under the Royal Sign Manual, counter-signed by the President of the Board of Control" which meant that the highest appointments also came under the control of the board.
4. A Church establishment was to be created at the expense of the Company in India.
5. The Act also provided special provisions for the administration of justice in cases in which Britishers and Indians were involved. Special penalties were provided for theft, forgery and coinage offences.

This Act asserted the sovereignty of the British Crown over the Indian territories held by the Company, and though it renewed the Charter of Company for 20 years, it deprived the Company of its Indian trade monopoly except for trade in tea and with China. The Charter also required the Company to maintain separate and distinct commercial and territorial accounts. It further helped in paving the path for the missionaries to India.

THE CHARTER ACT OF 1833

The Act of 1833 was significant in the sense that it brought about fundamental changes in the administrative system of India, which can be viewed as a stepping stone in the history of Constitutional development in India. The main provisions were:

1. The Act of 1833 renewed the Company's possessions in India for another 20 years "in trust for His Majesty and His Heirs." It renewed for another 20 years, the Company's political and administrative authority only.
2. The monopoly of the Company was abolished altogether, i.e., in 1813, the Company had the monopoly over Chinese trade, but this Act abolished monopoly in totality.

3. This Act centralized the administration of the country. The Governor-General of Bengal became the Governor-General of India. He was given the power to superintend and direct the civil and military affairs of the Company. Bombay, Madras and Bengal and other districts were placed under the complete control the Governor-General-in-Council.
4. Centralization was established in all legislative and financial matters.
5. The Governor-General was the only authority to make laws and regulations for the British possessions in India.
6. The laws passed by the Government of India were to be called Acts in place of earlier denomination known as regulations regarding the enactments of Bombay, Madras and Bengal Councils.
7. The Act added another member to the Executive Council of the Governor-General.
8. This Act laid down that "No native of the said territories nor any natural born subject of his Majesty, resident therein, shall by reason of his only religion, place of birth, descent, colour, or any of these be disabled from holding any office or employment under the Company." This was a great step, but no Indians had held high positions even after the passage of the Statute of 1833.

The significance of this Act lies in the fact that it established a central authority in place of three Councils which was authorized to pass laws for the entire British territory in India. It also abolished the trade monopoly of the Company and restricted it strictly to the political function, thereby separating the commercial from the political. It is usually upheld as an extensive measure between the Pitt's India Act of 1784 and the Queen's Proclamation of 1858.

THE CHARTER ACT OF 1853

This Act of 1853 was the last of this sort before the final surrender of the authority by the East India Company to the British Crown by the passage Government of India Act, 1858. The Act of 1853 carried out a separation if the Executive and Legislative authority which was again a significant step towards Constitutional development. The main provisions were:

1. The Act allowed the Company to govern "only until Parliament shall otherwise provide."
2. This Act extended the Executive Council of the Governor-General for legislative purposes. Legislation for the first time was treated as a special function of government requiring special machinery and special process.
3. The Legislative Council should consist of Governor-General, Executive Councillors, the Chief Justice and one of the judges of the Supreme Court of Bengal and four members drawn from the servants of the

Company and appointed by the Presidency governments and Lieutenant-Governors.

4. The consent of the Governor-General was made necessary for all legislative proposals.

This Act can be said to be ushering in parliamentary system in India. However, the greatest defect of the Act was the total exclusion of Indians in the Legislative Council.

THE GOVERNMENT OF INDIA ACT, 1858

The Charter of 1853 was not renewed as was the case with earlier Charters. Meanwhile, the Sepoy Mutiny of 1857 opened the door for curbing the activities of a trading company. The British Government decided to put an end to the Company rule in India. In February 1858, Lord Palmerstone introduced a Bill for liquidating the Company and transferring the administration of India to the Crown. However, there were protests by the Company, and J.S. Mill drafted a petition for the Company for the retention of the East India Company. Despite such protests, the Act for the Better Government of India, 1858 was passed which also came to be known as the Government of India Act, 1858. The main provisions of the Act were:

1. Vide the Act, the Government of India passed from the hands of the Company to the Crown. The Governor-General came to be known as the Viceroy.
2. The Board of Control and the Court of Directors were abolished and their powers were transferred to the Secretary of State for India and his India Council.
3. The Secretary of State was given the power to superintend, control and direct the Indian affairs. He was to sit in the Parliament and was to be assisted by a Parliamentary Under-Secretary. He was a Cabinet Minister of England, but his salary was to be paid out of the revenue generated from India.
4. The Act created an Indian Council of 15 members; seven of them were to be elected by the Court of Directors and the remaining eight were to be appointed by the Crown.
5. The Secretary of the State for India was to be the President of the Indian Council. He was given a vote and a casting vote in case of a tie.
6. Control over civil and military servants of the Crown was given to India Council.
7. Every year the Secretary of State was to present to the House of Commons a Report on the moral and material progress of India.
8. The Act of 1858 transferred the Government of India into hands of Parliament and the latter acquired full, formal and legal control over Indian affairs.

The Act on the whole formalized the process of the end of East India Company's rule and placed India under the direct control of the British Crown.

Queen Victoria's Proclamation, 1858

The assumption of the Government of India by the British crown was announced formally by a Proclamation of Queen Victoria on 1 November 1858. The Queen declared, "We hereby announce to the native Princes of India, that all treaties, and engagements made with them by or under the authority of the Hon'ble East India Company are by us accepted and will be scrupulously maintained. We shall respect the rights, dignity and honour of native Princes as our own."

INDIAN COUNCILS ACT, 1861

The Act of 1858 did not include any provision regarding the administrative set up in India. However, the 1857 mutiny was an eye-opener and the British realized that they have to pay some regard to the Indian public in order to avert such tragedies in future. Hence, the suggestion put forward by Sir Syed Ahmed seemed to be quite acceptable to the British Government. He suggested that there should be nomination of non-official Indians in the Council of the Governor-General. This was a major effort to include Indians in the Council, but it failed to provide the desired result and reflect true public opinion as mostly the Indian Princes, the *diwans*, the *zamindars* and the capitalist people were nominated. Nevertheless, it was quite an important step towards Constitutional development as it introduced legislative decentralization by amending the elements of centralism as introduced by the Act of 1833. The main features of the Act were:

1. As regards the Central Government a fifth member was added to the Executive Council of the Viceroy.
2. The Executive Council was to be strengthened by the addition of not less than six, and not more than 12 members, nominated by the Governor-General for the purpose of legislation.
3. The Governor-General was authorized to nominate a President who was to preside over the meetings of the Executive Council in his absence.
4. The Governor-General was given the power of making rules and regulations for the conduct of the business of the Executive Council.
5. Not less than half of the additional members were to be non-officials.
6. The function of the Council was strictly limited to legislation, and the Act expressly forbade the transaction of any other business and imposed certain restrictions on the legislative power also.

7. The Governments of Bombay and Madras were given the power to nominate the Advocate-General and not less than four and not more than eight additional members of the Executive Council for purposes of legislation. The consent of the Governor-General was made necessary for all legislation passed or amended by the Governments of Madras and Bombay.
8. The Governor-General was given the power to create new Provinces and to appoint Lieutenant-Governors for them. He was also authorized to divide or alter the limits of any Presidency, Province or territory.
9. The Act made no distinction between the Central and Provincial subjects, but measures concerning public debt, finances, currency, post-office, telegraph, religion, patents and copyrights were to be ordinarily considered by the Central Government.

The Indian Councils Act, 1861, has been considered by academicians as a landmark in the Constitutional history of India. It introduced the provisions of including the Indians in the legislative work of the Council, restored the law-making power to the Madras and Bombay Presidencies which had been deprived by the Act of 1833 and made provisions for Legislative Councils in other Provinces. By this it is thought that this Act had actually laid the foundations of the policy of legislative devolution in India.

INDIAN COUNCILS ACT, 1892

The Indian Councils Act of 1861 failed to meet the expectation of the Indian public who wanted to see more involvement of the Indians in the Councils, wielding huge influence on the policy decisions of the government. The atmosphere was charged up with the spirit of nationalism. Several factors added to the spread of nationalism and demand for larger share of Indians in the membership of the Councils. Spread of western education, repressive policies of the colonial power, the Vernacular Press Act introduced by Lord Lytton (condemned as the Gagging Act), Afghan policy of Lord Lytton, the Illbert Bill controversy, the indignant attitude of the colonial rulers towards the native, and above all the formation of the Indian National Congress in 1885 created discontent among the Indians and mounted the growing hatred against the British Government. Demands arose for reform and expansion of the Councils. The Congress, in its very first session, passed the resolution which Stated "That this Congress considers the reform and expansion of the Supreme and existing Local Legislative Councils by the admission of a considerable proportion of elected members (and the creation of similar Councils for the North-Western Provinces and Oudh, and also for Punjab) essential; and holds that all Budgets should be referred to these Councils for consideration, the members being more over empowered to interpellate the Executive in regard to all branches of the administration." Resolutions of similar nature containing similar demands of expansion and election of members to the Councils were made. Thus in 1888, Lord Dufferin, the then Governor-General, formed a Committee with a view to evolve ideas about reforms in the Councils. He had a scheme for enlargement of Provincial Councils and election of Indian members, but these could not be materialized as he had to leave India. Later, Lord Lansdowne gave full support to his views, but the proposals of the Government of India were not accepted by the Government of England. Even a Bill, which was introduced in the House of Lords for this purpose, was not acted upon immediately and was allowed to linger. Finally, only in 1892 the Indian Councils Act was passed. The major provisions of the Act were:

1. The Act enlarged the functions of the Legislative Councils. They were authorized to discuss the annual financial Statement under certain conditions and restrictions.
2. The members of the Councils were given the right of addressing questions to the government on matters of public interest.
3. The number of additional members in the Councils was increased. It was not to be less than ten and not more than sixteen in the case of supreme Legislative Council and not less than eight and not more than twenty in the case of Madras and Bombay. The maximum for Bengal was fixed at twenty and for North-Western Province and Oudh it was fifteen.
4. Due to continuous pressure form the Indian National Congress, the Government allowed elections to be held in India under the rules, though the members so elected could take their seats only after being nominated by the Government.
5. The Governor-General appointed the maximum number of ten non-official members.

The Indian Councils Act of 1892 was plagued with many shortcomings and defects and in a way could not be categorized as substantial gain for the people of India. The system of election was not a fair deal. The functions of the Legislative Council were circumscribed. The number of non-official members was small. Despite such defects, it can be said that this Act of 1892 introduced the principle of election for the first time, and gave the legislature some control over the executive and to some extent can be considered as a strong step towards, if not for Indian self-government, but for Indian participation in the highest administrative functions.

The Morley-Minto Reforms, 1909

The Indian Councils Act of 1892 could not meet the expectations of the people of India. There was rising demand for reforms and expansions of the

Councils. The split in the Indian National Congress between the moderates and the extremist created an atmosphere where the extremists did not have faith in the Constitutional methods proposed by the moderates mostly identified as the policy of prayer and petition, and they demanded *swaraj* and more action towards self-reliance rather than 'political mendicancy', i.e., begging for political advancement. This was followed by series of Acts like the Seditious Meetings Act and Explosives Act which were passed to suppress political crimes or terrorist attacks or movements all over India especially in Punjab and Bengal. The Regulating Act of 1818 was also frequently used by the colonial masters to suppress public outrage. Gradually, the extremist influence in the Congress began to grow, and under their influence in 1906 the Congress fixed self-government as its goal. In 1907, the Constitution of the Congress also incorporated the same objective. Further, the high-handedness of Lord Curzon and his notorious scheme of partition of Bengal had garnered the anti-British sentiment, and a desire for self-government in India. Meanwhile, the victory of the Liberals in 1906 in Britain had given a ray of hope of some reform movement to the Indians. Due to the charged situation all over India, Lord Morley and Lord Minto agreed that reforms were the demand of the day, but did not accept the idea of responsible government or self-government in India. Lord Morley in the House of Lords, on 8 December 1908 stated, "if I were attempting to set up a parliamentary system in India, or if it could be said that this chapter of reforms led directly or necessarily up to the establishment of a parliamentary system in India, I for one, would have nothing to do with it ... a parliamentary system is not at all the goal." Both Morley and Minto envisaged a plan to simply increase the scope of the Existing Councils. In the meantime, in October 1906 a Muslim deputation headed by H.H. Aga Khan met Lord Minto and put forward their claims for separate electorates and weightage of seats for the proper representation of their community under the reforms. In December 1906, the *Nawab* of Dacca appealed to the Muslims to form the All-India Muslim Confederacy which would protect the interests of their community whenever any reform would emanate form the government. Thus in 1906, the All-India Muslim League was formed. The colonial government recommended to the home government in Britain to accept the principle of giving separate representation to the Muslims. The home government accepted the proposal, and in December 1908, Lord Morley introduced his famous Bill in the House of Lords. The Bill was passed in 1909 as the Indian Councils Act. This Act for the first time introduced the policy of divide and rule in India by creating separate electorate for different communities. The major provisions of the Act of 1909 were:

1. The Act of 1909 enlarged the size of the Legislative Councils. The additional members of the Governor-General's Council were increased to a maximum of 60 and those of Madras, Bengal, U.P., Bombay and Bihar and Orissa to a maximum of 50 and those of the Punjab, Burma and Assam to 30.

2. The Central Imperial Legislative Council was expanded and came to consist of 37 officials and 32 non-officials.
3. The Act did not provide for any official majority in the provincial Legislative Councils. The majority of the members were non-officials.
4. According to the Government of India, territorial representation was not suited to the people of India. Representation by classes and interests was the only practicable method embodying the elective principle in the Constitution of the Indian Legislative Councils. Therefore, the Act provided for separate electorates for the due representation of the different communities, classes and interests. The remaining seats were allotted to the municipalities and district boards which were called general electorates.

   In the case of the Imperial Legislative Council, the total number of the elected seats was 27. Out of these, 6 were allotted to the landlords, 5 to the Mohamedans and 1 to the Muslim landlords and one each to the Bengal and Bombay Chambers of Commerce. The remaining 13 seats were filled by the non-official members of the Provincial Legislative Councils.
5. The functions of the Legislative Councils were increased.
6. The members were given the right of asking questions and supplementary questions for the purpose of further elucidating any point.
7. The members were given the power to move resolutions in the Councils.
8. Rules were also framed under the Act for the discussion of matters of general public interest in the Legislative Councils.
9. The Act raised the number of the Executive Council in Bombay, Bengal and Madras to 4.
10. In the Provinces, the University Senates, landlords, district boards, Municipalities and Chambers of Commerce were to elect members. Muslims were given separate representation. Muslim members of the legislatures were elected by the Muslims themselves.
11. Disqualifications were imposed on political offenders. They could not offer themselves for elections.

The Act of 1909 was notorious and full of confusion. It was notorious because it introduced the system of separate electorates for the Muslims. British rulers generally encouraged communal differences through these reserved seats, as the Muslim candidates did not have to appeal for Hindu votes and vice versa. Later on British Government transferred more powers to Indian politicians through the Acts of 1919 and 1935, but the Hindu-Muslim divisibility increased furthermore which hindered the natural harmony in India. The legacy was carried forward in the Act of 1919 when Sikhs got separate electorates. Further, the Act of 1935 gave separate representation to Indian Christians, Anglo-Indians, Europeans and *harijans*. These concessions for Muslim community brought about a constant conflict during the years 1909–1947.

The Act created confusion because although it introduced parliamentary reforms, but did not bestow responsibility equally. Even the size of electorate was small, and women were totally excluded. The system of election was indirect and there was no connection between the people and the members sitting in the Legislative Council. The Act was not intended to introduce democratic system in India, and hence, the changes in functions of the legislatures were made cautiously. It was to have the right of criticism and not to function as an independent law-making body. Thus, it was to serve as advisory bodies and the ultimate power and responsibility lied with the Government.

The Indian National Congress passed four resolutions against the reforms of 1909. In these resolutions, the Congress condemned the creation of separate electorate on the basis of religion, demanded the creation of Executive Councils to assist Lt. Governors of the United Province, Punjab, eastern Bengal, Assam and Burma, criticized the reforms regulations for Punjab, and expressed dissatisfaction at the non-establishment of a Council for the central Provinces and Berar.

K.M. Munshi observed, "The rising democracy having been stabbed. Minto promised separate electorates to the Muslims in the proposed reforms. A religious minority at the behest of the British authorities was accorded a political existence as a make-weight against the growing nationalism in the country, while the Councils established under the Minto-Morley reforms of course remained *gilded shams* with 'magnified non-entities whose Constituency was the Government House."

AUGUST DECLARATION, 1917

The Queen's Proclamation of 1858 formed the basis of British policy towards India for a long period of time only to be replaced by the August Declaration of 1917 which declared the establishment of Responsible Government in India. It is also known as the Magna Carta of India.

The Lucknow pact between the Congress and the Muslim League, and the beginning of the Home Rule Movement in India (1916) prompted Sir Edwin Samuel Montague, Secretary of State for India (1917–1922) to proclaim on 20 August 1917, a declaration in the House of Commons outlining the British policies in India which came to be known as August Declaration. This aimed at 'increasing association of Indians in every branch of the administration for progressive realization of responsible government in India as an integral part of the British empire'. The main point to be taken notice of is the inclusion of the keyword—Responsible Government, i.e., the rulers must be answerable to the representatives of the people. The Montague–Chelmsford reforms or the Act of 1919 was based on this declaration.

GOVERNMENT OF INDIA ACT, 1919: THE MONTFORD REFORMS

During the World War I, the British claimed that they stood for the protection of democracy around the world. Thus, the Indians, who fought for them in this war, demanded that democracy should also be introduced in their country. In his famous August Declaration presented before the House of Commons on 20 August 1917, Montague, the Secretary of State for Indian affairs said that in order to satisfy the local demands, his government was interested in giving more representation to the natives in India. New reforms would be introduced in the country to meet this objective. He came to India and stayed for six months. During this period he held meetings with different government and non-government people. Finally, in cooperation with the Governor-General, Lord Chelmsford, Montague presented a Report on the Constitutional reforms for India in 1918. The Report was discussed and approved by the British Parliament, and became an Act in 1919. This Act is commonly known as Montague-Chelmsford reforms. The Act was enacted for ten years from 1919 to 1929.

The following were the main features of the Act of 1919:

1. The Council of the Secretary of the State was supposed to comprise of 8 to 12 people, out of which 3 should be Indian, and at least half of them should have spent at least 10 years in India.
2. Some of the powers of Secretary of the State was taken away and given to a High Commissioner of India who was appointed and paid by the government of India. The High Commissioner who resided in London would represent India there in Great Britain. The Secretary of State was supposed to follow the advice of his Council.
3. Part of the expenses of the office of the Secretary of the State was to be met by the British Government. Earlier, he was paid from the revenues generated from India.
4. The Secretary of the State was not allowed to interfere in administrative matters of the Provinces concerning the transferred subjects and also in the matters on which Governor-General and his legislative were in agreement.
5. The Governor-General had the power to nominate as many members to his Executive Council as he wanted.
6. Members appointed to the Executive Council were to have served in India for at least 10 years.
7. The Central Legislature was to consist of two houses, i.e., the Council of the State (Upper House) and the Legislative Assembly (Lower House).
8. Council of the State was supposed to consist of 60 members out of which 33 were to be elected and 27 nominated by the Governor-General.

9. The Legislative Assembly was to consist of 145 members out of which 103 were to be elected and 41 to be nominated by the Governor-General. Out of the nominated members, 25 were officials and the rest were nominated. Out of the 103 elected members, 51 were elected by the general constituencies, 32 by communal constituencies (30 by Muslims and 2 by Sikhs), and 20 by special constituencies (7 by land-holders, 9 by Europeans and 4 by Indian Commerce).
10. The franchise was limited for both houses of the Central Legislature.
11. The tenure of the Upper House was five and of the Lower House was three years, but the duration could be extended by the Governor-General. The first speaker of the Assembly was nominated by the Government, but the subsequent speakers were elected by the members of the Assembly.
12. Both the houses had equal legislative powers. In case of a tie, the Governor-General was to call a joint meeting where the matter was to be decided by majority vote. The Governor-General was given the power to summon, prorogue and dissolve the chambers. He had also the right of addressing the members of the two houses.
13. The Executive Council of the Governor-General was not responsible to the legislature and the Governor-General had the right to refuse its advice. The Act of 1919 established a responsive, but not Responsible Government at the centre. The members of the Executive Council of the Governor-General were nominated members. The people were not involved in either their appointment or removal. No vote of no-confidence by the legislature could turn them out.
14. The Act of 1919 provided for two subjects, central subjects like defence, railways, customs, currency, post and telegraph, etc., and Provincial subjects like Local and Self Government, education, public works, law and order, health, transport and so on.
15. Provincial legislatures were to be unicameral.
16. Around 70 per cent members of the provincial Legislative Councils were to be elected and 30 per cent were to be nominated.
17. The Governors were given instrument of instructions which guided them in carrying out their administrative affairs.
18. The system of diarchy was introduced in the Provinces. The subjects to be dealt with by the Provincial Governments were divided into two parts: transferred and reserved subjects. The reserved subjects were administered by the Governor with the help of the Executive Council and the transferred subjects were dealt with by the Governor with the help of ministers. Members of the Executive Council were nominated by the Governor, the ministers were appointed by the Governor from the members of the legislature.
19. If the legislature brought any Bill on the transferred subjects, it could be finally passed subject to the approval of the Governor-General.

The Governor-General could cancel any Act passed by the Provincial Legislature on transferred subjects. The Provincial Legislature could not bring any Bill on the reserved subjects without prior approval of the Governor.

20. Besides the Muslims, other minorities including Sikhs, Anglo-Indians, Christians and Europeans were also given the right of separate electorate.

Montague-Chelmsford reforms were not accepted by most quarters in India as they fell far short of the expectations of the Indians. The Indian National Congress was not satisfied with this law and termed this as inadequate, unsatisfactory and disappointing. The major criticism against the Act of 1919 was that by the system of separate electorate, the national unity was destroyed which got reflected as the national events that followed in the later years.

NEHRU REPORT, 1928

The Government of India Act 1919, failed to bring about substantial gains for the Indians so much so that the Indian National Congress in its annual session in 1919 condemned the reforms of 1919 as inadequate, unsatisfactory and disappointing. The Rowlatt Act of 1919 was seen as another repressive act and immense agitation started against it. Mahatma Gandhi appealed to the people to offer *satyagraha* as a protest against the oppressive laws. *Hartals* took place all over the country. In Punjab, martial law was imposed, but on 13 April 1919, General Dyer ordered open fire on a peaceful crowd at Amritsar. This came to be known as the Jallianwala Bagh tragedy which stupefied the people of India. The launching of the non-cooperation movement in 1920 by the Congress under the leadership of Gandhi, which was the continuance of the *Khilafat* movement, and the role of the the revolutionaries in wrecking the working of legislatures from within and weakness of diarchy as a system, created the situation for another round of demand for giving full responsible government to the Indians. The Government of India was not in a mood to accept this demand and appointed a Committee under the Chairmanship of Sir Alexander Muddiman. This Committee did not submit a unanimous Report and the majority found nothing wrong with diarchy. Only the minority viewed the diarchy as a system an absolute failure, and considered it would never be successful in the future. In 1925, the government moved a resolution in the Assembly for acceptance of the principle underlying the majority view which was opposed by Pt. Motilal Nehru, and he moved an amendment which was carried out in the Assembly in spite of opposition of the government. However, the political agitation taking place all over India on a massive scale, forced the British Government to appoint a statutory Commission on 8 November 1927, two years before the expiration of, and 10 years after the passing of the Act of 1919 [Section 84 of the Government of India Act, 1919]. The Commission was to consist of 7 members of the British Parliament with Sir John Simon as its Chairman and no place for Indians in the Commission. The Commission was appointed "for the purpose of inquiring into the working of system of Government, the growth of education and development of representative institutions in British India and matters connected therewith" and reporting "as to whether and to what extent it is desirable to establish the principle of Responsible Government, or to extend, modify, or restrict the degree of Responsible Government then existing therein, including the question whether the establishment of second chambers of the local legislatures, is or is not desirable." The composition of the Commission was taken to be an insult to the dignity and national self-respect of India. Thus, the day on which the Commission landed in India the members were greeted with black flags and slogans like "Go back Simon."

Lord Birkenhead justified the exclusion of the Indians from the Commission and challenged the Indians to produce an agreed Constitution and submit the same to the British Parliament for consideration. Accepting this challenge an All Party Conference was held in Bombay on 19 May 1928. Dr. M.A. Ansari presided over the conference, and Pt. Motilal Nehru was appointed as a Chairman of the Committee to consider and determine the principles of the Constitution of India. The Nehru Report was framed on 10 August 1928, and the All Parties Conference met at Calcutta on 22 December 1928, to consider the Report. Jinnah on behalf of the All India Muslim League made several amendments to the Report. The main features of the Nehru Report were:

1. There was a compromise between two groups, one who favoured Dominion Status and those who favoured complete independence. The majority favoured dominion status not merely as distant goal but as "the next immediate step." It however, gave liberty of action to all those groups and parties which made complete independence as their goal.
2. Envisaging secularism as the basic feature of the Constitution, the Report proposed joint electorates with reservation of seats for minorities on population basis with the right to contest additional seats.
3. No seats were to be reserved for any community in Punjab and Bengal.
4. The people were to enjoy 19 fundamental rights.
5. The government was to derive its authority from the people.
6. The Federal structure was to be introduced involving a division of powers between the centre and the Provinces. The residuary powers were to be vested with the centre with a view to make it powerful.
7. Regarding the Provinces, the Report recommended the organization of the Provinces on linguistic basis and granting of Provincial autonomy in internal administration.
8. The Report demanded that full Responsible Governments should be established at the Central and Provincial levels.
9. The Governor-General was to be appointed by the British Government. He was to act on the advice of the Executive Council. The Prime

Minister was to be appointed by the Governor-General and other ministers were to be appointed on the advice of the Prime Minister.

10. The Report provided for a parliament with two houses, viz., Senate and House of Representatives. Senate was to be the Upper House and should comprise 200 members to be indirectly elected by the members of the Provincial Councils for a term of 7 years. House of Representatives was to be the Lower House, and was to have 500 members to be elected directly by people on the basis of universal adult franchise and secret ballot for a term of 5 years.
11. The Government of the Province was supposed to have a Governor appointed by the British Crown who was to get the pay out of the provincial revenues. He was to act on the advice of the Provincial Executive Council whose number was not to exceed 5—the Chief Minister and 4 other ministers. The Executive Council was to be responsible before the Provincial Legislature.
12. Regarding the Supreme Court, the Report held that it was to be the court of final appeal in India.

On the whole, it recommended the establishment of a parliamentary democracy in India both at the central and provincial levels.

The Nehru Report was submitted on 10 August 1928 and in the All Parties Conference in Calcutta in December 1928 after much deliberation and several amendments being proposed by Mr. Jinnah on behalf of the All India Muslim League and being rejected by those having Hindu point of view, the communal question prevented unanimity. The Congress at its Calcutta Session on 31 December 1928, accepted the Nehru Report. It also demanded the acceptance of the Report by the British Government on or before 31 December 1929, and threatened that they will instigate a non-violent non-cooperation movement by advising the people to withhold payment of taxes and other measures.

The Muslims were critical about the Report as the Report did not provide separate electorate as was given to them by the Acts of 1909 and 1919. Therefore, in response to the Nehru Report, Jinnah forwarded his 14-Point formula.

Jinnah's 14-Point Formula, 1929

Jinnah summoned a meeting of the All India Muslim League at Delhi in March 1929, and put forward his fourteen points as the minimum Muslim demands for any political settlement. Refuting the Nehru Report, the Resolution of the League laid that no scheme for the future Constitution of the Government of India will be acceptable to the Muslims of India until and unless the following basic principles are given effect to and provisions are embodied therein to safeguard their rights and interests:

1. The form of the future Constitution should be Federal with the residuary powers vested in the Provinces.

2. A uniform measure of autonomy shall be granted to all provisions.
3. All legislatures in the country and other elected bodies shall be constituted on the definite principle of adequate and effective representation of minorities in every Province without reducing the majority in any Province to a minority or even equality.
4. In Central Legislature the Muslim representation shall be one-third.
5. Representation of communal groups shall continue to be by separate electorates as at present provided; it shall be open to any community, at any time, to abandon its separate electorate in favour of joint electorates.
6. Any territorial re-distribution that might at any time be necessary shall not in any way affect the Muslim majority in the Punjab, Bengal and North-West Frontier Province.
7. Full religious liberty, i.e., liberty of belief, worship and observance, propaganda, association and education shall be guaranteed to all communities.
8. No Bill or resolution or any part thereof shall be passed in any legislature or any elected body if three-fourths of the members of any community in that particular body oppose such a Bill, resolution or part thereof on the ground that it would be injurious to the interests of that community or in the alternative method is devised as may be found possible and practicable to deal with such cases.
9. Sind should be separated from Bombay presidency.
10. Reforms should be introduced in the North-West Frontier Province and Baluchistan on the same footing as in other Provinces.
11. Provision should be made in the Constitution giving Muslims an adequate share along with other Indians in all the services of the State and in local self-government bodies having due regard to the requirements of efficiency.
12. The Constitution should embody adequate safeguards for the protection of Muslim culture and for the promotion of Muslim education, language, religion, personal laws and Muslim charitable institutions and for their due share in the grants-in-aid given by the State and by the self-governing bodies.
13. No cabinet either central or provincial should be formed without there being a proportion of at least one-third Muslim ministers.
14. No change shall be made in the Constitution of the Central Legislature except with the concurrence of the States constituting the Indian federation.

The Britishers neither accepted the Nehru Report nor Jinnah's fourteen points. The Britishers, in their zeal to further deepen communal divisions, came up with the Communal Award. The then Prime Minister of Britain, Ramsay Macdonald gave this Communal Award. According to it, separate representation was to be provided for the Muslims, Sikhs, Christians, Anglo-Indians, Europeans, and so on. The depressed classes were assigned a number of seats to be filled by election from special constituencies in which voters belonging to the depressed classes only could vote. Mahatma Gandhi started his agitation against this award. Finally, the Gandhi-Irwin pact was signed between Mahatma Gandhi and the then Viceroy of India, Lord Irwin on 5 March 1931, before the Second Round Table Conference in London. Before this, the Viceroy Lord Irwin announced a vague offer of Dominion Status for India in October 1929. The Indian National Congress was totally dissatisfied with the way things were taking shape, and they at the Lahore session passed a resolution declaring attainment of *Swaraj* or complete independence as its sole aim and authorized the All-India Congress Committee to start civil disobedience. From there on, 26 January 1930 was declared as India's Independence day, and civil disobedience started in March 1930 followed by repressions by the British Government.

SIMON COMMISSION REPORT, 1930

Amidst the charged atmosphere of the civil disobedience movement, the Simon Commission submitted its Report which published its Report in June, 1930.

The Simon Commission was appointed in November 1927 as a part of the Section 84 of the Government of India Act of 1919, which called for the formation of a statutory Commission "at the expiration of ten years after passing of the Act for the purpose of enquiring into the working of the system of government and the development of representative institutions in India, with a view to extend, modify or restrict the degree of responsible government then existing in India". However, under pressure from the rising momentum of the nationalist upsurge in India, the Commission was formed two years earlier under Sir John Simon. The Commission was landed in 1928 and faced black flags, boycotts and *hartals* and slogans like 'Go Back Simon'. Despite the protests by the Indians, the Simon Commission continued its work and submitted its Report in June 1930. The chief focus of the Report was the future Constitutional framework for India and the position the Provinces should enjoy. The important recommendations of the Commission were:

1. The future Constitutional development of India should be on Federal lines and can never be of a unitary type.
2. Diarchy should be abolished in the Provinces and the whole field of Provincial administration should be entrusted to ministers responsible to their legislatures.
3. Each Province should be like a mistress in its own house; the Governor was to be vested with over-riding powers over Legislature.
4. The size of the Provincial Legislative Councils should be enlarged.
5. The Upper House of the Central Legislature (Council of State) should remain as it is, while the size of the Lower House (Central Legislative

Assembly) be widened and its members be elected by the Provincial Legislative Councils.

6. There should be no Responsible Government at the centre. The Governor-General should be vested with powers to select and appoint the members of his Executive Council; his powers should be enlarged in some matters.
7. There should be reduction in the functions and membership of the Council of the Secretary of the State for India.
8. A Council of Greater India consisting of the representatives of the States and British India for consultative purposes should be set up.
9. A Provincial Financial Fund to ensure adequate resources to the Provinces should be created.
10. The High Courts should remain under the control of the Government of India.
11. Burma should be separated from India in the new Constitutional scheme.
12. The question of making Sindh and Orissa into separate Provinces should be given further consideration.
13. The presence of British troops and British officers in Indian regiments should be maintained for many years, but the Commander-in-Chief should not be a member of the Viceroy's Executive Council and that he should not be a part of Central Legislature.

The Report of the Simon Commission failed to meet the aspirations of the Indians. There was apprehensions that acceptance of this Report would make the Governor-General very powerful in the Central Legislature and the Governor in the Provinces. The Report also did not give any direction towards the future goal of India. The nationalists and even the Muslim League resented the Report and the racial arrogance shown by Lord Birkenhead. However, the British Government accepted the Report and called the First Round Table Conference (1930–1931) in London for discussing the future Constitutional reforms in India.

THE GOVERNMENT OF INDIA ACT, 1935

After the failure of the Third Round Table Conference, the British Government gave the Joint Select Committee the task of formulating the new Act for India. The Committee comprised of 16 members each from the House of Commons and House of Lords, 20 representatives from British India and seven from the Princely States. Lord Linlithgow was appointed as the President of the Committee. After a year and a half of deliberations, the committee finally came out with a draft Bill on 5 February 1935. The Bill was discussed in the House of Commons for 43 days and in the House of Lords for 13 days, and finally, after being signed by the King, was enforced as the Government of India Act, 1935, in July 1935.

The main features of the Act were:

1. A Federation of India was to be formed comprising both Provinces and States. The provisions of the Act establishing the Federal Central Government were not to go into operation until a specified number of rulers of States had signed instruments of accession. The functions of the Crown with regard to the Indian States were to be performed in India by his representative who was the Viceroy himself. Since, this did not happen, the Central Government continued to function in accordance with the 1919 Act, and only the part of the 1935 Act dealing with the Provincial Governments went into operation.
2. This Act of 1935 provided three lists: Federal List, Provincial List and the Concurrent List. The Federal Government was authorized to pass laws on the subjects given in the Federal Lists. The subjects given in the provincial list within the exclusive jurisdiction of the Provincial Legislature. As regards to the concurrent list both the Federal Legislatures and the Provincial Legislatures could pass laws on the subjects given in that list. However, if a law was passed by the Federal Legislature on any subject given in the concurrent list, the Provincial Legislature could not make law on the same subject afterwards. Regarding the residuary powers, the Governor-General, in his discretion, was given the power to decide as to which of three lists a particular subject was to be allotted. No finance Bill could be placed in the Central Legislature without the consent of the Governor-General.
3. The Governor-General remained the head of the central administration and enjoyed wide powers concerning administration, legislation and finance. The Governor-General was to be assisted by Council of Ministers in discharge of his functions and the number should not exceed beyond 10. By a separate instrument of instructions the Governor-General was instructed to secure representatives of the States who were nominees of their rulers and representatives of the important minorities.
4. Diarchy, which had been established in the Provinces by the Act of 1919, was to be established at the centre. However, it came to an end in the Provinces. Certain Federal subjects were reserved in the hands of the Governor-General to be administered by him with the assistance of not more than three counsellors to be appointed by him. The foreign policy, defence, tribal areas, ecclesiastical affairs and other important matters were to remain in his hands.
5. The Federal Legislature was to consist of two Houses, the Council of State (Upper House) and the Federal Assembly (Lower House). The term of the Federal Assembly was restricted to five years from the

date of his first meeting. After five years the term was to be dissolved automatically. However, the Governor-General was given the power to extend his tenure.

6. The Council of State was to consist of 260 members, out of whom 156 were to be elected by the British colonial powers and 104 to be nominated by the rulers of Princely States. This was considered as a permanent body in which one-third members were to retire after three years. The members from the States were to be nominated by the rulers. The representatives from British India were to be elected. The Hindu, Muslim and Sikh members were to be elected on communal lines.
7. The Federal Assembly was to consist of 375 members; out of which 250 were to be elected by the Legislative Assemblies of the British Indian Provinces while 125 were to be nominated by the rulers of the Princely States.
8. The Central Legislature had the right to pass any Bill, but the Bill required the approval of the Governor-General before it became a law. Also, the Governor-General had the power to frame ordinances.
9. The Indian Council of the Secretary of the State was abolished. In its place, few advisers were nominated to help the Secretary of the State for India who may or may not be consulted or whose advice may not be followed, except advice given with respect to the services.
10. The Secretary of the State was not expected to interfere in the matters dealt by the Governor with the help of Indian ministers.
11. The Provinces were given autonomy with respect to subjects delegated to them.
12. An important feature of the Act of 1935 was the electoral safeguards. The safeguards were of two kinds. In the first place there was a denial of legislative powers to the India legislatures in regard to a large number of subjects. In the second place, there was the grant of powers to the Governor-General or the Governors to override their ministers and legislators in certain circumstances including assumption of absolute dictatorial powers in the event of breakdown of the Constitution.
13. Two new Provinces Sindh and Orissa were created.
14. Reforms were introduced in the North-West Frontier Province as were in the other Provinces.
15. Separate electorates were to be continued as before.
16. In the Central Legislature, one-third of the Muslim representatives were permitted.
17. Autonomous Provincial Governments in 11 Provinces, under ministries responsible to legislatures, were setup.
18. Burma and Aden were separated from India and transferred to the control of the colonial office.

19. The Federal Court was established in the center with the jurisdiction over the States and the Provinces.
20. The Reserve Bank of India was established with a mutual consent of the Governor and fifteen Directors to control currency and keep financial stability in the country.

Both the Indian National Congress and the Muslim League opposed the Act, but participated in the Provincial elections of winter 1936–37, conducted under stipulations of the Act. At the time of independence, the two dominions of India and Pakistan accepted the Act of 1935, with few amendments, as their Provisional Constitution.

CRIPPS MISSION PROPOSALS, 1942

The Government of India Act was passed in 1935, but the provisions relating to the Provinces only came to be applied in 1937. Meanwhile, the Congress got majority in six Provinces and in two was in a position to form governments with the help of other parties, but did not want to form the government until and unless the Governor gave the assurance that he would not interfere with the working of the legislature. Finally, the Governor-General gave the assurance and Congress ministers came to power. The outbreak of the Second World War in 1939 gave rise to another deadlock. British India, without consulting the Indians, was dragged into the war as a belligerent country. The Congress Working Committee protested against such an action of the British Government and asked whether "the treatment of India as a free nation whose policy will be guided in accordance with the wishes of the people." The British refused to give such assurance and made vague promises. Under such circumstances the Congress High Command called the Congress Ministries in eight Provinces to resign and they did so in October 1939.

The discontent of the Indian public made Viceroy Lord Linlithgow present his offer on 8 August 1940, which came to be known as the "August offer." However, the offer remained unsuccessful as it failed to satisfy the demand of the Congress relating to the transfer of power at an early and also on a specific date. Therefore, under Gandhiji's direction, the Indians started individual *satyagraha*—a symbolic protest against the attitude of the government. In the meantime, the Japanese advances towards India made the British to look afresh at the situation. The British public and the Labour Party were all in favour of reconciling the Indian demands. It is under such circumstances that Cripps Mission was sent to India.

On 29 March 1942, Cripps addressed a Press Conference and then released the text of his draft proposals whose terms were as follows:

1. Immediately on the cessation of hostilities, steps shall be taken to set up in India, in the manner prescribed hereafter, an elected body charged with the task of framing a new Constitution.

2. Provision shall be made, as set out below, for the participation of Indian States in the Constitution-making body.
3. His Majesty's Government undertakes to accept and implement forthwith the Constitution so framed subject only to:
   (a) the right of any Province of British India that is not prepared to accept the new Constitution to retain its present Constitutional position, provision being made for its subsequent accession if it so decides.

   "With such non-acceding Provinces should they so desire, His Majesty's Government will be prepared to agree upon a new Constitution giving them the same full status as the Indian union and arrived at by a procedure analogous to that here laid down."

   (b) The signing of a treaty which shall be negotiated between His Majesty's Government and the Constitution-making body. This treaty will cover all necessary matters arising out of the complete transfer of responsibility from British to Indian hands; it will make provision, in accordance with undertakings given by His Majesty's Government, for the protection of racial and religious minorities, but will not impose any restriction on the power of the Indian union to decide in future its relationship to other member States of the British Commonwealth.

   Whether or not an Indian State elects to adhere to the Constitution, it will be necessary to negotiate a revision of its treaty arrangements so far as this may be required in the new situation.
4. The Constitution-making body shall be composed as follows unless the leaders of Indian opinion in the principal communities agree upon some other form before the end of hostilities.

   "Immediately on the result being known of provincial elections which will be necessary at the end of hostilities, the entire membership of the Lower House of Provincial Legislatures shall as a single electoral college proceed to the election of the Constitution-making body by the system of proportional representation. The new body shall be in number about one-tenth of the number of the electoral college."

   "Indian States shall be invited to appoint representatives in the same proportion to their total population as in the case of representatives of British India as a whole and with the same powers as British Indian members."
5. During the critical period which now faces India and until the new Constitution can be framed, His Majesty's Government must inevitably bear the responsibility for and retain the control and direction of the defence of India as a part of their world war effort; but the task of organizing the full military, moral and material resources of India must be the responsibility of the Government of India with the cooperation

> of the people of India. His majesty's Government would desire and invite the immediate and effective participation of the principal sections of the Indian people in the counsels of the country and of the Commonwealth nations. And that they will be enabled to give their active and constructive help to discharge a task which is vital and essential for the future freedom of India.

The Cripps proposal disappointed the Indians once again. Mahatma Gandhi termed them as "a post-dated cheque on a crashing bank". The nationalist section of the people viewed a plan of division of the country inherent in the Cripps proposal. The Congress outright rejected the proposal. Even the Muslim League opposed it and Jinnah observed that the idea of Pakistan embodied in the Cripps proposals was nebulous and serious impediments were placed in the path of achieving it. On the whole, Cripps proposal failed to achieve anything positive, and tended to strengthen the doubts and suspicions in the minds of political leaders that there was no genuine desire on the part of His Majesty's Government to part with power. It also became evident that the British Government were moving in the direction of eventual division of the country although ostensibly they did not make it explicit.

Hereafter, Viceroy Archibald Wavell called a meeting at Simla (also known as the Simla Conference) in June 1945 meeting between Viceroy and the major political leaders of India. It was convened to agree on and approve the Wavell plan for Indian self-government. However, differences arose between the leadership of the two parties on the issue of representation of the Muslim community. The Muslim League claimed that it was the only representative party of the Muslims in India, and thus, all the Muslim representatives in the Viceroy's Executive Council should be the nominees of the party. Congress, which had sent Maulana Azad as the leader of their delegation, tried to prove that their party represented all the communities living in India and thus should be allowed to nominate Muslim representatives as well. Differences cropped over a number of issues which ultimately resulted in a deadlock. On 14 July 1945, Wavell announced the failure of his efforts.

CABINET MISSION PLAN, 1946

After the victory of the Allied Powers in the Second World War, Britain though emerged victorious, but was devastated. It was difficult for her to retain her colonies. Besides, there was change of political situation in Britain. With the victory of the labour party, Clement Atlee, who was known to be a 'friend of India' became the Prime Minister. In the House of Commons, Mr. Atlee issued a statement on 15 March 1946, where he admitted the right of the Indians to self-determination and their right to frame a Constitution for free India. It was also announced that the British Government was sending a Cabinet Mission to India to resolve the political deadlock. Thus, on 23 March 1946, three cabinet members, Pethick-Lawrence, Sir Stafford Cripps and

Mr. A.V. Alexander arrived in India with the objective to negotiate a settlement, on the basis of which Indian Constitution would be framed, and setting up a national government in favour of which transferences of power would take place.

The Cabinet Mission held discussions with the leaders of all political parties including the representatives of the Princely States and submitted its scheme for a stable and practicable solution of the political crisis in India. The Cabinet Mission plan comprises three parts. The first relates to the Indian Union, the second to the Constituent Assembly and the third to the Interim Government. The summary of the plan is given as follows:

1. **Indian Union:** The Cabinet Mission plan recommended that
   (a) there should be a Union of India consisting of both British India and Princely States dealing with these subjects—defence, foreign affairs and communications—and in addition to that powers to raise the finances require for the above subjects;
   (b) the Union should have an executive and a legislature constituted from the representatives of British India and Indian States. Any question involving a major communal issue in the legislature should require for its decisions a majority of the representatives, present and voting, of each of the two major communities as well as absolute majority of all members, present and voting;
   (c) all other subjects and residuary items should be given to the Provinces of the proposed union;
   (d) the Provinces should be free to form groups with executives and legislatures and each group could determine the Provincial subjects to be in common;
   (e) the Constitution of the Union of the groups should contain a provision whereby any Province could by a majority vote of its Legislative Assembly, call for a consideration of the terms of the continuation after an initial period of ten years and at ten years' interval thereafter.

2. **Constituent Assembly:** For the formation of a Constituent Assembly in order to frame the Constitution without delay, the plan suggested:
   (a) to allot to each Province a total number of seats in proportion to its population roughly in the ratio of one to a million as the nearest substitute for representation by adult suffrage;
   (b) to divide the provincial allocation of seats between the main communities in each Province in proportion to their respective population;
   (c) to provide that the representative allotted to each community in a Province shall be elected by the members of the community in its Legislative Assembly;
   (d) that the method of selection in the case of the representatives of the Princely States was to be determined by consultation.

3. **Interim Government:** It was recommended that an Interim Government be set up immediately for the transference of power. It would consist of the representatives of main political parties. All portfolios would be vested in the hands of the Indian leaders having full cooperation of their people and the British Government will give full cooperation to this government thus formed in matters of administration and in bringing about as rapid and smooth a transition as possible.

The Cabinet Mission plan was appreciated, and all saw it as a great reconciliation between the stands taken by the Congress and the Muslim League. It also upheld the long demand of the Indians for setting up of a Constituent Assembly. Congress was happy because the plan ruled out a separate Pakistan and Muslim League got satisfaction from the provision of the grouping of Provinces coupled with the provision that all major communal issues would require for their decision a majority vote of the representatives of each of the major communities and that this plan would not be altered in the Constituent Assembly, nor any decision can be taken on major communal issues without the approval of the majority of the minority communities. But the Plan also laid the passage of Mountbatten Plan, then the Indian Independence Act of 1947, and the final partition of India.

MOUNTBATTEN PLAN, 1947

On the basis of the recommendation of the Cabinet Mission and after intense negotiation with the Muslim League and the Congress party, Lord Wavell was able to convince the Congress to form the Interim Government. However, the Muslim League initially refused to join the government, because they wanted a separate Pakistan. Jawaharlal Nehru formed the Interim Government on 2 September 1946, only to be joined by the Muslim League in October 1946. But they mainly joined to weaken the government and to secure support for creation of Pakistan. Alongside communal violence broke-out in different parts of India (Calcutta and Noakhali riots must be mentioned).

There arose serious differences between the Congress and the Muslim League regarding the grouping of Provinces according to the Cabinet Mission plan. So, when the Constituent Assembly met in its first session on 9 December 1946, the Muslim League boycotted the session. Ultimately, situation became so tensed that Congress demanded the resignation of the members of Muslim League from the Interim Government for not taking part in the proceedings, and Muslim League also demanded the resignation of the Congress nominees. The situation was such that pleasing one would offend the other. Thus, Prime Minister Atlee made a famous declaration on 20 February 1947, where he observed that "...the present state of uncertainty is fraught with danger and cannot be indefinitely prolonged. His Majesty's Government wish to take necessary steps to effect the transference of power to responsible Indian hands by a date not later than June 1948."

Atlee further stated that if a Constitution was not framed by a fully representative Constituent Assembly by June 1948, then "His Majesty's Government will have to consider to whom the powers of the Central Government in British India should be handed over, on due date, whether as a whole to some form of Central Government for British India, or in some areas to the existing Provincial Governments or in such other way as may seem most reasonable and in the best interests of the Indian people." It was also announced that Lord Mountbatten will succeed Lord Wavell as the Viceroy of India and he would be entrusted with the task of transfer of power to the Indians.

Lord Mountbatten took over the charge as the Viceroy from 24 March 1947. The day he arrived in India, i.e., 22 March 1947, was observed as the Pakistan day by the Muslim League. The political atmosphere in the country was tense and Hindu-Muslim distrust reached a point where a civil war became inevitable. Judging the gravity of the situation Lord Mountbatten forwarded his first plan which was rejected by all. He had proposed the partitioning of the Provinces of Bengal and Punjab with a view of separating the predominantly Muslim areas from the predominantly non-Muslim areas. He was also in favour of providing the option to the Muslim district of Sylhet to join the Muslim Province of Bengal. In the case of North-West Frontier Province, fresh election was to be held to ascertain the wishes of the people. The Plan also suggested that the transfer of power was to take place on the basis of Dominion Status to India and such other areas as wanted by to separate themselves from India and form another State.

When this Plan was rejected and even sent back by the home government to England with a number of changes, he left for London on 18 May 1947, and came back with the final Plan with the approval of the British Government which came to be known as "Statement Regarding the method of Transfer of Power, 3 June 1947."

The Plan provided for a clear division of the country. It stated that:

1. The applicability of the principle of self-determination for those parts of the country which did not desire to remain within the Indian Union and provision for similar rights was also granted to those parts of the Provinces which desired to remain within the Indian Union.
2. The Provinces of Punjab, Sindh, Baluchistan, North-West Frontier Province, Bengal and the Muslim majority district of Sylhet and in Assam were given the right to decide whether they wanted to remain in Indian Union or not. The Hindu majority districts of Bengal and Punjab were also given similar rights.
3. In Bengal and Punjab, the representatives of the Muslim and non-Muslim majority districts of their respective Legislative Assemblies were given the right to decide separately whether they opted for India or Pakistan.
4. In North-West Frontier Province and the Muslim majority district of Sylhet in Assam this was to be decided by a referendum.

5. In Sindh, the Assembly was to vote as a whole for the decision.
6. In Baluchistan, a joint meeting of the representative institutions was to be held for that purpose.
7. In the event of a decision for the partition of the Provinces of Punjab, Bengal and Assam independent boundary Commissions were to be appointed to fix the dividing lines between two parts of the Provinces.
8. An arrangement was also to be made for the distribution of assets and liabilities between the two dominions.
9. Both India and Pakistan were to be accorded Dominion Status with a right to leave British Commonwealth nations at a later date.

The Mountbatten plan was accepted both the Congress and the Muslim League. The Congress, accepted the terms of the plan and the possibility of partition under the compulsion of events. Upon the acceptance of the plan, the British Parliament passed the Indian Independence Act of 1947, and in the midnight of 14 August 1947, the country was partitioned with the creation of the two dominions of India and Pakistan.

THE INDIAN INDEPENDENCE ACT, 1947

To give effect to the Mountbatten Plan or the 3 June 1947, the Indian Independence Bill was introduced in the British Parliament on 4 July 1947 and passed on 18 July 1947.

1. The Act provided for the partition of India and the establishment of two dominions of India and Pakistan from the appointed day (15 August 1947). The Act also provided for the legislative supremacy of the two dominions.
2. The legislatures of the two dominions were given full power to make laws having extra-territorial jurisdiction.
3. The British Government was to have no control over the affairs of the dominions, Provinces, or any part of the dominions after 15 August 1947.
4. Until a new Constitution was framed for each dominion, the Act made the existing Constituent Assemblies the dominion legislatures for the time being. The Assemblies were to exercise all the powers which were formerly exercised by the Central Legislatures, in addition to its power regarding the framing of a new Constitution.
5. Pending the framing of a new Constitution, each of the dominion and all the Provinces were to be governed in accordance with the Government of India Act, 1935. Each dominion was authorized to make modifications in the Government of India Act, 1935 under the Indian Independence Act.

6. The Governor-General was given the power to modify or adapt the Government of India Act, 1935 as might be considered necessary till 31 March 1948. After that day, it was open to the Constituent Assembly to modify or adapt the same act.
7. The right of the King to veto laws or to reserve laws for his pleasure was given up and given to the Governor-General.
8. The Act provided for the termination of the suzerainty of the Crown over the Indian States. All treaties, agreements and functions exercisable by his Majesty with regard to States and their rulers were to lapse from 15 August 1947.
9. Agreements with the tribes of the North-Western Frontier Province of India were to be negotiated by the successor dominion.
10. The office of the Secretary of the State for India was to be abolished and his work was to be taken over by the Secretary of the State for Commonwealth Affairs.
11. The title of "Emperor of India" was to be dropped from the royal style and titles of the King of England.
12. It was provided that for each of the new dominions there shall be a Governor-General who shall be appointed by His Majesty and shall represent His Majesty for the purposes of the government of the dominions.

The Indian Independence Act gave India its long aspired freedom, but with it there came the tragic partition. Two countries were born—India and Pakistan. Formally, Pakistan became an independent State on and from 14 August 1947. On 15 August 1947, India became an Independent Sovereign State. Nehru observed, "At the stroke of midnight hour, when the world sleeps, India will awake to life and freedom. A moment comes, which comes but rarely in history, when we step out from the old to the new, when an age ends, and when the soul of a nation, suppressed, finds utterance..." The Constituent Assembly had begun its work of drafting a Constitution for free India since 9 December 1946. Finally, the Constitution was adopted on 26 November 1949, and was inaugurated on 26 January 1950. On this day, India was proclaimed as a Sovereign Democratic Republic. Dr. Rajendra Prasad (1884–1963) became the first President of India (26 January 1950–13 May 1962).

EXERCISES

I. Short Answer Questions: **(100 words)**

1. The Government of India Act, 1858
2. Queen's Proclamation, 1858
3. August Declaration, 1917

4. Nehru Report, 1928
5. Jinnah's Fourteen Points, 1929
6. Simon Commission Report, 1930
7. Cripps Mission, 1942

II. Long Answer Questions: **(1200 words)**

8. Analyze the Morley-Minto Reforms of 1909.
9. Discuss the Montague-Chelmsford Reforms of 1919.
10. Discuss the provisions of Government of India Act, 1935.
11. Analyze the various proposals of Cabinet Mission Plan, 1946.
12. Examine the Mountbatten Plan, 1947. How was it implemented in the form of Indian Independence Act, 1947?
13. Examine the Indian Independence Act, 1947.

REFERENCES

Cabinet Mission Plan, 1946.

Chandra, Bipan, et al., *India's Struggle for Independence,"* Viking, New Delhi, 1988.

Chandra, Bipan, Mukherjee, Mridula and Mukherjee, Aditya, *India After Independence*, Viking, New Delhi, 1999.

Chandra, Bipan, Tripathi, Amales and De, Barun, *Freedom Struggle,* National Book Trust, New Delhi, 2007.

Charter Acts, 1813, 1833 & 1853

Government of India Act, 1858

Government of India Act, 1909

Government of India Act, 1919

Government of India Act, 1935

Indian Councils Acts, 1861 & 1892

Indian Independence Act, 1947

Jinnah's Fourteen Point Formula

Majumdar R.C., Majumdar, D.K. (Eds.), *British Paramountcy and Indian Renaissance*, *Part* I, "The History and Culture of the Indian People", Bharatiya Bidya Bhavan, Bombay, 1963.

Majumdar R.C., Majumdar, D.K. (Eds.), *British Paramountcy and Indian Renaissance*, Part II, "The History and Culture of the Indian People", 2nd revised ed., Bharatiya Bidya Bhavan, Bombay, 1981.

Mountbatten Plan, 1947

Nehru Report, 1928

Pitts India Act, 1784

Proposals of Cripps Mission, 1942

Regulating Act, 1773

Report of Simon Commission, 1930

Robb, P.G., *The Government of India and Reform: Policies Towards Politics and the Constitution 1916–1921,* Heritage Publishers, New Delhi, 1986.

2

Framing of the Constitution of India—Demand, Formation and Working of the Constituent Assembly

INTRODUCTION

India became a Sovereign Democratic Republic with the Constitution of India coming into force on 26 January 1950, the day which is celebrated with much reverence and respect as the Republic Day of India. It was on this day that India ceased to be a dominion of the British Empire with the President of India becoming the head of the State. However, the grand Constitution was the product of the Constituent Assembly which drafted the Constitution for independent India, after it was formed in 1946 under the provisions of the Cabinet Mission Plan. The Constitution was passed and adopted on 26 November 1949, and was inaugurated on 26 January 1950. The framing of the Indian Constitution, formation of the Constituent Assembly, objectives and resolutions will be discussed in this Chapter.

DEMAND FOR A CONSTITUENT ASSEMBLY

The Cabinet Mission Plan (1946) embodied the provision for the formation of a grand Constituent Assembly. It was under tremendous pressure from the nationalists, the Congress and the Indian people, that the Britishers ultimately conceded to send a Cabinet Mission to India to chalk out the final procedures of transferring the power to the Indians. However, the demand for the formation of a Constituent Assembly had been raised many-a-times by the Indians long before. It was only after the Second World War that the Britishers conceded to the demand for a Constituent Assembly and the Cabinet Mission (1945) which contained the provisions for the establishment of a Constituent Assembly.

During the First World War the Indian Nationalists had demanded the right for the people of India to frame a Constitution for themselves, but this was outrightly rejected by the Britishers. In 1922, Mahatma Gandhi said "Let us see clearly what *Swaraj* with the British connection means. It means undoubtedly India's ability to declare her independence if she wishes. *Swaraj*, therefore, will not be a free gift of the British Parliament. It will be a declaration of India's full expression. That it will be expressed through an Act of Parliament is true. But it will be merely a courteous ratification of the declared wish of the people of India, even as it was in the case of the Union of South Africa."

Later, in 1922 and 1923 under the inspiration of Mrs. Annie Besant, another round of demand was raised by some moderate members of the central Legislative Assembly and they called a National Convention "in order to obtain for the Commonwealth of Indian Dominion Status in her external relations and *Swaraj* in her internal affairs."

In 1924 the *Swarajists* started their demand in the Central Legislative Assembly for convening a Round Table Conference or convention for recommending a scheme of a Constitution for India which after approval by the elected legislature could be placed in the British Parliament for its enactment as a statute. We have seen in the preceding chapter while discussing the circumstances under which the Simon Commission came to India, that Lord Birkenhead, the then Secretary of the State for India, threw a challenge to the *Swarajists* in the face of their above demand, "to produce a Constitution which carries behind it a fair measure of general agreement among the great people of India." The challenge was accepted and the outcome was the Nehru Report (1928). [refer Chapter 1 for details].

The demand for an Indian Constituent Assembly was raised for the first time by M.N. Roy. The Congress accepted the idea of Constituent Assembly in 1934, but many leaders within the Congress still had faith in the conference method. After the failures of the Indian Statutory Commission and the Round Table Conference, and as a counterpart to the White Paper Proposals of 1933 issued by the British Government, a demand for a Constituent Assembly in clear terms was made. The Congress Working Committee, while refusing the white paper proposals, upheld that "the only satisfactory alternative to the white paper is a Constitution drawn up by a Constituent Assembly elected on the basis of adult franchise or, as near as it is possible, with power, if necessary, to the important minorities to have their representatives elected exclusively by the electors belonging to such minorities."

In 1936, at its Faizpur session the Congress declared that "it reiterates its entire rejection of the Government of India Act, 1935, and the Constitution that has been imposed on India against the declared will of the people of the country. In opinion of the Congress, any cooperation with this Constitution is a betrayal of India's struggle for freedom and a strengthening of the hold of British Imperialism and a further exploitation of the Indian masses who have been already reduced to dire poverty under Imperialist domination. The Congress therefore, repeats its resolve not to submit to this Constitution or to co-operate with it, but to combat it, both inside and outside the legislatures, so as to end it...." In 1938, Jawaharlal Nehru gave a concrete form to the demand of a Constituent Assembly when he said, "The Indian National Congress stands for independence and a democratic State. It has proposed that the Constitution of free India must be framed, without outside interference, by a Constituent Assembly elected on the basis of adult franchise."

The Second World War dragged India into the war as a belligerent party. The Government of British India declared war against Germany without the consent of people or India or their representatives. The Congress withdrew cooperation from the British Government and demanded recognition of "India's independence and the right of her people to frame their Constitution through a Constituent Assembly." The Congress Ministries in various Provinces resigned, and on 14 September 1939, the Congress passed the resolution which demanded that "the Committee wish to declare again that recognition of India's independence, and the right of her people to frame their Constitution through a Constituent Assembly is essential in order to remove the taint of imperialism from Britain's policy and to enable the Congress to consider further co-operation." In subsequent sessions, the demand for Constituent Assembly was reiterated in order to frame a Constitution through a Representative Assembly elected on the basis of adult franchise.

On the face of persistent demand for a Constituent Assembly by the Indians, the British tried to appease the Indians by the August Offer. Lord Linlithgow, the then Viceroy of India declared the August Offer, which among the other things contained provisions for a Constituent Assembly after the Second World War. The August Offer was rejected by the nationalist Indians and the political atmosphere became charged with the demands for independence and creation of a Constitution for an Independent India. Quit India Movement of 1942 was a rejection of the British plans in the form of Cripps Proposal (1942) because it was considered like "a post-dated cheque of a failing bank". After the failure of the Cripps Mission, and a change in the Government in Britain, the demand for a Constituent Assembly saw the light.

FORMATION OF THE CONSTITUENT ASSEMBLY

After the Second World War in 1945, things started moving. The Labour party came to power with Mr. Atlee as the Prime Minister and a Cabinet mission was sent to India in 1945, which formally accepted the demand for the formation of a Constituent Assembly. Cabinet Mission proposals regarding the formation of the Constituent Assembly *inter alia* were:

1. to allot to each Province a total number of seats in proportion to its population roughly in the ratio of one to a million as the nearest substitute for representation by adult suffrage;
2. to divide the provincial allocation of seats between the main communities in each Province in proportion to their respective population;
3. to provide that the representative allotted to each community in a Province shall be elected by the members of the community in its Legislative Assembly;
4. the method of selection in the case of the representatives of the Princely States was to be determined by consultation.

The grouping of the Indian Provinces and the composition proposed for the Constituent Assembly is shown in Table 2.1.

From the table it becomes clear that according to the Cabinet Mission Plan, the Constituent Assembly was to consist of 389 members only: 187 from Section A, 35 from Section B and 70 from Section C—a total of 292 seats were allotted to British Indian Provinces and a maximum of 93 seats for Indian States and 4 Chief Commissioners Provinces.

Table 2.1 Indian Provinces and the composition

S. No.	*Provinces*	*Sections*	*Seats*			*Total*
			General	*Muslims*	*Sikhs*	
1.	Madras	A	45	4		49
2.	Bombay	A	19	2		21
3.	U.P.	A	47	8		55
4.	Bihar	A	31	5		36
5.	C.P.	A	16	1		17
6.	Orissa	A	9	0		9
		Total	167	20	4	187
7.	Punjab	B	8	16		28
8.	North-West Frontier Province	B	0	3		3
		B	1	3		4
9.	Sind	Total	9	22		35
10.	Bengal	C	27	33		60
11.	Assam	C	7	3		10
		Total	34	36		70

Total strength for Indian Provinces–292, Total strength for Indian States–93, Total strength for the Chief Commissioner Provinces–4, Grand Total–389

In July 1946, election to the Constituent Assembly took place with the participation of the Provincial Legislative Assemblies. The idea of indirect elections was accepted by the Congress as adult suffrage was regarded as too cumbersome and slow, and thus, it forsake its long-held demand for a Constituent Assembly created by adult suffrage. The representation of the

Provinces in the Assembly was to be in the ratio of one is to one million of their population approximately. The members of three communal categories in the legislatures Muslim, Sikh and General (Hindus and all other communities), would elect separately, according to their percentage of the population of the Provinces and their proportion of the provincial delegation. The Princely States according to the Cabinet Mission plan, were allotted 93 representatives in the Assembly, but the method for selecting them was left to consultation between the Assembly and the rulers of the States.

When the elections actually took place in July 1946, out of the total 1585 seats in the Provincial Assemblies, the Congress had won 923 seats in the elections which was almost 58% of the seats in the election of 1945. Thus, the Congress emerged victorious in the elections held for the Constituent Assembly. The Congress secured 203 out of 212 general seats (representing all communities except Muslims and Sikhs). In addition to this, Congress had put up 4 Muslims and 1 Sikh candidate who won and increased the number of seats won by Congress to 208 out of 292 seats allotted to the Provincial Legislative Assemblies. The Muslim League won 7 of the seats reserved for Muslims and the remaining 16 seats went to five small groups: Sikh and the Unionists (of Punjab) 3 each, 1 to the Communists, 1 to the Scheduled Castes federation and 8 to the independents. However, after the partition of the country the majority of the Congress party rose to 82%. The native Princely States nominated their 93 members who constituted the non-elected section of the otherwise democratically constituted body. There was a little change in the representation of the various communities and marginal readjustments of seats according to the new figures of the population of Punjab, Bengal and Assam as given by the Boundary Commission.

The election results however, disappointed the Muslim League and they withdrew their support, and declared to boycott the Assembly and resolved to resort to direct action for achieving a separate Pakistan. They also observed the Direct Action Day on 16 August 1946.

The Congress-League animosity and distrust heightened and could not be reconciled. Therefore, it was not until 20 November 1946, that Lord Wavell made an announcement that the Assembly would meet on 9 December 1946, but not much headway was made. Constituent Assembly was formally convened on the 9 December 1946, in the Hall of the Constitution which was attached to the Constitution House which had the residential quarters for most of the members of the Constituent Assembly. The First Session of the Constituent Assembly took place from 9 December to 23 December 1946. The deliberation started with Dr. Sachhidanand Sinha, the oldest member as the temporary Chairman. Dr. Rajendra Prasad was later on unanimously elected as President on 11 December 1946. In the absence of the Muslim League, the Congress commanded an overwhelming majority. It was on 3 June 1947 Lord Mountbatten declared his plan which contained the sinister design of partitioning the country with the final transfer of power on 15 August 1947. The Indian Independence Act was passed to give effect to the Mountbatten Plan, which became operative from 15 August 1947. With this, the Constituent Assembly became a legally sovereign body engaging itself in making of the Constitution of India. It was now relieved from the limitations placed by the Cabinet Mission Plan and came to have full freedom in framing the Constitution of India. Lord Mountbatten was appointed as the first Governor-General of India and Jawaharlal Nehru as the first Prime Minister of India. The Constituent Assembly was entrusted with two-fold functions. It was to enact the ordinary law of the land and also frame the new Constitution of free India. These two functions continued till the adoption of the Constitution on 26 November 1949.

The Constituent Assembly, when it met for the first time, was not a sovereign body and its power was circumscribed by the limitations set by the Cabinet Mission Plan. It was subjected to the authority of the British Parliament. It was not totally a representative body as the Muslim League boycotted the Assembly. Besides, the election procedure was also indirect through the members of Provincial Legislative Assemblies which were based on limited franchise. However, such shortcomings were not able to prevent the Constituent Assembly from functioning. Initially, the Assembly was involved in performing preliminary work of adopting an objective resolution, of electing Committees to begin drafting fundamental rights and a federal system, and of opening negotiations with the Princely States.

THE INDIAN CONSTITUTION: OBJECTIVES RESOLUTION, AND FRAMING

A historic **Objectives Resolution** was moved by Pt. Jawaharlal Nehru on 13 December, 1946, which envisaged the Indian union as an independent sovereign republic comprising autonomous units with residuary powers where the ideals of social, political and economic democracy would be guaranteed to all sections of people and adequate safeguards would be provided for minorities, backward and tribal areas, depressed and other backward classes.

The **Objectives Resolution** was adopted on 22 January 1947, and it embodied:

"The Constituent Assembly declares its firm and solemn resolve to proclaim India as an Independent, Sovereign, Republic and to draw up for her future government a Constitution:

WHEREIN the territories that now comprise British India, the territories that now form the Indian States and such other parts of India as are outside British India and the States, as well as such other territories as are willing to be continued into the independent, sovereign India, shall be a Union of them all; and

WHEREIN the said territories, whether with their present boundaries or with such others as may be determined by the Constituent Assembly and thereafter, according to the law of the Constitution shall possess and retain the status of autonomous Units, together with residuary powers and functions of government and administration save and except such powers and functions as are vested in or assigned to the Union or as are inherent or implied in the union or resulting therefrom; and

WHEREIN all powers and authority of the Sovereign, Independent India, its constituent parts and organs of Government, are derived from the people; and

WHEREIN shall be granted and secured to all the people of India, *justice*, social, economic and political, *equality* of status, of opportunity and before the law, *freedom* of thought, expression, belief, faith, worship, vocation, association and action, subject to law and public morality; and

WHEREIN adequate safeguards shall be provided for minorities, backward and tribal areas and depressed and other backward classes; and

WHEREIN shall be maintained the integrity of the territory of the Republic and its sovereign rights on land, sea and air according to justice and the law of civilized nation; and this ancient land attain its rightful and honoured place in the world and make its full and willing contribution to the promotion of the world peace and the welfare of mankind."

The Constituent Assembly also set up various Committees to Report on the various procedural and substantive aspects of the Constitution. They were:

(a) Committees on procedural affairs
   1. Rules of Procedure Committee
   2. Finance and Staff Committee
   3. Credentials Committee
   4. House Committee
   5. Press Gallery Committee
   6. Steering Committee
   7. Orders of Business Committee
   8. Hindi Translation Committee
   9. Urdu Translation Committee
   10. Committee to examine the effect of Indian Independence Act

(b) Committees on substantive affairs
   1. Committee for Negotiating with States
   2. Advisory Committee (with 5 Sub-Committees)
      (i) Committee on Fundamental Rights
      (ii) Minorities Committee
      (iii) Committee on North-East Frontier (Excluded and partially excluded areas of Assam)
      (iv) Committee on North-West Frontier (Outside Assam)
      (v) Committee on Excluded and Partially Excluded Areas (outside Assam)
   3. Union Powers Committee

4. Union Constitution Committee
5. Provincial Constitution Committee
6. Drafting Committee
7. Expert Committee on Financial Provisions
8. Committee on Chief Commissioners' Provinces
9. Special Committee appointed by the President to examine the Draft Constitution
10. Ad Hoc Committee on National Flag
11. Ad Hoc Committee on the Supreme Court
12. Commission on Linguistic Provinces.

The most important Committee was the drafting Committee. It was constituted on 29 August 1947 with Dr. B.R. Ambedkar as the Chairman. The other members were M.A. Ayyangar, Dewan Bahadur, N. Gopalswami Ayyangar, Dewan Bahadur, Alladi Krishnaswami Ayyar, Jairamdas Daulatram, Shankarrao Dattatraya Deo, Shrimati G. Durgabai, T.T. Krishnamachari, H.C. Mookerjee, K.M. Munshi, Benegal Narsing Rau, N. Madhava Rau, Saiyad Mohammed Saadulla, Satyanarayan Sinha and B. Pattabhi Sitaramayya.

The draft Constitution was published in January 1948, and eight months were given to elicit the public opinion of the Indian people and suggestions for further incorporation. It was on 4 November 1948, that the general discussion on the draft Constitution began in the Constituent Assembly, and continued till 9 November 1948. Between 15 November 1948 and 17 November 1949, thorough discussions were held and each clause of the draft Constitution was discussed. There were 7,635 amendments proposed and 2,473 amendments discussed by the Constituent Assembly. The draft was given the third and final reading from 14 November to 26 November, 1949. The new Constitution of India was adopted on 26 November 1949, and was enacted after it was signed by Dr. Rajendra Prasad as the President of the Constituent Assembly. The Constitution of India was inaugurated on 26 January 1950.

Austin observes that "With the adoption of the Constitution by the members of the Constituent Assembly on 26 November 1949, India became the largest democracy in the world. By this act of strength and will, Assembly members began what was perhaps the greatest political venture since that originated in Philadelphia in 1787."

Around 11 sessions of the Constituent Assembly were held, and it took 2 years, 11 months and 18 days to frame the Constitution, and the consideration of the draft Constitution took 114 days. After the Constitution came into force India became a Sovereign Independent Republic with Dr. Rajendra Prasad as the first President of India. The first general elections to the Lok Sabha since independence were held in India between 25 October 1951 and 21 February 1952. The Indian National Congress (INC) emerged victorious as the single largest party securing 364 out of the 489 seat. Jawaharlal Nehru became the first elected Prime Minister of the country with an absolute majority in the Lok Sabha.

EXERCISES

I. Short Answer Questions: **(100 words)**

1. Formation of the Constituent Assembly on the basis of Cabinet Mission Plan.
2. Objectives Resolution, 1947
3. Framing of the Indian Constitution.

II. Long Answer Questions: **(1200 words)**

4. Discuss the demand for a Constituent Assembly and its formation and the subsequent framing of the Indian Constitution.
5. What was the Objectives Resolution? Whose vision was it? Analyze by referring to the Objectives of the Resolution.
6. Discuss the formation of the Constituent Assembly with special reference to the Cabinet Mission Plan, 1946.

REFERENCES

Aggarwala, R.N., *National Movement and Constitutional Development of India (1857-1984)*, Metropolitan Book Co., Delhi, 1984.

Austin, Granville, *The Indian Constitution: Cornerstone of A Nation,* Oxford University Press, Bombay, 1972.

Bakshi, P.M., *The Constitution of India,* (with selective comments), Universal Law Publishing, Delhi, 2000.

Basu, Durga Das, *Introduction to the Constitution of India*, Prentice-Hall of India, New Delhi, 1992.

Government of India, *Constitution of India*

Kohli, Atul, (Ed.), *The Success of India's Democracy*, Cambridge University Press, New Delhi, 2001.

Mahajan, V.D, *Constitutional History of India,* S. Chand & Co., New Delhi, 1976.

Mishra, Shreegovind, *Constitutional Development and National Movement in India (1919-47)*, Janaki Prakashan, Patna, 1978.

Morris Jones, W.H., *The Government and Politics of India*, Hutchinson University Library, London, 1967.

Philip, A.T., and Shivaji Rao, K.H., *Indian Government and Politics*, Sterling Publishers, New Delhi, 1984.

Pylee, M.V., *India's Constitution*, S. Chand & Company, New Delhi, 1994.

Rao, K.V., *Parliamentary Democracy of India: A Critical Commentary*, The World Press, Calcutta, 1961.

Sikri, S.L., *Indian Government and Politics*, Kalyani Publishers, Delhi, 2004.

3

The Preamble

INTRODUCTION

The Constitution of India comprises the Preamble and it is divided into twenty-two parts containing 395 Articles, 12 Schedules of Indian Constitution, 104 Amendments and 5 appendices. The Constitution of India is a lengthy document, which is partly rigid and partly flexible and quasi-federal in nature. The voluminous document is a comprehensive account of the scheme of distribution of powers and functions among Central and the State Governments, the Union Territories, along with the Supreme Court, High Courts, other courts, the Election Commission of India and all other government bodies. It also details on the powers and functions of the Executive and Legislative bodies of Indian administration. Indian Constitution is an extensive document and its features are derived from some of the legal traditions followed by major Constitutions of the world like the British Constitution, the United States Constitution, the Irish Constitution, the French Constitution, the Canadian Constitution, the Australian Constitution and the Soviet Constitution. The Preamble of Indian Constitution, reflects the basic structure and the spirit of the Constitution. It contains the basic features of the Constitution. The essence of the Preamble is discussed in this chapter.

THE PREAMBLE AND ITS FEATURES

As shown in Figure 3.1, the Preamble of Indian Constitution States the following:

"WE, THE PEOPLE OF INDIA, having solemnly resolved to constitute India into a SOVEREIGN, SOCIALIST, SECULAR, DEMOCRATIC, REPUBLIC and to secure to all its citizens:

JUSTICE, social, economic and political;

LIBERTY of thought, expression, belief, faith and worship;

EQUALITY of status and of opportunity; and to promote among them all

FRATERNITY assuring the dignity of the individual and the unity and INTEGRITY of the Nation;

IN OUR CONSTITUENT ASSEMBLY this twenty-sixth day of November, 1949, do HERE BY ADOPT, ENACT AND GIVE TO OURSELVES THIS CONSTITUTION."

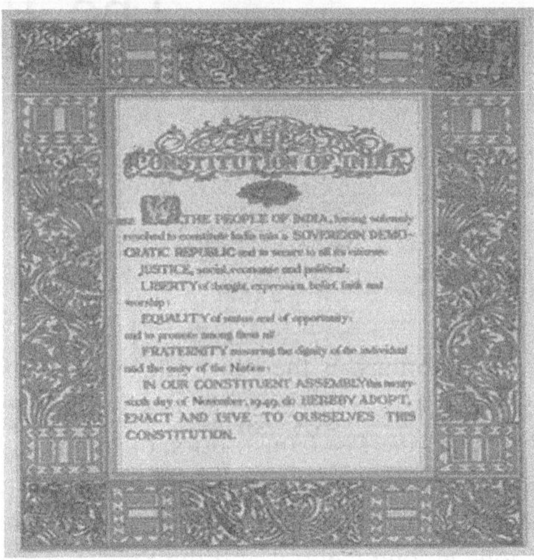

THE CONSTITUTION OF INDIA

WE, THE PEOPLE OF INDIA, having solemnly resolved to constitute India into a SOVEREIGN DEMOCRATIC REPUBLIC and to secure to all its citizens:

JUSTICE, social, economic and political;

LIBERTY of thought, expression, belief, faith and worship;

EQUALITY of status and of opportunity;

and to promote among them all

FRATERNITY assuring the dignity of the individual and the unity of the Nation;

IN OUR CONSTITUENT ASSEMBLY this twenty-sixth day of November, 1949, do HEREBY ADOPT, ENACT AND GIVE TO OURSELVES THIS CONSTITUTION.

Figure 3.1 The Preamble to the Constitution of India.

The Preamble Acts as the preface of the Constitution of India and lays down the fundamental values and philosophical ideas. It represents the essence of the Constitution in written words. The Preamble is significant because it highlights the type of society and government which the founders of the Constitution perceived to establish in India. The Preamble in every sense was influenced by the historic Objectives Resolution moved by Pt. Jawaharlal Nehru on 13 December 1947 (see Chapter 2 for details). The Preamble is considered to be the most precious part of the Constitution and a yardstick with which all the 395 Articles of the Constitution have to be measured. It is the soul of the Constitution—a key to understand the essence of the Constitution of India.

The text of the Preamble to some extent resembles the language of the Preamble to the American Constitution of 1787 which reads, "We the people of the United States, in order to form a more perfect Union, establish justice, insure domestic tranquility, provide for the common defence, promote the general welfare, and secure the blessings of liberty to ourselves and our posterity, do ordain and establish the Constitution for the United States of America." However, there are also some major differences in terms of domestic tranquility and common defence in the Preamble of the American Constitution as the words like 'Sovereign Democratic Republic' has not been included in the Preamble as it has been given preference in the case of Indian Constitution.

The Preamble to the Indian Constitution was adopted with the Constitution in the Constituent Assembly. It came into effect in 1950 along with the Constitution. The original draft of the Constitution opened with the words 'Sovereign Democratic Republic' in the first line. The words 'Socialist and Secular' were inserted later by the 42nd Amendment (1976). The same Amendment replaced the words unity of the nation into 'unity and integrity' of the nation. The significance of the Preamble of Indian Constitution lies in the "We, the people". These words emphasized that ultimately the powers are vested in the hands of the people of India. The expressions State that the Constitution is made by and for the people of India. In addition to that, the Preamble also lays down the essential national goals for every citizen which are justice, liberty, equality and fraternity.

According to the Preamble of Indian Constitution, the word 'Sovereign' occupies a vital role in the independent existence of the country. It means supreme or independent and expresses that India is independent internally and externally as far as decision-making and formulation and execution of its policies are concerned. It is free from the control of any foreign power. Furthermore, the country has a free government which is directly elected by the people, and makes laws that govern the people. The word 'Socialist' also has its own significance, as it implies social and economic equality. The word was added by the 42nd Amendment Act of 1976 during the emergency. In addition to that Social equality identifies the absence of discrimination on the grounds only of caste, colour, creed, sex, religion, or language. Besides, social equality also aims at equal status and opportunities for all. The Preamble also guarantees secularism. The word 'Secular' was also inserted into the Preamble by the 42nd Amendment Act of 1976, which implies equality of all religions and religious tolerance and does not identify any official State religion which upholds the fact that India is not a theocratic State.

Preamble of Indian Constitution also puts forth the terms, Democratic and Republic. It means that India should have a democratic form of Government. The people of India elect their governments at all levels such as Union, State and the Local Governments by a system of universal adult franchise. India is also a Republic, because it is a country where the Head of State is elected, directly or indirectly, for a fixed tenure. The President of India though is a titular head of the State, yet he is indirectly elected by the people of India and not appointed by/represents any foreign country.

Thus, the Preamble not only indicates the source of the Constitution of India, i.e., from where it derives its authority but also States the objectives, which the Constitution seeks to establish and promote.

However, the Preamble does not contain laws enforceable in a Court, but no law can also be enacted or amended in a manner that violates the spirit of the Preamble. Thus, the Preamble of the Constitution of India is unamendable or unalterable. The Preamble is the soul of our Constitution which according to former Chief Justice Mr. Hidayatullah, "lays down the pattern of our political society...It contains a solemn resolve which nothing but a revolution can alter." The features of the Preamble are discussed as follows:

FEATURES OF THE PREAMBLE

The Source of Authority

The expression 'We the People of India' truly recognizes the people of India as the source of ultimate sovereignty and the fact that the Constitution is the product of the consent or acquiescence of the people. It shows that the Constitution has its roots in the people of India and it derives its authority from the people. It is an embodiment of the fact that the people are the real source of all authority and that they themselves have declared India to 'be a Sovereign, Socialist, Secular and Democratic Republic.' The powers defined by the Constitution with respect to the Centre and State Governments are not dictated by the former colonial masters, Princely States or any particular section of the society. The Constitution of India has been framed by the people of India through their representatives in the Constituent Assembly, and can only be modified by the procedure laid down by the Constitution itself. The Constituent Assembly was made up of Indians, and it was not a body of Englishmen, but it comprised elected members like Jawaharlal Nehru, Dr. Rajendra Prasad, Sardar Vallabhbhai Patel, K.M. Munshi, Maulana Azad and Dr. B.R. Ambedkar among others, who can no way be said to be representing any interest of British Raj or the Princely States, but the voice of the people of India. Thus, the significance of 'We, the People of India' lies in the fact that the Constitution of India "eliminates the British King externally and the Indian Princes internally, from claiming any vestiges of sovereignty. While the former was explicit, the latter was to be made implicit, as, with the lapse of paramountcy on 15th August 1947, the Indian Princes became independent, and so sovereignty belonged to them as a matter of inherent right which had to be neutralized by some such declarations."

Nature of State

The features of the Indian State have been projected in the Preamble as Sovereign, Socialist, Secular, and Democratic Republic. These are discussed as follows:

Sovereign

Sovereignty is the supreme authority of a State which excludes any external intervention in the exercise of supreme power of the State, both internally and externally. In this sense, the Preamble declares India to be a Sovereign State with the power to take decisions without any external influence. It ceases to be the colony of a British empire, and even the Dominion Status conferred upon India by the Indian Independence Act of 1947 got terminated with the promulgation of the Constitution and declaration of India as a Sovereign Democratic Republic.

Serious doubts, however, rose immediately after the adoption of the Constitution regarding India's membership to the Commonwealth of Nations with the Queen of England as the symbolic head. Pt. Nehru clarified India's position and gave a suitable reply to all opposition by stating that "It is an agreement by free will, to be terminated by free will." India's membership to the Commonwealth is based on an extra-Constitutional contractual arrangement entered into at will and terminable at will, and the Crown of England is only to be regarded as a symbolic head of the Commonwealth and this has nothing to do with India's allegiance to the British Crown. It is a voluntary association and in no way it affects the sovereignty of the country.

Socialist

This term was inserted by the 42nd Constitution Amendment Act of 1976. But the term is vague and controversial. Simply looking at socialism from one angle, the term means a theory or policy which proposes no private ownership, but advocates the ownership of means of production, i.e., capital, land or property by the community as a whole. But the framers by socialism referred to democratic socialism which went a step forward and came to imply that the State would undertake the responsibility in eradication of poverty, removal of inequality by taking steps to foster economic progress along with preventing growth of monopoly. By the 45th Constitution Amendment Bill, the Janata Government tried to define what is meant by 'Socialist Republic'. The Bill explained that a 'Socialist Republic' is a republic in which there is freedom from all forms of exploitation, social, political or economic. But this could not be moved because of the strong opposition from the Rajya Sabha, and the definition had to be deleted. What can be said about the Indian brand of socialist idea is that by inserting the word socialist it is intended to give positive direction to the Government in formulating its policies. Hence, successive Governments have made efforts towards alleviation of poverty and minimization of inequalities. In keeping with the socialist spirit, the Right to Property had been deleted from the list of fundamental rights. Presently, this spirit of socialism seems to be a bit diluted in the face of globalization as India embraced the liberal model of market economy since the 1990s, which was followed by rapid de-regulation, privatization, de-nationalization, laying off the workers and foreign direct investment in different sectors. These have widened the gap between the rich and the poor quite contrary to the hopes of the makers of the Constitution when they envisaged an egalitarian society based on socialist ideals. Yet, the Indian State still finds itself committed to secure socio-economic equality amidst the rapid pace of globalization, though the process might not be smooth enough.

Secular

This term has also been added by the 42nd Constitution Amendment Act, 1976. Despite the insertion of the term Secular, nowhere is the term defined and also like the term Socialist, it is also vague and ambiguous. The 45th Constitution Amendment Bill defined 'Secular Republic' as a 'Republic in which there is equal respect for all religions.' But again it was vehemently opposed and rejected by the Rajya Sabha. The argument was that the definition given is restricted, and also gave improper meaning to what was meant by Secular Republic. In reality, what was cherished for was the separation between the State and the religion which was very much reflected in the Right to Religion under the fundamental rights contained in Part III of the Constitution. There is therefore, freedom, liberty of faith and worship of any religion whatever religion one belongs to. The State will not interfere with any religion, but would treat every religion equally and there would be no religious foundation of the State of India. There is no ecclesiastical department of the State. The State has no official religion. In other words, India is not a theocratic State like Pakistan, Bangladesh and Iran. No citizen of India, therefore, is discriminated on the basis of religion. Every citizen has the right to profess, practice and propagate any religion of their choice. (Read more in Chapter 4 on Fundamental Rights)

However, contemporary Indian political scenario is plagued with the problem of communalism and politicization of religion. The Ayodhya-Babri Masjid episode is well-known and the ensuing riots after demolition of Babri Masjid has been a stigma on Indian secularism which can never be wiped out. Further, the Godhra incident and religious assaults on Christians in Orissa have tainted the secular image of India.

Democratic

The Preamble declares India to be a democratic State. By democracy one simply means Government of the people, for the people and by the people. In other words, the people have a share in political power which they exercise through the representatives chosen by them. The universal adult suffrage ensures the political participation of the people. The State of India does not discriminate any person on the ground of religion, race, colour, place of residence, sex and the like while exercising one's suffrage or enjoying one's rights and liberties guaranteed by the Constitution of India. In India, there is indirect or representative democracy almost like the British model. The people vote in the general elections and choose their representatives who exercise the legislative function on their behalf by forming the government or becoming a part of the opposition. If the government turns out to be unfavourable or insensitive to the public sentiments, then the people can change the government in the next general election. Thus, the representatives of the people who form the Government and those who are in the opposition are responsible for the public well-being, at large. The people of India individually, collectively or by becoming a part of the civil society can oppose and prevent the government from doing excesses. Now-a-days, media and civil society have also come to play an active role in limiting the powers of the government. Further, the Supreme Court is the protector of the Constitution of India and it also can restrict the excesses done by the government. Presently, there is also a growing trend of judicial activism in India. The Right to Information (RTI) Act, 2005, is also a check on governmental powers.

Republic

There may be different meanings to the term Republic, but the architects of the Constitution generally meant that Republic is a State in which the supreme power rests with the people; and their elected representatives as opposed to hereditary monarchs or a British King as the Head of the State. Going by this meaning, India, has a democratically elected Government and the Head of the State is neither a nominated representative nor a hereditary monarch, but an elected Representative of the People even though the election may be indirect. The President of India is the head of the State who is elected by the members of the Parliament and State Legislative Assemblies for a fixed term of five years. Further all offices, from the lowest to the highest, (that of the President) will be open to all citizens without any distinction of caste, creed, religion, race, and sex. The membership to the Commonwealth of Nations, the United Nations or several other international organization no way hinders the status of India as a Republic. The heads of these respective organizations are merely symbolic, and do not affect the position of the President of India as the Head of State of India.

Objectives of the State

The Preamble underlies four objectives of the State of India. They are:

1. JUSTICE, social, economic and political;
2. LIBERTY of thought, expression, belief, faith and worship;
3. EQUALITY of status and of opportunity; and to promote among them all
4. FRATERNITY assuring the dignity of the individual and the unity and integrity of the Nation.

These are discussed as follows:

Justice

Justice has been used in the Preamble to ensure it in three different forms—social justice, economic justice and political justice. Chapters on Fundamental Rights and Directive Principles of State Policy have been included in the Constitution to achieve these objectives. Social justice aims at removing all social barriers on the basis of caste, class, creed, race, sex, religion and the like. It aims at establishing equality by prohibiting discrimination on the above grounds. Social barriers like untouchability have been declared unlawful by the Untouchability (Offences) Act (1955) which was amended and renamed as the

Protection of Civil Rights Act, 1955. Similarly, the Constitution has upheld reservation for backward classes to bring them at par with the mainstream. In order to prevent atrocities against the *dalits,* the Government has enacted The Scheduled Castes and Scheduled Tribes (Prevention of Atrocities) Act, 1989 and the Scheduled Castes and the Scheduled Tribes (Prevention of Atrocities) *Rules* of 1995 were framed. The rules for the Act were notified on 31 March 1995. Reservation for women in jobs and others are also permitted under the Constitution. Hence, the Constitution provides for 'protective discrimination' for Scheduled Caste, Scheduled Tribes and other weaker sections of society. On the whole, the objective of the consititution makers was to establish a welfare State in India. Though successive governments have tried to interpret these lofty ideals of social justice into reality, but subjection of *dalits* to severe persecution and politicization of social factors like caste and religion, have raised questions regarding the actualization of social justice in India.

Economic justice is very much related to social justice. If social justice aims at removal of differences/discrimination between citizens, economic justice also targets to abolish discrimination in the economic sphere by ensuring equal pay for equal work to all. It means providing equal opportunity to all in case of recruitment to public services. It means non-discrimination of citizens on the basis of economic values, i.e., ensuring equitable distribution of wealth, end of monopoly control over means of production and distribution. Thus, again it can be discerned from the essence of economic justice as visualized by the Constitution makers that all successive governments should make a whole-hearted effort to establish a welfare State in India. As Nehru during the Constituent Assembly Debates said, "I trust this Constitution itself will lead us to the real freedom that we have clamoured for and that real freedom, in turn, will bring food to our starving peoples, clothing for them, housing for them and all manners of opportunities of progress." However, it is doubtful whether economic justice has been secured in India especially after the phase of liberalization, disinvestment and privatization began in India from 1990s onwards.

Political justice means ensuring free and fair political participation to the citizens of India. This is guaranteed in India through universal adult suffrage (Article 326) which is secured without any discrimination on the basis of caste, class, sect, sex, religion and the like. Freedom of right to form associations, right to assemble freely, expression of opinion, participation in elections, and right to information are vital parts in the functioning of the Indian political system which is democratic. However, women have always been outside the purview of politics and to ensure their participation in politics and decision-making the Women's Reservation Bill was moved which was passed by the Rajya Sabha, but is still pending in Lok Sabha. This shows that India has a long way to go in achieving political justice for all sections of the society. Further, corruption and criminalization of politics have also hindered the Indian State to achieve the goal of political justice for all.

Liberty

Liberty is guaranteed in the Constitution in Part III under Fundamental Rights like Freedom of expression and thought, (Article 19) Religious freedom, (Article 25) Right to life and liberty, (Article 21). Therefore, the Constitution guarantees to all, the liberty of thought, expression, belief, faith and worship, and ensures the independence of judiciary for the proper protection of the Fundamental Rights guaranteed in its Part III.

Equality

Liberty without equality is totally meaningless. Therefore, the Constitution ensures equal status for all the citizens of India (in Part III of the Constitution under the Section on Fundamental Rights). Right to equality under Articles 14–18 provides equality in the eyes of law and equality before law and also abolish any distinction on basis of caste, class, religion, sex, colour and race. It also prohibits the practice of untouchability, and also the use of titles. All public offices are open to all the citizens of India and no discrimination is made on the grounds of religion, colour, sex, or caste. To ensure social equality, the Constitution permits the government to make reservations for women and the weaker sections or minority community.

Fraternity

National integration is an objective which every State aims to achieve. This can be aimed by establishing dignity of the individuals by fostering the spirit of fraternity. In a country with diverse culture, religion, languages, caste and community, to foster the spirit of brotherhood is essential to achieve national unity. To attain this objective, the Preamble was suitably amended in 1976 by the 42nd Constitution Amendment Bill, and the terms unity and integrity were inserted to create a greater sense of fraternity among the people of India. It also aims to ensure dignity of the individual. It seems that fraternity, as incorporated in Article 1 of the Universal Declaration of Human Rights of 1948, which upholds that, "All human beings are born free and equal in dignity and rights. They are endowed with reason and conscience and should act towards one another in a spirit of brotherhood" has been the driving force behind the adoption of the ideal of fraternity by the frames of the Constitution of India.

BASIC STRUCTURE DOCTRINE

The Preamble is the soul of the Indian Constitution. However, whether the Preamble can be amended or not under the provisions provided in Article 368 has been a point of controversy a number of times. In the *Shankari Prasad Case*, (1951) the validity of Constitution (1st Amendment) Act, 1951 which inserted inter alia, Articles 31-A and 31-B of the Constitution relating to Right to Property (saving of laws providing for acquisition of estates, etc.-31A & Validation of certain Acts and Regulations even if they take away or abridge

Fundamental Rights–31B) was challenged. The Amendment was challenged on the ground that it abridges the rights conferred by Part III, (Fundamental Rights) and hence was void. The Supreme Court, however, rejected the above argument, and held that power to amend including the fundamental rights is contained in Article 368. This verdict of the Supreme Court was reaffirmed in the *Sajjan Singh Case* (1965).

However, in the *Golaknath Case* (1967) the validity of 17th Amendment which inserted certain Acts in Ninth Schedule was again challenged. This time the Supreme Court ruled that the Parliament had no power to amend Part III of the Constitution and overruled its earlier decision in *Shankari Prasad* and *Sajjan Singh* cases. In order to remove difficulties created by the decision of Supreme Court in *Golaknath Case*, Parliament enacted the 24th Amendment Act (1971). By this Amendment Act, Articles 13 and 368 were amended and fundamental rights were made amendable under the procedure laid down in Article 368.

The Supreme Court recognized Basic Structure concept for the first time in the historic *Keshavananda Bharati Case* in 1973. In this case, validity of the 24th amendment was challenged. The 24th Amendment Act enlarged the scope of the Parliament by empowering it to make changes in Part III of the Constitution (the Fundamental Rights). The Apex Court, by majority, overruled the verdict of the *Golaknath Case*, which denied the Parliament the power to amend fundamental rights of the citizens. The Supreme Court declared that Article 368 did not enable Parliament to alter the basic structure or framework of the Constitution, and Parliament could not use its amending powers under Article 368 to damage, emasculate, destroy, abrogate, change or alter the basic structure or framework of the Constitution. This decision is not just a landmark in the evolution of Constitutional law, but a turning point in Constitutional history.

Further in the *Minerva Mills Case* (1980) the Supreme Court applying *Keshavananda* principle invalidated the Clauses (4) and (5) of Article 368 inserted by 42nd Amendment as violative of the basic structure of the Constitution. Therefore, as it stands today, the Parliament can amend every part of the Constitution, but cannot change the basic structure of Constitution. (See Chapter 14 for details)

SIGNIFICANCE OF THE PREAMBLE

What follows from the above judgements and views of legal luminaries that Preamble comprises the basic structure of the Indian Constitution. Chief Justice Hidayatullah Stated: "Preamble resembles the Declaration of Independence of the United States of America, but is more than a declaration. It is the soul of our Constitution which lays down the pattern of our political society which it States is Sovereign Democratic Republic. It contains a solemn resolve which nothing but a revolution can alter."

Former Chief Justice of India, P.B. Gajendragadkar observed: "It would, I think, be fairly accurate to say that the basic philosophy of the Constitution of India is to be found, in essence, in the Preamble itself. India is one country, and there is only one citizenship in India. India is committed to the ideal of the welfare State and must establish socio-economic justice. India is committed to democracy and respects individual liberty and India wants to give to all its citizen's equality of status and opportunity, thereby attempting to create a mighty brotherhood of Indian citizens which would assist the Sovereign Democratic Republic of India in reaching it proclaimed objectives. That, in substance, is the message of the Preamble."

Therefore, undoubtedly the Preamble is the cornerstone of the Indian Constitution. Though it is not binding upon the Government of India, but it is not possible either to ignore or to violate the pledges that have been enshrined in the Preamble. It embodies the spirit of the Indian polity which is to ensure justice, liberty, equality and fraternity and unity and integration of the nation, while it also upholds the nature of Indian polity which is Sovereign, Socialist, Secular, and Democratic Republic.

EXERCISES

I. Short Answer Questions: **(100 words)**

1. Write on any two features of the Preamble.
2. What are the objectives of the Indian State according to the Preamble?
3. Briefly State the Basic Structure Doctrine.
4. State briefly the significance of the Preamble.

II. Long Answer Questions: **(1200 words)**

5. Discuss the salient features of the Preamble while bringing out the significance of the Preamble with respect to the features.
6. Do you think that the Preamble embodies the philosophy of the Constitution of India? Argue.
7. Do you think that the Preamble is an integral part of the Constitution of India or just a preface to the Constitution? Argue?
8. Do you think that the Preamble is amendable in the ways prescribed under Article 368? In the light of *Keshavananda Bharati Case* (1973), argue your case for the Basic Structure Doctrine.
9. Discuss the objectives of the Constitution of India as enshrined in the Preamble and bring out their significance?

REFERENCES

Austin, Granville, *The Indian Constitution: Cornerstone of A Nation,* Oxford University Press, Bombay, 1972.

Bakshi, P.M., *The Constitution of India* (with selective comments), Universal Law Publishing, New Delhi, 2000.

Basu, Durga Das, *Introduction to the Constitution of India*, Prentice-Hall of India, New Delhi, 1992.

Golaknath v. *State of Punjab* (1967), 2 SCR 762: AIR 1967 SC

Government of India, *Constitution of India*

Kesavananda Bharati v. *State of Kerala*, AIR 1973 SC 1461

Kohli, Atul, (Ed.), *The Success of India's Democracy*, Cambridge University Press, New Delhi, 2001.

Mahajan, V.D., *Constitutional History of India,* S. Chand & Company, New Delhi, 1976.

Minerva Mills Ltd. v. *Union of India* (1980) 3 SCC 625.

Pylee, M.V., *India's Constitution*, S. Chand & Company, New Delhi, 1994.

Rao, K.V., *Parliamentary Democracy of India: A Critical Commentary*, The World Press, Calcutta, 1961.

Sajjan Singh v. *State of Rajasthan* (1965) 1 SCR 933: AIR 1965 SC 845

Shankari Prasad Singh v. *Union of India*, AIR 1951SC 458

Sikri, S.L., Indian Government and Politics, Kalyani Publishers, Delhi, 2004.

4

Fundamental Rights—Part III of the Indian Constitution

INTRODUCTION

Fundamental rights are integral part of any democratic political set-up. They are required for the overall development of an individual's personality. The Constitution of India also provides us with a number of Fundamental Rights. The Constituent Assembly which began its work on December 1946, created a special Committee under Sardar Patel, to deal with the problems of Fundamental Rights. They faced a stupendous job of identifying which rights would be essential for the people of India. Thus, they made a distinction between Directive Principles of State Policy and Fundamental Rights making the former non-enforceable, and the latter enforceable by the Courts of law. The Fundamental Rights are the 'conscience of the Constitution' and the very 'soul of the Constitution'.

FUNDAMENTAL RIGHTS: THE CHARACTERISTICS

The Constitution of India incorporated the idea of fundamental rights from various declarations and several Constitutions of leading liberal democracies of the world. On one hand, there is the French Declaration of Rights of Man as a Citizen, the Bill of Rights of the U.S. Constitution, the Irish Constitution of 1935, the post-war Constitutions of Japan and Burma, (now Myanmar), and on the other hand there is the Universal Declaration of Human Rights, which have influenced the framers of the Indian Constitution to prepare a list of basic rights for the people of India to ensure fullest development of their personalities. The experience of British colonial atrocities and sufferings under the regime and the diversities present in the Indian society, at large, to a great extent helped to give final shape to Part III of the Indian Constitution. Thus, we find provisions for protection of interests of minorities and scheduled caste and tribes have been included in this chapter.

The Fundamental Rights are universal, i.e., they are applicable to all the citizens of India irrespective of distinction of caste, colour, creed, sex and religion, for example, Articles 15, 16, 19 and Article 30. However, some fundamental rights are applicable to any person living in India, including both citizens and non-citizens like Articles 21, 23, 25, 27, 28, 31 and 32, whereas some fundamental rights like Article 29 applies to citizens only. Therefore, there is a clear distinction between citizens and non-citizens as far as the enjoyment of these rights are concerned.

Article 33, however, empowers the Parliament to modify the rights conferred by this Part shall in their application. It States:

Parliament may, by law, determine to what extent any of the rights conferred by this part shall, in their application to,

(a) the members of the Armed Forces; or
(b) the members of the Forces charged with the maintenance of public order; or
(c) persons employed in any bureau or other organization established by the State for purposes of intelligence or counter intelligence; or
(d) persons employed in, or in connection with, the telecommunication systems set up for the purpose of any force, bureau or organization referred to in clauses (a) to (c), be restricted or abrogated so as to ensure the proper discharge of their duties and the maintenance of discipline among them.

Article 34 puts restrictions on rights mentioned in Part III while martial law is in force in any area. Parliament may by law indemnify any person in the service of the Union or of State or any other person in respect of any act done by him in connection with the maintenance or restoration of order in any area within the Territory of India where martial law was in force or validate any sentence passed, punishment inflicted, forfeiture ordered or other act done under martial law in such area.

Part III and Part IV of the Constitution together provide a comprehensive list of rights available to the citizens of India. Part III refers to Fundamental Rights and Part IV refers to Directive Principles of State Policy. The Directive Principles contain noble ideals, the fulfillment of which would set-up a welfare State. But there is a significant difference between the Part III and Part IV. While Part III is justiciable and legally enforceable, Part IV is non-justiciable rights of the people. Economic rights and even the most basic right to education have not been included as a part of Part III of the Constitution rather they are included in Part IV, hence become non-justifiable. However, Right to Education was made a Fundamental Right by 86th Constitutional Amendment

Act 2002, and was incorporated under Article 21A. Even right to vote is not a Fundamental Right in India though it is contained in Article 326 of the Constitution. Right to Information Act (RTI) (2005) have been acknowledged as an important right under this Act, but has not been acknowledged as a Fundamental Right yet.

The Fundamental Rights can be classified as negative and positive. Some Fundamental Rights impose restrictions on actions of State like Article 14 which embodies that "The State shall not deny to any person equality before the law..." Articles 15(1), 16(2), 18(1), 20, 21, 22(1) and 28(1) can be said to impose similar prohibitions on actions of State. Therefore, they can be said to constitute negative rights. Some Fundamental Rights which constitute the positive aspect of rights and can be said to be directly conferred upon the citizens of India, without even containing any provision relating to the actions of the State, are Articles 19(1), 25, 29(1) and 30(1). The essence of these positive rights is best expressed in the words of former Chief Justice P.B. Gajendragadkar who upheld Fundamental Rights as "a legally enforceable right governing the relations between the State and the individual. It has both a negative and positive aspect. It must, as the words indicate, be fundamental. It does not mean a right of liberty permissible under law; it also means a Right of Liberty in a positive sense which enables an individual to develop his personality and his faculties and to live his life in his own interest and in the interests of the community as a whole."

The Constitution also provides an elaborate machinery to defend the rights in actual practice. Article 32 makes the Supreme Court the ultimate defender/guarantor of Fundamental Rights. Whenever, rights of individuals stand breached that can seek redress from the Supreme Court. It has been given the supreme authority by the Constitution of India to enforce the Fundamental Rights and the Supreme Court can issue writs or any order/directives to enforce the enjoyment of Fundamental Rights. Public Interest Litigations (PIL) and National Human Rights Commission and State Human Rights Commissions have further helped in protecting and securing the Fundamental Rights.

Fundamental rights are binding upon not only the State and agencies of State but also upon individuals/organizations. If untouchability or any sort of discrimination is practiced by any individual then that individual indulging in such practices is punishable under the law of the land. Article 12 gives the definition of State as including not only the executive and legislative organs of the Union and the States but also local bodies and other authorities. Even the act of any individual may become an act of the State if it is enforced or aided by any of the authorities mentioned above.

Certain Fundamental Rights are also available against private individuals like Article 15(2) [equality with regard to access to and use of places of public resort], Article 17 [prohibition of traffic in human beings], Article 18(3)–(4) [prohibition of acceptance of foreign title], Article 23 [prohibition of traffic in human beings] and Article 24 [prohibition of employment of children in hazardous employment].

Right to Property has been deleted from the list of Fundamental Rights by the 44th Constitutional Amendment Act, 1978. This was made a legal right under Article 300A inserted by the same amendment. It says, "No person shall be deprived of his property save by authority of law." The Right to Education at an elementary level has been included as one of the Fundamental Rights under Article 21A by the 86th Constitutional amendment of 2002. The Right to Information was passed in 2005 under which people have access to all information from Government departments and agencies. But this has not been made into a Fundamental Right either.

Fundamental rights are listed in Table 4.1.

Table 4.1 List of fundamental rights

Right to Equality	Equality before law and equal protection of law Prohibition of discrimination on grounds of caste, colour, creed, sex and religion Equal opportunity regarding employment Abolition of untouchability Abolition of titles
Right to Freedom	Freedom of speech and expression, Assembly, movement, residence and settlement and profession Protection in respect of condition for offences Protection of life and liberty Protection against arrest and detention in certain cases
Right against Exploitation	Prohibition of Traffic in Human beings and Forced Labour (beggar) Prohibition of employment of children in hazardous employment
Right to Freedom of Religion	Freedom of conscience and free profession Freedom to manage religious affairs Freedom as to payment of taxes for promotion of any particular religion Freedom as to attendance at religious instructions in certain educational institutions
Cultural and Educational Rights	Protection of language, script or culture of minorities Right of minorities to establish and administer educational institutions
Right to Constitutional Remedies	Remedies for enforcement of fundamental rights—writs of *Habeas Corpus*, *Mandamus*, *Prohibition*, *Certiorari* and *Quo Warranto*
Right to Property	Deleted by the Constitutional Amendment Act, 1978 (44th Amendment)

RIGHT TO EQUALITY (ARTICLE 14–ARTICLE 18)

The Constitution of India provides the Right to Equality to the citizens of India under Articles 14-18. Article 14 embodies: "The State shall not deny any person equality before the law or equal protection of the laws within the territory of India."

The above Article contains both a negative as well as a positive concept of equal rights. The positive aspect include the equal protection of all the citizens under equal circumstances and the negative aspect contained in the expression equality before the law implies the absence of privilege or favour towards any individuals irrespective of his rank or status. This negative concept of equality before law can be said to be derived from Dicey's concept of Rule of Law. Equality before law means, that among equals, the law should be equal, and should be administered and the like should be treated alike.

The Supreme Court of India while interpreting the scope of Article 14 in the *Charanjit Lal Choudhury* v. *The Union of India* (1950) upheld –

1. Equal protection means equal protection under equal circumstances
2. The State can make reasonable classification for purposes of legislation
3. Presumption of reasonableness is in favour of legislation
4. The burden of proof is on those who challenge the legislation

However, certain exceptions exist as far as Article 14 is considered. They are:

1. The President or the Governor of a State shall not be answerable to any court for the exercise and performance of the powers and duties of his office or any act done or to be done by him in the exercise and performance of those powers and duties.
2. No criminal proceeding shall be carried on against the President or a Governor in any court during his term in the office.
3. No civil proceeding in which relief is sought against the President or Governor of a State can be instituted during his term of office in any court in respect of any act done or to be done by him in his personal capacity whether before or after he entered upon his office as President or Governor of such State, until the expiration of two months next after notice in writing has been delivered to the President or the Governor, as the case may be, or left at his office stating the nature of the proceedings, the cause of action therefore, the name, description and place of residence of the party by whom such proceedings are to be instituted, and the relief which he claims (Article 361).

These would however, not prevent from moving impeachment proceedings against the President of India and suits or other appropriate proceedings against the Government of India or Government of a State.

Further, the legislature is entitled to make different treatment if there is a reasonable basis for classification which must be related to the object of legislation. Therefore, the basis of classification may be geographical, according to difference in time or may be based on the difference in the nature of the trade, calling or occupation, which is sought to be regulated by the legislation.

Article 15 ensures that

"(1) The State shall not discriminate against any citizen on grounds only of religion, race, caste, sex, place of birth or any of them.

(2) No citizen shall, on grounds only of religion, race, caste, sex, place of birth or any of them be subjected to any disability, liability, restriction or condition with regard to—

(a) access to shops, public restaurants, hotels, places of public entertainment or

(b) the use of wells, tanks, bathing *ghats*, roads and places of public resort maintained wholly or partly out of State funds or dedicated to the use of the general public

(3) Nothing in this Article shall prevent the State from making any special provision for women and children

(4) Nothing in this Article or in Clause (2) of Article 29 shall prevent the State from making any special provision for the advancement of any socially and educationally backward classes of citizens or for the Scheduled Castes and the Schedules Tribes." (added by the First Amendment Act, 1951)

The Clause (1) of Article 15 is the prohibition against State action and Clause (2) is against actions of individuals. This Article in simple terms means that no citizen of India on grounds of religion, race, caste, sex, place of birth or any of them be subject to any disability, liability, restriction or condition with regard to access to shops, public restaurants, hotels and places of public entertainment or the use of wells, tanks, bathing *ghats*, roads and places of public resort maintained wholly or partly out of State funds or dedicated to the use of the general public. As this Article is also applicable against actions of individuals it can be mentioned that Article 17 abolishing untouchability and other social discriminatory practices has been an advancement of the provision articulated in Article 15. However, there are two exceptions to the application of Article 15. The State can make special provisions for women and children as well as make special arrangements for the advancement of any socially and educationally backward classes of citizens or for the Scheduled Castes and the Scheduled Tribes.

Article 16 States that

"(1) There shall be equality of opportunity for all citizens in matters relating to employment or appointment to any office under the State.

(2) No citizen shall, on grounds only of religion, race, caste, sex, descent, place of birth or any of them, be ineligible for any office under the State."

The exceptions are given in the following clauses of Article 16. They are:

1. Residence within the State may be laid down by Parliament as a condition for particular classes of employment or appointment under any State or other local authority. [Article 16(3)]
2. The State may reserve any post or appointment in favour of any backward class of citizens who, in the opinion of the State, are not adequately represented in the services under that State. [Article 16(4)]
3. Offices connected with a religious or denominated institution may be reserved for members professing the particular denomination to which the institution relates [Article 16(5)].
4. The claims of the members of the Schedules Castes and Schedule Tribes shall be taken into consideration in the matter of appointment to services and posts under the Union and the States, as far as may be consistent with the maintenance of efficiency of the administration. [Article 335].

However, for the upliftment of the backward classes, in 1979, the Morarji Desai Government appointed the Mandal Commission with a mandate to "identify the socially or educationally backward". It was headed by Bindheshwari Prasad Mandal, and it was supposed to consider the question of seat reservations and quotas for people to redress caste discrimination, and use eleven social, economic, and educational indicators to determine backwardness. All the recommendations of the Report are not yet implemented. The recommendation of reservations for other backward classes (OBCs) in Government services was implemented in 1993. A decade after the Commission gave its Report, the then Prime Minister V.P. Singh, tried to implement its recommendations in 1989. It was followed by massive students' protests in colleges across the country against job reservations for backward castes in India followed by several self-immolations. However, in 1993, in the *Indra Sawhney* v. *Union of India*, the Supreme Court scrutinized the Article 16 and Clause 4, in particular, and made certain observations. Some notable observations were that it said that Article 16(4) is not an exception to Article 16(1) and it is an instance of classification inherent in Article 16(1). Article 16(4) is exhaustive of the subject of reservation in favour of backward classes though it may not be exhaustive of the very concept of reservation. It further said that the expression backward class in 16(4) takes in other backward classes as well and there is no Constitutional bar to the classification of backward classes and more backward classes for the purpose of Article 16(4).

Article 17 upholds that "Untouchability is abolished and its practice in any form is forbidden. The enforcement of any disability arising out of untouchability shall be an offence punishable in accordance with law."

This particular Article has to be read along with Article 35 which confers upon the Parliament the power to make laws for prescribing punishments for the perpetration of those offences as mentioned in Part III of the Constitution. Acting under this provision the Parliament enacted the Untouchability (Offences) Act, 1955 which has been amended and renamed in 1977 as the Protection of Civil Rights Act, 1955.

The Act declares punishments for those offences when they are done on the ground of untouchability. The following have been declared as offences under this Act:

1. Refusing admission to any person to public institutions, such as hospital, dispensary, educational institutions;
2. Preventing any person from worshipping or offering prayers in any place or public worship;
3. Subjecting any person to any disability with regard to access to any shop, public restaurant, hotel or public entertainment or with regard to the use of any reservoir, tap or other source of water, road, cremation ground or any other place where services are rendered to the public.

The scope of the Act was widened in 1976 following an amendment, practising which was considered as a serious offence. The amendments are as follows:

1. *Insulting* a member of a scheduled caste on the ground of untouchability
2. *Preaching* untouchability, directly or indirectly
3. *Justifying* untouchability on historical, philosophical or religious grounds or on the grounds of tradition of the caste system.

Further, a new provision that was included in this Act by the 1976 amendment was that any person convicted of untouchability offence would be disqualified for contesting elections.

Article 18 of the Indian Constitution abolishes the use of any sort of titles which once was very much linked to the British colonial rule and was abused most often. The Article reads as follows:

1. No title, not being a military or academic distinction, shall be conferred by the State.
2. No citizen of India shall accept any title from any foreign State.
3. No person who is not a citizen of India shall, while he holds any office of profit or trust under the State, accept without the consent of the President any title from any foreign State.
4. No person holding any office of profit or trust under the State shall, without the consent of the president, accept any present, emolument, or office of any kind from or under any foreign State."

The Constitution in order to prevent the creation of any sort of artificial distinctions in the society, seeks to prevent such abuse of titles by prohibiting the State from conferring any title at all. However, Universities or any other public institutions can confer titles or honours by way of honouring persons of merit or public leaders. The State is also not debarred from conferring military or academic distinctions which should however, may be used as titles. The State can also confer awards/distinctions for excellence in social, cultural, public service or exceptional services towards advancement of art, literature and science like Bharat Ratna, Padma Vibhushan, Padma Bhushan and Padma Shri, which cannot be used by the recipient as a title. Under Article 18, any Indian citizen is forbidden to accept titles from foreign States without the consent of the President of India. Article 18 can be said to have followed the essence of the Constitution of United States, 1787, which prohibited all titles of nobility in the United States conferred by the British monarchs.

RIGHT TO FREEDOM (INCLUDING RIGHT TO EDUCATION)

The right to freedom is one of the most important fundamental rights which constitute the very essence of liberty. This fundamental right is described in the Constitution under Article 19 as:

1. All citizens shall have the right:
   - **(a) To freedom of speech and expression;**
   - **(b) To assemble peaceably and without arms;**
   - **(c) To form associations or unions;**[1]
   - **(d) To move freely throughout the territory of India;**
   - **(e) To reside and settle in any part of the territory of India;**
     [Sub-clause (f) omitted by the Constitution Forty-fourth Amendment Act, 1978 which was related to the freedom of acquiring, holding and disposing of property.]
   - **(g) To practice any profession, or to carry on any occupation, trade or business.**
2. Nothing in sub-clause (a) of Clause (1) shall affect the operation of any existing law, or prevent the State from making any law, in so far as such law imposes reasonable restrictions on the exercise of the right conferred by the said sub-clause in the interests of the sovereignty and integrity of India, the security of the State, friendly relations with foreign States, public order, decency or morality, or in relation to contempt of court, defamation or incitement to an offence.
3. Nothing in sub-clause (b) of the said Clause shall affect the operation of any existing law in so far as it imposes, or prevent the State from making any law imposing, in the interests of the sovereignty and

[1] The 97th Amendment Act, 2012, added the words "or co-operative societies" after the word "or unions" in Article 19 (l)(c)

integrity of India or public order, reasonable restrictions on the exercise of the right conferred by the said sub-clause.

4. Nothing in sub-clause (c) of the said clause shall affect the operation of any existing law in so far as it imposes, or prevent the State from making any law imposing, in the interests of the sovereignty and integrity of India or public order or morality, reasonable restrictions on the exercise of the right conferred by the said sub-clause.
5. Nothing in sub-clauses (d)–(e) of the said clause shall affect the operation of any existing law in so far as it imposes, or prevent the State from making any law imposing, reasonable restrictions on the exercise of any of the rights conferred by the said sub-clauses either in the interests of the general public or for the protection of the interests of any scheduled tribe.
6. Nothing in sub-clause (g) of the said clause shall affect the operation of any existing law in so far as it imposes, or prevent the State from making any law imposing, in the interests of the general public, reasonable restrictions on the exercise of the right conferred by the said sub-clause, and, in particular, nothing in the said sub-clause shall affect the operation of any existing law in so far as it relates to, or prevent the State from making any law relating to-
   (i) the professional or technical qualifications necessary for practising any profession or carrying on any occupation, trade or business, or
   (ii) the carrying on by the State, or by a corporation owned or controlled by the State, of any trade, business, industry or service, whether to the exclusion, complete or partial, of citizens or otherwise.

No freedom can be unlimited. Therefore, to strike a balance between individual liberty and public order reasonable restrictions have been imposed under Article 19 in the Sub-clauses (2) to (6). In *Gopalan* v. *State of Madras*, the Supreme Court upheld that "there cannot be any such thing as absolute or uncontrolled liberty wholly freed from restraint for that would lead to anarchy and disorder. The possession and enjoyment of all rights ... are subject to be essential to such reasonable conditions as may be deemed to the governing authority of the country to be essential to the safety, health, peace, general order and morals of the community."

The Constitution of India however, does not specifically mention the freedom of press. *Express Newspaper* v. *Union of India* stated that freedom of the Press is included in the wider freedom of expression guaranteed by Article 19(a). The Preamble of the Indian Constitution ensures to all its citizens the liberty which includes freedom of expression too. Freedom of the press has been included as part of freedom of speech and expression under the Article 19 of the UDHR which says: "Everyone has the right to freedom of opinion and expression, this right includes freedom to hold opinions without interference and to seek, receive and impart information and ideas through any media and regardless of frontiers."

In *Romesh Thapar* v. *State of Madras*, the Supreme Court observed, "Freedom of speech and of the press lay at the foundation of all democratic organizations, for without free political discussion no public education, so essential for the proper functioning of the process of popular government, is possible" and also laid down that freedom of speech and expression included the propagation of ideas and that was possible only if freedom of circulation was guaranteed.

The Supreme Court observed in *Union of India* v. *As & Soacnioatthieorn for Democratic Reforms*, 2002 "One sided information, disinformation, misinformation and non information, all equally create an uninformed citizenry which makes democracy a farce. Freedom of speech and expression includes right to impart and receive information which includes freedom to hold opinions".

In *Indian Express* v. *Union of India*, 1986 it has been held that the press plays a very significant role in the democratic machinery. The courts have duty to uphold the freedom of press and invalidate all laws and administrative actions that abridge that freedom. Freedom of press has three essential elements. They are:

1. freedom of access to all sources of information,
2. freedom of publication, and
3. freedom of circulation.

In India, the press has not been able to exercise its freedom to express the popular views. In *Sakal Papers Ltd.* v. *Union of India*, 1962, The Daily Newspapers (Price and Page) Order, 1960, which fixed the number of pages and size which a newspaper could publish at a price was held to be violation of freedom of press and not a reasonable restriction under the Article 19(2). Similarly, in *Bennett Coleman and Co.* v. *Union of India*, 1973; the validity of the Newsprint Control Order, which fixed the maximum number of pages, was struck down by the court holding it to be violation of provision of Article 19 (1)(a) and not to be reasonable restriction under Article 19(2). The court struck down the plea of the government that it would help small newspapers to grow.

In *Romesh Thapar* v. *State of Madras* 1950, entry and circulation of the English journal *Cross Road*, printed and published in Bombay, was banned by the government of Madras. The same was held to be the violation of the freedom of speech and expression, as "without liberty of circulation, publication would be of little value". In *Prabha Dutt* v. *Union of India,* 1982, the Supreme Court directed the superintendent of Tihar jail to allow representatives of a few newspapers to interview Ranga and Billa, the death sentence convicts, as they wanted to be interviewed.

There are instances when the freedom of press has been suppressed by the legislature. The authority of the Government, in such circumstances, has been under the scanner of judiciary. In the case of *Brij Bhushan* v. *State of Delhi,* 1950, the validity of censorship previous to the publication of an English weekly of Delhi, the organizer was questioned. The court struck down the Section 7(1)(c) of the East Punjab Safety Act, 1949, which directed the editor and publisher of a newspaper "to submit for scrutiny, in duplicate, before the publication, till the further orders, all communal matters, all the matters and news and views about Pakistan, including photographs, and cartoons", on the grounds that it was a restriction on the liberty of the press. Similarly, prohibiting newspaper from publishing its own views or views of correspondents about a topic has been held to be a serious encroachment on the freedom of speech and expression.

Issue of calling of *bandhs*, came up in the case of *Communist Party of India (M)* v. *Bharat Kumar*, 1998, when the Supreme Court upheld that *bandhs* do not fall within the fundamental right of speech. A *bandh* is a warning to a citizen that if he goes for work or opens shop he would be prevented. Even if the legislature does not prohibit them, courts could intervene to protect the right to work or right to study. There cannot be any right to call or enforce *bandhs* which conflicts, with the exercise of the Fundamental Rights of other citizens, in addition to causing national loss in many ways. Therefore, the Supreme Court declared that calling for a *bandh* and enforcing of that call by it, is illegal and unconstitutional, and directed the officials of the State including the law enforcement agencies to do all that is necessary to give effect to this declaration.

The freedoms guaranteed by Article 19 are further sought to be protected by Articles 20–22. Article 20 provides protection from conviction for offences in certain respects, including the rights against ex post facto laws, double jeopardy and freedom from self-incrimination. Article 20 upholds:

1. No person shall be convicted of any offence except for violation of the law in force at the time of the Commission of the act charged as an offence, nor be subjected to a penalty greater than that which might have been inflicted under the law in force at the time of the Commission of the offence.
2. No person shall be prosecuted and punished for the same offence more than once.
3. No person accused of any offence shall be compelled to be a witness against himself.

Article 21 provides for protection of life and personal liberty. It says, "No person shall be deprived of his life or personal liberty except according to procedure established by law." The scope of these Articles, particularly with respect to the doctrine of due process, was heavily debated by the Constituent Assembly. The Constituent Assembly in 1948 omitted the phrase "due process" in favour of "procedure established by law". As a result, Article 21, which prevents the encroachment of life or personal liberty by the State except in accordance with the procedure established by law was, until 1978, construed narrowly as being restricted to executive action. However, in 1978, the Supreme Court in the case of *Maneka Gandhi* v. *Union of India*, 1978, extended the protection of Article 21 to legislative action, holding that any law laying down a procedure must be just, fair and reasonable, and effectively reading due process into Article 21. In the same case, the Supreme Court also ruled that "life" under Article 21, meant more than a mere "animal existence"; it would include the right to live with human dignity and all other aspects which made life "meaningful, complete and worth living". Subsequent judicial interpretation has broadened the scope of Article 21 to include within it a number of rights including those to livelihood, clean environment, good health, speedy trial and humanitarian treatment while imprisoned. **The Right to Education at elementary level has been made one of the fundamental rights under Article 21A by the 86th Constitutional amendment of 2002.** The newly inserted Article 21A reads, **"The State shall provide free and compulsory education to all children of the age of six to fourteen years in such manner as the State may, by law, determine." Right to Information Act, 2005,** provide for setting out the practical regime of right to information for citizens to secure access to information under the control of public authorities, in order to promote transparency and accountability in the working of every public authority, the Constitution of a Central Information Commission and State Information Commissions and for matters connected therewith or incidental thereto.

Article 22 provides specific rights to arrested and detained persons, in particular

1. the rights to be informed of the grounds of arrest,
2. consult a lawyer of one's own choice,
3. be produced before a magistrate within 24 hours of the arrest, and the freedom not to be detained beyond that period without an order of the magistrate.

The above safeguards are not available to (a) an enemy alien; (b) a person arrested or detained under a law providing for preventive detention. The Constitution also authorizes the State to make laws providing for preventive detention, subject to certain other safeguards present in Article 22. The provisions pertaining to preventive detention were discussed with skepticism and misgivings by the Constituent Assembly, and were reluctantly approved after a few amendments in 1949. Article 22 provides that when a person is detained under any law of preventive detention:

(a) the State can detain such person without trial for only three months, and
(b) any detention for a longer period must be authorized by an advisory board.

(c) the person being detained also has the right to be informed about the grounds of detention, and be permitted to make a representation against it, at the earliest opportunity.

Preventive Detention Act was passed by the Parliament in 1950. When this expired in 1969, it was replaced by Maintenance of Internal Security Act (MISA) in 1971, Conservation of Foreign Exchange and Prevention of Smuggling Activities Act (COFEPOSA) in 1974, the National Security Act (NSA) 1980 and The Prevention of Black Marketing and Maintenance of Supplies of Essential Commodities Act (ESMA), 1980. All these laws allow for preventive detention. Though MISA was subsequently repealed, the other laws continue to remain in existence along with State legislations of a similar nature and anti-terrorism laws that also provide for similar provisions.

The very first case that came up before the Indian judiciary subsequent to enacting the Indian Constitution was that in the *Gopalan* v. *State of Madras case*, 1950 in the Supreme Court in which the preventive detention law was challenged. The Court observed that the law of preventive detention could not be challenged on the ground that fundamental freedoms guaranteed under Article 19 of the Indian Constitution had been violated. This ruling was subsequently overturned in *Maneka Gandhi's Case* (1978). On the issue of preventive detention, some of the principles laid down by the courts are as follows:

- The power of preventive detention is a "necessary evil", and is tolerated in a free society in the larger interest of security of the State and maintenance of public order.
- A distinction exists between preventive and punitive detention as the former is a precautionary measure to prevent the person from doing.
- Preventive detention is a serious invasion of personal liberty and the safeguards in the Constitution must be zealously watched and enforced by the court.
- Law of preventive detention must pass the test of reasonable and fair procedure established by law for deprivation of personal liberty; such scrutiny would be done by the judiciary,
- Any unreasonable or unexplained delay in furnishing to the detained person the grounds of detention, with the basic documents, or in considering the person's representation, would vitiate the detention and entitle the detained person to be released.

Examples of State legislations providing for preventive detention are the Maharashtra Prevention of Dangerous Activities of Slum Lords, Bootleggers and Drug Offenders Act, 1981; Maharashtra Control of Organized Crimes Act (MCOCA) 1999; Gujarat Prevention of Anti-Social Activities Act, 1985; and A.P. Prevention of Dangerous Activities of Bootleggers, Dacoits, Drug Offenders, Goondas, Immoral Traffic Offenders and Land Grabbers

Act, 1986. Since the 1980s, certain laws were enacted to address the threats arising from terrorism/terrorist activities, but have raised criticisms from many quarters especially from human rights activists. These include the Terrorist and Disruptive Activities (Prevention) Act (TADA) 1987, the Prevention of Terrorism Act (POTA) 2002 and the amendments to Unlawful Activities (Prevention) Act (UAPA) in 2004 and 2008.

RIGHT AGAINST EXPLOITATION (ARTICLES 23–24)

Articles 23 and 24 are designed to prevent the exploitation of weaker sections of the society, and they guarantee rights of individuals against exploitation. Article 23 upholds:

1. Traffic in human beings and beggar and other forms of forced labour are prohibited, and any contravention of this provision shall be an offence punishable in accordance with law.
2. Nothing in this article shall prevent the State from imposing compulsory service for public purposes, and in imposing such service the State shall not make any discrimination on grounds only of religion, race, caste or class or any of them.

These provisions are almost similar to the 13th Amendment of the American Constitution by virtue of which slavery or involuntary servitude was abolished. Our Constitution, to make the ambit of Article 23 wider, has used the term 'traffic in human beings' rather than 'slavery' so that it not only prohibits slavery, but also any sort of traffic in women or children or the crippled for immoral or other purposes.

Article 24 contains provisions banning employment of children in factories and hazardous jobs. It States, **"No child below the age of fourteen years, shall be employed to work in any factory or mine or engaged in any other hazardous employment."** This Article can be said to be related to the Directive Principle of State Policy (before Right to education became a fundamental right) which calls upon the State to ensure universal compulsory and free primary education for all children upto the age of 14.

RIGHT TO RELIGION (ARTICLES 25–28)

The Preamble to the Constitution of India contains lofty ideals which declare India to be a secular State. Thus, there is neither a 'State religion' in India nor the Indian State endeavours to establish a religion of its own and patronizing any particular religion. Articles 25–28 further, endorses the religious neutrality and impartiality of the Indian State and also guarantees the rights of religious minorities.

Article 25 enshrines the freedom of conscience and free profession, practice and propagation of religion. It states that:

"(1) Subject to public order, morality and health and to the other provisions of this Part, all persons are equally entitled to freedom of conscience and the right freely to profess, practice and propagate religion.

(2) Nothing in this article shall affect the operation of any existing law or prevent the State from making any law—

(a) regulating or restricting any economic, financial, political or other secular activity which may be associated with religious practice;

(b) providing for social welfare and reform or the throwing open of Hindu religious institutions of a public character to all classes and sections of Hindus."

However, it must be remembered that though Article 25(1) gives the right to propagate and spread the tenets of one's religion, but it does not give the right to convert another individual. The wearing and carrying of *kripans* were to be deemed as part of the profession of the Sikh religion and the sub-clause (b) of (2) refers to Hindus which must include a reference to persons professing the Sikh, Jain or Buddhist religion, and the Hindu religious institutions must be construed accordingly. As far as restrictions are concerned in the *Acharya Jagadiswarananda Avadhuta* v. *Police Commissioner, Calcutta*, 1984 case or the Anand Margi, case the *tandav dance* with lethal weapons and human skulls were held not essential religious practice, and banning of the procession in public interest and public order and morality was considered to be a reasonable restriction by the Supreme Court.

Article 26 confers upon the religious groups the freedom to manage religious affairs. It reads as—"Subject to public order, morality and health, every religious denomination or any section thereof shall have the right—

1. to establish and maintain institutions for religious and charitable purposes;
2. to manage its own affairs in matters of religion;
3. to own and acquire movable and immovable property; and
4. to administer such property in accordance with law.

Article 27 relates to the freedom as to payment of taxes for promotion of any particular religion. It states "No person shall be compelled to pay any taxes, the proceeds of which are specifically appropriated in payment of expenses for the promotion or maintenance of any particular religion or religious denominations."

Article 28 refers to the freedom as to attendance at religious worship in certain educational institutions. It upholds

"(1) No religious instruction shall be provided in any educational institution wholly maintained out of State funds.

(2) Nothing in Clause (1) shall apply to educational institution which is administered by the State but has been established under any endowment or trust which requires that religious instruction shall be imparted in such institutions.

(3) No person attending any educational institution recognized by the State or receiving aid out of State funds shall be required to take part in any religious instruction that may be imparted in such institution or to attend any religious worship that may be conducted in such institution or in any premises attached thereto unless such person or if such person is a minor, his guardian has given his consent thereto."

Along with these provisions relating to freedom of religion there are also some general provision mentioned earlier under Articles 15 and 16 which read as follows:

Article 15(1) "the State shall not discriminate against any citizen on grounds only of religion, race, caste, sex, place of birth or any of them."

Article 15(2) "No Citizen shall on grounds only of religion, race, caste, sex, place of birth or any of them be subject to any disability, liability, restriction or condition with regard to–

(1) access to shops, public restaurants, hotels, places of public entertainment or

(2) the use of wells, tanks, bathing *ghats*, roads and places of public resort maintained wholly or partly out of State funds or dedicated to the use of the general public."

Article 16(2) "No citizen shall, on grounds only of religion, race, caste, sex, descent, place of birth or any of them, be ineligible for any office under the State."

Admission into any cducational institution maintained or aided by the State [Article 29(2)] and obviously the right to vote under Article 325 are some of the general provisions provided by the Constitution which also guarantees freedom of religion.

CULTURAL AND EDUCATIONAL RIGHTS (ARTICLES 29–30)

The Constitution of India guarantees cultural and educational rights to the citizens of India which are so very important for the preservation of one's own distinct language, script or culture. Article 29 underlines the protection of interests of the minorities. It states:

"(1) Any section of the citizens residing in the territory of India or any part thereof having a distinct language, script or culture of its own shall have the right to conserve the same.

(2) No citizen shall be denied admission into any educational institution maintained by the State or receiving aid out of State funds on grounds only of religion, race, caste, language or any of them."

Article 30 gives the rights to the minorities to establish and administer educational institutions. It underlines: [1] "All minorities, whether based on religion or language, shall have the right to establish and administer educational institutions of their choice.

[(1A) In making any law providing for the compulsory acquisition of any property of an educational institution established and administered by a minority, referred to in clause (1), the State shall ensure that the amount fixed by or determined under such law for the acquisition of such property is such as would not restrict or abrogate the right guaranteed under that clause.] (Inserted by the 44th Amendment Act, 1978)

(2) The State shall not, in granting aid to educational institutions, discriminate against any educational institutions on the ground that it is under the management of a minority, whether based on religion or language."

Several cases have come before the Supreme Court as well as State High Courts where the litigants felt that their rights under Article 29(2) were encroached upon. Remarkable among them were the *State of Madras* v. *Champakam Doaraijan Case* (1951) and *State of Bombay* v. *Bombay Education Society* (1954). In the former case, there was an appeal against a Communal G.O, which gave guidelines for filling up of seats in the medical as well as in the engineering colleges. The Supreme Court held that if a person has the required academic qualifications, but is refused admission into any such institutions on the grounds of religion, race, caste, language or any of them, then there is a clear breach of his fundamental right. In the later case, there was an appeal from the Bombay Education Society to the High Court of Bombay to issue a writ of *mandamus* restraining the State of Bombay from enforcing a circular which forbade any non-Anglo-Indian students from receiving education/admission in a school/class where English was used as a medium of instruction. The High Court issued the order, and the Supreme Court, where an appeal was made by the State of Bombay, upheld that under the Articles 29(1) and 30(1) the minority community like the Anglo-Indian community has the right to conserve its own language and script and the right to establish its own educational institutions and impart instruction in its own language to the children of its own community and the State by its police power cannot determine the medium of instruction in contravention to these fundamental rights. As regards Article 29(2) it must be read subject to Article 15(4) discussed above and as inserted by the First Amendment Act of 1951 permitting special provisions for backward classes which can be said to have overridden the judgment of in the *State of Madras* v. *Champakam Doaraijan Case* (1951).

RIGHT TO CONSTITUTIONAL REMEDIES (ARTICLE 32)

Rights without guarantees against infringement become meaningless. Therefore, the most conspicuous of all the fundamental rights conferred upon by the Constitution of India, without which the rights would just become mere embodiments of lofty ideals, is the right to Constitutional remedies. Remedies for enforcement of rights conferred by this part contains that

"1. The right to move the Supreme Court by appropriate proceedings for the enforcement of the rights conferred by this part is guaranteed.
2. The Supreme Court shall have the power to issue directions or orders or writs, including writs in the nature of *habeas corpus, mandamus, prohibition, quo warranto* and *certiorari*, whichever may be appropriate, for the enforcement of any of the rights conferred by this part
3. Without prejudice to the powers conferred on the Supreme Court by Clauses (1) and (2), Parliament may by law empower any other court to exercise within the local limits of its jurisdiction all or any of the powers exercisable by the Supreme Court under Clause (2).
4. The right guaranteed by this article shall not be suspended except as otherwise provided for by this Constitution."

Therefore, the Supreme Court has been made the guarantor and protector of fundamental rights. The power to issue writs for the enforcement of fundamental rights has been given by the Constitution to the Supreme Court and also to the High Courts. (Articles 32 and 226). Supreme Court, however, can issue writs under Article 32 only for the enforcement of the fundamental rights, whereas the High Courts acting under Article 226 can issue writs for enforcing fundamental rights as well as for redress of any injury or illegality arising out of violation of ordinary law. The right guaranteed by Article 32 shall not be suspended except during a Proclamation of Emergency in the manner laid down by the Constitution (Article 359).

Habeas Corpus

This is a Latin term meaning 'to have a body' or 'you may have the body'. Originally it is a concept under the law of England, and has been formalized in the *Habeas Corpus Act,* 1679. In India also the court secures the body of a person who has been detained/imprisoned to be brought before itself and secure release from confinement if that ground of detention is found to be unlawful. The writ can be issued by the Supreme Court and the High Courts. The writ of *habeas corpus* is in a form of direction to person given by the court to order him to bring the body of the person in his custody as a specified time to a specified place for a specified purpose. As under Article 21, "No person shall be deprived of his life and personal liberty except according to procedure established by law," but when the executive or its agencies unlawfully detains or arrests any person or the arrest contravenes the procedure established by law under which the arrests has been made, the Supreme Court and the High Courts may issue a writ of *habeas corpus* against the authority who has detained an individual unlawfully.

Mandamus

In Latin, *Mandamus* means 'we order'. It is an order of the Supreme Court and High Court commanding a person to perform some public or quasi-public duty which he has refused to do and there is no alternative legal remedy is available for its enforcement. The High Court may refuse to issue a writ of *Mandamus* if there is an alternative remedy available for redress of injury. A writ of *Mandamus* can be issued not only against officers or persons engaged in public duty, but also against the government itself (Articles 226 & 361).

Apart from enforcement of fundamental rights a writ of *Mandamus* can be issued by High Courts for the purposes of enforcement of the performance of a statutory duty of a public officer conferred upon him by a statute or Constitution, to compel a Court or Judicial Tribunal to exercise its jurisdiction which it has failed to do and to direct a public official or the Government not to enforce any law that may be unconstitutional.

Prohibition

Prohibition is a writ issued by the Supreme Court to restrain the lower/inferior courts from usurping jurisdiction or overstepping their jurisdiction in any proceedings before it. The writ of *Prohibition* is different from the writ of *Mandamus* for it demands inaction, whereas in case of the latter it commands action on the part of the public authority. Further, a writ of *Mandamus* is applicable against both judicial and administrative authorities, but a writ of *Prohibition* is applicable only against body exercising public functions of a judicial or quasi-judicial nature.

Certiorari

It is kind of prerogative writ which orders the removal of a suit from an inferior court to a higher court. A writ to *Certiorari* and *Prohibition* are sought together so that the inferior court or tribunal operates within its jurisdiction and does not usurp jurisdiction. Like *Prohibition,* a writ of *Certiorari* is opposite that of *Mandamus* which directs a judicial or administrative body to perform its duty and a writ of *Certiorari* is issued against only judicial or quasi-judicial authorities. By a writ of *Certiorari* a decision of an inferior court or tribunal is quashed when there is an error of law, or the subject matter is beyond the jurisdiction of the body or it assumes jurisdiction on the basis of a wrong decision or the inferior court or tribunal has violated the principles of natural justice. In these cases the High Court can issue a writ of *Certiorari* and quash a decision of the inferior court or tribunal and the Supreme Court can issue this writ of *Certiorari* if some fundamental rights have been infringed upon in such cases.

Quo Warranto

By a writ of *Quo Warranto*, a High Court or the Supreme Court may prevent a person from usurping a public office which he is not entitled to and may oust that person from it enjoyment and declare the office to be vacant. But a writ of *Quo Warranto* can only be issued when there is an usurpation of an office of public nature and an office which is substantive in nature, and there has been a contravention of the Constitution or a statute or statutory instrument in appointing that person to that particular office. This is a discretionary remedy and may be refused by the Court on the basis of evidences.

Article 32A (repealed by 43rd Amendment Act, 1977), inserted by the 42nd Amendment Act, 1976 States that the Constitutional validity of State laws are not to be considered in proceedings of the court under Article 32. Further Article 33 confers upon the Parliament the power to modify the rights provided by Part III in their application. Parliament by law can determine the extent to which these rights are applicable to members of armed forces, members of forces charged with the maintenance of public order, persons employed in any bureau or other organization established by the State for purposes of intelligence or counter intelligence and persons employed on or in connection with the telecommunication system set up for the purposes of any Force, bureau organization as mentioned above be restricted or abrogated so as to ensure the proper discharge of their duties and the maintenance of discipline among them. Further, Article 34 empowers that when martial law is enforced in any area, the Parliament to indemnify any person in the service of the Union or State for any act done by him in connection with the maintenance or restoration of order in such area or validate any sentence passed, punishment inflicted, forfeiture ordered or other act done under martial law in such area.

From the foregoing discussion therefore, it becomes evident that Part III of the Constitution is vital for the existence and personal development of each and every individual in India. Though these are sure limits on State encroachment on the rights of individuals, but their enjoyment is always with certain restrictions.

SUSPENSION OF FUNDAMENTAL RIGHTS

The fundamental rights may be regarded as the 'conscience of the Constitution', but they are not absolute and their enjoyment is subjected to certain restrictions. The State can impose by law reasonable restrictions on the exercise of any rights in the interests of the sovereignty and integrity of India, the security of the State, friendly relations with foreign States, public order, decency or morality, or in relation to contempt of court, defamation or incitement to an offence. The fundamental rights will also remain suspended with the proclamation of emergency made by the President under Article 352 (General Emergency). Even during normal times, several restrictions have been imposed upon the enjoyment of these basic rights like the Preventive Detention Act as mentioned under Article 22 in the form of MISA, NSA, ESMA, COFEPOSA, POTA, TADA and other restrictions of these genres. There can be easy misuse of these restrictions which may be equivalent to serious invasion of personal liberty and repugnant to democratic Constitutions.

AMENDMENT OF FUNDAMENTAL RIGHTS

The Fundamental Rights provided in the Indian Constitution are a guarantee against actions of State as well as individuals who might hinder the life and liberty of any citizen of India. However, a major debate that exists is that whether the fundamental rights are immune from Constitutional amendments or not as provided under Article 368 relating to the procedure of amendment of the Indian Constitution. Till the *Golaknath* v. *State of Punjab Case* (1967) came into limelight, the view that was commonly upheld was that no part of the Constitution was immune from amendment and the Parliament by passing a Constitutional Amendment Act as provided in Article 368 can amend any part of the India Constitution including the fundamental rights contained in Part III of the Constitution and Article 368 itself. In the *Golaknath Case* (1967) the Supreme Court upheld that the fundamental rights contained in Part III of the Constitution "had been given a transcendental position by the Constitution, so that no authority functioning under the Constitution, including the Parliament exercising the amending power under Article 368, was competent to amend fundamental rights." In order to remove difficulties created by the decision of Supreme Court in *Golaknath Case*, Parliament enacted the 24th Amendment Act (1971). By this Amendment Act, Articles 13 and 368 were amended, and fundamental rights were made amendable under the procedure laid down in Article 368.

However, this was overruled in the *Keshavananda Bharati Case* (1973). In the *Keshavananda* v. *State of Kerala*, 1973, the judgment upheld that the basic features are not amendable at all, though, curiously, fundamental rights are not included in the list of basic features as formulated by the majority and expressed in the Preamble. Next, the 42nd Amendment Act, 1976, inserted Clauses (4) and (5) in Article 368 which proclaimed that "no amendment of the Constitution (including the provisions of Part III, i.e., the fundamental rights) shall be called in question in the court on any ground." In the *Minerva Mill* v. *Union of India* (1980), the Supreme Court applying Keshavananda principle invalidated the Clauses (4) and (5) of Article 368 as violation of the basic features of the Constitution. Therefore, the Keshavananda judgment has been restored.

FUNDAMENTAL DUTIES OF CITIZENS OF INDIA

The Fundamental duties of citizens were added to the Constitution under Article 51A by the 42nd Amendment Act of 1976. Originally, they were ten in number, but later the duties were increased to eleven by the 86th Amendment in 2002, which added a duty on every parent or guardian to ensure that their child or ward aged between six years and fourteen years was provided with the opportunities for education. However, like the Directive Principles, these are non-justifiable, and thus, without any legal sanction in case of their violation or non-compliance. As India upholds the Universal Declaration of Human Rights and International Covenant on Civil and Political Rights, where there is some reference to such duties it can be said that Article 51A tries to strike a balance with these international treaties.

The following are the Fundamental duties prescribed by the Constitution of the nation under Part [IV-A] to its every citizen:

1. to abide by the Constitution and respect its ideals and institutions, the National Flag and the National Anthem
2. to cherish and follow the noble ideals which inspired our national struggle for freedom
3. to uphold and protect the sovereignty, unity and integrity of India
4. to defend the country and render national service when called upon to do so
5. to promote harmony and the spirit of common brotherhood amongst all the people of India transcending religious, linguistic and regional or sectional diversities; to renounce practices derogatory to the dignity of women
6. to value and preserve the rich heritage of our composite culture
7. to protect and improve the natural environment including forests, lakes, rivers and wild life, and to have compassion for living creatures
8. to develop the scientific temper, humanism and the spirit of inquiry and reform
9. to safeguard public property and to abjure violence
10. to strive towards excellence in all spheres of individual and collective activity so that the nation constantly rises to higher levels of endeavour and achievement

The 86th Constitutional amendment added the 11th fundamental duty in 2002, which States that every citizen "who is a parent or guardian, to provide opportunities for education to his child or, as the case may be, ward between the age of six and fourteen years".

EXERCISES

I. Short Answer Questions: **(100 words)**

1. The characteristics/features of the fundamental rights in India.
2. Right to Equality under Article 14
3. The limitations on the enjoyment of Right to Freedom under Article 19
4. The provisions of writ petition under Article 32.
5. The Constitutional provisions on Right against Exploitation.
6. Cultural and Educational Rights as guaranteed under the India Constitution.

7. Right to Education under Article 21A.
8. Conditions for suspension of fundamental rights.
9. Fundamental duties of the citizens of India.

II. Long Answer Questions: **(1200 words)**

10. Discuss the provisions related to the Right to Equality as provided by the Constitution of India.
11. Examine critically the Right to Freedom.
12. Examine the Preventive Detention Acts and their effects on the enjoyment of fundamental freedom as provided by the Constitution.
13. Discuss elaborately the provisions related to the Right against Exploitation.
14. Critically discuss the Right to Religion by bringing out practical examples where you think that the secularism in India is endangered.
15. Discuss the provisions as provided under the Cultural and Educational Rights.
16. Do you think that Right to Constitutional Remedies is vital for our enjoyment of fundamental rights? Argue by bringing in the discussion about various writs under Article 32.
17. Discuss how the fundamental rights in India can be protected in the light of Article 32.
18. Discuss in the light of various judgements, the amendability of Part-III of the Constitution on the fundamental rights.

REFERENCES

Bakshi, P.M., *The Constitution of India*, (with selective comments), Universal Law Publishing, Delhi, 2000.

Basu, Durga Das, *Introduction to the Constitution of India*, Prentice-Hall of India, New Delhi, 1992.

Bennett Coleman and Co. v. *Union of India*, AIR 1973 SC 106.

Brij Bhushan v. *State of Delhi,* AIR 1950 SC 129.

Charanjit Lal Choudhury v. *The Union of India*, 1950, SCR 869.

Communist Party of India (M) v. *Bharat Kumar*, AIR 1998 SC 184.

Express Newspaper v. *Union of India,* AIR 1958 SC 578.

Golaknath v. *State of Punjab*, (1967) 2 SCR 762: AIR 1967 SC.

Gopalan v. *State of Madras* (1950) SCR 88/AIR 1950 SC 27.

Goyal, O.P., *Indian Political System*, Macmillan India, New Delhi, 1985.

Indian Express v. *Union of India*, 1986 SC 515.

Indra Sawhney v. *Union of India*, AIR 1993 SC 477.

Keshavananda Bharati v. *State of Kerala*, AIR 1973 SC 1461.

Mahajan, V.D., *Constitutional History of India*, S. Chand & Co., New Delhi, 1976.

Maneka Gandhi v. *Union of India*, AIR 1978 SC 597.

Minerva Mills Ltd. v. *Union of India*, 1980 3 SCC 625.

Prabha Dutt v. *Union of India*, 1982 AIR 1982 SC 6.

Pylee, M.V., *India's Constitution*, S. Chand & Company, New Delhi, 1994.

Romesh Thapar v. *State of Madras*, AIR 1950 S.C. 124 SCR 594.

Sakal Papers Ltd. v. *Union of India*, AIR 1962 SC 305.

State of Bombay v. *Bombay Education Society* (1955), 1SCR 568: AIR 1954 SC 561.

State of Madras v. *Champakam Doaraijan case* (1951), AIR 1951 SC 226.

Union of India v. *As & Soacnioatthieorn for Democratic Reforms* 2002 RD-SC 244.

5

Directive Principles of the State Policy—Part IV of the Indian Constitution

INTRODUCTION

Part III of the Indian Constitution deals with Fundamental Rights, and Part IV of the Constitution embodies broad principles of Directive Principles of State Policy. These are lofty ideals which are fundamental for the governance of the country. The framers of the Constitution drew their inspiration from the Declaration of the Rights of Man and the Citizen proclaimed by Revolutionary France in 1789, and the Declaration of Independence by the American colonies (July 4, 1776), the Charter of the United Nations and also the Universal Declaration of Human Rights (10 December 1948). But the most obvious influence was of the Constitution of the Irish Republic which contains a chapter on "Directive Principles of Social Policy". One should also not forget the Instruments of Instructions which were issued to the Governor-General and the Governors under the Government of India Act, 1935 (see Chapter 1). However, unlike the Fundamental Rights they are non-justifiable. Despite this shortcoming, one must acknowledge that they are valuable guiding principles for the Government.

DIRECTIVE PRINCIPLES OF STATE POLICY

Articles 36 to 51 laid down the broad principles which can be seen as the positive directions to the State to strive to promote the welfare of people by securing social, economic and political justice for all. The State shall direct its policy in such a manner that the ideals as embodied in the Preamble of the Indian Constitution are realized.

The Directive Principles can be seen as directions to realize the ideals of social, economic and political justice to ensure liberty, equality and fraternity. As far as economic justice is concerned, Directive Principles try to secure the right of all men and women to an adequate means of livelihood, equal pay for equal work and to make effective provisions for securing the right to work, education and to public assistance in the event of unemployment, old age, sickness and disablement. The State shall endeavour to secure to workers a living wage, humane conditions at work, a decent standard of life, and full involvement of workers in management of industries (Articles 41-42). Further, the State is to direct its policy in such a manner that it secures distribution of ownership and control of material resources of community to subserve the common good, and to ensure that operation of economic system does not result in concentration of wealth and means of production to common detriment (Article 39).

As far as social justice is concerned, important directives relate to provisions of opportunities and facilities for children to develop in a healthy manner, free and compulsory education for all children upto the age of 14, promotion of education and economic interests of Scheduled Castes, Scheduled Tribes and other weaker sections. Some Gandhian principles relate to organization of village panchayats, promotion of cottage industries, prohibition of the consumption of intoxicating drinks and drugs, organization of agriculture and animal husbandry, and to take steps for preserving and improving the breeds, and prohibiting slaughter of cows and calves and other milch and draught cattle. Miscellaneous provisions include separation of judiciary from executive, promulgation of a uniform civil code for whole country, protection of national monuments, promotion of justice on a basis of equal opportunity, provision of free legal aid, protection and improvement of environment and safeguarding of forests and wildlife of the country; promotion of international peace and security, just and honourable relations between nations, respect for international law, treaty obligations, and settlement of international disputes by arbitration.

Directive Principles, therefore, on the whole, are like a yardstick to measure the performance of the government. The Directive Principles are however, non-justiciable rights of the people. Article 31C, inserted by the 25th Amendment Act of 1971, seeks to upgrade the Directive Principles. If laws are made to give effect to the Directive Principles over Fundamental Rights, they shall not be invalid on the grounds that they take away or abridge any of the rights conferred by Article 14, Article 19 and Article 31 of Fundamental Rights. In case of a conflict between fundamental rights and Directive Principle, if the Directive Principles aim at promoting larger interest of the society, the Courts shall try to uphold the principle of harmonious construction so as to give effect to both.

The Directive Principles though are non-justiciable, i.e., they cannot be enforced in the courts of law, yet they are fundamental in the governance of the country. It shall be the duty of the State to apply these principles in making laws. Besides, all executive agencies should also be guided by these principles. Even the judiciary has to keep them in mind while deciding cases. Later two more amendments were passed adding **Article 45**, which ensures Provision for free and compulsory education for children, (86th Amendment Act, 2002) and **Article 48-A**, which ensures *Protection and improvement of environment and safeguarding of forests and wild life* (42nd Amendment Act, 1976).

Difference between Directive Principles and Fundamental Rights

The Fundamental Rights are in the nature of negative and the Directive Principles can be said to be positive direction for the State. If the Fundamental Rights demand inaction on the part of governmental authorities, i.e., set limits to the actions of governments, the Directive Principles command actions on the part of the State to achieve certain goals. Fundamental rights are not absolute, because they are subjected to certain limitations, but Directive Principles have no such limitations and can be realized to the fullest extent if the resources are available to the government backed by its political will.

Fundamental rights are enforceable, but Directive Principles require proper legislation to become a reality. As long as there is no law in place, it is difficult to execute the Directive Principles into action. Like the 73rd Amendment to the Indian Constitution gave expression to the Gandhian principles of organizing Panchayati Raj in India. The 74th Amendment Act restructured the municipal institutions.

During the Proclamation of an Emergency, the fundamental rights can be suspended under Article 352, but again restored immediately after the withdrawal of the emergency. Many scholars have been of the opinion that due to the very character of the Directive Principles, i.e., non-justifiability, they stand in a State of perpetual suspended animation, until and unless they are implemented through proper legislation.

Directive Principles are not enforceable in the Courts of Law, whereas the Fundamental Rights have Constitutional guarantees in the form of Right to Constitutional Remedies provided under Articles 32 and 226 of the Indian Constitution which empower the Supreme Court and High Courts to protect the Fundamental Rights of the citizens of India. Nevertheless, **Article 37** of the Directive Principles uphold that **the provisions contained in this Part shall not be enforced by any court, but the principles therein laid down, are nevertheless fundamental in the governance of the country, and it shall be the duty of the State to apply these principles in making laws.**

A major question that has been confronted in the Indian political scenario is that in the event of conflict between the two, the Fundamental Rights and the Directive Principles, which one prevails over the another? Undoubtedly, Directive Principles are by far a much greater embodiment of social and economic ideals, yet they do not enjoy a superior position when compared with the fundamental rights as mentioned in Chapter III of the Indian Constitution. From the preceding discussion, it becomes evident that Directive Principles are non-enforceable, and the courts cannot declare any law as void if they clash with the Directive Principles. However, the courts can strike down any law which contravenes any of the fundamental rights. This only relegates the Directive Principles to a secondary position. Even the Supreme Court in the *State of Madras* v. *Champakam Case*, (1951), held that the Directive Principles cannot override the fundamental rights and that the chapter on fundamental rights is sacrosanct and not liable to be abridged by any legislative or executive act or order except to the extent provided in the appropriate Articles in Part III. Further, it held that the Directive Principles must conform and run subsidiary to the fundamental rights. The First Constitutional Amendment (1951) tried to create more scope for Directive Principles and it inserted Clause (4) in Article 15 which provided that the government can take special steps for making special provisions for scheduled castes and scheduled tribes, notwithstanding anything contained in Article 29(2) which prevents discrimination in admission to educational institutions maintained by the State or receiving aid out of State funds on the grounds of religion, race, caste or language. This Amendment also added Articles 31A and 31B in the Constitution by which Ninth schedule was inserted, and provided that none of the Acts and Regulations mentioned in this Schedule shall be void on the ground that they are inconsistent with or take away/ abridge any of the Fundamental Rights. Thus, in some cases the Supreme Court upheld the value of Directive Principles for serving 'public purpose'.[*] The 24th Amendment Act (1971) and 25th Amendment Act (1971) are also important, because while the former made the Fundamental Rights amendable by making an attempt to nullify the decision of the Supreme Court in the *Golaknath* v. *State of Punjab Case,* (1967) which declared the Fundamental Rights as unamendable and the latter substituted the word 'amount' in place of the word 'compensation' in Article 31 (**Regarding Compulsory acquisition of property**, Repealed by the Constitution Forty-fourth Amendment Act, 1976) on the one hand, and inserted Article 31(C) on the other, which made Fundamental Rights mentioned in Articles 14, 19 and 31 subordinate to Article 39, Clause (b) and (c). But in the *Keshavananda Bharati* v. *State of Kerala*, (1973) that part of the 25th Amendment was struck down which subordinated Articles 14, 19 and 31 to Clauses (b) and (c) of Article 39 dealing with Certain principles of policy to be followed by the State. The 42nd Amendment Act (1976) again subordinated the Fundamental Rights guaranteed under Articles 14, 19 and 31 to all Directive Principles contained in Part IV and limited the power of judicial review. To establish a primacy of Directive Principles, Article 31C was amended by the 42nd Amendment Act which Stated that though the Directives

[*]*State of Bombay* v. *F.N. Balsara,* AIR, 1951, SC 318

themselves are not directly enforceable in the Courts, if any law is made to implement any of the Directives contained in Part IV of the Constitution, it would be totally immune from unconstitutionality on the grounds of contravention of the Fundamental Rights conferred by Articles 14 and 19. However, in the *Minerva Mills* v. *Union of India* (1980) in which some of the provisions of the 42nd Amendment Act was challenged, the primacy of the Fundamental Rights was upheld and the court struck down the widening of Article 31C to include any or all of the Directives in Part IV, and also the newly inserted Clauses (3), (4) and (5) in Article 368 on the ground that such total exclusion of judicial review would offend the basic structure of the Constitution. Thus, Article 31C was restored to its previous position which meant that a law would only be protected by Article 31C only if it has implemented the directive in Article 39(b)-(c) and not any of the other Directives included in Part IV. Therefore, the Directive Principles have been made subordinate to the fundamental rights and this position continues still. Finally, Article 31 containing provisions regarding right to property has been deleted by the 44th Constitutional Amendment Act (1978). (See Chapter 2 and Chapter 3 for more).

Therefore, it becomes evident that Directive Principles are just high sounding ideals whose realization solely depends on the political will of the Government running the State of India. Still Directive Principles cannot be said to be without any value as the Government while formulating public policy or even the courts while determining the Constitutional validity of any law or in cases of interpretation of statute have given due regard to the Directive Principles.

The Constitution has been amended several times like the First, Fourth, Seventeenth, Twenty-fifth, Forty-second and Forty-fourth amendments to modify 'those' Fundamental Rights by reason of whose existence the State was facing difficulty in introducing reforms in agrarian, economic and social sectors as embodied in the Directive Principles.

DIRECTIVE PRINCIPLES AS ENSHRINED IN THE CONSTITUTION OF INDIA

Directive Principles are classified as Gandhian, economic and socialistic, political and administrative, legal, environmental, protection of monuments and international peace and security. The Directive Principles as laid down in the Constitution of India are:

Article 36: Definition

In this part, unless the context otherwise requires, "the State" has the same meaning as in Part III.

Article 37: Application of the principles contained in this Part

The provisions contained in this part shall not be enforced by any Court, but the principles therein laid down are nevertheless fundamental in the governance of the country and it shall be the duty of the State to apply these principles in making laws.

Article 38: State to secure a social order for the promotion of welfare of the people

The State shall strive to promote the welfare of the people by securing and protecting as effectively as it may a social order in which justice, social, economic and political, shall inform all the institutions of the national life.

The State shall, in particular, strive to minimise the inequalities in income, and endeavour to eliminate inequalities in status, facilities and opportunities, not only amongst individuals but also amongst groups of people residing in different areas or engaged in different vocations. [added by the 44th Amendment Act]

Article 39: Certain principles of policy to be followed by the State

The State shall, in particular, direct its policy towards securing—

1. that the citizen, men and women equally, have the right to an adequate means of livelihood;
2. that the ownership and control of the material resources of the community are so distributed as best to subserve the common good;
3. that the operation of the economic system does not result in the concentration of wealth and means of production to the common detriment;
4. that there is equal pay for equal work for both men and women;
5. that the health and strength of workers, men and women, and the tender age of children are not abused and that citizens are not forced by economic necessity to enter avocations unsuited to their age or strength;
6. that children are given opportunities and facilities to develop in a healthy manner and in conditions of freedom and dignity, and that childhood and youth are protected against exploitation and against moral and material abandonment.

Article 39A: Equal justice and free legal aid

The State shall secure that the operation of the legal system promotes justice, on a basis of equal opportunity, and shall, in particular, provide free legal aid, by suitable legislation or schemes or in any other way, to ensure that opportunities for securing justice are not denied to any citizen by reason of economic or other disabilities.

Article 40: Organization of village panchayats

The State shall take steps to organise village panchayats, and endow them with such powers and authority as may be necessary to enable them to function as units of self-government.

Article 41: Right to work, to education and to public assistance in certain cases

The State shall, within the limits of its economic capacity and development, make effective provision for securing the right to work, to education and to public assistance in cases of unemployment, old age, sickness and disablement, and in other cases of undeserved wants.

Article 42: Provision for just and humane conditions of work and maternity relief

The State shall make provision for securing just and humane conditions of work and for maternity relief.

Article 43: Living wage, etc., for workers

The State shall endeavour to secure, by suitable legislation or economic organisation or in any other way, to all workers agricultural, industrial or otherwise, work, a living wage, conditions of work ensuring a decent standard of life and full enjoyment of leisure and social and cultural opportunities and, in particular, the State shall endeavour to promote cottage industries on an individual or co-operative basis in rural areas.

Article 43A: Participation of workers in management of industries

The State shall take steps, by suitable legislation or in any other way, to secure the participation of workers in the management of undertakings, establishments or other organisation engaged in any industry.

Article 44: Uniform civil code for the citizens

The State shall endeavour to secure for the citizens a uniform civil code throughout the territory of India.

Article 45: Provision for free and compulsory education for children

The State shall endeavour to provide, within a period of ten years from the commencement of this Constitution, for free and compulsory education for all children until they complete the age of fourteen years.

Article 46: Promotion of educational and economic interests of scheduled castes, scheduled tribes and other weaker sections

The State shall promote with special care the educational and economic interests of the weaker sections of the people, and in particular, of the scheduled castes and the scheduled tribes, and shall protect them from social injustice and all forms of exploitation.

Article 47: Duty of the State to raise the level of nutrition and the standard of living and to improve public health

The State shall regard the raising of the level of nutrition and the standard of living of its people and the improvement of public health as among its primary duties and, in particular, the State shall endeavour to bring about prohibition of the consumption except for medicinal purpose of intoxicating drinks and of drugs which are injurious to health.

Article 48: Organisation of agriculture and animal husbandry

The State shall endeavour to organise agriculture and animal husbandry on modern and scientific lines and shall, in particular, take steps for preserving and improving the breeds, and prohibiting the slaughter, of cows and calves and other milch and draught cattle.

Article 48A: Protection and improvement of environment and safeguarding of forests and wild life of the country

The State shall endeavour to protect and improve the environment and to safeguard the forests and wild life of the country.

Article 49: Protection of monuments and places and objects of national importance

It shall be the obligation of the State to protect every monument or place or object of artistic or historic interest, declared by or under law made by Parliament to be of national importance, from spoliation, disfigurement, destruction, removal, disposal or export, as the case may be.

Article 50: Separation of judiciary from executive

The State shall take steps to separate the judiciary from the executive in the public services of the State.

Article 51: Promotion of international peace and security

The State shall endeavour to–

1. promote international peace and security;
2. maintain just and honourable relations between nations;
3. foster respect for international law and treaty obligations in the dealings of organised people with one another; and
4. encourage settlement of international disputes by arbitration.

Significance and Implementation of Directive Principles of State Policy

The current status of the Directive Principles are secondary to the fundamental rights, and the latter enjoy a legal superiority over the former. This does not, for one moment, make the Directive Principles, unnecessary or less important. The crux of several Amendments and Supreme Court verdicts thrust the responsibility on the Government of the day to implement the Directive Principles in such a way that they do not contravene the Fundamental Rights or there arise a need for further Constitutional amendment. What is required is a harmonious balancing of both. The Directive Principles and fundamental rights complement each other and must be read together. If this is done then the objective of the makers of the Constitution can be realized. As Austin says, "By establishing these positive obligations of the State, the members of the Constituent Assembly made it the responsibility of future Indian governments to find a middle way between individual liberty and the public good, between preserving the property and the privilege of the few and bestowing benefits on many in order to liberate the powers of all men equally for contributions to the common good." Therefore, the Directive Principles are no less significant than the Fundamental Rights.

The implementation of Directive Principles is a monumental job for any government, because non-implementation or failure to implement the Directive Principles can cost the Governments heavily. Therefore, the Directive Principles should not just remain as pious principles enshrined in the Constitution, but must be translated into reality. The Governments over the year have made efforts to give expressions to some of the Directive Principles, yet lot has to be done if the benefit of social welfare and economic justice is to percolate into the bottom most level of the society.

The State has made many efforts to implement the Directive Principles. With the aim of providing universalization of education, the Government works with the objective to provide elementary education free of cost to all children upto the age of 14 years which has always been a priority for the Government. The 86th Constitutional Amendment of 2002 inserted a new Article, Article 21A, into the Constitution, that seeks to provide free and compulsory education to all children aged from 6 to 14 years. The Government has made great effort so that the percentage of drop-outs from the schools decreases every year. Mid-day meals are also provided for their nutrition as well as added incentive to come to school. The Government since 2002 has embarked upon a policy of *Sarva Shiksha Abhiyan* (education for all) to ensure primary and compulsory education for the children aged from 6 to 14 years. Efforts have also been made to introduce programmes for adult education and women education. Scholarships and financial assistance are provided by both Central and State Governments to weaker sections of the society as well as minorities.

Welfare schemes for the weaker sections are being implemented both by the central and the State Governments. The year 1990-1991 was declared as the "Year of Social Justice" in the memory of B.R. Ambedkar. In order to prevent atrocities against the *dalits* (scheduled castes and scheduled ribes), the government has enacted The Scheduled Castes and Scheduled Tribes (Prevention of Atrocities) Act, 1989 and the Scheduled Castes and the Scheduled Tribes (Prevention of Atrocities) *Rules* of 1995 were framed. The rules for the Act were notified on 31 March 1995. The 1989 Act aimed at preventing and punishing atrocities against the *dalits*. Besides, the Government provided for reservation in educational institutions, public jobs and tries to ensure access to health facilities. The Other Backward Classes (OBCs) and Economically Backward Classes (EBCs) are also being brought under the purview of reservation. The aim is to bridge the gap of inequality whether social or economic, and thereby, secure justice for all.

Another noteworthy development was the 73rd Amendment Act, 1992 which is a landmark amendment towards decentralization and setting up of Local Self Government in India and this amendment inserted Part IX to make provisions for Constitution, election, financing and functioning of Panchayati Raj bodies. The 74th Amendment Act, 1992, inserted Part IXA to make provisions for Constitution, election, financing and functioning of Municipal bodies. These two were a great step towards decentralization and establishment of Local Self Governments.

As far as poverty alleviation and creation of employment opportunities are concerned, several programmes have been initiated by the Government of India like, Community Development Programme, 1952; Mahatma Gandhi National Rural Employment Guarantee Act (MGNREGA), 2005; Swarnjayanthi Gram Swarozgar Yojana, 1999; Food for Work Programme, 2001; Pradhan Mantri Gram Sadak Yojana, 2000; Sampoorna Grameen Rozgar Yojana (programme was implemented through the Panchayati Raj institutions), 2001; Jawahar Rozgar Yojana, 1989; Jawahar Gram Samridhi Yojana (restructuring the Jawahar Rozgar Yojana), 1999; Integrated Rural Development Porgramme (IRDP), 1980; and various other schemes under the development and employment programmes in India.

Several Land Reform Acts were enacted to provide ownership rights to poor farmers. Now, Jagirdari system has been abolished and Zamindari Abolition Acts are in place. Land has been distributed to scheduled castes, scheduled tribes and the landless poor. The thrust of banking policy in India has been to improve banking facilities in the rural areas. Banks have been mobilized to provide agrarian loans to farmers directly or through cooperatives. The Zamindari Abolition Acts and other land reforms enacted by different States have all been put under Ninth schedule to make them immune to judicial scrutiny. The Urban Land Ceiling Act was passed in 1976.

As far as rights of women are concerned, several legislations have been enacted for securing their rights. Like The Suppression of Immoral Traffic

In Women and Girls Act, 1956, Dowry Prohibition Act, 1961; Indecent Representation of Women (Prohibition) Act, 1986; National Commission for Women Act, 1990; Protection of Women from Domestic Violence Act, 2005; Protection of Women against Sexual Harassment Bill, 2007; Equal Remuneration Act, 1976; Maternity Benefit Act, 1961 and a host of other Acts. Besides there are also several laws relating to marriage and divorce, maintenance, property, succession, inheritance, guardianship and adoption, abortion and the like. One-third of the total number of seats has been reserved for women in Panchayats at every level and in the case of Bihar, half the seats have been reserved for women. As far as representation of women in the Parliament is concerned, the Bill has been forwarded on the same regards, but is still pending as it is caught between politics of pro and anti-reservationists.

To protect the right of child, the Indian Government has also passed several Acts, like Child Labour (Prohibition & Regulation) Act, 1986; Child Marriage Restraint Act, 1929; Children Act, 1960; Children (Pledging of Labour) Act, 1933; Commissions for the Protection of Child Rights Act, 2005; Commissions for Protection of Child Rights (Amendment) Act, 2006; and so on.

Legal aid at the expense of the State has been made compulsory in all cases pertaining to criminal law, if the accused is too poor to engage a lawyer. Law Commission has been appointed for monitoring this service. To this effect National Legal Service Authority (NALSA) has been created. In 2005, NALSA launched the first National Literacy Mission (2005-2010) to provide legal education to the underprivileged people. By several other devices like Right to Information Act (RTI), Public Interest Litigation (PIL) Petition, Lok Adalats, Consumer Protection Forums and Human Rights Commission, the legal rights of the people have been secured. There has been a continuous demand for Lok Pal, and at present the demand still persists under the civil society mobilization of people at large in order to fight corruption. As far as the uniform civil code is concerned, it has not been implemented and is much a debated issue involving political parties and religious communities having their own personal laws.

There are several national laws and many more State-level labour laws in India. Some important labour laws are The Contract Labour Act (1970); Minimum Wages Act, 1948; Weekly Holidays Act, 1942; Beedi and Cigar Workers Act, 1966; The Payment of Wages Act, 1936; The Workmen's Compensation Act, 1923; The Factories Act, 1948; and many more. The concept of bonded labour has been abolished.

Small scale and cottage industries play a vital role in the growth of the economy. The basis for this distinction between the small-scale and cottage industries was laid down by the Fiscal Commission in 1950, when it stated that "A cottage industry is thus one which is carried on wholly or primarily with the help of members of the family either as a whole or a part-time occupation. A small scale industry on the other hand, is one which is operated mainly with hired labour, usually 10 to 50 hands." The well-known organization like Khadi and Village Industries Commission (KVIC) is working towards the development and endorsement of cottage industries in India. Other premier organizations are Central Silk Board, Coir Board, All India Handloom Board and All India Handicrafts Board, and organizations like Forest Corporations and National Small Industries Corporation which are also playing an active promotion and expansion of cottage industries in India. Despite several attempts by these organizations, the cottage industries and small-scale industries still face threats of extinction under inadequate monetary and technological support from Government.

Nationalization of banks, and insurance sectors were other significant steps towards realization of Directive Principles in India. In the year 1955, bank nationalization was initiated when the Imperial Bank of India became the State Bank of India, under the SBI Act of 1955. The nationalization of banks continued thereafter. The next level of nationalization was achieved with the nationalization of the seven subsidiary banks of SBI with deposits over 200 crore rupees, on 19th July 1960. The next major nationalization of banks was done in the year 1969 under the Central Government led by Indira Gandhi, when the Government nationalized 14 major commercial banks in India. Thereafter, another round of nationalization was done in the year of 1980, in which six more banks were nationalized with the deposits over 200 crore rupees. With this, the Government of India held a control over 91% of the banking industry in India.

To translate the Directive Principles into action, the Government of India has initiated national Five Year Plans for which a Planning Commission has been formed. The Planning Commission of India was set up on March 15 1950, under the Chairmanship of Jawaharlal Nehru, by a resolution of Union Cabinet for formulation of plans for the most effective and balanced utilization of country's resources. Till date, 12 plans have been implemented, and the Twelfth Plan (2012–2017) was the last in the line of the Five-Year Plans. From 1947 to 2017 India had a planned economic development based on allocations made through the Five-Year Plans. Since the dissolution of the Planning Commission which was replaced by NITI Aayog (see Chapter 23) there has not been any further Five-Year Plan.

India's Foreign Policy, has also to some degree, been influenced by the Directive Principles. India has always reposed great faith in the United Nations (UN) and has always upheld its basic principles and objectives. It has also taken part in a number of peace-keeping activities under the auspices of the United Nations. India, since the days of Nehru, has put great faith in the purposes and principles as upheld in the UN Charter. Even the salient principles of Indian foreign policy may be seen as a reflection of the UN principles. India, has always believed in establishment and maintenance of international peace and security, non-alignment, freedom and welfare of its people, elimination of racial discrimination, poverty, disease, ignorance, promotion of human rights and economic development not only for India but also for the newly emerging nations for which India has always extended her support to all UN efforts.

Despite such steps taken by the Government of India, at both the State and the Central levels, a lot is to be done as the conditions of women, children, weaker sections of the society and the poor have not shown significant difference even with such lofty measures and Acts in place.

EXERCISES

I. Short Answer Questions: **(100 words)**

1. Concept of Directive Principles of State Policy.
2. Difference between Fundamental Rights and Directive Principles.
3. Any Five Directive Principles of State Policy.
4. The significance of the Directive Principles.

II. Long Answer Questions: **(1200 words)**

5. Analyze the significance of the Directive Principles in comparison with the Fundamental Rights as guaranteed under the Constitution of India.
6. How far do you think the Indian State has been successful in implementing the Directive Principles of the State Policy?
7. Examine the various Directive Principles as provided under the Constitution of India.
8. Discuss the importance of the Directive Principles while discussing the various Directive Principles of State Policy.

REFERENCES

Austin, Granville, *The Indian Constitution: Cornerstone of A Nation,* Oxford University Press, Bombay, 1972.

Bakshi, P.M., *The Constitution of India,* (with selective comments), Universal Law Publishing, Delhi, 2000.

Basu, Durga Das, *Introduction to the Constitution of India,* Prentice-Hall of India, New Delhi, 1992.

Bijoy Cotton Mills v. *State of Ajmer,* AIR, 1955, SC 33

Government of India, *Constitution of India.*

M.H. Qureshi v. *State of Bihar,* AIR, 1958, SC 731

Siwach, J.R., *Dynamics of Indian Government and Politics,* Sterling Publishers Pvt. Ltd., New Delhi, 1985.

State of Bombay v. *F.N. Balsara,* AIR, 1951, SC 318

6

The Indian Federation

INTRODUCTION

Article 1 of the Constitution of India lays down that India shall be a Union of States. Nowhere is the word federation been used in the Constitution, but a closer study of the Constitution and the working of the Indian political system reveals the federal traits of the India Polity. However, in its entirety, mostly unitary features are noticeable alongside the federal features. Thus, it is sometimes argued that the Indian polity is a federation with strong unitary tendencies or federalism with a centralizing tendency, and sometimes it is ascribed as being quasi-federal. Unlike the American Federation, the Indian Federation is not the product of any agreement among the constituent units of a federation. Under the 1935 Government of India Act, the constituent units of Indian Federation were given an autonomous status and not full-fledged independence, and they all were under the British paramountcy until India gained her independence on 15 August 1947. These constituent units gained independence as a whole after 15 August 1947. Following independence there had been problems of integration of some of the constituent units like the Princely States which had to be forcibly integrated into the Indian Federation. Therefore, there was no Declaration of Independence as done by the 13 American colonies. The Constituent Assembly was the representative of the Indian people and not of the constituent units. Therefore, India is a Union of States where the States have no right to secede and Central Government has a more powerful position in comparison to the Governments of the constituent States. The argument that is given is that while India has federal features it has also a strong centralizing tendency.

PART I (ARTICLES 1–3): THE UNION AND ITS TERRITORY

Article 1 of the Indian Constitution proclaims that India, that is Bharat, shall be a Union of States. The territory of India comprises the territory of the States, the Union Territories mentioned in the First Schedule and such other territories as may be acquired.

Article 2 lays down that regarding the establishment or admission of new States, the Parliament may by law admit into the union, or establish, new States on such terms and conditions as it thinks fit.

Regarding the formation of new States and alteration of areas, boundaries or names of existing States under **Article 3**, the Parliament by law can form a new State by separating the territory of any State or by uniting two or more States or parts of States or by uniting any territory to a part of any State; increase the area of any State; diminish the area of any State; alter the boundaries of any State or alter the name of any State. This can be done only when such Bill is introduced in either of the houses on the recommendation of the President, and where there is a proposal contained in the Bill that affects the area, boundaries or name of any State, the Bill has to be referred by the President to the Legislature of that State for expressing its views within a particular period as may be specified by the President.

Article 4 says that to give effect to the laws made under Article 2 and Article 3, the First and the Fourth Schedule as may be necessary can be amended and may come to contain certain supplemental, incidental or consequential matters for this purpose. No such law however, will be seen as an amendment of the Constitution under Article 368.

REORGANIZATION OF STATES

India comprises 28 States and 8 Union Territories. The Government of India Act, 1935 Stated that a federation of India was to be formed comprising both Provinces and States. The provisions of the Act establishing the federal Central Government were not to go into operation until a specified number of rulers of States had signed Instruments of Accession. The problem arose with regard to the integration of the Princely States when the White Paper was released on 12 May 1946. It said "...His Majesty's Government will cease to exercise the power of paramount. This means that the rights of the States which flow from their relationship to the Crown will no longer exist, and that the rights surrendered by the States to the paramount power will return to the States. Political arrangements between the States on the one side, and the British Crown on the other will thus be brought to an end." On the basis of this the Indian Independence Act, 1947, provided that "as from the appointed day, the suzerainty of His Majesty over the Indian States lapses and, with it, all treaties and agreements in force at the date of the passing of this Act between His Majesty and the rulers of the Indian States, all functions exercisable by

His Majesty at the date towards Indian States or the rulers thereof, and all powers, rights, authority or jurisdiction exercisable by His Majesty at the date or relation to Indian States by treaty, grant, usage, sufferance or otherwise..." Even before the Indian Independence Act 1947 was passed, negotiations had started for integration of Princely States into the Indian Union through accession. Most of the Princely States agreed to accede to the Indian union except Junagarh, Hyderabad and Kashmir which were later integrated under the able Statesmanship of Sardar Patel. The integration of the Princely States took place in the manner mentioned in Table 6.1. There was a fourfold scheme of classification of States. They were:

1. 216 States having a population over 19 million were merged with the neighbouring provinces (former British Provinces) and were designated as Part A States.
2. 275 States with a population of about 35 million were integrated to create new administrative units, namely Part B States of the Indian Union; some very big States like those of Hyderabad, Mysore and Jammu & Kashmir were also placed in this category.
3. 61 States having a population of about 7 million were constituted into Part C States and were declared as Centrally Administered Areas.
4. The Islands of Andaman and Nicobar were placed in Part D of the Indian Union.

Table 6.1 Categories of Indian States and Centrally Administered Areas

Part A States	*Part B States*	*Part C States*	*Part D States*
Assam	Hyderabad	Ajmer	Andaman & Nicobar Islands
Bihar	Jammu & Kashmir	Bilaspur	
Bombay	Mysore	Bhopal	
Madhya Pradesh	Patiala and East Punjab States Union (PEPSU)	Coorg	
Madras	Rajasthan	Delhi	
Orissa	Saurashtra	Himachal Pradesh	
Punjab	Travancore-Cochin	Kutch	
U.P.		Manipur	
West Bengal		Tripura	
Andhra Pradesh (A.P. was created by separating a part of the then Madras)		Vindhya Pradesh	

The integration of the Princely States was an ad hoc arrangement, and therefore, arose a need to give a fresh look at the approach towards the problem of reorganization of States. The Government of India appointed a Commission under the Chairmanship of S.K. Dar to examine the case of the reorganization of the Indian States on linguistic basis. In December 1948, the Dar Commission submitted its 56 page Report which recommended the reorganization of the component units of the Indian federation for the sake of administrative convenience, and not at all on the basis of linguistic composition of the area. The Dar Commission Report was not at all accepted. Therefore, another Committee was formed, the JVP Committee (Jawaharlal Nehru, Vallabhabhai Patel and Pattabhi Sitaramayya) which was set to re-examine the issue of the linguistic re-organization of the Indian States. The JVP Report was dismissed in 1949 and was followed by protests. Thereafter in December 1953, Nehru announced the appointment of a Commission for a rethinking about the reorganization of States in the Parliament. Thus, a States Reorganization Commission (SRC) was appointed with three members—Fazl Ali (Chairman), K.M. Panikkar and Pt. H.N. Kunzru. The SRC submitted its Report on 30 September 1955. The Commission recommended the abolition of A, B, C and D categories of the units of the Indian Union, and instead proposed the formation of 16 States and 3 Centrally Administered Areas.

The proposal of the Commission was accepted, and with minor modifications the State Reorganization Act of 1956 was passed which created 14 States and 5 Union Territories. The 14 States were Andhra Pradesh, Assam, Bihar, Bombay, Jammu & Kashmir, Kerala, Madhya Pradesh, Madras, Mysore, Odisha, Punjab, Rajasthan, Uttar Pradesh and West Bengal. The 5 Union Territories were Delhi, Himachal Pradesh, Manipur, Tripura and Andaman & Nicobar, Laccadive, Aminidive and Minicoy islands.

Even after the passage of the State Reorganization Act of 1956, problems continued and reorganization of States also continued. A deed of transfer was signed with the government of France in May 1956, by virtue of which former French possessions of Chandernagore, Mahe, Yanam and Karekal were merged with the Indian States, while Pondicherry was given the status of a Union Territory. In December 1961, India acquired the territories of Goa, Daman and Diu by means of police action, and thus Goa, Daman and Diu formed another Union Territory. In 1960, due to struggle on the basis of language, the bi-lingual Bombay State was bifurcated into Maharashtra (Marathi-speaking) and Gujarat (Gujarati speaking). In 1963, Nagaland was formed out of Assam. In 1966, State of Punjab was bifurcated into Punjab (Punjabi speaking) and Haryana (Hindi speaking) States. The city of Chandigarh remained unsettled. In 1969, the State of Assam was further disintegrated to create the State of Meghalaya. In 1971, Himachal Pradesh got the status of a State and the north-eastern region of India was re-organized in a way that Meghalaya became a full-fledged State, the Union Territories of Manipur and Tripura got statehood and the Union Territories of Mizoram and Arunachal Pradesh (former NEFA) came into being. Sikkim became an Associate State in 1974, and it became a full-fledged State in 1975.

Mizoram got Statehood in 1986. Further, in 1987 Arunachal Pradesh and Goa got Statehood. In 2000, three new States were formed, which were Uttarakhand (out of U.P.), Jharkhand (out of Bihar) and Chhattisgarh (out of Madhya Pradesh). The demand for the State of Telangana (out of Andhra Pradesh) created turbulence in the State. The State of Telangana was officially formed on 2 June 2014 and it became the 29th State of India. Hyderabad will remain as the joint capital of both Telangana and Andhra Pradesh for a period of 10 years. The **Jammu and Kashmir Reorganisation Act, 2019** reconstituted Jammu and Kashmir into two Indian-administered union territories, one to be called Jammu and Kashmir, and the other Ladakh, on 31 October 2019.

States and Union Territories of India

Currently, India has 28 States and 8 Union Territories including the National Capital Territory of Delhi as shown in the Figure 6.1 and Table 6.2.

Figure 6.1 Map of India showing the States and Union Territories.

Table 6.2 List of States of India and Union Territories

S.No.	Names of States	Capital
1.	Andhra Pradesh	Amaravati
2.	Arunachal Pradesh	Itanagar
3.	Assam	Dispur
4.	Bihar	Patna
5.	Chhattisgarh	Raipur
6.	Goa	Panaji
7.	Gujarat	Gandhinagar
8.	Haryana	Chandigarh
9.	Himachal Pradesh	Shimla
10.	Jharkhand	Ranchi
11.	Karnataka	Bengaluru
12.	Kerala	Thiruvananthapuram
13.	Madhya Pradesh	Bhopal
14.	Manipur	Imphal
15.	Maharashtra	Mumbai
16.	Meghalaya	Shillong
17.	Mizoram	Aizwal
18.	Nagaland	Kohima
19.	Odisha	Bhubaneshwar
20.	Punjab	Chandigarh
21.	Rajasthan	Jaipur
22.	Sikkim	Gangtok
23.	Tamil Nadu	Chennai
24.	Telangana	Hyderabad
25.	Tripura	Agartala
26.	Uttarakhand	Dehradun
27.	Uttar Pradesh	Lucknow
28.	West Bengal	Kolkata
S.No.	*Union Territories*	*Capital*
1.	Andaman & Nicobar Islands	Port Blair
2.	Chandigarh	Chandigarh
3.	Dadra & Nagar Haveli and Daman & Diu	Daman
4.	Delhi (NCT)*	Delhi
5.	Jammu and Kashmir	Srinagar (Summer), Jammu (Winter)
6.	Ladakh	Leh, Kargil
7.	Lakshadweep	Kavaratti
8.	Puducherry	Puducherry

* Delhi: Officially the National Capital Territory of Delhi, is a city and a Union Territory of India. The Chief Minister is Shri Arvind Kejriwal, and the Lt. Governor is Vinai Kumar Saxena.

RELATIONS BETWEEN THE UNION AND STATE GOVERNMENTS

The relations between the Union and the States are laid down in details in Part XI and XII of the Constitution. The Legislative and Administrative relations are laid down in Part XI under Chapters 1 and 2, respectively while the financial relations are laid down in Chapter XII. From the analysis of the distribution of powers in these parts of the Constitution, it can be said that the relations between the Union and the States are not purely federal in nature, rather a mixture of federal and unitary features. It has been pointed out for long that the Central Government enjoys a lion's share of power in comparison to the State Governments.

Legislative Relations

1. Explicitly, by the provisions mentioned under Part XI, Chapter I, the Central Government has been vested with huge powers. Article 245 draws up the scope of the laws made by the Parliament and the Legislature of a State. It says that subject to the provisions of the Constitution of India, the Parliament may make laws for the whole or any part of the country and the Legislature of a State may make laws for the whole or any part of the State. No laws made by the Parliament shall be deemed to be invalid on the ground that it would have extra-territorial operation. However, there are certain limitations to the powers of Parliament as well as Legislatures of State. They may be summed up as follows:
   (a) The federal scheme of distribution of legislative powers
   (b) Fundamental rights and other provision of the Constitution
   (c) Constitutional provisions as to prior sanction or approval of the President or Governor with respect to certain Bills.
   (d) The rule that the State Legislature cannot legislate extra-territorially—though the Parliament can do so under Article 245(2).
   (e) The doctrine that the Legislature cannot delegate matters of policy
   (f) The doctrine that the legislation must not be a fraud of the Constitution
   (g) The doctrine that the legislature must make a 'law'. Its function is neither adjudicatory nor executive, but only legislative.
2. When it comes to the law-making the most important issue is what should be the subject matters of law making by the Parliament, and the Legislature of a State. Article 246 lays down clearly three lists pertaining to law making by the Union and the State. The lists are Union List, State List and the Concurrent List. Originally, there were 97 items in the Union List, 66 in the State List and 47 in the Concurrent List. As a result of subsequent amendments of the Constitution, the number of entries in the Union List and the Concurrent List has increased to

99 and 52, respectively; while the number of entries in the State List has decreased to 62. The Parliament has exclusive jurisdiction over the subject matters mentioned in the Union List. The States can make laws on the subject matters mentioned in the State List. As far as Concurrent List is concerned, it contains items of common importance of both the Union and the States. The items contained in Union List are defence, foreign affairs, currency and coinage, war and peace, atomic energy, natural resources, preventive detention, citizenship, post and telegraph, railways, ports, navigation and shipping, foreign trade, inter-State trade and commerce, banking, insurance, National highways, patents and copyrights, etc., which are the matters of National importance. The items mentioned in State List are public order, police, jails, agriculture, public health and sanitation, land, Local Self-Government, fisheries, markets and fairs, and so on. Concurrent List deals with the matters like marriage and divorce, infants and minors, adoption and succession, civil and criminal law and procedure, education, economic and social planning, trade unions, labour welfare, social security, and so on.

3. Under Article 248, all residuary powers of legislation have been given to the Parliament which is to enjoy exclusive jurisdiction as far as law-making is concerned on subjects not mentioned in either Concurrent List or State List. Such power includes the power of making any law imposing tax not mentioned in either of those lists.
4. All powers discussed till now are explicit powers of the Union Government and the State Governments as far as legislations are concerned. The Parliament however, can make-in roads into the State List in different way and, in the subsequent provisions, it can be seen that a primacy has been given to the Union Government even with respect to matters mentioned in the State List in the national interest.
   (a) Article 249 lays down that the Council of States or Rajya Sabha can declare by a resolution supported by not less than two-third of the members present and voting, that it is necessary or expedient in national interest that Parliament should make laws with respect to a matter enumerated in the State List specified in the resolution. This can remain in force for one year, provided that, if another resolution providing for the continuance of the resolution is passed in the same manner in the Rajya Sabha, then the resolution shall continue to be in force for another one year. Such a law may remain in force for six months at the most after the revocation of the resolution.
   (b) During a period of emergency, the Parliament enjoys wide powers to legislate with respect to any matter in the State List. Article 250, in unambiguous terms, lays down that while a Proclamation of Emergency is in operation, the Parliament shall have the power

to make laws for the whole or any part of the Territory of India with respect to matters enumerated in the State List in case of emergencies are declared under Article 352 (National emergency) or under Article 356 (State emergencies). The State laws remain suspended to the extent that it is repugnant to the Union law. However, the Union law shall not remain in operation beyond six months, at the most, after the Revocation of Emergency.

(c) Article 251 again establishes supremacy of Union laws. It enumerates that nothing in Article 249 and Article 250 shall restrict the power of the Legislature of a State to make any law which under the Constitution is given in the State List. What is important is that if any provision of a law made by the Legislature of the State is repugnant to or comes into conflict with any provision of a law made by the Parliament, before or after the law made by the State Legislature, then the Union law should prevail, and the law made by the State Legislature becomes inoperative to the extent of being repugnant to the law of the Centre. Again under Article 254, if there is any inconsistency between the laws made by the Parliament and the laws made by the Legislatures of the State with respect to items mentioned in Concurrent List, the laws made by the Parliament, whether before or after the laws have been made by the Legislatures of the States shall prevail. However, where a law made by the State Legislature with respect to one of the matters enumerated in the Concurrent List contains any provision repugnant to the provisions of an earlier law made by Parliament or an existing law with respect to that matter, the law made so by the Legislature of such State shall, if it has been reserved for the consideration of the President and has received his consent prevail in that State. However, Article 254 also specifies that the Parliament can enact any law any time with respect to similar matters including a law adding to, amending, varying or repealing the law so made by the Legislature of the States.

(d) The Parliament further vide Article 252 can legislate for two or more States by consent and adoption of such legislation by any other State with regard to matters mentioned in State List. Such resolutions have to be passed by all the Houses of the Legislatures of the concerned States, and then it shall be lawful for the Parliament to pass an Act for regulating that matter accordingly. The Act thus passed will become applicable for the States concerned as well as for any other State which may afterwards adopt by resolution passed by the House/Houses of the same. Any Act passed by Parliament to this effect may be amended or repealed by another Act of Parliament passed or adopted in the same manner on request by the concerned Legislatures of the States.

(e) Under Article 253, the Parliament has the power to make any law for the whole country or any part of the Territory of India for implementing any treaty, agreement or convention with any other country or countries or any decision made at any International Conference, association or other body.

5. Another primacy of the Union Government has been established under Article 200. It says that certain Bills passed by the State legislatures can be reserved for consideration by the President of India by the Governor of that State. The President may either give his assent or withhold his consent, i.e., veto it or may return to the State Legislature for reconsideration with his recommendations after seeking the advice of the Supreme Court, if he so desires.

Administrative Relations

Just like Legislative Relations, the Administrative Relations between the Centre and the State need a scrutiny. Chapter 2 of Part XI of the Constitution gives us the idea of the distribution of administrative powers between the Centre and the State. The scheme of distribution is given as follows:

1. Article 256 states the obligation of the States and the Union in the sense that the executive power of every State shall be so exercised as to ensure compliance with the laws made by Parliament, and any existing laws which apply in that State, and the executive power of the Union shall extend to giving such directions to a State as may appear to the Government of India necessary for that purpose.
2. Article 257 contains provisions for the control of the Union over States in certain cases. It says that the executive power of every State shall be so exercised as not to impede or prejudice the exercise of the executive power of the Union, and the executive power of the Union shall extend to the giving of such directions to a State as may appear to the Government of India to be necessary for that purpose or for construction and maintenance of the means of communications declared in the direction to be national and military importance.
3. Article 258 states certain powers of the Union to confer powers, etc., on States in certain cases. It says that the President, may, with the consent of the Governor of the State entrust either conditionally or unconditionally to that Government or to its officers functions in relation to any matter to which the executive power of the Union extends. A law made by the Parliament which applies in any State may, notwithstanding that it relates to the matter with respect to which the Legislature of a State has no power to make law, confer powers and the imposition of duties or authorize the conferment of powers and the imposition of duties on the State or officers and authorities thereof. By Article 258A, the

Governor of a State may with the consent of the Government of India, entrust either conditionally or unconditionally to that Government or its officers functions in relation to any matter to which the executive power of the State extends. Regarding the payment of extra-costs of administration, this shall be solved by mutual agreement. In case of a dispute, the matter shall be decided by an arbitrator appointed by the Chief Justice of India.

4. Article 260 states the jurisdiction of the Union in relation to territories outside India. The Government of India, may, in agreement with the Government of any Territory not being part of the Territory of India, undertake any executive, legislative or judicial functions vested in the Government of such Territory, but every such agreement shall be subject to and governed by any law relating to the exercise of foreign jurisdiction from the time being in force.
5. Article 261 relates to Public Acts, records and judicial proceedings. It states that full faith and credit shall be given throughout the territory of India to Public Acts, records and judicial proceedings of the Union and of every State. The manner in which and the conditions under which the Acts, records and proceedings shall be proved, and the effect thereof determined shall be provided by law made by Parliament. Final judgments or orders delivered or passed by civil courts in any part of the territory of India shall be capable of execution anywhere within that territory according to the law.
6. Article 262 provides for adjudication of disputes relating to waters of inter-State rivers or river valleys. It says that the Parliament may by law provide for the adjudication of any dispute or complaint with respect to the use, distribution or control of the waters of, or in, any inter-State river or river valley.
7. Article 263 contains provisions for the formation of inter-State Council for coordination among States. The President, at any time, if he thinks that the public interests would be served by the establishment of a Council charged with the duty of
   a. inquiring into and advising on disputes which may have arisen between the States;
   b. investigating and discussing subjects in which he by order may establish such a Council, and define the nature of its duties to be performed by it along with its organization and procedure.
8. Again, Article 355 empowers the Union Government to take necessary steps to protect every State against external aggression and internal disturbances and to ensure that the Government of every State is carried on in accordance with the provisions of the Constitution.
9. The Union has also been given a superior position by virtue of Article 356 or provisions regarding the imposition of President's Rule in a

State, due to the breakdown of Constitutional machinery. During the operation of an emergency, the State is expected to follow the directions and instructions of the Union Government.

10. The officers of the Indian administrative service and the Indian police service are recruited by the Union Public Service Commission (UPSC) and they are given to serve the State Governments. While they draw their salaries and allowances from the State Governments, their grades and emoluments are determined by the centre alone. Moreover, any disciplinary action against an officer of these categories can be taken only by the union home ministry working in consultation with the UPSC. Article 312 authorizes the Rajya Sabha may pass a special resolution thereby empowering the Parliament for the creation of an All-India Service common to the Union and State.
11. The Union Government also has the power to appoint Inquiry Commissions against any Chief Minister for charges of corruption or malpractices or any Act of Commission or omission. Such inquiry Commissions have been appointed, which has, to some extent, be given the power of controlling the State Governments by the Union. Some of the prominent Commissions were Das Commission in 1963 for investigating charges against Chief Minister of Punjab Sardar Pratap Singh Kairon, the Chhangani Commission in 1972, against Punjab Chief Minister S. Prakash Singh Badal, Sarkaria Commission in 1976, against the Chief Minister of Tamil Nadu, Karunanidhi, Vimal Dalal Commission against Vengal Rao of Andhra, Durman Commission in 1979, against S.M. Sengupta in Tripura, Ray Commission in 1981 for investigating the spirit scandal in Tamil Nadu. Such Commissions are surely a powerful tool in the hands of the Union Government, which it can use to flex its muscle vis-à-vis the State Government.
12. The President appoints the Governor of the States of the Indian Union. He also has the power to dismiss the Governor. In reality, this is practiced by the President in consultation with the union cabinet. The convention is that the Chief Minister or the State Governments must be consulted while making such appointments. Usually, the Central Government has the major say in such appointments and removals. In 2004, the UPA-I Government was able to get the Governors of Goa, Gujarat, Haryana and U.P. removed by a Presidential decree. Further, the Governor is seen as the agent of the Centre, because at any time he can send a Report to the President regarding the failure of Constitutional machinery in the State and recommend President's rule under Article 356. The Governor can also reserve a Bill for the consideration of the President. When the emergency is in operation, the Governor becomes the real head of the State and during the National Emergency under Article 352 he becomes the agent of the Centre, and secure the implementation of the orders in the State.

Financial Relations

Chapter II of Part XI of the Constitution deals with the Financial relations between the Union and the States. This is most controversial of all relations. In matters of financial autonomy the States enjoy none. The important aspects of financial relations are:

1. Article 265 lays down that no tax shall be levied or collected except by authority of law. Article 266 embodies provisions for creation of 'Consolidated Funds', and public accounts of India and of the States. Parliament under Article 267 may, by law, establish a contingency fund for the purposes of meeting unforeseen expenditure pending authorization of such expenditure by Parliament by law under Article 115 and Article 116.
2. Regarding the distribution of revenues under Article 268, there are certain duties which shall be levied by the Union, but collected and appropriated by the States like stamp duties and duties of excise on medicinal and toilet preparations as mentioned in the Union List. These shall be levied by the Union Government but collected:
   (a) in the case where such duties are leviable within any Union Territory by the Union Government and
   (b) in other cases by the States within which such duties are respectively leviable.

   There are also certain taxes levied and collected by the Union assigned to the States under Article 269. These are duties in respect of succession to property other than agricultural land, State duty in respect of property other than agricultural land, State duty in respect of property other than agricultural land, terminal taxes on goods or passengers carried by railway, sea, or air, taxes on railway fares and freights, taxes other than stamp duties on transactions in stock-exchanges and future markets, taxes on the sale or purchase of newspapers and on advertisements published therein, taxes on the sale or purchase of goods other than newspapers, where such sale or purchase takes place in the course on inter-State trade or commerce and taxes on the consignment of goods.

   There are certain taxes that are levied and collected by the Union and distributed between the Union and the States under Article 270. These are taxes on income other than agricultural income which shall be levied and collected by the Government of India and distributed between the Union and the States, and under Article 272 Union duties of excise other than such duties of excise on medicinal and toilet preparations as are mentioned in the Union List shall be levied and collected by the Government of India. Article 271 States that notwithstanding anything in Articles 269 and 270, the Parliament may at any time increase any of the duties or taxes referred to in those articles by a surcharge for purposes of the Union and the whole proceeds of any such surcharge shall form part of the consolidated fund of India.

Then again there are certain taxes which are levied and collected by the States and become the sources of State revenues. These are land revenues, taxes on agricultural income or succession to agricultural land, estate duty on agricultural land, lands and buildings, mineral rights, excise on opium and alcoholic liquors and narcotics, consumption or sale or electricity, sale and purchase of goods other than newspapers, goods and passenger tax, vehicles, animals and boats, tolls, capitations, professions, trades, calling and employments, luxuries and entertainments, betting and gambling, stamp duty and fees in respect of any matter in the Concurrent List, but not including fees taken in any court.

There are certain taxes which are levied and collected by the Union Government which are related to the Union List like railways, post and telegraph, telephones, wireless, broadcasting and other form of communications, property of the Union and the revenue therefrom, public debt of the union. Foreign exchange, currency, coinage and the legal tender, foreign loans, Reserve Bank of India, post office savings bank, lotteries, taxes on income other than agricultural, customs and export duties, excise on tobacco, alcoholic, liquors, corporation tax, taxes on the capital value of assets, death duty and taxes on any item covered in the Union List.

3. Regarding the grants-in-aid of the Union Government to the States, Article 273 lays down that there shall be a charge on the consolidated fund of India, each year as grants-in-aid of the revenues of the States of Assam, Bihar, Orissa and West Bengal in lieu of assignment of any share of the net proceeds in each year of export duty on jute and jute products to those States such sums as may be prescribed. The sums of such grants shall be determined by the President and be paid to the States so long as the export duty on jute and jute products continues to be levied by the Government of India or until the expiry of ten years since the commencement of the Constitution, whichever is earlier. Under Article 275, the Parliament by law can provide such grants as it may deem necessary for giving financial assistance to any State which is in need of such help. The Union Parliament can also provide grants for financing the welfare schemes of weaker sections of people like the Scheduled Castes and Scheduled Tribes in a particular State. Under Article 282, the Union and the State can make grants for any public purpose, notwithstanding that the purpose is not one with respect to which the Parliament or the Legislature of a State as the case may be, may make laws.
4. It is also provided that after the deduction of sums attributable to the Union Territories, and to the Union emoluments, the net proceeds of the income tax shall be divided between the Union and the States as

per the orders given by the President after considering the Report of the Finance Commission.

5. Article 292 and Article 293 of Chapter II of Part XII contains provisions for borrowing by the Union Government and the State Governments. The Union Government can borrow money on the security of the consolidated fund of India, subject to the limitation laid down by the Act of the Parliament. A State Government can borrow only within India, and cannot raise a new loan without the consent of the Union Government if there already exists outstanding any part of a previous loan granted by the Union or owed to it. The Union Government may make loans to the States subject to the condition laid down by an Act of the Parliament, or may guarantee loans to the States provided that the limits set by the Parliament to the Union loans have not exceeded.
6. The Comptroller and Auditor-General of India is appointed by the President of India and the Parliament can entrust him with the duties and such power in relation to State accounts as may deem proper. In the absence of such legislation, but with the prior approval of the President, the Comptroller and Auditor-General may prescribe the form in which State accounts are to be maintained.
7. Article 280 provides for the appointment of a Finance Commission. Article 280(1) enjoins on the President to constitute a Finance Commission, within two years of the commencement of the Constitution, and thereafter at the expiration of every fifth year or before, if it is considered necessary. Clause 2 of that Article empowers Parliament to determine by law the requisite qualifications of its members and the manner of their selection. Clause 3 of the same Article enumerates the duties of the Finance Commission. It reads that it shall be the duty of the Commission to make recommendations to the President as —
   (a) the distribution between the Union and the States of the net proceeds of taxes which are to be, or may be, divided between them under this Chapter and the allocation between the States of respective shares of such proceeds
   (b) the principles which should govern the grants-in-aid of the revenues of the States out of the consolidated fund of India
   (c) any other matter referred to the Commission by the President in the interests of sound finance
8. Centralized planning is a feature in India political system. There is a centralized Planning Commission and the Prime Minister is the Chairman of this Commission. The Planning Commission is the primary body which formulates plans and allocates plan resources to the States. The States can at best lobby to get the maximum plan allocation for their respective States.

Nature of the Indian Federation

Article 1 describes India as a 'Union of States'. These States are specified in the First schedule to the Constitution. Articles 2, 3 and 4 enable Parliament by law to admit a new State, increase, diminish the area of any State or alter the boundaries or name of any State. A special aspect of the Indian Union is that the Union is indestructible, but this is not the case with the Indian States; their identity can be altered or even obliterated. Another distinctive aspect of the Indian Constitution is that it provides for a single citizenship for the whole of India. There is no dual citizenship, one of the Union and the other of the States as in the case of American federation. There is a written Constitution and Article 368 lays down the special procedure for the amendment of the Constitution which makes the amendment procedure partly rigid. The Constitution is the supreme law of the land, and there is the Supreme Court which Acts as the guardian of the Constitution. There are two sets of Government—at the Centre and in the States. There also is an elaborate distribution of Governmental powers whether Legislative, Administrative or Financial, between the Union and the States. The Union Legislature or the Parliament has two Houses, the Council of States (Rajya Sabha) and the House of the People (Lok Sabha). Unlike in most federations, representation in both is on the basis of population, through indirect election in the former and direct election in the latter. The Council of States has been given some special functions regarding matters affecting States (see Chapter 9 for special powers of Rajya Sabha), while the House of the People has been given some special role regarding financial matters, especially relating to Money Bills. States have been given some flexibility about having bicameral or unicameral Legislatures.

Despite such federal arrangements, the framers of the Indian Constitution made the Central Government stronger than the State. The Union enjoys dominant and relatively larger powers. The subjects of Legislative power have been classified under three lists—the Union List (List I), the State List (List II) and the Concurrent List (List III) under the Seventh Schedule of the Constitution. Parliament has the exclusive power to legislate in respect of matters in the Union List. Similarly, exclusive power has been conferred on the State Legislatures with respect to matters in the State List. Parliament and the State Legislatures also have power to make laws on any matters in the Concurrent List (Articles 245 and 246 read with the Seventh Schedule). Residuary powers of legislation have been vested in Parliament (Article 248 read with entry 97, List I). The Constitution makes a distribution of taxing powers between the Union and the States. The fields of taxation have been enumerated either in the Union List or in the State List. There is no subject of taxation in the Concurrent List. The Constitution makes provisions for funds for States as it clearly states that certain tax revenues will be raised by the Union, but to be shared with the States. It provides not only for their distribution between the Union and the States but also among the States on the recommendations of the Finance Commission (Articles 268 to 281).

In the matters of law-making, if the Rajya Sabha declares by a resolution supported by not less than two-third of the members present, and voting that it is necessary or expedient in national interest then the Parliament can make laws with respect to a matters enumerated in the State List specified in the resolution. Where, with respect to a matter, there is irreconcilable conflict or overlapping as between the three lists, the laws made by the Parliament shall prevail over the laws made by the Legislatures of the States. A law made by a State Legislature, repugnant to a law made by Parliament or an existing law applicable in that State, in regard to any matter enumerated in the Concurrent List, shall be void to the extent of repugnancy. Every citizen in a State is subject to the operation of the laws of the Union and the States. If a State fails to comply with any valid executive direction of the Union Government, it shall be lawful (under Article 365) for the President to hold that a situation has arisen in which the Government of a State cannot be carried on in accordance with the provisions of the Constitution and, therefore, warrants action under Article 356.

The Governor is also appointed by the President but here the will of the union prevails. The Governors also continue their office as long as they enjoy the pleasure of the President, but again that is theoretically true as in reality, the President just carries out the wishes of the Union Government. The Governor Acts as the head of the State as well as the agent of the centre in the State. The President also appoints the Comptroller and Auditor-General to verify and check the accounts of the Union and the States. The Election Commission also conducts elections for Lok Sabha and Legislative Assemblies of States. The Planning in India is also a centralized planning through the Planning Commission in which the Prime Minister is the ex-officio Chairman of the Planning Commission.

From the foregoing discussion on the fiscal relations between the Union and the States we have seen that the union government enjoys a superior position than the State Governments. The State Governments can also be placed in a discomfortable position by the appointments of inquiry Commissions against the Chief Minister of a particular State.

Therefore, what can be discerned from the above discussion is that though certain features of federal form of Government are present, the Indian polity exhibits signs of unitarianism. As the tendency towards centralization continues tensions arise in the Union-State relations.

Tension Areas in Union-State Relations

Financial relations

Mobilization, sharing and utilization of financial resources play a very crucial role in Centre-State relations. The Indian Constitution contains provisions (Article 280) for the creation of the Finance Commission, which is set up periodically, for advising/recommending to the President of India on matters pertaining to the division of certain tax revenues raised by the Union, between the Union and the States.

The Planning Commission also advises the Union Government regarding the desirable transfer of resources to the States over and above those recommended by the Finance Commission. Its recommendations cover, among other things, feasible changes in tax rates and efforts by both, quantum and allocation of borrowings between the Union and the States. Bulk of the transfer of revenue and capital resources from the union to the States is determined largely on the advice of these two Commissions. Apart from these, the Union Government also makes certain other transfers to the States.

The resources allocated to the States are inadequate particularly for the State Governments, as they are handicapped when it comes to the creation of social infrastructure, which involve large investments with minimum direct return. These include development of roads, generation and distribution of power, and so on or taking up programmes for socio-economic development like working towards rural development, education, medical and public health facilities, welfare of Scheduled Castes and Scheduled Tribes, etc. Apart from these, the State have to incur huge expenditure on maintenance of law and order, especially those States suffering from disturbances, insurgencies and uprisings of various types. The States want more financial autonomy which by far has been ignored. Further what is accused by certain States that there are certain factors which determine how much fund will be allocated to a particular State. These factors are as follows:

1. **Alignment factors:** Central assistance to the State Governments is often made on the consideration of party politics. Governments at State level constituted by the same party at the Centre or their coalition partners very often receive more central assistance.
2. **Swing factor (voters):** This refers to the response of the electorate. If the chances of swing is more, i.e., if the prospect of the party at the centre or its coalition partners seems to be favourable in the forthcoming elections, then more funds are allocated to that particular State to win voters.
3. **Lobbying (number of MPs at ministerial level):** If the number of MPs from a particular State at the ministerial level is more or have the capacity to influence the decision regarding the distribution of funds, undoubtedly, that State Government is bound to receive more Central assistance.

Besides, lobbying another crucial factor also determines the amount of central fund to be allocated. The amount of fund for a particular State is determined also by the utilization of previous year's fund. The financial relations have been the most debated and conspicuous area of interaction between the Central Government and the State Governments.

Use/misuse of Article 356

The most controversial provision in the Constitution is Article 356 related to imposition of President's Rule in a State. When in the initial years the ruling party was Congress both at the Centre and the States, frictions were less. The non-congress States of PEPSU in 1953, and Kerala in 1957–1959, however, had a chequered relationship. After 1967, when as many as 9 States formed non-Congress Governments, tensions between the Centre and the State became a regular affair. In 1951, emergency under Article 356 was imposed for the first time in the State of Punjab. In 1959, the Kerala was put under the President's Rule. There have been many cases of Proclamation State Emergencies due to 'Constitutional breakdown' like in Orissa in 1961, Haryana in 1967, U.P. in 1970, Tamil Nadu in 1976 and nine States of Punjab, Haryana, U.P., Bihar, West Bengal, Madhya Pradesh, Himachal, Rajasthan and Karnataka in 1977. In 1978, Pondicherry, in 1979 Manipur and in 1980 again another nine States were brought under President's Rule like U.P., Bihar, Rajasthan, M.P., Punjab, Gujarat, Odisha, Maharashtra and Tamil Nadu. The State of Assam has been also put under President's Rule in 1980. In 1986, emergency was imposed in Jammu and Kashmir due to terrorism and insurgency. Punjab and Kerala have been subjected to President's Rule for a number of times. In all, there are more than hundred times that emergency has been imposed in various States for one reason or the other. However, after 1995, the use of this provision has rarely been made. It was used by the United Front Government for imposing President's Rule in Gujarat and U.P. between 1996 and 1997. In 2002, again President's Rule was imposed in U.P., as there was no party to form a stable Government. In 2005, the UPA-I Government imposed Article 356 in Goa and Bihar. In the case of Goa, President A.P.J. Abdul Kalam approved the imposition of President's Rule in the State as recommended by the Union Cabinet. The Union Cabinet had recommended that Goa be brought under President's Rule and the Assembly kept under suspended animation, even though the Rane government earlier won a kind of vote of confidence in the House. With regard to Bihar, since neither the RJD-led alliance nor the NDA came forward with the support of 122 MLAs required for majority, therefore, the Governor recommended imposition of President's Rule under Article 356 of the Constitution to end the political uncertainty. Thus, President's Rule was imposed in Bihar. There has been use misuse of Article 356 by all the parties whichever one has come to form the Government at the Centre. The Sarkaria Commission had recommended that Article 356 should be sparingly used.

Law and order in the State and the Centre

The deployment of the central forces in the States without the permission of the State Governments, non-implementation of Central Laws and Central Directives, use of All-India Services and C.B.I. have led to tensions between the Centre and the States. The States have complained that maintenance of law and order is very much within the purview of the State Government as it is under State List, but there have been occasions when the Union Government has deployed para-military forces like Border Security Forces (BSF), Central Industrial Faculty Force (CISF) and Central Reserve Police (CRP) without consulting the States sometimes in the name of protecting Central Government's undertakings and property.

The establishment of National Counter Terrorism Centre (NCTC) can be seen as the infringement of the State Government's powers and violation of federal structure. The NCTC, a body that will coordinate operations against terror groups, has been constituted under the Ministry of Home Affairs and has been granted special powers to arrest and search anyone/ any place under suspicion, without prior consultation with State Governments. The move was supposed to become operational from 1 March 2012. The officers of the operations divisions of the NCTC shall have the power to arrest and power to search under Section 43A of the Unlawful Activities (Prevention) Act, 1967. Vehement criticisms and oppositions came from the Chief Ministers of different States. The Chief Ministers of West Bengal, Tamil Nadu, Bihar and Odisha have been most vocal against NCTC. During the Budget Session (2012) when this was placed in the Parliament there was a furor over NCTC. However, the UPA-II Government got a relief over the fiercely contested National Counter Terrorism Centre (NCTC) when three amendment motions moved by the opposition on the anti-terror intelligence hub were defeated in the Lok Sabha and in Rajya Sabha with the help of the Samajwadi Party (SP), the Bahujan Samaj Party (BSP) and absence of Trinamool Congress members, the government defeated the opposition backed amendments on the National Counter Terrorism Centre (NCTC) in the Rajya Sabha despite lacking majority in the House. It is to be seen how the execution of NCTC affects the centre-State relations. In a meeting held on 5 May 2012, with the Chief Ministers of different State, organized to finalize the NCTC was inconclusive with no final decision being taken as there were vehement criticisms from some Chief Ministers.

From the above discussion we can conclude by saying that Indian polity exhibits more of unitary characteristics than federal features. As K.C. Wheare observes, "The Indian Constitution established a system of government which is almost quasi-federal, almost devolutionary in character, a unitary State with subsidiary federal features rather than federal States with unitary features." C.N. Joshi is of the view that "The Union is not strictly a federal polity but a qausi-federal polity with vital and important element of unitariness."

INTEGRATION MECHANISMS

From the above discussion it becomes clear that there have always been tensions between the relation of the Union and the State. There have also been efforts for further integration between the Centre and the State. Therefore, with that aim, the National Development Council (NDC) was formed. Further, in 1969, the Administrative Reforms Commission, constituted by the Government of India, had submitted its Report, substantial parts of which had focused on the steps to be taken for maintaining harmonious Centre-State relations. The Rajamannar Committee, appointed by the Government of Tamil Nadu, likewise had given its Report in 1971, recommending greater autonomy for the States in legislative and fiscal matters. The Shiromani Akali Dal in Punjab, the Telugu Desam Party in Andhra Pradesh, the State Governments of West Bengal, Tamil Nadu and the North-East had all been demanding review of the overall Constitutional scheme of Centre-State relations. Under tremendous pressure from the States, Prime Minister Indira Gandhi, in 1983, declared the Constitution of the first Commission on Centre-State relations. It was to be headed by Justice R.S. Sarkaria, a retired Judge of the Supreme Court of India. Based on the recommendations of the Sarkaria Commission, inter-State Council has been set up on 28th May 1990, under Article 263 of the Constitution for co-ordination of Inter-State matters. Some of the mechanisms of integration are discussed as follows:

National Development Council

The Rashtriya Vikas Parishad or the National Development Council (NDC) came into existence on 6 August 1952. The draft outline of the very first Five Year Plans (July 1951) had expressed the need for creation of a body consisting of the representatives of the Central Government, the constituent units of a Federal Union and others equally interested and qualified for the job. This proposal was accepted by the Government of India, and thus, the Rashtriya Vikas Parishad was created. The main objective of NDC has been to strengthen and mobilize the efforts and resources of the nation in support of the Five Year Plans, to promote common economic policies in all vital spheres and to ensure the balanced and rapid development of all parts of the country.

Composition

The Council comprises the Prime Minister, all the Union Cabinet Ministers, Chief Ministers of all States or their substitutes, representatives of the Union Territories and the members of the Commissions. There have been occasions when the Reserve Bank Governor and other experts have been invited to address the meetings. The large membership of the Council, which at one time rose to 50, reduced the utility of the Council for discussion as a compact body and in November 1954, a Standing Committee was established with only nine Chief Ministers and a few Union Ministers as members. In addition, the Council has been appointing Committees from time-to-time for a detailed examination of certain problems. The Prime Minister is the Chairman of the Council and the Secretary to the Commission Acts as its Secretary and the Commission furnishes the Council with administrative and other assistance.

The Council ordinarily meets twice a year. A point to be noted is that in the Council ordinarily no resolution is passed formally. The practice is to have a complete record of discussion, and from it highlighting the general trends directing towards particular conclusions. The decisions are usually unanimous. The Fiftieth meeting of the NDC was held on 21 December 2002, which marked the Golden Jubilee of NDC meetings. On this occasion, the Planning Commission brought out the Summary Record of Discussions of the 50 meetings of the NDC in five volumes.

Functions of National Development Council

In October 1967, on the recommendations of the Administrative Reforms Commission, the Council was reconstituted and its functions were redefined. The functions are:

1. Prescription of guidelines for the formulation of National Plan, including the assessment of resources for the plan;
2. Consideration of National Plan as formulated by the Planning Commission;
3. Considering important questions of social and economic policy affecting national development; and
4. The review of working of the plan from time-to-time, and recommending such measures as are necessary for achieving the aims and targets to secure the active participation and cooperation of the people, improving the efficiency of the administrative services, ensuring the fullest development of the less advanced regions and sections of the community and, through sacrifice, borne equally, by all citizens, build up resources for national development.

It was envisaged that the NDC would advise and make its recommendations to the Central and State Governments. Since its inception, it has been functioning as an important consultative body for the implementation of the Five Year Plans and advising on important problems being faced the Indian economy.

The prime function of the Council is to act as a kind of bridge between the Union Government, the Planning Commission and the State Governments. It helps in the coordination not only of policies and programmes of plans, but also other matters of national importance. It provides a viable forum for discussion and exchange of views. Striking a balanced economic development in all the States is the prime motive of NDC. (Details given in Chapter 22).

Inter-State Council

Article 263 of the Constitution of India provides as under:

"If at any time it appears to the President that the public interest would be served by the establishment of a Council charged with the duty of–

1. inquiring into and advising upon disputes which may have arisen between States;
2. investigating and discussing subjects in which some or all of the States, or the Union and one or more of the States, have a common interest; or
3. making recommendations upon any such subject and in particular, recommendations for the better co-ordination of policy and action with respect to that subject, it shall be lawful for the President by order to establish such a Council, and to define the nature of the duties to be performed by it and its organization and procedure."

Based on the recommendations of the Sarkaria Commission, Inter-State Council has been set up on 28th May 1990 under Article 263 of the Constitution for co-ordination of Inter-State matters.

The Inter-State Council Secretariat is headed by the Secretary to the Government of India who looks into the affairs of the Inter-State Council and its Standing Committees. In addition, Inter-State Council Secretariat also is the Secretariat for Commission for Centre-State relations.

Composition

The Council was set up vide Presidential order given on 28th May 1990. Paragraph 2 of the Presidential order provides for the composition of the Council. According to this, the Council shall consist of Prime Minister as the Chairman and as members, Chief Ministers of all States, Chief Ministers of Union Territories having a Legislative Assembly and administrators of Union Territories not having a Legislative Assembly and Governors of States under President's Rule (Governor's rule in the case of J&K), 6 Ministers of Cabinet rank in the Union Council of Ministers to be nominated by the Prime Minister.

In October 2011, the Centre has reconstituted the Inter-State Council and its standing committee, incorporating new members in these panels. The changes were made following the reshuffle in the Union Cabinet and States, since the body was last reconstituted over two years ago.

The ISC, which was set up in 1990 following the recommendation of the Sarkaria Commission on Centre-State relations, is empowered to discuss matters concerning one or more States and Union Territories. While the Inter-State Council is chaired by Prime Minister Manmohan Singh, and has all the Chief Ministers as its members, the reconstituted Standing Committee now consists of nine Chief Ministers, including Narendra Modi, Mayawati, J. Jayalalithaa, Ashok Gehlot, Naveen Patnaik, Manik Sarkar, Oommen Chandy, Lal Thanhawla and Prakash Singh Badal. The Standing Committee that was set up in 1996 is meant for continuous consultation for the Council's consideration. Union Home Minister P. Chidambaram heads the panel. Besides 9 Chief Ministers, the Committee has 6 Union Cabinet Ministers—Pranab Mukherjee, Sharad Pawar, M. Veerappa Moily, M.K. Alagiri, Salman Khursheed and

Dinesh Trivedi as its members as reconstituted in 2011, and might be changed following reshuffle of Union Cabinet and Pranab Mukherjee becoming the President of India in July 2012.

Sarkaria Commission

Sarkaria Commission was set up in June 1983 by the Government of India. The Sarkaria Commission's Charter was to examine the relationship and balance of power between State and Central Governments in the country and suggest changes within the framework of Constitution of India. The Commission was so named as it was headed by Justice Rajinder Singh Sarkaria, a retired judge of the Supreme Court of India. The other two members of the committee were Shri B. Sivaraman and Dr. S.R. Sen.

The Commission after conducting several studies, eliciting information, holding discussions and after detailed deliberations submitted its 1600-page Report in January 1988. The Report contains 247 recommendations spreading over 19 Chapters. Chapter 0. Introduction Chapter I. Perspective Chapter II. Legislative Relations Chapter III. Administrative Relations Chapter IV. Role of the Governor Chapter V. Reservation of Bills by Governors for President's consideration and Promulgation of Ordinances Chapter VI. Emergency Provisions Chapter VII. Deployment of Union Armed Forces in States for Public Order Duties Chapter VIII. All India Services Chapter IX. Inter-Governmental Council Chapter X. Financial Relations Chapter XI. Economic and Social Planning Chapter XII. Industries Chapter XIII. Mines and Minerals Chapter XIV. Agriculture Chapter XV. Forests Chapter XVI. Food and Civil Supplies Chapter XVII. Inter-State River Water Disputes Chapter XVIII. Trade, Commerce and Inter-course within the Territory of India Chapter XIX. Mass Media Chapter XX. Miscellaneous Matters Chapter XXI. General Observations Chapter XXII and Appendices.

In spite of the large size of its Reports—the Commission recommended, by and large, status quo in the Centre-State relations, especially in the areas, relating to legislative matters, role of Governors and use of Article 356.

Key Recommendations of the Sarkaria Commission

1. On administrative relations, Sarkaria Commission, while making recommendation keeping in mind the provisions of Article 256 and 257 (discussed above) and Article 356 pertaining to Declaration of Emergency on the ground of failure of Constitutional Machinery, observed that non-compliance by any State, the application of Article 356 must be a careful and cautious decision. As for Article 356, it was recommended that it should be used very sparingly, in extreme cases, as a measure of last resort, when all other alternatives fail to prevent or rectify a breakdown of Constitutional machinery in the State.

2. As far as legislative relations between the Union and the States are concerned the Commission recommended that the residuary powers of legislation in regard to taxation matters should remain exclusively in the competence of Parliament, while the residuary field other than that of taxation should be placed on the Concurrent List. The enforcement of Union laws, particularly those relating to the Concurrent List there should be prior consultation not only with the State Governments individually, but also collectively with the inter-governmental Council.
3. Regarding the financial relations between the Union and the State, the Commission made a number of recommendations for sharing of taxes, levy of surcharge, decentralization of planning process, improvement for working of finance Commission, Planning Commission and National Development Council and various others.
4. While deploying central forces for reasons other than the request of the State Government or declares an area within a State as disturbed, the Commission observed that necessary consultation with the State Governments must be held wherever, it is feasible even though the prior consultation with the State Government is not obligatory.
5. The Commission also recommended that State Governments should avoid the wrong practice of mechanical and repeated promulgation of an Ordinance without caring to get replaced by an Act of the Legislature. Any such decision of promulgation and repromulgation of an Ordinance should be taken on the basis of Stated facts necessitated such action collectively taken by the State Council of Ministers.
6. Regarding Article 200 under which the Governor can reserve Bills for Presidential assent, the Commission recommended that the Presidential assent should not be withheld only on the ground that the Union government is in the process of exploring the possibilities of a law on the same subject. Further, the Governor should not reserve the Bill for his personal dissatisfaction over the provisions of the Bill. Only under exceptional circumstances Bills should be reserved and while considering any Bill, the Governor must act according to the advice of the Council of Ministers.
7. The Commission also recommended criteria for selecting a Governor of a State and also observed that his tenure of five years in a particular State should not be disturbed except under exceptional circumstances. While appointing Governors of the States, the Commission recommended that the Chief Minister of the concerned state should be consulted and for this necessary amendment of the Constitution must be made by amending Article 155. The Vice-President and the Speaker of the Lok Sabha may also be consulted. The Commission further recommends criteria which can be kept in the mind of Governor while making appointment of a Chief Minister of a State.

8. The Sarkaria Commission also recommended the establishment of a permanent Inter-State Council under Article 263 of the Constitution.
9. The Commission did not recommend a drastic change in the basic structure of the Constitution, but improvement and reform of a number of aspects cannot be ruled out.

In 2007, two decades after Sarkaria Commission submitted its Report on the subject, the centre decided to have another look at Centre-State relations by setting up a four-member Commission. It was headed by former Chief Justice of India, Justice Madan Mohan Punchhi and it was framed to look into matters concerning 'federal crime' as well as the deployment of Central Forces in States when needed. Members of the Commission included two former Union Home Secretaries — Dhirendra Singh and V.K. Duggal. Former director of the National Law School of India, Bangalore, N.R. Madhava Menon, was the fourth member of the panel. The Commission on June 2009 was given a nine-month extension upto 31 March 2010. The Commission submitted its Reports on March 2010.

In the seven volumes of the Report, the present Commission has tried to address a range of complex issues which have come up in Centre-State relations in the context of social and economic developments that have taken place over the years since the Report of the Sarkaria Commission of 1988. The focus of the Commission during its numerous deliberations has been on 'as to what framework of relationship between the Centre and the States will strengthen the unity and integrity of the country and ensure India's stability, security and economic growth and the welfare of her people'.

The National Commission to Review the Working of the Indian Constitution (NCRWC) or the Venkatachallaih Commission constituted in 2000, identified major areas of Centre-State relations which require review especially use of Article 356 and imposition of President's Rule in any State.

EXERCISES

I. Short Answer Questions: **(100 words)**

1. Article 1 of the Constitution.
2. The reorganization of Indian States since the formation of the Dar Commission.
3. The Centre-State legislative relations (any four provisions)
4. The Centre-State administrative relations (any four provisions)
5. The Centre-State financial relations (any four provisions)
6. Inter-State Council
7. Sarkaria Commission
8. National Development Council

II. Long Answer Questions: (1200 words)

9. Examine the tension areas in the relationship between the Centre and the State.
10. Discuss critically the Centre-State legislative relations.
11. Discuss critically the Centre-State administrative relations.
12. Discuss critically the Centre-State financial relations.
13. Discuss some of the key integration mechanisms to strike a balance between Centre and the State.
14. Discuss the nature of Indian Federation. Do you think that it is more of a unitary character? Argue.

REFERENCES

Awasthy, S.S., *Indian Government and Politics*, Har-Anand Publications, Revised Edition, New Delhi, 2006.

Bakshi, P.M., *The Constitution of India* (with selective comments), Universal Law Publishing, Delhi, 2000.

Basu, Durga Das, *Introduction to the Constitution of India*, Prentice-Hall of India, New Delhi, 1992.

Jain, M.P., *Indian Constitutional Law*, Wadhwa & Company, Nagpur, 1999.

Rao, K.V., *Parliamentary Democracy of India: A Critical Commentary*, The World Press, Calcutta, 1961.

Sarkar, Siuli, *Public Administration in India,* PHI Learning, New Delhi, 2010.

Singh, M.P. and Saxena Rekha, *Indian Politics: Constitutional Foundations and Institutional Functioning,* PHI Learning, New Delhi, 2008.

Siwach, J.R., *Dynamics of Indian Government and Politics*, Sterling Publishers, New Delhi, 1985.

7

The Union Executive—The President of India

INTRODUCTION

India is a Democratic Republic, and hence has a democratically elected government, and the head of the State is neither a nominated representative nor a hereditary monarch, but an elected representative of the people even though the election may be indirect. The President of India, is the head of the State and occupies the highest office in India. He is elected by the elected members of the Parliament and State Legislative Assemblies for a fixed term of five years. However, he has to act according to the aid and advice given to him by the Council of Ministers and the Prime Minister. There is a debate regarding the actual position of the President for he is the nominal executive or the Constitutional head, the actual power being exercised by the Prime Minister and the Council of Ministers who are the real executive. The 12th President of India was Her Excellency Pratibha Devi Singh Patil who was sworn in as the President of India on 25 July 2007. She is the first woman to serve in the office whose tenure ended on 25 July 2012. The Fourteenth President of the Indian Republic is Shri Ram Nath Kovind.

PRESIDENT OF INDIA

Qualifications to Become a President

Article 58 of the Constitution sets the principle qualifications, which one must meet to be eligible to the office of the President. They are as follows:

1. He must be a citizen of India
2. He must have completed 35 years of age

3. He must be qualified to become a member of the Lok Sabha
4. A person shall not be eligible for election as President if he holds any office of profit under the Government of India or the Government of any State or under any local or other authority subject to the control of any of the said Governments. [Article 58(2)]

Certain office-holders, however, are also permitted to stand as Presidential candidates. They are:

1. The current Vice President
2. The Governor of any State
3. A minister of the Union or of any State (Including Prime Minister and Chief Ministers)

In situations where the Vice President, a State Governor or a Minister is elected as a President, they are considered to have vacated their previous office on the date they begin serving as President.

Under Article 59 he should not be a member of either House of the Parliament or of a House of a State Legislature. "... if a member of either House of Parliament or of the Legislature of any State be elected President, he shall be deemed to have vacated his seat in that House on the date on which he enters upon the office as President." Article 59(2) also states that the President must not hold any other office of Profit.

Further, Article 59 enumerates that The President shall be entitled without payment of rent to the use of his official residences and shall be also entitled to such emoluments, allowances and privileges as may be determined by Parliament by law and, until provision in that behalf is so made, such emoluments, allowances and privileges as are specified in the Second Schedule which cannot be diminished during his term of office. The President of India resides in an estate in New Delhi known as the Rashtrapati Bhavan (Raisina Hill, New Delhi) and the Presidential retreats are The Retreat Building, Mashobra in Shimla and Rashtrapati *Nilayam* (President's Place) Bolarum in Hyderabad. The President of India used to receive ₹10,000 per month as per the Constitution. The Government of India increased the salary of the President of India to ₹50,000 per month in 1998. On 11 September 2008, the Government of India increased the salary of the President to ₹1.5 lakh per month. Currently the President of India receives a salary of ₹500,000 and other allowances fixed to the President of India.

Term of Office and Removal

Article 56 upholds that the President of India shall hold office for a term of five years from the date on which he enters upon his office. The President may be removed before the expiry of his or her term through impeachment or if the President by in his own writing addressed to the Vice-President submits his resignation [Article 56(1) (a), (b) and Article 61 of the Constitution of India]. Under both these cases the President shall continue to hold office till his successor enters upon the office [Article 56(c)].

Article 61 describes the procedure for impeachment of the President. It says that when a President is to be impeached, the charge must be leveled either of the two Houses of the Parliament. The charges are contained in a resolution which has to be signed by at least one-fourth of the total members of that house, and moved after at least fourteen days of notice. A resolution to impeach the President has to be passed by a two-third majority of the total members of the originating House. It is then sent to the other House and the other House then investigates the charges or cause of such charges that have been made. During this process, the President has the right to defend himself/herself through an authorized counsel. If the second House also approves the charges made by two-third majority again, the President stands impeached, and is deemed to have vacated his/her office from the date when such a resolution stands passed. No President has faced impeachment proceedings till date. Hence, the above provisions have never been used.

Article 57 provides that a person who holds, or who has held, office as President shall, subject to the other provisions of the Constitution, be eligible for re-election to that office.

Succession

In the event of a vacancy created for the President's post due to death, resignation, removal, and so on, Article 65 of the Indian Constitution says that the Vice President will have to discharge his duties. The Vice President reverts to his office when a new President is elected and enters his office. When the President is unable to act owing to his absence, illness or any other cause, the Vice President discharges the President's functions for a temporary period until the President resumes his duties.

When the Vice President acts as, or discharges the functions of the President, he has all the powers and immunities of the President and is entitled to the same emoluments, allowances and privileges as the President.

Parliament has, by the President (Discharge Of Functions) Act, 1969 made provisions for the discharge of the functions of the President when vacancies occur in the offices of the President and of the Vice President simultaneously, owing to removal, death, resignation of the incumbent or otherwise. A crisis occurred in 1969, when the Office of the President of India fell vacant due to the death of Dr. Zakir Hussain, and the Vice President V.V. Giri decided to contest the election, the office of the President of India remained vacant. Thus, the Parliament hurriedly passed the 1969 Act to fill in the gap which provided that in such an eventuality, the Chief Justice, or in his absence, the senior most Judge of the Supreme Court of India available, discharges the functions of the President until a newly elected President enters his office or a newly elected Vice President begins to act as President under Article 65 of the Constitution, whichever is the earlier.

Immunities of the President of India

The President under Article 361, shall not be answerable to any court for the exercise and performance of the powers and duties of his office or for any act done or purporting to be done by him in the exercise and performance of those powers and duties. No criminal proceedings, whatsoever, shall be instituted or continued against the President during his term of office. No process for the arrest or imprisonment of the President shall be issued from any court during his term of office. No civil proceedings in which relief is claimed against the President cannot be also instituted during his term of office in any court in respect of any act done or purporting to be done by him in his personal capacity whether before or after he takes upon his office as President until the expiration of two months next after notice in writing has been delivered to the President.

Method of Election of the President of India

Detailed provisions regarding the election are contained in the Presidential and Vice-Presidential Elections Act, 1952 (No. 31 of 1952) and the rules made there under *The Presidential and Vice-Presidential Elections Rules*, 1974. An Ordinance was also promulgated on 5th June 1997 to further amend The Presidential and Vice-Presidential Elections Act, 1952, which was later converted into an Act. These Acts introduced various important provisions relating to the mode and manner of elections to the offices of the President and Vice-President. A prospective Presidential candidate should get his nomination paper subscribed by at least fifty electors as proposers, and at least fifty electors as seconders. In the case of prospective Vice-Presidential candidate, the nomination paper should be subscribed by at least twenty electors as proposers, and at least twenty electors as seconders. No elector shall subscribe whether as proposers or as seconder, more than one nomination paper at the same election and if he does so, his signature shall be inoperative on any paper other than the one first delivered.

Not more than four nomination papers can be filed by or on behalf of a candidate or received by the Returning Officer. A prospective candidate should deposit a sum of ₹15000 as security deposit. This amount is liable to be forfeited if at the election where the poll has been taken the candidate is not elected and the number of valid votes polled by such candidate does not exceed one-sixth of the votes necessary to secure the return of a candidate at such election.

An election petition calling in question an election to the office of the President may be presented, within 30 days from the date of publication of the declaration of the result of election, to the Supreme Court by any candidate at such election or any twenty or more electors joined together as petitioners; and in the case of the election to the office of the Vice-President, by any candidate at such election or by ten or more electors joined together as petitioners.

Electoral College

Under Rule 40 of the Presidential and Vice-Presidential Elections Rules, 1974, the Election Commission is required to maintain a list of members of the Electoral College referred to in Article 54 of the Indian Constitution. Article 54 contains reference to the composition of the Electoral College which according to this Article consists of the elected members of both Houses of Parliament and the elected members of the Legislative Assemblies of the State. The list of members of Electoral College therefore, contains the names of elected members of the Rajya Sabha, Lok Sabha and the elected members of State Legislative Assemblies [including National Capital Territory of Delhi and the Union Territory of Puducherry vide the Constitution (Seventieth Amendment) Act, 1992]. The nominated members of either House of Parliament or the Legislative Assemblies of State are not eligible to be included in the Electoral College. The names will be numbered in a continuous series and arranged in alphabetical order of the State/Union Territory. By convention, the Secretary General of Lok Sabha and the Secretary General of Rajya Sabha are appointed as the Returning Officers by rotation aided by two other Assistant Returning Officers. As provided by the Election Commission of India for the Presidential Election of 2007 the composition of the Electoral College was:

Total number of electors

The total number of members in the Electoral College for the Presidential election in 2007 was 4896, shown as follows:

S.No.	*House*	*Seats*
1.	Rajya Sabha	233
2.	Lok Sabha	543
3.	State Assemblies	4120
	Total	4896

Formula of uniformity in the election of the President

The Constitution while stipulates the creation of an Electoral College under Article 54, under Article 55 provides for the formula of uniformity, in the scale of representation of the different States at the election. For securing such uniformity among the States as well as parity between the States as a whole and the Union, a formula-based on the population of each State is given in the Constitution for determination of the value of vote which each elected Member of Parliament and of the Legislative Assembly of each State is entitled to cast. The Constitution (Eighty-fourth) Amendment Act, 2001 provides that until the relevant population figures for the first census to be taken after the year 2026 have been published, the population of the States for the purposes of calculation of value of votes for the Presidential election shall mean the population as ascertained at the 1971-census. The value of votes is calculated in the following manner:

$$\text{Total number of votes of an elected MLA} = \frac{\text{Population of the States}}{\text{Total number of elected MLA's}} + 1000$$

Illustration

Total population of Andhra Pradesh (1971 census): 43,502,708

Total no. of elective seats in the State Assembly: 294

Number of votes for each member:

$$= \frac{43,502,708}{1000 \times 294}$$

$$= 147.96 \text{ or } 148$$

Total value of votes of all members of each State Assembly is worked out by multiplying the number of elective seats in the Assembly by the number of votes for each member, e.g., 294 × 148 = 43,512 for Andhra Pradesh. The total value of votes of all the States added together is divided by the total number of elected members of Parliament [Lok Sabha (543) + Rajya Sabha (233)] to get the value of votes per each Member of Parliament.

Therefore, the value of votes of each elected member of Parliament will be the total number of the votes of all the elected MLA's of the country divided by the total number of elected MP's and 1 should be added to the quotient in case the remainder is more than half of the total strength of the elected members of Parliament.

$$\text{Total number of votes of an elected MP} = \frac{\text{Total number of votes assigned to all elected MLA's}}{\text{Total number of the elected Members of Parliament}}$$

System of proportional representation by means of single transferable vote

The election of the President shall be held in accordance with the system of Proportional Representation by means of the single transferable vote and the voting at such election shall be by secret ballot (Rule 17 of the Presidential and Vice-Presidential Elections Rules, 1974). The ballot paper does not contain any election symbol. There are two columns in the ballot paper. Column 1 of the ballot paper contains the heading **Name of Candidate** and column 2 contains the heading **Mark order of preference**. Each elector shall have as many preferences as there are candidates, but no ballot paper shall be considered invalid solely on the ground that all such preferences are not marked. An elector in giving his vote shall place Figure 1 in the space opposite the name of the candidate whom he chooses for his first preference and may, in addition, mark as many subsequent preferences as he wishes by placing on his ballot paper the Figures 2, 3, 4 and so on in the spaces opposite the names of other candidates, in order of preference.

The value of vote of each elector is pre-determined by using the formula of uniformity worked out with the help of illustration of the value of votes of Andhra Pradesh above which is 148. The value of votes for the members of each Legislative Assembly varies as in case of Uttar Pradesh it is 208 and Sikkim it is 7. The value of vote of each Member of Parliament is 708. After calculating the total value of votes polled by each candidate, the Returning Officer totals up the value of all valid votes polled. The quota for declaring a candidate as elected is determined by dividing the total value of valid votes by 2 and adding one to the quotient, ignoring the remainder, if any. For example, assuming the total value of valid votes polled by all candidates is 1,00,001. Therefore, the quota required for getting elected is:

$$\text{Electoral quota} = \frac{\text{Total Number of Valid Votes Polled}}{\text{Total Number of Seats to be filled } +1} + 1$$

Illustration

$$\frac{1,00,001}{2} + 1 = 50,000.50 + 1 \text{ (Ignore 0.50)}$$

$$\text{Quota} = 50,000 + 1 = 50,001$$

After ascertaining the quota, the Returning Officer has to see whether any candidate secured the quota for being declared as elected on the basis of the total value of first preference votes polled by him/her. If no candidate gets the quota on the basis of first preference votes, then the Returning Officer proceeds further to second round of counting during which the candidate having lowest value of votes of first preference is excluded and his votes are distributed among the remaining candidates according to the second preference marked on these ballot papers. The other continuing candidates receive the votes of excluded candidate at the same value at which he/she received them in the first round of counting. The Returning Officer will go on excluding the candidates with lowest number of votes in subsequent rounds of counting till either one of the continuing candidates gets the required quota or till only one candidate remains in the field as the continuing candidate and shall declare him/her as elected. In case no aspiring candidate gets the required quota in the first count done on the basis of First Preference votes secured by each candidate then the candidate with the lowest number of votes polled gets eliminated, and his votes are transferred to the remaining candidates on the basis of Second Preferences as recorded by his voters. This process continues till one candidate secures the required quota.

A problem arose during the Fifth Presidential Election and the system of transfer of votes had to be used. Dr. Zakir Hussain, the Third President of India, passed away suddenly on 3 May 1969. Under Article 65(1) of the Constitution, the Vice-President Shri V.V. Giri assumed office to act as President. However, Shri V.V. Giri, resigned on 20th July, 1969 as Vice-President and also as the acting President. As under Article 62(2) of the Constitution, an election to fill a vacancy in the office of the President occurring by reason of his death, resignation, etc., is required to be held in any case within 6 months from the date of the occurrence of the vacancy, necessary steps to hold the election were taken immediately. The quota fixed for election was 4,18,169 votes. As no candidate could secure the required quota in the first count, candidate after candidate was excluded till only two candidates, namely, Shri V.V. Giri (with 4,20,077 votes) and Shri N. Sanjeeva Reddy (with 4,05,427 votes) remained in the field. Shri V.V. Giri who secured the quota was declared elected by the Returning Officer on 20 August 1969, and he assumed office of the President on August 24, 1969.

Table 7.1 gives us a statement of value of votes of elected members of the State Legislative Assemblies and both Houses of Parliament under the Article 55 of the Constitution of India for the Presidential Election of 2022.

Table 7.1 Presidential elections, 2022

Statement of value of votes of elected members of the State Legislative Assemblies and both Houses of Parliament as per Provisions of Article 55(2) of the Constitution of India

S. No.	*Name of State*	*Number of Assembly Seats (Elective)*	*Population (1971 Census)*	*Value of Vote for Each MLA*	*Total Value of Votes for the State*
1	Andhra Pradesh	175	27800586	159	159 × 175 = 27825
2	Arunachal Pradesh	60	467511	8	008 × 060 = 480
3	Assam	126	14625152	116	116 × 126 = 14616
4	Bihar	243	42126236	173	173 × 243 = 42039
5	Chhattisgarh	90	11637494	129	129 × 090 = 11610
6	Goa	40	795120	20	020 × 040 = 800
7	Gujarat	182	26697475	147	147 × 182 = 26754
8	Haryana	90	10036808	112	112 × 090 = 10080
9	Himachal Pradcsh	68	3460434	51	051 × 068 = 3468
10	Jharkhand	81	14227133	176	176 × 081 = 14256
11	Karnataka	224	29299014	131	131 × 224 = 29344
12	Kerala	140	21347375	152	152 × 140 = 21280
13	Madhya Pradesh	230	30016625	131	131 × 230 = 30130
14	Maharashtra	288	50412235	175	175 × 288 = 50400
15	Manipur	60	1072753	18	018 × 060 = 1080
16	Meghalaya	60	1011699	17	017 × 060 = 1020
17	Mizoram	40	32390	8	008 × 040 = 320
18	Nagaland	60	516449	9	009 × 060 = 540
19	Odisha	147	21944615	149	149 × 147 = 21903
20	Punjab	117	13551060	116	116 × 117 = 13572
21	Rajasthan	200	25765806	129	129 × 200 = 25800
22	Sikkim	32	209843	7	007 × 032 = 224

(Contd.)

Table 7.1 Presidential elections, 2022 (*Contd.*)

S. No.	*Name of State*	*Number of Assembly Seats (Elective)*	*Population (1971 Census)*	*Value of Vote for Each MLA*	*Total Value of Votes for the State*
23	Tamil Nadu	234	41199168	176	176 × 234 = 41184
24	Telangana	119	15702122	132	132 × 119 = 15708
25	Tripura	60	1556342	26	026 × 060 = 1560
26	Uttarakhand	70	4491239	64	064 × 070 = 4480
27	Uttar Pradesh	403	83849905	208	208 × 403 = 83824
28	West Bengal	294	44312011	151	151 × 294 = 44394
29	NCT of Delhi	70	4065698	58	058 × 070 = 4060
30	Puducherry	30	471707	16	016 × 030 = 480

The value of votes of the elected members of State Legislative Assemblies and both Houses of Parliament is governed by Article 55(2) of the Constitution. The total value of votes for MLAs for 16th Presidential Election is 543231. The total value of votes for MPs is 543200. The total value of vote of electors for the Presidential Election, 2022 is 1086431 as shown below.

Value of vote of each MP:

The total value of votes of all the states added together is divided by the total number of elected MPs of Parliament

Lok Sabha (543) + Rajya Sabha (233) = 776

$$\text{Value of each Vote} = \frac{543200}{776} = 700$$

The total value of votes for MPs was 700 × 776 = 543200.

The total value of votes for MLAs for 16th Presidential Election was 543231.

The total value of vote of electors for the Presidential Election, 2022 is 543200 + 543231 = 1086431.

In 2007, Smt. Pratibha Devi Singh Patil secured 638116 number of votes and became the Twelfth President of the Republic of India (this was the thirteenth Presidential election, but Pratibha Devi Singh Patil was sworn in as the Twelfth President of the Republic of India as Dr. Rajendra Prasad had been in the office of the President for two consecutive terms). She took office as India's first woman President on 25 July 2007. Shri Pranab Mukherjee secured 713,763 votes in the 2012 Presidential election and he defeated P.A. Sangma who secured 315,987 votes. Shri Mukherjee assumed office on 25th July 2012 as the Thirteenth President of India. Shri Ram Nath Kovind assumed the office of the President of India in 2017. He was able to secure 7,02,044 votes in the 2017 Presidential election and became the fourteenth President of India.

With each MP having a vote value of 700 in this presidential election, Murmu had a total vote value of 5,23,600 which is 72.19 per cent of the total valid vote count of MPs polled.

The oath of office for the President of India

The candidate who secures the required quota or surpassing it gets elected. The result is notified in the Gazette of India. According to Article 60, every President and every person acting as President or discharging the functions of the President shall, before entering upon his office must take an oath or affirmation. The oath of office of the President is administered by the Chief Justice of India and in his absence, the senior most Judge of the Supreme Court available. The oath is as follows:

"I, ..., do swear in the name of God (or solemnly affirm) that I will faithfully execute the office of President (or discharge the functions of the President) of the Republic of India, and will to the best of my ability preserve, protect and defend the Constitution and the law, and that I will devote myself to the service and well-being of the people of Republic of India."

Table 7.2 shows the list of Presidents of India from Independence to till date.

Table 7.2 List of Presidents of India

S. No.	*President*	*Tenure*
1.	Dr Rajendra Prasad (1884–1963)	26 January 1950–13 May 1962
2.	Sarvepalli Radhakrishnan (1888–1975)	13 May 1962–13 May 1967
3.	Zakir Hussain (1897–1969)	13 May 1967–3 May 1969
	Varahagiri Venkata Giri* (1894–1980)	3 May 1969–20 July 1969
	Muhammad Hidayatullah* (1905–1992)	20 July 1969–24 August 1969
4.	Varahagiri Venkata Giri (1894–1980)	24 August 1969–24 August 1974
5.	Fakhruddin Ali Ahmed (1905–1977)	24 August 1974–11 February 1977
	Basappa Danappa Jatti* (1912–2002)	11 February 1977–25 July 1977
6.	Neelam Sanjeeva Reddy (1913–1996)	25 July 1977–25 July 1982
7.	Giani Zail Singh (1916–1994)	25 July 1982–25 July 1987
8.	Ramaswamy Venkataraman (1910–2009)	25 July 1987–25 July 1992
9.	Shankar Dayal Sharma (1918–1999)	25 July 1992–25 July 1997
10.	Kocheril Raman Narayanan (1920–2005)	25 July 1997–25 July 2002
11.	A.P.J. Abdul Kalam (1931–2015)	25 July 2002–25 July 2007
12.	Pratibha Patil (1934–)	25 July 2007–22 July 2012
13.	Pranab Mukherjee (1935–2020)	25 July 2012–25 July 2017
14.	Ram Nath Kovind (1945–2020)	25 July 2017–25 July 2022
15.	Droupadi Murmu (1958–)	25 July 2022–

*Acting Presidents

THE POWERS OF THE PRESIDENT OF INDIA

Executive Powers

Article 53 of the Indian Constitution confers executive powers on the President of the Indian Republic. It states that the executive power of the Union shall be vested in the President and shall be exercised by him directly or through officers subordinate to him in accordance with the Constitution. Therefore, all the executive functions are performed by the government in the name of the President. For the running of the administration he makes rules and also allocates portfolios to the Ministers.

Being the Chief Executive of the Union, the President has the power to make a number of major appointments. He has the sole power to appoint the Prime Minister and the Council of Ministers on the advice of the Prime Minister. However, in the event of the death of Prime Minister, the President can use his judgment in appointing a successor to the office of the Prime minister of India. In three consecutive cases of deaths of Prime Ministers of India, Pandit Nehru in 1964, Lal Bahadur Shastri in 1966 and Indira Gandhi in 1984, the two Presidents, Dr. Sarvepalli Radhakrishnan and Giani Zail Singh conducted the Prime Ministerial succession in different manners. In the first two cases, President Radhakrishnan had sworn in the senior most cabinet colleague of the late Prime Minister pending the election of the regular leader of the Congress Parliamentary Committee. In the third case President Zail Singh ignored the seniormost Cabinet Minister Pranab Mukherjee and sworn in Rajiv Gandhi, the son of Indira Gandhi as the Prime Minister. Another period of crisis had cropped up in the Indian political scenario around the late 1990s with governments begin formed and dissolved in quick successions, and in all these cases the President played a notable role. In May 1997, the 13 day old BJP government under Atal Bihari Vajpayee failed to secure a majority in the Lok Sabha, and hence had to tender his resignation. The President then called upon the thirteen party coalition of United Front under H.D. Deve Gowda getting support from outside of Congress(I) and the Left to form the Government. This government could function for ten months and collapsed with the withdrawal of support of Congress (I) in March 1997, and failed to secure the confidence vote from the Lok Sabha in April 1997. Thereafter the United Front selected I.K. Gujral as the leader, and Congress (I) again extended its support and the President invited Gujral to form the Government in April 1997. This government also collapsed, and the President in March 1998 invited Atal Bihari Vajpayee to form the government which he did and the BJP led Government proved its majority in March 1998. Thereafter, when the 13th Lok Sabha election was held in 1999, the BJP-led alliance, the National Democratic Alliance (NDA) secured a simple majority and the President K.R. Narayanan invited Atal Bihari Vajpayee to form the government. Such a situation henceforth has not arisen in the later years. In the 14th Lok Sabha election held in 2004 the President A.P.J Abdul Kalam appointed Dr. Manmohan Singh as the Prime Minister of India and in the 15th Lok Sabha election held in 2009, President Pratibha Devi Singh Patil appointed again Dr. Manmohan Singh, the leader of Congress-led UPA, as the Prime Minister of India. In the 16th Lok Sabha elections, President Pranab Mukherjee appointed Shri Narendra Modi, leader of BJP-led NDA, as the 14th Prime Minister of India.

Besides Prime Minister, The President appoints, on the advice of Prime Minister, the Attorney-General of India, Comptroller and Auditor-General of

India, Chief Justices and other judges of the Supreme Court and, ambassadors, envoys, Governors of State, Lt. Governors, Chief Commissioners of the Union Territories, Chairman and Members of Union Public Service Commission, Election Commission, Finance Commission, Official Language Commission, Commission for Scheduled Castes and Scheduled Tribes, Commission of enquiry, etc. As he is the chief appointing authority, he also has the power to dismiss/remove them under certain circumstances. He can dismiss a judge of Supreme Court or a High Court after a special address of impeachment is passed by the Parliament. The President can also dismiss a member of the UPSC after on affirmation of guilt on the basis of an enquiry Report from a judge of the Supreme Court. The Prime minister and the Ministers hold office during "the pleasure of the President". The President can accept the resignation of the Prime Minister and the Union Ministers or may dismiss them if they forfeit his pleasure. However, it must be remembered that any step in such direction has to be taken by the President on the aid and advice of the Prime Minister and his Council of Ministers to avert Constitutional crisis.

Article 77 lays down that all executive actions of the Government of India shall be expressed to be taken in the name of the President. Article 299 also lays down that all contracts made in the exercise of the executive power of the Union or the State shall be expressed to be made by the President, or by the Governor of the State, as the case may be, and all such contracts and all assurances of property made in the exercise of that power shall be executed on behalf of the President or the Governor by such persons and in such manner as he may directing authorize. Further, neither the President nor the Governor shall be personally liable in respect of any contract or assurance made or executed for the purposes of the Constitution or for the purposes of any enactment relating to the Government of India hereto in force, nor shall any person making or executing any such contract or assurance on behalf of any of them be personally liable in respect thereof.

Article 78 states that it shall be the duty of the Prime Minister to communicate to the President all decisions of the Council of Ministers relating to the administration of the affairs of the Union and proposals for legislation and also must supply information on any legislative proposals if the President asks for it. The President can also ask the Prime Minister to submit a decision of any minister for the consideration of the Council of Ministers in order to have the decision of the cabinet which has not been considered by the Council of Ministers.

The President being the Chief Executive authority and the Head of the State, all foreign relations are conducted in his name. He accredits ambassadors and envoys to other countries. All treaties and international agreements are signed in his name though they become effective only after ratification by the Parliament.

The President vide Article 53(2) is the Supreme Commander of the Armed forces of India—Army, Navy and Air Force. However, under Article 53(3) it is stated that "Nothing in this article shall—

(a) be deemed to transfer to the president any functions conferred by any existing law on the Government of any State or other authority; or

(b) prevent Parliament from conferring by law functions on authorities other than the President."

In other words, although the President is the Supreme Commander of the Armed Forces, he cannot declare war or pursue peace at his own will. The authority of the Parliament especially the decision of the Cabinet, the Prime Minister, the Union Defence Minister, Secretary of Union Defence Ministry and also the Chiefs of the three wings of the armed forces are required.

The President has the power of making rules pertaining to joint sessions of the Parliament, appointment of the officers of the Supreme Court, administrative powers of the CAG, recruitment to Union Services and also fixing the strength of the UPSC, appointment of the ad hoc judges of Supreme Court, etc. The President has also the power with regard to the administration of the Union Territories under Part VIII Article 239 of the Constitution. He administers the Union Territories through Governors or Chief Commissioners or authorities whom he thinks are fit to be appointed. He might also appoint the Governor of a State as administrator of an adjoining Union Territory, and where a Governor is so appointed, he shall exercise his functions as such administrator independently of his Council of Ministers. The President also appoints the Lieutenant Governor for National Capital Territory (Delhi) vide the Sixty-ninth Amendment Act, 1991 under the Article 239. Under Article 240, the President has been conferred the power to make regulations for the peace, progress and good government of the Union Territory of the Andaman and Nicobar Islands, Lakshadweep, Dadra and Nagar Haveli, Daman and Diu and Puducherry. Under the Fifth Schedule the President has the power to administer Scheduled Castes areas and Scheduled Tribes. He may also, by order, declare as area to be Scheduled Areas or Tribal Areas. Under Article 263, the President, if he feels it necessary in the public interest may order the establishment to inquire and advise disputes arising between the States. Based on the recommendations of the Sarkaria Commission, Inter-State Council has been set up on 28th May 1990 under article 263 of the Constitution for co-ordination of inter-State matters.

Finally, the most extensive and conspicuous executive power of the President is with regard to State Government and their functioning. The President can give directives to the State Governments which the State Governments must follow, and he can ensure compliance also. As we have discussed (in the Chapter on the Union-State relations) that the President with the consent of the State Government can entrust duties of the Union Government to the officers of the State and also give directions to the State with regard to the maintenance and construction of means of communications of national importance and also railways (Article 258). Further, in the case of failure of Constitutional machinery the President can declare State emergency by invoking Article 356.

Legislative Powers

As India is a Parliamentary form of Government designed following the Westminster pattern of government of Britain, the President is an integral part of the Parliament as much as the British Monarch. The legislative powers must be seen to be intertwined with the exercise of the President's executive power. The legislative powers of the President can be enumerated as:

1. The President has the power to summon and prorogue the session of the Parliament. He can also dissolve the Lok Sabha. He can also summon joint session of the Parliament in case of a deadlock regarding any particular non-money Bill.
2. The President has the power to address and send messages to either or both the Houses. The first session of the Parliament after a general election and the first session of every new year open with the inaugural address of the President. However, the speech is prepared by the Council of Ministers and outlines the broad objectives and future activities of the present Government.
3. Money Bills cannot be introduced in the Lok Sabha without the prior consent of the President. Bills seeking alterations of State boundaries or changes in the names of State again has to be introduced in the Parliament with the prior consent of the President.
4. The Bills passed by the Parliament can only become laws after the President has given his assent to them. But here the President of India enjoys the power to *veto* any Bill, i.e., he may withhold his assent or he may also return the Bill to the Parliament for reconsideration. However, if the Bill is passed again by the Parliament with or without the changes suggested, the President cannot withhold his consent. The President also does not enjoy no veto power over money Bills, and Constitutional amendment Bills. He also does not have *pocket veto* like the US President.
5. The President has very important **ordinance making power**. When the Parliament is not in session, but a certain special situation as it may rise might require the proclamation of an ordinance which has the force and effect of the law. Such ordinances are issued on the aid and advice of the Council of Ministers. The 42nd Amendment (1976) had made *Presidential Satisfaction* immune from judicial review, but it was later repealed by the 44th Amendment (1978). The President may at any time, withdraw the ordinance or such ordinances need to be placed before both the Houses of the Parliament when their session commences otherwise ordinances will cease to operate after the expiry of six weeks from the reassembly of the Parliament.
6. The President lays the Reports and recommendations of several important bodies/Commissions before the Parliament like the UPSC, Finance Commission, CAG, etc.

7. The President also enjoys absolute veto powers over State Bills which may be *essential* by the Parliament, or may be in conflict with the Union legislation already in force, or with any policy matter considered essential by the Governor of the State and he has reserved such a Bill for the consideration of the consent of the President (Article 200).
8. The President nominates 12 members to the Rajya Sabha from fields of Arts, Science, Literature or Social Service. He can also nominate two persons of the Anglo-Indian community to the Lok Sabha if there are sufficient reasons for him to find that the community is not adequately represented in the Lower Chamber.

Financial Powers

Special provisions relating to financial Bills are given in Article 117. It stipulates that a Bill or amendment making provision for any of the matters as given in Article 110 pertaining to Money Bills cannot be introduced or moved except on the recommendation of the President, and a Bill making such provision shall not be introduced in the Council of States. Further a Bill which, if enacted and brought into operation, would involve expenditure from the consolidated fund of India, shall not be passed by either Houses of the Parliament unless the President has recommended to that Houses for consideration of the Bill.

The Annual Financial Statement is laid before both the Houses of Parliament showing the annual estimated receipts and expenditure of the Government of India for that year by the President of India for their approval (Article 112).

The President has the control over the Contingency Fund of India and he can order advances out of it to meet unforeseen expenditure pending its authorization by the Parliament (Article 267).

The President has also been given the power to constitute a Finance Commission at the expiration of every fifth year or at such earlier time as the President considers necessary which shall comprise a Chairman and four other members appointed by the President (Article 280).

Judicial Powers

First and the foremost, the President has the power to appoint the Chief Justices and other judges of Supreme Court and High Courts. He can also dismiss them only after an address by each House of Parliament supported by a majority of the total membership of that House and by majority of not less than two-third of the members of the House present and voting has been presented to the President in the same session for such removal on the ground of proved misbehaviour or incapacity [Article 124(4)].

Article 72 gives the President of India the power to grant pardons, reprieves, respites or remissions of punishment or to suspend, remit or commute the sentence of any person convicted in cases of

1. punishment or sentence by a Court Martial,
2. punishment or sentence for an offence against any law relating to a matter to which the executive power of the Union extends, and
3. death sentence.

The effects of a series of decisions of the Supreme Court and of some High Courts[1] too have upheld that:

1. the exercise of the power by the President under Article 72 is primarily a matter for his discretion, and the courts would not interfere with his actual decision on the merits.
2. Courts exercise a very limited power of judicial review, to ensure that the President considers all relevant materials before coming to his decision.
3. the President can, in the exercise of this power, examine the evidence afresh without sitting as a court of appeal. His power is independent of the judiciary. He can, therefore, afford relief not only from a sentence which he regards as unduly harsh, but also from an evident mistake.
4. the President is not bound to hear a petitioner for mercy before he rejects the petition.

Miscellaneous Powers

There are also some other miscellaneous powers of the President. They are:

1. He may refer any question of public importance involving a question of law to the Supreme Court
2. He may make regulations determining the number of members of the UPSC including their tenure and conditions of service and the like
3. He has some important powers in relation to the administration of Jammu and Kashmir.

Emergency Powers

Part XVIII of the Indian Constitution provides a detailed description of the Emergency Provisions which is the most critical and debatable part of the Constitution. Articles 352, 356 and 360 deal with three kinds of emergency situations in India—General Emergency, State Emergency and Financial Emergency which can be proclaimed by the President of India.

Article 352 contains provisions relating to General Emergency. It states that if the President is satisfied that a grave emergency exists whereby security of India or any part of the territory thereof is threatened, whether by war or

[1] *Nanvati* v. *State of Bombay*, AIR 1961 SC 122
Godse v. *State of Maharashtra*, AIR 1961 600
Kehar Singh v. *Union of India*, (1988) 4 SCC 693: AIR 1989 SC 653

external aggression or armed rebellion, he may, by Proclamation, make a declaration to that effect in respect of the whole of India or of such part of the territory thereof as may be specified in the Proclamation.

This Article suggests that such a Proclamation can be revoked or a varied Proclamation can also be issued. However, the decision of the Cabinet Ministers (Council consisting of the Prime Minister and other Ministers of Cabinet rank under Article 75) to issue such a Proclamation must be sent to the President in written form prior to his issuance of the same. According to the Article, all such Proclamations should be presented to both the Houses of the Parliament except where it is a Proclamation revoking a previous Proclamation, cease to operate at the expiration of one month unless before the expiration of that period it has been approved by resolutions of both Houses of Parliament.

However, if any such Proclamation is issued at a time (not being a Proclamation revoking a previous Proclamation) when the House of the People has been dissolved, or place during the period of one month referred to in this clause, and if a resolution approving the proclamation has been passed by the Council of States, but no resolution with respect to such Proclamation has been passed by the House of the People before the expiration of that period, the Proclamation shall cease to operate at the expiration of thirty days from the date on which the House of the People first sits after its reconstitution, unless before the expiration of the said period of 30 days a resolution approving the Proclamation has been also passed by the House of the People. If the Proclamation is not accepted after the passing of a second resolution, then it will become ineffective after the expiry of 6 months from the date of the passing of the second resolution. It is also mentioned in the Article that not less than two-thirds of the members of any of the Parliamentary Houses should be required to pass a resolution. There are certain rules specified in this Article regarding the power of the President for revoking or issuing a varied Proclamation during emergency.

Further, the discontinuance of such national emergency can take place where a notice in writing signed by not less than one-tenth of the total number of members of the House of the People has expressed their intention to move a resolution for disapproving or as the case may be for disapproving the continuance in force of, a Proclamation issued under this Article to the Speaker if the House in session or to the President if the House is not in session. A special sitting of the House shall be held within 14 days from the date on which such notice is received by the speaker or as the case may be by the President for the purpose of considering such resolution.

The President has also been conferred with the power by this Article to issue different Proclamations on different grounds being war or external aggression or armed rebellion or imminent danger, whether or not, there is a Proclamation already issued by the President under this Article and such Proclamation is in operation.

Article 353 specifies the effect of Proclamation of Emergency. This Article states that during the Proclamation of Emergency the executive power of the Union shall extend to the giving directions to any State as to the manner in which the executive power thereof is to be exercised. The Parliament, as per this Article, can confer the power to make laws conferring powers and imposing duties on the union or officers and authorities of the union as respects that matter, notwithstanding that it is one which is not enumerated in the Union List.

Article 354 deals with the application of provisions relating to distribution of revenues while a Proclamation of Emergency is in operation. The President may while a Proclamation of Emergency is in operation by order direct that all or any of the provisions of Articles 268 to 279 shall, for such period, not extending in any case beyond the expiration of the financial year in which such Proclamation ceases to operate as may be specified in the order have effect subject to such exceptions or modifications as he thinks fit. Information about all such orders must be conveyed to both the Houses of Parliament.

Article 355 lays down the duty of the Union to protect States against external aggression and internal disturbance and provides that the Union or Center is solely responsible for defending the various States from all types of violence and aggressions erupting from outside and disturbances occurring within the nation's Territory.

Article 356 deals with the provisions in case of failure of Constitutional machinery in States. The President of India can take charge of a State if the Reports submitted to him by the Governor suggest that the government of the State has become incapable of exercising the Constitutional powers.

The President may by Proclamation—

1. assume to himself all or any of the functions of the Government of the State, and all or any of the powers vested in or exercisable by the Governor or any body or authority in the State other than the Legislature of the State;
2. declare that the powers of the Legislature of the State shall be exercisable by or under the authority of Parliament;
3. make such incidental and consequential provisions as appear to the President to be necessary or desirable for giving effect to the objects of the Proclamation, including provisions for suspending in whole or in part the operation of any provisions of this Constitution relating to any body or authority of the State.

This Article also upholds that any such Proclamation may be revoked or varied by a subsequent Proclamation. It is also required that any such Proclamation issued under this Article except where it is a Proclamation revoking a previous Proclamation, cease to operate at the expiration of two months unless before the expiration of that period it has been approved by resolutions of both Houses of Parliament. A Proclamation, so approved, shall unless revoked, cease to operate on the expiration of a period of six months from the date of its issue. Further, if the dissolution of the House of the People takes place during any such period of six months and a resolution approving the continuance in force of such Proclamation has been passed by the Council of States, but no resolution with respect to the continuance in force of such Proclamation has been passed by the House of the People during the said period, the Proclamation shall cease to operate at the expiration of 30 days from the date on which the House of the People first sits after its reconstitution unless before the expiration of the said period of thirty days, a resolution approving in force of the Proclamation has also been passed by the House of People.

The Article further states that a resolution with respect to the continuance in force of a Proclamation approved for any period beyond the expiration of one year from the date of issue of such proclamation shall not be passed by either House of Parliament unless a Proclamation is in operation in the whole of India or as the case may be in the whole or any part of the State at the time of passing of such resolution. Further, the Election Commission until certifies that the continuance in force of the Proclamation is necessary on account of difficulties in holding elections to the Legislative Assembly of the State concerned.

Article 357 deals with the exercise of legislative powers under Proclamation issued under Article 356. It states that where such an emergency is declared under Article 356, the powers of the legislature of the State shall be exercised by the Parliament during Emergency.

1. The Parliament is authorized to confer on the President the power of the legislature of the State to make laws and to authorize the President to delegate subject to such conditions as he may think fit to impose, the power so conferred to any other authority to be specified by him on his behalf;
2. The Parliament is competent to make laws conferring powers and imposing duties the union or officers and authorities thereof. This might be done by the President or any authority in whom such legal power is vested.
3. When the House of the People is not in session, the President is to authorize expenditure form the Consolidated Fund of the State pending the sanction of such expenditure by Parliament.
4. Any law made in exercise of the power of the legislature of the State under the authorities competent to make such laws under Articles 356 and 357 shall be in force until altered repealed or amended by a competent legislature or other authority.

Article 358 relates to suspension of provisions of Article 19 during emergencies. Any provision under Article 19 will not be effective during emergency, and the States can make law and undertake executive action. However, only those laws and executive actions that do not contain recital to the effect that such laws are in relation to the Proclamation of Emergency in operation remain untouched and nothing contained in Article 358 would apply to them (inserted by 44th Constitutional Amendment Act, 1978).

Article 359 contains provisions regarding suspension of the enforcement of the rights conferred by Part III during emergencies. Where there is a Proclamation of Emergency is in operation, The President by order may suspend the right to move any court for the enforcement of such of rights conferred by Part III as may be mentioned in the order and all proceedings pending in any court for the enforcement of the rights so mentioned shall remain suspended for the period during which the Proclamation is in force or for such shorter period as may be specified in the order. The State can also make law or take any executive action pertaining to Part II during such emergency, but such laws would cease to have effect as soon as the order aforesaid ceases to operate. Every order made under such Article must be laid before each House of Parliament.

Article 359A has been repealed under 63rd Constitutional Amendment Act (1989).

Article 360 contains provisions regarding Financial Emergency. If the President is satisfied that a situation has arisen whereby the financial stability or credit of India or any part of the territory thereof is threatened he may proclaim Financial Emergency. Such a Proclamation can be revoked and has to be presented in both the Houses of the Parliament. The Proclamation thus issued, will cease to operate at the expiration of two months if the same is not approved through a resolution passed by the houses of Parliament. In case the Houses are not in session, the Article suggests certain specific guidelines regarding the Proclamation. This Article also includes provisions relating to the salary and allowance reduction of those who are employed with Union and State departments. A provision relating to Money Bills and other financial Bills passed by the State legislature is mentioned in the Article. This provision States that all such Bills have to be considered by the President during financial instability.

CHANGES INTRODUCED BY THE 44th CONSTITUTIONAL AMENDMENT (1978)

The 44th Constitutional amendment substantially altered the emergency provisions of the Constitution to rectify the misgivings of the 42nd Amendment Act, 1976. It also restored certain changes that were done by 42nd amendment. The following are important points of these amendments-

1. "Internal disturbance" was replaced by "armed rebellion" under Article 352.
2. The decision of proclamation of emergency must be communicated by the cabinet in writing was made compulsory.
3. Proclamation of emergency must be approved by the Houses within one month, and so also should be the continuation of the emergency which must be re approved by the Houses every six month.

4. Emergency can be revoked by passing a resolution to that effect by a simple majority of the Houses present and voting. One-tenth of the members of a House can move such a resolution.
5. When Emergency is proclaimed, the suspension of provisions of Article 19 under Article 358 should be applicable only on declaration of war or external aggression and not on armed rebellion.
6. Suspension of the enforcement of the rights conferred by Part III during emergencies under Article 359, will not include art 20 and 21.
7. Reversed the term of Lok Sabha from 6 to 5 years.

Assessment of the Emergency Provisions

National Emergency has been declared in our country three times so far. For the first time, emergency was declared on 26 October 1962 after China attacked the Indian borders in the North-east. This National Emergency lasted till 10 January 1968. For the second time, it was declared on 3 December 1971 in the wake of the second India-Pakistan War, and was lifted on 21 March 1977. While the second emergency, on the basis of external aggression, was in operation, third National Emergency (called internal emergency) was imposed on 25 June 1975. This emergency was declared on the ground of internal disturbances.

Emergency under Article 356, was first imposed in 1951 in the State of Punjab. In 1959, the Kerala State was put under the President's rule. There have been many cases of Proclamation State emergencies due to 'Constitutional breakdown' like in Odisha in 1961, Haryana in 1967, U.P. in 1970, Tamil Nadu in 1976, and nine States of Punjab, Haryana, U.P., Bihar, West Bengal, Madhya Pradesh, Himachal, Rajasthan and Karnataka in 1977. In 1978 Pondicherry, in 1979 Manipur and in 1980 again another nine States were brought under President's rule like U.P, Bihar, Rajasthan, M.P., Punjab, Gujarat, Orissa, Maharashtra and Tamil Nadu. The State of Assam has been also put under President's rule in 1980. In 1986, emergency was imposed in Jammu and Kashmir due to terrorism and insurgency. Punjab and Kerala have been subjected to President's rule for a number of times. Emergency has been imposed in various States for one reason or the other for more than hundred times. However, after 1995 the use of this provision has rarely been made.

Till date Financial Emergency has never been proclaimed in India. The Emergency Provisions under the Constitution of India has come under scanner for its undemocratic and anti-federal nature. With the Proclamation of Emergency the country is transformed into a centralized unitary political structure with the power of the Central Government being maximized and stretching to making laws under State subjects. The enforcement of Fundamental Rights under Article 32 is suspended during Proclamation of Emergency. However, the 44th Amendment included that under Article 359, suspension of the right to move courts for violation of Part III will not include

Articles 20 and 21. Still there is every possibility of the Emergency Provisions being misused by the ruling Government of the day.

The Preventive Detention Act was passed in 1950 and later on the Defence of India Act, the Maintenance of Internal Security Act (MISA promulgated in 1971 also provided for preventive detention. The Government arrested opposition leaders and opposition party workers including most of the leaders of the Janata Party under the Defence of India Rules (1971) and the Maintenance of Internal Security Act. Among the prominent leaders who were arrested were Jay Prakash Narayan, Raj Narain, Morarji Desai, Charan Singh, Jivatram Kripalani, Atal Bihari Vajpayee, L.K. Advani and several other Communist party leaders and workers. Shortly after, the Janata Government came to power in 1977, the Parliament passed the 44th Amendment, which introduced Constitutional amendments especially pertaining to Article 352 which now justified Proclamation of an Emergency on the grounds of "armed rebellion" rather than "internal disturbance". During Janata rule, Parliament also repealed the Defence of India Rules and the Maintenance of Internal Security Act. However, after the Congress (I) returned to power in 1980, Parliament passed the National Security Act (NSA) in 1980 authorizing security forces to arrest individuals without warrant for suspicion of action that subverts national security, public order, and essential economic services. The Essential Services Maintenance Act (ESMA), 1981 permits the government to prohibit strikes and lockouts in sixteen economic sectors providing critical goods and services. The 59th Amendment, passed in 1988, stated that Article 352 may be suitably amended in its application to the State of Punjab to include "internal disturbance" as one of the grounds of declaring emergency. It was to be justified on the ground that the integrity of India is threatened by internal disturbance in any part of the territory of India and this would facilitate taking of action under this Article in future as the expression "armed rebellion" included in that article as one of the grounds for declaration of Emergency may not be appropriate in the prevailing situation in Punjab to declare a Proclamation in that State. Thus "internal disturbance" was restored as a ground for declaring emergency. The 59th Amendment also increased the period by stating that an emergency can be in effect without legislative approval from six months to three years without any assurance of due process and protection of life and liberty guaranteed under Articles 20 and 21. These rights were restored in 1989 by the 63rd Amendment.

Though some might justify the Proclamation of Emergency for national security reasons, it cannot be denied that these provisions can be misused despite the Constitutional safeguards provided by 44th Amendment (1978).

Constitutional position of the President

As far as the Constitutional position of the President of India is concerned, it is argued that though the President is the Nominal Executive almost similar to the British Monarch, yet there is ample room for Presidential assertion.

Though the Presidential discretionary powers are not clearly enumerated in the Constitution, and it is true that Article 53 vests all executive authority in the President which must be exercised by him directly or indirectly, but that is highly circumscribed by Article 74 which states that the President shall act on the aid and advice of the Council of Ministers. Yet, this leaves ample scope for exercising his prerogative powers. He can use his judgment and reason if a Constitutional crisis arises like that of 1979 where a section of the Janata Party broke away and formed Janata(S) and its leader Charan Singh staked his claim to be the Prime Minister. Here the President gave the first opportunity to the leader of the opposition, Y.B. Chavan of Congress (S) to stake his claim. When he refused, the President weighed the claims of Janata and Janata (S), and finally invited Charan Singh to form the Government. Certain situations can be explored where the President can actually, if he wishes, act on his own without the aid and advice of the Council of Ministers. For example, if the Council of Ministers loose the confidence of the House shall the President refrain from acting simply because the Prime Minister does not advise him? Or if the current Prime Minister's party looses the election and a new Prime Minister has to be appointed, then is the President bound by the advice of the Prime Minister whose Party has lost the election? Or in matters of dissolution of the Lok Sabha can the President sometimes act according to his own judgment? These grey areas still leave marginal powers in the hands of the President.

The 42nd Amendment Act (1976) and 44th Amendment Act (1978) have circumscribed the power of the President to a great extent. Before 1976, Article 74(1) stated that the Council of Ministers is to 'aid and advise' the President in the exercise of his functions and Article 74(2) declared that this advice tendered to the President cannot be inquired in any court. However, the 42nd Amendment Act inserted the word *shall* thus making the advice of the Council of Ministers binding upon the President. The 44th Amendment while retaining the language of the Article 74(1) as amended by the 42nd Amendment Act, added another provision:

"Provided that the President may require the Council of Ministers to reconsider such advice, either generally to otherwise, and the President shall act in accordance with the advice tendered after such reconsideration."

Thus, sending advice was a new power added to the list of the powers enjoyed by the President though this could be done by him only once. Never-the-less, if a Bill is send for reconsideration that will itself have an impact on the activity of the government. The President vide his position can act as a guardian of the Indian political system, and he can exercise his right to advise, to encourage, get information, send messages and Bills for reconsideration. A dynamic President like A.P.J Abdul Kalam has been a motivational figure for the youth and he established links with the people via e-mails which could be directly send to the President. He also created an instance when he returned the Office of Profit Bill to the Union Parliament for reconsideration in 2006.

Therefore, the President of India is not just a mere rubber stamp. No President till date however, has exceeded his authority and has asserted himself/herself. Most of the Presidents have played constructive role and have guided the Indian Government meaningfully. However, it cannot be doubted that the real executive power lies in the Prime minister and his Council of Ministers, and the President is the only formal executive. A number of decisions of the Supreme Court have accepted this formal position of the President of India. In cases like *Ram Jawaya* v. *Punjab*, 1955, *U.N.R Rao* v. *Indira Gandhi*, 1971, *R.C. Cooper* v. *India*, 1970, and *Samsher Singh* v. *Punjab,* 1974, the Supreme Court upheld the position of the President as the mere Constitutional head, who normally acts in all matters including the promulgation of an ordinance on the advice of the Council of Ministers. Therefore, in a Parliamentary democracy like India, a President is required to become a dictatorial yet a democratic President whose duty is to use his judgment and reason to keep the democratic and representative government of the country functioning.

VICE-PRESIDENT OF INDIA

The Vice-President of India is the second highest Constitutional rank in the country. The Vice-President holds his office for a term of five years, but he can continue to be in office, notwithstanding the expiration of his term until his successor assumes office (Article 67). Articles 63-69 deal with provisions relating to the position and election of the Vice-President of India.

The Constitution is silent on who performs the duties of the Vice-President, when a vacancy occurs in the office of the Vice-President of India, before the expiry of his term, or when the Vice-President acts as the President of India. The only provision in the Constitution is with regard to the Vice-President's function as the Chairperson of the Council of States (Rajya Sabha), which is performed, during the period of such vacancy, by the Deputy Chairperson of the Rajya Sabha, or any other member of the Rajya Sabha authorized by the President of India. However, the Parliament has passed the President (Discharge of Functions) Act 1969, to fill in this gap which provides that in case the office of the Vice President also falls vacant, the Chief Justice, or in his absence, the senior most Judge of the Supreme Court of India available discharges the functions of the President until a newly elected President enters upon his office or a newly elected Vice President begins to act as President under Article 65 of the Constitution, whichever is the earlier.

The current Vice-President of India is Shri Jagdeep Dhankhar, who has been elected on 11 August 2022.

Qualifications of the Vice-President of India

A person to be elected as the Vice-President must:

1. be a citizen of India
2. has completed 35 years of age
3. is qualified for election as a member of the Council of States (Rajya Sabha)

A person shall not be eligible if he holds any office of profit under the Government of India or of any State Government or any subordinate local authority subject to the control of governments whether State or Central.

Term of Office and Removal

Article 67 lays down the provisions for the term of office of the Vice-President. It says that the Vice-President shall hold office for a period of five years from the date on which he enters upon his office. He may by writing addressed to the President resign his office or may be removed from his office by a resolution of the Council of States passed by a majority of all the then members of the Council and agreed to by the House of the People. Such resolution cannot be moved unless at least fourteen days' notice has been given of the intention to move the resolution.

A Vice-President shall notwithstanding the expiration of his term continue to hold office until his successor enters upon his office.

Article 68 stipulates that an election to fill a vacancy caused by the expiry of the term of office of Vice-President is completed before the expiry of the term. It also enumerates that an election to fill a vacancy in the office of Vice-President occurring by reason of his death, resignation or removal, or otherwise shall be held as soon as possible after the occurrence[2] of the vacancy, and the person elected to fill the vacancy shall, subject to the provisions of Article 67, be entitled to hold office for the full term of five years from the date on which he enters upon his office.

Election of the Vice-President of India

The Vice-President is elected by an electoral college consisting of members of both Houses of Parliament, in accordance with the system of proportional representation by means of the single transferable vote and the voting in such election is by secret ballot.[3] The Vice-President shall not be a member of either House of Parliament or of a House of a Legislature of any State. If he is a member of either House of Parliament or of a House of a Legislature of any State and is elected as Vice-President, he is deemed to have vacated his seat in that House on the date he/she enters his office as a Vice-President.

The Election Commission of India conducts the election to the office of the Vice-President. The election of the next Vice-President is to be held within 60 days of the expiry of the term of office of the outgoing Vice-President. Any dispute regarding the election of the Vice-President are enquired into and

[2] The Constitution provides an outer limit of six months (Article 62) for election to the office of the President of India under these circumstances

[3] The Electoral College for electing the President of India comprises only the elected members of Parliament and State Legislative Assemblies.

decided by the Supreme Court of India and the decision of the Apex Court is final.

Salaries and Allowances

Article 97 contains provisions relating to the salaries and allowances of the Chairman and Deputy Chairman and the Speaker and Deputy Speaker. It states that there shall be paid to the Chairman and the Deputy Chairman of the Council of States, and to the Speaker and the Deputy Speaker of the House of the People, such salaries and allowances as may be respectively fixed by Parliament by law and, until provision in that behalf is so made, such salaries and allowances as are specified in the Second Schedule. The current salary of Vice-President is ₹ 400,000 per month only under capacity of *ex-officio* Chairman of Rajya Sabha. However, when the post of the President becomes vacant, and the Vice-President discharges the duties of the President then that person is entitled for the salary and privileges of the President of India. But during this period, that person is not entitled to receive the salary of the Chairman of Rajya Sabha. The pension is 50% of the salary.

Oath or Affirmation by the Vice-President

Article 69 states that every Vice-President shall before entering upon his office make and subscribe, before the President, or some person appointed by him, an oath or affirmation. The oath/affirmation of the Vice President is as follows:

"I, ... do swear in the name of God/solemnly affirm that I will bear true faith and allegiance to solemnly affirm the Constitution of India as by law established and that I will faithfully discharge the duty upon which I am about to enter."

Powers and Functions of the Vice-President of India

The powers and functions conferred upon the Vice-President of India as enumerated in the following subsections.

Vice-President as the Ex-officio chairperson of the Council of States (Rajya Sabha)

Article 64 enumerates that the Vice-President is the *ex-officio* Chairperson of the Council of States (Rajya Sabha) and does not hold any other office of profit provided that during any period when the Vice-President acts as President or discharges the functions of the President under Article 65, he shall not perform the duties of the office of Chairman of the Council of States, and shall not be entitled to any salary or allowance payable to the Chairman of the Council of States under Article 97. During any period when the Vice-President acts as, or discharges the functions of the President, he does not perform the duties of the office of the Chairperson of the Council of States (Rajya Sabha) and, is not entitled to any salary or allowances payable to the Chairperson, Rajya Sabha.

Article 89 also upholds that the Vice-President of India shall be *ex-officio* Chairman of the Council of States. Being the Chairman of the Council of States, the Vice-President is the presiding officer of the House and is charged with the prime duty of maintaining decorum in the House and ensuring that the proceedings of the House are carried out smoothly. The Council of States shall, as soon as may be, choose a member of the Council to be Deputy Chairman thereof and, so often as the office of Deputy Chairman becomes vacant, the Council shall choose another member to be Deputy Chairman thereof. Article 92 states that the Chairman or the Deputy Chairman not to preside while a resolution for his removal from office is under consideration. While any resolution for the removal of the Vice-President from his office is under consideration, at any sitting of the Council of States, the Chairman, or while, any resolution for the removal of Deputy Chairman from his office is under consideration, the Deputy Chairman shall not, (though he is present) preside, and the provisions of Clause (2) of Article 91 shall be applied in relation to every such sitting as they apply in relation to a sitting from which the Chairman, or, as the case may be, the Deputy Chairman is absent. Article 91 states that the power of the Deputy Chairman or other person to perform the duties of office of, or to act as Chairman under the above situations.

The Chairman shall have the right to speak in, and otherwise to take part in the proceedings of the Council of States while any resolution for the removal of the Vice-President from his office is under consideration in the Council, but, notwithstanding anything in Article 100, shall not be entitled to vote at all on such resolution or on any other matter during such proceedings. The Chairman exercises only a casting vote in the case of equality of votes in ordinary sessions of the house. If at any time during a meeting of a House there is no quorum, it shall be the duty of the Chairman to either adjourn the house or suspend the meeting till there is a quorum.

Various other powers are conferred on the Chairman under the Rules of Procedure of the Rajya Sabha in connection with the proceedings of the House, Committees and such other matters as questions, calling attention, motions, resolutions, amendments to Bills, authentication of Bills, petitions, papers to be laid on the table and so on. He has the prime function of maintenance of order in the House. He, as the Chairman, has been vested with all the necessary disciplinary powers under the rules for the purpose, such as checking irrelevance or repetition in the speech of a member, intervening when a member makes an unwarranted or defamatory remark by asking him to withdraw the same.

As the Chairman of the Rajya Sabha, he may permit a member to address the House in his mother tongue. In case of resignation of a member from the House, if the Chairman is satisfied that the resignation it is voluntary, otherwise he may refuse to accept the resignation. Under the Tenth Schedule of the Constitution, the Chairman determines the question as to disqualification of a member of the Rajya Sabha on ground of defection.

Principal Spokesperson of the House

The Vice-President as the principal spokesperson of the Rajya Sabha communicates the decisions of the Houses to the public, and also communicates messages received by him from foreign countries and legislatures. As the Chairman of the House, he also communicates to the President of India in the form of a formal address after a motion has been made and carried by the House like the motion of thanks on the President's address to the two Houses of Parliament assembled together, after its adoption by the House, is conveyed to the President by the Chairman. The President also communicates his messages to the Chairman of the Rajya Sabha which the Chairman communicates to the members of the House. He also issues warrants to execute the orders of the House, wherever necessary.

Powers relating to Bills passed in Rajya Sabha

Under the Rules of Procedure of the Rajya Sabha, the Chairman has the authority to correct patent errors in a Bill after it has been passed by the House and to make such other changes in the Bill consequential on the amendments accepted by the House. After a Bill is passed by the Lok Sabha, and thereafter, lies with the Rajya Sabha, the Chairman authenticates the Bill with his signature after it is passed by the House before presenting it to the President for his assent.

Discharge functions of the President in the event of vacancy in the office of the President

Under Article 65 the Vice-President acts as the President, during casual vacancy in the office of the President by reason of death, resignation or removal or otherwise, until a new President is elected as soon as practicable and, in no case, later than six months from the date of occurrence of the vacancy. When the President is unable to discharge his functions owing to absence, illness or any other cause, the Vice-President discharges those functions till the President resumes office. During this period, the Vice-President has all the powers, immunities and privileges of the President and receives emoluments and allowances payable to the President.

Miscellaneous functions

Other than the above mentioned functions, there are several functions which have been conferred upon the Vice President from time-to-time by passing statutes like rules made under the Salary, Allowances and Pension of Members of Parliament Act, 1954. The Act do not take effect until they are approved and confirmed by the Chairman and the Speaker. Even under the Judges (inquiry) Act, 1968, the Chairman has to Constitute a Committee on receipt of a motion for the removal of a Judge of the Supreme Court or of a High Court, for investigation into the grounds on which the removal of a Judge is prayed for.

The Vice-President as the Chairman of the Rajya Sabha may from time-to-time nominate members of the Rajya Sabha on various bodies such as Courts of Banaras Hindu University, Jawaharlal Nehru University, North-Eastern

Hill University, Pondicherry University, Haj Committee, Press Council of India, Samsad (Court) of Visva Bharati, and the like, all set up under the relevant statutes. The Chairman also nominates members of the Rajya Sabha on other bodies like General Assembly of the Indian Council for Cultural Relations, General Body of the Central Social Welfare Board, General Council of the School of Planning and Architecture, Hindi Shiksha Samiti, Institute of Constitutional and Parliamentary Studies and the like.

From the above discussion it might follow that the office of the Vice-President has been created just to fill in certain position (that of the President) in case of unforeseen situations. But from an analysis of the powers and functions of the Vice-President, we can conclude that he is not totally a person of insignificance as he is the Chairman of the Rajya Sabha, and he occupies an honourable position. Therefore, in the scheme of Parliamentary system of Government in India many Vice-Presidents have later on become Presidents of Indian Republic.

EXERCISES

I. Short Answer Questions: **(100 words)**

1. State the qualifications as prescribed in the Constitution to become the President of India.
2. Write briefly about how the President of India is elected.
3. What is the method of removal of the President of India?
4. What are the Presidential Immunities?
5. Briefly state the Executive powers of the President.
6. Make a brief assessment of the Legislative Powers of the President of India.
7. Write briefly about the Emergency Powers of the President of India.
8. Write a note on the election of Vice-President of India.

II. Long Answer Questions: **(1200 words)**

9. Discuss the powers and functions of the President of India.
10. Examine the method of election of the President of India.
11. Discuss critically the emergency powers of the President of India.
12. In the light of the powers and functions of the President of India assess the Constitutional position of the President of India.
13. In the light of the powers and functions of the President of India, do you think that in reality he is just a 'titular' head of the State and the actual power lies elsewhere? Argue.
14. Discuss the powers and functions of the Vice-President of India.
15. Do you think that the Vice-President plays an effective role in Indian political system? In the light of his position as the *ex-officio* Chairman of Rajya Sabha argue your case.

REFERENCES

Bakshi, P.M., *The Constitution of India* (with selective comments), Universal Law Publishing, Delhi, 2000.

Basu, Durga Das, *Introduction to the Constitution of India*, Prentice-Hall of India, New Delhi, 1992.

Election Commission of India, *Election to the Office of President of India, 2007*, New Delhi, 2007 (www.eci.gov.in).

Jain, M.P., *Indian Constitutional Law*, Wadhwa & Company, Nagpur, 1999.

Rao, K.V., *Parliamentary Democracy of India: A Critical Commentary*, The World Press, Calcutta, 1961.

R.C. Cooper v. *India,* AIR 1970 SC 564.

Samsher Singh v. *Punjab,* AIR 1974 SC 2192.

Singh, M.P and Saxena, Rekha, *Indian Politics: Contemporary Issues and Concerns,* Prentice-Hall of India, New Delhi, 2008.

Siwach, J.R., *Dynamics of Indian Government and Politics*, Sterling Publishers, New Delhi, 1985.

44th Constitutional Amendment, 1978.

Ram Jawaya v. *Punjab*, AIR 1955 SC 549.

U.N.R. Rao v. *Indira Gandhi,* AIR 1971 SC 1002.

8

The Union Council of Ministers and the Prime Minister of India

INTRODUCTION

India follows a Westminster pattern of Government, and in such a model the Prime Minister performs a pivotal role which cannot be denied. In India too, the nominal executive is the President and the real executive power is exercised by the Prime Minister, and his Council of Ministers. Most striking feature of the Constitution of India is that, there is no mention about the position or role of the Prime Minister. Only certain duties of the Indian Prime Minister are mentioned in the Constitution. Even then, over the years, the way the Prime Ministers have acted have surely pointed to the direction that the Office of the Prime Minister is significant as well as commands great respect and authority in relation to his Cabinet, Council of Ministers, Parliament as well as the President of India.

PRIME MINISTER OF INDIA

In our Constitution the Part V titled 'The Union' and under it Chapter I titled 'The Executive' the basic framework for the systematic functioning of the Indian Parliamentary democracy is explained. As Articles 52 and 53 and subsequent Articles deal with the power and position of the President of India, under Article 74, the Constitution provides information for the Council of Ministers and the Prime Minister. The Article reads as "There shall be a Council of Ministers with Prime Minister at the head to aid and advise the President who shall, in the exercise of his functions, act in accordance with such advice."

Further, Article 75 lays down that the Prime Minister shall be appointed by the President and the other Ministers shall be appointed by the President on the advice of the Prime Minister. The Ministers shall hold office during the pleasure of the President.

Appointment of the Prime Minister

The Prime Minister is appointed by the President of India. But the pertinent question that can be raised is can the President use his discretion in the appointment of the Prime Minister? If, after the Lok Sabha elections, one party emerges with an absolute majority, then the President has a little choice, but to invite the leader of the majority Party to form the Government. If a coalition of different parties wins the election then the President can invite the leader chosen by the coalition as the Prime Minister. In the first Five General elections held in 1951, 1957, 1962, 1967 and 1971, the Congress Party had a thumping victory so the President appointed in the first three cases Jawaharlal Nehru and in the next two cases Indira Gandhi as the Prime Ministers of India. In the sixth General elections immediately after the emergency in 1977 the Lok Dal (Janata Secular) was victorious and therefore, the President invited Morarji Desai to form the Government. The Janata Party was an amalgam of Bharatiya Lok Dal, Socialist Congress, Congress for Democracy CFD, Bharatiya Jana Sangh and others. There were rival claimants to the post of the Prime Minister. Charan Singh withdrew and among Morarji Desai and Jagjiwan Ram, the consensus was more or less in favour of Morarji Desai, so his name was proposed as the Prime Minister of India and the President just performed the formality.

A critical situation arose when the Janata Party experienced a split in 1979 and Morarji Desai resigned. The President could have asked the leader of the opposition party (Y.B. Chavan) to form the Government. The President asked the leader of the opposition to explore the possibilities of forming a cohesive and stable Government and also indicated the type of persons to be inducted in the Cabinet. The President was informed by Y.B. Chavan that he was not in a position to form the Government and therefore, he declined from the race of Prime Minsitership. Subsequently, the President asked Charan Singh and Morarji Desai to submit their list of respective supporters in the Lok Sabaha. On the basis of the lists submitted, the President invited Charan Singh to form the Government, and he was given a time of three months to prove his majority in the Lok Sabha. When Charan Singh resigned without proving his majority, Jagjiwan Ram placed his claim to form the Government. After assessing the situation and talks with Jagjiwan Ram and Chandra Shekhar, the President dissolved the Lok Sabha.

Another critical situation arose in 1989, 1996 and 1998. In 1989 election (Ninth Lok Sabha), the Congress emerged as a single largest party, but it did not stake the claim to form the Government. President Venkataraman thereafter invited V.P. Singh to form the Government. It was a conglomeration of the opposition parties which formed together a minority National Front Government under V.P. Singh with the help of the Left Parties and Bharatiya Janata Party, which supported it from outside. V.P. Singh held office for slightly less than a year, from 2 December 1989 to 10 November 1990. After he resigned his rival, Chandra Shekhar who broke away from the Janata Dal with 64 MPs and formed the Samajwadi Janata Party in 1990, became the 11th Prime Minister of India. He got outside support from the Congress. He finally resigned on 6 March 1991, when Congress withdrew support and fresh elections had to be held. These are difficult and unstable situations in which the President has to guide the Indian political system in the right direction. In 1991, elections to the 10th Lok Sabha were held. No party could get a majority, so a minority Government under the Indian National Congress with the help of Left Parties was formed under P.V. Narasimha Rao as the Prime Minister. This Government, however, lasted for the next 5 years.

In 1996, General elections to the 11th Lok Sabha were held. The result of the election was a hung-Parliament, which would see three Prime Ministers in two years and which forced the country back to the polls in 1998. The BJP became the largest party within the Lok Sabha, a first for a non-Congress party, although it secured enough seats it needed more to prove a parliamentary majority. The then President, Shankar Dayal Sharma invited Atal Bihari Vajpayee as leader of the BJP to form a Government. Sworn in on 15 May, the new Prime Minister was given two weeks to prove majority support in the Parliament. Before the confidence vote on 31 May, the BJP attempted to build up the much needed support. However, on 28 May, Vajpayee conceded that he could not arrange support from more than 200 of the 545 members of Parliament, and thus resigned rather than face the confidence vote, ending his 13 day Government. The second largest party, the Indian National Congress, declined to form a Government, instead chose to support a United Front Government headed by H.D. Deve Gowda, the then Chief Minister of Karnataka, to the post of the Prime Minister. When the President was assured that Deve Gowda would be in a position to form the Government, and would be able to command a majority in the House, the President formally invited him to form the Government. Thus, the United Front, was created and got support from 332 members out of the 545 seats in the Lok Sabha, resulting in H.D. Deve Gowda from the Janata Dal becoming the 14th Prime Minister of India who continued his office till April 1997. Again when the Congress withdrew its support from the United Front Government, it collapsed in April 1997. In order to avoid elections, a compromise was reached and the Congress decided to support another United Front Government under a new leader, I.K. Gujral. Thus, in the similar manner as in the above cases, the President invited I.K. Gujral to form the government on 21 April 1997. The Congress party finally withdrew support from this government on 28 November 1997, and Gujral resigned following this withdrawal. Prime Minister Gujral continued in the office for over 11 months, including 3 months as a caretaker Prime Minister. In March 1998, Atal Bihari Vajpayee was appointed as the Prime Minister, and was asked to prove his majority in the House which he did successfully but he failed to secure the confidence of the House in April 1999 and had to resign. In 1999, General Elections to the 13th Lok Sabha was held. This was for the first time that a united front of parties managed to attain a majority and form a Government, which lasted a full-term of five years. The BJP led National Democratic Alliance (NDA) formed the government and Atal Bihari Vajpayee was invited by the President to become the Prime Minister.

In the 14th and 15th Lok Sabha elections, the Congress led United Progressive Alliance (UPA) formed the Government. Gone are those days when a party like the Indian National Congress was able to secure an absolute majority. Coalition politics is now more or less a common phenomenon. If the coalition parties are able to elect a leader and propose his name then the job of the President becomes easier. However, if the number of ambitious candidates are many, the President will face a tough situation in selecting the appropriate candidate for the post of the Prime Minister. In the 16th Lok Sabha elections the BJP-led NDA had a landslide victory, with the BJP alone winning 282 seats. After a long gap a single party was able to win majority seats in the Lok Sabha. Shri Narendra Modi became the 14th Prime Minister of India. In the 16th Lok Sabha elections, the BJP-led NDA had a landslide victory with the BJP alone winning 282 seats. After as long gap a single party was able to win majority seats in the Lok Sabha. Shri Narendra Modi became the 14th Prime Minister of India. The 17th Lok Sabha elections of 2019 was a big win for the NDA with the BJP getting 303 seats alone and NDA total of 353 seats. Shri Narendra Modi became the Prime Minister of India for the second term. In the 18th Lok Sabha elections BJP could secure only 240 seats. The NDA garnered support from Telegu Desam Party and Janata Dal (United) as two main allies and various other smaller partners to confirm the support of around 293 MPs in the Lok Sabha and place its case for formation of the government. Therefore, Sri Narendra Modi became the Prime Minister for the third term but this time heading a truly coalition government as BJP solely failed to reach the 272 majority mark.

Qualification

Article 84 of the Constitution of India, which in general, lays down the qualifications for membership of the Parliament, which also is applicable in case of judging the eligibility of a person to the office of the Prime Minister. A Prime Minister must be:

1. a citizen of India
2. should be a member of the Lok Sabha
3. he should not hold any office of profit under the Government of India or the Government of any State, other than declared by Parliament by law not to disqualify its holder. (Article 102)

When a person who has been appointed as a Prime Minister is not a member of Lok Sabha, by convention he gets elected himself as soon as possible as the member of Lok Sabha. After the death of Lal Bahadur Shastri, Indira Gandhi was appointed as the Prime Minister, and at that time, she was the member of Rajya Sabha. She soon got herself elected as a Lok Sabha member. Same was the case with P.V. Narasimha Rao in 1991. However, for H.D. Deve Gowda in 1996 and I.K. Gujaral in 1997 both were Rajya Sabha members, but continued to remain so and did not contest elections to become a member of Lok Sabha. Former Prime Minister Dr. Manmohan Singh was a member of Rajya Sabha. Therefore, as nowhere it is mentioned in the Constitution that the Prime Minister has to belong to the Lok Sabha, it is almost an accepted convention that he may belong to either of the Houses, but he must become member of any one of the Houses within a maximum period of six months from his appointment as the Prime Minister.

Tenure

The Prime Minister and his Council of Ministers usually are elected for five years. They continue their office as long as they enjoy the pleasure of the President of India. Jawaharlal Nehru was the longest serving Prime Minister and next was Indira Gandhi. Narasimha Rao, Rajiv Gandhi and Atal Bihari Vajpayee (after the 1999 election) all completed their term of five years. From the above discussion we have seen that how India faced troubled phases in politics with the resignation of Prime Ministers like V.P. Singh, Chandra Shekhar, H.D. Deve Gowda, I.K. Gujral and Atal Bihari Vajpayee, who could not complete the term of five years in their office. Till date, no President has ever dismissed any Prime Minister of India. The President may ask the Prime Minister, if he thinks that the Ministry has lost its confidence, to prove their majority in the Lok Sabha, failing the test, the Ministry has to resign.

Oath of Office

"I, <name>, do swear in the name of God/solemnly affirm that I will bear true faith and allegiance to the Constitution of India as by law established, that I will uphold the sovereignty and integrity of India, that I will faithfully and conscientiously discharge my duties as Prime Minister for the Union and that I will do right to all manner of people in accordance with the Constitution and the law, without fear or favour, affection or ill-will."

—*Constitution of India, Third Schedule, Part I*

Oath of Secrecy

"I, <name>, do swear in the name of God/solemnly affirm that I will not directly or indirectly communicate or reveal to any person or persons any matter which shall be brought under my consideration or shall become known to me as Prime Minister for the Union except as may be required for the due discharge of my duties as such minister."

—*Constitution of India, Third Schedule, Part II*

Salary and Allowances

By Article 75 of the Constitution of India, remuneration of the Prime Minister as well as other ministers are to be decided by the Parliament, and is to be renewed from time-to-time. At present, the salary of the Prime Minister of India is ₹ 200,000. He also receives the Constituency Allowance and a monthly Sumptuary Allowance.

Powers and Functions of the Prime Minister

As pointed out earlier, the Constitution does not confer on the Prime Minister of India any specific powers and functions. However in reality, the Prime Minister of India performs a wide range of functions and enjoys a wide array of powers. In fact the executive powers assigned to the President of India are performed by the Prime Minister in the name of the President. The broad range of powers of the Prime Minister is as follows:

1. The leader of the party securing maximum seats in the Lok Sabha is elected as the Prime Minister. He is not only the leader of the Majority Party, but is also the leader of the Parliament. Every single policy decision of the Government to be discussed by the Parliament is decided by him. He also sets the agenda of the Lok Sabha along with the Speaker. He also advises the President as regard to the summoning and proroguing of the Parliament. He is answerable to the Parliament for all policy decisions of his Government and his Ministers. He has to ensure that his Ministers satisfy the queries of the opposition parties in the Parliament. The Prime Minister can recommend the President to dissolve the Lok Sabha if he feels so. He plays an important role in the formation of Parliamentary Committees as well.
2. The most important function of the Prime Minister is the formation of the Council of Ministers. The President appoints the Ministers on the recommendations of the Prime Ministers. A Prime Minister of a single majority party has a freedom of choice of his Council of Ministers. A Prime Ministers of coalition parties and alliances have to work under coalition pressures and have little room for making his own choice. The Congress-led UPA-I and UPA-II and before that the BJP-led NDA Government had to work under pulls and pressures of coalition partners. The Prime Minister allocates different portfolios/departments among the Ministers. While generally the work of the Government is divided into various Ministries, the Prime Minister may retain certain portfolios
3. As the leader of the Cabinet, the Prime Minister presides over its meetings. All major decisions are chalked out in the Cabinet meetings. The Ministers must follow the line of the Prime Minister who may, on the other hand, be guided by party line. The Prime Minister coordinates the policies of his Ministers. In case of a conflict, he tries to resolve it and when it is not possible to resolve the Prime Minister may ask

that particular Minister to resign. The coordinating work is generally allocated to the Cabinet Secretariat who in turn, acts as a nodal agency for the functioning of the various Ministries. Therefore, the Ministers though according to the Constitution can continue in the office as long as they enjoy the pleasure of the President but in reality, it is the pleasure of the Prime Minister. The Prime Minister can from time to time reshuffle and remove some of this Ministers and induct new persons as Ministers. Coalition partners may also create pressure upon the Prime Minister to change a particular minister.

4. The Prime Minister plays a decisive role as far as appointments to several important positions are concerned. The appointments are all made by the President, but on the recommendations of the Prime Minister like, the Chief Justice of India and other judges of the Supreme Court and High Courts, the Attorney-General of India, the Chiefs of Army, Navy and Air force, Governors of the States, Ambassadors and High Commissioners, Chairman and members of various Commissions, the Chief Election Commissioner and other members of Election Commission and the like.
5. The Prime Minister is the link between the President and the Council of Ministers. He is responsible for aiding and advising the President in distribution of work of the Government to various Ministries and offices and also in terms of the *Government of India (Allocation of Business) Rules, 1961.* According to Article 78, it is the duty of the Prime Minister to communicate to the President all decisions of the Council of Ministers, and also furnish information relating to the administration of the affairs of the Union and proposals for legislation if asked for by the President. If the President requires to submit for the consideration of the Council of Ministers, any matter on which a decision has been taken by a Minister, but which has not been considered by the Council.
6. The Prime Minister is the Chief Spokesperson of the Government. The Prime Minister is collectively responsible for all the policies of the Government and also the errors of omission and Commission by his Ministers to the Lok Sabha. If the Prime Minister and his Ministers are not able to defend their policies, they can face a no-confidence motion which might result in the premature death of the Government.
7. As far as the Planning Commission in India was concerned the Prime Minister was the ex-officio Chairman of the Planning Commission and now currently is the Chairperson of NITI Aayog. Undoubtedly, the priorities of each of the five-year plans were largely influenced by the Prime Minister. Since the dissolution of the Planning Commission which was replaced by NITI Aayog (see Chapter 23) there has not been any further Five-Year Plan. However, the Prime Minister of India is the Chairperson of NITI Aayog.
8. The Prime Minister is also the Chief Spokesperson in the external relations of India. International Conferences, Summits, Meetings of heads of Governments are attended by the Prime Minster like the G-20, SAARC, NAM, ASEAN, IBSA, BRICS and others.

9. The Prime Minster is the leader of the Nation. All major decisions about war and peace are taken by him. The Prime Minister has to take responsibility of any debacle or failures and also praises for any of controversial policies. Nehru had to take the blame for the disastrous Indo-China war of 1962, Narasimha Rao for demolition of disputed structure at Ayodhya, Vajpayee for 1998 Pokhran explosion and consequent international sanctions.
10. An emergency under Article 352 is declared by the President on the advice of the Prime Minister and his Council of Ministers. During the Proclamation of Emergencies under Article 352, the Prime Minister becomes all powerful. Indira Gandhi passed the 42nd Amendment which has been one of the controversial amendments of all times. The Power of Parliament enhanced for amending the Constitution including the Part III of the Constitution. The power of Judicial Review was restricted. The Fundamental Duties Part IVA was inserted. Duration of Lok Sabha and State Legislative Assemblies were extended during National Emergency (six years). It also Stated that no quorum shall be required for conducting the meeting of the Lok Sabha and the State Legislative Assemblies. Several Preventive Detention Acts like MISA, COFEPOSA were misused by the Government. So at times of emergency, the Prime Minister can become the real dictator.
11. The Prime Minister is fully responsible for the success and the failure of his Government. He has to keep in mind the Principle of Collective Responsibility while discharging his functions as well as coordinating the functions of his Council of Ministers.
12. The Prime Minister is assisted in the discharge of his functions by several committees and Councils like:
    (a) The Economic Advisory Council
    (b) High Level Committee on Manufacturing
    (c) PM's Council on Micro, Small and Medium Enterprises (MSMEs)
    (d) Delivery Monitoring Unit
    (e) PM's Council on Climate Change
    (f) PM's National Council on Skill Development
    (g) The Trade and Economic Relations Committee
    (h) PM's National Council on India's Nutrition Challenges
    (i) PM's Council on Trade and Industry

Prime Minister's Office (PMO)

Prime Minister's Office (PMO) is located at South Block, Raisina Hill, New Delhi. The PMO provides secretarial assistance to the Prime Minister. It is headed by the Principal Secretary to Prime Minister. The PMO includes the anti-corruption unit and the public wing dealing with grievances. The subject-matter of files required to be submitted to the Prime Minister depends on whether he is holding direct charge of the Ministry or whether there is a Cabinet Minister or Minister of State (independent charge) in-charge of the Ministry. Prime Minister's office also includes anti-corruption unit. He is responsible for the Planning Commission (now NITI Aayog) and the PMO gets relevant files for clearance. Prime Minister Office directly operates National Defence Fund (NDF) and Prime Minister's National Relief Fund (PMNRF). All the important policy issues are submitted at the Prime Minister's office to get information and orders. In cases where the Prime Minister is the Minister-in-Charge, all matters requiring Ministerial approval not delegated to the Minister of State/ Deputy Minister, if any, are submitted for orders. The Prime Minister has traditionally been the Minister-in-charge of the departments of Space, Atomic Energy, and Ministry of Personnel, Public Grievances and Pensions. L.K. Jha, P.N. Haksar, P.N. Dhar, R.K. Dhawan, Amar Nath Verma, Brajesh Mishra, Dr. P.K. Mishra, Ajit Doval KC, Amit Khare, and Tarun Kapoor are a few powerful and influential persons to be acting as the Prime Minster's Secretary.

Position of the Prime Minister

The Prime Minister is the most powerful person in the Indian political system. His position can be summed up as:

1. The Prime Minister is the real executive authority;
2. The Prime Minister is the ex-officio Chairman of the Planning Commission, National Development Council, National Integration Council and Inter-State Council;
3. The President convenes and prorogues all sessions of Parliament in consultation with the Prime Minister;
4. The Prime Minister can recommend the dissolution of Lok Sabha before expiry;
5. The Prime Minister recommends the names to the President for the appointment of the Council of Ministers;
6. The Prime Minister enjoys dominant position in the Cabinet
7. The Prime Minister allocates portfolios to his Ministers and can ask a Minister to resign, and if he is unwilling then the Prime Minister can get him dismissed by President;
8. The Prime Minister can recommend to the President to declare emergency on grounds of war, external aggression or armed rebellion;
9. The Prime Minister advises the President about the imposition of President's Rule in any State or emergency due to financial instability or even national emergency
10. The Prime Minister is the leader of the House and also represents the nation internationally.

As coalition politics becomes the trend in Indian Politics, the undisputed dominant position of the Prime Minister now comes under question. With regard to reference being made about to the National Counterterrorism

Centre (NCTC) in the Presidential speech there were objections from the allies of UPA-II, and they wanted an amendment. It is another thing that the UPA-II had a face saver when the Lok Sabha adopted the motion of thanks on the President's address after a huge number of amendments moved by the opposition were negative. The then Lok Sabha Speaker Meira Kumar declared, "The motion is passed...all the other amendments are negative." Therefore, a Prime Minister can command his cabinet and pilot all legislations in the Parliament provided that he has a clear majority in the House. Table 8.1 gives list of Prime Ministers of India from Independence to till date.

Table 8.1 List of Prime Ministers of India

S. No.	*Prime Ministers*	*Period*
1.	Jawaharlal Nehru	15 August 1947–27 May 1964
2.	Gulzarilal Nanda*	27 May–9 June, 1964 and 11–14 January 1966
3.	Lal Bahadur Shastri	9 June 1964–11 January 1966
4.	Indira Gandhi	24 January 1966–24 March 1977 and 14 January 1980–31 October 1984
5.	Morarji Desai	24 March 1977–28 July 1979
6.	Charan Singh	28 July 1979–14 January 1980
7.	Rajiv Gandhi	31 October 1984–2 December 1989
8.	Vishwanath Pratap Singh	2 December 1989–10 November 1990
9.	Chandra Shekhar	10 November 1990–21 June 1991
10.	P.V. Narasimha Rao	21 June 1991–16 May 1996
11.	H.D. Deve Gowda	1 June 1996–21 April 1997
12.	Inder Kumar Gujral	April 21, 1997–19 March 1998
13.	Atal Bihari Vajpayee	16 May 1996–1 June 1996 and 19 March 1998–22, May 2004
14.	Manmohan Singh	22 May 2004–26 May 2014 [UPA-I & UPA-II]
15.	Narendra Modi	26 May 2014 – till date

RELATION BETWEEN THE PRESIDENT AND PRIME MINISTER OF INDIA

In a Parliamentary Democracy like India, the division of executive into real and nominal leaves very little room for the nominal executive to manipulate or manoeuvre the functioning of the Government. Therefore, the President being the nominal executive can only function with the aid and advice of the real executive, i.e., the Prime Minister and his Council of Ministers. Article 74 lays down that the Prime Minister and his Council of Minister are to aid and advice the President of India. The same Article also lays down that such advice is a binding on the President of India. It says that the President shall

*Gulzarilal Nanda became the interim Prime Minister twice.

in the exercise of his functions act in accordance with such advice. The first President Dr. Rajendra Prasad refused sometimes to listen to such advice. Dr. Rajendra Prasad raised objections about the hasty legislation of the Hindu Code Bill, disagreed on the Government's proposals to impose ceiling on land holdings and to introduce cooperative farming and to resort to State trading in food grains. Dr. Rajendra Prasad went to install the deity in Somnath Temple and attended the funeral of Sardar Patel much against the advice of the Prime Minister. Most of the other Presidents however, have listened to the advice of the Prime Minister.

According to Article 78, it is the duty of the Prime Minister to communicate to the President all decisions of the Council of Ministers and also furnish information relating to the administration of the affairs of the Union and proposals for legislation if asked for by the President. As far as this duty of the Prime Minister is concerned, many times it has been found that the President has been kept in the dark. There were major irritants between President Rajendra Prasad and Nehru over certain appointments of highest State officials and even Governors and ambassadors. The President came to know about certain top level appointments from the daily newspaper. He protested against such practices of ignoring the President, because it was setting 'bad precedents'. President Rajendra Prasad also criticized the Treaty of 1954 on Tibet with China. Again relation between the President Giani Zail Singh and Rajiv Gandhi became strained, because the President felt that he was not being informed about the State of affairs by the Prime Minister. At one time, the President was exploring the possibilities of dismissing the Government. In both the above two cases at one point both the Prime Ministers had started avoiding or ignoring their respective Presidents.

Mostly, the other Presidents like Zakir Hussain, V.V. Giri, F.A. Ahmed, R. Venkataraman, Shankar Dayal Sharma stuck to their Constitutional role and the relations between them and the Prime minister did not enter into any controversy. President Zail Singh also did not give his assent to the Indian Post Office Amendment Bill which was again refused by President R.Venkatraman. President K.R. Narayan also sent back the Cabinet's advise to impose Article 356 or President's rule in the State of Bihar. President A.P.J Abdul Kalam again in many cases earned the wrath of the Prime Minister on many occasions. On assuming office, he wanted to address the members of Parliament, but that was refused by the Cabinet on the ground that there were no such provisions in the Constitution. His official visit to riot-hit Gujarat was not appreciated by the Government. The President also sent back the Poll Ordinance for reconsideration but had to sign it after it was passed for the second time. He also sent back the Office of Profit Bill in 2006. After him Pratibha Devi Singh Patil performed her role according to the Constitutional provisions, and during her entire tenure there has been no friction between the Government and the President.

On the whole, it can be said that only in the matters of appointment of the Prime Minister there is a little scope for the President can use his discretion and that too again when no party enjoys clear majority. However, if the President is ambitious then he can search for opportunities to assert himself as Dr. Rajendra Prasad refused to accept the position of the President of India like the Queen of England. President K.R. Narayanan also stated that the President of India is not an appellate or supervisory authority over the Prime Minister, he is like an emergency lamp which becomes active when power fails, and becomes dormant when power is restored. The Office of the President maintains continuity in the administration and enables a smooth change-over from the fall of one Cabinet to the establishment of another.

UNION COUNCIL OF MINISTERS

Article 75 provides that:

1. The Prime Minister shall be appointed by the President, and the other Ministers shall be appointed by the President on the advice of the Prime Minister.
2. The Ministers shall hold office during the pleasure of the President.
3. The Council of Ministers shall be collectively responsible to the House of the People.
4. Before a Minister enters his office, the President shall administer to him the oaths of office and of secrecy according to the forms set out for the purpose in the Third Schedule.
5. A Minister who for any period of six consecutive months is not a member of either House of Parliament shall at the expiration of that period cease to be a Minister.
6. The salaries and allowances of Ministers shall be such as Parliament may from time-to-time by law determine, and until Parliament so determines, shall be as specified in the Second Schedule.

Immediately after the election, when the leader of the party or coalition of parties securing a majority, is appointed as the Prime Minister by the President of India, he selects his Council of Ministers, recommends their names to the President, who in turn appoints them. As pointed out earlier, if the Prime Minister commands a party with absolute majority, then he has a freedom to choose his Council of Ministers especially Cabinet Ministers. In case of a Prime Minister heading a Coalition Government, the compulsions of coalition politics prohibits him to exercise a free choice. The compulsions of Morarji Desai, H.D. Deve Gowda, I.K. Gujral and Manmohan Singh in his UPA-I and UPA-II are well-known.

Composition of Council of Ministers

It is stipulated that the total number of Ministers, including the Prime Minister, in the Council of Ministers of India shall not exceed fifteen per cent of the total number of members of the House of the People. The Council of Ministers is a larger body comprising 50-60 Ministers as against the Cabinet which consists of 15-20 senior and important Ministers. The real decisions are taken in the Cabinet and not the Council of Ministers. The Council of Ministers in India comprises three different categories that include—Cabinet Ministers, Ministers of State and Deputy Ministers. The Indian Constitution does not mention anything about the Cabinet Ministers except in Article 352 where Cabinet is defined as the Council consisting of the Prime Minister and other Ministers of Cabinet rank under Article 75. However, in India it is the Cabinet led by the Prime Minister which takes all the policy decisions and advises the President. Besides them, the Minister of State has an independent charge of a Ministry. The Deputy Ministers, on the other hand, act as assistants to their chiefs, and look after their work in their absence. The number of Ministers may vary according to the volume and variety of work of the Central Government.

However, in the formation of the Council of Ministers, the Prime Minister has to keep in mind certain points. They are:

1. The total number of Ministers, including the Prime Minister cannot exceed fifteen per cent of the total number of Lok Sabha members.
2. A Member of Parliament who is disqualified from the membership under the anti-defection law (Tenth Schedule of the Constitution) cannot be made a Minister till the term of his membership expires. But if he is re-elected to the Parliament, then he can be made a Minister.
3. He has to include the important leaders of his party.
4. Approximately all the States should be represented in the Council of Ministers.
5. The Scheduled Castes, Scheduled Tribes, and women should also be represented.

Functions of Council of Ministers

1. The main function of the Council of Ministers is mainly to aid and advise the President in the exercise of his functions. Since the Ministry is the highest organ of the Government of India, it determines all the policies relating to the country's administration like high level appointment, removal, imposition of emergencies and the like. For all these actions, the decision of the Cabinet is necessary which is only executed in the name of the President. It also has the responsibility of formulating internal and foreign policies. The success and failure of any Government/Policy of the Government is to a great extent the responsibility of the Prime Minister and his Council of Ministers.

2. The Ministers are the head of the executive departments allocated to them. Usually, they are persons who occupy key positions in the structure of the party forming the Government. The Council of Ministers also plays a key role in determining the major policies of the Government whether, financial, social and welfare or political or even international. The Council of Ministers have an important role to play in the functioning of the total administrative machinery of the Central Government. Therefore, the Council of Ministers becomes collectively responsible to the Lok Sabha, and Council may have to face a vote/motion of no-confidence for every act of their omission or commission.
3. India being a Parliamentary Democracy, the executive powers vested by the Constitution of India upon the President are actually exercised by the Council of Ministers headed by the Prime Minister. Article 74 of the Constitution lays down that the President if, in the exercise of his functions, act in accordance with the advice tendered by the Council of Ministers. The President appoints Governors, Ambassadors and other diplomatic representatives, the Chief Justice and other judges of the Supreme Court, High Courts, Attorney-General and Auditor-General of India and various Commissions such as the Finance Commission of India and the Election Commission of India. All these appointments are suggested by the Cabinet which is the main body of the Council of Ministers and on the basis of such recommendations the President makes all appointments to the posts mentioned above. The President has the power to remove the Attorney-General of India, the Governors of the States, etc. But in removing these officers he has to act on the advice of the Council of Ministers.
4. Certain legislative powers are also exercised by the Council of Ministers especially the Cabinet in the name of the President. The President summons and prorogues the Indian Parliament and dissolves the Lok Sabha on the advice of the Prime Minister. He addresses Parliament and sends messages to it. The addresses and messages are prepared by the Cabinet. It is the Cabinet that prepares the Annual Budget and supplementary budgets, if any. They are laid before Parliament by the Finance Minister on behalf of the President. The President promulgates ordinances when Parliament is not in session. He does it on the advice of the Cabinet. Joint sittings of Parliament are summoned by the President on the advice of the Council of Ministers. Twelve members to the Rajya Sabha and two Anglo-Indians to the house of the People are nominated by the President on the advice of the Council of Ministers. Most Bills are prepared and submitted to Parliament by the Council of Ministers.
5. The President exercises his power of pardon, reprieve on the advice of the Council of Ministers.

6. The President has the authority to use emergency powers (Article 352-360). Decision of declaration of Emergencies, whether arising out of war, aggression or armed rebellion, emergency arising out of failure of Constitutional machinery in a State and Financial Emergency are done are exercised by the cabinet in the name of the President. The President can declare emergency only under the written advice of the Cabinet especially the Prime Minister.
7. The executive power relating to foreign affairs is exercised by the Council of Ministers in reality. All treaties and international agreements are negotiated and concluded by the Council of Ministers in the name of the President. Declaration of war and conclusion of peace are performed by the Council of Ministers in the name of the President.

Relation between the Council of Ministers and the President of India

The Council of Ministers are the real power house in the Indian political system. Though the President is the head of the State, but the head of the Government is the Prime Minister. Though it is stated in Article 74 that the Council of Ministers with the Prime Minister will be there to aid and advise the President, but it is also given that the President is bound to accept that advice whether he likes it or not.

Further, as discussed earlier, all the executive functions of the President are performed by the Prime Minister and his Council of Ministers. The Legislative functions of the President are guided by the advice of the Prime Minister, but the President also has a hold on the Government. The Presidential consent is required for a Bill to become an Act. The President can give assent to a Bill or withhold his assent or send back the Bill for reconsideration. This can act as an influence on the Government policy. The Government might disregard his recommendations and pass the Bill for the second time, but if there are merits in the recommendations of the President, then public opinion can go against the Government which no Government can ignore.

Article 78 makes it the duty of the Prime Minister to communicate all decisions of the Council of Ministers to the President, but it so happens that often the Prime Minister and Council of Ministers do not inform the President regarding the affairs of administration of the Union.

Article 75, as discussed above, states that the Council of Ministers are collectively responsible to the Lok Sabha and not the President. This makes the Prime Minister and the Council of Ministers accountable to the Lok Sabha and not to the President. This makes evident that the actual charge-de-affairs is the Prime Minister and the Council of Ministers. The same Article states that the Ministers shall hold office during the pleasure of the President, but the real fact is that the ministers can be installed and removed from their position by the President on the advice of the President. Even the dissolution of a Lok Sabha by the President is advised by the Prime Minister.

However, use of discretion of the President becomes important during the formation of a new Government. The appointment of Prime Minister becomes crucial, if no party wins majority and when suddenly the Government loses majority in the House due to defection or split, then it is upto the President to assess the situation and dissolve the Lok Sabha and call for fresh elections. On the whole, the Council of Ministers led by the Prime Minister are the actual players in the Government of India. The relation between the Council of Minister and the President largely depends on the charisma and lack of ambition on the part of the President and the personality of the Prime Minister, for he commands his Council of Ministers.

Relation between the Council of Ministers and the Parliament

The Parliament is the bastion of democracy in India. The people of India send their representatives to the Parliament, thus it is obvious that the working of the Parliament is directly linked with the demands and aspirations of the people of India. Every Minister is a member of Parliament, either the Lok Sabha or the Rajya Sabha. The Ministers are bound by the rules and procedures of the Parliament. It is not possible for the ruling government to disregard the Parliament. However, the real fact is that sometimes the Parliament is hijacked by the Council of Ministers, mostly when the ruling party enjoys an absolute majority in the House as was the case during the primeminsitership of Nehru or Indira Gandhi. The Prime Minister and his Council of Ministers can pilot a Bill in the House in such situations by using party whip to secure the voting of its party members in the House/s. In 1977 during emergency, the power of the Parliament was enlarged and also the term of the Parliament (six years). It was some sort of cabinet dictatorship that was experienced during this phase of Indian politics.

In case of a coalition of parties, the Council of Ministers do not always command the affairs in the Parliament. The recent experience with the FDI Bill in the Lok Sabha in the winter session of 2011 showed how not only the opposition, but coalition partners created problems for the ruling party and the Prime Minister. As far as UPA-I is concerned the ruling Government wanted to pass the nuclear Bill, but the Left Parties which were supporting from outside withdrew the support, and the Government survived a collapse by garnering the much required support with great difficulty. Therefore, whatever the Council of Ministers, more precisely, the Cabinet formulates as government policies, the recent trends in Indian politics show that the Council of Ministers do not have the final say.

Further, the Parliament especially the Lok Sabha enjoys a greater power in the sense that the Council of Ministers is collectively, and also individually responsible to it. Thus, for any error of omission and commission the Parliament can become a ground of debate and even leading to passage of no-confidence motion. The opposition parties can also bring cut motions on the annual budget and thereby exercise control over Governmental decisions. Further, the Members of Parliament can pass adjournment motion, call attention motion, censure motion, cut motion as well as keep a check on Governmental policies by asking questions, supplementary questions to the Prime Minister or to the concerned ministers. If the budget gets rejected or a Bill gets defeated in Lok Sabha, then this tantamounts to the loss of confidence of the Government in the House and the Government might have to resign. Given the current trend of coalition politics in India, the Parliament has come to occupy an important position when compared to the Council of Ministers.

EXERCISES

I. Short Answer Questions: **(100 words)**

1. Write a note on Prime Minister's Office (PMO).
2. Briefly state the relation between the Prime Minister of India and the President of India.
3. Write a note on the Union Council of Ministers.
4. Discuss briefly the relation between the Union Council of Ministers and President of India.
5. State briefly the relation between the Union Council of Ministers and the Parliament.

II. Long Answer Questions: **(1200 words)**

6. Discuss the powers and functions of the Prime Minister of India.
7. Examine the relation between the Prime Minister of India and the President of India.
8. In the light of the powers and functions of the Prime Minister discuss the Constitutional position of the Prime Minister.
9. Analyze the composition, powers and functions of the Union Council of Ministers. In this connection examine the relation between the Union Council of Ministers and the Parliament.
10. Examine the relation between the Union Council of Ministers and the President of India.

REFERENCES

Awasthy, S.S., *Indian Government and Politics*, Revised Edition, Har-Anand Publications, New Delhi, 2006.

Bakshi, P.M., *The Constitution of India*, (with selective comments), Universal Law Publishing Co., Delhi, 2000.

Basu, Durga Das, *Introduction to the Constitution of India*, Prentice-Hall of India New Delhi, 1992.

Jain, M.P., *Indian Constitutional Law*, Wadhwa & Company, Nagpur, 1999.

Rao, K.V., *Parliamentary Democracy of India: A Critical Commentary*, The World Press, Calcutta, 1961.

Singh, M.P. and Saxena Rekha, *Indian Politics: Contemporary Issues and Concerns,* Prentice-Hall of India, New Delhi, 2008.

Siwach, J.R., *Dynamics of Indian Government and Politics*, Sterling Publishers, New Delhi, 1985.

9

The Union Parliament

INTRODUCTION

India follows a Westminster Model of political system; hence India has a bicameral legislature composed of Rajya Sabha and Lok Sabha. To a large extent, the Parliament is a non-sovereign authority whose power is circumscribed by the provisions of the Constitution as contained in the provisions of judicial review. Though the President is not a member of either House, yet like the British King-in-Parliament, the Indian President forms an integral part of the Parliament (Article 79) in a sense that he summons and prorogues the sessions, may dissolve the Lok Sabha, delivers inaugural address, sends messages and authenticates Bills passed by the parliament by putting his signature on them. A detailed discussion on the Parliamentary Democracy is a must for any student of Indian Government and Politics.

A BICAMERAL PARLIAMENT: COMPOSITION OF RAJYA SABHA AND LOK SABHA

The Preamble to the Constitution of India gives us the very essence of the nature of Indian polity when it declares in clear terms that **"WE, THE PEOPLE OF INDIA, having solemnly resolved to constitute India into a SOVEREIGN, SOCIALIST, SECULAR, DEMOCRATIC, REPUBLIC and to secure to all its citizens...** IN OUR **CONSTITUENT ASSEMBLY** this twenty-sixth day of November, 1949, do **HERE BY ADOPT, ENACT AND GIVE TO OURSELVES THIS CONSTITUTION."** It acclaims the republican character of the polity and sovereignty of the people. The democratic character as proclaimed in the Preamble is upheld by the Constitutional provisions ensuring universal adult suffrage, democratically elected people's representation and responsibility of the Executive to the Legislature whether in the Centre or in the State.

Part V, Chapter I of the Indian Constitution contains provisions relating to the power and functions of the executive (The President, Vice-President and the PM and the Council of Ministers). Chapter II deals with the composition, powers, privileges and legislative procedures of the Parliament. Article 79 speaks about the composition of the Parliament of India which says that it shall consist of the President and the two Houses which are to be known as the Council of States (**Rajya Sabha**) and the House of People (**Lok Sabha**). The Lok Sabha is a directly elected popular and powerful lower chamber and the Rajya Sabha is indirectly elected upper chamber. The Speaker is the Chairman and the presiding officer of the Lok Sabha. Every citizen of India, who is over 18 years of age, irrespective of gender, caste, religion or race and possesses such other qualifications as may be prescribed in that behalf by or under any law made by Parliament, is eligible to be elected as a member of the Lok Sabha. The Constitution provides that the maximum strength of the Lok Sabha should be 550. However, subsequently it had been raised, and the maximum strength of Lok Sabha stood at 552 (530 to be elected from States, 20 from Union Territories and 2 members of the Anglo-Indian community to be nominated by the President). Currently, the strength is 543 (as of April 2020). 2 seats reserved for Anglo-Indian community has been removed by the 104th amendment (25 January, 2020). The term of Lok Sabha is five years unless dissolved prematurely (Article 83). To be eligible for membership in the Lok Sabha, a person must be a citizen of India and must be 25 years of age or older, mentally sound, should not be bankrupt, should not be criminally convicted and should not hold any Office of Profit (Article 84). The Parliament (Prevention of Disqualification) Amendment Bill, 2006 sought to bring changes in the 1959 Act by exempting more posts from the purview of the office of profit. The Bill was passed by voice vote amid opposition by the National Democratic Alliance with some of its members staging a walkout. Around 40 parliamentarians and 200 legislators faced disqualification petitions on the office of profit issue. The then President A.P.J. Abdul Kalam wanted "comprehensive and generic" criteria for the exemptions. He observed while returning the Bill that the criteria should be "fair and reasonable" and applicable in a "clear and transparent" manner across all States and Union Territories. Signing the Office of Profit Bill was the "toughest" decision Dr. A.P.J. Abdul Kalam had taken during his tenure as the President. There are also some other criteria which have been laid down in the Representation of People Act, 1951 for the qualification and disqualification of membership of the Parliament like disqualification—

1. for conviction for certain offences,
2. on grounds of corrupt practices,
3. for dismissal for corruption or disloyalty
4. expressing interests for Government contracts, etc.

5. holding an office under any corporation in which the Government has any financial interest and
6. for failure to lodge account of election expense.

The Rajya Sabha is a permanent body, and is not subject to dissolution. Each member has a term of 6 years and elections are held for one-third of the seats after every 2 years. Its members are indirectly elected by members of legislative bodies of the States. The Rajya Sabha can have a maximum of 250 members in all. Around 238 members are to be elected from States and 2 Union Territories, and 12 are to be nominated by President of India, who usually are persons having special knowledge or practical experience in the fields of literature, science, art and social service (Article 80). At present, there are 245 members in Rajya Sabha (233 are representatives of States and Union Territories of Delhi and Puducherry + 12 are nominated members). The Vice-President of India is the *ex-officio* Chairman of the Rajya Sabha. One-tenth of the total number of members of Rajya Sabha constitutes the quorum for a meeting of the House. All questions are decided by majority vote (Article 100). The Chairman or person acting as such, shall not vote in the first instance, but shall have and exercise a casting vote in the case of an equality of votes (Article 100).

Detailed provisions relating to the composition, duration of the Houses of the Parliament, sessions of Parliament and qualification for membership of Parliament are given in Articles 80–85. Article 105 embodies the powers, privileges and immunities of Parliament and its members. The Legislative procedures including Joint Sessions of the Parliament are given in Articles 107–117. Article 85 contains provisions regarding Right of the President to summon each House of the Parliament, prorogue the Houses or either House and dissolve the Lok Sabha and Article 86 deals with right of President to address either House of Parliament or both Houses assembled together and send messages to either House. Rights of Ministers and Attorney-General as respects Houses are contained in Article 88. The powers and functions of Officers of Parliament, i.e., the Chairman and Deputy Chairman are contained in Articles 89–92. The powers and functions of Speaker and Deputy Speaker are contained in Article 93–96 of the Constitution. The Voting procedure in Houses is given under Article 100. Articles 101 and 102 deal with the provisions for disqualification of membership to the Parliament. It is needless to say that the Union Parliament must be seen along with the Prime Minister and his Council of Ministers who are the ones who actually run the Union Government in India. However, a nod of the Parliament is necessary for various public policies which the Union Government wants to adopt. Hence, it is undeniable that the Union Parliament is a powerful Legislature.

The Union Parliament though primarily a Legislative body, performs several executive as well as judicial functions. As far as the Legislative power of the Union Parliament is concerned, it makes laws over the subjects mentioned in the Union List, the Concurrent and the residuary subjects. Further, the Union Parliament can also make laws on subjects under State list if:

1. Rajya Sabha passes a resolution;
2. For the entire part of the country or any part thereof if there is a National Emergency under Article 352;
3. For a particular State where there is emergency under Article 356;
4. If there is a request by two or more States and;
5. If there is the implementation of some international treaty or convention.

The Executive powers of the Union Parliament under Article 75 provides that the Council of Ministers with the Prime Minister 'shall be collectively responsible to the Lok Sabha'. The Council of Ministers will have to resign in case a vote of censure is passed amounting to no-confidence in the Government. The adoption of Annual Budget is also an important financial function of the Parliament. It also exercises control over the Contingency Fund of India. It also studies the Reports of the Estimates Committee and Public Accounts Committee. Further, the Parliament acts as an Electoral College for the election of the President. The Vice-President of India is also elected by the two Houses. The Union Parliament also enjoys the power to impeach a President or any Judge of the Supreme Court and the State High Court. The Union Legislature also acts as the Board of Directors for the Public Sector Undertakings.

POWERS AND FUNCTIONS OF RAJYA SABHA

We have read how Constitutional development took place gradually in India through various Acts and reformative measures. If we look into the origins of the Rajya Sabha or the Council of States, we will find the roots in various Acts of the Colonial era like the Montague-Chelmsford Report of 1918. The Government of India Act, 1919, which provided for the creation of a Council of State as a second chamber of the then legislature with a restricted franchise actually came into existence in 1921. The Government of India Act, 1935, hardly made any changes in its composition. The powers of the Rajya Sabha can be broadly categorized as Executive, Legislative, Financial, Judicial, Electoral and Special Powers.

Executive Powers

In comparison to the Lok Sabha, the Rajya Sabha does not enjoy a huge array of Executive powers. Though the Council of Ministers is collectively responsible to the Lok Sabha, it does not mean that the Rajya Sabha has no power over it. Rajya Sabha cannot pass the vote of no-confidence, but it can exert control over the Council of Ministers by means of asking questions, supplementary questions, tabling important motions, introducing resolutions and calling attention motions and also demanding half-an-hour discussions and also moving adjournment motions. A member of the Rajya Sabha can also become the Prime Minister of India as in case of Mr. H.D. Deve Gowda in 1996, Mr. I.K. Gujral in 1997 and Manmohan Singh in 2004 and 2009.

Legislative Powers

As far as ordinary Bills are concerned, Rajya Sabha enjoys almost equal powers with the Lok Sabha. A Bill can be introduced in either House of Parliament. A Bill has to pass through three stages in each House of Parliament, and receive Presidential assent before it becomes an Act of Parliament (as discussed below). In the event of a deadlock between the two Houses on a Bill other than a Money Bill or a Constitution Amendment Bill, the issue is resolved at a joint sitting of the two Houses.

The Constitution has classified the subjects for legislation into three Lists, namely—the Union List, the State List and the Concurrent List. (Discussed in details in Chapter 6). With regard to the State List, over which the States have exclusive jurisdiction, Parliament can assume authority, if

1. Rajya Sabha declares by a resolution supported by not less than two-thirds of the members present and voting that such legislation is in national interest, or
2. two or more States mutually agree that Parliament may do so, or
3. it is necessary to implement treaties or international conventions.

Further, when a Proclamation of Emergency is in operation, Parliament is competent to legislate on matters included in the State List (Articles 249-253).

Financial Powers

No Money Bill can be introduced in the Rajya Sabha, and regarding Money Bills, Rajya Sabha is empowered to make only recommendations. If a Money Bill which is transmitted to Rajya Sabha for its recommendations is not returned to Lok Sabha within fourteen days, it is deemed to have been passed by both Houses at the expiration of the said period in the form it was passed by Lok Sabha. If the House of People does not accept the recommendations of the Rajya Sabha, the Money Bill then also will be deemed to have been passed by both Houses in the form in which it was passed by the Lok Sabha without the amendments recommended by the Rajya Sabha (Article 109).

A Bill which, if enacted and brought into operation that would involve expenditure from the Consolidated Fund of India is also called a Financial Bill. Such a Bill, however, can be introduced in Rajya Sabha and in case of financial Bills, Rajya Sabha has full power like an ordinary legislation. The annual budget of the Government is also laid before Rajya Sabha, but the budget speech is made in Lok Sabha only. Rajya Sabha has no powers to vote on the demands for grants of the Ministries/departments as this is the exclusive domain of Lok Sabha.

Judicial Powers

The Rajya Sabha enjoys co-equal power in the election and removal of the President. It can pass special address to remove the Chief Justice and judges of the Supreme Court and the High Courts or some high officer like the Comptroller and Auditor-General of India, Attorney-General of India and the Chief Election Commissioner.

Electoral Powers

The members of the Rajya Sabha form the Electoral College for the election of President and Vice-President of India. The Rajya Sabha also elects its own Deputy Chairman from amongst its members.

Constitution Amending Powers

The Rajya Sabha has equal powers with regard to amendment of the Constitution where it is required that the Bill must be passed by both the Houses. Such a Bill might originate in any of the Houses of the Parliament.

Special Powers

Rajya Sabha being a federal chamber enjoys certain special powers under the Constitution. As discussed all the subjects/areas regarding legislation have been divided into three Lists—Union List, State List and Concurrent List. Union and State lists are mutually exclusive—one cannot legislate on a matter placed in the sphere of the other. However, if Rajya Sabha passes a resolution by a majority of not less than two-thirds of members present and voting saying that it is necessary or expedient in the national interest that Parliament should make a law on a matter enumerated in the State List, Parliament becomes empowered to make a law on the subject specified in the resolution, for the whole or any part of the Territory of India. Such a resolution remains in force for a maximum period of one year, but this period can be extended by one year at a time by passing a similar resolution further.

Under the Constitution, the President is empowered to issue Proclamations in the event of national emergency, in the event of failure of Constitutional machinery in a State, or in the case of Financial Emergency. Every such Proclamation has to be approved by both Houses of Parliament within a stipulated period. Under certain circumstances, however, Rajya Sabha enjoys special powers in this regard. If a Proclamation is issued at a time when Lok Sabha has been dissolved or the dissolution of Lok Sabha takes place within the period allowed for its approval, then the Proclamation remains effective, if the resolution approving it is passed by Rajya Sabha within the period specified in the Constitution under Articles 352, 356 and 360.

Under Article 312 the Rajya Sabha is empowered to create an All-India Service if it adopts a resolution by its two-third majority stating that it is necessary or expedient in the national interest common to the Union and the States, Parliament becomes empowered to create by law such services.

Powers and Functions of Lok Sabha

The Constitution of India came into force on 26 January 1950, and the first general elections under the new Constitution were held during the year 1951–52. The first elected Parliament came into being in April 1952, the second Lok Sabha in April 1957, the third Lok Sabha in April 1962, the fourth Lok Sabha in March 1967, the fifth Lok Sabha in March 1971, the sixth Lok Sabha in March 1977, the seventh Lok Sabha in January 1980, the eighth Lok Sabha in December 1984, the ninth Lok Sabha in December 1989, the tenth Lok Sabha in June 1991, the eleventh Lok Sabha in May 1996, the twelfth Lok Sabha in March 1998, thirteenth Lok Sabha in October 1999, fourteenth Lok Sabha in April-May 2004, the fifteenth Lok Sabha in April-May 2009, sixteenth Lok Sabha May 2014 and seventeenth Lok Sabha in May 2019. The regular tenure of Lok Sabha is for five years if not disturbed due to some emergencies as in the case of Proclamation of Emergency when the tenure will be extended for one year. However, while a declaration of Emergency is in operation, this period may be extended by Parliament by law for a period not more than one year at a time and not extending, in any case, beyond a period of six months after the declaration has ceased to function.

The Lok Sabha performs a wide array of functions. These are discussed as follows:

1. As far as the Legislative Power of the Lok Sabha is concerned, its primary function is to make laws as contained in the Union List or (if need be) in the Concurrent List. Matters related to Ordinary Bills, after it is passed by the originating House (that is either Lok Sabha or Rajya Sabha) if is sent to the other House, where it can be kept for a maximum period of 6 months time. If the other House rejects the Bill or 6 months pass or the suggestions made by the other House is not acceptable to the originating House, it results in a situation of deadlock. This is resolved by the President by calling a joint session of both Houses which is presided over by the Speaker of the Lok Sabha and decided by a simple majority. Since the Lok Sabha has greater numerical strength, it is in a position of advantage. A very recent case which raised furore in public was the Lokpal Bill which could not be

passed in the Monsoon Session (2011) and finally, almost at the fag end of an extended Winter Session (2011) the Lok Sabha passed a feeble Lokpal Bill, but the Constitutional Amendment Bill was defeated. The Bill was caught in a limbo when the Rajya Sabha was adjourned *sine die* and the Bill got deferred. Sometimes a joint sitting of the Parliament can help to overcome a logjam as was the case with POTO Bill in 2002, which resolved the crisis and finally POTA was passed and then terminated in 2004.

2. The Executive Power of the Lok Sabha extends to the control of the executives through various devices like calling attention motion, questions and supplementary questions, half an hour discussion, No Confidence Motions and other means. Article 75(3) lays down that "The Council of Ministers shall be collectively responsible to the House of the People." The Council of Ministers, if they lose the confidence of the House must resign. In other cases, if the House disapproves the budget, or rejects any official policy of the Government or a Bill gets defeated or includes revisions to any Bills (as in case of the Lok Pal Bill 187 alterations was suggested by BJP-led NDA coalition in 2011 Winter Session) then it can show the lack of trust of the House on the Government. Lok Sabha approves various acts of Government like Proclamation of Emergencies which cannot be declared by the President unless the decision of the Union Cabinet (Council consisting of the Prime Minister and other Ministers of Cabinet rank under Article 75) is communicated to him in writing. Every such Proclamation of Emergency shall be laid before each House of the Parliament. In case the Lok Sabha is dissolved before the declaration of Emergency, Rajya Sabha becomes the sole *de facto* and *de jure* Parliament which has to approve the Proclamation of Emergency.
3. As far as the Financial Power of the Lok Sabha is concerned, Money Bills can only be introduced in the Lok Sabha and can be deliberated to Rajya Sabha for fourteen days. If it is not rejected by Rajya Sabha or the period lapse after 14 days from the day of introduction without any action or recommendations made by the Rajya Sabha is not accepted by Lok Sabha, then it is considered passed. Also, the budget of the year is presented by the Finance Minister in the Lok Sabha. However, whether a particular Bill is a Money Bill or not is to be decided by the Speaker of the Lok Sabha, whose decision is the final and cannot be challenged by either the Lok Sabha or the Rajya Sabha. The annual budget of the Government is before Rajya Sabha and the Lok Sabha, but the budget speech is made in Lok Sabha only. Rajya Sabha has no powers to vote on the Demands for Grants of the Ministries/departments as this is the exclusive domain of Lok Sabha.
4. Among the Judicial Powers, the Lok Sabha possesses certain equal powers with Rajya Sabha. This includes initiating and passing of any

Bill on Constitutional Amendments; equal powers in electing as well as passing a motion on the impeachment of the President by two-third membership of the total membership of the House, and equal powers in initiating and passing of impeachment against the Judges of Supreme Court and State High Courts by a majority of the membership of the House and at least two-thirds majority of the members present and voting). It also has power of removal of Comptroller and Auditor-General, Chief Election Commission and others.

5. Some miscellaneous functions of Lok Sabha pertains to approval of Ordinances issued by the President, changes of boundaries of States, creation of new States and changes in the names of States, revision of salary and allowances of the members of Parliament, setting up of Joint Public Service Commission for two or more States and the like. It shares equal power with Rajya Sabha in discussing Reports submitted by autonomous agencies like the Union Public Service Commission, Comptroller and Auditor-General of India, Finance Commission, Language Commission, Minorities Commission, Scheduled Castes and Scheduled Tribes Commission and so on.

In addition to the Legislative powers of Lok Sabha, the powers and functions of Lok Sabha members include being part of many Parliamentary Committees. Parliamentary Committees are of two kinds: Standing Committees and Ad hoc Committees (discussed in the later sections). The Lok Sabha also performs some electoral functions as it elects the President and Vice-President of India along with the Rajya Sabha and its Speaker and Deputy Speaker.

PARLIAMENTARY PROCEDURE IN INDIA

The first hour of every sitting is called the **Question hour**. It is during the Question hour that the members of Parliament may ask questions on different aspects of administration and Government policy in the national as well as international spheres. Questions are of three types—Starred, Unstarred and Short Notice. A Starred Question is one to which a member desires an oral answer in the House and which is distinguished by an asterisk mark. An Unstarred Question is one which is not called for oral answer in the House and on which no Supplementary Questions can consequently be asked. An answer to such a question is given in writing. Minimum period of notice for Starred/Unstarred question is 10 days. A Short Notice Question may only be answered on short notice if so permitted by the Speaker and the Minister concerned is prepared to answer it at shorter notice. A Short Notice Question is taken up for answer immediately after the Question hour.

After the question hour there can be **Half-an-Hour discussion**, on matters of sufficient public importance which has been the subject of a recent question, oral or written and the answer to which needs elucidation on a matter of fact. Questions of public importance can also be raised during **Zero hour**.

Since this session starts at 12.00 noon it is called as **Zero hour**. **Special Mention** is yet another device through which a member can raise an issue of public importance in the House. A member may move an **Adjournment Motion** of urgent public importance having a definite and factual basis with the prior notice being given to the Speaker or the Minister or the Secretary-General. The concept of **Calling Attention** is another device which combines the asking of a question for answer with supplementaries and short comments in which different points of view are expressed concisely and precisely. A member may with the prior permission of the Speaker call attention of a Minister on any matter or urgent public importance. This gives an opportunity to the members of Parliament to highlight the failure/misgivings or inadequate action of government on a matter of urgent public importance. Another device of utmost importance is **No Confidence motion**. As the Council of Ministers is collectively responsible to the Lok Sabha, once they lose the confidence of the House a motion of this sort can be moved with prior notice being given to the Speaker. A **Censure Motion** contains specific charges against the Government and no leave of the House is required to move it.

Regarding debates in the Lok Sabha and Rajya Sabha members may have discussions on matters of urgent public importance with the permission of the Speaker. Such discussions may take place on two days in a week. After the member who initiates discussion on an item of business has spoken, other members can speak on that item of business in such order as the Speaker may call upon them. Only one member can speak at a time and all speeches are directed to the chair. A matter requiring the decision of the House is decided by means of a question put by the Speaker on a motion made by a member.

Sessions of Parliament

The parliament has three sessions each year:

1. Budget session: February to May
2. Monsoon session: July to August
3. Winter session: November to December

Procedure Relating to an Ordinary Bill in the Union Parliament

Legislative proposals are brought before in either Houses in the form of a Bill. A Bill is the draft of a Legislative proposal, which, when passed by both Houses of Parliament and assented to by the President, becomes an Act of Parliament. There are Government Bills and private members' Bills. Bills may also be classified as Public Bills and Private Bills. A Public Bill is one referring to a matter applying to the public in general, whereas a Private Bill relates to a particular person or corporation or institution.

There are three stages through which a Bill other than the Money Bill has to be passed in one House of the Parliament. The First reading of any Bill other than Money Bill is Introduction of the Bill by a Minister or by a private member only after a notice of his intention. A minister or member-in-charge of the Bill seeks the leave of the House to introduce a Bill. The Second reading is the Discussion stage, and this is further divided into three stages as follows:

1. the Bill may be taken into consideration, may be referred to a select Committee or a Joint Committee of both the Houses, or it may be circulated for eliciting public opinion.
2. The next stage is the discussion on the Report. This consists of a clause-by-clause consideration of the Bill as reported by the Committee. When all the clauses have been put to vote and disposed of, the Second reading of the Bill is over.
3. Next changes or amendments to the Bill can be made only in this stage. Amendments become a part of a Bill if they are accepted by a majority of the members present and voting.

The Third reading is the voting stage. The debate on the Third reading of a Bill is of a restricted character. It is confined only to arguments either in support of the Bill or for its rejection, without referring to its details. When all the amendments are disposed of, the Bill is finally passed. After the Bill is passed, it is sent to the other House for consideration where it goes through the same procedure and the different stages. The House has three alternatives before it:

(a) it might pass it in the same form as sent by the originating House,
(b) it might amend or altogether reject the Bill, and the Bill may be returned to the originating House,
(c) it may not return it at all within six months after the receipt of the Bill, which will mean the same as rejection.

In case of a deadlock between the two Houses or in case where more than six months have lapsed in the other House, the President may summon a Joint Session of the two Houses which is presided over by the Speaker of the Lok Sabha and the deadlock is resolved by simple majority.

When a Bill has been finally passed, it is sent to the President for his/her assent. The President can assent or withhold his/her assent to a Bill or he/she can return a Bill, other than a Money Bill, with his/her recommendations. If the President gives his/her assent, the Bill becomes an Act. If he/she withholds his assent, the Bill is dropped, which is known as pocket veto. If the President returns it for reconsideration, the Parliament must do so, but if the Houses pass the Bill again with or without amendments and the Bill is presented to the President for his assent. After such reconsideration, the President shall have no power to withhold his assent from the Bill. In the case of a Constitutional Amendment Bill, the President is bound to give his/her assent.

Procedure Relating to a Money Bill in the Union Parliament

A Money Bill cannot be introduced in the Council of States or Rajya Sabha. When a Money Bill is passed by House of People or Lok Sabha, it is sent to Rajya Sabha for its recommendations. The Rajya Sabha within a period of 14 days from the date of receipt of the Bill return the Bill to the Lok Sabha with its recommendations. The Lok Sabha may either accept or reject all or any of the recommendations, and in either case the Bill is considered to have passed by both the Houses in the form in which it was passed by the Lok Sabha. If the Money Bill is not returned by Rajya Sabha to Lok Sabha within the said period of 14 days, it shall be deemed to have been passed by Houses at the expiration of the said period.

Powers, Privileges and Immunities of the House and Members

Parliamentary privileges in India are not codified. Some of the privileges and immunities of the Houses of Parliament, the members and Committees thereof are specified in the Constitution under Article 105 while some are contained in certain statutes and the Rules of Procedure of the Houses and also in conventions which have grown over the years.

A few important privileges and immunities are:

1. Freedom of speech in Parliament and immunity of a member from any proceedings in any court in respect of anything said or any vote given by him in Parliament or any Committee thereof
2. Immunity to a person from proceedings in any court in respect of the publication by or under the authority of either House of Parliament of any Report, paper, votes or proceedings
3. Prohibition on the Courts to inquire into proceedings of Parliament
4. Freedom from arrest of members in civil cases during the continuance of the session of the House and forty days before the commencement and forty days after its conclusion
5. Exemption of a member from initiation of a legal process civil or criminal and arrest within the precincts of the House without obtaining permission of the Speaker

RELATION BETWEEN RAJYA SABHA AND LOK SABHA

As India follows the Westminster model of Parliamentary democracy and thereby consists of a Bicameral Legislature a serious discussion regarding the interrelation of the Houses is much needed.

Legislative Process

As far as passage of Bill is concerned, if it is an ordinary Bill both the Houses enjoy equal power. The Constitution does not make any distinction between the Houses in this regard. Every Minister has the right to speak and take part in the proceedings of either House, but he is entitled to vote only in the House of which he is a member. If a deadlock arises with respect to a certain Bill, then it can be resolved by summoning a Joint Session of the Parliament. Issues in joint sitting are decided by a majority of the total number of members of both Houses present and voting. The joint sitting is held in the Central Hall of Parliament House presided over by the Speaker of the Lok Sabha.

As regards a Constitution Amendment Bill, it has been provided in the Constitution that such a Bill has to be passed by the specific majority, as prescribed under Article 368 of the Constitution, by both Houses. There is, therefore, no provision for resolving a deadlock between the two Houses in regard to a Constitution Amendment Bill.

President's ordinances are laid before both the houses, and it lapses if both the Houses pass a resolution disapproving it. The power of the two houses, therefore is co-ordinate in this matter.

With regard to the powers, privileges and immunities of the Houses of Parliament, their members and Committees thereof, the two Houses are placed absolutely on equal footing by the Constitution.

Executive Powers

Under Article 75(3) of the Constitution, the Council of Ministers is collectively responsible to Lok Sabha which means Rajya Sabha cannot make or unmake the Government. It can, however, exercise control over the Government and this function becomes quite prominent, particularly when the Government does not enjoy majority in Rajya Sabha.

Both Houses enjoy equal powers like election and impeachment of the President, election of the Vice-President, approving the Proclamation of Emergency, the Proclamation regarding failure of Constitutional machinery in States and Financial Emergency. In respect of receiving Reports and papers from various statutory authorities, etc., both Houses have equal powers.

Financial Legislation

Money Bills can only originate in the Lok Sabha. Ruling of the Speaker of the Lok Sabha is final whether a particular Bill is a Money Bill or not. However, in the case of a Money Bill, there is no provision in the Constitution for a joint sitting of both Houses as Lok Sabha clearly enjoys pre-eminence over Rajya Sabha in financial matters. Rajya Sabha can delay the Bill for a period of 14 days and after the expiration of the said period it is deemed to have been passed by both the Houses of the Parliament and send to the president for his assent.

Emergency Powers

Declaration of emergency is laid before both the Houses and it cannot remain in force for more than one month unless, before the expiry of that period, if it is approved by both Houses.

It is with much evident that the framers of the Constituion of India did not wanted to make Rajya Sabha a non-entity. It is thus, clear that except in the case of collective responsibility of the Council of Ministers and certain financial matters, which fall in the domain of Lok Sabha only, both Houses enjoy equal powers. But the Rajya Sabha also enjoys two special powers which have been discussed above (Special Powers of Rajya Sabha). They are declaration of a State subject of national importance and creation or abolition of All India Services. In actual practice, the Rajya Sabha, though a prestigious chamber, enjoys a less powerful position than the Lok Sabha.

SPEAKER OF LOK SABHA

According to Article 93 the House of the People (Lok Sabha) shall choose two members of the House to be respectively Speaker and Deputy Speaker and if the office of the Speaker or Deputy Speaker becomes vacant, the House shall choose another member to be Speaker or Deputy Speaker as the case may be. Article 95 contains that while the office of Speaker is vacant, President may appoint a member from the House of the People for the purpose. The members of Parliament represent the individual constituencies, and the Speaker represents the full authority of the House itself.

In India, through the Constitution, through the Rules of Procedure and Conduct of Business in Lok Sabha and through the practices and conventions, adequate powers are vested in the office of the Speaker to help him in the smooth conduct of the Parliamentary proceedings and for protecting the independence and impartiality of the office. The Constitution of India provides that the Speaker's salary and allowances are not to be voted by Parliament and are to be charged on the Consolidated Fund of India.

Term of Office and Removal

Under Article 94 the Speaker holds office from the date of his election till immediately before the first meeting of the Lok Sabha after the dissolution of the one to which he was elected. He is also eligible for re-election. On the dissolution of the Lok Sabha, although the Speaker ceases to be a member of the House, he does not vacate his office until the first meeting of the House of people is held after dissolution. The Speaker may, at any time, resign from office by writing a resignation letter in his own handwriting addressed to the Deputy Speaker. The Speaker can be removed from office only on a resolution of the House passed by a majority of all the then members of the House. Such a resolution has to satisfy some conditions provided that it should be specific with respect to the charges and it should not contain arguments, inferences, ironical expressions, imputations or defamatory Statements, etc. Not only should these, discussions be confined to charges referred to in the resolution. It is also mandatory to give a minimum of 14 days' notice of the intention to move the resolution.

Balram Jakhar is till date the longest serving speaker, who served for 9 years, 10 months, and 27 days. He served as Speaker of Lok Sabha from 1980 to 1989.

Election of Speaker

In the Lok Sabha, the Lower House of the Indian Parliament, both the Speaker and the Deputy Speaker are elected from among its members unanimously by a simple majority of members present and voting in the House (Article 93). As such, no specific qualifications are prescribed for being elected as the Speaker. Usually the qualifications required to be eligible for membership of Lok Sabha are applicable in case of a Speaker of Lok Sabha. The Constitution only requires that he should be a member of the House. Usually, a member belonging to the ruling party is elected as the Speaker. However, in most cases the ruling party generally nominates its candidate after informal consultations with the leaders of other parties in the House. There are also instances when members not belonging to the ruling party or coalition were elected to the office of the Speaker. Somnath Chatterjee had been associated with the Communist Party of India (Marxist) for most of his life, though he is currently an independent candidate. He was the Speaker of the Lok Sabha from 2004 to 2009 when UPA(I) was in power and the Left Parties had extended support from outside. Once a decision on the candidate is taken, his name is normally proposed by the Prime Minister or the Minister of Parliamentary affairs.

Proterm Speaker

The first meeting, after election in which Speaker is elected by the members of Lok Sabha, is held under the senior most member of Parliament who is commonly known as *Proterm* Speaker. The Speaker *proterm* presides over the sitting in which the Speaker is elected, if it is a newly constituted House.

Powers and Functions of the Speaker of Lok Sabha

The Speaker is the presiding officer of the Lok Sabha. He has been vested with several powers to maintain discipline in the House and ensure its dignity. The Speaker in his task is guided by the provisions of the Constitution and the Rules of Procedure and Conduct of Business in Lok Sabha. He also benefits from the directions issued by his predecessors which are compiled periodically. As the conventional head of the Lok Sabha and as its principal Spokesman, the Speaker represents its collective voice.

Presiding Officer of Lok Sabha

He is the spokesman of the Lok Sabha, and he represents it in all ceremonial functions. In the Lok Sabha chamber, the Speaker's chair is distinctively placed and, from his seat, he gets a commanding view of the entire House. As the presiding officer, he/she decides the admissibility of a question; the form in which amendments may be moved to the motion of thanks to the President's Address and the like. With regard to moving amendments to a Bill, the permission of the chair is required. The Speaker decides whether any amendment is to be moved to various clauses of the Bill or not which is pending in the House. The Speaker of the Lok Sabha also presides over joint sittings called in the event of disagreement between the two Houses on any legislation under consideration. The Speaker being the Presiding Officer has the power to adjourn the House and can also suspend its meeting in the absence of quorum which is one-tenth of the members of the House (Article 100).

As regards regulating discussions in the House, it is the Speaker who decides as to when a member shall speak and how long he shall speak. It is left to him to ask a member to discontinue his speech or even decide that what a particular member said may not go on record as part of the proceedings. On matters regarding interpretation of Constitutional provisions relating to the House or the Rules of Procedure, he often gives rulings which must be respected by members and they are binding in nature. In case of Money Bills if a dispute arises as to whether a Bill is a Money Bill or not, the decision is made by the Speaker. This decision is final and cannot be challenged outside the House. The Speaker protects the rights and privileges of the House, its Committees and members. It depends solely on the Speaker to refer any question of privilege to the Committee of privileges for examination, investigation and Report. The Speaker can direct a member to withdraw from the House for a specific period of time, if that member tries to disrupt the proceedings of the House for the Speaker is empowered to maintain discipline in the House. A member who flouts his orders or directions may be named by the Speaker and in such cases, that member may have to withdraw from the House. Following the 52nd Constitution Amendment, the Speaker is vested with the power relating to the disqualification of a member of the Lok Sabha on grounds of defection. The

Speaker is also the main channel of communication between the President and the Lok Sabha.

Casting Vote

Normally, the Speaker does not take part in voting in the House. But in case of a tie, he exercises his right of casting vote. His casting vote would decide the issue. In such a case his vote would normally go in favour of the party to which he belongs. Further, when a resolution for the removal of the Speaker is put to vote in the House, he/she has the right to cast his vote (Article 100).

Role of the Speaker Regarding the Committees

The Speaker is the ex-officio Chairman of certain Committees like the Business Advisory Committee, the General Purposes Committee and the Rules Committee. Other than these, all Committees of the House are constituted by him and function under his overall direction. The Chairman of all Parliamentary Committees of Lok Sabha are nominated by him.

Administrative Functions

The Lok Sabha Secretariat functions under the control and direction of the Speaker. The Speaker's authority over the Secretariat staff of the House, its precincts and its security arrangements is supreme. All strangers, visitors and press correspondents are subject to his discipline and orders. No alternation or addition can be made in the Parliament House, and no new structure can be erected in the Parliament Estate without the Speaker's permission.

Miscellaneous Functions

As the Speaker is the spokesman of the Lok Sabha and he represents it in all ceremonial functions of the Lok Sabha. He is the *ex-officio* President of the Indian Parliamentary Group (IPG), set up in 1949, which functions as the National Group of the Inter-Parliamentary Union (IPU) and the Main Branch of the Commonwealth Parliamentary Association (CPA). In that capacity, members of various Indian Parliamentary Delegations going abroad are nominated by him after consulting the Chairman of the Rajya Sabha. Most often, the Speaker himself leads such delegations. Besides, he is the Chairman of the Conference of Presiding Officers of Legislative Bodies in India.

Position of the Speaker

The office of the Speaker in India is not without significance and at times helps to address the problems in the working of Parliament. The Speaker is the Constitutional and ceremonial head of the House. From the above discussion about the role of the Speaker it is quite evident that his office is a dignified one and must be respected. What is important is that while discharging his function, the Speaker must be impartial and neutral. The Speaker is like the guardian of the Lok Sabha, and he with his expertise and dignity of his chair, guides the proceedings of the Lok Sabha which helps to maintain the continuation of representative democracy in India. Pt. Jawaharlal Nehru, while commenting on the position of the Speaker said, "The Speaker represents the House. He represents the dignity of the House, the freedom of the House and because the House represents the Nation, in a particular way, the Speaker becomes a symbol of Nation's freedom and liberty. Therefore, it is right that, that should be an honoured position, a free position and should be occupied always by men of outstanding ability and impartiality".

Table 9.1 Gives a list of the Speakers of India from the beginning to the date.

Table 9.1 List of the Speakers of Lok Sabha

Name of the Speaker	*Term*
Sh. G.V. Mavalankar	(15 May 1952–27 February 1956)
Sh. M.A. Ayyangar	(8 March 1956–10 May 1957) & (11 May 1957–16 April 1962)
Sardar Hukam Singh	(17 April 1962–16 March 1967)
Sh. N. Sanjeeva Reddy	(17 March 1967–19 July 1969) & (26 March 1977–13 July 1977)
Sh. G.S. Dhillon	(8 August 1969–17 March 1971) & (22 March 1971–1 December 1975)
Sh. Bali Ram Bhagat	(15 January 1976–25 March 1977)
Sh. K.S. Hegde	(21 July 1977–21 January1980)
Sh. Balram Jakhar	(22 January 1980–15 January 1985) & (16 January 1985–18 December 1989)
Sh. Rabi Ray	(19 December 1989–9 July 1991)
Sh. Shivraj V. Patil	(10 July 1991–22 May 1996)
Sh. P.A. Sangma	(23 May 1996–23 March 1998)
Sh. G.M.C. Balyogi	(24 March 1998–19 October 1999) & (22 January 1999–3 March 2002)
Sh. Manohar Joshi	(10 May 2002–2 June 2004)
Sh. Somnath Chatterjee	(4 June 2004–31 May 2009)
Smt. Meira Kumar	(4 June 2009–18 May 2014)
Smt. Sumitra Mahajan	(6 June 2014–17 June 2019)
Sh. Om Birla	19 June 2019–

PARLIAMENTARY COMMITTEES

The work of the Union Legislature is massive and time-consuming, and sometimes, may need some special expertise/attention for a particular matter.

Therefore, for smooth functioning of the Legislature in the process of law-making, the Parliament has created several Committees, as discussed below which are sometimes referred to as Mini Legislature.

Ad hoc Committees

Ad hoc Committees are appointed for a specific purpose and they cease to exist when they finish the task assigned to them and submit a Report. The principal Ad hoc Committees are the select and Joint Committees on Bills which are formed for a particular purpose.

Select and Joint Committees

When a Bill is taken up for general discussion, then it is up to the House to refer it to either a select Committee of the House or a Joint Committee of the two Houses. For this, there must be a motion moved and adopted to this effect in the House in which the Bill originates. In case the motion adopted is for reference of the Bill to a Joint Committee, the decision is conveyed to the other House requesting them to nominate members of the other House to serve on the Committee. After consideration by the select or the Joint Committee then amendments can be moved to various clauses by members of the Committee. Thereafter, the Committee submits its Report to the House which referred to the matter to that Committee.

Some of the important Joint Parliamentary Committees in which members of both the Houses are represented are:

1. Committee on the Welfare of Scheduled Castes and Scheduled Tribes;
2. Committee on Offices of Profit;
3. Committee on Empowerment of Women;
4. Library Committee;
5. Committee on Food Management in Parliament House Complex;
6. Committee on Installation of Portraits/Statues of National Leaders and Parliamentarians in the Parliament House complex;
7. Committee on Security Matters in Parliament House complex and others.

Standing Committees

Each House of Parliament has Standing Committees. These Committees are elected by the House or nominated by the presiding officer each year or from time-to-time, and they are permanent in nature. They can be Financial Committees like the Estimates Committee, Public Accounts Committee and Committee on Public Undertakings. There can be House Committees as Business Advisory Committee, Committee on the Absence of Members from sittings of the House and so on. There can be Enquiry Committee as Committee on Petitions, Privileges Committee. There are also Scrutiny Committees on

Government Assurances, Committees on Subordinate Legislation, Committee on Papers Laid on the Table of the House, Committee on the Welfare of Scheduled Caste and Scheduled Tribes. There are also Service Committees such as General Purposes Committee, House Committee, Library Committee, Joint Committee on Salaries and Allowances of MPs.

Some important Standing Committees

Some important Committees which act as Parliament's watch dogs and thereby perform necessary surveillance over the executive are:

1. The Committees on Subordinate Legislation
2. The Committee on Government Assurances
3. The Committee on Estimates
4. The Committee on Public Accounts and
5. The Committee on Public Undertakings and Departmentally Related Standing Committees (DRSCs).

The Committee on Estimates, the Committee on Public Accounts, the Committee on Public Undertakings and DRSCs play an important role in exercising a check over Governmental expenditure and Policy formulation. [Public Accounts Committee and Estimates Committee are discussed in details in Chapter 22]

Departmentally related Standing Committees

A new system of 17 departmentally related Standing Committees came into being in April, 1993. As a result of which 17 Standing Committees were formed. They are:

1. Committee on Commerce;
2. Committee on Home Affairs;
3. Committee on Human Resource Development;
4. Committee on Industry;
5. Committee on Science & Technology, Environment & Forests;
6. Committee on Transport, Culture and Tourism;
7. Committee on Agriculture,
8. Committee on Information Technology;
9. Committee on Defence;
10. Committee on Energy;
11. Committee on External Affairs;
12. Committee on Finance;
13. Committee on Food, Civil Supplies and Public Distribution;
14. Committee on Labour and Welfare;
15. Committee on Petroleum and Chemicals;

16. Committee on Railways and
17. Committee on Urban and Rural Development.

Out of the 17 Committees, 6 Committees (from 1 to 6) are looked after by the Rajya Sabha Secretariat and 11 Committees (from 7 to 17) by the Lok Sabha Secretariat. The Chairmen of 6 Committees serviced by the Rajya Sabha are appointed by the Chairman of the Rajya Sabha and the Chairman of 11 Committees serviced by the Lok Sabha are appointed by the Speaker of the Lok Sabha.

Each of these Standing Committees consists of not more than 45–30 members to be nominated by the Speaker from amongst the members of Lok Sabha and 15 to be nominated by the Chairman, Rajya Sabha from amongst the members of Rajya Sabha. A Minister is not eligible to be nominated to these Committees. The term of members of these Committees is one year. The functions of the Committees with reference to the Ministries/departments under their purview pertain to consideration of demands for grants, examination of Bills referred to by the Chairman, Rajya Sabha or the Speaker, Lok Sabha as the case may be or even consideration of Annual Reports, but not matters related to the everyday administration of the concerned Ministries/Departments.

Now, we will specifically go into the discussion of the Committee System of both the Houses.

Committees of Rajya Sabha

Rajya Sabha possesses an elaborate system of Committees. Some are Ad hoc Committees and others are Standing Committees. Everything related to the appointments, term of office, functions and procedure for conducting business in these Committees is regulated under the provisions of the rules and directions given by the Chairman of the Rajya Sabha from time-to-time. Some important Ad hoc Committees formed were an Ad hoc Committee to consider its Rules of Procedure in 1962, a Committee was appointed to enquire into the conduct of a sitting member of the House in 1976 and many others.

The Standing Committees of the Rajya Sabha may be divided in terms of their functions and can be classified under four broad heads like Committees to Enquire, Committees to Scrutinize and Control, Committees Relating to day-to-day Business of the House and House Keeping Committees. Under the **Committees to Enquire**, there are Committee on Petitions; Committee of Privileges; and Ethics Committee. Certain Committees are under **Committees to Scrutinize and Control** like Committee on Government Assurances; Committee on Subordinate Legislation; and Committee on Papers Laid on the Table. Under **Committees relating to day-to-day Business of the House** there are Committees on Business Advisory Committee; and Rules Committee. Finally, under the **House Keeping Committees**, there are House Committee; General Purposes Committee; and Committee on Provision of Computers to Members of Rajya Sabha.

There are also Joint Parliamentary Committees which have been mentioned above. The members of Rajya Sabha are present in some of the Financial Committees of the Lok Sabha too like the Committee on Public Accounts, the Committee on Public Undertakings, the Committee on Offices of Profit and the Committee on the Welfare of Scheduled Castes and Scheduled Tribes and they are elected by the House, while members of the other Joint Committees are nominated by the Chairman of Rajya Sabha. The proportion of number of members of the two Houses in these Committees is approximately in the ratio of 2 members of Lok Sabha to 1 of Rajya Sabha.

COMMITTEES OF THE LOK SABHA

Some important Committees of the Lok Sabha are discussed as follows:

Business Advisory Committee

The Business Advisory Committee of Lok Sabha consists of 15 members including the Speaker who is the ex-officio Chairman. The members are nominated by the Speaker. The function of the Committee is to recommend the time that should be allotted for the discussion of a particular legislative matter like time to be allotted for discussion on a particular Bill and other business as the Speaker, in consultation with the leader of the House, may direct to be referred to the Committee. The Committee generally meets at the beginning of each session, and thereafter, as and when necessary.

Committee on Private Members' Bills and Resolutions

This Committee consists of 15 members, and generally, the Deputy Speaker is its Chairman. The members of the Committee is nominated by the Speaker. The functions of the Committee are to allot time to private members' Bills and resolutions and to examine private members' Bills before their introduction in Lok Sabha. Before a private member Bills are taken up for consideration in the House, this Committee classifies them according to its importance into two categories namely, category A and category B as Bills which are of greatest importance and as those which are less important.

Rules Committee

The Rules Committee consists of 15 members nominated by the Speaker with the Speaker as the *ex-officio* Chairman of the Committee. The Committee considers matters of procedure and conduct of business in the House and recommends changes/amendments to the Rules of Procedure and Conduct of Business in Lok Sabha, if necessary.

Committee of Privileges

This Committee consists of 15 members nominated by the Speaker. If there are cases of violation/breach of privileges of the members of the Parliament, the matter is then referred to it by the House or by the Speaker. It determines whether there has been a breach of privilege, and makes suitable recommendations in its Report.

Committee on Papers Laid on the Table

This Committee consists of 15 members nominated by the Speaker. Its function is to examine all Papers Laid on the Table of the House by Ministers. The Committee after its consideration Reports to the House if there has been compliance of the provisions of the Constitution, Act, rule or regulation under which the paper has been laid or whether there has been any unreasonable delay in laying the paper or even whether both the Hindi and English versions of the paper have been laid on the Table. The Speaker from time-to-time may also assign certain functions to the Committee related to matters falling within its purview.

Committee on Petitions

The Committee consists of 15 members nominated by the Speaker. A minister is not nominated to this Committee. The function of the Committee is to consider and Report on petitions presented to the House. It scrutinizes the petitions and sends them to the respective departments with or without their recommendations.

Committee on Subordinate Legislation

The Committee consists of 15 members nominated by the Speaker. The function of the Committee is related to what is commonly known as delegated legislation or subordinate legislation. The main function of the Committee is to scrutinize and Report to the House whether the powers to make regulations, rules, sub-rules, by-laws conferred by the Constitution or delegated by Parliament are being properly exercised by the Executive within the scope of such delegation.

Committee on Government Assurances

This Committee consists of 15 members nominated by the Speaker. A Minister is not nominated to this Committee. While replying to questions in the House or during discussions on Bills, resolutions, motions etc., Ministers, at times, give assurances or undertakings either to consider a matter or to take action or to furnish the House further information later. The functions of this Committee are to scrutinize the assurances, promises, and undertakings given by the Ministers from time-to-time, and to Report to Lok Sabha on the extent to which such assurances have been implemented and to see whether such implementation has taken place within the minimum time necessary for the purpose.

Committee on Absence of Members

The Committee consists of 15 members who hold office for one year. The members are nominated by the Speaker. This Committee considers all applications from members for leave of absence from the sittings of the House and examines every case where a member has been absent for a period of 60 days or more, without permission, from the sittings of the House which might also be equivalent to declaring that particular seat to be vacant as has been specified in the Constitution.

Estimates Committee

This Committee consists of 30 members who are elected by the Lok Sabha every year from amongst its members. A Minister is not eligible for election to this Committee. The term of the Committee is one year. The main function of the Committee on estimates is to:

1. Report what economies, improvements in organization, efficiency, or administrative reform, consistent with the policy underlying the estimates may be effected;
2. Suggest alternative policies in order to bring about efficiency and economy in administration.
3. Examine whether the money is well laid-out within the limit of the policy implied in the estimates and any other matters referred to it by the Speaker or the House. [details in Chapter 22]

Committee on Public Undertakings

The Committee on Public Undertakings consists of 22 members out of which 15 members are elected by the Lok Sabha and 7 members by the Rajya Sabha. A Minister is not eligible for election to this Committee. The term of the Committee is one year.

The main functions of the Committee on Public Undertakings relate examination:

1. of the Reports and accounts of Public Undertakings;
2. of the Reports, if any, of the Comptroller and Auditor-General on the Public Undertakings;
3. in the context of the Autonomy and efficiency of the Public Undertakings whether the affairs of the Public Undertakings are being managed in accordance with sound business principles and prudent commercial practices; and

This Committee also performs such other functions which have been vested on the Committee on Public Accounts and the Committee on estimates in relation to the public undertakings, but are not covered by the above clauses. The Committee may also perform functions as may be allotted to the Committee by the Speaker from time-to-time.

Public Accounts Committee

This Committee consists of 22 members, out of which 15 members are elected by the Lok Sabha and 7 members are elected from the Rajya Sabha. A Minister is not eligible for election to this Committee. The term of the Committee is for one year.

The main duty of the Committee is to examine whether the money granted by Parliament has been spent by Government within the scope of the demand. The Committee is not concerned with questions of policy. It is concerned only with the execution of the policy laid down by Parliament and its results. The main function of the PAC is to examine and verify the accounts of the Government involving financial transactions and also scrutinizes all appropriations and make suitable recommendations for future expenses. [Details given in Chapter 22]

CIVIL SOCIETY ACTIVITIES: A RISING CHALLENGE TO PARLIAMENTARY DEMOCRACY IN INDIA

The loopholes in the functioning of both the Executive and the Legislature have created discontent among the people, and this frustration is now being utilized by the civil society to vent the discontent of the common people. In doing so, the civil society has become hyper-active and in the face of anti-corruption movement, and Anna Hazare's series of fast, a question that is coming to every Indian's mind is whether the seat of law-making would shift from the Indian Parliament to the *Ramlila* Ground?

Civil society has been active in India for quite a long time, and the Indian polity has experienced several social movements like the *Narmada Bachao Andolan* and *Chipko* movement led by the civil society. However, nowhere these movements could assume such a dimension as in the case of Anti-Corruption movement. The Anti-Corruption movement has been successful to convert itself to a nation-wide protest movement, and garner nation-wide supporters. It is for the media coverage and also the social media which helped the movement to come into focus. It has even drawn international attention. The social web instruments of the present day like the Facebook, Orkut, Twitter and the web, in general, have played a phenomenal role in the Anti-Corruption movement spearheaded by Anna. The movement gradually assumed such a dimension that it came to be dubbed as India's Second National. Though, it is claimed that the movement could mobilize only the middle class, and not the underprivileged population, yet it can be said that the Anti-Corruption movement sounded a warning bell to the Government and all the political parties.

Therefore, when the Lok Pal Bill was being tabled in the Parliament an agitation continued outside the Parliament simultaneously. The Parliament with its elected representatives are there to debate and discuss but, every now and then, if the civil society expresses its displeasure over the provisions of the Lokpal Bill, Government cannot go on appeasing them. Anna through his series of fast was holding the Parliament and the legislators to ransom. If this continues, then the future of Parliamentary democracy in India is at stake.

Parliament must be allowed to work and discharge its duty with due respect to public sentiment. Healthy debates over any public policy or major reform Bills in the Houses of the Parliament are always welcome and this is the normal Parliamentary procedure in India.

India should not head towards a near-anarchy situation. The sanctity of the Parliament must be reaffirmed. Parliament should not become a symbol of decline of India's democracy, but it should be the bastion of India's democracy.

EXERCISES

I. Short Answer Questions: **(100 words)**

1. Write a short note on the Composition of Rajya Sabha.
2. Write a short note on the Composition of Lok Sabha.
3. Briefly state the special powers of the Rajya Sabha.
4. Write on:

   (a) Question hour (b) Half-an-hour discussion (c) Zero hour
5. State briefly the Legislative procedure for passage of Money Bill.
6. State briefly the Legislative procedure for passage of Ordinary Bill.
7. Briefly state the powers and privileges of the members of the Parliament.
8. Write briefly on the role of the Speaker of the Lok Sabha.
9. Write briefly on the role of the Chairman of the Rajya Sabha.
10. Write on Committees of Lok Sabha (any four).
11. Write on Committee system of Rajya Sabha.
12. Write briefly on challenges of civil society to the functioning of Parliamentary democracy in India.

II. Long Answer Questions: **(1200 words)**

13. Discuss the composition, powers and functions of the Rajya Sabha.
14. Discuss the composition, powers and functions of the Lok Sabha.
15. Analyze the Parliamentary procedure in India.
16. Examine the relation between the Rajya Sabha and Lok Sabha.
17. Discuss the powers and position of Speaker of the Lok Sabha.
18. Examine the powers and functions of both Houses of the Parliament and bring out their relation.
19. Discuss the composition of the Indian Parliament and examine the relation between the two Houses. Do you think the Lok Sabha to be more powerful than the Rajya Sabha? Argue.
20. Discuss the Committee system of the Indian Parliament.
21. Write on the Committees of Rajya Sabha.
22. What are the Committees of Lok Sabha? Discuss.

REFERENCES

Bakshi, P.M., *The Constitution of India* (with selective comments), Universal Law Publishing, Delhi, 2000.

Basu, Durga Das, *Introduction to the Constitution of India*, Prentice-Hall of India, New Delhi, 1992.

Government of India, *Constitution of India.*

Jain, M.P., *Indian Constitutional Law*, Wadhwa & Company, Nagpur, 1999.

Rao, K.V., *Parliamentary Democracy of India: A Critical Commentary*, The World Press, Calcutta, 1961.

10

The Governor

INTRODUCTION

The Government at the State level in India is a replica of the Government at the Central level. At the centre there is the President on whom all the executive powers of the Union is vested. Similarly, at the State level there is the Governor on whom all the Executive powers at the State level is vested. As there is the Prime Minister and the Council of Ministers to aid and advise the President, at the State level too there is the Chief Minister and the Council of Ministers to aid and advise the Governor. However, the Governor is not just a mere figurehead, but he is supposed to play a constructive role in the administration of the affairs of the States. He has therefore vital roles to play; one as the executive head of the Government of the State and the other a link between the Centre and State Government which becomes very vital during the Proclamation of Emergency under Article 356.

APPOINTMENT OF GOVERNOR

Much had been debated in the Constituent Assembly, and there were three proposals which came up for consideration. They are:

1. The Governor should be directly elected by the people on the basis of adult suffrage
2. He should be appointed by the President from a panel of four candidates to be elected by the members of the State Legislature in accordance with the system of proportional representation by means of single transferable vote
3. The Governor should be directly appointed by the President, and there was no need to provide for a panel of candidates for such appointment.

After much debate and discussion, the third proposal was accepted for the first two proposals seemed to open up a host of problems which would hamper the working of the State administration. If vide the first proposal, a Governor became elected representative of the people, then it is needless to say that there would be constant tension and friction between the Chief Minister and the Governor. If one accepts the second proposal, then the Governor if he is to be selected by the State Legislature, must be a partyman and a nominee of the Chief Minister. Therefore, the third proposal is more rational, and hence, vide Article 155, the Governor of any State is appointed by the President by warrant under his hand and seal.

Normally, each State has its own Governor, but under the Seventh Amendment Act, 1956, the same person can be appointed as Governor of one or more States or Lt. Governor of the Union Territory.

Qualification for Appointment as a Governor

Article 157 lays down the qualifications required to become the Governor of any State, and Article 158 provides for conditions of Governor's office. On the whole, a person to become the Governor of a State must:

1. be a Citizen of India
2. have completed 35 years of age
3. should not be a member of either House of Parliament or of a House of the State Legislature. If a member of either House of Parliament or of a House of the Legislature of any State be appointed Governor, he shall be deemed to have vacated his seat in that House on the date on which he enters upon his office as Governor
4. must not hold any office of profit

The Sarkaria Commission has suggested that a person to become a Governor should fulfill the following criteria:

1. He should be eminent in some walk of life.
2. He should be a person from outside the State.
3. He should be a detached figure and not too intimately connected with the local politics of the State;
4. He should be a person who has not taken too great a part in politics, in general, and in the recent past, in particular.

In selecting a Governor in accordance with the above criteria, the Commission recommended that persons belonging to the minority groups should continue to be given a chance as earlier.

Emoluments

The salary of the Governor is charged from the Consolidated Fund of the State and at present the salary is ₹3,50,000 per month, and is not subject to the vote of the State Legislature. When the same person is appointed as the Governor of two or more States, the emoluments and allowances payable to him shall be allocated among the States in such proportion as the President of India may by order determine. The emoluments and allowances of the Governor cannot be diminished during his term of office [Article 158(4)].

Term of Office

Article 156 lays down the term of office of the Governor. It states:

1. The Governor shall hold Office during the pleasure of the President.
2. The Governor may, by writing under his hand addressed to the President, resign his office.
3. Subject to the foregoing provisions of this Article, a Governor shall hold for a term of five years from the date on which he enters his office:

Provided that a Governor, notwithstanding the expiration of his term, continue to hold office until his successor takes over his office.

Therefore, the usual term of office of the Governor is 5 years and he may be asked to continue for more until his successor takes charge. The Legislature of a State or High Court has no role in the removal of the Governor. The Governor, if he loses the pleasure of the President, may have to resign or else be removed. This happened in the cases of the Governor of Tamil Nadu in 1980, Prabhu Das Patwari and Governor of Rajasthan in 1981, Raghukul Tilak, Governor of West Bengal, T.N. Singh was forced to resign in 1982 under the threat of withdrawal of pleasure of the President. On the other hand, Governor of Haryana, B.N. Chkaravarti, remained in the office for another three years after the expiration of his actual term of five years, which was a clear violation of Constitutional provision for the Union and the State Government should have made the arrangements for the election of his successor before the expiry of five years for continuation of office till the successor takes over means only for certain emergency situations like delay in swearing in of the new Governor and the like.

Transfer of Governors

There are no provisions in the Constitution of India, but there have been instances when Governors have been transferred from one State to another. Transfer of Governors are violation of the Constitution, because whenever they are transferred, they have to take fresh oath, and thereby, start a fresh tenure for another five years. There have been certain cases of transfers of Governors like The Governor of Rajasthan, Dr. Chenna Reddy was transferred to Tamil Nadu, Former Governor of Himachal Pradesh, Bali Ram Bhagat was transferred to

Rajasthan, former Governor of Goa, Ramesh Bhandari was transferred to U.P. These are some of the examples of transfer of Governors.

OATH OR AFFIRMATION BY GOVERNOR

Article 159 lays down that every Governor and every person discharging the functions of the Governor before taking up the responsibilities of his office must take an oath of affirmation before the Chief Justice of the concerned State High Court, and in his absence the senior-most Judge of that Court. The oath or affirmation of the Governor is:

"I, ..., do swear in the name of God/solemnly affirm that I will faithfully execute the office of Governor (or discharge the functions of the Governor) of ... (name of the State) and will to the best of my ability preserve, protect and defend the Constitution and the law and that I will devote myself to the service and well-being of the people of ... (name of the State)."

IMMUNITIES OF A GOVERNOR

Under Article 361, the Governor of any State enjoys certain immunities. They are:

1. He is not answerable to any Court for the exercise of duties of his office
2. No civil or criminal proceedings can be instituted or continued against him in any Court so long as he is in office
3. No process for his arrest or imprisonment can be issued by any Court against him

POWERS AND FUNCTIONS OF THE GOVERNOR

The Governors of Indian States and Lieutenant-Governors of the Territories of India have similar powers and functions at the State level as that of the President of India at Union level. On the other hand, it should be observed that in conformity with the provisions of the Indian Constitution, the Governor acts as the nominal head, whereas the real power remains within the ambit of the Chief Minister and his Council Ministers. As D.D. Basu observes that the Governor possesses executive, legislative and judicial powers analogous to those of the President except diplomatic or military powers and emergency powers like the President. This is because the Indian Constitution has bestowed similar powers and functions to the Governors of States and Lieutenant Governors of Union Territories as enjoyed by the President of India at the Union level. Governors are appointed in States by the President for a term of 5 years. In the Union Territories and in Capital City, Delhi, Lieutenant Governors are also appointed by the President for the same period.

The Governor of any Indian State or Lt. Governors of any Union Territory enjoys executive powers, legislative powers and also the discretionary powers which are discussed as follows:

Executive Powers

Article 154 embodies that the Executive Power of the State shall be vested in the Governor, and shall be exercised by him either directly or through officers subordinate to him in accordance with this Constitution. Article 166 embodies that all executive action of the Government of a State shall be expressed to be taken in the name of the Governor. According to Article 164(1), the most important executive function of the Governor is the appointment of the Chief Minister and other Ministers on the advice of the Chief Minister. He may also ask the Chief Minister to prove his majority in the Assembly within a specified period. When in any Assembly election a party secures a majority, the Governor faces no problem in inviting the leader of the majority party to form the Government. Difficulty arises when none of the political parties win an absolute majority. In such cases, the Governors of different States have over the years followed two practices:

1. the principle of non-assessment
2. the principle of assessment

According to the first Principle, when none of the political parties has secured an Absolute Majority, the Governor might invite the leader of the largest party to form the Government as was done in the States of Madras, PEPSU, Travancore-Cochin in 1952, Orissa in 1957 and Rajasthan in 1967. This was also done in the first instance in Bihar, Punjab and West Bengal in 1967, and when they refused only then the Governors invited the leaders of other parties to form the Government.

When none of the parties has a clear majority in the Assembly elections, then according to the second Principle, the Governor should make his own assessment and find out which party can form the Government. This Principle was applied for the first time in Travancore-Cochin in 1954, Kerala in 1957 and 1965, Rajasthan in 1967, Bihar in 1969, Orissa and West Bengal in 1971, Nagaland in 1974, Gujarat in 1975, Maharashtra in 1978, and in Karnataka in 1982.

If the Governor has the power of appointment of the Chief Minister, he also has the power of dismissal of the Chief Minister if he feels that the Chief Minister no longer enjoys the confidence of the Assembly or is not working according to the provisions of the Constitution. This might happen if there is a large scale defection from the ruling party as it happened in Haryana, U.P. and West Bengal in 1967 and Punjab, Bihar and Madhya Pradesh in 1968. Sometimes, a Governor who may be charged with favouritism/nepotism, can without giving a scope to the Chief Minister to prove his majority in the Assembly, might ask him to resign as in the case of Farooq Abdullah in J&K and with N.T. Rama Rao in 1984. While again, The Governors of West Bengal in 1967, Punjab in 1970, Orissa in 1971, Manipur in 1973, Bihar and Manipur in 1979 asked the Chief Ministers to prove their majority as political defection were taking place, the Governors of Bihar in 1967, U.P. in 1969, Bihar in 1970, Punjab and Bihar in 1971, Orissa in 1973 and Assam in 1981 ignored the defections and did not ask the respective Chief Ministers to prove their majority.

The Governor also has the powers of appointing and dismissing Ministers on the recommendation of the Chief Minister. The Governor has the power to appoint the Advocate-General and the members of the State Public Service Commission and Vice-Chancellors of the universities on the recommendations of the Chief Ministers. The Advocate-General and the Ministers hold their office as long as they enjoy the pleasure of the Governor. However, the Governor cannot remove the members of State Public Service Commission as they can only be removed only by the President on the Report of the Supreme Court and, in some cases, on the grounds of certain disqualifications as provided under Article 317. The Governor also has no power to appoint the judges of the State High Court, but he is entitled to be consulted by the President in such matters (Article 217). As far as the upper chamber of the State Legislature is concerned (where the State Legislature has two chambers), the Legislative Council, the Governor has the power of nominating one-sixth of its members having outstanding achievements and accomplishments in literature, science, arts and so on (Article 171). He can, in some States, also nominate one member of the Anglo-Indian community in the Legislative Assembly if that community is not adequately represented (Article 333). It is also his duty to administer oath to the newly-elected members (Article 188).

Article 163 mentions that the Chief Minister and the Council of Ministers is to aid and advise the Governor and keep him informed (Article 167) about all decisions of the Council of Ministers and proposals for legislations. The Governor can also seek information from the Chief Minister about certain issues of concern to the State administration or proposals for legislation [Article 167(b)]. The Governor has to act according to aid and advise of the Chief Minister and his Council of Ministers except where he can use his discretionary powers (see details in the next section).

Legislative Powers

Although the Governor is not a member of the State Legislature, but he is an integral part of it just like the President who is an integral part of the Union Parliament. He summons, prorogues [Article 174(1)]& dissolves the State Legislature [Article 174(2)(b)]. He also addresses the first session of State Legislature after election and at the beginning of each new session. Ordinarily, the State Legislature is summoned on the advice of The Council of Ministers, but under difficult situations where the ruling party is facing defections, then they might not want to summon the session, because they might fear losing their confidence in the Assembly. This happened when Governors of West Bengal in 1967, Punjab in 1970, Orissa in 1971, Manipur in 1973, Bihar and Manipur in 1979 asked the respective Chief Ministers to prove their strength, but when they disagreed to summon the Assembly within a stipulated time given by the Governor, the Chief Ministers were dismissed. The Governor can dissolve the Assembly, but on the advice of the Chief Minister. In a situation where the Chief Minister has lost a majority in the Assembly or has a doubtful majority and the Governor is of the opinion that an alternative Ministry is possible, the Governor may not accept the recommendation of the Chief Minister to dissolve it. The Governors of Haryana, Punjab in 1967 and Gujarat in 1971 rejected the advice of the Chief Ministers to dissolve the Assembly.

The Governor also can address either House or both assembled together and may also send messages to them for consideration. In the first session of the State Legislature after an Assembly election and the first session of a new year, the Governor delivers his inaugural address.

The Governor may nominate a member of the Anglo-Indian community to the Legislative Assembly in case he finds that the community is not suitably represented in the Legislative Assembly. Where there is also a Upper Chamber of the State Legislature, there the Governor can nominate one-sixth members of the Upper House from among persons having special knowledge of or expertise in the fields of Science, Arts, Literature, Social Service and the like.

Another Legislative power of the Governor is giving assent to the Bills passed by the State Legislature. As no Bill can become an Act unless he gives his assent. When a Bill is passed by the State Legislature, it is sent to the Governor and during that time he may exercise certain options. The options are, he

1. can give his assent to the Bill;
2. can withhold his assent;
3. can return it, if it is not a Money Bill, for reconsideration suggesting alternations. But such Bills when passed again have to be given assent;
4. He may reserve the Bill for the assent of the President (Article 200) affecting the powers and position of High Court as to endanger the position which that Court is by this Constitution designed to fill.

The Governor can also send messages to State Legislature on Bills pending before it.

Another important Legislative power of the Governor is the power to issue ordinances when the State Legislature is not in session (Article 213). Usually the ordinances are issued on the advice of the Chief Minister, but it has happened that the Governor might not listen to that advice as was done in U.P., in 1979. In the case, the then Governor G.D. Tapase, refused to issue an ordinance recommended by the Ministry for the nationalization of private homeopathic colleges. Governor can issue ordinance only in respect of those subjects mentioned in State List. The ordinance will lapse if not approved by the State Legislature at the expiration of six weeks from the reassembly of the Legislature.

Financial Powers

The Governor also enjoys some Financial powers. A Money Bill cannot be introduced in the State Legislature without his prior recommendation. He ensures that the Annual Budget is laid. The Contingency Fund of the State is at his disposal, and he can make advances out of it to meet unforeseen expenditure pending authorization of the Sate Legislature. However, in exercising all these powers he has to be advised by the Chief Minister.

Judicial Powers

The President consults Governor while appointing the Chief Justice and other judges of High Court. The Governor appoints judges of Courts lower than the High Court and can grant pardon reprieve or remission of punishment for offense against State laws (Article 161) but he cannot grant pardon in cases of death sentences. He also enjoys immunity from all civil and criminal proceedings during his term in office.

Emergency Powers

The most important and controversial power of the Governor is related to his Emergency Powers under Article 356. The Governor has the power to recommend in case of failure of the constitutional machinery in the State "if the State is not being carried on in accordance with the provisions of the Constitution," and can send reports to the President under such circumstances, and recommend the President's Rule (Article 356). Such report may or may not be based on Ministerial advice. When the President's Rule is in progress, he becomes the agent of the Union Government in the State. He takes over the administration of the State directly and runs the State with the aid of the Civil Servants. Such emergency has been declared a number of times and has triggered-off controversies like in PEPSU in 1953, Kerala in 1959, Haryana in 1967, Karnataka in 1977 where State Governments were dismissed when they had a majority in the Assembly. Some non-Congress parties were also prevented from forming Government after election like in Kerala in 1955 and Rajasthan in 1967 on the ground that Stable Government was not possible. Sometimes, it is adopted to deny opportunity to the opposition to form the Government when the ruling party is sure or anticipates its defeat on the floor of the House as was done in Pondicherry in 1968, Orissa in 1973, Nagaland in 1975, Manipur in 1981, Kerala in 1982 and Sikkim in 1984. Therefore, the misuse of Article 356 is possible, because nowhere in the Constitution the exact meaning or definite of the failure of Constitutional machinery of a State is given.

Discretionary Powers

Besides the above-mentioned powers of the Governor, he also has some discretionary powers where he can act his own without the aid and advice of the Chief Minister and his Council of Ministers. They are:

1. The Governors of Assam (Article 371B & Sixth Schedule), Meghalaya, Tripura, Mizoram (Sixth Schedule), Manipur [Article 371C(1)], Sikkim [Article 371F(g)] and Andhra Pradesh (Article 371D) have discretionary powers with regard to the administration of tribal areas of the States.
2. In case the President appoints a Governor as the administrator of an adjoining Union Territory, he shall exercise his functions independently.
3. The Governor of Nagaland has been entrusted with responsibilities to be discharged vide his discretionary powers in order to combat disruptive activities of Nagas [Article 371A(1)(b)].
4. The Governor may study a situation of a State with regard to the breakdown of Constitutional machinery and may send Report to the President with his recommendations conforming to the advice of his Council of Ministers or not.
5. He may reserve a Bill passed by the State Legislature on the plea that it is likely to be in conflict with any Union law or policy of the Union Government.
6. Before promulgating ordinances, the Governor seeks instructions from the President.
7. He might dissolve the Vidhan Sabha on the advice of the Council of Ministers or according to his assessment of the situation.
8. He can also permit initiation of criminal proceedings against serving or former Chief Ministers involved in some alleged offences.

It is clearly stated in Article 163(2), that if any question arises whether any matter is or is not a matter as respects which the Governor is by or under this Constitution required to act in his discretion, the decision of the Governor in his discretion shall be final. In other cases, the Governor is to act on the advice of the Ministers.

Miscellaneous Powers

Among other powers, the Governor can receive and table the Report of State Auditor-General and the Report of State Public Service Commission. He also acts as Chancellor of State Universities and appoints Vice-Chancellors.

POSITION OF THE GOVERNOR OF AN INDIAN STATE

Governors are the Nominal Executive, whereas the real power is in the hands of the Chief Ministers and the Council of Ministers of respective States. (As we have a clear idea about the executive, legislative and discretionary powers of the Governor from the above discussion.)

The Governor exercises executive powers in appointing the Chief Minister of the State and his Council of Ministers. He also appoints the Advocate-General, the Chairman and the Members of the State Public Commission. The Governor has formal Legislative Powers over the dissolving of Vidhan Sabha and summoning of both the Houses of the State Legislature. While exercising these powers, he always has to act on the advice of the Chief Minister and Council of Ministers. A Bill that has been passed by the State Legislature will become a law after the consent of the Governor. Though he cannot reject a Money Bill, he can send back other Bills for reconsideration. He does not have the authority to reject a Bill for the second time. At the same time, no Money Bill can be introduced in the Legislative Assembly except on the Governor's recommendation. He may reserve any Bill for the assent of the President.

The Governor uses his discretionary powers in certain situations. In the Vidhan Sabha elections if no party secures a majority, the Governor has the authority to act on his own and ask the leader of the single largest party or the chosen leader of two or more parties to form the Government. He then appoints that leader as the Chief Minister. Again when the State machinery breaks down due to improper administration the Governor can send a report to the President and ask him to impose President's Rule in the State. The Constitution authorizes the Governor to promulgate ordinances during the period when the State Legislature is not in session (Article 213).

Some Governors who have been assertive have caught themselves up in major conflicts with the real executive. Executive powers, we learnt in the appointment of Chief Ministers, how different Governors under certain circumstances have used their reason and judgment while appointing Chief Ministers, whereas some have been charged of being biased. As in case of Kerala in 1957 and 1965, West Bengal in 1971 and Haryana in 1982 when the non-Congress party alliances were barred from forming the Governments.

Even in the dismissal of the Ministry, the discretionary powers of the Governors are also not beyond criticisms. The most controversial action was that of the Governor of West Bengal, Dharma Vira in 1967. A United Front Ministry was a conglomeration of fourteen parties and it formed the Government in March 1967. However, in November 1967 some members defected and informed the Governor that they had withdrawn support from the Ministry. The Congress informed the Governor of its support to a new Ministry if it is formed by the leader of the new party.

Under such circumstances the Governor asked the Chief Minister Ajoy Mukherjee to prove the majority by calling an early session of the Assembly. However, the Ministry wanted to delay it by six weeks. Consequently, the Governor dismissed the Ministry and installed another Ministry. He justified his action by stating that the Ministry support in the Assembly and it was unconstitutional for the Ministry to continue to be in the office. The Governor's dismissal of the United Front Ministry raised a storm of criticisms for Constitutional experts. In February 2005, the Governor of Goa dismissed the 32-month old BJP-led Government of Manohar Parrikar even though the Government won the vote of confidence and the confidential Report of the voting was yet to be send to the Governor. This was seen as a violation of the Constitution and sparked-off controversy.

There are also instances when some Governors have misused their ordinance-making power on the recommendations of the Chief Ministers. In *D.C. Wadhwa* v. *State of Bihar Case (1987)* regarding the repeated promulgation of the same Ordinance(s) the petitions under Article 32 of the Constitution raised the question relating to the power of the Governor under Article 213 of the Constitution to repromulgate ordinances from time-to-time without getting them replaced by Acts of the Legislature. The question was—can the Governor go on repromulgating Ordinances for an indefinite period of time, and thus, takeover to himself the power of the Legislature to legislate even after knowing that power was conferred on him under Article 213 only for the purpose of enabling him to take immediate action when the Legislative Assembly of the State, and if there is a Legislative Council also in the State, are not in session. The writ petitions were filed by four petitioners challenging the practice of the State of Bihar in promulgating and repromulgating Ordinances on a massive scale and in particular they challenged the Constitutional validity of three different Ordinances issued by the Governor of Bihar, namely, (i) Bihar Forest Produce (Regulation of Trade) Third Ordinance, 1983, (ii) Bihar Intermediate Education Council Third Ordinance, 1983, and (iii) The Bihar Bricks Supply (Control) Third Ordinance, 1983. In *D. C. Wadhwa* v. *State of Bihar* (*1987*) it was brought to the notice of the Supreme Court that between 1967–1981, the Governors of Bihar promulgated 256 ordinances. Some ordinances were kept alive for periods ranging from 1 to 14 years by repromulgating them again and again. The Supreme Court considered such promulgation as an abuse of the power and a fraud on the Constitution. Whereas we have also seen how some Governors have resisted the pressures from their respective Chief Ministers in issuing ordinances like the Governor of U.P., G.D. Tapase in 1979.

Recent incidents which have invited many controversies are like the nod from the Governor of Tamil Nadu, in 1995, to Dr Subramaniam Swamy to launch prosecution proceedings against Ms. Jayalalitha on charges of corruption.

Dr Subramaniam Swamy, President of Janata party, filed a private complaint before the Court against Ms. Jayalalitha for the alleged Commission of offences under Section 11, 13(1)(c) and (d) of Prevention of Corruption Act, 1988 stating that the latter while she was the Chief Minister, along with others contravened the various provisions of law and indulged in some transaction of the property owned by the Government and so on (*Dr. Subramanian Swamy* v. *J. Jayalalitha,* 20 August, 1996). The Jayalalitha-led AIADMK lost power in the 1996 elections, when it won 4 of the 168 seats that they contested, and Jayalalitha was herself defeated by the DMK candidate in Bargur constituency. The reason cited for this defeat is mostly anti-incumbency votes in the wake of so many charges of corruption. But issue here is the role of the Governor which sparked-off controversy. Further Jayalalitha was barred from contesting election in the 2001, because she had been found guilty of criminal offences, including allegedly obtaining property belonging to a State-operated agency called TANSI. Although she appealed to the Supreme Court, having being sentenced to five years' imprisonment, the matter had not been resolved at the time of the elections. Despite this, the AIADMK won a majority and she was installed as Chief Minister as a non-elected member of the State Assembly on 14 May 2001. Her appointment was legally voided in September 2001 when the Supreme Court ruled that she could not hold it whilst convicted of criminal acts. O. Panneerselvam, a Minister in her party, was subsequently installed as the Chief Minister. Subsequently, in March 2002, Jayalalitha assumed the position of Chief Minister once more, having been acquitted of some charges by the Madras High Court.

Another very recent controversy and muscle flexing that took place was between Karnataka Chief Minister Yeddyurappa and the Governor H.R. Bhardwaj. When Yeddyurappa became the Chief Minister on 30 May 2008 trouble started with the Governor. It was Governor Bhardwaj who first gave signs of his intention to dislodge Yeddyurappa. In 2010 also, Chief Minister and the Governor were caught up in a tussle. On October 11, B.S. Yeddyurappa faced a trust vote to prove his party's continuing majority after 11 rebel MLAs from the party and 5 independent MLAs showed signs of reaching out to the opposition parties in the State. Before the trust vote could begin, Speaker K.G. Bopaiah dismissed the 16 rebel MLAs from the Karnataka Assembly under the anti-defection Act in response to Yeddyurappa's petition. Soon after, the floor test was won by the Chief Minister B.S. Yeddyurappa, Governor of the State H.R. Bhardwaj stated that the disqualification of the MLAs was illegal and that President's Rule be imposed in the State. The 16 MLAs then approached the High Court where a specially constituted Bench headed by Chief Justice J.S. Kehar and Justice N. Kumar, heard their petition. The Chief Minister was again saved this time as a third judge of the Karnataka High Court upheld the disqualification of the rebel BJP MLAs. Justice V.G. Sabhahit who heard the matter when an earlier bench consisting of Chief Justice J.S. Kehar and Justice N. Kumar gave a split verdict regarding the disqualification of the rebel MLAs.

Again in May 2011, the two were involved in a bitter war of words where the Governor wanted to impose President's Rule in the State and the Chief Minister alleged that Bhardwaj was working as an agent of the Congress high-command. Even the Chief Minister had on May 17 marched his MLAs to the President of India for showing his majority in the State Assembly. The move was a reaction to the Governor's letter to Prime Minister in which he had asked for the imposition of President's Rule in Karnataka. However, at the end the two hugged each other at a public event and made up. Ultimately, Yeddyurappa resigned in July 2011 following his indictment by the Karnataka Lokayukta N.Santosh Hegde on illegal mining.

Under the Parliamentary system of Government, there is need for a Nominal Executive, because the tenure of the real executive though is fixed for five years, the stability of a particular Government can never be guaranteed. With the fall of the cabinet a vacuum may be created in the administrative field if there is no provision for the post of Governor. It is he who maintains continuity in administration and enables a smooth change-over from the fall of one Cabinet to the establishment of another. The Sarkaria Commission suggested that the Chief Minister should be consulted while appointing the Governor, and active politicians must be kept out of the race. Further, the Commission suggested that there is no need to remove the post of Governor. Table 10.1 gives a list of Governors of India till 2024.

Table 10.1 List of Governors of States and Union Territories of India (December 2024)

State	*Name of Current Governors*
Andhra Pradesh	Shri Justice (Retd.) S. Abdul Nazeer
Arunachal Pradesh	Lt. General Kaiwalya Trivikram Parnaik, PVSM, UYSM, YSM (Retired)
Assam	Shri Gulab Chand Kataria
Bihar	Shri Rajendra Vishwanath Arlekar
Chhattisgarh	Shri Biswa Bhusan Harichandan
Goa	Shri P.S. Sreedharan Pillai
Gujarat	Shri Acharya Dev Vrat
Haryana	Shri Bandaru Dattatraya
Himachal Pradesh	Shri Shiv Pratap Shukla
Jharkhand	Shri C.P. Radhakrishnan
Karnataka	Shri Thaawarchand Gehlot
Kerala	Shri Arif Mohammed Khan
Madhya Pradesh	Shri Mangubhai Chhaganbhai Patel
Maharashtra	Shri Ramesh Bais
Manipur	Sushri Anusuiya Uikye
Meghalaya	Shri Phagu Chauhan

(*Contd.*)

Table 10.1 List of Governors of States and Union Territories of India (December 2024) (*Contd.*)

State	*Name of Current Governors*
Mizoram	Dr. Kambhampati Haribabu
Nagaland	Shri La. Ganesan
Odisha	Shri Raghubar Das
Punjab	Shri Banwarilal Purohit
Rajasthan	Shri Kalraj Mishra
Sikkim	Shri Lakshman Prasad Acharya
Tamil Nadu	Shri R. N. Ravi
Telangana	Shri C.P. Radhakrishnan (Addl. Charge)
Tripura	Shri Indra Sena Reddy Nallu
Uttar Pradesh	Smt. Anandiben Patel
Uttarakhand	Lt. Gen. Gurmit Singh, PVSM, UYSM, AVSM, VSM (Retd.)
West Bengal	Dr. C.V. Ananda Bose
Union Territories	*Current Lieutenant Governors and Administrators*
Andaman and Nicobar Islands (UT)	Admiral D. K. Joshi (Retd.)(Lieutenant Governor)
Chandigarh (UT)	Shri Banwarilal Purohit (Administrator)
Dadra and Nagar Haveli and Daman and Diu (UT)	Shri Praful Patel (Administrator)
Delhi (NCT)	Shri Vinai Kumar Saxena (Lieutenant Governor)
Jammu and Kashmir (UT)	Shri Manoj Sinha (Lieutenant Governor)
Ladakh (UT)	Brig. (Dr.) Shri B.D. Mishra (Retd.) (Lieutenant Governor)
Lakshadweep (UT)	Shri Praful Patel (Administrator)
Puducherry (UT)	Shri C.P. Radhakrishnan (Addl. Charge) (Lieutenant Governor)

EXERCISES

I. Short Answer Questions: (100 words)

1. Method of appointment of the Governor.
2. Constitutionality of the transfer of the Governors of the State.
3. The immunities of the Governor.
4. The discretionary powers of the Governor.

II. Long Answer Questions: (1200 words)

5. Discuss the powers and functions of the Governor of a State.

6. In the light of the powers and functions of the Governor of a State analyze the Constitutional position of the Governor.
7. Examine the actual position of the of the Governor of a State by bringing in examples of actions of the Governor which show that at times he can assert himself as the real executive.

REFERENCES

Bakshi, P.M., *The Constitution of India* (with selective comments), Universal Law Publishing, Delhi, 2000.

Basu, Durga Das, *Introduction to the Constitution of India*, Prentice-Hall of India, New Delhi, 1992.

D.C. Wadhwa v. *State of Bihar* (1987) 1 SCC 37.

Dr. Subramanian Swamy v. *J. Jayalalitha,* 1996.

Jain, M.P., *Indian Constitutional Law*, Wadhwa & Company, Nagpur, 1999.

Rao, K.V., *Parliamentary Democracy of India: A Critical Commentary*, The World Press, Calcutta, 1961.

Singh, M.P. and Saxena, Rekha, *Indian Politics: Contemporary Issues and Concerns,* Prentice-Hall of India, New Delhi, 2008.

11

Chief Minister and the State Council of Ministers

INTRODUCTION

In a Parliamentary set-up at the Union level, there is the President in Parliament as the nominal executive and the real executive being the Prime Minister and his Council of Ministers. Similarly, at the State level, there is the Governor in Legislature as nominal executive and the real executive is the Chief Minister and his Council of Ministers. The leader of the party who commands absolute majority in the Legislative Assembly or the Vidhan Sabha is appointed by the Governor as the Chief Minister. When no party secures the required majority, the Governor uses his discretion in appointing the Chief Minister.

THE CHIEF MINISTER

Article 164(1) of the Constitution provides that the Chief Minister shall be appointed by the Governor and the other Ministers shall be appointed by Governor on the advice of the Chief Minister. The Ministers shall hold their office during the pleasure of the Governor. It is for the Chief Minister to determine the size of his Council of Ministers. The number of Ministers is not fixed. The Council of Ministers is collectively responsible to Legislative Assembly of the state. A Governor may face tough situations while appointing a person as the Chief Minister. If a party secures an absolute majority then the Governor has no alternative, but to invite the leader of the majority party to form the Government. Problem arises when no party secures a majority. In that case, the Governor uses his judgment and reason while making such appointment (for details see Chapter 10). In case, a coalition of political parties formed before the general election, manages to secure clear majority in the Assembly, and they present the name of their chosen person whom they want to be appointed as the Chief Minister, the Governor has no choice but to accept their choice of candidate and make such appointment. Therefore, in case a coalition of parties secures an absolute majority in the elections of the Legislative Assembly, the Governor appoints the leader of the coalition as the Chief Minister. Again there may be post-electoral alliance on the basis of common minimum agenda and a name commonly accepted by them may be proposed, then the Governor has to appoint that person as the Chief Minister. In certain cases, the Governor may seek the advice of the Advocate-General of the State. In case the Governor finds out that no party secures a majority and there are also no chances of post-electoral coalitions, then the Governor may recommend for the imposition of half-state emergency, but this action is controversial. This happened when the U.P. Governor, in 1970, advised the President to invoke Article 356 when he dismissed the Charan Singh Ministry on the plea that the Congress had withdrawn their support from the BKD-led Ministry. Then he invited T.N. Singh to form another coalition Ministry soon after. Even a full-fledged emergency can be imposed if the Governor is sure that no stable Government is possible, he may recommend to the President his proposal of placing the State under Centre's rule as was done in U.P. in 1968, with the fall of the first Charan Singh Ministry. Due to the death or sudden resignation of the Chief Minister, the Governor may appoint a Chief Minister *Proterm*. He may also appoint the person selected by the ruling party which has a majority in the Assembly as the Chief Minister. In case there are several aspirants, then he has to wait and watch until the leadership controversy is resolved.

The Chief Minister is usually a member of the Legislative Assembly, though there is no constitutional bar to his being a member of the Legislative Council.

Eligibility

The Constitution of India sets the principle qualifications one must meet to be eligible to the office of the Chief Minister. This is the usual qualifications for membership of any person to the State Legislature. To become a Chief Minister a person must be:

1. a citizen of India
2. should be a member of the State Legislature. If a person is elected Chief Minister who is not a member of the Legislature, then he/she must become a member within six months
3. should be of or above 25 years of age.

Oath

The Chief Minister is appointed by the Governor and thus the swearing in is done before the Governor of the state.

The oath of office

"I, <Name of Minister>, do swear in the name of God/solemnly affirm that I will bear true faith and allegiance to the Constitution of India as by law established, that I will uphold the sovereignty and integrity of India, that I will faithfully and conscientiously discharge my duties as a Minister for the State of <Name of the State> and that I will do right to all manner of people in accordance with the Constitution and the law without fear or favour, affection or ill-will."

—*Constitution of India, Schedule 3, Para 5*

The oath of secrecy

"I, <Name of Minister>, do swear in the name of God/solemnly affirm that I will not directly or indirectly communicate or reveal to any person or persons any matter which shall be brought under my consideration or shall become known to me as a Minister for the State of <Name of the State> except as may be required for the due discharge of my duties as such Minister ."

—*Constitution of India, Schedule 3, Para 6*

Term

Usually under Article 172 the life of the State Legislature is five years, this means that the Chief Minister will also have a usual term of five years. It is stated however, under Article 164(1) that the Chief Minister and the Council of Ministers shall hold office during the pleasure of the Governor. If there is a vote of no-confidence passed against the Government, then the Chief Minister has to resign with his Council of Ministers. Even the Governor can dismiss the Chief Minister if he loses its majority support. How the Governor uses this is sure to raise controversies as was the case with the Ajoy Mukherjee Ministry which was dismissed by the West Bengal Governor Dharma Vira in 1967 (details in Chapter 10). The Chief Minister can always contest for re-elections.

Powers and Functions

The powers and functions of the Chief Minister are, in most respects, similar to those of the Prime Minister at the centre. The only difference lies in the jurisdiction over which they exercise their powers. The Chief Minister who is also the leader of the ruling party chooses the members of his Council and allots portfolio to them, presides over all meetings, and is the prime spokesman of the Government.

The Chief Minister is the pivot of the State executive in the real sense and its chief architect. It is the Chief Minister who maintains the link between the State Government and the Union Government. He maintains the relation between the State Legislature, the Council of Ministers and the Governor.

1. According to Article 163 there shall be a Council of Ministers with Chief Minister as the head to aid and advise the Governor in the exercise of his functions except in the cases where Governor Acts in his own discretion.
2. The Chief Minister presides over the meetings of his Council of Ministers. The Chief Minister allocates the portfolios among his Ministers and decides who will be Cabinet Minister or a Minister of State or a Deputy Minister. He may ask a particular Minister to resign for his Acts of Commission and omission for he has to remember that the principles of collective responsibility makes him and his Council of Ministers answerable to the Legislative Assembly and are responsible to it for all its actions and decisions. For that, he may advise the Governor to dismiss a Minister whose action might cause trouble for the survival of the Government.
3. The Chief Minister also communicates to the Governor all the decisions of his Council of Ministers relating to matters of administration of the State and proposals of legislation. He is the communication link between the Governor and the Council of Ministers. He must also furnish such information relating to the administration of the affairs of the State and proposals for Legislation. If the Governor so requires, the Chief Minister has to submit for the consideration of the Council of Ministers any matter on which a decision has been taken by a Minister, but has not been considered by the Council (Article 167).
4. The Chief Minister is the sole channel of communication between his Ministers and the Legislature. It is the Chief Minister who pilots all the Bills and also directs as to what should be the position of Ministers in the Assembly regarding any of their policy. He also coordinates the working his Ministers and in case of deadlocks and conflicts his decisions are final.
5. It has become a convention that the Union Government consults Chief Minister before nominating the Governor.
6. The Chief Minister might tender his resignation at any time, and then advise the Governor either to dissolve the House or advise the Governor to summon such and such person for the installation of another Ministry or dissolve the House, and thereby place the State under President's rule. It is up to the Governor to accept such advice or not.
7. The Chief Minister is the leader of the Legislative Assembly. If he is the leader of majority party then his position is quite strong than a Chief Minister of a Coalition Government.

Constitutional Limitations of the Chief Minister

There are certain constitutional limitations, and the Chief Minister has to function under those limitations:

1. Article 164(1) states that the Ministers shall hold office during the pleasure of the Governor.
2. The Governor, under Article 163(2), can exercise his power in his discretion without seeking the advice of the Council of Ministers.
3. Governor may recommend the imposition of Article 356 relating to the invocation of President's Rule due to failure of the Constitutional machinery. On the basis of the Report submitted by the Governor or on the basis of the Report received from other sources, the President can dissolve the Council of Ministers of a State under Article 356 on the ground of the failure of the Constitutional machinery in the State.
4. The enjoyment of the confidence of the Legislative Assembly is a condition for the continuance of the office of the Chief Minister and his Council of Ministers. Unless the Chief Minister is always backed by a stable majority in the Assembly, he cannot go ahead taking the confidence of the Legislative Assembly for granted.
5. The Constitution of India assigns very limited power to the States as specified in the State List in the Seventh Schedule. This limited power assigned to the State imposes restriction in becoming a real head by the Chief Minister as in many cases his activities are circumscribed by the dictates of the Union Government, which frequently results in friction between the Centre and States.

COUNCIL OF MINISTERS

According Article 163 of the Constitution provides that there shall be a Council of Ministers with Chief Minister as the head to aid and advise the Governor in the exercise of his functions except in the cases where Governor Acts in his own discretion. The Governor appoints the Chief Minister and other Ministers on the advice of the Chief Minister. The Minister holds office during the pleasure of the Governor. The number of Ministers is not fixed. It is for the Chief Minister to determine the size of his Council of Minister and the number of Minister he wants in his cabinet. The Council of Ministers are collectively responsible to Legislative Assembly of the State. There are different categories of Ministers like Cabinet Ministers who are in charge of important portfolios like finance, commerce, health, home and other departments, Ministers of State who are attached to the departments under the Cabinet Ministers and do not participate in the cabinet meetings and Deputy Ministers who assist the Ministers in the discharge of their functions.

Term

The usual tenure for the Council of Ministers is also five years but their existence largely depends on the pleasure of the Governor. However, it is largely on the pleasure of the Chief Minister, because if the Chief Minister is dissatisfied with a certain Minister he can request the Governor to dismiss the Minister if that particular person refuses to resign. The Chief Minister from time-to-time reshuffles his Ministers as he wishes to do and induct new persons as Ministers. Any Minister on his own may also tender his resignation from the Council. Further, the Council of Minister is collectively responsible to the Legislative Assembly and it can be removed if the Assembly passes a vote of no-confidence against it or rejects any Bill or cuts the funds of the Government.

Salary and Allowances

According to Article 195, the salaries and allowances of the State Legislature including that of the Speaker and Deputy Speaker and Chairman and Deputy Chairman are fixed by the Legislature of the State by law. The salaries and allowances are charged from the Consolidated Fund of the State. The salaries and allowances differ from State to State.

Powers and Functions of the Council of Ministers

The Council of Ministers is the most powerful body in the machinery of the State. Within the Council of Ministers again the Chief Minister and his Cabinet wield the actual power. The Governor is the nominal executive and the real executive in practice is the Chief Minister and his Cabinet and obviously the other Ministers too. The powers and functions of the Council of Ministers are quite wide ranging from formulation of State policies to running the administration as well as performing important financial functions of the State. They are discussed as follows:

1. The first and foremost function of the Council of Ministers is related to the legislative process of the State. The policies are formulated at the behest of Council of Ministers, especially in the Cabinet meetings in the presence of the Chief Minister. The view-point is obviously of the Chief Minister, and in some cases the party line is the last word. The Bills are moved by the Ministers in the State Legislature, and if the Ministry commands a majority in the House, the Bills can be easily passed.
2. Administration of affairs of the State is done by the Cabinet Ministers holding different portfolios helped by Ministers of State and Deputy Ministers. Each Minister is individually responsible for his errors of omission and commission which might create problems for the survival of the Government.

3. The Council of Ministers actually is run by the Chief Minister and he recommends the names of his Ministers to the Governor for their appointment. The appointments made by the Governors like the Vice-Chancellors of different universities, Advocate-General, Chairman and members of the State Public Service Commission, Chairman of various corporations and various Boards, made by the Governors on the basis of recommendations of the Chief Minister and his Council of Ministers. Chief Ministers play a key role in the choice of candidates as pointed out above.
4. In the financial matters of the State, the Council of Ministers play major role. The annual financial statement, i.e., budget is prepared by the ministry concerned and passed by the State Legislature. The annual budget is the reflection of the estimates of expenditure to be incurred in the coming financial year and also the expenditure charged upon the Consolidated Fund of the State. Money Bills are also drafted by the Council of Ministers and piloted by the Ministers in the Legislature.
5. Other than regular law-making, the Council of Ministers can use to its convenience the ordinance making power of the Governor under Article 213. An Ordinance promulgated under this Article has the same force and effect as an Act of Legislature of the State assented to by the Governor when the Assembly is not in session. When the Assembly reassembles, then such ordinances can be passed by the Legislature and given the effect of law.
6. Under Article 163, the Council of Ministers and the Chief Minister is there to aid and advise the Governor in the exercise of his functions, except in so far as he is by or under this Constitution required to exercise his functions or any of them in his discretion.

GOVERNOR AND THE COUNCIL OF MINISTERS

The appointment of the Chief Minister and the other Ministers on the recommendation of the Chief Minister is done by the Governor. The Council of Ministers also aid and advise the Governor and also furnish information to the Governor from time-to-time. However, there are some exceptions to these functions. In the appointment of Chief Minister the Governor can use his assessment if no party secures majority or there is no possibility of a stable Government. Sometimes, while using his discretionary powers, the Governor may or may not accept such advise. The Governor can also sent report to the President of India if there is a failure of Constitutional machinery with or without the consent of the Ministry or Chief Minister in particular. The Governor may also reserve a Bill for the consideration of the President under Article 200. The Governor can also dissolve the Assembly if a vote of no-confidence is passed or if the Chief Minister asks him to do so. Sometimes in the past, certain Governors sparked-off debates by dissolving Ministry on the assumption that the Ministry has lost the majority without going to the actual test of strength in the Assembly as was done by West Bengal Governor, Dharma Vira in 1967. As D.D. Basu observes that the relation between the Governor and his Ministers is similar to that between the President and his Ministers with this important difference that while the Constitution does not empower the President to exercise any function 'in his discretion' it authorizes the Governor to exercise some functions 'in his discretion'. On the whole, the Governor is a nominal executive and the real executive powers rests on the Chief Minister and the Council of Ministers. However, except certain exceptional circumstances mostly the Governors have stuck to their constitutional position and therefore, the Chief Minister and his Council of Ministers emerge as the real executive.

Advocate-General

Advocate-General is a Constitutional post. Article 165 of the Constitution of India lays down the provisions relating to the appointment, powers and functions of the Advocate-General:

Under Article 165:

1. the Governor of each State shall appoint a person who is qualified to be appointed a judge of a High Court to be Advocate-General for the State.
2. It shall be the duty of the Advocate-General to give advice to the Government of the State upon such legal matters, and to perform such other duties of a legal character, as may from time-to-time be referred or assigned to him by the Governor, and to discharge the functions conferred on him by or under this Constitution or any other law for the time being in force.
3. The Advocate-General shall hold office during the pleasure of the Governor, and shall receive such remuneration as the Governor may determine.

EXERCISES

I. Short Answer Questions: (100 words)

1. State briefly the procedure of appointment of the Chief Minister of a State.
2. Examine briefly the Constitutional limitations placed on the powers of Chief Minister of a State.
3. Write on the Advocate-General of a State.

II. Long Answer Questions: (1200 words)

4. Discuss the appointment, powers and functions of the Chief Minister of a State.

5. Discuss the composition, powers and functions of the Council of Ministers.
6. Examine the relationship between the Governor and the Council of Ministers.

REFERENCES

Awasthy, S.S., *Indian Government and Politics*, Har-Anand Publications Revised Edition, New Delhi, 2006.

Bakshi, P.M., *The Constitution of India*, (with selective comments), Universal Law Publishing, New Delhi, 2000.

Basu, Durga Das, *Introduction to the Constitution of India*, Prentice-Hall of India, New Delhi, 1992.

Jain, M.P., *Indian Constitutional Law*, Wadhwa & Company, Nagpur, 1999.

Rao, K.V., *Parliamentary Democracy of India: A Critical Commentary*, The World Press, Calcutta, 1961.

Singh, M.P and Saxena Rekha, *Indian Politics: Constitutional Foundations and Institutional Functioning*, PHI Learning, New Delhi, 2008.

Siwach, J.R., *Dynamics of Indian Government and Politics*, Sterling Publishers, Delhi, 1985.

12

The State Legislature

INTRODUCTION

The State Legislatures in India resemble broadly the Legislature at the Union level. The difference lies in the fact that some of the State Legislatures are unicameral, whereas some are bicameral. Other than that as there is a President-in-Parliament, there is also the Governor-in-Legislature. The State Legislatures of Uttar Pradesh, Jammu & Kashmir, Karnataka, Bihar, Maharashtra and Andhra Pradesh are bicameral while the others have a unicameral State Legislature. The Upper House of a bicameral State Legislature is commonly known as Vidhan Parishad or the Legislative Council and the Lower Chamber is known as the Vidhan Sabha or the Legislative Assembly. The Legislative Assembly is by far more powerful than the Legislative Council.

THE STATE LEGISLATURE

The Constitution provides for a Legislature for every State, but there is no hard and fast rule that every State should have a bicameral Legislature. The Upper Chamber is known as the Legislative Council or Vidhan Parishad and the Lower Chamber which is popularly elected is known as the Vidhan Sabha.

Legislative Council (Vidhan Parishad): Composition

Article 171 lays down that the total strength of the Legislative Council (Vidhan Parishad) of a State shall not exceed [one-third] of the total number of members in the Legislative Assembly (Vidhan Sabha) of that State provided that the total number of members in the Legislative Council of a State shall in no case be less than forty. Article 169 contains provisions for abolition and creation of Legislative Councils of States. It states that the Parliament may by law provide for the abolition or creation of the Legislative Council of a State after a resolution to this effect is passed by the Vidhan Sabha of the State with a majority of not less than two-third of the members of the Assembly present and voting.

The composition of Legislative Council is provided by Article 171(3). It says:

(3) Of total number of members of the Legislative Council of a state:

(a) as nearly as may be, one-third shall be elected by electorates consisting of members of municipalities, district boards and such other local authorities in the State as Parliament may by law specify;

(b) as nearly as may be, one-twelfth shall be elected by electorates consisting of persons residing in the State who have been for at least three years graduates of any university in the territory of India or have been for at least three years in possession of qualifications prescribed by or under any law made by Parliament as equivalent to that of a graduate of any University;

(c) as nearly as may be, one-twelfth shall be elected by electorates consisting of persons who have been for at least three years engaged in teaching in such educational institutions within the state, not lower in standard than that of a secondary school, as may be prescribed by or under any law made by Parliament;

(d) as nearly as may be one-third shall be elected by the members of the Legislative Assembly (Vidhan Sabha) of the State from amongst persons who are not members of the Assembly;

(e) the remainder shall be nominated by the Governor in accordance with the provisions of Clause (5).

Under 171(5) some members of Legislative Council are nominated by the Governor who are persons having special knowledge or practical experience in different fields like Literature, Science, Art, co-operative movement and social service.

The actual strength of each House is however fixed by Parliament as far as the Legislative Council is concerned like for Uttar Pradesh it is 108, for Maharashtra it is 78, for Bihar it is 96, for Karnataka it is 75, for Jammu & Kashmir it is 36 and Andhra Pradesh it is 90.

Qualifications of Membership

According to Article 173 a person shall not be qualified to be chosen to fill a seat in the Legislature of a State unless he—

1. is a citizen of India, and makes and subscribes before some person authorized in that behalf by the Election Commission an oath or

affirmation according to the form set out for the purpose in the Third Schedule;
2. is, in the case of a seat in the Legislative Assembly, not less than twenty-five years of age and in the case of a seat in the Legislative Council, not less than thirty years of age; and
3. possesses such other qualifications as may be prescribed in that behalf by or under any law made by Parliament.

No one can be a member both the Houses of the State Legislature simultaneously including the Parliament at one and same time.

Term

The Legislative Council of a State is a continuing Chamber and can be ascribed as a quasi-permanent body. One-third of the members retire every second year. Each member has tenure of six years.

The Chairman and Deputy Chairman

According to Article 182, the Legislative Council of every State must choose two members of the Council to be respectively Chairman and Deputy Chairman. In case the office of the Chairman or Deputy Chairman becomes vacant, the Council shall choose another member as the Chairman or the Deputy Chairman as the case may be. Article 183 lays down that a Chairman or a Deputy Chairman may vacate his office if he ceases to be a member of the Council or may any time by writing under his hand resigns his office or may be removed from his office by a resolution of the Council passed by a majority of all the then members of the Council. The Chairman and the Deputy Chairman can preside over all the sessions of the Legislative Council except a session where a resolution for the removal of Chairman or Deputy Chairman is under consideration. The Chairman cannot participate in the voting, but can exercise his casting vote.

Powers and Functions of the Legislative Council

We can broadly categorize the powers and functions of the Legislative Council of a State as falling under legislative powers, control over executive and financial powers.

Legislative Powers

According to Article 196, an ordinary Bill may originate in either House of the State Legislature of a State which has a Legislative Council. A Bill pending in the Legislature shall not lapse due to prorogation of the House or Houses. A Bill pending in the Legislative Council of a State which has not been passed by the Legislative Assembly shall not lapse on a dissolution of the Assembly, but a Bill which is pending in the Legislative Assembly of a State, or which having been passed by the Legislative Assembly and pending in the Legislative Council shall lapse on a dissolution of the Assembly. Article 197 further lays down certain restrictions on powers of the Legislative Council as to Bills other than Money Bills. It stipulates that if after a Bill has been passed by the Legislative Assembly of a State having a Legislative Council and transmitted to the Legislative Council the Bill may be

(a) rejected by the Council; or
(b) more than three months elapse from the date on which the Bill is laid before the Council without the Bill being passed by it; or
(c) the Bill is passed by the Council with amendments to which the Legislative Assembly does not agree. In such a case the Legislative Assembly may pass the Bill again in the same or in any subsequent session with or without such amendments, if any, as have been suggested by the Legislative Council, and then transmit the Bill to the Legislative Council for reconsideration.

If however, after a Bill has been passed for the second time by the Legislative Assembly and transmitted to the Legislative Council, the Bill whether is rejected again, or more than one month lapses from the date on which the Bill is laid before the Council or the Bill is passed by the Council with amendments which the Legislative Assembly does not agree then the Bill shall be deemed to have been passed by the Legislature of the State in the form in which it was passed by the Legislative Assembly for the second time with or without the amendments suggested by the Legislative Council.

Control over Executive

The Legislative Council exercise minimum Control over the Executive of a State when compared to the Legislative Assembly. The Council of Ministers headed by the Chief Minister is collectively responsible to the Assembly and not to the Council. The Legislative Council can hardly do anything more than asking questions or criticizing the Ministers for acts of omission and commission. In every case the will of the Legislative Assembly prevails.

Financial Powers

As far as the financial matters are concerned, Money Bill cannot be introduced in the Legislative Council. If a Money Bill is sent to the Council for consideration after it is passed by the Legislative Assembly, the Council can only delay the Bill by fourteen days. Within fourteen days the Bill must be returned to the Assembly.

The Legislative Council is a weak chamber without any effective powers. Therefore, most of the states have opted for a Unicameral Legislature.

LEGISLATIVE ASSEMBLY (VIDHAN SABHA): COMPOSITION

The State Legislative Assembly or the Vidhan Sabha is the popular chamber which is directly elected by the people of the concerned State. Under Article 170, the Legislative Assembly of each State shall consist of not more than 500 and not less than 60 members chosen by direct election from territorial Constituencies in the State. Provisions have been made for reservation of seats in various Legislative Assemblies for women and Scheduled Castes and Scheduled Tribes. The Governor also has been given the authority to nominate a member of the Anglo-Indian community in case he finds that the community has an inadequate representation in the House. However, this provision has been removed by the 104th Amendment of the Constitution of India (25 January, 2020). The membership to the Legislative Assembly or the Vidhan Sabha is on the basis of population of the State. The strength of members of Legislative Assembly of West Bengal is 294, Tamil Nadu is 234, Andhra Pradesh is 175, Punjab is 117, Union Territory of Puducherry is 30, National Capital of Delhi is 70, and so on.

Qualifications of Membership

According to Article 173, a person shall not be qualified to be chosen to fill a seat in the Legislature of a State unless he—

1. is a citizen of India, and makes and subscribes before some person authorized in that behalf by the Election Commission an oath or affirmation according to the form set out for the purpose in the Third Schedule;
2. is, in the case of a seat in the Legislative Assembly, not less than twenty-five years of age and in the case of a seat in the Legislative Council, not less than thirty years of age; and
3. possesses such other qualifications as may be prescribed in that behalf by or under any law made by Parliament.

No one can be a member of both the Houses of the State Legislature simultaneously including the Parliament at one and same time.

Term

Article 172 states that every Legislative Assembly of every State, unless dissolved, shall continue for five years from the date of appointment for its first meeting. However, when an emergency is proclaimed, the period of the Assembly can be extended by a law of the Parliament for a period of one year, and not extending in any case beyond a period of six months after the Proclamation has ceased to operate.

The Speaker and Deputy Speaker

According to Article 178, the Legislative Assembly of every State must choose two members of the Assembly to be the Speaker and the Deputy Speaker, respectively. In case the office of the Speaker or Deputy Speaker becomes vacant, the Assembly shall choose another member as the Speaker or the Deputy Speaker. Article 179 lays down that a Speaker or a Deputy Speaker may vacate his office if he ceases to be a member of the Assembly or may any time by writing under his hand resigns his office or may be removed from his office by a resolution of the Council passed by a majority of all the then members of the Assembly. The Speaker and the Deputy Speaker can preside over all the sessions of the Legislative Assembly except a session where a resolution for the removal of Speaker or Deputy Speaker is under consideration. The Speaker cannot participate in the voting, but can exercise his casting vote.

There are two extraordinary cases where the Speakers had used considerable discretion even exceeding their limits and adjourned the House. In the case of West Bengal, Speaker Bijoy Kumar Banerjee adjourned the house *sine die* soon after a new ministry was formed by Dr. P.C. Ghosh after the Governor Dharma Vira dismissed the Ajoy Mukherjee Government in 1967 before he could prove his strength in the Assembly. As soon as the session of the House was summoned, the Speaker adjourned the House *sine die* as he thought that the appointment of Dr. P.C. Ghosh as Chief Minister and summoning the House on his advice was unconstitutional. The Speaker prevented the Assembly from working, and when the Vidhan Sabha met in February 1968 following violent disturbances which was preventing the Governor to read out his advice, he readjourned the House *sine die* for the second time. The Speaker of Punjab Assembly, Joginder Singh Mann also adjourned the House for two months in March 1968 to prevent the tabling of a motion of no-confidence against him and subsequent passage and his removal. These incidents are rare and the Speaker of the Assembly usually performs his functions within constitutional limits without raising controversies.

Quorum

Article 189(3) stipulates that until it is provided by the Legislature of the State by law the quorum to constitute a meeting of a House of the Legislature of a State shall be one-tenth of the total number of members of the House, whichever is greater.

Sessions

The Governor according to Article 174 shall form time-to-time summon the House or each House of the Legislature of the State to meet but six months should not intervene between its last sitting in one session and the date appointed for its first sitting in the next session. The Governor has the power to prorogue the House or either of the House, and also has the power to dissolve the Legislative Assembly.

Powers and Functions of Legislative Assembly

The powers of the Legislative Assembly are as follows:

Legislative Powers

The Assembly can make laws on any subject provided in the State List as well as Concurrent List provided does not conflict with the laws made by the Parliament. As far as the legislative process is concerned we have seen in the above discussion of the legislative powers of the Legislative Council of a State, that the real power is wielded by the Assembly, the Council can just delay an ordinary Bill by (3+1) four months and Money Bill by 14 days.

Control of Executive

More than the Council, the Assembly exercise control over the Council of Ministers headed by the Chief Minister. Besides, asking questions, introducing resolutions, motions, the Assembly can pass a vote of censure to dismiss the Government. This is equivalent to no-confidence motion against the Ministry. The Council of Ministers are individually and collectively responsible to the Assembly for all their Acts, policies and decisions. By passing a no-confidence vote, the Assembly can bring down the Government. It can also show its lack of confidence by rejecting any policy, any law or budget of the Government.

Financial Powers

The financial control is also in the hands of the Legislative Assembly of a State. Article 265 lays down that no tax can be levied except by authority of law; no appropriations can be made except by law; no money is granted and no tax can be increased and Money Bill or Financial Bill can be introduced without the consent of the Governor. In a Unicameral Legislature, the passage of the Money Bill is easier than a Bicameral Legislature. Money Bill can only be introduced in the Assembly and not in the Council. After the Money Bill is passed by the Assembly, it is sent to the Council for its consideration and recommendations. The Council has fourteen days to decide on the Bill. The Assembly may or may not accept the recommendations and over that if the Council fails to return the Bill to the Assembly within 14 days, the Bill is deemed to have been passed by the Assembly and the Council in the form it was originally passed by the Assembly. Like an ordinary Bill a Money Bill has to be send to the Governor for his assent.

Amending Powers

The State Legislative Assembly also enjoys some powers with regard to the amendment of the Constitution. Under Article 368, a Bill of Constitutional amendment, after being passed by the Parliament is referred to the States for ratification. The Legislative Assembly has the power of passing a resolution by its simple majority showing approval or disapproval of that particular Bill. The President also can refer to the Legislature, the Legislative Assembly of a concerned State a proposal (desiring alteration of its boundary lines or its reorganization) to elicit its view before he recommends such Bill to be introduced in the Parliament.

Electoral Functions

The Legislative Assembly of the State performs some electoral functions too. It is part of the electoral college for the election of the President. It also elects its own Speaker and Deputy Speaker.

Therefore from the foregoing discussion, it is clear the Legislative Assembly is the real law-making body which also controls the finance and working of the Council of Ministers.

Privileges

The powers, privileges of the House of Legislatures and of members and Committees provided under Article 194 are similar to the legislative privileges of the House of Parliament. Article 194 guarantees freedom of speech in the State Legislature, and immunizes a member of a Legislature from any proceedings in any court for anything said or any vote in the Legislature or a Committee thereof or for publication under the authority of a House of any Report, paper, votes or proceedings. Further, this Article authorizes the State Legislature to make a law to define the powers and privileges and immunities of each House, and its members and Committees. Article 208 empowers each House of the State Legislature to make rule for regulating, subject to the provisions of the Constitution, its procedure and the conduct of its business.

Relations between the Two Houses of the State Legislature

The relation between the two Houses of the State Legislature (where there are two chambers) is one of primacy of one in comparison with the other. In other words, who prevails over whom is the main concern as far as matters of legislations are taken into consideration. In case of an Ordinary Bill, it can originate in any of the Houses. Here the Legislative Council can delay it only for a period of three months in the first instance. In the second instance, it can hold it only for a month and then return it to the Lower House. Then it is up to the will of the Legislative Assembly either to make necessary changes as recommended by the Council or pass the Bill in its original form with or without the changes. Due to the strength of the Lower House, it is the will of the latter that prevails. A Money Bill can only be introduced in the Legislative Assembly. The Council can only delay it for 14 days. The Chief Minister and his Council of Ministers are responsible to the Legislative Assembly, and not to the Legislative Council. The Legislative Council is just a delaying chamber and the actual power is wielded by the Legislative Assembly.

EXERCISES

I. Short Answer Questions: **(100 words)**

1. Write on the composition of the Vidhan Sabha.
2. Write on the composition of the Vidhan Parishad.
3. State the qualifications of the members of State Legislature.
4. Comment on the role of the Speaker of the State Legislative Assembly.
5. Comment on the role of the Chairman of the Legislative Council.

II. Long Answer Questions: **(1200 words)**

6. Discuss the composition, powers and functions of Legislative Council of a State.
7. Discuss the composition, powers and functions of Legislative Assembly of a State.
8. Discuss the composition and functions of the State Legislature and examine the relationship between the two Houses of the State Legislature.

REFERENCES

Awasthy, S.S., *Indian Government and Politics*, Har-Anand Publications, Revised Edition, New Delhi, 2006.

Bakshi, P.M., *The Constitution of India*, (with selective comments), Universal Law Publishing, New Delhi, 2000.

Basu, Durga Das, *Introduction to the Constitution of India*, Prentice-Hall of India, New Delhi, 1992.

Jain, M.P., *Indian Constitutional Law*, Wadhwa & Company, Nagpur, 1999.

Rao, K.V., *Parliamentary Democracy of India: A Critical Commentary*, The World Press, Calcutta, 1961.

Singh, M.P. and Saxena, Rekha, *Indian Politics: Contemporary Issues and Concerns*, Prentice-Hall of India, New Delhi, 2008.

Siwach, J.R., *Dynamics of Indian Government and Politics*, Sterling Publishers, New Delhi, 1985.

13

The Judiciary in India

INTRODUCTION

The judiciary plays an important part in the life of the Indian polity. The judiciary has an important role as the interpreter of the Constitution and as the guardian of the Constitution with the prime objective of safeguarding the supremacy of the Constitution, enforcing the Fundamental Rights of the people guaranteed by the Constitution of India and as an arbiter of disputes between the Centre and State. At present, the dismal performance by the Executive and the Legislature in India and the administration being fraught with corruption and neglect of public welfare, the judiciary is the sole hope for the people to seek justice. The judiciary gives directions to the State and its agencies to work in accordance with the law and the Constitution. India has a unified judiciary with Supreme Court at its apex and the High Courts and other subordinate Courts like Criminal Courts, Civil Courts and Revenue Courts below it.

THE SUPREME COURT

The Supreme Court is the apex court and is the supreme interpreter of the Constitution and the Guardian of the Fundamental Rights of the People of India. The Supreme Court is the Court of Appeal in all Civil and Criminal matters and the protector of the law of the land. Supreme Court Rules, 1966 are framed under Article 145 of the Constitution to regulate the practice and procedure of the Supreme Court. Under Article 130, the seat of the Supreme Court shall be at Delhi, but with the approval of the President, under the same Article, the Chief Justice of India may allow the sittings of the Courts in other places as well.

Composition of the Supreme Court

The composition of the Supreme Court is mentioned in Article 124 of the Constitution. The number of Judges has now been raised to 31 (30 Judges + 1 Chief Justice of India) including the Chief Justice. The Judges of Supreme Court and the Chief Justice are appointed by the President under his hand and seal. There is a convention that the senior most Judge of the Supreme Court is appointed as the Chief Justice of India. The other Judges, at present, are appointed by the President after consultation with the Chief Justice of India. Article 124 states that "**There shall be a Supreme Court of India consisting of a Chief Justice of India and, until Parliament by law prescribes a larger number, of not more than seven (25 vide Act 22 of 1986 Sec. 2 and 30 at present by the Constitutional Amendment Act, 2008) other Judges**."

Appointment of Judges

Article 124(2) states that "**Every Judge of the Supreme Court shall be appointed by the President by warrant under his hand and seal after consultation with such of the Judges of the Supreme Court and of the High Courts in the States as the President may deem necessary for the purpose and shall hold office until he attains the age of sixty-five years.**"

In case of appointment of other Judges of the Supreme Court and the High Courts, the President can consult the Chief Justice of India if he deems that to be necessary. The President makes such appointment on the advice of the concerned Minister usually the Law Minister. Generally, the Judges are appointed by taking into consideration their age. The senior-most Judge of the Supreme Court is appointed as the Chief Justice whenever there is a vacancy. However, the Law Commission suggested that more than age, capability and experience should be the criteria for making such appointment. Strict adherence to this rule has created sometimes, certain situations where the Chief Justice has held office for a few months before his retirement like C.J. Jayantilal Chhotalal Shah (35 days), C.J.E.S. Venkataramiah (181 days), C.J. Lalit Mohan Sharma (85 days) and Gopal Ballav Pattanaik (41 days). However, sometimes controversies have also resulted when the rule has been violated. In 1977, the Government appointed Justice Beg as the Chief Justice by-passing Justice Khanna who was senior to him at that time. As a result, Justice Khanna resigned in protest. In 1973, the Government again broke the convention and Justice A.N. Ray was appointed superseding three senior Judges, Justice J.M. Shelat, Justice K.S. Hegde and Justice A.N. Grover. In protest these three senior Judges resigned. During the tenure of Janata Government, the seniority principle was revived and the senior most Judge, Justice Yeshwant Vishnu Chandrachud was appointed as the Chief Justice. The decisions of the Supreme Courts are taken by majority. However, minority opinion may be recorded in the judgment. As far as the appointment and transfers of judges to the higher judiciary are concerned a 'Collegium' system is followed. A 'Collegium' comprising the Chief Justice of India and a forum of four senior-most judges of the Supreme Court recommends appointments and transfers of judges. The 99th Amendment, 2014, to the Indian Constitution replaced the 'Collegium' system by the National Judicial Appointments Commission (NJAC). However, the Constitutional Bench of the Supreme Court in 2015 quashed the 99th Amendment and NJAC Act and restored the 'Collegium' system.

Qualifications

Article 124(3) provides certain qualifications for a person to be appointed as the Judge of Supreme Court. They are:

1. He must be a citizen of India;
2. A distinguished jurist in the opinion of the President;
3. Has been a High Court Judge for at least 5 years or two or more such courts in succession; or
4. Has been an advocate of a High Court (or two or more such courts in succession) for at least 10 years.

Tenure and Removal

Article 124(2) provides that a Judge of the Supreme Court shall hold office till he attains the age of 65 years. However, by the same Article and subsequent Clauses, a Judge may resign at any time before his term of office is completed by submitting his resignation to the President. A Judge of the Supreme Court may be removed by an order of the President passed after an address of the each House of Parliament supported by a majority of the total membership of that House and by a majority not less than two-thirds of the members voting and present in the House. This majority is also known as special majority. The procedure is known as impeachment.

A Judge of the Supreme Court can be removed only on the grounds of *proved misbehaviour or incapacity*. The Judges Inquiry Act, 1968 provides for the inquiry of the conduct of a Judge to prove the charges against him. It should be noted that the same procedure is followed for the removal of a Judge of High Court. So far, no Judge of either court has been removed by Parliament through impeachment except for Justice Sen who was impeached by Rajya Sabha, but resigned before being impeached by Lok Sabha to avoid ignominy.

The first Judge to face an impeachment proceeding was Justice Soumitra Sen of Calcutta High Court. The Rajya Sabha passed the motion making him the first Judge to have been impeached by the Upper House for misconduct. CPI(M) leader Sitaram Yechury was asked by the Chair, Hamid Ansari to move the motion in August 2011. Thus, the power invested in the House contained in Article 217 with Clause (4) of Article 124 to present an address to the President for removal of a Judge was invoked. Justice Sen was found guilty of misappropriating US $ 33,22,8000 as sale proceeds of goods in a case between Steel Authority of India and Shipping Corporation of India. An Inquiry Committee was appointed by the Chairman of Rajya Sabha which found Justice Sen guilty. Chief Justice K.G. Balakrishnan wrote to the Prime Minister recommending his impeachment.

Before, the Lok Sabha moved a motion of impeachment, Justice Sen tendered his resignation.

Salary and Allowances

Currently the Chief Justice of India is paid a salary of ₹2,80,000 lakh per month and other Judges are paid a monthly salary of ₹2,50,000. Further, by Article 125, the salary and other allowances of Judges cannot vary to their disadvantage during their term of office; except during the enforcement of the financial emergency under Article 360. Every Judge shall be entitled to such privileges and allowances and to such rights in respect of leave of absence and pension as may from time-to-time be determined by or under law made by Parliament and, until so determined, to such privileges, allowances and rights as are specified in the Second Schedule.

Oath of Affirmation

The President of India administers the oath of office to the Judges of Supreme Court. The format of oath is given in the Third Schedule of the Constitution.

"I, (name), having been appointed Chief Justice of the Supreme Court of India do swear in the name of God/solemnly affirm that I will bear true faith and allegiance to the Constitution of India as by law established, that I will uphold the sovereignty and integrity of India, that I will duly and faithfully and to the best of my ability, knowledge and judgment perform the duties of my office without fear or favour, affection or ill-will and that I will uphold the Constitution and the laws."

—*Constitution of India, Third Schedule, Part IV*

APPOINTMENT OF AN ACTING CHIEF JUSTICE

When the office of Chief Justice of India is vacant or when the Chief Justice is, by reason of absence or otherwise, unable to perform the duties of the office, his duties will shall be performed by one of the other Judges of the Court as the President may appoint for the purpose (Article 126). If the post of both the President and the Vice-President falls vacant, the Chief Justice of India discharges the functions of the President till new incumbent is elected to the office of the President. M. Hidayatullah is the only Chief Justice who acted as President in 1969.

APPOINTMENT OF *Ad Hoc* JUDGES

Article 127 provides that if at any time there should not be a quorum of the Judges of the Supreme Court available to hold or continue any session of the Court, the Chief Justice of India may, with the previous consent of the President and after consultation with the Chief Justice of the High Court concerned, request in writing the attendance at the sittings of the Court, as an *ad hoc* Judge, for such period as may be necessary, of a Judge of a High Court duly qualified for appointment as a Judge of the Supreme Court to be designated by the Chief Justice of India. It shall be the duty of the Judge, so designated, to give priority to his duty to attend the sittings of the Supreme Court rather than other duties at the time and period for which his attendance is required in the Supreme Court. At that time he shall have all the jurisdiction, powers and privileges, and shall discharge the duties, of a Judge of the Supreme Court. The Chief Justice of India, with the prior consent of the President, may request a retired Judge of the Supreme Court or the High Court to sit and Act as a Judge of Supreme Court (Article 128).

INDEPENDENCE OF INDIAN JUDICIARY

The Constitution seeks to ensure the independence of Supreme Court Judges in various ways. A Judge of the Supreme Court cannot be removed from office except by an order of the President passed after an address in each House of Parliament and supported by a majority of the total membership of that House and by a majority of not less than two-thirds of members present and voting, and presented to the President in the same Session for such removal on the ground of proved misbehaviour or incapacity. A person who has been a Judge of the Supreme Court is debarred from practising in any court of law or before any other authority in India. The independence of the Supreme Court Judges can be summarized as:

1. The President is the appointing authority of the Judges, and he acts in this case with the advice of the Council of Ministers, but arbitrary decisions are checked by insertion of the provision of consultation with the Chief Justice of India.
2. There are definite qualifications laid down for Judges, who are appointed by the President in consultation with a collegium of Judges.
3. The procedure for the removal of Judges is difficult as it is not possible to mobilize the support of special majority in each House of Parliament. This ensures their functioning without fear and prejudice. [Article 124(4)]. The salary and allowances of Judges cannot be reduced to their disadvantage during the term of their office. [Article 125(2)] However, the President has the power to override such guarantee when a Financial Emergency has been proclaimed in the Country by Article 360(4)(b).
4. It is also provided that the administrative expenses of the Supreme Court, salaries and allowances, etc., of the Judges as well as of the staff of the Supreme Court will be charged upon the Consolidated Fund of India and shall not be subject to vote in Parliament [Article 146(3)].
5. It is provided in Article 144 of the Constitution that all civil and judicial authorities shall act in the aid of Supreme Court.
6. The Court has the power to punish persons and authorities for contempt of itself.

7. The Supreme Court has power to lay down the rules of procedure for its functioning. These rules can be changed or modified by the Supreme Court only.
8. The Supreme Court has the power to exercise administrative control over the employees working in the court. This power covers the authority for the appointment and removal of such employees.
9. It is forbidden by Article 121 that no discussion of the conduct of a Judge of the Supreme Court (or a High Court) in Parliament, except upon a motion for an address to the President for the removal of the Judge.
10. Article 124(7) lays down that after retirement a Judge of the Supreme Court shall not plead or act in any Court or before any authority within the territory of India.

JURISDICTION OF THE SUPREME COURT

It should also be noted that the Supreme Court is the highest Court of the land. It is the highest Court of appeal against the decisions of subordinate courts. The Apex Court also functions as a Federal Court, which resolves the disputes arising out of the functioning of federal system. There are three kinds of jurisdictions of the Supreme Court: original jurisdiction, appellate jurisdiction and advisory jurisdiction.

The Supreme Court of India enjoys *three types of Jurisdiction which are discussed as follows:*

[1] Original Jurisdiction (Article 131)

The Supreme Court holds the primary jurisdiction with respect to the disputes between the States or the Union and the States. Original jurisdiction refers to those cases/disputes which can be initiated, at the first stance, only at the Supreme Court, and not in any other court. Under Article 131, the Supreme Court shall have primary jurisdiction in any dispute—

1. between the Government of India and one or more States; or
2. between the Government of India and any State or States on one side and one or more other States on the other; or
3. between two or more States, if and in so far as the dispute involves any question (whether of law or fact) on which the existence or extent of a legal right depends.

However, the jurisdiction of the Supreme Court does not extend to:

1. a dispute arising out of any Treaty, Agreement, covenant, engagement, *sanad*, or other similar instrument which, having been entered into or executed before the commencement of the Constitution, continues to be in operation after such commencement or which provides that the said jurisdiction shall not extend to such a dispute.

2. a dispute arising out of any treaty, etc. which provided that the original jurisdiction of the court would not apply to any dispute arising under the treaty, etc., i.e., agreements which provides that the Supreme Court's original jurisdiction shall not extend to such a dispute.

Other provisions in the Constitution which are excluded from the original jurisdiction of the Supreme Court are:

1. Disputes specified in the Provision to Article 131 and 363(1)
2. Complaints as to interference with Inter-State water supplies, referred to the statutory tribunal mentioned in Article 262, if Parliament so legislates
3. Matters referred to the Finance Commission (Article 280)
4. Adjustment of certain expenses as between the Union and the States under Articles 257(4) and 258(3)
5. Adjustment of certain expenses as between the Union and the States under Article 290.

Very few cases have come up for their resolution in the Supreme Court regarding settlement of disputes between the Union and the States. One prominent among them is *Bihar* v. *India*, 1970, where the State of Bihar filed a suit against the Government of India as the owner of railways and Hindustan Steel Ltd., a Government Company, claiming damages for short supply of iron and steel ordered by the State for the Gandak Project. Another significant case was *West Bengal* v. *India* 1963, where the State of West Bengal filed a suit against the centre seeking a declaration that a central law, the Coal Bearing Areas (Acquisition and Development) Act, 1957 was unconstitutional but this was dismissed by the Supreme Court. In the words of Justice Chandrachud, "The purpose of Art 131 is to afford a forum for the resolution of disputes which depend for their decision on the existence or extent of a legal right. It is only when a legal, not a mere political, issue arises touching upon the existence or extent of a legal right that Art 131 is attracted."

[2] Appellate Jurisdiction

The appellate jurisdiction consists of three kinds of appeals.

1. **Appeals in Constitutional Matters (Article 132):** An appeal shall lie in the Supreme Court from any judgment, decree or final order of the High Court in the territory of India, whether in a civil, criminal or other proceeding, if the High Court certifies under Article 134A that the case involves a substantial question of law which requires the interpretation of the Constitution.
2. **Appeals in Civil Matters (Article 133):** An appeal shall lie to the Supreme Court from any judgment, decree or final order in a civil proceeding of a High Court in the territory of India, if such High Court certifies under Article 134A:

(a) that the case involves a substantial question of law of general importance, and

(b) that in the opinion of the High Court the said case needs to be decided by the Supreme Court.

3. **Appeals in Criminal Matters (Article 134):** An appeal, in a criminal matter, against the decision of the High Court shall lie in the Supreme Court, if the High Court:

   (a) has on appeal reversed the order of the acquittal of the accused person and sentenced him to death, or

   (b) has withdrawn for trial before itself any case from any subordinate court and convicted the accused person and sentenced him to death; or

   (c) certifies under Article 134A that the case is a fit case for appeal to the Supreme Court.

Appeal by Special Leave

This is the special power of the Supreme Court to admit any appeal against any court, even if it is not covered in the appellate jurisdiction of the court. Thus, under **Article 136** of the Constitution, the Supreme Court may, in its discretion, grant special leave (permission) to appeal from any judgment, decree, determination, sentence, or order in any cause or matter passed or made by any court or tribunal in the territory of India. However, this power does not apply to the appeals against any order or judgment, determination, sentence or order passed by any court or tribunal constituted by or under any law relating to the Armed Forces.

There are also provisions for **Statutory Appeals** under Section 23 of the Consumer Protection Act, 1986 provides for an appeal to the Supreme Court from an order made by the National Commission, entertaining complaints where the value of the goods or services and compensation, if any, claimed exceeds Rupees One Crore. Section 116-A of the Representation of People Act, 1951 provides for an appeal to the Supreme Court on any question, whether of law or fact, from every order passed by a High Court under Section 98 or Section 99 of the said Act and the like. There are also provisions for appeals under Section 379 of the Code of Criminal Procedure, 1973, Section 130E of the Customs Act, 1962, Section 35L of the Central Excise and Salt Act, 1944, Section 19(1)(b) of the Contempt of Courts Act, 1971, Section 38 of the Advocates Act, 1961, Section 10 of the Special Court (Trial of offences relating to Transactions in Securities) Act, 1992, Section 55 of the Monopolies and Restrictive Trade Practices Act, 1969, Section 18 of the Telecom Regulatory Authority of India Act, 1997, Section 15(z) of the Securities and Exchange Board of India Act, 1992, Section 261 of the Income-Tax Act, 1961, Section 19 of the Terrorist and Disruptive activities (Prevention) Act, 1987 and Section 53T of the Competition Act, 2002.

[3] Advisory Jurisdiction of the Supreme Court

The Supreme Court of India also enjoys the advisory jurisdiction which is discussed as follows:

1. Under **Article 143**, if at any time it appears to the President that any question of law or fact has arisen or is likely to arise, which is of such a nature and of such public importance that it is expedient to obtain the opinion of the Supreme Court upon it, he may refer the question to the Supreme Court to seek its legal opinion on such question. It should be noted that neither the court is bound to give its legal opinion on a question referred to it by the President nor the President is bound to accept the legal advice given by the court in any case.
2. **Article 317** provides that the Chairman or any other member of a Public Service Commission can be removed from his office by order of the President, on the ground of misbehaviour, after the Supreme Court on reference being made to it by the President, has on inquiry, Reported that the Chairman or the case may be ought on any such ground to be removed.
3. **Section 53K of the Competition Act, 2002** provides for removal and suspension of Chairperson and Members of Appellate Tribunal in consultation with the Chief Justice of India on any of the grounds specified in Clauses (a) to (f) of Sub-section (1) of Section 53K after an enquiry by a Judge of the Supreme Court of India.

Jurisdiction Regarding Electoral Disputes

Article 71 provides that all doubts and disputes arising out of or in connection with the election of a President or Vice-President shall be inquired into and decided by the Supreme Court whose decision shall be final.

Power of the Supreme Court to Review its Own Judgment

Under the Supreme Court Rules, the Apex Court may review its judgment or order, but no application for review is to be entertained in a civil proceeding except on the grounds mentioned in rules of the Code of Civil Procedure and in a criminal proceeding except on the ground of an error apparent on the face of the record.

Miscellaneous Jurisdiction

Article 138 pertains to enlargement of the jurisdiction of the Supreme Court. It upholds that the Supreme Court shall have such further jurisdiction and powers with respect to any of the matters in the Union List as Parliament may by law confer. It also states that the Supreme Court shall have such further jurisdiction, and powers with respect to any matter as the Government of India and the

Government of any State may by special agreement confer, if Parliament by law provides for the exercise of such jurisdiction and powers by the Supreme Court.

Article 142 provides the jurisdiction for enforcement of decrees and orders of Supreme Court as is necessary for doing complete justice in any cause or matter pending before it. Any order or decree so passed or order so made shall be enforceable throughout the territory of India in such a manner as may be prescribed by or under any law made by Parliament, and until provision in that behalf is so made in such manner as the President may by order prescribe. Further, under any law made by the Parliament, the Supreme Court shall have the power throughout the territory of India to make any order for the purpose of securing the attendance of any person, the discovery or production of any documents, or investigation or punishment of any contempt to itself.

Article 146 empowers the Supreme Court regarding the appointments of Officers and servants of the Supreme Court which shall be made by the Chief Justice of India or such Judge or Officer of the Court as he may direct. Subject to the provisions of any law made by the Parliament, the conditions of service of Officers and servants of the Supreme Court shall be such as may be prescribed by rules made by the Chief Justice of India or by some other Judge or Officer authorized by the Chief Justice of India.

The administrative expenses of the Supreme Court including all salaries, Allowances and pensions payable to or in respect of the offices and servants of the Court shall be charged on the Consolidated Fund of India, and any fees or other moneys taken by the Court shall form part of that Fund.

Transfer of Cases

Article 139A(1) provides that where cases involving the same or substantially the same questions of law are pending before the Supreme Court and one or more High Courts or before two or more High Courts, and the Supreme Court is satisfied, on its own motion, or on an application made by the Attorney-General for India or by a party to any such case, such questions are substantial questions of general importance, the Supreme Court may withdraw the case or cases pending before the High Court or the High Courts and dispose of all the cases itself.

Article 139A(2) provides that the Supreme Court may, if it deems it expedient so to do for the ends of justice, transfer any case, appeal or other proceedings pending before any High Court to any other High Court.

Supreme Court as the Court of Record

According to Article 129, the Supreme Court shall be a court of Record and shall have all the powers of such courts including the power to punish for contempt of itself. The Supreme Court has a summary jurisdiction to punish contempt of its authority. This power is exercised only in the public interest to punish an Act which might interfere in the administration of justice. The Court exercises this power "cautiously, wisely and with circumspection." The Court can punish its contempt by fine or imprisonment. The court may take action (a) *Suo motu*, or (b) on a petition made by Attorney-General, or Solicitor General, or (c) on a petition made by any person, and in the case of a criminal contempt with the consent in writing of the Attorney-General or the Solicitor General.

Supreme Court as the Court of Appeal

The Supreme Court of India is the final appellate authority. The Appellate jurisdiction of the Supreme Court is provided under Articles 132–134. Appeals from the High Court in civil cases are dealt under Articles 133 which has been amended by the 13th Constitutional Amendment Act, 1972, and it states that an appeal from the decision of a High Court in a civil matter will lie to the Supreme Court only if the High Court **certifies** that the case involves 'a substantial question of law of general importance' and that 'the said question needs to be decided by the Supreme Court.' Article 134 provides the provisions dealing with appellate jurisdiction of Supreme Court in regard to criminal matters.

Supreme Court as a Protector of Fundamental Rights

Under Article 32 of the Constitution, the Supreme Court has the power to issue writs in the nature of *habeas corpus, mandamus, prohibition, quo warranto* and *certiorari* for the enforcement of fundamental rights. The cases related to the violation of fundamental right may be brought before the court both under original and appellate jurisdiction. Again, the power of High Courts to issue above writs is more wide in comparison to Supreme Court as the High Court (Article 226) can issue such writs to enforce all rights including the fundamental rights, whereas the Supreme Court can issue these writs only for the enforcement of fundamental rights. [For a detailed discussion on writs see Chapter 4 on Fundamental Rights]

Supreme Court and the Power of Judicial Review

The Constitution of India is the Supreme Law of the land and the Indian Judiciary with the Supreme Court at its apex is the protector/guardian of this Constitution. This implies that anything which violates or goes against the provisions of the Constitution can be declared null and void by the Supreme Court. Such is the power of judicial review that the Court can declare null and void those orders of the executive and those laws passed by the Legislatures, which violate any provision of the Constitution, because the Constitution is the fundamental law of land.

However, the concept of Judicial Review or provisions of Judicial Review is nowhere mentioned in the Constitution. From the provisions of certain Articles that the Supreme Court and the High Courts derive their power of Judicial Review. Article 13 while embodying the principle regarding the inconsistency of law with or in derogation with fundamental rights in Clause (2) upholds that "The State shall not make any law which takes away or abridges the rights conferred by this Part (Fundamental Rights) and any law made in contravention of this clause shall, to the extent of the contravention, be void."

Further, Article 32 which spells out the remedies for the enforcement of rights conferred by the Part III of the Constitution gives the right to move to the Supreme Court by appropriate proceedings for the enforcement of the rights conferred under Part III. The Supreme Court has been vested with the power by this same Article to issue directions or orders or writs for the enforcement of any rights conferred by this Part III on Fundamental Rights. Again Article 131 (pertaining to disputes between the Union and the States or between two or more States) and Article 132 (pertaining to appeals from any judgment, decree or final order of a High Court in civil, criminal or other proceedings) give ample scope for judicial review to the Supreme Court under its original and appellate jurisdictions, respectively. Article 226 confers upon every High Court the power to issue to any person or authority, including in appropriate cases, any Government, directions, orders or writs or any of them, for enforcement of any of the rights conferred by Part III of the Constitution.

Article 13(2) provides the power of judicial review with respect to the provisions related to the Fundamental Rights. However, the courts have enlarged the mandate of this Article to cover the entire provisions of the Constitution under the power of Judicial Review by applying the theory of implied powers. However, the power of Judicial Review cannot be exercised on its own until a case has not been brought before the court by the affected party. The power of Judicial Review can be adjudged from various landmark judgments of the Supreme Court and the effort of the Parliament to claim its sovereignty by limiting the power of Judicial Review. This has been the source of hot debates for years.

The first encounter which came into light between the Parliament and the Judiciary was when the Court overturned State laws redistributing land from *Zamindar* (see Chapter 14 for details on Constitutional Amendments) estates on the grounds that the laws violated the *Zamindars*' Fundamental Rights. Parliament passed the First (1951), Fourth (1955), and Seventeenth Amendment Acts (1964) to protect its authority to implement land redistribution. The Supreme Court countered these amendments in 1967 when it ruled in the *Golaknath* v. *State of Punjab* case that Parliament did not have the power to abrogate the Fundamental Rights, including the provisions on private property. On February 1970, the Supreme Court invalidated the government-sponsored

Bank Nationalization Bill that had been passed by Parliament in August 1969. The Supreme Court also rejected as unconstitutional a Presidential order of September 1970 that abolished the titles, privileges, and privy purses of the former rulers of India's old Princely States.

In reaction to Supreme Court's decisions, in 1971, Parliament passed the Twenty-fourth Amendment empowering it to amend any provision of the Constitution, including the Fundamental Rights, the Twenty-fifth Amendment, making legislative decisions concerning proper land compensation non-justiciable, and the Twenty-sixth Amendment, which added Article 363A abolishing princely privileges and privy purses. On 24 April 1973, the Supreme Court gave its historic ruling in the *Keshavananda Bharati* v. *The State of Kerala, Case* 1973, that although these amendments were constitutional, the Court still reserved for itself the discretion to reject any Constitutional Amendments passed by Parliament by declaring that the Amendments cannot change the Constitution's *basic structure*.

During the 1975–77 Emergency, Parliament passed the Forty-second Amendment in January 1976, to overcome the obstacle arising out of the ruling in the *Keshavananda* case which prevented the Supreme Court from reviewing any constitutional amendment with the exception of procedural issues concerning ratification. The Forty-second Amendment deprived the Supreme Court of its power of judicial review to a great extent. However, the Forty-third (1977) and Forty-fourth (1978) amendments, passed by the Janata Government reversed the position and restored the power of Judicial Review to the Supreme Court. In the *Minerva Mills* case of 1980, the Supreme Court reaffirmed its authority to protect the basic structure of the Constitution. Later, there have been innumerable cases where the Apex Court has exercised its power of Judicial Review. However, there is also some who are critical about the court's role as far as Judicial Review is concerned, and they view it as a hindrance to the law-making power of the Parliament, and may turn out to be a source of conflict between the two pillars of Indian democracy. Some have feared that Judicial Review in many cases may lead to judicial activism in India. Judiciary becomes active when there is a problem in governance and the Parliament or the Government or its agents fail to deliver good to the people. Currently the Indian Judiciary plays a dignified role though sometimes it gives some verdicts which are path breaking. The Supreme Court gave its verdict on tackling the return of the inter-state workers who are suffering as a result of country-wide lockdown due to Covid 19 pandemic outbreak and are unable to return to their states in May 2020. It was a late response never-the-less it gave a little hope to the inter-state workers. The Supreme Court took *suo motu* proceedings on the basis of media reports and representations from senior advocates. It pointed out inadequacies and lapses on the part of both the Central and State governments in addressing the crisis of inter-state workers. The Court asked the Centre and States to address the problem of transportation and food for the distressed inter-state workers.

Judicial Activism

The recent trend of judicial activism in India has drawn great attention from different quarters. The common question is that whether the Courts have power to make law or to restrict itself to interpreting the law as it is. Justice Bhagwati opines "It is for the Judge to give meaning to what the Legislature has said and it is this process of interpretation which constitutes the most creative and thrilling function of a Judge" and "The Judge infuses life and blood into the dry skeleton provided by the Legislature and creates a living organism appropriate and adequate to meet the needs of the society." The first case of judicial activism can be seen in case of the *Keshavananda Bharati case* (1973) or the Fundamental Rights case where the Court gave the verdict that a Constitutional amendment duly passed by the Legislature was invalid as damaging or destroying its basic structure. There have been a whole lot of cases where the Court has played an active role. Some important cases are like *S.P. Gupta* v. *Union of India*, 1982, where through public interest litigation the Court has granted access to persons inspired by public interest to invite judicial intervention against abuse of power or misuse of power or inaction of the Government, *Vineet Narain* v. *Union of India,* 1996 the Apex Court took upon itself the task of monitoring the investigations pertaining to the hawala transactions and in *Common Cause* v. *Union of India,* 1996, and the Supreme Court cancelled the allotment of petrol pumps made by the then Minister of State of Petroleum and Natural Gas, Captain Satish Sharma on the ground of nepotism and malafide and passed severe strictures against the Minister. In a recent landmark judgment in February 2012, the Supreme Court has canceled 122 telecommunications licenses awarded to companies in 2008 related to the 2G Spectrum scam.

Several environmental-friendly judgments/pronouncements have been given by the Courts. Some are like for ensuring green belts and open spaces for maintaining ecological balance; forbidding stone-crushing activities near residential complexes; earmarking a part of the reserved forest for *adivasis* to ensure their habitat and means of livelihood; compelling the municipal authorities to perform their statutory obligations for protecting the health of the community; compelling the industrial units to set-up effluent treatment plants; directing installation of air-pollution-controlling devices for preventing air pollution; directing closure of recalcitrant factories in order to save the community from the hazards of environmental pollution and various others.

The Public Interest Litigation (PIL) has given even the most ordinary man access to the Courts. Large numbers of cases under PIL have been made under social action groups, law professionals, journalists, social scientists and even the have-nots have got access to the court. The Courts have issued several landmark directives in Public Interest Litigation (PIL) on a variety of matters such as road safety, pollution, illegal structures in VIP zones, unpaid dues by former and serving legislators, nursery admissions, and admissions in institutions of higher learning. Lok Adalat, which are voluntary mediation agencies have given a new direction to the alternative dispute resolution in the judicial system in India. These would take cases pending in the lowest courts and attempt to secure a settlement. The free legal aid service which means that free legal aid would be given from the Supreme Court Legal Aid Committee to the less privileged (mentioned below) also has given access to the have-nots to seek justice against wrong done.

Many are of the opinion that the Judiciary must not be overly active and must stick to its constitutionally assigned functions. But the lack of governance in India and large scale corruption, misappropriations, absence of Lok Pal to heed to citizen's grievances, neglect of inclusive development and widening gap between the rich and the poor coupled with these are the environmental hazards and displacement of population due to mega projects and industrialization bids, have forced the Citizen's to take recourse to law and move the courts through PIL when they have found that the administration has become unresponsive and non-performing, and this has resulted in enlarging the field for judicial intervention

The Parliament must become active and relieve the Supreme Court of its legislative function. The sanctity of Indian Parliamentary Democracy must be restored by rebuilding the faith of the people of India on the Governmental system in India. There is no alternative to infusing greater accountability into political institutions such as the Legislature and the executive. Parliament must act to strengthen the grievance redressal systems at various levels. There is no doubt that the Courts are essentially meant for adjudication and certainly not for administration. Judicial Activism is no substitute for good governance.

Public Interest Litigation

Although the proceedings in the Supreme Court arise out of the judgments or orders made by the Subordinate Courts including the High Courts, but of late, the Supreme Court has started entertaining matters in which interest of the public at large is involved and the Court can be moved by any individual or group of persons either by filing a Writ Petition at the Filing Counter of the Court or by addressing a letter to the Chief Justice of India highlighting the question of public importance for invoking this jurisdiction. Such concept is popularly known as 'Public Interest Litigation'.

Two Justices of the Supreme Court, Justice V.R. Krishna Iyer and P.N. Bhagwati recognized the possibility of providing access to justice to the poor and the exploited people by relaxing the rules of locus standi. In a series of path-breaking pronouncements, for instance, *S.P. Gupta* v. *Union of India,* 1982, the Supreme Court of India, through public interest litigation, has granted access to persons inspired by public interest to invite judicial intervention against abuse of power or misuse of power or inaction of the Government. Justice P.N. Bhagwati in this case articulated the concept of PIL. He observed that "where a legal wrong or a legal injury is caused to a person or to a determinate class of persons by reason of violation of any constitutional or legal right or any burden is imposed in contravention of any constitutional or legal provision or without authority of law or any such legal wrong or legal injury or illegal burden is threatened and such person or determinate class of persons by reasons of poverty, helplessness or disability or socially or economically disadvantaged position unable to approach the court for relief, any member of public can maintain an application for an appropriate direction, order or writ in the High Court under Article 226 and in case any breach of fundamental rights of such persons or determinate class of persons, in this court under Article 32 seeking judicial redress for the legal wrong or legal injury caused to such person or determinate class of persons."

Not only was the requirement of *locus standi* (that a person, whose right is infringed alone can file a petition, has been considerably relaxed by the Supreme Court in its recent decisions) was widened along with it justiciability so as to include within judicial purview actions or inactions that were not considered to be capable of resolution through judicial process according to traditional notions of justiciability. The Supreme Court of India gave its verdict in different PIL cases for under-paid workers (*People's Union for Democratic Rights* v. *Union of India*, 1982), bonded labour (*Bandhua Mukti Morcha* v. *Union of India,* 1984), prisoners (*Sunil Batra* v. *Delhi Administration*, 1978), pavement dwellers (*Olga Tellis* v. *Bombay Municipal Corporation*, 1985), under-trial detenues (*Hussainara Khatoon* v. *State of Bihar*, 1979), inmates of protection homes (*Upendra Baxi* v. *State of U.P.,* 1983), victims of Bhopal gas disaster (*Union Carbide Corporation* v. *Union of India*, 1991) and may others. The first Reported case of PIL in 1979 focused on the inhuman conditions of prisons and under trial prisoners in the *Hussainara Khatoon* v. *State of Bihar*, 1979. Some pronouncements for ensuring gender justice have been in a landmark judgment of the Supreme Court in *Delhi Domestic Working Women's Forum* v. *Union of India*, (1995), where the Court issued guidelines for rehabilitation and compensation for the rape on working women. In *Vishaka* v. *State of Rajasthan and others* (1997), the Supreme Court has laid down exhaustive guidelines for preventing sexual harassment of working women in place of their work.

Other important Public Interest Litigations cases related to environment are Taj Pollution Matter (*M.C. Mehta* v. *Union of India* (UOI) & Ors. W.P. (C) No.13381/1984), Ganga Pollution Matter [Writ Petition (Civil) No. 3727/1985 (*M.C. Mehta* v. *UOI & Ors.*)], Vehicular Pollution in Delhi [Writ Petition (Civil) No.13029/1985 (*M.C. Mehta* v. *UOI & Ors.*)] and others.

In *Guruvayur Devaswom Managing Committee and Anr.* v. *C.K. Rajan and Ors,* J.T. 2003, the Supreme Court held "Public interest litigation has come to stay and its necessity cannot be overemphasized. The courts evolved a jurisprudence of compassion. Procedural propriety was to move over giving place to substantive concerns of the deprivation of rights. The rule of *locus standi* was diluted. The Court in place of disinterested and dispassionate adjudicator became active participant in the dispensation of justice." In essence, the PIL develops a new jurisprudence of the accountability of the State for Constitutional and legal violations adversely affecting the interests of the weaker elements in the community.

Position of the Supreme Court

The Supreme Court in India is the ultimate interpreter of the Constitution and the laws of the land. When the Supreme Court decides disputes between the Union and the States, it acts as a Federal Court. It should be noted that in the cases involving the violation of Fundamental Rights, the Supreme Court enjoys both the original and appellate jurisdiction, which means such cases can be either directly initiated at the Supreme Court or may be brought to it through the appeal against the order of the High Court. The Supreme Court has also a very wide appellate jurisdiction over all Courts and Tribunals in India in as much as it may, in its discretion, grant special leave to appeal under Article 136 of the Constitution from any judgment, decree, determination, sentence or order in any cause or matter passed or made by any Court or Tribunal in the territory of India. The Supreme Court is also empowered to give advisory opinions on issues referred to it by the President. It also functions as a court of record and supervises every High Court. As we have seen the 42nd Amendment Act, 1976 restricted the power of judicial review which has been however, restored by the 44th Amendment Act of 1978.

Legal Aid

Under the **Legal Services Authorities Act, 1987**, a member of Scheduled Caste or Scheduled Tribes; a person whose annual income is not more than ₹50,000/- for cases before Supreme Court and ₹25,000/- in other Courts; a person victim of trafficking in human beings or beggar; disabled, including mentally disabled; a woman or child; a victim of mass disaster, ethnic violence, caste atrocities, flood, drought, earthquake, industrial disaster and other cases of undeserved want; an industrial workman; a person in custody including protective custody; a person facing charge which might result in his imprisonment; a person unable to engage a lawyer and secure legal services on account of reasons such as poverty and indigence can get free legal aid from the Supreme Court Legal Aid Committee. The aid so granted by the Committee includes cost of preparation of the matter and all applications connected therewith, in addition to providing an advocate for preparing and arguing the case. The Committee after ascertaining the eligibility of the person provides necessary legal aid to him/her.

Amicus Curiae

In case a party is unrepresented who may be in jail or accused in any other criminal matter or in case or civil matters too, then if he files a petition, then an Advocate is appointed as *amicus curiae* by the Court to defend and argue the case of the accused. The Court can also appoint *amicus curiae* in any matter of general public importance or in which the interest of the public at large is involved.

Concept of Lok Adalats

The concept of *Lok Adalat* (Peoples' Court) comprises a new direction in Indian jurisprudence as it has introduced the concept of the ADR (Alternate Dispute Resolution) system in India. **Legal Services Authorities Act, 1987** contains provisions to constitute legal services authorities to provide free and competent legal services to the weaker sections of the society to ensure that opportunities for securing justice are not denied to any citizen by reason of economic or other disabilities, and to organize *Lok Adalats* to secure that the operation of the legal system promotes justice on a basis of equal opportunity.

The Legal Services Authorities Act, 1987 provides statutory status to the legal aid movement, and it also provides for setting up of Legal Services Authorities at the Central, State and District levels. These authorities will have their own funds. Further, *Lok Adalats* which are at present informal agencies will acquire statutory status. Every award of *Lok Adalats* shall be deemed to be a decree of a civil court or order of a Tribunal and shall be final and binding on the parties to the dispute. It also provides that in respect of cases decided at a *Lok Adalat*, the court fee paid by the parties will be refunded.

Jurisdiction of Lok Adalat

According to the Act of 1987, a *Lok Adalat* shall have jurisdiction to determine and to arrive at a compromise or settlement between the parties to a dispute in respect of:

1. any case pending before; or
2. any matter which is falling within the jurisdiction of, and is not brought before, any court for which the *Lok Adalat* is organised

The *Lok Adalat* can compromise and settle even criminal cases, which are compoundable under the relevant laws.

Organization of Lok Adalat

The State Authority and District Authority, Supreme Court Legal Services Committee, High Court Legal Services Committee and Taluk Legal Services Committee (mentioned in Section 19 of the Act) can organize *Lok Adalat* at such intervals and places as may be deemed fit. Every *Lok Adalat* so organized shall consist of: (a) Serving or retired judicial officers, (b) other persons, as may be specified.

The experience and qualification of "other persons" in a *Lok Adalat* conducted by Supreme Court Legal Services Committee shall be prescribed by the Central Government in consultation with the Chief Justice of India. At present, Rule 13 of the National Legal Services Authorities Rules, 1995 prescribes such experience and qualifications as:

1. A member of the legal profession; or
2. A person of repute who is specially interested in the implementation of the Legal Services Schemes and Programmes; or
3. An eminent social worker who is engaged in the upliftment of weaker sections of people, including Scheduled Castes, Scheduled Tribes, women, children, rural and urban labour.

The experience and qualification of other persons mentioned in Clause (b) shall be prescribed by the State Government in consultation with the Chief Justice of High Court.

Powers of Lok Adalat

1. The *Lok Adalat* shall have the powers of a civil court under the Code of Civil Procedure, 1908, while trying a suit, in respect of the following matters:
   (a) Power to summon and enforce the attendance of any witness and to examine him/her on oath
   (b) Power to enforce the discovery and production of any document
   (c) Power to receive evidence on affidavits
   (d) Power for requisitioning of any public record or document or copy thereof or from any court
   (e) Such other matters as may be prescribed
2. Every *Lok Adalat* shall have the power to specify its own procedure for the determination of any dispute coming before it.
3. All proceedings before a *Lok Adalat* shall be deemed to be judicial proceedings within the meaning of Sections 193, 219 and 228 of IPC
4. Every *Lok Adalat* shall be deemed to be a Civil Court for the purpose of Sec 195 and Chapter XXVI of Cr.P.C.

Passing of the Award

1. Every award of *Lok Adalat* shall be deemed to be a decree of a civil court.
2. Every award shall be signed by all the parties to the dispute and the panel constituting the *Lok Adalat*.
3. Every award shall form part of the judicial records.
4. Every award shall be categorical and lucid.
5. Every award shall be in the regional language or in English.
6. A certified copy of the award will be given free of cost, to all the parties.
7. Every award made by *Lok Adalat* shall be final and binding on all the parties to the dispute, and no appeal shall lie to any court against the award.
8. If a pending case is settled at *Lok Adalat*, any court fee already paid will be refunded as provided by the Court Fees Act, 1870.

Permanent Lok Adalat (PLA)

The Central or State Authorities may establish by notification, Permanent *Lok Adalat* at any place, for determining issues in connection to Public Utility services. It consists of a person as a Chairman who is or has been a District Judge or Additional District Judge or has held judicial office higher in rank than that of a District Judge. There will be two more members who must have adequate experience in Public Utility Service to be nominated by Central Government on the recommendation of central authority and by the State Government on the recommendation of the State Authority. PLA have the same powers that are vested on the *lok adalat*, mentioned under Section 22(1) of the Legal Services Authorities Act, 1987.

Fast Track Courts

There are 1,734 (according to the recommendations of the Eleventh Finance Commission) such courts in the country, dealing mainly with cases that are over five years old. Trial courts have the largest number of pending cases, of over 2.5 crore, followed by 1.5 lakh cases in the High Courts and 50,000 in the Supreme Court. The average time taken to dispose of cases in trial courts is over 10 years.

Five fast-track courts were envisaged to be set up in every district to clear the backlog. The scheme functions under the respective High Courts, and the infrastructure is provided by the State Governments. The Supreme Court, acting on a petition filed by Brij Mohan Lal, (2005), has been monitoring the functioning of such courts since they were set up. The Supreme Court expressed unhappiness over the fact that several states had still not created the sanctioned number of such courts. The Court also asked the Centre to make fresh budgetary allocations to expedite the process.

Most of these Fast Track Courts were created under a centrally-funded scheme on 1 April 2001, and were expected to lapse within five years. They have since been given repeated extensions. In 2005, the Supreme Court directed the Government to continue the Fast Track Courts, and accordingly, the Government gave an extension to 1562 Fast Track Courts operational at that time for another five years, i.e., 2010. The Supreme Court has ruled in 2010 again that Fast Track Courts, set up to ease the load of pending cases in subordinate courts, will continue to function in all States until further orders. A bench headed by Chief Justice of India K.G. Balakrishnan gave this order.

As of 2010, West Bengal, has so far only created 120 of the 151 courts sanctioned, whereas in Assam, all 20 Fast Track Courts have started functioning, as also in other North-Eastern States and other States are yet to create the sanctioned number of courts like Gujarat (sanctioned 166, created 65), Andhra Pradesh (sanctioned 108, created 71), Orissa (sanctioned 72, created 44), Uttarakhand (sanctioned 36, created 26), Maharashtra (sanctioned 187, created 115), Madhya Pradesh (sanctioned 85, created 68) and Delhi (sanctioned 20, created 8).

HIGH COURTS OF STATES

Article 214 states **that there shall be a High Court for each State**. The High Court stands at the top of a State's judicial administrative set up. The Parliament under Article 231 may by law establish a common High Court for two or more States and a Union Territory. There are 21 High Courts in the country, some having jurisdiction over more than one State. Among the Union Territories Delhi alone has a High Court of its own. Other six union territories come under the jurisdiction of different State High Courts.

Composition of High Court

Under Article 216, every High Court shall consist of a Chief Justice and such other Judges as the President may, from time-to-time, appoint. The Chief Justice of a High Court is appointed by the President in consultation with the Chief Justice of India and the Governor of the State (Article 217).

Appointment of Judges

Article 217 lays down the procedure of appointment of the Judges. It states that every **Judge of a High Court shall be appointed by the President by warrant under his hand and seal after consultation with the Chief Justice of India, the Governor of the State, and, in the case of appointment of a Judge other than the Chief Justice of a High Court.** They hold office until the age of 62 years and are removable in the same manner as a Judge of the Supreme Court. Article 220 restricts any persons who have held office as a permanent Judge of a High Court to plead or Act in any Court or before any authority in India except the Supreme Court and the other High Courts.

Qualifications

To be eligible for appointment as a Judge one must be a citizen of India, and has held a judicial office in India for ten years or must have practised as an Advocate of a High Court or two or more such Courts in succession for a similar period [Article 217(2)].

Tenure and Removal

The Judges shall hold Office until they attain the age of 62 and in case of additional or acting Judges as provided under Article 224, the age specified is 62 years for retirement. However, a Judge may by writing under his hand addressed to the President, resign his office. A Judge can only be removed from his office by the President in the manner as mentioned above with respect to removal of Judges of Supreme Court, passing of impeachment motion under Article 124(4).

The office of a Judge shall be vacated by his being appointed by the President to be a Judge of the Supreme Court or by his being transferred by the President to any other High Court within the territory of India. [Article 217(1)(c)]

Oath of Affirmation

Every person to be appointed as a Judge of a High Court shall before he enters upon his Office take an oath of affirmation before the Governor of the State, or some person appointed by the Governor on his behalf, according to the form set out for the purpose in the Third Schedule.

"I, name, having been appointed Chief Justice (or A Judge) of the High Court at (or of) .... do swear in the name of God/solemnly affirm that I will bear true faith and allegiance to the Constitution of India as by law established, that I will uphold the sovereignty and integrity of India, that I will duly and faithfully and to the best of my ability, knowledge and judgment perform the duties of my office without fear or favour, affection or ill-will and that I will uphold the Constitution and the laws."

—Constitution of India, Third Schedule, Part VIII

Salaries and Allowances

The Judges of the Supreme Court and the Chief Justices of the High Courts draw a salary of ₹2,50,000 per month, and allowances thereon whilst the Judges of the High Court will draw a salary of ₹2,25,000 per month and allowances. The salaries and pension shall not be varied by Parliament to his disadvantage after his appointment (Article 221) except under a Proclamation of Financial Emergency [Article 360(4)(b)].

Transfer of Judges

Article 222 contains provisions for transfer of Judges from one High Court to another. It states that the President may after consultation with the Chief Justice of India, transfer a Judge from one High Court to any other Court.

Appointment of Acting Chief Justice

According to Article 223 when the office of the Chief Justice of a High Court is vacant or when any such Chief Justice is, by reason of absence or otherwise, unable to perform the duties of his office, the duties of the office shall be performed by a Judge of the Court as the President may appoint.

Appointment of Additional and Acting Judges

Under Article 224, if due to temporary increase in the business of the High Court or there are huge number of cases pending, then the President may increase the number of Judges if he finds that there is a paucity of Judges to handle the existing load of cases. The President may appoint duly qualified persons to be additional Judges of the Court for such period not exceeding two years as he may specify.

When any Judge of a High Court other than the Chief Justice is by reason of absence or for any other reason unable to perform the duties of his office or is appointed to Act temporarily as Chief Justice, the President may appoint a duly qualified person to Act as a Judge of that Court until the permanent Judge resumes his duty. However, no person appointed as additional or acting Judge of a High Court shall hold office after attaining 62 years of age.

Appointment of Retired Judges

The Chief Justice under Article 224A may at any time with the consent of the President request any person who has held the office of Judge of that Court or of any other High Court to sit and act as a Judge of the High Court for that State. While this person is sitting and acting, he will be entitled to such allowances as the President may by order determine and have all the jurisdiction powers and privileges of a Judge of the High Court which he would not have otherwise enjoyed.

Independence of the Judges of High Court

The Constitution provides provisions for ensuring independence of the Judges of the High Court just like the Judges of the Supreme Court. They can be summarized as follows:

1. The procedure for removal of the Judges of the High Court which requires an address of each House of Parliament (passed by a special majority) to the President on the ground of misbehaviour or incapacity.
2. The salaries and allowances of the Judges are charged from the Consolidated Fund of the State [Article 229(3)]
3. The salaries and pension shall not be varied by Parliament to his disadvantage after his appointment (Article 221) except under a Proclamation of Financial Emergency [Article 360(4)(b)]
4. After retirement a permanent Judge of High Court shall not plead or act in a Court or before any authority in India, except the Supreme Court and a High Court other than the High Court in which he had held his office (Article 220).

However, in many respects the Union Government exerts control over the High Courts. They are summed up as follows:

1. Appointment under Article 217, transfer under Article 222 from one High Court to another and removal and determination of dispute as to age [Article 217(3)) of the Judges of the High Court.
2. The Constitution and organization of High Courts and the power to establish a common High Court for two or more states and to extend the jurisdiction of High Court to or to exclude its jurisdiction from a Union Territory are all the exclusive powers of the Union Parliament.

Territorial Jurisdiction of High Courts

Except where Parliament establishes a common High Court for two or more States under Article 231 or extends jurisdiction of a High Court to a Union Territory, the jurisdiction of the High Court of a State is co-terminus with the territorial limits of the State. Table 13.1 gives an idea of jurisdiction and seats of High Courts in India.

The Calcutta High Court is the oldest High Court in India. It was established on 1st July 1862, under the High Court's Act, 1861. The High Court building was designed by Mr. Walter Granville, Government Architect, on the model of the *Stadt-Haus* or Cloth Hall at Ypres, in Belgium.

Jurisdiction of High Courts

[1] Original Jurisdiction

The Courts of Calcutta, Bombay and Madras has an original jurisdiction both civil and criminal over cases arising within the respective Presidency towns. They are authorized to hear civil cases of more than ₹2000 and in criminal cases (referred to them by the Presidency Magistrates and other cases of revenue). The original criminal jurisdiction of the High Courts has been completely taken away by the Criminal Procedure Code, 1973. The Other High Courts have limited original jurisdiction in cases relating to admiralty, will, divorce, marriage, company laws and contempt of Court.

[2] Jurisdiction to Issue Writs

The Constitution of India conferred **original writ jurisdiction** under Article 226 of the Constitution of India upon the High Court. No other Court subordinate to High Court has got the power to issue such prerogative writs. Under Article 226 of the Constitution of India, the High Court has got the power, throughout the territories in relation to which it exercises its jurisdiction, to issue to any person or authority, including in appropriate cases, any Government, within those territories, directions, orders or writs including writs in the nature of

Table 13.1 Jurisdiction and Seat of High Courts

S. No	*Name*	*Year*	*Territorial establishment jurisdiction*	*Seat*
1.	Allahabad	1866	Uttar Pradesh	Allahabad (Bench at Lucknow)
2.	Andhra Pradesh	1956	Andhra Pradesh	Hyderabad
3.	Bombay	1862	Maharashtra, Goa, Dadra and Nagar Haveli and Daman and Diu	Bombay (Benches at Nagpur, Panaji and Aurangabad)
4.	Calcutta	1862	West Bengal	Calcutta (Circuit Bench at Port Blair)
5.	Delhi	1966	Delhi	Delhi
6.	Guwahati	1948	Assam, Manipur, Meghalaya, Nagaland, Tripura, Mizoram and Arunachal Pradesh	Guwahati (Benches at Kohima, Aizwal & Imphal. Circuit Bench at Agartala & Shillong)
7.	Gujarat	1960	Gujarat	Ahmedabad
8.	Himachal Pradesh	1971	Himachal Pradesh	Shimla
9.	Jammu & Kashmir	1928	Jammu & Kashmir	Srinagar & Jammu
10.	Karnataka	1884	Karnataka	Bangalore
11.	Kerala	1958	Kerala & Lakshadweep	Ernakulam
12.	Madhya Pradesh	1956	Madhya Pradesh	Jabalpur (Benches at Gwalior and Indore)
13.	Madras	1862	Tamil Nadu & Pondicherry	Madras
14.	Orissa	1948	Orissa	Cuttack
15.	Patna	1916	Bihar	Patna
16.	Punjab & Haryana	1975	Punjab, Haryana & Chandigarh	Chandigarh
17.	Rajasthan	1949	Rajasthan	Jodhpur (Bench at Jaipur)
18.	Sikkim	1975	Sikkim	Gangtok
19.	Chhattisgarh	2000	Chhattisgarh	Bilaspur (Chhattisgarh)
20.	Jharkhand	2000	Jharkhand	Ranchi
21.	Uttarakhand	2000	Uttarakhand	Nainital

habeas corpus, mandamus, prohibition, quo warranto and *certiorari* or any of them for the enforcement of fundamental rights conferred by Part III of the Constitution and for any other purpose. In fact, the power of the High Court to issue writs is larger than that of the Supreme Court as Supreme Court can issue writs under Article 32 of the Constitution of India in cases where the fundamental rights of a person have been violated, whereas the High Court can issue writs in respect of the violation of fundamental rights or in respect of cases where the legal rights of the persons have been jeopardized. Article 226 reads as:

1. Notwithstanding anything in Article 325, every High Court shall have powers, throughout the territories in relation to which it exercises jurisdiction, to issue to any person or authority, including in appropriate cases, any Government, within those territories directions, orders or writs, including (writs in the nature of, *habeas corpus, mandamus, prohibition, quo warranto* and *certiorari*, or any of them, for the enforcement of any of the rights conferred by Part III and for any other purpose.)
2. The power conferred by Clause (1) (to issue directions, orders or writs to any Government, authority or person) may also be exercised by any High Court exercising jurisdiction in relation to the territories within which the cause of action, wholly or in part, arises for the exercise of such power, notwithstanding that the seat of such Government or authority or the residence of such person is not within those territories.
3. Where any party against whom an *interim* order, whether by way of injunction or stay or in any other manner, is made on, or in any proceedings relating to, a petition under Clause (1), without—
   (a) furnishing to such party copies of such petition and all documents in support of the plea for such interim order; and
   (b) giving such party an opportunity of being heard, makes an application to the High Court for the vacation of such order and makes an application to the High Court for the vacation of such order and furnishes a copy of such application to the party in whose favour such order has been made or the counsel of such party, the High Court shall dispose of the application within a period of two weeks from the date on which it is received or from the date on which the copy of such application is so furnished, whichever is later, or where the High Court is closed on the last day of that period, before the expiry of the next day afterwards on which the High Court is open; and if the application is not so disposed of, the interim order shall, on the expiry of that period, or, as the case may be, the expiry of the said next day, stand vacated.
4. The power conferred on a High Court by this article shall not be in derogation of the power conferred on the Supreme Court by Clause (2) of Article 32.

Appellate Jurisdiction

The Appellate Jurisdiction of the High Court extends to both Civil and Criminal cases.

A. On the Civil side and Appeal can be either a First Appeal or a Second appeal.

   [1] Appeal from the decisions of the District Judges and from those of subordinate Judges in cases of a higher value lie direct to the High Court on questions of fact as well as law.

   [2] Under various Central and State enactments, the High Court has been conferred with appellate as well as revisional jurisdiction. An appeal when it is a creation of the statute can be filed by a person only in case the law provides for the same. No one has got a right to file an appeal. As per Section 100 of the Code of Civil Procedure, an aggrieved party can file an appeal to the High Court from every decree passed in appeal by any court subordinate to the High Court, if the High Court is satisfied that **the case involves a substantial question of law.**

Even under the fiscal statutes, such as Income-tax Act, the High Court exercises appellate jurisdiction. Section 260A of the Income-Tax Act, 1961 confers the right of an appeal against any order passed in appeal by the Income Tax Appellate Tribunal, if the High Court is satisfied that the case involves a substantial question of Law.

Further, under Section 115 of the Code of Civil Procedure, the High Court may call for the record of any case, which has been decided by any court subordinate to the High Court and in which no appeal lies thereto, if it appears to the High Court that the subordinate court has exercised a jurisdiction not vested in it by law or has failed to exercise the jurisdiction so vested or has acted in the exercise of its jurisdiction illegally or with material irregularity.

The High Court can also withdraw any suit, appeal or other proceeding pending in any Court subordinate to it and try or dispose of the same or transfer the same for trial or disposal to any court subordinate to it and competent to try or dispose of the same or re-transfer the same for trial or disposal to the court from which it was withdrawn.

B. On the Criminal side, the Appellate Jurisdiction of the High Court consist of appeals from:

   [1] A Sessions Judge or an Additional Sessions Judge where the sentence of imprisonment, exceeding 7 years.

   [2] An Assistant Sessions Judge, Metropolitan Magistrate or other Judicial Magistrates in certain specified cases other than 'petty' cases.

Power of Certification

The Constitution under Article 132 regarding Appellate Jurisdiction of the Supreme Court specifies that any appeal can go to the Supreme Court only after the High Court certifies under Article 134A that the case involves a substantial question of law as to the interpretation of this Constitution.

Court of Record

The High Court is a Court of Record and has power to punish for its contempt. The 42nd Amendment Act of 1976 curtailed the jurisdiction of the High Courts in various spheres. However, the 44th Amendment Act of 1979 restored the original jurisdiction and position of the High Courts.

Power of Superintendence: Control over Subordinate Courts

The High Court also exercises superintendence over all **subordinate Courts** situated within its jurisdiction by virtue of Article 227 of the Constitution. Article 227 reads as:

(1) Every High Court shall have superintendence over all courts and tribunals throughout the territories in relation to which it exercises jurisdiction.

(2) Without prejudice to the generally of the foregoing provisions, the High Court may
   (a) call for returns from such courts;
   (b) make and issue general rules and prescribe forms for regulating the practice and proceedings of such courts; and
   (c) prescribe forms in which books, entries and accounts shall be kept by the officers of any such courts.

(3) The High Court may also settle tables of fees to be allowed to the sheriff and all clerks and officers of such courts and to attorneys, advocates and pleaders practising therein.

    Provided that any rules made, forms prescribed or tables settled under Clause (2) or Clause (3) shall not be inconsistent with the provision of any law for the time being in force, and shall require the previous approval of the Governance.

(4) Nothing in this article shall be deemed to confer on a High Court powers of superintendence over any court or tribunal constituted by or under any law relating to the armed forces.

The High Court supervises the working of all subordinate Courts and frames rules and regulations for the transaction of business. It can examine the records of subordinate Courts. The High Court may call for returns from such Courts, make and issue general rules and prescribe forms for regulating the practice and proceedings of such courts and prescribe forms in which books, entries and accounts shall be kept by the officers of any such courts. There are two types of law courts in every district—Civil and Criminal Courts. Besides the District Court, there are courts of sub-Judges, munsiff courts and courts of small causes. Below the Session Courts are the courts of First Class Magistrates. In metropolitan cities like Kolkata, Chennai, Mumbai and Delhi, these Magistrates are known as metropolitan Magistrates. Apart from this, there are courts of Second Class and Third Class Magistrates also. They function under the superintendence and control of the High Court of that particular State.

Jurisdiction over Administrative Tribunals

Administrative Tribunals which are statutory bodies and which have quasi-judicial functions regarding settlement of disputes in connection with the administration of laws either because the ordinary Courts are already overburdened to take up these new matters or disputes are of such a technical nature that they can be decided only by experts with working knowledge on the provisions of the Act under which it arises. Such Tribunals whose decisions are binding upon the disputing parties must be kept under the control or supervision of some authority and the High Courts exercise jurisdiction over these Tribunals under Articles 32, 226 (issuing writs) and Article 227 (general power of superintendence over all Tribunals).

Position of High Court

The High Court is also the protector of the fundamental rights guaranteed by the Constitution of India. High Courts have the power to issue to any person within its jurisdiction directions, orders, or writs including writs which are in the nature of *habeas corpus*, *mandamus*, *prohibition*, *quo warranto* and *certiorari* for enforcement of Fundamental Rights and for any other purpose. High Court also has the powers of superintendence over all subordinate Courts and Administrative Tribunals except Military Tribunals within its jurisdiction. The High Courts of India exercises original Jurisdiction and Appellate Jurisdiction. Under its Appellate Jurisdiction, the High Court is the highest court of appeal in respect of any criminal or civil cases of the State. An appeal can only go to the Supreme Court when the High Court certifies it under Article 134A. The Union Parliament has been empowered to either enlarge or restrict the jurisdiction of the High Court. The High Court has the authority of making laws regarding the appointment of its own officials and other internal affairs. There can be a common High Court for two or more State or for two or more States and a Union Territory as specified by a law of the Parliament.

EXERCISES

I. Short Answer Questions: **(100 words)**

1. Write a note on composition of Supreme Court of India.
2. Briefly discuss the Independence of Indian Judiciary.
3. State the Original Jurisdiction of Supreme Court.
4. Discuss briefly the Appellate Jurisdiction of Supreme Court.
5. State the Advisory Jurisdiction of Supreme Court.
6. Give the essence of Judicial Review in India.
7. Provide an idea about *Lok Adalats* in India.
8. Examine the process of removal of Supreme Court and High Court Judges.

II. Long Answer Questions: **(1200 words)**

9. Discuss the composition, and various jurisdictions of the Supreme Court of India.
10. Examine the 'original', 'appellate' and 'advisory' jurisdictions of the Supreme Court of India.
11. Analyze the power of the Supreme Court regarding the protection of fundamental rights of the people of India.
12. Elucidate Supreme Court's power of Judicial Review. Do you think that this has given rise to Judicial Activism? Argue.
13. Discuss the concept of Public Interest Litigation in India. Do you think that PIL has empowered the people at large? Argue.
14. In the light of Legal Services Authorities Act, 1987, discuss the powers and functions of *Lok Adalat.*
15. Examine the jurisdictions of High Courts of States in India.
16. Discuss the composition and functions of High Courts of States in India.
17. Discuss the position of High Courts in the light of jurisdictions and other powers and functions of High Courts.

REFERENCES

Bakshi, P.M., *The Constitution of India* (with selective comments), Universal Law Publishing, Delhi, 2000.

Basu, Durga Das, *Introduction to the Constitution of India*, Prentice-Hall of India, New Delhi, 1992.

Dutta, Satyabrata, *Constitution Review: Venkatachaliah Commission,* Progressive Publishers, Kolkata, 2004.

Government of India, *Constitution of India.*

Jain, M.P., *Indian Constitutional Law*, Wadhwa & Company, Nagpur, 1999.

Pylee, M.V., *India's Constitution*, S. Chand & Company, New Delhi, 1994.

Siwach, J.R., *Dynamics of Indian Government and Politics*, Sterling Publishers, New Delhi, 1985.

Legal Services Authorities Act, 1987.

http://www.supremecourtofindia.nic.in/jurisdiction.htm, Official Website of the Supreme Court of India.

Fast Track Courts, *The Telegraph*, March 4, 2010, Kolkata, http://www.telegraphindia.com/1100304/jsp/nation/story_12175598.jsp

Bandhua Mukti Morcha v. *Union of India*, AIR 1984 SC 802.

Bihar v. *India*, AIR 1970 SC 1446.

Common Cause v. *Union of India*, AIR 1996 SC 3538.

Delhi Domestic Working Women's Forum v. *Union of India* (1995) 1 SCC 14.

Golaknath v. *State of Punjab* (1967) 2 SCR 762: AIR 1967 SC.

Guruvayur Devaswom Managing Committee and Anr. v. *C.K. Rajan and Ors.*, J.T. 2003 (7) S.C. 312.

Hussainara Khatoon v. *State of Bihar*, AIR 1979 SC 1360.

Keshavananda Bharati v. *State of Kerala*, AIR 1973 SC 1461.

Minerva Mills Ltd. v. *Union of India* (1980) 3 SCC 625.

Olga Tellis v. Bombay Municipal Corporation (1985) 3 SCC 545.

People's Union for Democratic Rights v. *Union of India*, AIR 1982 SC 1473.

State of West Bengal v. *Union of India*, AIR 1963 SC 1241.

S.P. Gupta v. *Union of India*, AIR 1982 SC 149.

Sunil Batra v. *Delhi Administration*, AIR 1978 SC 1675.

Upendra Baxi v. *State of U.P.* (1983) 2 SCC 308 (1986) 4 SCC 106.

Union Carbide Corporation v. *Union of India* (1991) 4 SCC 584.

Vineet Narain v. *Union of India*, AIR 1996 SC 3386.

Vishaka v. *State of Rajasthan and others* (1997) 6 SCC 241, AIR 1997 SC3011, (1998) BHRC 261, (1997) 3 LRC 361, (1997) 2 CHRLD 202.

14

Amendment of the Constitution

INTRODUCTION

The Indian Constitution was formally inaugurated on 26 January 1950. It has travelled a long course and has faced many challenges emanating from the implementation/interpretation of the provisions of the Constitution. Time is changing too fast especially in the Post-1990s with the country opening up for liberalization. This makes it necessary to take up amendment/review of certain clauses/provisions of the Constitution. Till date, more than 90 amendments have been made to the Constitution of India. A Constitution Review Committee under the Chairmanship of Former Chief Justice of India was constituted in 2000, to review the working of the Constitution and make recommendations.

PROCEDURE OF AMENDMENT

PART XX of the Indian Constitution contains provisions relating to the amendment of the Constitution. Specifically Article 368 gives us the procedure of amendment. According to Article **368 the Parliament of India has the power to amend the Constitution and it states:**

1. Notwithstanding anything in this Constitution, Parliament may in exercise of its constituent power amend by way of addition, variation or repeal any provision of this Constitution in accordance with the procedure laid down in this Article.
2. An amendment of this Constitution may be initiated only by the introduction of a Bill for the purpose in either House of Parliament, and when the Bill is passed in each House by a majority of the total membership of that House and by a majority of not less than two-thirds

of the members of that House present and voting, it shall be presented to the President who shall give his assent to the Bill and thereupon the Constitution shall stand amended in accordance with the terms of the Bill:

Provided that if such amendment seeks to make any change in—

(a) Article 54, Article 55, Article 73, Article 162 or Article 241, or
(b) Chapter IV of Part V, Chapter V of Part VI, or Chapter I of Part XI, or
(c) any of the lists in the Seventh Schedule, or
(d) the representation of States in Parliament, or
(e) the provisions of this Article

the amendment shall also require to be ratified by the Legislatures of not less than one-half of the States by resolutions to that effect passed by those Legislatures before the Bill making provision for such amendment is presented to the President for assent.

3. Nothing in Article 13 shall apply to any amendment made under this Article.

*4. No amendment of this Constitution (including the provisions of Part III) made or purporting to have been made under this Article whether before or after the commencement of Section 55 of the Constitution (Forty-second Amendment) Act, 1976] shall be called in question in any Court on any ground.

5. For the removal of doubts, it is hereby declared that there shall be no limitation whatever on the Constituent power of Parliament to amend by way of addition, variation or repeal the provisions of this Constitution under this Article.

From the above provisions it can be discerned that the Union Parliament is the only body which can move any amendment of the Indian Constitution. Some provisions of the Constitution like those dealing with citizenship, delimitation of constituencies, privileges of Members of Parliament, creation or abolition of an Upper Chamber in a State, Official Language of India, fixing of salaries and allowances of Members of Parliament and the like, can be amended in the ordinary process of law by the Union Parliament (by simple majority). For the other provisions, two specific methods of amending the Constitution have been mentioned under Article 368. **Firstly**, an amendment Bill has to be passed by each of the two Houses by a majority of its total membership and by a two-thirds majority of members present and voting. For this, the consent of the

* [Clauses (4) and (5) were ins. "in article 368 by s. 55 of the Constitution (Forty-second Amendment) Act, 1976. This section has been declared invalid by the Supreme Court in *Minerva Mills Ltd. and Others* v. *Union of India and Others* (1980) 2 S.C.C. 591.]

States of the Indian Union are required. **Secondly**, some key features of the Constitution as mentioned under Article 368 can be amended when the Bill is passed by both the Houses by a majority of the total membership and a two-third majority members present and voting in each House. However, in such cases, the amendment Bills passed by the Union Parliament can only become effective after they secure ratification from at least half of the several State Legislatures and assent of the President. By the 24th Amendment Act, 1971, the Presidential assent has become obligatory as the President's power to veto has been curtailed by inserting the words '*shall* give his assent' in Clause (2) of Article 368.

Therefore, though there is an element of flexibility in the process of amendment of the Indian Constitution, but in most part it is a rigid method and difficult to achieve if no single majority party is in power. This was seen in the recent Lokpal Bill case during the Winter Session of the Year 2011 when it was passed in the Lok Sabha by a minimum majority, but a Constitutional Amendment making it a Constitutional Body like the Election Commission was defeated in Lok Sabha.

AMENDMENT AND THE BASIC STRUCTURE DOCTRINE

As discussed in Chapter 3, we have seen how several cases have come up before the Supreme Court regarding the Power of the Parliament to amend the *Basic Structure* of the Indian Constitution as early as 1951. It was for the first time that in the backdrop of the Government enacting various laws in several States with the aim of reforming land ownership and tenancy structures that there was a necessity to amend the Constitution (**The First and Fourth amendments** 1951 and 1955 respectively). The First Amendment, 1951 amended inter alia Article 31 pertaining to Right to Property and also inserted the *Ninth Schedule* pertaining to acquisition of private property and compensation payable for such acquisition. The main purpose of this amendment was that such laws cannot be challenged in a Court of law on the ground that they violated the Fundamental Rights of citizens, i.e., to remove the Fundamental Rights from the purview of judicial review. An analysis of the Ninth Schedule would reveal the existence of several laws passed by State Legislatures with the aim of regulating the size of land holdings and abolishing various tenancy systems. The Fourth Amendment, 1955 further amended **Article 31 and 31-A** (Right to Property) and also amended the *Ninth Schedule*.

In 1952, *Shankari Prasad Singh Deo* v. *Union of India* and in 1955, *Sajjan Singh* v. *Rajasthan*, the Supreme Court upheld the power of Parliament to amend any part of the Constitution including that which affects the Fundamental Rights of citizens which could be done just by a majority party in the Parliament. In the *Golaknath* v. *State of Punjab* case, 1967, the Apex Court reversed it earlier position taken in the above Cases. The Supreme Court observed that the Fundamental Rights included under Part III of the Constitution cannot by very nature be subject to the process of amendment provided under Article 368. It also observed that the amending power and legislative powers of Parliament were essentially the same. Therefore, any amendment of the Constitution must be deemed law as understood in **Article 13(2)** which states that "The State shall not make any law which takes away or abridges the rights conferred by this Part and any law made in contravention of this clause shall, to the extent of the contravention, be void".

The Supreme Court recognized **Basic Structure** concept for the first time in the historic *Keshavananda Bharati* (1973) case. In this case the validity of the Twenty-fourth Amendment Act (1971) was challenged. The Twenty-fourth Amendment Act enlarged the scope of the Parliament by empowering it to make changes in Part III of the Constitution—the Fundamental Rights. This case which is popularly known as the **Fundamental Rights case**, the court by majority overruled the verdict of the *Golaknath Case* which denied the Parliament the power to amend Fundamental Rights of the citizens. The majority in this case upheld the validity of the Twenty-fourth amendment. The Apex Court upheld that it is competent for the Parliament to amend Fundamental Rights under Article 368 which does not make any exception in favour of Fundamental Rights and a Constitution Amendment Act passed by Parliament is not 'law' within the meaning of Article 13(4) ["Nothing in this article, shall apply to any amendment made under Article 368"]. The Supreme Court, however, declared that Article 368 did not enable Parliament to alter the *basic structure* or *framework of the Constitution* and Parliament could not use its amending powers under Article 368 to 'damage', 'emasculate', 'destroy', 'abrogate', 'change' or 'alter' the 'basic structure' or framework of the Constitution. This decision is not just a landmark in the evolution of Constitutional law, but a turning point in Constitutional history.

Soon after the declaration of National Emergency, the Congress at the centre constituted a committee under the Chairmanship of Swaran Singh to study the question of amending the Constitution in the light of past experiences/ verdicts of the Apex Court. Based on its recommendations, the Government incorporated several changes to the Constitution through the **Forty-second Amendment** (passed in 1976 and came into effect on January 3, 1977). Among other things the amendment:

(a) gave the Directive Principles of State Policy precedence over the Fundamental Rights contained in **Article 14** (Right to Equality before Directive Principles of State Policy), Article 19 (various freedoms like freedom of speech and expression, right to assemble peacefully, right to form associations and Unions, right to move about and reside freely in any part of the country and the right to pursue any trade or profession) and **Article 21** (Right to Life and Personal Liberty). **Article 31C** was amended to prohibit any challenge to laws made under any of the directive Principles of State Policy;

(b) laid down that amendments to the Constitution made in the past or those likely to be made in future could not be questioned in any court on any ground;

(c) removed all amendments to Fundamental Rights from the scope of judicial review and

(d) removed all limits on Parliament's power to amend the Constitution under Article 368.

With the Janata Government in power in the post-emergency phase, the Forty-Third (1978) and Forty-Fourth Amendment (1979) were passed which restored the power of judicial review over all laws and amendments along with the deletion of the Right to Property from the list of Fundamental Rights. With this it was thought that there would be an end to the conflict between Fundamental Rights and Directive Principles. The Forty-second Amendment was again challenged before the Supreme Court, but in the *Minerva Mills Case* (1980) the Supreme Court applying *Keshavananda* principle invalidated the Clauses (4) and (5) of Article 368 inserted by 42nd Amendment as violative of the basic structure of the Constitution. Overall the status quo which prevailed after the *Keshavananda Bharati Case* (1973) was restored.

The debate on the basic structure of the Constitution was taken up by the National Commission to Review the Working of the Constitution (NCRWC), formed by the National Democratic Alliance Government (formed by a coalition of 24 national and regional level parties). This Committee stated that the *basic structure* of the Constitution would not be tampered and Justice M.N. Venkatachaliah, Chairman of the Commission, emphasized on several occasions that an inquiry into the *basic structure* of the Constitution lay beyond the scope of the Commission's work. While the idea that there is such a thing as a basic structure to the Constitution is well-established what constitutes the *basic structure* cannot be completely determined with any measure of finality. Nevertheless, from various judgments and opinions of jurists, it can be said that the basic structure can be considered to constitute *inter alia* the sovereign, democratic and secular character of the polity, rule of law, independence of the judiciary and Fundamental Rights of citizens which are some of the essential features of the Constitution that have time and again been upheld in the various judgments of the Supreme Court.

LIST OF AMENDMENTS

1. **First Amendment Act, 1951,** amended Articles 15, 19, 85, 87, 174, 176, 341, 342, 372 and 376 and inserted Articles 31A and 31B and also Schedule 9. This amendment set to restrict Right to Equality, Liberty and Property in public interest. A new constitutional device, called Schedule 9 was introduced to protect laws that are contrary to the constitutionally guaranteed fundamental rights.

2. **Second Amendment Act, 1952,** set to amend Article 81 regarding representation of States in the Parliament. This amendment of Article 81(1)(b) of the Constitution fixed the limits of Parliamentary constituency between 850,000 and 650,000 voters.
3. **Third Amendment Act, 1954,** amended the Seventh foodstuffs, including edible oil seeds and oils; cattle fodder, including oilcakes and other concentrates; raw cotton whether ginned or unginned, and cotton seeds; and raw jute were included in the Concurrent List.
4. **Fourth Amendment Act, 1955,** amended Articles 31, 31A and 305 and Schedule 9. It puts restrictions on property rights and lead to the inclusion of related Bills in Schedule 9 of the Constitution.
5. **Fifth Amendment Act, 1955,** amended Article 3 and provided for a new mechanism for ascertaining the will of the States in matters relating to the amendments to the territorial matters and in the re-naming of the State.
6. **Sixth Amendment Act, 1956,** amended Articles 269 and 286 and also Schedule 7 dealing with inter-State Sales tax.
7. **Seventh Amendment Act, 1956,** amended Articles 1, 49, 80, 81, 82, 131, 153, 158, 168, 170, 171, 216, 217, 220, 222, 224, 230, 231 and 232 and inserted Articles 258A, 290A, 298, 350A, 350B, 371, 372A and 378A and amended Part 8 and also Schedules 1, 2, 4 and 7. This mainly dealt with reorganization of States as this brought about comprehensive changes in the reorganization of States, a large number of consequential changes also had to be made which made this amendment quite exhaustive.
8. **Eighth Amendment Act, 1960,** amended Article 334 regarding the reservation of states in Legislatures in favour of Scheduled Castes and Scheduled Tribes by another ten years, i.e., 1970.
9. **Ninth Amendment Act, 1960,** amended Schedule which sought to settle certain boundary disputes between the Governments of India and Pakistan relating to the borders of the States of Assam, Punjab and West Bengal, and the Union territory of Tripura like Berubari Union, Khulna 24 Parganas—Jessore Boundary disputes, Assam-East Pakistan Boundary and the like.
10. **Tenth Amendment Act, 1961,** amended Article 240 and Schedule 1 which led to the incorporation of Dadra and Nagar Haveli as a Union Territory, consequent to acquisition from Portugal.
11. **Eleventh Amendment Act, 1961,** amended Articles 66 and 71 regarding the electoral process of the Vice President of India. It stated that the election of Vice President by Electoral College consisting of members of both Houses of Parliament, instead of election by a Joint Sitting of Parliament. The election of the President and Vice President

shall not be challenged on the ground of existence of any vacancies in the Electoral College or for whatever other reasons in the appropriated Electoral College.

12. **Twelfth Amendment Act, 1962,** amended Article 240 and also Schedule 1 to incorporate Goa, Daman and Diu as a Union Territory, consequent to acquisition from Portugal.
13. **Thirteenth Amendment Act, 1962,** amended Part 21 relating to the formation of State of Nagaland, with special protection under Article 371A. The amendment also vested certain responsibilities to the Governor of Nagaland.
14. **Fourteenth Amendment Act, 1962,** amended Articles 81 and 240 and inserted Article 239A and also amended Schedules 1 and 4 to incorporate Pudducherry into the Union of India and creation of Legislative Assemblies for Himachal Pradesh, Tripura, Manipur and Goa, Daman and Diu and Pudducherry.
15. **Fifteenth Amendment Act, 1963,** amended Articles 124, 128, 217, 222, 224, 226, 297, 311 and 316 and inserted Article 224A also amended Schedule 7. By this amendment the retirement age of the Judges of High Courts was raised to 62 years from 60 years with provision for re-employment of the retired Judges and also the jurisdiction of the High Courts was extended. However, this amendment Act restricted the scope of Government servants to appeal against Government decisions in disciplinary matters.
16. **Sixteenth Amendment Act, 1963,** amended Articles 19, 84 and 173 and Schedule 3 making it obligatory for seekers of public office to swear their allegiance to the Indian Republic and prescribe the various obligatory templates before a person authorized by the Election Commission. He must take the oath of affirmation that he will bear true faith and allegiance to the Constitution and will uphold the sovereignty and integrity of India.
17. **Seventeenth Amendment Act, 1964,** amended Article 31A and Schedule 9. It redefined the term estate in Article 31-A to include lands held under *ryotwari settlement* and also other lands in respect of which provisions are normally made in land reform enactments.
18. **Eighteenth Amendment Act, 1966,** amended Article 3 which brought about some Technical Amendment to include Union Territories in Article 3, and hence, permitted reorganization of Union Territories. It created two new states of Punjab Suba and Haryana as a result of reorganization of the former State of Punjab and the Union Territory of Himachal Pradesh.
19. **Nineteenth Amendment Act, 1966,** amended Article 324 leading to the abolition Election Tribunals and enabling trial of election petitions by regular High Courts.

20. **Twentieth Amendment Act, 1966,** inserted Article 233A validating appointment, posting or promotion of a person as a District Judge, if such appointment was illegal or void by reason of its not being in accordance with Article 233 or 235.
21. **Twenty-first Amendment Act, 1967,** amended Schedule 8 and included Sindhi Language in the Eighth Schedule of the Constitution.
22. **Twenty-second Amendment Act, 1969,** amended Article 275 and inserted Articles 244A and 371B for making provision to form autonomous hill State of Meghalaya within the State of Assam.
23. **Twenty-third Amendment Act, 1969,** amended Articles 330, 332, 333 and 334 and extended the reservation of seats for schedules castes and scheduled tribes and Anglo-Indian community for another 10 years.
24. **Twenty-fourth Amendment Act, 1971,** amended Articles 13 and 368 and gave the power to the Parliament to amend any part of the Constitution including the Fundamental Rights.
25. **Twenty-fifth Amendment Act, 1971,** amended Article 31 and inserted Article 31C restricting property rights and compensation in case the State takes over private property and also the Fundamental Rights were made subordinate to the Directive Principles as given under Article 39.
26. **Twenty-sixth Amendment Act, 1971,** amended Article 366 and inserted article 363A and removed Articles 291 and 362 resulting in the abolition of privy purse paid to former rulers of princely states which were incorporated into the Indian Republic.
27. **Twenty-seventh Amendment Act, 1971,** amended Articles 239A and 240 and inserted Articles 239B and 371C for reorganization of Mizoram into a Union Territory with a Legislature and Council of Ministers.
28. **Twenty-eighth Amendment Act, 1972,** inserted Article 312A and removed Article 314 to rationalize Civil Service rules to make it uniform across those appointed prior to independence and post independence and to abolish the protection given to the ICS officers' conditions of service and privileges.
29. **Twenty-ninth Amendment Act, 1972,** amended Schedule 9 and placed the Kerala Land Reforms (Amendment) Act, 1969 and the Kerala Land Reforms (Amendment) Act, 1971 under the Ninth Schedule to protect these Acts from judicial review under Article 31-B relating to land reform Acts and amendments to these Act under Schedule 9 of the Constitution.
30. **Thirtieth Amendment Act, 1972,** amended Article 133 which changed the basis for appeals in Supreme Court of India in case of Civil Suits from value criteria to one involving substantial question of law
31. **Thirty-first Amendment Act, 1973,** amended Articles 81, 330 and 332 which increased the uper limit of elective seats of the Lok Sabha from 525 to 545 seats.

32. **Thirty-second Amendment Act, 1974,** Amended Article 371 and inserted Articles 371D and 371E and also amended Schedule 7. By this amendment sought to implement the 6-point programme for the State of Andhra Pradesh.
33. **Thirty-third Amendment Act, 1974,** amended Articles 101 and 190 creating provision for resignation by members of Parliament and State Legislatures and the procedure for verification and acceptance of resignation by the Speaker of the House.
34. **Thirty-fourth Amendment Act, 1974,** amended Schedule 9 to provide Constitutional protection to 20 Acts passed by various States as Land Reforms.
35. **Thirty-fifth Amendment Act, 1974,** amended Articles 80 and 81 and inserted Article 2A and Schedule 10 to provide associates State status to Sikkim.
36. **Thirty-sixth Amendment Act, 1975,** amended Articles 80 and 8, inserted Article 371F, removed Article 2A, amended Schedules 1 and 4 and removed Schedule 10 and gave full statehood to Sikkim as 22nd state.
37. **Thirty-seventh Amendment Act, 1975,** amended Articles 239A and 240 creating provision for the Constitution of the Legislative Assembly and the Council of Ministers in Arunachal Pradesh.
38. **Thirty-eighth Amendment Act, 1975,** amended Articles 123, 213, 239B, 352, 356, 359 and 360 making the declaration of Emergency by the President and Promulgation of Ordinances by the President, Governors and Administrative Heads of Union Territories non-justiciable.
39. **Thirty-ninth Amendment Act, 1975,** amended Articles 71 and 329, inserted Article 329A and amended Schedule 9 and placed the election of President, Vice-President, Prime Minister and the Speaker beyond judicial scrutiny.
40. **Fortieth Amendment Act, 1976,** amended Article 297 and Schedule 9 to place land reform and other Acts and amendments to these Act under schedule 9 of the Constitution thus making them immune from judicial scrutiny.
41. **Forty-first Amendment Act, 1976,** amended Article 316 and raised the retirement Age Limit of Chairman and Members of Union and State Public Commissions from sixty to sixty two.
42. **Forty-second Amendment Act, 1976,** amended articles 31, 31C, 39, 55, 74, 77, 81, 82, 83, 100, 102, 103, 105, 118, 145, 150, 166, 170, 172, 189, 191, 192, 194, 208, 217, 225, 226, 227, 228, 311, 312, 330, 352, 353, 356, 357, 358, 359, 366, 368 and 371F. It also inserted Articles 31D, 32A, 39A, 43A, 48A, 131A, 139A, 144A, 226A, 228A and 257A, Parts 4A and 14A and amended Schedule 7. This has

been one of the controversial amendments of all times. It added the words Secular, Socialist and Integrity to the Preamble. The Power of Parliament enhanced for amending the Constitution including the Part III of the Constitution. The power of Judicial Review was restricted. The Fundamental Duties Part IV-A was inserted. Duration of Lok Sabha and State Legislative Assemblies were extended during National Emergency (six years). It also stated that no quorum shall be required for conducting the meeting of the Lok Sabha and the State Legislative Assemblies. Delimitation of the constituencies of the Lok Sabha and the Legislative Assemblies of the States shall be on the basis of the population of 1971 till the year 2001.

43. **Forty-third Amendment Act, 1977,** amended Articles 145, 226, 228 and 366 and removed Articles 31D, 32A, 131A, 144A, 226A and 228A. This amendment was passed after revocation of internal emergency in the country and some of the misgivings of the 42nd Amendment Act were repealed. Protection of the rights and powers of the judiciary, power of Judicial Review was restored and provisions relating to the power of Parliament to deal with anti-national activities were repealed.
44. **Forty-fourth Amendment Act, 1978,** amended Articles 19, 22, 30, 31A, 31C, 38, 71, 74, 77, 83, 103, 105, 123, 132, 133, 134, 139A, 150, 166, 172, 192, 194, 213, 217, 225, 226, 227, 239B, 329, 352, 356, 358, 359, 360 and 371F. It inserted Articles 134A and 361A and removed Articles 31, 257A and 329A. It also amended Part 12 and Schedule 9. This was passed after the revocation of the emergency. It aimed to correct some of the atrocities of the 42nd Amendment Act. It, first and foremost removed the Right to Property under Article 30A. The term of Lok Sabha and State Legislative Assemblies were restored to five years. The provisions of quorum was restored to pre-42nd amendment. The Right to Life and Personal Liberty and the freedom of press were restored. In Article 352, the words "internal disturbance", were substituted for the words "armed rebellion", Article 356 was also amended to reduce the period of President's Rule in a State from one year to six months at a time and the total period not to exceed one year. Power of Judicial Review was also restored.
45. **Forty-fifth Amendment Act, 1980,** amended Article 334 to extend reservation for SC/ST and nomination of Anglo-Indian members in Parliament and State assemblies for another ten years, i.e. up to 1990.
46. **Forty-sixth Amendment Act, 1982,** amended Articles 269, 286 and 366 amended Schedule 7 to plug loopholes and sales tax and also to bring about some uniformity in tax rates in case of certain items.
47. **Forty-seventh Amendment Act, 1984,** amended Schedule 9 to place some Land Reform Acts and amendments to these Act under Schedule 9 of the Constitution.

48. **Forty-eighth Amendment Act, 1984,** amended Articles 356 to extend the period of emergency in the State of Punjab. The Proclamation issued by the President under Article 356 of the Constitution on the 6th day of October, 1983 with respect to the State of Punjab cannot be continued in force for more than one year unless the special conditions mentioned in Clause (5) of Article 356 of the Constitution are satisfied. Therefore, by this amendment "any period beyond the expiration of one year" shall be construed as a reference to "any period beyond the expiration of two years".
49. **Forty-ninth Amendment Act, 1984,** amended Article 244 and amended Schedules 5 and 6 to recognize Tripura as a tribal State and enable the creation of a Tripura Tribal Areas Autonomous District Council.
50. **Fiftieth Amendment Act, 1984,** amended Article 33 so as to determine how much the Parliament was empowered to enact laws determining to what extent any of the rights conferred by Part III of the Constitution shall, in their application to the members of the Armed Forces or the Forces charged with the maintenance of public order, be restricted or abrogated so as to ensure the proper discharge of their duties and the maintenance of discipline among them. Article 33 was amended as to bring within its scope:
    (i) the members of the Forces charged with the protection of property belonging to, or in the charge or possession of, the State; or
    (ii) persons employed in any bureau or other organization established by the State for purposes of intelligence or counter intelligence; or
    (iii) persons employed in, or in connection with, the telecommunication systems set up for the purposes of any Force, bureau or organization. Experience has revealed that the need for ensuring proper discharge of their duties and the maintenance of discipline among them is of paramount importance in the national interest.
51. **Fifty-first Amendment Act, 1984,** amended Articles 330 and 332 to provide reservation to Scheduled Tribes in Nagaland, Meghalaya, Mizoram and Arunachal Pradesh Legislative Assemblies.
52. **Fifty-second Amendment Act, 1985,** amended Articles 101, 102, 190 and 191 and inserted schedule 10 to provide disqualification of members of Parliament and Assembly in case of defection from one party to other, expulsion from the party which set him as a candidate in the election or joining of a political party by an independent member of the House after expiry of six months from the date on which the takes seat in the House.
53. **Fifty-third Amendment Act, 1986,** inserted Article 371G. On the 30th June 1986, a Memorandum of Settlement on Mizoram was signed by the Government of India and the Government of Mizoram

with the Mizo National front which envisages among other things the conferment of statehood on the Union Territory of Mizoram subject to the other stipulations contained in the Memorandum. To give effect to this Article 371G was inserted in the Constitution.

Article 371G contains special provision with respect to the State of Mizoram. "Notwithstanding anything in this Constitution. It states:

(a) no Act of Parliament in respect of—
   (i) religious or social practices of the Mizos,
   (ii) Mizo customary law and procedure,
   (iii) administration of civil and criminal justice involving decisions according to Mizo customary law,
   (iv) ownership and transfer of land shall apply to the State of Mizoram unless the Legislative Assembly of the State of Mizoram by a resolution so decides:

Provided that nothing in this clause shall apply to any Central Act in force in the Union territory of Mizoram immediately before the commencement of The Constitution (Fifty-third Amendment) Act, 1986;

(b) the Legislative Assembly of the State of Mizoram shall consist of not less than forty members.

54. **Fifty-fourth Amendment Act, 1986,** amended Articles 125 and 221 and amended Schedule 2 to increase the salary of Chief Justice of India and other Judges and to provide for determining future increases without the need for constitutional amendment. This Act amended Part 'D' of the second schedule to the Constitution to give effect to the increase in salaries of Judges and to make an enabling provision in Articles 125 and 221 to provide for changes in salaries of Judges in future by Parliament by law.
55. **Fifty-fifth Amendment Act, 1986,** inserted Article 371H and the Government of India conferred statehood on the Union territory of Arunachal Pradesh and it became the 24th State of the Union of India. Special powers were given to the Governor of Arunachal Pradesh consequent to formation of State of Arunachal Pradesh.
56. **Fifty-sixth Amendment Act, 1987,** inserted Article 371I for transition provisions for the formation of the State of Goa.
57. **Fifty-seventh Amendment Act,** amended Article 332 to provide effective reservation for scheduled tribes in Nagaland, Meghalaya, Mizoram and Arunachal Pradesh Legislative Assemblies.
58. **Fifty-eighth Amendment Act, 1987,** inserted Article 394A and amended Part 22 to make provisions to publish authentic Hindi translation of Constitution as on date and provision to publish authentic Hindi translation of future amendments.

59. **Fifty-ninth Amendment Act, 1988,** amended Articles 356 and 352 and inserted Article 359A to permit President's rule up to three years in the State of Punjab, Articles 352 and Article 359A amended to permit imposing emergency in the State of Punjab or in specific districts of the State of Punjab.
60. **Sixtieth Amendment Act, 1988,** amended Article 276 so as to increase the ceiling of taxes on professions, trades, callings and employment from two hundred and fifty rupees per annum to two thousand and five hundred rupees per annum.
61. **Sixty-first Amendment Act, 1988,** amended Article 326 lowering the age of voting from twenty-one to eighteen.
62. **Sixty-second Amendment Act, 1989,** amended Article 334 extending reservation for SC / ST and nomination of Anglo-Indian members in Parliament and State Assemblies for another ten years.
63. **Sixty-third Amendment Act, 1989,** amended Article 356 and removed Article 359A repealing applicability of emergency powers to State of Punjab, accorded in Article 359A as per 59th Amendment regarding the right to life and liberty.
64. **Sixty-fourth Amendment Act, 1990,** amended Article 356 extending the duration of President's Rule in Punjab for another six months.
65. **Sixty-fifth Amendment Act, 1990,** amended Article 338 forming the National Commission for Scheduled Castes and Scheduled Tribes with its statutory powers specified in the Constitution. In other words it was given a Constitutional Status.
66. **Sixty-sixth Amendment Act, 1990,** amended Schedule 9 and added a further group of land reforms enactments passed by different State Legislatures to the Ninth Schedule.
67. **Sixty-seventh Amendment Act, 1990,** amended Article 356 to permit President's Rule up to four years in the State of Punjab.
68. **Sixty-eighth Amendment Act, 1991,** amended Article 356 to permit President's rule up to five years in the State of Punjab.
69. **Sixty-ninth Amendment Act, 1991,** inserted Articles 239AA and 239AB to provide for a Legislative Assembly and Council of Ministers for Federal National Capital of Delhi. Delhi continues to be a Union Territory.
70. **Seventieth Amendment Act, 1992,** amended Articles 54 and 239AA to include within the scope of term 'State'. *The National Capital of Delhi and the Union Territory of Pondicherry and also included* National Capital of Delhi and Union Territory of Pondicherry in Electoral College for Presidential Election.
71. **Seventy-first Amendment Act, 1992,** amended Schedule 8 to include Konkani, Manipuri and Nepali as National Languages.

72. **Seventy-second Amendment Act, 1992,** amended Article 332 to fix number of seats to be reserved for Scheduled Tribes in Tripura State Legislative Assembly.
73. **Seventy-third Amendment Act, 1992,** a landmark amendment towards decentralization and setting up of local self Government in India and this amendment inserted Part 9 to make provisions for Constitution, election, financing and functioning of Panchayati Raj bodies.
74. **Seventy-fourth Amendment Act, 1992,** inserted Part 9A to make provisions for Constitution, election, financing and functioning of Municipal bodies.
75. **Seventy-fifth Amendment Act, 1993,** amended Article 323B for setting up of state-level rent tribunals for speedy disposal of disputes by reducing the tiers of appeal and to exclude jurisdiction of all courts except that of Supreme Court under Article 136 of the Constitution.
76. **Seventy-sixth Amendment Act, 1994,** amended Schedule 9 Enabling the continuance of 69% reservation in Tamil Nadu by including the relevant Tamil Nadu Act under 9th schedule of the Constitution and by including it under Ninth Schedule it made it free from the purview of judicial scrutiny.
77. **Seventy-seventh Amendment Act, 1995,** amended Article 16 to protect reservation to SC/ST employees in promotions in public services.
78. **Seventy-eighth Amendment Act, 1995,** amended schedule 9 with a view to put entries 257–284 land reform Acts and amendments to these Act under Schedule 9 of the Constitution in proper order.
79. **Seventy-ninth Amendment Act, 1999,** amended Article 334 to extend reservation for SC/ST and nomination of Anglo-Indian members in Parliament and State Assemblies for another ten years.
80. **Eightieth Amendment Act, 2000,** amended Articles 269 and 270 and removed Article 272 to implement tenth Finance Commission recommendation to simplify the tax structures by pooling and sharing all taxes between States and The Centre.
81. **Eighty-first Amendment Act, 2000,** amended Article 16 to protect SC/ST reservation in filling backlog of vacancies.
82. **Eighty-second Amendment Act, 2000,** amended Article 335, permitting relaxation of qualifying marks and other criteria in reservation in promotion for SC/ST candidates to any class or classes of services or posts in connections with affairs of the Union or a State.
83. **Eighty-third Amendment Act, 2000,** amended Article 243M for exempting Arunachal Pradesh from reservation for Scheduled Castes in Panchayati Raj institutions

84. **Eighty-fourth Amendment Act, 2002,** amended Articles 5, 81, 82, 170, 330 and 332 for extending the usage of 1971 national census population figures for State wise distribution of Parliamentary seats.
85. **Eighty-fifth Amendment Act, 2002,** amended Article 16 restoration of reservation to protect seniority in case of promotions of SC/ST employees.
86. **Eighty-sixth Amendment Act, 2002,** amended Articles 45 and 51A and inserted Article 21A by which Right to Education was made the Fundamental Right and fundamental duty has been fixed to the parents and guardians to provide opportunities for education to their children between age group of 6–14 years.
87. **Eighty-seventh Amendment Act, 2003,** amended Articles 81, 82, 170 and 330 for making provisions so that each State shall be divided into territorial Constitutions in such a manner that the ratio between the population as per 2001 census and not 1991 census, of each constituency and number of seats allotted to it is so far as practicable, the same throughout the State.
88. **Eighty-eighth Amendment Act, 2003,** amended Article 270, inserted Article 268A and amended schedule 7 to extend statutory cover for levy and utilization of Service Tax.
89. **Eighty-ninth Amendment Act, 2003,** amended Article 338 and inserted Article 338A creation for separate Commission for Scheduled Castes. The National Commission for Scheduled Castes and Scheduled Tribes was bifurcated into The National Commission for Scheduled Castes and The National Commission for Scheduled Tribes.
90. **Ninetieth Amendment Act, 2003,** amended Article 332 making room for reservation in Assam Assembly relating to Bodoland Territory Area.
91. **Ninety-first Amendment Act, 2003,** amended Articles 75 and 164, inserted Article 361B and amended Schedule 10 for restricting the size of Council of Ministers to 15% of legislative members and to strengthen Anti-Defection laws.
92. **Ninety-second Amendment Act, 2003,** amended Article 270, inserted Article 268A and amended Schedules 7 and 8 to enable Levy of Service Tax and include Bodo, Dogri, Santali and Maithili as National Languages in the Eighth Schedule.
93. **Ninety-third Amendment Act, 2005,** amended Article 15 which now has to be read as—

    In Article 15 of the Constitution, after Clause (4), the following clause shall be inserted, namely:

    "(5) Nothing in this article or in sub-clause (g) of Clause (1) of Article 19 shall prevent the State from making any special provision, by law, for the advancement of any socially and educationally backward classes of citizens or for the Scheduled Castes or the Scheduled Tribes in so far as such special provisions relate to their admission to educational institutions including private educational institutions, whether aided or unaided by the State, other than the minority educational institutions referred to in Clause (1) of Article 30."

94. **Ninety-fourth Amendment Act,** 2006, amended Article 164 to provide for a Minister of Tribal Welfare in newly created Jharkand and Chhattisgarh States.
95. **Ninety-fifth Amendment Act,** 2010, amended Article 334 to extend the reservation of seats for SCs and STs in the Lok Sabha and states assemblies from sixty years to seventy years.
96. **Ninety-sixth Amendment Act,** 2011, amended Article to substitute "Odia" for "Oriya" in the Eighth Schedule.
97. **Ninety-seventh Amendment Act,** 2012, amended Art 19 and added Part IX-B of the Constitution. This Amendment Act added the words "or co-operative societies" after the word "or Unions" in Article 19(l) (c), inserted Article 43B which now provides that "The State shall endeavour to promote voluntary formation, autonomous functioning, democratic control and professional management of co-operative societies." and added Part IX-B entitled 'The Co-operative Societies' which contains provisions for incorporation, election, Constitution, suspension of members, auditing and various other measures for the functioning of co-operative societies.

Till September 2016 there have been 101 amendments to the constitution of India. The 101st amendment has been made with regard to Goods and Services Tax Bill (GST) which came into force from 1 April 2017.

Between 2016 and 2019 there have been three amendments. 102nd amendment related to the constitutional status of National Commission for Backward Classes. 103rd amendment is related to amendment to Article 15 and 16. Clause [6] was added to both related to maximum of 10% Reservation for Economically Weaker Sections (EWSs) of citizens of classes other than the classes mentioned in clauses (4) and (5) of Article 15. 104th Amendment is related to Article 334 in order to extend the reservation of seats for SCs and STs in the Lok Sabha and States Assemblies from Seventy years to Eighty years and remove reserved seats for Anglo Indian community. 105th Amendment relates to Article 338B, 342A and 366 and it aims at restoration of the power of the state governments to identify Other Backward Classes (OBCs) that are socially and educationally backward. 106th Amendment pertains to reservation of seats for women. It amended article 239AA and inserted of articles 330A, 332A, 334A. It reserved one-third of the seats in the Lok Sabha (330A), state legislative assemblies (332A) and Delhi Legislative Assembly (239AA) for women for a period of 15 years after coming effect (334A).

NATIONAL COMMISSION TO REVIEW THE WORKING OF THE CONSTITUTION (NCRWC): VENKATACHALIAH COMMISSION

A debate about the review of the Constitution has always been there in the political circle, but it gained momentum when the BJP-led National Democratic Alliance came to power in 1999. A resolution of the Government of India, Ministry of Law, Justice and Company Affairs dated 22 February 2000 stipulated that "the Commission shall consist of a whole time Chairperson who shall be a person of distinction with knowledge and expertise of constitutional issues and in the working of the democratic institutions of the nation." This led to the creation of an eleven membered Commission headed by Justice M.N. Venkatachaliah, former Chief Justice of India. However, the whole issue about constitutional review soon got embroiled in a countrywide hot debate. Even the President of India, K.R. Narayanan, strongly reacted to this idea, and posed a question before the nation whether it was "the Constitution that has failed us or whether it is we who have failed the Constitution." All other major opposition parties also opposed the idea of review of the Constitution. Even the constitutionality of the Review Commission was questioned. The Commission itself held that the Parliament should be associated from the initial stage itself in the matter of formulating proposals for constitutional amendments. It also said that a standing committee of the two Houses of Parliament would be appropriate body to review the working of the Constitution. With three extensions, the Commission finally submitted its 1976 page report to the Government. The main areas of concern of the Commission were:

1. Strengthening the institutions of Parliamentary democracy like the working of the Legislature, the Executive and the Judiciary and exploring the possibilities of stability within the discipline of Parliamentary democracy.
2. Electoral reforms and standard in political life.
3. Assurance of social and economic rights; "how fair? How fast? How equal?"
4. Promoting literacy, generating employment, ensuring social security, alleviation of poverty and the like.
5. Union-State relations.
6. Decentralization, devolution and strengthening of Panchayati Raj institutions.
7. Enlargement of Fundamental Rights.
8. Effectuation of Fundamental Duties.
9. Effectuation of Directive Principles and achieving the "preambular objectives of the Constitution."
10. Legal control of fiscal and monetary policies, public audit mechanism.
11. 'Administrative system' and 'standard in public life'.

For effective functioning the Commission constituted eleven advisory panel of experts for each of the constitutional issue identified by it. Each Advisory Panel was chaired by an eminent person with distinguished and scholarly achievements. The Panels were:

1. Enlargement of Fundamental Rights
2. Union-State Relations
3. Strengthening of the Institutions of Parliamentary Democracy
4. Effectuation of Directive Principles
5. Pace of Socio-Economic Change and Development under the Constitution
6. Electoral Reforms
7. Promoting Literacy, generating employment and poverty alleviation
8. Decentralization and devolution, empowerment and strengthening of Panchayati Raj Institutions
9. Effectuation of Fundamental Duties
10. Legal control of fiscal and monetary policies, public audit mechanism and standard in public life
11. Administrative System

The Commission circulated 22 consultation papers to elicit public opinion. Alongside seven background papers were utilized by the Commission in order to initiate a proper review of the Constitution. It was not an easy task for the Commission to review the working of the Constitution. As it was a multi-membered Commission, after its final report came into light, differences of opinion among the members and in the final report there were attached four notes of dissent. Former Lok Sabha Speaker P.A. Sangma of the Nationalist Congress Party resigned even before the completion of the Commission's work, because his plan debarring foreign-born Indian nationals from holding key constitutional position was not accepted by the Commission. Justice B.P. Jeevan Reddy, Dr. Subhash C. Kashyap, C.R. Irani and Sumitra Gandhi Kulkarni all appended separate notes to the final report. Much furore was raised after the report was published. Hence, the discussions of the report were kept at a low key.

The Constitution of India is a reflection of lofty socio-economic and political ideals envisaged by our Founding fathers. However, with globalization, the nature of demand on the polity and impact of international political economy on the domestic front necessitates every now and then to translate the provisions of the Constitution in a way that the provisions can relate to the present needs. In the face of rising corruption, a strong *Lokpal* is the need of the hour, but if the *Lokpal* is to become a constitutional body like the Election Commission, then necessary amendments to the Constitution has to be made. In the Winter Session of 2011 the Lok Sabha passed a feeble Lokpal Bill but the Constitutional Amendment Bill was defeated which wanted to give a constitutional status to Lokpal.

EXERCISES

I. Short Answer Questions: **(100 words)**

1. Briefly State the Constitutional provisions regarding the amendment of the Constitution of India.
2. Write a short note on Venkatachaliah Commission.

II. Long Answer Questions: **(1200 words)**

3. Examine the procedure of amendment of the Constitution of India.
4. Critically discuss the 'Basic Structure' of the Constitution and amendment.
5. Discuss the significance of the Venkatachaliah Commission.

REFERENCES

Bakshi, P.M., *The Constitution of India* (with selective comments), Universal Law Publishing, Delhi, 2000.

Basu, Durga Das, *Introduction to the Constitution of India*, Prentice-Hall of India, New Delhi, 1992.

Dutta, Satyabrata, *Constitution Review: Venkatachaliah Commission,* Progressive Publishers, Kolkata, 2004.

Golaknath v. *State of Punjab* (1967) 2 SCR 762: AIR 1967 SC.

Government of India, *Constitution of India.*

Keshavananda Bharati v. *State of Kerala*, AIR 1973SC 1461.

Minerva Mills Ltd. v. *Union of India* (1980) 3 SCC 625.

Pylee, M.V., *India's Constitution*, S. Chand & Company, New Delhi, 1994.

Shankari Prasad Singh v. *Union of India*, AIR 1951SC 458.

Sajjan Singh v. *State of Rajasthan* (1965) 1 SCR 933: AIR 1965 SC 845.

15

Local Government in India

INTRODUCTION

The 73rd and the 74th Amendments (1992) of the Indian Constitution can be termed as milestones in the establishment of Local Self Governments in India. While the 73rd Amendment established Panchayati Raj Institutions (PRIs), the 74th Amendment established Municipal bodies. The Directive Principles of State Policy in Article 40 which is Gandhian in essence embodies the principle that *the State shall take steps to organize Village Panchayats and endow them with such powers and authority as may be necessary to enable them to function as units of self-government.* The functioning of the Indian polity necessitated a proper enactment to institutionalize the PRIs and Municipal bodies in India. In that sense, the year 1992 can be regarded as the year of great achievement when these Two Amendments created the third tier in the administrative set up in India, and thereby making an attempt to establish grassroots democracy.

THE 73RD AMENDMENT AND THE PANCHAYATI RAJ INSTITUTIONS IN INDIA

In India from the ancient times there have been some sort of local governance systems. References of *Gram Sangha* can be found in the writings of Manu and even in the epics like *Mahabharata*, *Ramayana*, and Kautilya's *Arthashastra* and Sukracharyas's *Nitishastra.* Panchayat literally means a "council of five". From the ancient times, Panchayats, comprising residents of a village (usually village elders) had been performing essential administrative as well as judicial functions.

During the British rule, in the initial years there was not much concern about the Local Government. It was only after the 1857 uprising when the administration faced a financial crunch that they undertook 'compelled' decentralization but that too with respect to municipal administration. A real push was given to the local self government by Lord Ripon's resolution of May 1882. In this resolution, he highlighted two reasons for the necessity of local self-government. They are: administrative efficiency and political education. Under stiff resistance form Colonial Government this resolution could not meet its objectives and decentralization remained a far-fetched dream. Next landmark was the formation of the Royal Commission on Decentralization 1907, under the Chairmanship of C.E.H. Hobhouse which recognized the importance of Panchayats at the village level. The Commission recommended that "it is most desirable, alike in the interests of decentralization and in order to associate the people with the local tasks of administration that an attempt should be made to constitute and develop Village Panchayats for the administration of local village affairs." Montague-Chelmsford Reforms 1919, included local self-government as a provincial transferred subject, under the domain of Indian Ministers in the Provinces. Fiscal constraints prevented a full-fledged introduction of Panchayat that were truly democratic. However, by 1925, eight Provinces had passed Panchayat Acts, and by 1926, six native states had also passed Panchayat laws. The Government of India Act, 1935 can be said to be the benchmark in the evolution of the Panchayat system in India. Yet, these reforms failed to yield positive outcome.

During the drafting of the Indian Constitution the local-self Government also failed to draw commendable attention and after much debate, it was placed under the Part IV of the Constitution, i.e., the Directive Principles of the State Policy which are the non-justiciable part of the Constitution under Article 40. In 1952, the launching of the Community Development Programme with the focus on popular participation can be seen to set the ball into motion for the organization of Panchayati Raj System in India. In 1953, the National Extension Service was introduced to secure the involvement of the rural people in the rural development. However, none of these programmes could achieve even a minimum degree of success during the First Five-Year Plan period. Hence, to assess the failure of the Community Development porgrammes and make recommendations for democratic decentralization, the Balwant Rai Mehta Committee was constituted. Later on, K. Santhanam Committee 1963; Ashok Mehta Committee, 1978; G.V.K. Rao Committee, 1985; and L.M. Singhvi Committee, 1986 were constituted for looking into the issue of democratic decentralization and introduction of PRIs in India. Let us now look into the recommendations of these Committees which can be regarded as the preparatory stages for the ultimate passage of 73rd and 74th constitutional Amendment Acts 1992.

Balwant Rai Mehta Committee

In 1957, the Government of India appointed a Committee to examine the functioning of the Community Development Programme (1952) and the National Extension Service (1953) and to suggest measures for their better performance. The Committee submitted its report in November 1957, and recommended the establishment of the scheme for democratic decentralization, which ultimately came to be known as the 'Panchayati Raj'.

The recommendations made by the Balwant Rai Mehta Committee are:

1. An early establishment of a three-tier Panchayati Raj System which includes *Zila Parishad* at the District Level, *Panchayat Samiti* at the Block Level and *Gram Panchayat* at the Village Level, organically linked together through a device of indirect elections.
2. The Village *Panchayat* should be constituted with directly elected representatives, whereas the *Panchayat Samiti* and the *Zila Parishad* should be constituted with indirectly elected members.
3. There should be genuine transfer of power to these local bodies to enable them to discharge their responsibilities.
4. All welfare and developmental activities upto the district level should be entrusted to these bodies.
5. Adequate resources should be transferred to these bodies for their effective performance of functions.
6. The *Panchayat Samiti* should be the executive body while the *Zila Parishad* should be the advisory, coordinating and supervisory body.
7. The District Collector should be the Chairman of the *Zila Parishad.*
8. There should be a genuine transfer of power and responsibility to these democratic bodies.
9. The Panchayati Raj System should facilitate further devolution of authority in future.

These recommendations were accepted by the National Development Council in January 1958. The Council did not insist on a single rigid pattern and left it to the States to evolve their own patterns suitable to the local conditions. But the basic principles and the broad fundamentals should be identical throughout the country. Rajasthan was the first State to establish the institution of *Panchayati Raj.* The scheme was inaugurated by the then Prime Minister Jawahar Lal Nehru on 2 October 1959, in Nagaur District, Rajasthan, which was followed by Andhra Pradesh which also adopted the system in 1959. Rajasthan adopted a three-tier system, Tamil Nadu adopted a two-tier system and West Bengal adopted a four-tier system.

K. Santhanam Committee

The K. Santhanam Committee was appointed primarily to look into the issue of fiscal decentralization in 1963. It was to look into the issues related to sanctioning of grants to PRIs by the State Government, evolving mutual financial relations between the three tiers of PRIs, gifts and donation, handing over revenue in full or part to PRIs. The important recommendations are:

1. Panchayats should have special powers to levy special tax on land revenues and home taxes, etc.
2. People should not be burdened with too many demands (taxes),
3. All grants and subventions at the State level should be mobilized and sent in a consolidated form to various PRIs
4. A Panchayat Raj Finance Corporation should be set up to look into the financial resources of PRIs at all levels, provide loans and financial assistance to these grassroots level Governments, and also provide non-financial requirements of villages.

Ashok Mehta Committee

In December 1977, the Janata Government appointed a Committee on Panchayati Raj institutions under the chairmanship of Ashok Mehta. It submitted its report in August 1978 and made 132 recommendations to revive and strengthen the declining Panchayati Raj System in the country.

Its main recommendations are:

1. The district is a viable administrative unit for which planning, coordination and resource allocation
2. The *Panchayati Raj* Institutions must be made into a two-tier system with *Mandal Panchayat* at the base and *Zila Parishad* at the top.
3. The *Zila Parishad* should be the executive body and be made responsible for planning at the district level.
4. There should be an official participation of the political parties at all the levels of *Panchayat* elections.
5. There should be representation of Scheduled Caste and Scheduled Tribes in the elections to PRIs on the basis of their population.
6. There should be participation of political parties in the elections.
7. A Minister for the Panchayati Raj should be appointed in the State Council of Ministers to look after the affairs of the Panchayati Raj institutions.

Due to the collapse of the Janata Government before the completion of its term, no action could be taken on the recommendations of the Ashok Mehta committee at the Central level. The three States of Karnataka, West Bengal and

Andhra Pradesh took steps to revitalize the Panchayati Raj, keeping in view some of the recommendations of the Ashok Mehta Committee. The States of Karnataka, Andhra Pradesh and West Bengal passed new legislation on the basis of the report of this Committee.

GVK Rao Committee

The main recommendations of the G.V.K. Rao Committee, 1985 were:

1. PRIs have to be activated and provided with all the required support to become effective organizations.
2. PRIs at district level and below should be assigned the work of planning, implementation and monitoring of rural development programmes
3. The Block Development Office should be the spinal cord of the rural development process.

LM Singhvi Committee

In 1986, Rajiv Gandhi Government appointed a Committee on the 'Revitalization of the Panchayati Raj Institutions for Democracy and Development' under the Chairmanship of L.M. Singhvi. The major recommendations are:

1. The Panchayati Raj Institutions should be constitutionally recognized, protected and preserved. For this purpose, a new chapter should be added in the Constitution of India. It also suggested some constitutional provisions to ensure regular, free and fair elections to the Panchayati Raj bodies.
2. Non-involvement of political parties in Panchayat elections
3. *Nyaya Panchayats* should be established for a cluster of villages.
4. The villages should be organized to make the *Gram Panchayats* more viable. It also emphasized the importance of the *Gram Sabha* and called it as the embodiment of direct democracy.
5. The *Village Panchayats* should have more financial resources.
6. The Judicial tribunals should be established in each State to eradicate controversies about election to the Panchayati Raj Institutions, their dissolution and other matters related to their functioning.

Attempts were made to Act upon the recommendations of these various Committees. In May 1989, the then Prime Minister Rajiv Gandhi introduced the 64th Amendment Bill to give Constitutional Status to the Local Self-Governments which got defeated in the Rajya Sabha, and thereafter, the entire PRI movement lost momentum and Rajiv Gandhi lost the elections too. In 1989, another attempt to introduce Constitutional Amendment Bill to give Constitutional Status to the Local Self-Governments was made but this Bill could not become an Act because of the dissolution of the Lok Sabha. Finally, the Narsimha Rao Government introduced the Constitutional Amendment Bill in the Lok Sabha in September 1991. It was passed by the Lok Sabha on 22 December 1992, and by the Rajya Sabha on December 23. Later, it was approved by the 17 State Assemblies and received the assent of the President of India in April 1993.

73RD CONSTITUTIONAL AMENDMENT: INTRODUCTION OF PANCHAYAT SYSTEM IN INDIA

Seventy-third Amendment Act, 1992 was a landmark amendment towards decentralization and setting up of local self Government in India, and this amendment inserted Part 9 to make provisions for Constitution, election, financing and functioning of Panchayati Raj bodies. A three-tier system was introduced. The 73rd Amendment reads as:

PART IX of the Constitution envisages a three-tier system of Panchayats, namely, The village level; at the district level and at intermediate level which stands between the village and district Panchayats in the States where the population is above 20 lakhs (Article 243B).

Composition

Article 243C(2) states that all the seats in a Panchayat shall be filled by persons chosen by direct election from territorial constituencies in the Panchayat area. The same Article states that the Chairperson of each Panchayat at village level shall be elected according to the law passed by a State and such State law shall also provide for the representation of Chairpersons at Village and intermediate levels and those not having Panchayats at Intermediate level and in the District level, as well as members of the Union and State Legislature in the Panchayats above the village level.

Reservation of Seats for Schedule Castes and Scheduled Tribes

Article 243D provides that seats are to be reserved for Scheduled Castes, and the Scheduled Tribes. The reservation shall be in proportion to their population in that Panchayat area. Out of the seats so reserved not less than one-third of the seats shall be reserved for women belonging to Scheduled Castes and Scheduled Tribes, respectively.

Reservation for Women

Article 243D also upholds that not less than one-third of the total number of seats to be filled by direct elections in every Panchayat shall be reserved for women.

Reservation of Offices of Chairpersons

Article 243D also provides that State may by law make provision for similar reservation of the offices of Chairpersons in the Panchayats at the village and other levels. Legislature of a State may by law also reserve seats or offices of Chairpersons in the Panchayat at any level in favour of backward classes of citizens.

Duration of Panchayat

Article 243E stipulates that every Panchayat shall continue for five years from the date of its first meeting. But it can be dissolved earlier in accordance with the procedure prescribed by State Law. Elections must take place before the expiry of the above period. In case it is dissolved earlier, then the elections must take place within six months of its dissolution. A Panchayat reconstituted after premature dissolution (i.e., before the expiry of the full period of five years) shall continue only for the remainder of the period. But if the remainder of the period is less than six months it shall not be necessary to hold elections.

Qualification for Membership

Article 243F provides grounds for disqualification which can be interpreted in a different way to provide us the necessary qualifications for membership. It provides that all persons who are qualified to be chosen to the State Legislature shall be qualified to be chosen as a member of a Panchayat. The only difference is that a person who has attained the age of 21 years will be eligible to be a member, whereas in case of State Legislature, the prescribed age is 25 years (Article 173). If a question arises as to whether a member has become subject to any disqualification, the question shall be referred to such authority as the State Legislature may provide by law.

Powers, Authority and Responsibilities of Panchayats

Articles 243G-243H provide that the State Legislatures have power, to confer on the Panchayats such powers and authority as may be necessary to enable them to function as institutions of self-government. They may be entrusted with the responsibility of preparing plans for economic development and social justice, implementation of schemes for economic development and social justice, and in regard to matters listed in the **Eleventh Schedule*** (inserted by the 73rd Amendment). The list contains 29 items like land improvement, minor irrigation, animal husbandry, fisheries, education, women and child development etc.

*The Eleventh Schedule is discussed in detail in the later section of this chapter.

Powers to Impose Taxes and Financial Resources

Under Article 243H, a State may by law authorize a Panchayat to levy, collect and appropriate taxes, duties, tolls, etc. It can also assign to a Panchayat various taxes, duties, and so on collected by the State Government and provide Grants-in-aids may be given to the Panchayats from the Consolidated Fund of the State and the State by law may also provide for Constitution of such funds for creating all money received, respectively, by or on-behalf of the Panchayats, and also for withdrawal of such money therefrom.

Panchayat Finance Commissions

Article 243I states that within one year from the commencement of the Constitution (Seventy-third Amendment) Act, 1992, and thereafter at the expiration of every fifth year the State Government shall appoint a Finance Commission to review the financial position of the Panchayats and to make recommendations as to:

1. the distribution between the State and the Panchayats of the net proceeds of taxes, duties, tolls and fees leviable by the State which may be divided between them, and how allocation would be made among various levels of Panchayats;
2. determination of taxes, duties, tolls and fees which may be assigned to the Panchayats;
3. Grants-in-aid to the Panchayats from the Consolidated Fund of the State
4. The measures needed to improve the financial position of the Panchayats
5. Any other matter referred to the Finance Commission by the Governor in interests of sound finance of the Panchayats

The Legislature of a State may, by law, provide for the composition of the Commission, the qualifications which shall be requisite for appointment as members thereof and the manner in which they shall be selected.

The Report of the Commission, together with a memorandum of Action taken on it, shall be laid before the State Legislature. These provisions are modelled on Article 280 which contains provisions regarding appointment of a Finance Commission for distribution of finances between the Union and the States.

Audit of Accounts

Article 243J lays down that the Legislature of a State may, by law, make provisions with respect to the maintenance of accounts by the Panchayats and the auditing of such accounts.

STATE ELECTION COMMISSION

Article 243K is designed to ensure free and fair elections to the Panchayats. Article 243K provides that the superintendence, direction and control of the preparation of electoral rolls for and the conduct of elections to the Panchayats shall be vested in a State Election Commission consisting of a State Election Commissioner to be appointed by the Governor. To ensure the independence of the Commissioner it is laid down that State Election Commissioner can be removed only in the same manner and on the same grounds as Judge of a High Court. The Governor of a State shall when so requested by the State Election Commission make available to them such staff as may be necessary for the discharge of the functions conferred on the State Election Commission. The State Legislatures have the power to legislate on all matters relating to elections to Panchayats.

Continuance of Existing Laws and Panchayats

Article 243N provides that any law relating to Panchayat in force in a State immediately before the commencement of the Constitution (73rd Amendment) Act, 1992, which is inconsistent with the provisions in Part IX of the Constitution shall continue to be in force until amended or repealed by a competent Legislature, other competent authority or until expiration of one year from such commencement, whichever is earlier.

Bar to Interference by Courts in Electoral Matters

Article 243O provides that the Courts shall have no jurisdiction to examine the validity of a law, relating to delimitation of constituencies or the allotments of seats, made under Article 243K. An election to a Panchayat can be called in question only by an election petition which should be presented to such authority and in such manner as may be prescribed by or under any law made by the State Legislature.

ELEVENTH SCHEDULE (ARTICLE 243-G): POWERS, AUTHORITY AND RESPONSIBILITIES OF PANCHAYATS

1. Agriculture, including agricultural extension
2. Land improvement, implementation of land reforms, land consolidation and soil conservation
3. Minor irrigation, water management and watershed development
4. Animal husbandry, dairying and poultry
5. Fisheries
6. Social forestry and farm forestry

7. Minor forest produce
8. Small-scale industries, including food processing industries
9. *Khadi*, village and cottage industries
10. Rural housing
11. Drinking water
12. Fuel and fodder
13. Roads, culverts, bridges, ferries, waterways and other means of communication
14. Rural electrification, including distribution of electricity
15. Non-conventional energy sources
16. Poverty alleviation programme
17. Education, including primary and secondary schools
18. Technical training and vocational education
19. Adult and non-formal education
20. Libraries
21. Cultural activities
22. Markets and fairs
23. Health and sanitation, including hospitals, primary health centres and dispensaries
24. Family welfare
25. Women and child development
26. Social welfare, including welfare of the handicapped and mentally retarded
27. Welfare of the weaker sections, and in particular, of the Scheduled Castes and the Scheduled Tribes
28. Public distribution system
29. Maintenance of community system

STRUCTURE OF PANCHAYATI RAJ INSTITUTIONS

The basic objective of Panchayati Raj being the evolution of a system of democratic decentralization, the Panchayati Raj system has a three-tier structure: (i) the Village Panchayats, (ii) the *Panchayat Samitis* and (iii) the *Zila Parishad.*

Village Panchayats/Gram Panchayat

Gram Sabha

The State Government, by notification, may establish a Gram Sabha by name for every area declared as Gram Sabha area. This is the lower-tier of the Panchayati Raj Institution, and comprise as members all villagers—men and women living in that particular area, who have attained the age of 18 years, and whose name has been entered as voter on the electoral roll prepared by the State Election Commission for the time being in force to the area of a *Gram Sabha*. The *Gram Sabha* meets twice a year in general meetings. Meetings of the *Gram Sabha* are convened to ensure the development of the people through their participation and mutual co-operation. In one year at least two meetings of the *Gram Sabha* are held. In its first meeting (*Sawni* meeting: in the month of December, at the time of harvesting of the Sawni Crop) the *Gram Sabha* considers the budget of the *Gram Panchayat*. In its second meeting (*Hari* meeting: in the month of June after the harvesting of the Hari Crop) it considers the annual reports of progress of preceding year and development programme proposed to be undertaken in the current year of the *Gram Panchayat*. The *Sarpanch,* at any time, may call an extraordinary general meeting where within thirty days of the receipt of a requisition in writing of the Panchayat Samiti or of not less than 150 of the total number of members of the *Gram Sabha* has been received by the *Sarpanch*. A *Gram Sabha* elects the members of its Panchayat and also the Chairperson of Panchayat/*Sarpanch*. Every meeting of the *Gram Sabha* shall be presided over by the *Sarpanch* of the *Gram Panchayat*, and in his absence by any *Panch* (member) to be elected at the time of the meeting. The annual budget and the development schemes for the village are placed before the *Gram Sabha* for consideration and approval by the Gram Panchayat. All decisions of community development should take in *Gram Sabha* only. The quorum for any meeting of the *Gram Sabha* is one-fifth of the total number of members.

Functions of Gram Sabha

The main functions of *Gram Sabha* are:

(a) to review the annual statement accounts and annual progress report of the Panchayat
(b) to discuss and audit administrative reports of its Panchayat and schemes for Panchayat works
(c) to approve the annual budget and plan development programme
(d) to render assistance in the implementation of the development projects
(e) to mobilize voluntary labour and contributions in kind or cash or in both for the community welfare programme
(f) to seek clarifications from the *Sarpanch* and the *Panches* of the *Gram Panchayat* about anything related to income, expenditure or any activity or schemes under the Panchayat.

Gram Panchayat

The executive arm of the *Gram Sabha* is the Village Panchayat or *Gram Panchayat*. The *Gram Panchayat* comprises elected representatives of the people. Membership varies from 5–31. Seats are also reserved for scheduled castes, scheduled tribes, and women community. The Chairman is elected from among its members, known as *Sarpanch*. The Panchayat is accountable for all its actions to the *Gram Sabha*, the general body of villagers, and consists of all the adults residing within the jurisdiction of the Panchayat. The Government may also nominate two members from among women and scheduled castes if the latter two are not represented at all. The members must not be salaried persons under the Government or co-operative society. Persons convicted for crimes for more than six months are also debarred from membership.

Sarpanch/Chairperson

The *Sarpanch* or Chairperson is the head of the *Gram Panchayat*. The elected members of the *Gram Panchayat* elect from among themselves a *Sarpanch*, and a Deputy *Sarpanch* for a term of five years. In some places they are also known as *Pradhan and Upa-Pradhan.* The *Pradhan* and in his absence *Upa-Pradhan* presides over the meetings. In some places the Panchayat President is directly elected by the villagers. The *Sarpanch* presides over the meetings of the *Gram Panchayat* and supervises its working. He implements the development schemes of the village. The *Deputy Sarpanch*, who has the power to make his own decisions, assists the *Sarpanch* in his work.

Source of Income and Power to Tax

Taxes and fees constitute its main source of income. It can levy rates and taxes on Houses and lands, professions and business within the village. Fees on litigation from *Nyaya Panchayat*, water supply, lighting of roads may be collected. Conservancy taxes may also be levied by it. The Panchayat also-derives its income from schools, dispensaries and its own properties. Its income may also be supplemented by grants from the *Panchayat Samiti* and *Zila Parishad*. Other sources of income include professional tax, taxes on pilgrimage, animal trade, grant received from the State Government in proportion of land revenue and the grants received from the *Zila Parishad*, loan for State Governments. Beside, *Gram Panchayat* can impose fees for registering vehicles, water fare, lighting charges and taxes on shops. With permission from the State Government a *Gram Panchayat* may take loans from bank or any other financial institution on the basis of a specific project of its own. The *Gram Panchayat* has to prepare a budget every year for every financial year which has to be placed before the *Panchayat Samiti*.

Meetings and Quorum

The meeting of *Gram Panchayat* shall be in public and must be held once a month. The *Gram Panchayat* carries out its work by passing resolutions. The *Sarpanch* convenes and presides over the meetings of the Panchayat. A majority of members of the Panchayat constitutes the quorum. Consensus or majority takes all decisions. *Sarpanch* can cast a vote in case of a tie. The *Sarpanch,* when required in writing by taking the consent of majority of the the *Panches*, shall convene a meeting within three days and failing this the *Panches* shall, with the previous approval of the prescribed authority, be entitled to call a meeting after giving a week's notice through the Panchayat Secretary, and such officers as the State Government may prescribe, to the *Sarpanch* and the other *Panches.*

Committees of the Gram Panchayat

The *Sarpanch* exercises control over Panchayat administration. The Panchayat functions through its four or five Committees like the Production Committee, the Social Justice Committee, the Amenities Committees and the like. The *Sarpanch* is an *ex-officio* member and President/Chairman of each Committee. The other members of Committees are elected by the *Panches* from amongst themselves.

Tenure

The *Gram Panchayat* is elected five years. Before the expiration of their tenure, election to a new Panchayat has to be arranged. The 73rd amendment Act provides that under abnormal situation, the State Government can extend the tenure upto a maximum of six months. If another six months, a proposal must be placed the State Legislature before such notifications. Under the circumstances that there are serious allegations about abuse of power by the *Gram Panchayat* or it is not competent to perform or make dismal performances as far as its activities are concerned or disregards any direction given by the *Panchayat Samiti* or *Zila Parishad* or the State Government, then the State Government can dissolve the *Gram Panchayat* by an order being published in the Official Gazette.

Powers and Functions of Gram Panchayat

The functions of the *Gram Panchayat* can be classified as general functions, construction, repair and maintenance of community assets, agriculture, social and farm forestry, minor forest produce fuel and fodder, rural housing, rural electrification including distribution of electricity providing for maintenance of lighting of public streets and other places, poverty alleviation programmes, adult and non-formal education-promotion of adult literary, cultural activities, fairs and festivals, public health and family welfare, women and child development, social welfare including welfare of the handicapped, mentally retarded, welfare of weaker sections especially the Scheduled Castes and Scheduled Tribes and public distribution system. The *Gram Panchayats* must also perform those functions which might be assigned by notification by the State Government and also some delegated functions of *Panchayat Samiti* or *Zila Parishad* if it is required by the State Government.

Among the general functions, the *Gram Panchayat* performs function like preparation of annual plans for the development of the Panchayat area; preparation of annual budget; mobilizing reliefs in natural calamities including relief to the poor; removal or encroachments on public properties; organizing voluntary labour and contribution for community works; maintenance of essential statistics of village; rendering assistance and implementation of development schemes pertaining to the village through its *Gram Sabha*; promotion of unity and harmony among all the sections of society in the village; exercising general supervision over the working of the Panchayat and laying down necessary guidelines for its working and performing functions pertaining to rule-making, rule implementation and to some extent judicial functions.

A Village/*Gram Panchayat* works for satisfying the needs of its area in respect of the following matters:

1. upkeep of public places, sanitation and drains
2. wells, water pumps, springs, ponds and tanks for the supply of drinking water and washing and bathing *ghats*
3. burial and cremating the grounds
4. building for accommodation of travellers
5. ponds for animals
6. the relief for poor
7. public health and sanitation
8. organization and celebration of public festivals other than religious festivals
9. improvement of the breeds of animals used for agricultural or domestic purpose
10. public gardens, playgrounds, establishment and maintenance or recreation parks, organization of games and spots, supply of sports materials and holding of tournaments
11. libraries and read the rooms
12. registration of the sales of cattle's
13. development of agriculture and village industrics
14. starting and maintaining a grain fund for the cultivators and lending them seeds for sowing purposes
15. construction, repair and maintenance of public places and buildings of public utility
16. allotment of places for preparation and conservation of manure
17. supply of water for domestic use and for cattle
18. the organization of 'Young Farmers Club' and 'Mahila Mandal' for the organization of games and sports and execution of development, social and cultural works in the *Sabha* area
19. planting and preservation of trees
20. measures to promote the moral, social and material well-being or convenience of the inhabitants of the *Sabha* area

21. community listening
22. organizing of village voluntary force for watch and ward and for assisting the executive in the discharge of its functions

A *Village Panchayat* has the power to make necessary rules. It can levy some taxes and collect some fees. It also earns income from Panchayat property. *Gram Panchayat* has also the power to settle small disputes among the people of the village.

The State Governments may by notification also assign other functions to it, such as, primary and vocational education, charitable dispensary and health centres, arrangement of ferry services, irrigation, grow more food campaign, rehabilitation of refugees, plantation of trees, introduction of co-operative fanning, improvement of cattle, establishment of libraries and reading rooms, sinking of tube-wells and excavation of tanks, development of cottage industries, open markets, prevention of theft and robberies, construction of hotels and rest-houses, etc.

The *Gram Panchayat* also has the power to make general order on a number of matters of importance to the village. Some of them are:

1. Prohibit the use of a well, pond or other excavation suspected to be dangerous to the public health
2. Regulate or prohibit the watering of cattle or bathing or washing at or near wells, ponds, or other excavations, reserved for drinking water
3. Regulate or prohibit the steeping of hemp or any other plant in or near ponds or other excavations within 220 yards of the residential area of a village
4. Regulate or prohibit the dyeing and tanning of skins within 440 yards of the residential area of a village
5. Regulate or prohibit the excavation or earth
6. Regulate or prohibit the establishment of brick kilns and charcoal kilns within 880 yards and pottery kilns within 220 yards of the residential area of the village
7. Regulate the construction of new buildings or the extensions or alterations of any existing building or the *abadi*
8. Regulate with the previous permission of the State Government the parking of public vehicles

The *Gram Panchayats* may also from time-to-time pass by-laws for carrying out its functions. Among other functions of the *Gram Panchayats*, they also have the power of naming of streets and numbering of buildings.

Judicial Functions

The judicial functions of the *Gram Panchayats* extends only to offences as mentioned in Schedule B of the Gram Panchayat Act, 1952 and over to cases/ offence falling under the provisions of Sections 178 to 181 of the Code of

Criminal Procedure, 1973. Certain cases are excluded from the purview of the *Gram Panchayat* like those offence under the Indian Penal Code, 1960, in which either the complainant or the accused is a public servant or such criminal cases where hearing on substantially the same facts against the same person is going on in another competent Court and the like.

Cognizance of criminal cases by the *Gram Panchayats* are taken on receipt of a complaint in writing and on payment of fee prescribed in the Act of 1952 by presenting it in person to the *Sarpanch*, and in his absence to any *Panch* or by sending it by registered post to the *Gram Panchayat.*

The *Gram Panchayat* on receipt of the complaint may examine the complaint and the witnesses, if any, and after such enquiry if it deems it to be necessary may dismiss the complaint or summons the accused. It may also dismiss the case if the complainant is absent on any day fixed for hearing of the case or for want of prosecution. If the complainant however, satisfies the *Gram Panchayat* that his absence was on sufficient cause, that is there were valid reasons for his absence, then the *Gram Panchayat* can revive the proceedings.

The *Gram Panchayat* at any time, if it appears to it that the offence is one for which the verdict/sentence which the *Gram Panchayat* is competent to pass would be inadequate, it can send the record of the case by order in writing to the Chief Judicial Magistrate.

If the accused fails to appear or cannot be found, the *Gram Panchayat* shall report the facts to the Magistrate having jurisdiction over the area. The Magistrate then shall issue summons or warrant for the arrest of the accused and in case of a warrant, shall direct by endorsement on the warrant that if such person executes a bond in certain amount with or without sureties for his attendance before himself under Section 71 of the Code of Criminal Procedure, 1973, he shall be released from custody. When the accused appears before the Magistrate he may direct him to execute a bond with or without sureties in the amount to be named to appear before the *Gram Panchayat* at its next meetings and it shall be the duty of such accused to enquire the date and time of the next meeting of the *Gram Panchayat.* On the failure to execute such a bond by him, if required to do so, the Magistrate shall order that the accused may be produced in custody before the *Gram Panchayat* at its next meeting. Further, if the accused fails to appear before the *Gram Panchayat* after executing a bond, the *Gram Panchayat* shall report the fact to the Magistrate before whom the bond was executed and such Magistrate shall proceed to compel the attendance of the accused amount of bond under Chapter XXXIII of the Code of Criminal Procedure, 1973.

Any *Gram Panchayat* may, on conviction, sentence the accused to a fine, discharge him after due admonition, may require him to execute within such time as *Gram Panchayat* may fix a bond with or without sureties, and in case, where the accused is under eighteen years of age the *Gram Panchayat* may require the father/guardian to execute within a given time the bond with or without sureties.

There are certain jurisdictions of the *Gram Panchayat* regarding civil, revenue and judicial functions. A *Gram Panchayat* may try cases like:

1. suits for the recovery of movable property or the value of such property;
2. suits for money or goods due on contracts or price thereof;
3. suits for compensation for wrongfully taking or injuring movable property; and
4. suits mentioned in Clauses (i), (k), (l) and (n) of the Sub-section (3) of Section 77 of the Punjab Tenancy Act, 1887.

However, there are certain limits to the jurisdiction of the *Gram Panchayat*. The *Gram Panchayat* cannot try the suits like:

1. On a balance of a partnership account;
2. For a share or a part of share under an intestacy or for a legacy or part of legacy under a Will;
3. By or against the Central Government or a State Government or local authority or a public servant or a Gram Panchayat or any other party who is in the opinion of the *Gram Panchayat* a necessary party;
4. By or against a minor or a person of unsound mind or when any such person is in the opinion of the *Gram Panchayat* a necessary party.
5. By or against a minor or a person of unsound mind or when any such person is in the opinion of the *Gram Panchayat* a necessary party.
6. Against an insolvent for a claim pertaining to the time prior to the admission of his insolvency petition;
7. In which the matter directly and substantially in issue is pending for decision or has been heard and finally decided by a Court of competent jurisdiction in a former suit between the same parties.

Panchayat Samiti

Panchayat Samiti is the second and middle tier of the Panchayati Raj. In different States it is known by different names. Madhya Pradesh calls it the *Janapada Panchayat*, Assam the *Anchalik Panchayat*, Tamil Nadu it is called the Panchayat Union Council, and U.P. the *Kshetra Samiti*. The Taluka level body is known as *Taluka Panchayat* in Gujarat and in Karnataka as the Taluka Development Board. Its most popular name however, happens to be *Panchayat Samiti*. A *Panchayat Samiti* is created at the block level. Each block consists of the areas of several Panchayats.

Composition

The *Panchayat Samiti* is the main executive body which operates at the block level. The block, comprising multiple villages is administered through a *Panchayat Samiti*, consisting of indirectly elected members of Village

Panchayat. Membership of *Panchayat Samiti* comprises six or ten members who are elected directly by the voters of all the constituencies falling within the area of the *Panchayat Samiti*. One member of the *Panchayat Samiti* is elected for a population unit of 15000, elected representatives of the *Sarpanch*s of the Panchayats of the Block, Local MLAs and MLCs and women representatives, Scheduled Castes and Scheduled Tribes whose seats stand reserved. In every *Panchayat Samiti*, seats are reserved for women and people belonging to Scheduled Castes and Scheduled Tribes and OBCs. Not more than one-third of all seats stand reserved for SC/ST are reserved for women belonging from Scheduled Castes and Scheduled Tribes.

Chairman and Vice Chairman of the Panchayat Samiti

In the very first meeting, each *Panchayat Samiti* elects two of its members as Chairman and Vice-Chairman. They are also known as *Sabhapati* and *Saha-Sabhapati* in certain places. Chairmanships of at least one-third *Panchayat Samitis* stand reserved for women members. Likewise, some of the offices of Chairman stand reserved for members belonging to SCs. The tenure of the Chairman is equal to the tenure of the *Panchayat Samiti*. The members of a Panchayat Samiti can remove the Chairman by passing a resolution supported by two-third majority. A Block Development and Panchayat Officer (BDO/BDPO) and a term of Block Extension officers help every *Panchayat Samiti* in its work.

Funds of a Panchayat Samiti

The main source of fund of the *Panchayat Samiti* can be said to the proceeds of taxes and fees which a *Panchayat Samiti* may levy on share in the land or local fee and duty on transfer of property, community development grants, funds allotted by the State Government or *Zila Parishad*, loans granted by the Central Government or loans collected by the *Samiti* keeping its own property as bond. It also comes from the ad hoc grants from or through the *Zila Parishad*, donations and contributions, funds from schemes transferred by the Government to the *Panchayat Samiti* as an agency for execution and various other sources.

Tenure

The term of each *Panchayat Samiti* is five years in all States except the *ex-officio* members. If a member of the *Samiti* voluntarily resigns or is discharged or dies, the concerned seat lies vacant. Any member of the *Samiti* can be removed on the grounds as applicable to the members of a *Gram Panchayat*. The same procedure is followed regarding the extension of tenure of a *Panchayat Samiti* as that of a *Gram Panchayat*.

Meeting and Quorum

A meeting of *Panchayat Samiti* is either ordinary or special. The date of every meeting is fixed by the Chairman of the *Panchayat Samiti* and in his absence by the Vice-Chairman and the notice has to be served before seven days of meeting, but an emergent meeting can be convened within a prior notice three days. The quorum of the meeting requires the presence of one-fourth of total members. In case the presence is less than the minimum required, the meeting of the *Panchayat Samiti* cannot take any decision. The *Sabhapati* may put his or her casting vote in case of tie.

Powers of a Panchayat Samiti

To prepare plans and to make the arrangements including financial assistance regarding agriculture, animal husbandry, fisheries, rural health, sanitation programme, cottage industries, rural debt, primary and adult education including student welfare and the like. It helps in:

1. construction, repairs and maintenance of inter village roads and culverts on such roads and other means of communication
2. supply of drinking water
3. opening of drains and soakage pits
4. establishment of primary health and maternity centres
5. making provisions for medical and health services
6. making provisions for primary and basic schools, adult literacy and education centres
7. establishment of the community information, recreation centres, establish youth organizations, *Mahila Mandals*, Farmer Clubs, Village Clubs
8. establishment and popularization of libraries
9. encouragement for physical and cultural activities
10. promotion and strengthening of industrial, irrigation, farming and other cooperative societies.

The other important functions of the *Panchayat Samiti* pertaining to the fulfillment of the development programmes are:

1. execution of all programmes under community development
2. multiplication and distribution and popularization of improved manure and fertilizers
3. reclamation of land and conservation of soil
4. providing credit for agricultural purposes
5. providing irrigation facilities
6. planting of trees and growing of village forests
7. introducing improved fodder
8. prevention and cure of disease among cattle
9. dairying and milk supply
10. opening and development of cooperative societies in various fields

11. development of cottage, village and small-scale industries
12. establishment and maintenance of production-cum-training centres

Panchayat Samiti coordinates among developmental plans and projects taken by different *Gram Panchayats* within the block. It also examines and approves the budgets of *Gram Panchayats*.

Zila Parishad

The *Zila Parishad*, is at the apex of the Panchayati Raj Institution, and it functions at the district level. It is responsible for making executing and coordinating the programmes of rural development for the entire district. It looks after the development of the rural areas of the district. It has the power to acquire, hold and dispose of property. It can enter into contracts. It elects its Chairman from amongst its members. It is known in some parts of India as in Andhra Pradesh, Bihar, Gujarat, Maharashtra, Punjab, Rajasthan, West Bengal as *Zila Parishad*, in Assam as *Mohkuma Parishad* (sub-divisional level), in Gujarat as District Panchayat and in Tamil Nadu and Karnataka as District Development Council.

Composition of Zila Parishad

It has the 10 to 25 directly elected members from all the constituencies falling within the rural area covered by a *Zila Parishad*. Approximately 50,000 rural people elected one representative. All Chairmen of *Panchayat Samitis* are falling within the area of the *Zila Parishad*. The names MPs and MLAs stand registered as voters in any constituency of the area of *Zila Parishad*. In every *Zila Parishad* some seats are reserved for Scheduled Castes and Scheduled Tribes and OBCs, and women. The ratio of reserved seat is in proportion to the population of SCs. One-third directly elected seats are reserved for women. In the case of OBCs, one seat is reserved in case their population living in the *Zila Parishad* area in 20% or more of the total population.

Chairman and Vice Chairman of Zila Parishad

In the first meeting of the *Zila Parishad*, the members elect from amongst themselves, one Chairman and one Vice Chairman who are also sometimes known as *Sabhapati* and *Saha-Sabhapati*. The main function of the *Zila Parishad* Chairman is to preside over the meetings of the *Zila Parishad*. He exercises administrative supervision and control over the chief executive officer and other officials of the *Zila Parishad*. The *Zila Parishad* can assign him any duty. He supervises the financial administration of the *Zila Parishad*. The *Sabhapati* and *Saha-Sabhapati* can be removed from their posts if proposals of their removal are passed by a majority in a specially convened meeting of the *Parishad* for that purpose. In that meeting, the accused person cannot preside over.

Tenure

The term of each *Zila Parishad* is five years in all States except the *ex-officio* members. If a member of the *Parishad* voluntarily resigns or is discharged or dies, the concerned seat lies vacant. Any member of the *Samiti* can be removed on the grounds as applicable to the members of a *Gram Panchayat* and *Panchayat Samiti*. The presence of *ex-officio* members ensures the organic unity of all the three-tier of the Panchayat system. A member who has been disqualified has a right of appeal for justice to the authority appointed by the State Government within thirty days of his or her discharge from the membership of the *Zila Parishad*.

Sources of Income

There is a fund in each *Zila Parishad* where income from different sources are deposited. The funds come from part of land revenue given by Central Government or State Government, the grants received from the Central and State Governments, loan received from them, income collected from road tax and toll tax, income from cesses, fees, etc. income earned from schools, hospitals, dispensaries, houses, institutions and factories run and maintained by the *parishad*, income from donation or financial assistance or from the *Panchayat Samiti* or any other trust or professional institutions and other sources too. Funds of the *Zila Parishad* are kept in the Government treasury or sub-treasury or in a bank. The Secretary of the *Zila Parishad* signs all order of expenditure or cheques against the *Zila Parishad* funds.

Quorum for Meetings

The *Zila Parishad* meets once in three months. Its special meeting can also be held when requested in writing by one-third of its members. The Chairman has to call such a special meeting within 15 days of receipt of such a request. The majority of total membership of a *Zila Parishad* is the quorum for its meeting.

Committees of the Zila Parishad

The *Zila Parishad* functions through a number of standing committees. Each Committee is in charge of specified subjects and comprises five members. The members of these Committees are elected from amongst the members of the *Zila Parishad*. The Chairman of the *Zila Parishad* is an *ex-officio* member of all the Standing Committees. No member can be a member of more than two Committees. The five main Standing Committees are the General Committee, the Finance, Audit and Planning Committee, Social Welfare Committee, Education and Health Committee and Agriculture and Industry Committee.

Functions of the Zila Parishad

Main functions of *Zila Parishad* are development of agriculture, setup and maintain warehouses, train the farmers, land reclamation and conservation, development of irrigation, water utilization in an optimum way, rural electrification, development of animal husbandry, develop of cold storage facilities, small scale and cottage industries, spreading of education, celebration of national festivals, encouragement of small savings and to perform such functions as may be given to it by the State Government. The functions can be summed up as:

1. Development of agriculture
2. Setting up and maintenance of warehouses
3. Training the farmers
4. Land reclamation and conservation
5. Development of irrigation
6. Water utilization in an optimum way
7. Rural electrification
8. Distribution of essential commodities to the people
9. To collect and publish data regarding Panchayats, *Panchayat Samiti* and *Zila Parishad*
10. Developing marketing network for marketing agricultural produce
11. Conservation and development of forests
12. Looking after the development of Animal Husbandry, Dairy and Fisheries
13. Organization of health facilities
14. Construction and maintenance of roads
15. Developing of cold storage facilities
16. Encouragement to small scale and cottage industries
17. Spreading of education
18. Welfare of weaker sections of society
19. Celebration of national festivals
20. Encouragement of small savings
21. Performance of such functions as may be given to it by the State Government

The *Zila Parishad* being a supervisory body and an advisory body it also has certain other functions like:

1. Examination and approval the budget of the *Panchayat Samitis*
2. Issuing directions to *Panchayat Samitis* for performing their functions efficiently
3. Coordination development plans prepared by the *Panchayat Samitis*, coordinating inter-block activities
4. Advising the State Government on all matters relating to the development of the district
5. Distribution State-allocated funds to the *Panchayat Samitis* in the district

6. Informing the District Collector and the Divisional Commissioner about irregularities committed by the *Panchayat Samitis* in the district
7. Collection of statistics relating to the activities of local authorities in the district
8. Advising the State Government regarding the allocation of work to be made among *Panchayats* and *Panchayat Samitis* in the district
9. Exercising such powers and performs such functions as may be conferred by the State Government

Initially, the 73rd Amendment did not apply to Scheduled Tribes area in the States of Andhra Pradesh, Madhya Pradesh, Rajasthan, Gujarat, Maharashtra, Himachal Pradesh, Odisha and Bihar. Subsequently, the Panchayat (Extension to the Scheduled Areas) Act, 1996 was passed by the Parliament and vide this Act, tribal bodies have been granted vast amount of power.

WOMEN PARTICIPATION IN PANCHAYATS

Undoubtedly, the 73rd Constitutional Amendment has created a lot of political space for women. Indeed there has been a steady rise of women participation in PRIs as revealed in a study which showed that 36.7% women were present in most of the Panchayat bodies and 42.9% in Karnataka alone. Kerala also shows that women participation in women-headed Panchayats is more than male-headed Panchayats. Studies conducted by Participatory Research in Asia (PRIA) in several Indian States like Madhya Pradesh, Gujarat, Haryana, Uttar Pradesh in 1997, and other organizations conducting researches over female participation in Panchayat bodies in Maharashtra, Rajasthan, Odisha have shown that in some cases though the female participation is encouraging, but the story is almost similar everywhere except Kerala. In Rajasthan, the women in Panchayats are just there for namesake and their husbands or in-laws are the de facto people in the Panchayat bodies. In Uttar Pradesh, the husbands of the *Pradhans* popularly who come to be identified as *Pradhanpatis* wield the power of their wives and influence the village politics. In West Bengal, though many women have come forward to take upon their responsibilities in the Panchayat bodies, yet, most often, face financial constraints which prevent them from attending meetings or someone has to accompany them, either a husband or a relative to the meeting place. Some sort of insecurity, is thus, prevalent which debars active participation of women in politics. Sexual harassment and in subordination are also faced in some places. In most of the Panchayat bodies, headed by a male, women feel neglected. The women folks rarely attend the meetings and participation is low. Most of the women are illiterate and suffer from the fear of social restrictions and are also shy to come out into the world and participate in politics. As Prabhat Dutta points out that the inhibiting factors of women participation are:

1. Literacy and low educational level
2. Compliance with social restricts
3. Shyness and submissiveness
4. Lack of comprehensive understanding of their roles and responsibilities
5. Weak articulation skills

Certain other factors which contribute to the non-participation of women are:

1. Male family members/spouses assume the role of *Sarpanch*
2. Support of other Panchayat members divided along caste and gender considerations
3. Indifferent attitude of Government officials and functionaries
4. Misguidance by the Panchayat Secretary in conducting Panchayat activities.

Another deplorably alarming case is the *Caste Panchayat* or the *Khap Panchayats* which can be found in Haryana, Western Uttar Pradesh and parts of Rajasthan and which frequently issue *diktas* which are not only illegal but also have adopted heinous means to implement them at any cost like *honour killing*. In Maharashtra, there are traditional Panchayats like *Gavki* which comprises upper caste people, the village patriarchs and obviously women are excluded. The *Gavki* functions side by side the constitutionally mandated Panchayats and in most cases prevails over the Panchayats. These are certain developments which impedes the full-fledged participation of women in PRIs. Family support and education will improve the women's aptitude of decision-making so that she can mobilize the community participation. Here the support of voluntary organizations/community groups is very important. Needless to say that an overall change in attitude of the society is required so that the status of women gets uplifted and she no longer is considered as a weaker sex.

74TH CONSTITUTIONAL AMENDMENT AND THE MUNICIPAL CORPORATIONS AND MUNICIPAL COUNCIL, MUNICIPALITIES AND PLANNING COMMITTEES

PART IXA gives a Constitutional foundation to the Local Self-Government units in urban areas. Some of the provisions are similar to those contained in Part IX, e.g., Reservation of Seats, Finance Commission, Election Commission and others. Article 243Q lays down clearly that institutions of self-government, called by a general name municipalities are of three types:

1. Nagar Panchayat, for a transitional area, i.e., an area which is being transformed from a rural area to an urban area
2. Municipal Council for a smaller urban area
3. Municipal corporation for a larger urban area

Article 243Q makes it obligatory for every State to constitute such units. But if there is an urban area or part of it where municipal services are being provided or proposed to be provided by an industrial establishment in that area, then considering the size of the area and other factors the Governor may specify it to be an industrial township. For such an area it is not mandatory to constitute a Municipality.

Composition of Municipalities

Article 243R provides that the members of a municipality would generally be elected by direct election. The Legislature of a State, may by law, provide for representation in a municipality of persons having special knowledge or experience in municipal administration, Members of Lok Sabha, State Assembly, Rajya Sabha and Legislative Council, and the Chairpersons of Committees constituted under Clause (5) of Article 243S. The Chairperson shall be elected in the manner provided by the Legislature.

Wards Committee

Article 243S upholds that there shall be constituted *Wards Committees* consisting of one or more wards comprised within the territorial area of a municipality having a population of three lakh or more it would be obligatory to constitute *Wards Committees*. The State Legislature shall make provision with respect to its composition, territorial area and the manner in which the seats in a *Wards Committees* shall be filled. As far as the Constitution of other Committees are concerned it is open for the State Legislature to constitute Committees in addition to the *Wards Committees*.

Reservations of seats for Scheduled Castes and Scheduled Tribes

Article 243T provides that as in Part IX reservations of seats are to be made in favour of the Scheduled Castes and Scheduled Tribes in every Municipality.

Reservation for Women

Article 243T(2) provides that out of the total number of seats to be filled by direct elections at least one-third would be reserved for women. This includes the quota for women belonging to Scheduled Castes and Tribes.

Reservation of offices of Chairpersons

It has been left to the State Legislature to prescribe by law the manner of reservation of the offices of the Chairpersons of Municipalities. It is permissible for a State Legislature to make provisions for reservation of seats or offices of Chairpersons in favour of backward classes.

Duration of Municipalities

Article 243U provides that every Municipality shall continue for five years from the date of its first meeting. But it may be dissolved earlier according to law. Article 243U further prescribes that before dissolution, a reasonable opportunity of being heard must be given to the Municipality elections to constitute a municipality shall be completed before the expiry of the period of five years. If the Municipality has been superseded before the expiry of its term, the elections must be completed within six months of its dissolution. A Municipality constituted after its dissolution shall continue only for the remainder of the term. But if the remainder of the period is less than six months it shall not be necessary to hold elections. It has been provided that no amendment of the law in force shall cause dissolution of a Municipality before the expiry of the five years term.

Qualification for Membership

Article 243V lays down that all persons who are qualified to be chosen to the State Legislature shall be qualified for being a member of a Municipality. There is an important difference. Candidates who have attained the age of 21 years will be eligible to be a member while the constitutional requirement for election to the State Legislature of a State, is that a person must have attained the age of 25 years [Article 173].

Powers, authority and responsibilities of Municipalities

Article 243W lays down that the Legislatures of States have been conferred all such power and authority to confer on the Municipalitics such powers and authority which are necessary to enable them to function as institutions of self-government. It has specifically been mentioned that they may be given the responsibility of preparation of plans for economic development and social justice, implementation of schemes as may be entrusted to them, and in regard to matters listed in the **12th Schedule**.* This Schedule contains 18 items, e.g., Urban Planning, Regulation of Land Use, Roads and Bridges, Water Supply, Public Health, Fire Services Urban Forestry, Slums and so on.

Powers to impose taxes and financial resources

Article 243X empowers the State Legislature to authorize, by law, a Municipality to levy, collect and appropriate taxes, duties, tolls and so on. The law may lay down the limits and prescribe the procedure to be followed. It can also assign Municipality various taxes, duties, etc. collected by the State Government. Grants-in-aid may be given to the Municipalities, from the Consolidated Fund of the State.

---

* 12th Schedule is discussed later in the chapter.

Finance Commission

Article 243Y provides that the Finance Commission appointed under Article 243I shall also review the financial position of the Municipalities and make recommendations as to:

1. the distribution between the State and the Municipalities of the net proceeds of taxes, duties, tolls and fees leviable by the State which may be divided between them and how allocation of shares amongst various levels of Municipalities.
2. the taxes, duties, tolls and fees may be assigned to the Municipalities.
3. grant-in-aid to the Municipalities
4. the measures needed to improve the financial position of the Municipalities.
5. any other matter that may be referred to it by the Governor.

Additional duties have been assigned to the Finance Commission under Article 280 which states that the Commission will make recommendations in regard to the measures needed to augment the Consolidated Fund of a State to supplement the resources of the municipalities in the State on the basis of the recommendations made by the State Finance Commission.

Elections of Municipalities

Article 243ZA provides that the State Election Commission appointed under Article 243K shall have the power of superintendence, direction and control of the preparation of electoral rolls for, and the conduct of all elections to the Municipalities. State Legislatures have been vested with necessary power to regulate by law all matters relating to elections to Municipalities.

Bar to interference by courts in electoral matters

Article 243ZG embodies that the Courts shall have no jurisdiction to examine the validity of a law, relating to delimitation of constituencies or the allotment of seats made under Article 243ZA. An election to a Municipality can be called in question only by an election petition which should be presented to such authority and in such manner as may be prescribed by or under any law made by the State Legislature.

Committees for District Planning (Article 243ZD) and Metropolitan Planning (Article 243ZE)

Apart from giving constitutional recognition to Municipalities the 74th Amendment lays down that in every State two committees shall be constituted.

1. At the district level a District Planning Committee [Article 243ZD].
2. In every metropolitan area a Metropolitan Planning Committee [Article 243ZB].

The composition of the Committees and the manner in which the seats are to be filled are to be provided by a law to be made by the State Legislature. It has been laid down that:

1. In case of the District Planning Committee at least 4/5th of the members shall be elected by the elected members of the district level Panchayat and of the municipalities in the district from amongst themselves. Their proportion would be in accordance with the ratio of urban and rural population of the district. The State Legislature would by law make provision with respect to the functions relating to district planning that may be assigned to the district committees the manner in which the Chairperson of a district committee may be chosen. While preparing draft development plan the District Committees must have regard to matters of common interest between the Panchayats and the municipalities including spatial planning, sharing of water and other physical and natural resources, the integrated development of infrastructure and environmental conservation and the extent and type of available resources whether financial or otherwise. These Committees must consult such institutions and organizations as the Governor may by order specify.
2. In case of Metropolitan Planning Committee at least two-third of the members of the Committee shall be elected by the members of the municipalities and Chairpersons of the Panchayats in the metropolitan area from amongst themselves. The proportion of seats to be shared by them would be based on the ratio of the population of the Municipalities and the Panchayats in the area. The State Legislature would by law make provision with respect to composition of Metropolitan Planning Committee, manner in which seats are to be filled, representation in such Committees, functions relating to planning and coordination for the metropolitan area, the manner in which the Chairpersons of such Committees shall be chosen. The Committees shall prepare and forward the development plan to the State Government. In regard to the Metropolitan Planning Committee which is to prepare a development plan for the whole Metropolitan by giving full regard to the plans prepared by the Municipalities and the Panchayats, matters of common interest between the municipalities and the Panchayats, including spatial planning, sharing of water and other physical and natural resources, the integrate development of infrastructure and environmental conservation and overall objectives and priorities set by the Government of India and the Government of the State, the extent and nature of investments likely to be made in the Metropolitan area by agencies of the Government of the State and other available resources whether financial or otherwise. The Committees must also consult such institutions and organizations as the Governor may by order specify.

Twelfth Schedule (Article 243W): Powers, authority and responsibilities of Municipalities

1. Urban planning including town planning
2. Regulation of land use and construction of buildings
3. Planning for economic and social development
4. Roads and bridges
5. Water supply for domestic, industrial and commercial purposes
6. Public health, sanitation conservancy and solid waste management
7. Fire services
8. Urban forestry, protection of the environment and promotion of ecological aspects
9. Safeguarding the interests of weaker sections of society, including the handicapped and mentally retarded
10. Slum improvement and upgradation
11. Urban poverty alleviation
12. Provision of urban amenities and facilities such as parks, gardens, playgrounds
13. Promotion of cultural, educational and aesthetic aspects
14. Burials and burial grounds, cremation, cremation grounds and electric crematoriums
15. Cattle ponds; prevention of cruelty to animals
16. Vital statistics including registration of births and deaths
17. Public amenities including street lighting, parking lots, bus stops and public conveniences
18. Regulation of slaughter Houses and tanneries

Municipal Corporations

The 74th Amendment Act has been a landmark in setting up of local-self Governments in urban areas. The Municipal Corporation is at the apex of the urban local self Government. There are various forms of local Governmental bodies. They are:

1. Municipal Corporations
2. Municipal Councils or Municipalities
3. Notified Area Committees
4. Town Area Committees
5. Cantonment Boards
6. Townships

Existing notified area committees and town area committees have now been put under the rubric of N*agar Panchayat*. After the 74th Amendment was enacted there are only three categories of urban local bodies:

1. Nagar Nigam (municipal corporation) for a larger area
2. Nagar Palika (municipality) for a smaller urban area and
3. Nagar Panchayat (city council) for a transitional area, that is to say an area transition from a rural area to an urban area

Whether an area should be classified as a transitional area, a smaller urban area, or a larger urban area depends on how the Governor may deem fit specify notification on the basis of population of the area, the density of the population therein, the revenue generated for local administration, the percentage of employment in non-agricultural activities, the economic importance or other factors. The following criteria that have been laid down in the 1991 Census:

1. All statutory towns, i.e., all places with a corporation, municipality, cantonment, township, notified area committee, town area committee, etc.
2. The following criteria is to classify all other places which have:
   (a) A minimum population of 5,000
   (b) 75% of the male working population engaged in non-agricultural activity
   (c) A density of population of at least 400 per sq. km.

Every Municipal Corporation is set up by special statute adopted in the respective State Legislature. To meet the demands of the growing population and urbanization in various cities of India the local governing body work for providing necessary community services like health centers, educational institutes and matters related to housing and property tax. The municipal elections are held once in five years directly by the people. The aim behind its creation was to provide the convenient services to the people as it caters to their daily problems and holds a central importance in the entire State departments. The Municipal Corporations of Bombay, Madras and Calcutta have been borne out of special legislations. The Municipal Corporations in KAVAL towns covering Kanpur, Agra, Varanasi, Allahabad and Lucknow in Uttar Pradesh have been set up by UP Mahapalika Adhiniyam, 1959. The Municipal Corporations of GIRJ towns covering Gwalior, Indore, Raipur and Jabalpur have been set up by the MP Municipal Corporation Act, 1956. The oldest Municipal Corporations are in Kolkata, Mumbai and Madras. The largest Municipal Corporations in India currently are Mumbai, followed by Delhi, Kolkata, Bangalore, Chennai, Hyderabad and Ahmedabad. Corporation of Chennai is the oldest Municipal Corporation in the world outside UK.

Composition of the Municipal Corporation is fixed by the size of the population of the city as determined by laws passed by the State Legislature. The members are directly elected by the people. The Corporation area is divided into wards and every ward elects one member. Along with this, the members of the Legislative Assemblies of the State represent constituencies which comprise wholly or partly the Municipal areas. There are also provisions for reservation of seats for Scheduled Castes and Scheduled Tribes and not less than one-third of the total number of seats should be reserved for women including women belonging to the Scheduled Castes or as the case may be the Scheduled Tribes.

The tenure of Municipality is five years, and shall continue unless dissolved by law for the time being in force. Otherwise the Municipal Corporation will continue for five years from the date of commencement. A Municipal Corporation constituted upon dissolution of one such Corporation, shall continue only for the remainder of the period (if less than six months it shall not be necessary to hold any election) for which the dissolved Corporation would have continued.

The Municipal Corporation elects from themselves, after the first meetings of the Corporation after a Municipal election one **Chairman** and one **Deputy Chairman** popularly known as **Mayor** and **Deputy Mayor**. A Mayor is the highest ranking officer in a Municipal Government of local town or large urban city. Mayor presides over the meetings. He is elected by the Councilors including the aldermen from among themselves for a term of five years. However, the Mayor and Deputy Mayor can be removed from office before the expiry of their term by passing a resolution to that effect by two-third majority. The Council comprises the Councillors who are directly elected by the people from the ward to which he/she belongs to. They are also elected for a term of five years. The Council is the legislative wing of the corporation. West Bengal has a Mayor-in-Council consisting of the Mayor, the Deputy Mayor and not more than 10 other elected members of the Corporation.

The Mayor generally lacks executive authority. Councillors act by committee, the most powerful being the Standing Committee with its role of the steering committee exercising executive, supervisory, financial and personnel powers. It is composed of elected members varying in number between seven and sixteen through a system of proportional representation of Councillors.

Meetings are held once in a month usually, but emergency meetings can be held if written request are made by members of a Municipal Corporation. Decisions in a meeting are taken by a majority of members present and voting. In case of a tie, the Mayor can give his casting vote.

A **Municipal Commissioner** is the Chief Executive Officer of the corporation. He is an administrative staff of the Municipal Corporation, implement the decisions of the corporation and prepare its annual budget. In Kolkata Corporation, he prepares the annual report and is responsible for the custody of all records of the corporation. He is a professional high ranking officer who is appointed by the State Government usually of IAS rank to assist in the administrative works. The Commissioner can be withdrawn at any time. He has the right to speak in the meetings of the Council and its Committees without the right to vote.

Apart from the Mayor and the Commissioner, some Municipalities also have Standing Committees which form policies, and direct the functioning of the corporation. The elected councillors recommend policies to govern the municipal area to the administrative organization led by the Commissioner, and have supervisory as well as financial powers. These powers are clearly defined by State legislations. Among these powers are deciding which taxes are to be imposed, and in what proportion, formulating and passing a budget and raise loans if required, formulation of bye-laws relating to water supply, building and construction, public markets, regulation and use of public streets, control and supervision of slaughter houses etc., and preparation of draft development plans.

Functions of Municipal Corporations

The functions of Municipal Corporation can be classified as obligatory functions and discretionary functions.

Important Obligatory functions of the Municipal Corporation include roads and transport service; water supply; supply of electricity; construction, maintenance; naming and numbering of public places; scavenging; removal and disposal of filth and rubbish; records of births and deaths; sanitation that includes waste management, sewage, drainage and flood control; public safety services like fire and ambulance services, gardens and maintenance of buildings, provisons of primary education, publication of annual reports and returns on administration of the Corporation, control and regulation of eating places and eatables and many more functions which are necessary for the maintenance and development of a particular area under the Corporation.

The discretionary functions are like construction of public parks, gardens, libraries, museums, theatres, *akharas*, and stadiums; public housing, plantation of tress; registration of marriages, survey buildings and lands, organization and management of fairs, and so on.

The **Twelfth Schedule of Constitution** (Article 243W) provides an illustrative list of *eighteen functions*, which are entrusted to the municipalities (mentioned above).

Besides the traditional core functions of municipalities, it also includes development functions like planning for economic development and Social justice, urban poverty alleviation programmes and promotion of cultural, educational and aesthetic aspects.

The sources of income of the Corporation are property tax, entertainment tax, octroi, tax on vehicle and animals, tax on advertisements (other than newspapers), profession tax, education tax, theatre tax, tax on consumption and sale of electricity, license fees, rents from rest Houses and other buildings and others. The Corporation also receives grants from Governments, and can raise loans also from Government and Governmental institutions.

The 74th Constitutional Amendment Act as pointed out earlier embodies provisions for formation of a Finance Commission in each State. The Finance

Commission is entitled to lay down rules for distribution of taxes between State Government and Municipal Corporations, the determination of taxes, duties, tolls and fees which may be assigned to, or appropriated by the Municipal Corporations and also grants-in-aid from the consolidated fund of the State.

However, various legislations enacted by the different State Governments indicate wide variations in the composition, powers and functions of the Municipal Corporations. Some States like Bihar, Gujarat, Himachal Pradesh, Haryana, Manipur, Punjab and Rajasthan have included all the functions as enlisted in the Twelfth Schedule in their amended State municipal laws. Andhra Pradesh has not made any changes in the existing list of municipal functions. States like Karnataka, Kerala, Madhya Pradesh, Maharashtra, Orissa, Tamil Nadu, Uttar Pradesh and West Bengal have amended their municipal laws to add additional functions in the list of municipal functions as suggested in the Twelfth schedule. There is a lot of difference in the assignment of obligatory and discretionary functions to the municipal bodies among the states. Besides these State level agencies, City Improvement Trusts and Urban Development Authorities, like Delhi Development Authority (DDA), have been set up in a number of cities. These agencies usually undertake land acquisition and development works, and take up remunerative projects such as markets and commercial complexes, etc.

Nagar Panchayats

Transitional areas which are fast changing from rural to urban area or very small urban areas are to constitute Nagar Panchayats for local governance. The particular State Legislature by law fix the strength of the members as well as the tenure and powers and functions. Usually the tenure is five years and if it is dissolved before that then fresh elections must be held to elect a new body which continues for the rest of the tenure of the last Nagar Panchayat. Nagar Panchayats elect their own President and Vice-President. There are also provisions for reservation for Scheduled Caste, Scheduled Tribes and Women.

Municipal Councils

The Governor of a State has the power to notify any area as a smaller urban area for which a Municipal Council must be set up. Usually, factors such as the population or the economic importance of such an area are considerations for creating a Municipal Council. Members of Municipal Councils are elected directly, and the number of members in a particular Council is decided in proportion to the population of that area.

The members, who are an integral part of the Municipal Council, are its President, the committee and the Chief or the Executive Officer. The Municipal Council elects from among the Councillors one of its members as the President and another one as the Vice-President. Though the **President** is the elected head similar to a Mayor, his powers are much broader. The President not only presides over all the meetings, he is also required to watch over the financial and executive functioning of the Council. The President can be removed from office before the expiry of his term by passing a resolution to that effect by two-third majority. The Council is a larger body which includes all the elected members known as Councillors. There are also provisions for reservation of seats for Scheduled Caste, Scheduled Tribes and women including women belonging to scheduled caste or scheduled tribes.

The President has a substantive position in the municipal administration and enjoys significant authority and power both in the deliberative and executive arms of the municipality. The powers and functions of the Municipal Council committees are the same as those of the Municipal Corporation. President is helped in the discharge of his functions by an **executive officer** usually appointed by the State Government. In some states the Council makes the appointment, but his or her independence has been confirmed by making removal from office difficult—generally by a three-quarter majority vote.

Powers and Functions of the Municipal Council

The powers and functions of Municipal Councils are almost similar to those of Municipal Corporations. Municipal Councils may also have to discharge duties under some other Acts, which may be specified by the State Government. West Bengal has created a Chairman-in-Council for municipal Councils, similar to the Mayor-in-Council for municipal corporations.

While a Municipal Corporation takes care of a large area, Municipal Councils work for a comparatively smaller area. The Municipal Councils are governed directly by State statutes and therefore, they vary from one State to other depending on the size and population of the state. The municipal Councils also have discretionary and obligatory functions that have to be carried out and are almost similar to the functions of Municipal Corporations and Municipalities.

The **obligatory functions** performed by the Municipal Councils are supply of pure and wholesome water, construction and maintenance of public streets, lighting and watering public streets, cleansing public streets, places and sewers, regulation of offensive, dangerous or obnoxious trades, callings or practices, maintenance and support of public hospitals, registration of births and deaths, establishment and maintenance of primary schools, naming streets and numbering Houses and various other functions.

The discretionary functions include laying out of areas; securing or removing dangerous buildings or places; construction and maintenance of public parks, gardens, libraries, museums, rest Houses, leper homes, orphanages and rescue home for women; planting and maintenance of roadside and other trees; housing for low income groups; promotion of welfare of municipal employees and others.

It also performs certain **administrative functions** like framing bye-laws within the framework of the corresponding Municipal Act, imposing fines for violation of rules, purchase and sell of lands, levy and collect taxes and so on.

The sources of income are property tax, profession tax, octroi, animal and vehicle tax, entertainment tax, water tax, lighting tax, latrines and drainage tax, grants from Central and State Governments.

With passage of time, new steps have been taken up to update and upgrade the municipal system in the country. Many modern mechanisms have been applied to these local bodies so that their efficient functioning is ensured, and quality of services they provide improves.

The 73rd and the 74th Amendments Acts (1992) are milestones in the evolution of local self governments in India. Much work has to be done in order to fully realize the aims and objectives of these two amendments. Never-the-less they are significant stepping stone towards establishment of grassroots democracy.

EXERCISES

I. Short Answer Questions: **(100 words)**

1. Write a note on Balwant Rai Mehta Committee.
2. Write a note on K. Santhanam Committee.
3. Write a note on Ashok Mehta Committee.
4. Write a note on L.M. Singhvi Committee.
5. Gram Panchayat.
6. Panchayat Samiti.
7. Functions of Panchayats under the Eleventh Schedule
8. Write a note on the judicial functions of Gram Panchayat.
9. Functions of Municipalities under the Twelfth Schedule.

II. Long Answer Questions: **(1200 words)**

10. Discuss the evolution of Panchayati Raj System in India.
11. In the light of 73rd Amendment discuss the basic features of the Panchayati Raj Institution in India.
12. Discuss the structure of Panchayati Raj structures in India.
13. Examine the participation of women in Panchayats in India.
14. Discuss in the light of 74th Amendment the basic features of Municipal administration in India.
15. Discuss the composition, powers and functions of Municipal Corporations.
16. Discuss the composition, powers and functions of Municipal Councils.

REFERENCES

Avasthi, A. and S. Maheshwari, *Public Administration*, The Premier Press, Agra, 1985.

Awasthy, S.S., *Indian Government and Politics*, Har Anand Publications, New Delhi, 2006.

Bakshi, P.M., *The Constitution of India* (with selective comments), Universal Law Publishing, Delhi, 2000.

Dutta, Prabhat Kumar, "Daughters of the Seventy Third Amendment of the Constitution in action: Problems and Possibilities" International Seminar on Women's Political Participation: Quotas or Not, organized by Women's Studies Research Centre, Calcutta University, Kolkata, 2011.

Government of India, *Constitution of India.*

Raina, Ramendra K., *Panchayati Raj System in India*, Mohit Publications, New Delhi, 2010.

Sarkar Siuli, *Public Administration in India*, PHI Learning, New Delhi, 2010.

73rd Constitutional Amendment Act, 1992.

74th Constitutional Amendment Act, 1992.

16

Party System in India—Major National Parties

INTRODUCTION

India is a representative democracy, and the true essence of this democracy is sustained by way of representation of the people of India through various political parties in the Parliament or in the Legislatures of the State. India has a multi-party system, which can be broadly divided into two categories—the National Parties and the Regional Parties. National parties usually are those that are recognized in four or more states, and the Election Commission of India accords this status to them. Some recognized political parties in India are Indian National Congress, Bahujan Samaj Party, Bharatiya Janata Party, All India Forward Bloc, All India Trinamool Congress, Communist Party of India (CPI), Communist Party of India (Marxist), Indian National Conference, All India Anna Dravida Munnetra Kazhagam (AIADMK, Communist Party of India (Marxist-Leninist) Liberation, Dravida Munnetra Kazhagam, Indian Union Muslim League, Jammu and Kashmir National Conference, Janata Dal (Secular), Janata Dal (United), Samajwadi Party, Shiromani Akali Dal, Shiv Sena, Telangana Rashtra Samithi, Telugu Desam Party, All India Majlis-e-Ittehadul Muslimen, Jammu and Kashmir People's Democratic Party, Jharkhand Mukti Morcha, Kerala Congress, Rashtriya Janata Dal and others. From a single party majority, the Indian political scenario is now a game of coalitions. From the last few general elections, India has had a hung Parliament, and therefore, no single party has had the numbers to form the Government on their own and have been forced to make alliances with other parties to get the majority mark. In fact, parties these days form pre-poll alliances to enable their coalition to come up with the required numbers. The same scenario of coalition Governments is being witnessed in many States too.

FEATURES OF PARTY SYSTEM IN INDIA

The first and foremost feature of the Indian party system is that it is a multi-party system. There is a huge presence of political parties, big or small at national or regional level. National parties put up their candidates for elections usually all over India, and Election Commission also gives them such recognition. Some prominent national level parties are Indian National Congress, Bhartiya Janata Party, Bahujan Samaj Party, Samajwadi Party, Communist Party of India, Communist Party of India (Marxist) and so on. Regional parties are political parties which, participate in different elections but only within one State or in a particular region like Shiv Sena in Maharashtra, Telugu Desam in Andra Pradesh, Akali Dal in Punjab, Dravida Munnetra Kazhagam (DMK) and All India Anna Dravida Munnetra Kazhagam (AIADMK) in Tamil Nadu, to mention a few.

The next feature can be identified as the existence/origin of some of the parties prior to independence. Some parties started as movements and then gradually converted themselves into a political party like Indian National Congress, Forward Bloc, Akali Dal, and National Conference. Some of these parties were either social or political organization before India's independence, and they became political parties after independence.

Further, some parties were formed after splits from larger parties. In the 1960s, Lok Dal emerged from a split from the Indian National Congress. All India Trinamool Congress (AITMC) and the Nationalist Congress Party (NCP) are breakaway groups from Indian National Congress. Communist Party of India (Marxist) was established after the split in Communist Party of India in 1964. AIADMK was formed out of DMK. Telugu Desam broke up into two parts after N.T. Rama Rao's death. The two factions were Telugu Desam and NTR Telugu Desam (formed by Laxmi-Parvati, widow of NTR). Some parties also emerge after mergers like Janata Dal which emerged with the conglomeration of Janata Party factions, the Lok Dal, Congress (S) and the Jana Morcha led by V.P. Singh in 1988. Earlier Lok Dal had separated itself from Janata Party in 1979.

In Indian politics there are also many independent candidates. These candidates participate in election constituencies independently without the support of any party. In the 1952 Lok Sabha elections, independents secured 42 seats. In 1971, 1977 and 1980 elections independents secured 11, 9 and 3 seats in Lok Sabha elections respectively. In 1989, 1991, 1996, 1998, 1999, 2004 and 2009 the independents won 12, 1, 9, 6, 6, 5 and 9 seats, respectively.

Charisma/personality of a leader has also been a determining factor in case of many parties. Indira Gandhi had a charisma which compelled the party workers and even the public to follow her. N.T. Rama Rao being a film personality and having a huge fan following created an image of himself which helped the party to win votes. Atal Bihari Vajpayee and L.K. Advani have images to pull electorates during election time. Congress President Sonia Gandhi and Rahul Gandhi have their distinctive personality which enables them to control the party and influence the voters. Bal Thackeray, the Shiv Sena chief has his own style of functioning in Maharashtra, and is quite capable of retaining a large section of voters. At present, another trend is also being noticed. Political parties, whether national or regional, involve celebrities from all walks of life like authors, painters, singers, film actors, theatre personalities, academicians and the like to woo voters. These people not only make public appearances and campaign for the political parties/party candidates, but also participate as candidates in the elections.

Many of the large national parties have a pre-election agreement/alliance with smaller parties on joint candidates in some constituencies. This candidate belongs to one of the parties and the other party supports this candidate to prevent the splitting of the votes of their wing and losing the constituency to the rival wing. This was witnessed recently in the 2011 in the West Bengal Assembly elections where Trinamool Congress worked out a pre-electoral alliance with Congress to prevent the division of votes.

The most outstanding feature of the party system in India is that although India is a multi-party democracy, but in the period immediately after independence from 1951–1967, there has been one party dominance system with the Indian National Congress as the single largest party in the Parliament and in most of the States. The parties in the opposition were incapable of providing an alternative form of Government and limited themselves to criticisms and not in opposition for opposition's sake and sometimes even went to the extent of influencing like minded factions within the Congress. Thus, Rajni Kothari talks about Congress as a "party of consensus" and the opposition parties as "parties of pressure". The Communist Party of India has been the major opposition force in the Parliament, but very feeble to influence Government policies in its own way in the immediate post-independence phase. After 1967 however, there was a transformation of the party structure. The Congress failed to secure majority in eight States and managed to win 283 seats out of 520 losing nearly 60 seats in the Lok Sabha. This was the end of one-party dominance in India as the Congress under Indira Gandhi during 1967–71 formed a minority Government with the support extended by the Communists. In 1971 Lok Sabha elections, the Congress again revived its position only to lose to the Janata Party in 1977 due to the proclamation of emergency by Indira Gandhi. However, in 1977, to form a unified opposition, seven political parties including the Swatantra Party, the Utkal Congress, the Bharatiya Kranti Dal, and the Socialist Party came together to form the Bharatiya Lok Dal under Charan Singh. With these Jan Sangh, BLD and Congress (O) joined to form the Janata Party which deposed the Congress Government and came to power in 1977. This was the first Coalition Government since independence, which broke the long continuation of one-party dominance of Congress. Again in 1980 and 1984, the Congress witnessed successive victories. But this cannot be said to be return of one party dominance as other parties too by that time had come to existence, only the mood or sympathy of the voters were with the Congress. In 1980, it was the public disgust shown towards the factionalism in the Janata Dal which got reflected in the election results, and in 1984, the assassination of Indira Gandhi aroused sympathy among the voters which helped Rajiv Gandhi to get a landslide victory. However, in 1989 elections again, the situation was changed and though the Congress emerged as the largest party it refused to form the Government and instead sat in the opposition. From then onwards a new episode started in the Indian political scenario.

The year 1989 marked the beginning of coalition politics at national level. A non-Congress coalition, the National Front which was a conglomeration of parties like Janata Dal, Dravida Munnetra Kazhagam, Telugu Desam, Asom Gana Parishad and Indian Congress (Socialist) under V.P. Singh formed the Government succeeded by Chandra Shekhar of Samajwadi Janata Party in 1990, which resigned in 1991. As the Governments were short lived so elections to Lok Sabha were held in 1991 and no party could secure majority in the Parliament. A minority Government was formed by the Congress with the help of left parties which could complete the term for next 5 years under Narasimha Rao. The BJP emerged as the second largest party with 120 seats and got the recognition as the opposition party. In the 1996 Lok Sabha elections, again there was a hung Parliament, which would see three Prime Ministers in two years and fresh polls had to take place in 1998. First, BJP staked a claim and under Atal Bihari Vajpayee formed a Government which survived for 13 days and next in quick succession two coalition Governments were formed the United Front-I and United Front-II and the Congress was in the opposition. 1998 signalled the beginning of end of dominance of one party as a non-Congress coalition Government was formed under BJP-led National Democratic Alliance (NDA). Since then, no national party has been successful in obtaining absolute majority on its own and forming the Government at the centre. As in 2004 and 2009 the Congress could form Government with its coalition partners. Thus, it is not Congress alone but United Progressive Alliance I&II which is in power, and the Congress though commands a maximum number of seats, yet, it is not in the driver's chair. The Congress has to operate under pulls and pushes of its coalition partners.

Coalition is the rule of the day in the elections to the State Legislative Assemblies as well. In 2011 West Bengal Assembly elections, Trinamool and Congress forged an alliance which are also coalition partners in the

UPA-II. The Left Front Government from 1977–2011 in West Bengal was also a conglomeration of several left parties. In 2007, Shiromani Akali Dal came to power in Punjab in coalition with BJP. Congress shared power in Maharashtra with Nationalist Congress Party (NCP) in 1999 although both competed against each other in the State elections. The Biju Janata Dal (BJD) won a majority of seats in the State Legislative Assembly in the 2000 and 2004 elections in alliance with BJP in Odisha. So at State and National level coalition politics is becoming more prevalent as the electorate has become aware of the performance of different political parties. Moreover, media is so active that nothing escapes the media. Investigative journalism has unearthed many scandals and scams, and public therefore, has become more informed. Thus, the multi-party coalitions formed since 1990s are regarded as a kind of accommodative politics with all varieties of parties coming together in broad coalitions with national parties as the verdict of the electorate sways from time-to-time on the basis of issues and performance of political parties and one particular political party fails to emerge with an absolute majority.

Weak party discipline and consequent defections are prevalent in the Indian Party system. Sometimes, if a party line is unacceptable or election tickets are refused to some persons or may be someone's willingness to leave one party and join some other or float a different party, members may defect. Defection has caused splits in party, factionalism, rivalry, conflicts within party as such have led to weakness of party system. Party discipline sometimes has to be forcefully enforced through suspension or removal from membership. To tackle the problem of defection the Anti Defection Law was enacted through the 52nd constitutional Amendment Act, 1985, and was inserted as the Tenth Schedule in the Constitution, which provides for qualified defection, which means that a mass defection involving at least one-third of the members of the member of a party who decide to form a new party or join with other parties in the political process will result in a split and not defection and thus will be valid and legal.

MAJOR NATIONAL POLITICAL PARTIES IN INDIA

The Election Commission has provided criteria for recognition of parties as national or state level parties. Generally, inter alia, a political party shall be eligible for recognition as a State Party in a state, if, in the last general election to the Legislative Assembly of the State, the candidates sent up by the party have secured not less than six percent of the total valid votes polled in the State and in addition the party has won at least two seats to the Legislative Assembly of that State at such general election or at the last general election to the Legislative Assembly of the State, the party has won at least three percent of the total number of seats in the Legislative Assembly, or at least three seats in the Assembly, whichever is more.

A Political party is usually recognized as National Party, if, the candidates sent up by the party, in any four or more States, at the last general election to the House of the People, or to the Legislative Assembly of the State concerned and have secured not less than six percent of the total valid votes polled in each of those states at that general election; and, in addition, it has won at least four seats to the House of the People at the aforesaid last general election from any State or States; or at the last general election to the House of the People, the party has won at least two percent of the total number of seats in the House of the People and the Party's candidates have been elected to that House from not less than three States; or the party is recognized as State party in at least four States.

Some of the major political parties at the national level are discussed below:

Indian National Congress (INC)

Indian National Congress (INC) is one of the major political parties in India. Indian National Congress was established in 1885, under the initiative of A.O. Hume. Some earliest prominent leaders of the party were Dadabhai Naoroji, Dinshaw Wacha, Womesh Chandra Bonnerjee, Surendranath Banerjee, Mahadev Govind Ranade among others. The Indian National Congress (INC) was at the forefront of the nationalist movement in India. National movements between 1920 and 1947 like the Non-cooperation Movement (1920–1922), the Civil Disobedience Movement (1931–1932), and the Quit India movement (August 1942) made the Congress more acceptable to the people of India at large. This was reflected in the elections of 1936–1937 following the lines of Government of India Act 1935 where the Congress won seven of the eleven Provinces. Since the independence of India, the Congress, an all-embracing national movement, emerged as the ruling party, and it maintained power uninterrupted for almost three decades (1947–1977). However, the party has experienced a number of splits since it came into existence. Parties like the All India Trinamool Congress (AITMC) and the NCP (Nationalist Congress Party), are breakaway groups from INC.

Post-independence, the Congress under the leadership of Jawaharlal Nehru, India's first Prime Minister (1947–1964), the Congress controlled 70% of seats in Parliament and held power in most states between 1951 and 1967. This period of one-party dominance has been referred to as the "Congress system" in Indian politics. However, after the general elections of 1967, the Congress got a jolt and lost most of its seats in the Parliament as well as it could not secure majority in many states. This was followed by a phase of centralization of the party organization by Indira Gandhi. The party suffered a split in 1969 following a power struggle between Indira Gandhi and the Congress organization (especially Morarji Desai). The majority followed Mrs. Gandhi and her "New Congress" or "Congress (R)" (*R* for "ruling"), which was recognized by the election Commission as the "real" Indian National Congress. With the support from Socialist and Communist Parties, the Congress under Mrs.Gandhi could continue for the next two years after the split in 1969. To tide over internal tensions, Indira Gandhi's leadership witnessed the de-institutionalization of the party as she undermined the federal character of the party by stopping party elections for years and concentrated power in her own hands.

With the declaration of emergency and the human rights violations following mass arrests of opposition leaders and misuse of Preventive Detention Acts, the Congress lost its dominant position with a huge margin for the first time in the 1977 elections. The Janata Party formed the Government with Morarji Desai as the Prime Minister. Faced with criticism of her leadership, Mrs. Gandhi split the party for a second time, in 1978, and formed the breakaway Congress (I) (*I* for "Indira"). The Congress (I) returned to power in 1980, but Mrs. Gandhi was assassinated in 1984. Mrs. Gandhi was succeeded by her son Rajiv Gandhi (1944–1991), who lost power in the 1989 elections. Following the assassination of Rajiv Gandhi, although the party held power from 1991 to 1996, the Congress was in decline as a national party. The Congress again faced a split when a small number of Congress (I) leaders led by Sharad Pawar formed a breakaway party in 1999 (the Nationalist Congress Party) on the question of the possibility of Mrs. Sonia Gandhi, a foreign-born, becoming Prime Minister. In 2004 Parliamentary elections, the Congress won, but could not secure the majority mark. Thus, it had to form a coalition Government with the support of left parties—The United Progressive Alliance-I (UPA-I). Sonia Gandhi, however, declined to become Prime Minister and remained the Party President, and Manmohan Singh became the Prime Minister. In the 2009, General elections again the Congress could not secure the majority mark and formed a coalition Government, the UPA-II. However, there were charges of corruption like the 2-G scam, the Commonwealth Scam and a host of other charges of corruption coupled with the anti-corruption movement and demand for a strong Lokpal Bill have put the Government under pressure. Along with this, in certain cases, the Government has to succumb to pressure from coalition partners. Therefore, unlike the initial years immediately after the independence of India, Congress now has to do tight-rope walking with the risk of being toppled at any time. The UPA faced an electoral debacle in the 2014 and 2019 Lok Sabha elections. The BJP-led NDA had a landslide victory in both the Lok Sabha elections.

List of Indian Prime Ministers from the Indian National Congress

1. Jawaharlal Nehru (1947–1964)
2. Gulzarilal Nanda* (May–June 1964, January 1966)

*Caretaker Prime Minister

3. Lal Bahadur Shastri (1964–1966)
4. Indira Gandhi (1966–1977, 1980–1984)
5. Rajiv Gandhi (1984–1989)
6. P.V. Narasimha Rao (1991–1996)
7. Manmohan Singh (2004–2014)

If the performance of the Congress in the General elections since 1951 is analyzed, it can be safely concluded that till 1967, it was the single largest party and it came to occupy maximum number seats in the Lok Sabha. In the First General elections, the Indian National Congress had a stupendous victory by winning 364 out of the 489 seat. In the Second Lok Sabha (1957) elections again the Congress won 371 seats from a total of 490 seats. The party also secured 47.78 per cent majority winning a total of 57,579,589 votes. In the Third Lok Sabha elections (1962), the Congress won 361 seats out of 494 seats winning about 44.72% of total votes. The Fourth General elections (1967) was a poll debacle for the Congress as the election took place at a time when the country was suffering from inflation, severe scarcities due to drought and the fall out of the 1962 and 1965 wars causing hardships to the people at large. The Congress managed to win 283 seats out of 520 seats, losing nearly 60 seats. Coupled with this, the non-Congress Governments came to power in the States of Bihar, Kerala, Orissa, Madras, the Punjab and West Bengal. The ruling Congress Party won 352 seats out of total 518 total seats in the Fifth General election (1971) winning about 43.68% of the total votes. Before the country went for another round of elections, i.e., the Sixth Lok Sabha elections, Indira Gandhi had proclaimed National Emergency twice in India. Thus, the State of Emergency declared by the Congress Government was the core issue in the 1977 elections. Civil liberties were suspended during the National Emergency from 25 June 1975 to 21 March 1977, and Prime Minister Indira Gandhi assumed vast powers. This was reflected in the poll results. Four opposition parties, the Organization Congress, the Jan Sangh, the Bharatiya Lok Dal and the Socialist Party, decided to fight the elections as a single party, called the Janata Party. The Congress lost the elections for the first time in independent India and Janata Party leader Morarji Desai, who had been released from prison two months before the elections, won 298 seats and a Janata alliance formed the Government taking their strength in the Lok Sabha to 345. The Congress won 187 seats which were down by 217 seats. In 1978, there was again a split in the Congress and Congress (I) was born. Morarji Desai however, lost a trust vote in Parliament and resigned. Charan Singh, who had retained some partners of the Janata alliance, was sworn in as Prime Minister in June 1979. Congress promised to support Singh in Parliament, but later backed out. Therefore, fresh elections had to be held in 1980. In the Seventh Lok Sabha elections, (1980) The Congress (I) and its allied parties won 374 Lok Sabha seats and the Janata Party alliance won 34 seats. The Congress won 351 seats alone. So again it could emerge as the single largest party. The Eighth Lok Sabha elections (1984) took place soon after the assassination of previous Prime Minister, Indira Gandhi. The Congress won again with a huge margin where it claimed about 48.1% of the votes except Jammu & Kashmir, Andhra Pradesh and Sikkim. The Congress-I won 414 seats, and a majority of 295 in the 533-seat Parliament. The Ninth Lok Sabha Elections (1989) saw the defeat of Congress and The National Front formed the Government under V.P. Singh. The Congress won only 197 seats with 39.53% of the total votes. In the year 1991, Lok Sabha elections to the Tenth Election had to be held as V.P. Singh could not survive for five years. The 1991 election result showed that the Congress could win 244 seats. However, no party could get a majority, so a minority Government was formed by the Congress with the help of left parties which could complete the term for next 5 years, under Prime Minister P.V. Narasimha Rao. Eleventh Lok Sabha (1996) again witnessed a hung Parliament, which saw three Prime Ministers in two years and fresh polls had to take place in 1998. Before the elections the Congress Government under Prime Minister P.V. Narasimha Rao came under scanner due to scandals and accusations of mishandling. The Congress could secure only 140 seats which meant only 28.80% of the total votes. The Congress declined to form the Government and agreed to sit in the opposition. Atal Bihari Vajpayee of BJP was invited to form the Government. He failed to prove his majority and had to resign after 13 days. Thereafter, in quick succession India had two persons as Prime Ministers of non-Congress coalition Government—one under H.D. Deve Gowda heading the First United Front Government and the other under I.K. Gujral heading the second United Front Government both collapsed like a pack of cards. Thereafter, in 1998 the Twelfth General Elections were held. The result was a hung Parliament again. However, Vajpayee was appointed as the Prime Minister and was asked to prove his majority in the House which he did successfully but he failed to secure the confidence of the House in April 1999 and had to resign. Thereafter, General Elections to the Thirteenth Lok Sabha took place. The Congress and its allies could secure only 144 seats which is 26.14% of the total votes. BJP alone picked up 270 seats. Therefore, BJP-led National Democratic Alliance (NDA) with partners like Telugu Desam, secured a large majority in the Lok Sabha. Atal Bihari Vajpayee became the Prime Minister of India and completed his five year term. The Fourteenth Lok Sabha Elections took place in 2004. The Congress was able to put together a comfortable majority of more than 335 members out of 543 with the help of its allies. The Congress-led United Progressive Alliance secured external support from the Bahujan Samaj Party (BSP), Samajwadi Party (SP), Kerala Congress (KC) and the Left Front. (support from outside). Dr. Manmohan Singh became the Prime Minister of India. The fourteenth Lok Sabha elections (2004) saw a re-emergence of Congress in the Lok Sabha polls. BJP-led

National Democratic Alliance (NDA) faced a set back and lost the elections. In the Fifteenth Lok Sabha elections, 2009, the UPA was able to put together a comfortable majority with support from 322 members out of 543 members of the House. Congress alone won 262 seats which was better than compared to Fourteenth Lok Sabha where it won 218 seats. The coalition partners were All India Trinamool Congress, Dravida Munnetra Kazhagam, Nationalist Congress Party, National Conference, Jharkhand Mukti Morcha, Indian Union Muslim League, Viduthalai Chiruthaigal Katchi, Kerala Congress (Mani), All India Majlis-e-Ittehadul Muslimeen and Republican Party of India (Athvale). In the 2014 general elections the Congress could secure only 44 seats in the Lok Sabha and UPA secured altogether 60 seats. In the 2019 Lok sabha elections the Indian National Congress won 52 seats and UPA secured 91 seats.

In the 2024 Lok Sabha elections, the Indian National Congress formed the INDIA alliance and was able to secure for itself 99 on its own and around 235 for the INDI 'Gatbandhan'.

The Congress Manifesto 2024 was entitled as 'Nyay Patra'. The manifesto focuses on 'Youth Justice', 'Gender Justice', 'Farmers' Justice', 'Workers' Justice', and 'Equity Justice', 'economy', 'Federalism', 'National Security', 'Environment' and 'Defending the Constitution' among other electoral pledges for the 18th Lok Sabha elections.

Bharatiya Janata Party (BJP)

The Bharatiya Janata Party (BJP) is the most prominent member of the Sangh Parivar. The Rashtriya Swayamsevak Sangh (RSS), the first of the Parivar (family) was founded by Dr. Hedgewar in 1925, and consolidated by Shri Guruji after 1940. The next in the line was the Bharatiya Jana Sangh (BJS) which was formed under the leadership of Dr. Shyama Prasad Mookerjee in 1951. The BJS later reorganized itself as the Bharatiya Janata Party. The Election Commission recognized BJP as a national party with Lotus as its symbol in April 1980. The BJS began its political career after India's independence with only three members in the first elections held in 1952. The Bharatiya Janata Party (BJP) a direct successor of erstwhile Bharatiya Jana Sangh (BJS) was founded in 1980, as a major political party of India. Table 16.1 gives an idea about the emergence of BJP from Jana Sangh to its present form. The Philosophy of BJP is *Hindutva* (Cultural Nationalism) which represents the BJP's conception of Indian nationhood.

Table 16.1 Timeline of Emergence of BJP

Bharatiya Jana Sangh	1951–1977
Janata Party	1977–1979
Bharatiya Janata Party	1980

In the 1962 elections, the Jana Sangh won 3 seats (3.06% of total votes) whereas the Akhil Bharatiya Hindu Mahasabha won 4 seats. In the second General elections the Jana Sangh secure 4 seats (5.97% of total votes). In the Fourth General elections (1967) the BJS gradually was consolidating its position, and won 14 seats (6.44% of total votes). The BJS in the fourth General elections won about 35 seats (9.31% of total votes). The Fifth General elections (1971) however, did not fetch increased number of seats for Jana Sangh. It had to be contended with 22 which showed a decline from its past poll perfromane. Post emergency polls in the year 1977 saw four opposition parties, the Organization Congress, the Jan Sangh, the Bharatiya Lok Dal and the Socialist Party, come together to fight the elections as a single party, called the Janata Party. The Congress lost the elections for the first time in independent India, and Janata Party won 298 seats and a Janata Alliance formed the Government taking their strength in the Lok Sabha to 345. Morarji Desai became the first non-Congress Prime Minister of India, but he lost a trust vote in Parliament and resigned. Charan Singh, who had retained some partners of the Janata alliance, was sworn in as a Prime Minister in June 1979. Congress promised to support Singh in Parliament, but later backed out. Therefore, fresh elections were held in 1980. In the Seventh Lok Sabha elections (1980) The Congress (I) and its allied parties won 374 Lok Sabha seats and the Janata Party alliance won 34 seats. The Eighth Lok Sabha elections (1984) saw an unprecedented victory of the Congress. The other parties were just whitewashed. The sentiment of the public after the assassination of Indira Gandhi was with the Congress. The election for the first time was fought by the BJP and not as a part of the Jana Sangh, and it secured only 2 seats securing 7.74% of the total votes. The Ninth Lok Sabha Elections (1989) saw the defeat of Congress and The National Front formed the Government under V.P. Singh which was a minority Government. It collapsed in November 1990 and Chandrashekar became the Prime Minister. However, he too could not complete his term and he resigned in March 1991. In this election the BJP had won 85 seats. Thereafter, in 1991 the Tenth Lok Sabha elections had to be held to form a Government. The result of the election was that no party could get a majority so a minority Congress Government under P.V. Narasimha Rao with the support of the Left Parties was formed. BJP was able to secure 120 seats (20.04% of the total votes). BJP thus emerged as the second largest party in the Lok Sabha next after the Congress. As a result it got the recognition as the opposition party and L.K. Advani, later on A.B.Vajpayee got the status of the leader of the opposition in the Lok Sabha. Eleventh Lok Sabha elections (1996) again witnessed a hung Parliament, but the BJP emerged as the second party winning 161 seats alone. The then, President Shankar Dayal Sharma invited A.B. Vajpayee as the leader of the BJP to form a Government. Sworn in on May 15, the new Prime Minister was given two weeks to prove majority support in the Parliament. Before the confidence vote on May 31, the BJP attempted to build up the much needed support. However, on May 28, Vajpayee conceded that he could not arrange support from more than 200 of the 545 members of Parliament, and thus resigned. This was the shortest period served by any Government as the Government collapsed after 13 days. Thereafter, in quick succession India had two persons one H.D. Deve Gowda heading the first United Front Government and I.K. Gujral heading the Second United Front Government. But Gujral's Government collapsed in April 1997, and he continued as a caretaker Prime Minister for sometime. Thereafter, the Twelfth General Election was held in 1998. Vajpayee was appointed as the Prime Minister and was asked to prove his majority in the House which he did successfully but he failed to secure the confidence of the House in April 1999, and had to resign. Although the BJP managed to get support from 286 members out of 545, the Government collapsed when the AIADMK, with its 18 seats, withdrew their support, leading to new elections in 1999. Thereafter, General Elections to the Thirteenth Lok Sabha were held a few months after the Kargil War in September. BJP alone picked up 270 seats. Therefore, BJP-led NDA with partners like Telugu Desam, secured a large majority in the Lok Sabha. Atal Bihari Vajpayee became the Prime Minister of India. In the fourteenth Lok Sabha elections the Bharatiya Janata Party (BJP) -led National Democratic Alliance conceded defeat. It could secure 181 seats which were short by 89 seats. In the fifteenth Lok Sabha elections 2009, the UPA-II formed the Government. NDA could secure 159 seats (24.63% of total votes). In both Fourteenth and Fifteenth General Elections the Congress-led UPA formed the Governments.

As far as elections to the Legislatures of different States of India are concerned in Assembly Elections of Delhi in 1993, and Gujarat and Maharashtra in March 1995, the BJP showed a good performance as well as in the elections to the Karnataka Assembly in December 1994. In Andhra Pradesh and West Bengal too the vote percentage of BJP rose. In 1992, BJP secured 6 seats in Punjab Vidhan Sabha elections. In 1998, the BJP was a coalition partner in States like Uttar Pradesh, Haryana, Himachal Pradesh and Maharashtra and in Delhi and Rajasthan it had formed its own Government all by itself. However, from 2000 onwards the popularity of BJP started declining. It lost to Congress in Rajasthan in 2000 and a bit later in Maharashtra too. In 2002 in Uttar Pradesh, Punjab, Uttarakhand and Manipur Vidhan Sabha it lost miserably. In 2003, BJP again lost in Himachal Pradesh and Delhi, but fortunately managed to win in Rajasthan, Madhya Pradesh and Chattisgarh. But the popularity was already on the negative side and this got reflected in the General Elections of 2004 where the BJP-led NDA alliance suffered a huge defeat and Congress-led UPA came to power and formed the Government.

BJP as of 2022 is in power in Uttarakhand, Gujarat, Uttar Pradesh, Tripura, Arunachal Pradesh, Madhya Pradesh, Manipur, Assam, Karnataka, Goa and

Himachal Pradesh. In Haryana, BJP shares power with Jannayak Janta Party and the Chief Minister Sri Manohar Lal Khattar is from BJP. BJP shares power in Mizoram, Meghalaya, Nagaland, Sikkim and Maharashtra.

The main problem with the party is the tag that has been added to it as that of a "communal" party. Since 1998, the BJP has managed to form alliances and even Governments at Centre and States, but will have more difficulties because of its philosophy of *Hindutva* and the attitude/policies of the parties to profess it at national and State levels.

The BJP-led NDA had a landslide victory with the BJP alone securing 282 seats and the alliance securing 336 seats. Shri Narendra Modi became the Prime Minister of India for a term of 2014–2019. The 2017 Assembly elections in Uttar Pradesh, Uttarakhand, Manipur and Goa revealed positive results for BJP. In Uttar Pradesh, BJP secured a huge number of seats (312) and formed the government. The BJP won 303 seats in the 2019 Lok Sabha elections and on the whole NDA secured 353 seats.

In the 18th Lok Sabha elections BJP solely could not cross the 272 majority mark. It solely secured 240 seats and NDA could manage around 293 to form the government. Sri Narendra Modi became the Prime Minister for the third term.

BJP's manifesto or **'Sankalp Patra'**, Titled "Modi's Guarantee: Developed India 2047," revolves around the theme of BJP's commitment to the the country's development, prosperity, and welfare across various segments, including women, youth, the underprivileged, and farmers.

The 'Sankalp Patra' contains an account of **'10 Years of Good Governance and Vikas'** and Modi Ki Guarantee for the following:

- Garib Parivar Jan
- Middle-Class Parivar Jan
- Nari Shakti
- Young Citizens
- Senior Citizens
- Kisan Samman
- Fishermen Families
- Shramik Samman
- MSME, Small Traders and Vishwakarmas
- Sabka Saath Sabka Vikas
- Vishwa Bandhu Bharat
- Surakshit Bharat
- Prosperous Bharat
- Global Manufacturing Hub
- World-Class Infrastructure

- Ease of Living in Cities
- Virasat Bhi, Vikas Bhi
- Good Governance
- Swastha Bharat
- Quality Education
- Sports Development
- Balanced Regional Development
- Technology and Innovations
- Sustainable Bharat

Communist Parties in India

At the national level, the two parties the Congress and the BJP, have a rightist bend, whereas on the other end of the spectrum parties with a leftist bend or Left parties also come to play important role in Indian politics. There are several parties adhering to the Marxist-Leninist ideology, but here we will discuss the two most significant of them—The Communist Party of India (CPI) and the Communist Party of India—Marxist (CPI-M).

Communist Party of India (CPI)

The CPI was formed as a part of Communist International at the enthusiasm of some Indian revolutionaries. There are debates around the exact timeline of formation of the Party. The foundation day as it is celebrated is 26 December, 1925. It is said that the CPI was founded in Tashkent on October 17, 1920, soon after the Second Congress of the Communist International. M.N. Roy, Abani Mukherji, Mohammad Ali (Ahmed Hasan), Mohammad Shafiq Siddiqui and M.P.B.T. Acharya were the founding members of the party. It was because of the initiative of M.N. Roy that small communist groups were formed in Bengal led by Muzaffar Ahmed, in Bombay led by S.A. Dange, in Madras led by Singaravelu Chettiar, in United Provinces led by Shaukat Usmani and in Punjab led by Ghulam Hussain. The first Kerala unit of Communist Party of India was founded in 1937, at a clandestine meeting in Calicut in the presence of prominent personalities like E.M.S. Namboodiripad, Krishna Pillai, N.C. Sekhar, K. Damodaran and S.V. Ghate.

The Communist Party of India was legalized in July 1942. They also strengthened their control over the All India Trade Union Congress (AITUC). In 1946, the Communist Party of India for the very first time contested the Provincial Legislative Assembly elections on its own. They won 8 seats out of 1585 seats. They had contested for three seats from Bengal and won all of them. CPI candidate Somanth Lahiri was nominated to the Constituent

Assembly. In 1946, the Tebhaga Movement in Bengal was launched by the party. It was a militant campaign against feudalism. (See Chapter 20) The CPI led armed struggles in Tripura, Telangana and Kerala.

After independence, the Communist Party emerged as the main opposition in the first General Election of 1951, where the Congress secured a landslide victory. CPI secured 16 seats and 3.9% of total votes. Though their numbers were less, yet the CPI played a formidable role in Indian politics with their critical outlook of Governmental policies. The Communist Party of India emerged as the largest opposition party in the general elections held in the year 1957. In 1957, CPI won the State elections in Kerala and this led the party to win control over an Indian State for the first time. E.M.S. Namboodiripad became Chief Minister. In the second and third Lok Sabha, elections 1962 the CPI secured 27 seats and 8.9% votes and 29 seats with 9.94% of the total votes, respectively.

At this juncture, the Communist Party of India experienced a rift within with regard to the Sino-Indian War (1962). In this with regard to the war, a section of the Indian communists rallied their support towards the Indian Government and others affirmed looked at it as a conflict between a socialist and a capitalist state, and thus, took a pro-Chinese position. The CPI got divided into factions with prominent leaders like S.A. Dange, Nayar, Yogender Sharma, Dr. Ahmed who supported Nehru's policies and more 'leftists' like A.K. Gopalan, E.M.S. Namboodiripad, B.T. Ranadive, Sundarayya, P.C. Joshi, Basavapunniah, Jyoti Basu, and Harkishan Singh Surjeet were amongst those who backed China. These kinds of ideological divergences contributed to the split in the party in 1964. In the wake of the Chinese invasion, the National Council wanted to condemn the Chinese aggression which was resented by the 'leftists', and they resigned in protest. In 1964, the 'left' attempted to oust the Party Chairman Dange, but without much success. Namboodiripad and Jyoti Basu staged a walk-out and the Party finally split in 1964 when all the signatories to the appeal to repudiate Dange and the reformist line were suspended from the party. The Communist Party of India and the Communist Party of India (Marxist) thus born.

In the Fourth (1967), Fifth (1971) and Sixth (1977) Lok Sabha elections the CPI captured 23 seats (5.0% of the total votes), 23 seats (4.7% of total votes and 7 seats (2.8% of total votes) respectively. Thus, one can perceive the decline in the influence of the party. During 1970–77, the Communist Party of India rallied behind the Congress party. The CPI-leader Achutha Menon became the Chief Minister and formed a Government together with the Congress in Kerala. Later, after the collapse of Indira Government in the post-emergency election, the CPI again oriented itself with Communist Party of India (Marxist). In the seventh (1980), Eighth, Ninth (1984–85), Tenth (1989) and Eleventh (1991) Lok Sabha elections they managed to get 11, 6,

12, 13 and 12 seats respectively. In the Twelfth (1998) Lok Sabha elections it secured 9 seats (1.75% of total votes) and in the Thirteenth (1999), Fourteenth (2004) and Fifteenth (2009) Lok Sabha elections they could capture 8, 10 and 4 seats respectively. A point to be noted is that the CPI was a partner in the United Front-I under H.D. Deve Goda which was formed following the collapse of the 13 day BJP Government formed after the 1996 elections and also the United Front-II Government under I.K.Gujral after the fall of United Front-I Government. Even before that the Communists supported the National Front Government of V.P. Singh from outside. They supported the Indian National Congress-led United Progressive Alliance (I), 2004 from outside. The Communist Party of India in West Bengal is an alignment of several Leftist and other Communist Parties, popularly ascribed as the Left Front-Government. They were also a part of Manipur Government and Left Democratic Front in Kerala before the Assembly elections of 2012 and 2011, respectively. It is part of the Progressive Democratic Alliance in Tamil Nadu. However, their position has continued to become weaker. It cannot be denied that they have pockets of influence in Assam, Bihar, Himachal Pradesh, Karnataka, Kerala, Madhya Pradesh, Maharashtra, Manipur, Meghalaya, Orissa, Punjab, Rajasthan, Tamil Nadu, Tripura, Uttar Pradesh and West Bengal. The CPI traditionally has strongholds in West Bengal, Kerala and Tripura.

CPI has some principal mass organizations like, All India Trade Union Congress; All India Youth Federation; All India Students Federation; National Federation of Indian Women; All India Kisan Sabha (peasants organization); Bharatiya Khet Mazdoor Union (agricultural workers); and All India State Government Employees Federation (State Government employees). Ardhendu Bhushan Bardhan was the General Secretary of CPI till 2012, and was succeeded by S. Sudhakar Reddy who was in office till 2019. Doraisamy Raja, the national secretary of the Communist Party of India (CPI) from 1994 to 2019 became the General Secretary in 2019.

Communist Party of India (Marxist) [CPI(M)]

As we have seen in the forgoing discussion that the Communist Party of India (CPI) experienced a split, in 1964. The Communist Party of India (Marxist) was thus born. It was mainly due to ideological differences regarding the CPI's disposition towards Soviet and Chinese Communists and their policy towards Congress. The CPM has established its stronghold in Kerala, West Bengal, Tripura, Andhra Pradesh and Assam, though its influence has been declining over the years. Over the years, the party had toned down its Marxian ideology and had fought elections in alliance with other left parties including its parent party, the CPI. In the 1970s till 1977, the CPI maintained proximity with the Congress and even aligned with the Congress in West Bengal to prevent the

CPI (M) out of power. From 1980s however, there was a shift in policy, and as we have seen above the two parties moved closer. In West Bengal the CPI (M) and its allies formed the Left Front Government in West Bengal. CPI was a partner and still remains a partner of the Left Front. The CPI (M) had registered victory in 1982, 1991 and 1996 elections, and Jyoti Basu was the Chief Minister till he retired in 2000. Thereafter, from 2000 to 2011, Buddhadeb Bhattacharjee was the Chief Minister of West Bengal. It is only in Tripura that the Left Front is in power with it gaining 49 out of 60 seats in the Assembly, 46 of which went to the CPI (M).

In West Bengal, the CPI and CPI (M) moved closer in 1967 when the United Front was formed. It was political coalition shortly after the 1967 West Bengal Legislative Assembly election through the joining together of the United Left Front (ULF) and the People's United Left Front (PULF), along with other parties. Thus, the United Front was able to depose the Congress from power in West Bengal. Ajoy Mukherjee became the Chief Miniter and Jyoti Basu the Deputy Chief Minister. [In Chapter 10 we have seen how Governor of West Bengal Dharma Vira dismissed the United Front Government without even giving Mukherjee a chance to prove his majority in the Assembly]. However, in West Bengal, the CPM-led Left Front Government has been in power since 1977, and was dislodged only in 2011 Assembly elections by Trinamool Congress. In Kerala, the Front led by CPM has been on and off in power as of now after 2011 Assembly Elections it is in opposition. In Kerala, CPI (M) led Left Democratic Front coalition with 68 seats lost to Indian National Congress led United Democratic Front's 72 seats in a tough fight in the Assembly elections.

At the all India level in the Lok Sabha elections, in 1967 CPI (M) secured 19 seats, in 1971 it got 25 seats, in 1977 it secured 22 seats, in 1980 it got 37 seats, in 1984 it got 22 seats, in 1985, it got 5 seats in Assam and Punjab, in 1989, it secured 33 seats, in 1991 it got 35 seats (in 1992–0 seats in Punjab), in 1996 it got 32 seats, in 1998 it got 32 seats, in 1999 it got 33 seats, in 2004 it secured 43 seats and in 2009 it secured 16 seats. The Communists also supported the National Front Government of V.P. Singh from outside in 1989. In 1996, it helped form a United Front of like-minded parties to install a Government with H.D. Deve Gowda as Prime Minister and then I.K. Gujral. In 2004, CPI (M) gave support to the Congress-led UPA-I, but it withdrew its support because of differences over the nuclear deal with the US. The UPA-I survived a vote of confidence in the Parliament on 22 July 2008 after left parties withdrew their support. UPA survived a vote of confidence mainly because of the Samajwadi party extended its support. In the 2014 General Elections, 9 CPI(M) candidates were elected and 2 CPI(M) supported independents. In the 2019 Lok Sabha elections the Left Front managed to win only five seats CPI (M) won 3 seats and CPI won 2 seats. In the 2024 Lok Sabha elections CPI(M) won 4 seats.

Bahujan Samaj Party (BSP)

Bahujan Samaj Party (BSP) or Majority People's Party is one of the prominent national political parties in India. The ideology of the Bahujan Samaj Party (BSP) is *Social Transformation and Economic Emancipation of the Bahujan Samaj*, which comprises the Scheduled Castes (SCs), the Scheduled Tribes (STs), the Other Backward Classes (OBCs) and Religious Minorities such as Sikhs, Muslims, Christians, Parsis and Buddhists and account for over 85% of the country's total population.

In 1978, Shri Kanshi Ram formed the Backward (SC/ST and OBC) and Minority Community Employees Federation (BAMCEF). The BAMCEF was purely non political, Non Religious and Non Agitational organization. Later on, he formed another Social organization known as Dalit Shoshit Samaj Sangharsh Samiti or DS4. He started his attempt of unifying the *Dalit* vote bank in 1981 and by 1984 he founded the Bahujan Samaj Party (BSP).

The BSP acknowledges the contributions of leaders of the downtrodden communities like Mahatma Jyotiba Phule, Chhatrapati Shahuji Maharaj, Narayana Guru and Periyar E.V. Ramaswami who have been in the forefront of the fight against the *Manuwadi* system which had secured higher social status for the upper caste Hindus under this system. The struggle of Baba Saheb Dr. Bhimrao Ambedkar, have also been acknowledged along with that of Kanshi Ram. On 15 September 2003, after Sri. Kanshi Ram's health suffered a serious setback, the entire responsibility of the party fell on Mayawati (*Behen Ji*). Later, on 18 September 2003, the party, through a consensus and in keeping with its Constitution, made her its National President.

Aims and Objectives

The chief aim and objective of the party shall be to work as a revolutionary social and economic movement of change with a view to realize, in practical terms, the supreme principles of universal justice, liberty, equality and fraternity enunciated in the Constitution of India, to be followed by State in governance, and in particular summed up in the following extract from the Preamble of the Constitution.

The Party shall regard its ideology as a movement for ending exploitation of the weaker sections and suppression of the deprived through social and economic change in keeping with the above stated chief aim, and its political activity and participation in governance as an instrument of furthering such a movement and bringing in such a change.

This being the chief aim of the Party, the strategy of the Party in public affairs will be governed by the following general principles:

1. that all citizens of India being equal before law are entitled to be treated as equal in true sense and in all matters and all walks of life, and where equality does not exist it has to be fostered and where equality is denied it has to be upheld and fought for;

2. that the full, free, uninhibited and unimpeded development of each individual is a basic human right and State is an instrument for promoting and realizing such development;
3. that the rights of all citizens of India as enshrined in the Constitution of India and subject to such restrictions as are set out in the Constitution, have to be upheld at all costs and under all circumstances;
4. that the provisions of the Constitution requiring the State at Center and in States to promote with special care and protect the socio-economic interests of the weaker sections of the society denied to them for centuries, have to upheld and given practical shape in public affairs as a matter of prime most priority;
5. that economic disparities and the wide gaps between the 'haves' and the 'have nots' must not be allowed to override the political principle of "one man, one vote, one vote, one value" adopted by our republic;
6. that unless political empowerment is secured for the economically deprived masses they will not be able to free themselves from the shackles of economic and social dependence and exploitation.

In particular and without prejudice to the generality of the aims stated above the party will work specially towards the following objectives:

1. The Scheduled Castes, the Scheduled Tribes, the Other Backward Castes, and the minorities, are the most oppressed and exploited people in India. Keeping in mind their large numbers, such a set of people in India is known as the Bahujan Samaj. The party shall organize these masses. The party shall work for these down trodden masses to:
   (a) remove their backwardness;
   (b) fight against their oppression and exploitation;
   (c) improve their status in society and public life;
   (d) improve their living conditions in day-to-day life;
2. The social structure of India is based on inequalities created by caste system and the movement of the party shall be geared towards changing the social system and rebuild it on the basis of equality and human values. All those who join the party with the commitment to co-operate in this movement of social change shall be ingratiated into the fold of the party.

Towards the furtherance of the above-noted aims and objectives the organizational units of party as designated in this Constitution, shall be empowered to:

1. purchase, take on lease or otherwise acquire, and maintain, moveable or immovable property for the Party and invest and deal with monies of party in such a manner as may from time to time be determined;

2. raise money with or without security for carrying out any of the aims and objectives of the Party;
3. to do all other lawful things and Acts as are incidental or conducive to the attainment of any of the aforesaid aims and objectives.

Provided that none of these activities will be undertaken without the express approval of the National President.

The electoral performance of the BSP has shown some ups and downs. The party came into notice when it won 3 seats in the 1989 Ninth Lok Sabha elections getting about 2.07% of the total votes. In the subsequent Tenth, Eleventh, Twelfth, Thirteenth, Fourteenth and Fifteenth Lok Sabha elections, the BSP secured 2, 11, 5, 14, 19 and 21 seats, respectively.

As far as Assembly elections are concerned, the BSP could win 13 seats in the UP Legislative Assembly elections in 1989. In the subsequent UP Vidhan Sabha elections in 1991, it won 12 seats, but the seats increased dramatically to 67 in both the elections of 1993 and 1996. In 2002, BSP secured 98 seats and 23.06% of total votes and the BSP tied up with the BJP and Mayawati became the first *Dalit* woman Chief Minister. In August 2003, this coalition fell as the BJP withdrew support. The speaker recognized the split of the BSP legislative party, which gave Mulayam Singh Yadav an opportunity to become Chief Minister with rebel support. The greatest victory came in 2007 when the BSP stormed to power and formed the Government by securing 206 seats and securing 30.43% of votes. However, in the 2012 Assembly elections BSP faced a defeat and Samajwadi Party has come to the power to form the Government. BSP secured just 80 seats which is about 25.91% of total votes. In Punjab Vidhan Sabha Elections, the BSP secured 9 seats in 1992 and in the 1997 elections it secured one vote and in the rest of the elections it could not open any account in Punjab. BSP also has shown its presence in Bihar, Chhattisgarh, Delhi, Haryana, Himachal Pradesh, Madhya Pradesh, Maharashtra, Rajasthan, Uttarakhand among others. However, in most of these States it has exhibited dismal performance and in many States it has failed to secure any seat over the years. The greatest jolt came to BSP in the 2012 Assembly elections with its massive defeat in the election. Now, it has to again to build up its base and regain the confidence of the people. BSP was the third most voted party in the 2014 elections, but it failed to secure any seat in the Lok Sabha. It has 6 seats in the Rajya Sabha. In 2017 UP State Assembly elections, BSP could win only 19 seats. In 2022 UP Legislative Assembly elections, BSP won 1 seat.

EXERCISES

I. Short Answer Questions: (100 words)

1. State any two features of political parties in India.
2. Write a note on Indian National Congress.

3. Write a note on Bharatiya Janata Party.
4. Write a note on the Communist Parties in India.
5. Write a note on the Bahujan Samaj Party.
6. Write a note on Trinamool Congress.

II. Long Answer Questions: **(1200 words)**

7. Discuss the main features of political parties in India.
8. Examine the electoral performance of Indian National Congress since the First General Election of 1951.
9. In the light of the 2019 election Manifesto of the Indian National Congress examine the ideology of the party.
10. Examine the electoral performance of Bharatiya Janata Party since 1980.
11. In the light of the 2019 election Manifesto of the Bharatiya Janata Party examine the ideology of the party.
12. Examine the electoral performance of the CPI since the first General Elections of 1951. 13. In the light of the 2019 election Manifesto of the CPI (M) examine the ideology and programmes of the party.
14. Examine the electoral performance of Bahujan Samaj Party in Uttar Pradesh.

REFERENCES

Election Manifesto of Bharatiya Janata Party, 2019.

Election Manifesto of Indian National Congress, 2019.

Election Manifesto of Trinamool Congress, 2011.

Awasthy, S.S., *Indian Government and Politics*, Har Anand Publications, New Delhi, 2006.

Brass, Paul R., *The Politics of India Since Independence*, Cambridge University Press, Delhi, 2004.

Fadia, Babulal, *State Politics in India*, Vol. 1, Radiant Publishers, New Delhi, 1984.

Manor, James, "Parties and Party System," in Chatterjee, Partha (Ed.), *State and Politics in India*, Oxford University Press, Delhi, 2007.

Ray Amitabha, "The State of Political Parties: Regional," in Chatterjee Rakhahari (Ed.), *Politics India: The State Society Interface*, South Asian Publishers, New Delhi, 2004.

Sharma, Aditi Dey, "The Party System: National," in Chatterjee Rakhahari (Ed.), *Politics India: the State Society Interface*, South Asian Publishers, New Delhi, 2004.

Singh, M.P. and Saxena, Rekha, *Indian Politics: Contemporary Issues and Concerns*, Prentice-Hall of India, New Delhi, 2008.

Sikri, S.L., *Indian Government and Politics*, Kalyani Publishers, New Delhi, 2004.

Siwach, J.R., *Dynamics of Indian Government and Politics*, Sterling Publishers, Delhi, 1985.

17

Regional Parties in India

INTRODUCTION

Parties in India, play an important role in political aggregation, articulation, socialization and participation. Political parties have been important components of the Indian political system. India is a multi-party democracy and new parties are formed, now and then, either by splits or breakups from larger parties or are absolutely new emerging out of different political aspirations. Political parties may spring up suddenly, put up their candidates in general elections, and disappear quickly, or merge with similar groups or move in and out of electoral arrangements. Among those parties, operating at a particular time, some can be found to operate at the national level and their activities encompass a number of States and not particularly restricted to a particular region or State, then they can be classified as national level political parties. In the preceding chapter, we have discussed a part of the structure of party system in India, i.e., the political parties at national level. On the other hand, there are a number of parties which may be restricted in their area of operation geographically, and thus, have a regional existence, but never-the-less are important as they come to influence national politics also. This is true as currently India is witnessing Coalition Government and in this, the coalition partners are mostly regional parties.

Regional parties are parties whose main holds are in one particular State/ region, and mostly, they participate in the elections only within that State/region. Some prominent regional parties are Dravida Munnetra Kazhagam (DMK) and All Indian Anna Dravida Munnetra Kazhagam (AIADMK) in Tamil Nadu, Telugu Desam Party (TDP) in Andhra Pradesh, Shiromani Akali Dal (SAD) in Punjab, Shivsena in Maharashtra, National Conference in Kashmir, Haryana Vikas Party in Haryana, Manipur People's Party in Manipur, Maharashtrawadi Gomantak in Goa, Sikkim Democratic Front in Sikkim, Mizo National Front in

Mizoram, and many other parties. Break away groups from the Indian National Congress founded some regional parties like the Trinamool Congress, Tamil Manila Congress, Kerala Congress. There are also some Communist parties whose base is mostly strong in certain States.

FEATURES OF REGIONAL PARTIES

Regional parties in State politics are a great force to reckon with as they have captured the Governmental power from the hands of the all India parties in States like Punjab, Tamil Nadu, Sikkim, Nagaland, Jammu and Kashmir and very recently West Bengal after the Assembly elections of 2012. Some of the regional parties started their journey at the regional level, but gradually solidified their bases and gradually tend to become national parties like the Trinamool Congress in West Bengal. BJP-led NDA and Congress-led UPA-I and II have to rely heavily on the regional parties for their existence to avoid a test of confidence in the Lok Sabha. In 1977 and 1980, regional parties won 52 and 35 seats, respectively. Even before that in 1969, when there was a split in the Congress, the Congress Government under Indira Gandhi had to garner the support of regional parties like DMK to stay in power. In 1991, 1996, 1998 and 1999 elections to the Lok Sabha, the regional parties secured 36, 85, 90 and 105 seats, respectively which show that their strength is growing with simultaneous decline of popularity of national parties.

A political party is usually considered to be regional if it is naturally territorial in its operation. By its very nature a regional party restricts its area of action to a single region or a State. A party can come into existence in a particular State or region on the basis of articulating or defending a regionally based ethnic or religion-cultural identity like the DMK and AIADMK. A regional party may be primarily concerned with exploiting local sources of discontent or on pressing a variety of demands which are linked to their electoral destiny in their respective regions. Sometimes they also lead to demands for separate statehood, State autonomy, or movements based on regional language or regional sentiments or even caste and also may be sometimes communal in their outlook. The linguistic reorganization of States of Andhra Pradesh, Mumbai, Gujarat and Punjab show how powerful languages can become a factor in Indian politics (see Chapter 20 for details).

The regional parties are more concerned with the interests of certain groups than with the All India issues. They are limited in their aggregative potential by being identified with the interests of a particular ethnic, linguistic or religious group. Parochial or regional parties have grown considerably in India since independence many of these differences were, of course, submerged in the national movement. Often the national level parties fail to address the regional cause whether it is Congress or non-Congress Parties like CPI, CPI(M), BJP or others. Soon after independence, Congress was able to accommodate variety of forces and also regional interests into its fold, but gradually from late

1960s its hold over regional politics started slipping and almost the party got delinked from the regional players. This is because in the first two decades of independence the Congress party remained in power in the Centre, and in most of the States which paved the way for its hegemony in the Centre as well as in most of the States. In most cases this led to the neglect of the sentiments of the States. This provided a fertile ground for the regional parties to germinate and grow.

Demand for political autonomy in a federation has led to the formation of regional parties and groups. In their pursuit to bargain with the Centre in a better way regional parties strive to get more allocation of resources for regional development. N.T. Rama Rao and his Telugu Desam Party (TDP) wanted greater restructuring of the Centre-State relations and opposition to highly centralized nature of Indian federation. Post-1967 election debacle, deinstitutionalization of the party along with centralization of power in the hands of Indira Gandhi led to discontent among the State units of the Congress. The Congrėss party increasingly treated its State units, not as autonomous units, but as subordinate branches of the central congress party. This led to discontent within different ranks of the Congress at State level and apathy started growing among the people at large. High handed behaviour of the Central command often led to creation of regional parties to counter such pressure.

Lopsided development in various States have also been the reasons for growth of regional parties. Though through Planning Commission, Finance Commission, the Inter-State Council and certain other mechanisms a parity has been tried to be reached as far as development of all the States of India are concerned yet the gap still remains between developed regions/States and undeveloped or under-developed regions/States. This creates inter-regional disputes and tensions which might even give rise to regional aspirations and therefore, regionalism and regional parties to articulate it.

Some regional parties in India may be short-lived and often formed for ad-hoc purpose as a bargaining counter and either they have vanished from the political scene or have merged with bigger parties or have been ripped apart by factionalism to such an extent that it is difficult to identify which is the original party like the Bangla Congress, the Kerala Congress, the Utkal Congress and the Telangana Praja Samiti. Some parties are formed as part of identity movements and work towards more visibility in Indian politics and obtaining more concessions from the centre, and even demand for separate statehood or secession like the Naga National Council (NNC), the Mizo National Front (MNF) and the All Party Hills Leaders Conference (APHLC) and even the DMK and even the Shiromani Akali Dal.

The regional parties whether singly or in coalition have given the electorate an option to vote for some non-Congress Party which aspires to protect regional interests. The greatest weakness is that they cannot build a strong cohesive force as they are diverse in their agenda and different in their ways of functioning. The regional parties are fragmented and for the most part weak.

Never-the-less they have been instruments for the stimulation of political consciousness and have expanded political participation. At present, their presence at the national level, as coalition partners of ruling Government is significant. They hold the reins of the stability of the Government. It is being talked about widely that in the future, there might emerge a Fourth Front comprising regional parties.

Post-independence, almost for more than two decades there existed, only one strong national party and a very weak opposition. From late 1960s, gradually many parties began to arrive at the political scene mainly because of splits and gradually a not so strong yet challenging opposition started to grow. The year 1977 was the beginning of coalition politics with national parties getting weaker and regional parties emerging stronger. Though the Congress formed the Government at the centre, the UPA-II, but the reliance on coalition partners, mostly regional parties show that the space of national parties has shrunk considerably. In the 2014 and 2019 Lok Sabha elections BJP emerged as the largest partner in the NDA coalition. It alone won 282 seats in 2014 and 303 seats in 2019. Therefore, reliance on regional parties has become minimized. Even in majority of the states either BJP alone or in alliance with regional parties are running governments currently. Therefore, again it can be said to be the return of one party domination as of now. Future trends need to be watched carefully whether regional parties would be a deciding factor in the national as well as state elections.

MAJOR REGIONAL PARTIES IN INDIA

Dravida Munnetra Kazhagam (DMK)

The Dravida Munnetra Kazhagam (DMK) was founded by Dr. C.N. Annadurai, usually hailed as Anna on 17 September 1949 and is regarded as the successor of the Anti-Brahmin Dravidian Movement. The launch of the South Indian Welfare Association popularly known as **Justice Party** in November 1916 by Sir P. Thiagarayar and others to promote social, economic and political interests of the Non-Brahmins was the nucleus of the Dravidian movement. They became associated with attacks against the Brahmins and attempts were made to do away with the service of Brahmin priests. The Justice Newspaper a mouthpiece of non-Brahmin demands was launched in 1917. The *Purohit Maruppu Sangam* (Association for the Elimination of Priests) was formed and Self-Respect Marriages took place where no Brahmin priests were engaged. The movement got a boost when Periyar E.V. Ramasamy left the Congress in 1925 and spearheaded the **Self Respect Movement** in the 30s and 40s, which was later transformed into a liberation movement named Dravidar Kazhagam (DK) in 1944. Due to differences with Periyar over certain policies and programmes, Anna with his band of followers left DK and formed DMK on 17th September, 1949. Anna became the General Secretary. After Anna, since 1969, DMK is headed by M. Karunanidhi, popularly called Kalaignar (Connoisseur of letters).

The DMK was formed to liberate the Dravidian race from the shackles of superstition and religious dogmas, to revive and restore the ancient heritage of Tamil and Tamil Nadu, and to protect the Tamil language from Hindi imperialism. DMK upheld the Tamil national pride. The Dravidian movement demanded the formation of *Dravida Nadu* so DMK lodged a demand for it initially. The language movement witnessed violent protests in Tamil Nadu under the aegis of DMK. The introduction of Hindi as Official Language of India was vehemently opposed by the people of the South and this opportunity was seized by DMK to catapult itself to a prominent position. The party members also regarded the Tamil Brahmans as agents of North India who immigrated to South India to enforce to north Indian Aryan culture on the South Indians. The party demanded to reserve the Government jobs for Dravidians and not to immigrant Brahmans. While it took time to dilute the Tamil sub-nationalism from the party's agenda, yet with the changes of time, the party accommodated various other issues in its agenda like the restructuring of Centre-State relations and the like. However, DMK has been very sensitive to the Sri Lankan Tamil issue during Rajiv Gandhi's time and also at present. It has also insisted that the Central Government should not, on any account, support the Sri Lankan Government, when the Resolution tabled before the Human Rights Council of the U.N. was put to vote in 2012. In 1972, this party split and a new party was founded by M.G. Ramachandaran, and it was named All India Anna Dravida Munnetra Kazhagam (AIADMK).

An analysis of the electoral performance of the DMK would show how the party has grown from strength to strength. In 1959, DMK won the Madras City Corporation Elections with the help of the independents from the Congress. In 1967, it tasted a major victory when in the Madras Assembly Election it won 137 seats as compared to 50 seats in the 1962 Assembly elections. Thus, in 1967 it emerged as the ruling party and consequently it tended to solidify its base which got reflected in the Lok Sabha elections too. In 1967, it won 25 Lok Sabha seats as compared to 7 seats in the 1962 Lok Sabha elections. In the Tamil Nadu Assembly elections of 1971 again it secured 184 seats. However, facing a split in the party in 1972, its popularity showed a decline as in 1977 it lost power when it secured just 48 seats and in the next Assembly elections in 1980 it could manage just 37 seats and in 1984, 24 seats. Thereafter, in 1989 it again stormed into power by capturing 150 seats. DMK faced a poll debacle in 1991 by just winning 2 seats. It recovered its lost position in the Assembly elections of 1996 when it secured 173 seats. Again the party could not fare well in the 2001, 2006, 2011 Assembly elections, when it secured just about 31 seats, 96 seats and 23 seats respectively. The Government obviously has been formed by AIADMK with Kumari Jayalalitha as the Chief Minister.

Simultaneously, the performance of the DMK at the Lok Sabha elections also witnessed ups and downs. In 1962, 1967, 1971, 1977 and 1980 Lok Sabha elections the DMK secured 7 seats, 25 seats, 23 seats, 2 seats, and 16 seats respectively. In the 1989 and 1991 Lok Sabha elections DMK could not secure any seat. In 1996, 1998, 1999, 2004 and 2009, Lok Sabha elections DMK secured 17 seats, 5 seats, 12 seats, 16 seats and 18 seats, respectively.

One surprising element in all these elections whether Lok Sabha or State Assembly Elections, the DMK has switched its alliances on the basis of its calculation of interests. It has on a number of occasions aligned itself with the Congress which was once viewed as its arch rival and sometimes with NDA and sometimes with Third front and others. In the 1971, 1980 and 2011 Assembly elections DMK aligned with the Congress, in 1984 and 1991with left parties, 1996 with Tamil Maanila Congress, and in 2001, with NDA. Similarly, in the Lok Sabha elections in 1971 it aligned with Congress, in 1977 with Janata Party, 1980 with Congress, 1984 with left parties, Tamil Nadu Congress and Janata Party, 1989 with Janata Party and left parties, 1991 with National Front, 1996 and 1998 with United Front, 1999 with NDA and 2009 with UPA-II. In the 2014 Lok Sabha elections DMK failed to secure any seat. In Rajya Sabha DMK has 4 seats. In the 2019 General election, DMK became the third largest party in the Lok Sabha with 24 seats. In the 2021 State Legislative Assembly elections DMK won 133 seats out of 234 and formed the government. Currently, M.K. Stalin is the Chief Minister of Tamil Nadu. In the 2024 Lok Sabha election DMK secured 22 seats. In Rajya Sabha it has 10 setas. In Tamil Nadu Legislative Assembly it has 132 seats. In Puducherry Legislative Assembly, it has 6 seats.

All India Anna Dravida Munnetra Kazhagam (AIADMK)

DMK as pointed out above experienced a split in 1972, and thus, AIADMK was born. M.G. Ramachandran (MGR) due to differences of opinion with Karunanidhi, eventually leading to the dismissal of MGR from the post of Party Treasurer, launched the Anna Dravida Munnetra Kazhagam (ADMK) on 17 October 1972, with Anna's profile on the flag. On 16 May 1976, the name was changed to All India Anna Dravida Munnetra Kazhagam (AIADMK). On 31 January 1976, the Central Government, dismissed the Karunanidhi Government and instituted a Commission of inquiry headed by Justice Sarkaria. In the Assembly elections that followed the AIADMK emerged victorious. The party remained in power for the next 10 years. After the illness of MGR, and his death in 1987, the party was divided into two with one under Janaki Ramachandran and the other under J. Jayalalitha, a former film star and associate of MGR. The two factions led by Jayalalitha and Janaki merged in 1988 under the Jayalalitha's leadership.

Tamil Nadu has been a typical case where either the DMK or the AIADMK has been in power since the later's birth in the year 1972. The electoral performance of AIADMK also has seen ups and down except those 10 years of MGR's rule. In 1977, AIADMK stormed to power in Tamil Nadu by securing 132 seats. In the 1980 and 1984 Assembly elections it could hold on to its success and secured 129 seats and 134 seats respectively. In the 1989 elections however, it lost to DMK when Janaki could just manage to get 2 seats and Jayalalitha got 27 seats. In 1991 Assembly elections, it again secured a major victory by fetching 164 seats. 1996 was again a disappointment for AIADMK when it just got 4 seats. It was seen to be an anti-incumbency vote as well as several allegations of corruption and malpractices against her government and herself, as well as criticism for the arrangement of a lavish wedding for her foster son, V. Sudhakaran. The 2001 Assembly election results brought a relief when again AIADMK secured 132 seats. Jayalalitha was however, barred from standing as a candidate in the 2001 elections, because she had been found guilty of criminal offences, including allegedly obtaining property belonging to a state-operated agency called TANSI. In March 2002, Jayalalitha assumed the position of Chief Minister once more, having been acquitted of some charges by the Madras High Court. The year 2006 was another year of disappointment when it could fetch only 61 seats in the Assembly elections. 2011 saw much better performance by the AIADMK when it secured a massive 150 seats and formed the Government.

The Lok Sabha election results also have similar kind of reflections of the Assembly polls. In 1977 it won 17 seats, in 1980–2 seats, 1984–12 seats, 1989–11 seats, 1991–11 seats, in 1996 they could not get any, 1998 and 1999 they got 18 and 10 seats, 2004–again none, 2009–9 seats. In 1979, AIADMK became the first Dravidian and non-congress party to be part of the Union Cabinet, when two AIADMK Members of Parliament, Satyavani Muthu and Aravinda Bala Pajanor, joined the short-lived Charan Singh ministry which followed the Morarji Desai-led Janata Party Government of 1977–79.

As in case of DMK, AIADMK also shifted its alliance partners. In 1998, it made an alliance in the Parliamentary elections with Marumalarchi Dravida Munnetra Kazhagam (MDMK) and in 1998–1999 shared power with BJP in the Atal Bihari Vajpayee headed Government formed after the twelfth General Elections. In fact, AIADMK had been the deciding factor. Atal Bihari Vajpayee garnered support from 286 members out of 545, but the Government collapsed again in late 1998 when the AIADMK, with its 18 seats, withdrew their support, leading to Thirteenth Lok Sabha elections in 1999. In the 2014 Lok Sabha elections AIADMK secured 37 seats. With the death of Jayalalitha on 5 December, 2016, the leadership passed on to her close aide V.K. Sasikala. However, she was convicted by the Supreme Court due to corruption charges. Edappadi K. Palanisamy of AIADMK became the Chief Minister of Tamil Nadu. AIADMK could win only 1 seat in the 2019 Lok Sabha elections. After the 2021 State Legislative Assembly elections, AIADMK is the main opposition party with 66 seats. In the 2024 Lok Sabha election AIADMK could not secure any seat. In Rajya Sabha it has 3 setas. In Tamil Nadu Legislative Assembly it has 62 seats.

Telegu Desam Party (TDP)

In Andhra Pradesh, Telugu Desam was founded in 1982 by Telegu film actor, N.T. Rama Rao (NTR). On 28 March 1982, a Steering Committee consisting of 13 members was formed and NTR was the founder President of the new Party. The TDP aimed to protect the dignity and self respect of Telegu people.

Chandrababu Naidu, the present party chief broke away in 1995 due to differences of opinion with his father-in-law regarding his new wife, Lakshmi Parvathi. After NTR's death, the party merged and Chandrababu Naidu took over as party chief. The main driving point of the TDP was restructuring of the Centre-State relations and opposition to highly centralized nature of Indian federation. In other words in different fora like the conclaves of non-Congress parties between 1983–1984, NTR made it clear that TDP stood for greater State autonomy. Along with this NTR emphasized the pride of the Telugu people and their culture which was being hurt by Centre's interference in the internal affairs of the State.

A survey of the electoral performance of the TDP shows that the party did quite well in the elections both at the State and Central level. In 1983, TDP got the people's mandate to form the Government with an astounding 202 seats out of 294 seats. However, the Government was deposed by the Centre, but it again stormed to power after the mid-term polls of 1985 and retained the same number of seats, which was, 202. However, the party suffered badly at the 1989 election and this time the congress formed the Government and TDP jolt managed to get 74 seats. In the Lok Sabha elections of 1984, 1989 and 1991, TDP secured 30, 2 and 13 seats respectively. In 1994 Assembly elections, NTR registered a huge victory with 219 votes. He had used many populist measures to win over popular votes like the promise of providing rice at ₹2/kg. However, at this juncture TDP suffered a split with a conflict over NTR's marriage to Lakshmi Parvathi. His son-in-law Chandrababu Naidu left TDP with 150 MLAs. In 1995, thus the party was split into two, one under Chandrababu Naidu and other headed by Lakshmi Parvathi which came to be known as NTR Telegu Desam. Thereafter, in the Assembly elections of 1995, Chandrababu with the support of CPI and CPI (M) became the Chief Minister. In the 1996 Lok Sabha elections, with a hung Parliament, the TDP with 16 seats became a determining factor in the formation of Government at the centre. NTR Telegu Desam was erased off from the political arena as it could not secure a single vote in 1996 elections. Chandrababu Naidu's TDP won the next Assembly election of 1999 too. As during this period India was witnessing hung Parliament in every Lok Sabha elections till 1998, the regional parties became a determining factor in the formation of Government at the centre. The TDP garnered the support of AGP, DMK, Tamil Maanila Congress behind the United Front Government which formed the Government at the centre for a brief period. In 1998, TDP won 12 seats in the Lok Sabha elections. In 1999, the number of seats rose to 29 and supported the BJP-led NDA from outside in the Lok Sabha. As far as Assembly elections are concerned, after the 1999 elections, Chandrababu Naidu stayed in power for nine years as Chief Minister until 2004 when he was defeated by the Indian National Congress whose State leader Y.S. Rajasekhara Reddy became the Chief Minister who was sworn in for a second term on 20 May 2009 after the Assembly Elections of 2009. TDP just managed to get 92 seats. TDP won 16 seats in the 2014 general elections. In the April 2019 Andhra Pradesh Legislative Assembly polls TDP won 23 seats only. In Telengana Assembly polls of 2018 it won 2 seats only. TDP managed to win only 3 seats in the 2019 Lok Sabha elections. After 2024 polls TDP has 16 seats in the Lok Sabha and is part of the NDA. With its support the BJP-led NDA could cross the majority mark in the Lok Sabha elections held in 2024.

Shiromani Akali Dal (SAD)

Akali Dal has its main hold in Punjab. The Shiromani Akali Dal established on 14 December 1920, is the oldest regional party of the country. With the establishment in November 1920 of Shiromani Gurdwara Parbandhak Committee (SGPC), the need arose for developing a system to co-ordinate the work of regional *Jaththas* (structured groups or bands of men and women) to free the Gurdwaras from the clutches of the corrupt *Mahants* and Britishers. Initially therefore, the Akali Dal functioned as a task force for the SGPC, mobilizing and providing volunteers when required.

Shiromani Akali Dal was formed on 14 December 1920 which is generally the accepted date of the formation of SAD. The title Shiromani was added later through a resolution passed by the Dal on 29 March 1922. Akali Dal can be claimed as a religio-political party. The first election of the party held on 23–24 January 1921. The current party to be recognized by the Election Commission of India is the one led by Parkash Singh Badal.

Post-independence, under pressure of mass influx of Hindu and Sikh refugees, the economic opportunities for the local Sikhs became dim. Therefore, Shiromani Akali Dal decided to press for the formation of a linguistic State coterminous with Punjabi language. Master Tara Singh reactivated the Shiromani Akali Dal, and launched the campaign which came to be known as the Punjabi *Suba* movement. The movement for Punjabi *Suba* continued unabated under the leadership of Sant Fateh Singh which ultimately compelled the Government of India to agree to redraw the boundaries of Punjab and the Punjab re-organization Bill was introduced in the Parliament on 3 September 1966. Punjab was consequently divided into two states—Punjab and Haryana and the Hill district were merged with Himachal Pradesh.

Akali Dal came to power in Punjab, but many a times the SAD Governments were dismissed due to internal conflicts and minority mandate in its favour. In the first election to the State Legislature in the newly reorganized State of Punjab (1967), the Shiromani Akali Dal secured 26 seats in a House of 104, and Gurnam Singh, on 28 March 1967 formed the Government with the support of some small parties like Jana Sangh, the Communists and the independent candidate. But the ministry fell soon owing to internal dissensions. Open rebellion by Harcharan Singh and Lachhman Singh Gill, who sided with the Congress during a no-confidence vote placed the ministry in a difficult position. Though, the ministry survived the motion, but there was a split in the Akali Dal and Gurnam Singh Government became a real minority. Thereafter, Lachhman Singh Gill formed, with the support of Congress a new ministry which subsequently fell on 21 August 1968, when the Congress withdrew its support. The crisis led to the dissolution of the State Legislature and the State was placed under President's rule (July 1968–November 1969) and a mid-term poll had to be held in 1969.

The two factions of the Shiromani Akali Dal merged and emerged victorious in the mid-term polls emerging as the largest single party with 43 seats. Congress got 38, Jana Sangh—8, Communists—5, and others—11 seats. Gurnam Singh again formed a ministry in coalition with the Jana Sangh and the Communists supporting it from outside. This ministry collapsed on 25 March 1970 by internal party dissension. Prakash Singh Badal, then formed the Government on 27 March 1970. This Akali Government too had a short tenure and Punjab was again put under President's rule (June 1971–March 1972). In a fresh Punjab Assembly election which took place in March 1972, the Shiromani Akali Dal could secure only 24 seats out of total of 117, and the Government was formed by Congress under Giani Zail Singh (1972–1977). After this poll debacle the Working Committee of the SAD at its meeting held at Anandpur Sahib on 16–17 October 1973, adopted a statement of aims and objectives. This statement, known as the Anandpur Sahib resolution has, since then, been the cornerstone of Akali politics and strategy. The resolution outlines seven objectives:

1. The transfer of the federally administered city of Chandigarh to Punjab
2. The transfer of Punjabi speaking and contiguous areas of Punjab
3. Decentralisation of states under the existing Constitution, limiting the central Government's role
4. The call for land reforms and industrialization of Punjab, along with safeguarding the rights of the weaker sections of the population
5. The enactment of an all-India Gurdwara (Sikh House of worship) Act
6. Protection for minorities residing outside Punjab, but within India
7. Revision of Government's recruitment quota restricting the number of Sikhs in armed forces

In 1977, when National emergency was imposed, the SAD opposed the emergency vehemently. In 1977, after the emergency, in the Punjab, the Akali Dal entered into an electoral alliance with Janata Party and the Janata-Akali Dal-CPM alliance won all the Lok Sabha seats in Punjab. Subsequently, the Akalis formed an alliance again with the Janata Party and the CPM contested the Assembly elections in June 1977. Together they won 91 seats against 17 of the Congress. The Akalis alone won 58 out of 117 seats and Sardar Prakash Singh Badal led the Coalition Ministry.

However, soon after the victory of Congress party in the Parliamentary elections of 1980 the Akali Coalition Government was unconstitutionally dismissed and President's Rule was imposed. However, protests against such moves of the central Government gradually took an extremist turn and secessionist activities increased. The Congress formed the Government under Darbara Singh (June 1980–October 1983) which also had a short span. However, Punjab was again put under President's rule from October 1983 to September 1985. In the mean time, the Operation Blue Star in June 1984 in which the Golden Temple was stormed and ultimately the militants were flushed out of the Temple resulted in many casualties too. This also led to severe unrest in Punjab and ultimately, the assassination of Indira Gandhi was also seen as the outcome of her handling of Punjab politics.

When Rajiv Gandhi came to the power in 1984 matters came to a rest and the SAD signed the Punjab Accord or the Rajeev-Longowal accord (March 1985). Unfortunately, soon after this, Sant Harchand Singh Longowal himself was assassinated in August 1985. Attempts to restore peace and harmony were again made, and thus, elections were held in Punjab in September 1985. The Akalis won 73 seats out of 117, getting over 38% of the total votes. Sardar Surjit Singh Barnala was sworn in as the Chief Minister on 29 September after nearly two years of President's rule in Punjab.

However, certain issues in the Rajeev-Longowal Accord including the transfer of Chandigarh to Punjab led to the derailment of the Accord and as a result of this Punjab plunged into a fresh era of violence and killings. In 1987, due to a police action on Golden Temple the Longowal Akali Dal was split and the Barnala Ministry was dismissed on 12 May 1987, and Punjab was once again placed under President's rule (June 1987–February 1992). Violence escalated in Punjab during the President's rule and continued unabated till 1992. Fresh elections were held in Punjab in February 1992, and the Akalis boycotted these elections. The leader of the Punjab Congress, Sardar Beant Singh, claimed that he had the popular mandate, and thus, became the third Congress Chief Minister in the post-1966 Punjab.

The elections did not stop militancy and the Congress Government under Beant Singh also started losing its mandate and as a result lost key by-elections to the Akali Dal. In 1995, Beant Singh himself was assassinated. From 1995–1997 there were two Congress Ministries within this short span of time under Harcharan Singh Brar and Rajinder Kaul Bhattal. In 1996 Lok sabha elections, with an alliance with Bahujan Samaj Party (BSP), SAD won 11 seats out of 13 with Akalis securing 8 seats alone. Akali Dal under Prakash Singh Badal came back to power in 1997 and continued till 2002. In 1998 and 1999 Lok Sabha elections in alliance with BJP, the Akali Dal won 8 and 2, seats respectively. From 2002–2007 it was again a Congress Government under Captain Amarinder Singh in Punjab. In 2004 Lok Sabha elections, SAD won 8 seats only. SAD returned to power after the 2007 Punjab State Elections in which Akali Dal won 48 of the 117 seats, and became the largest party in the Punjab Legislative Assembly. However, in 2009 Lok Sabha elections SAD did miserable and it was down by 4 seats from the previous Lok Sabha elections. In 2009, it could manage only 4 Lok Sabha seats. However, SAD came back to power after the 2012 Punjab Assembly elections and was led by Prakash Singh Badal with the Bharatiya Janata Party as a coalition partner. In the 2014 general elections SAD managed to secure 4 seats. In 2017 Punjab Assembly elections, SAD could win just 15 seats and BJP earned 3 seats. In 2019 General Elections SAD won only 2 seats in the Lok Sabha. It could secure only 1 seat in the Lok Sabha election of 2024.

Asom Gana Parishad (AGP)

Asom Gana Parishad (AGP) in Assam/Asom is a political party that came into existence because of the discriminatory feelings of the local 'sons of soil' population. AGP started off as a movement later transformed itself into a political party. The backdrop was prepared by the 'anti-foreigner' agitation in Assam in the 1970s and 1980s. Here foreigners meant Muslim immigrants from Bangladesh who entered Assam after 1971. The demographic pattern of Assam was slowly undergoing change due to the presence of the immigrant population. The fear of enfranchisement of this huge section of immigrant Bengali Muslim population created violent protests all over Assam as the original Assamese feared a submersion by the majority Bengali-Muslim population and would become a minority in their own State. The All Assam Students' Union (AASU) and other organizations demanded disenfranchisement of the immigrants. Later the All Assam Gana Sangram Parishad (AAGSP) was formed which was a conglomeration of several different organizations working towards the similar agenda—anti-foreigner campaign. It was disturbing periods in Assam politics as Governments collapsed and President's Rule declared frequently. Ultimately, the signing of Assam accord between the Central Government and the AAGSP restored stability in Assam. Thereafter, the movement transformed itself into a political party, namely, Asom Gana Parishad with an agenda to give back Assam to the Assamese people.

The electoral performance of AGP shows that immediately after the Assam accord, the 1985 Assembly elections were won by the AGP. It won 64 seats out of 126, and replaced the Congress Government which was in power in the State. In 1991 however, AGP suffered a poll debacle and the Congress came to power getting the support of Bengali speaking population mainly the Muslims who were being repressed by the anti-foreigner movement of the AGP. In 1996, the AGP aligned itself with the CPI and CPI (M) and at the Assembly elections defeated the congress and the BJP winning 59 seats alone and together the alliance got 70 seats out of 122. Prafulla Kumar Mahanta became the Chief Minister. It was a partner of the United Front Government I & II formed during 1996–1998.

Since 1991, AGP has experienced several splits and break-ups as General Secretary, Bhrigu Kumar Phukan, former M.P. Dinesh Goswami, speaker Pulakesh Barua and others formed the Natun Asom Gana Parishad which again merged with the original party in 1992. In 2000, Atul Bora moved away and formed Trinamool Gana Parishad. Finally in 2008, all the groups merged under one umbrella.

Shiv Sena

After the linguistic Reorganization of State of Bombay in 1960, it was divided into Maharashtra and Gujarat. Bombay the cultural capital of the Marathis and the Gujaratis was made the capital of Maharashtra. After Maharashtra was established, a general feeling among many Marathis, was that Bombay is being ruled and governed by foreigners. Their main targets were not the Gujarati business communities, but immigrants who arrived from all over India and settled in Bombay. The popular grievance was that of the urban middle class Marathis, was that they were not being able to grab the white-collar jobs. These feeling snowballed and led to the formation of the Shiv Sena (SS) party in 1966. This party which began as a protest movement of the Marathis in Bombay and slowly became popular all around Maharashtra. The Sthaniya Lokadhikar Samiti (SLS) was formed under this party with the aim of securing preferential job opportunities mainly the white collar sector for the Marathi speaking. The party ideology was intertwined with Hindu-Marathi nationalist pride. It drew its inspiration from the great national hero, Shivaji. On the one hand, the Shiv Sena publicly supported the Babri Masjid demolition, and on the other hand, they were vehemently against the reservation policy, and attacked the recommendations of the Mandal Commission. When it was not in power it had undertaken demonstrations, *Bandhs* and strikes. To some extent it was militant in its activities. According to the party policy, many places in Maharashtra were renamed with Marathi oriented names. For example, Bombay was renamed back to its original name Mumbai. Its Hindu-nationalistic ideology helped it to nurture closeness with BJP which yielded results in the Assembly and Lok Sabha elections.

The Shiv Sena' political career began with its success in the Mumbai Municipal Election in 1985. In 1990, the Shiv Sena won 52 seats in the Assembly elections in Maharashtra but the Government was formed by Indian National Congress. The following year in 1991 Lok Sabha Elections, they won 4 seats which were 9.45% of the total votes, and BJP won 5 seats. In 1995, there was a major success for this alliance when in the Assembly elections the BJP-Sena alliance defeated the ruling Congress party and captured power in the State of Maharashtra. The alliance won 138 seats with BJP getting 65 and Shiv Sena securing 73 seats individually. The following year, in 1996, this result was repeated when the Shiv Sena won 15 seats in the Lok Sabha. In 1998 Lok Sabha elections, Shiv Sena won 6 seats and in 1999 the number increased to 15. However, in 1999 the BJP-SS alliance suffered a major setback in the Assembly elections and was defeated at the polls. The Government was formed by a post-poll alliance forged between Nationalist Congress Party and Congress. In the subsequent two Assembly elections of 2004 and 2009 Shiv Sena again lost to Nationalist Congress Party. Currently, Shiv Sena has 19 seats in the Lok Sabha and 3 in the Rajya Sabha. After the 2019 Legislative Assembly elections in Maharashtra, Shiv Sena left its long ally BJP and with NCP and Congress formed the government under a new alliance Maha Vikas Aghadi (MVA). Uddhav Thakeray became the Chief Minister of Maharashtra. The MVA lost its power and Shiv Sena faced a rift between Uddhav Thakeray and Eknath Shinde. Finally, Eknath Shinde garnered support of 2/3rd of Shiv Sena MLAs and along with BJP support became the Chief

Minister and formed a government on 30 June 2022. It could secure only 7 seats in the Lok Sabha election of 2024 and is a part of the NDA.

Samajwadi Party (SP)

Samajwadi Party came into existence on 4 October 1992 in Lucknow, under the leadership of Mulayam Singh Yadav. The party gives immense importance to the development of common man and adopted the bicycle as its symbol. The party is founded on the principle socialism, democracy and equality. Samajwadi Party believes in communal harmony and endeavours to create special opportunities for backward sections of society, Muslims and women.

Ideology

The Samajwadi Party believes in creating a socialist society, which works on the principle of equality and the party has a secular and democratic outlook. The Samajwadi Party believes in continuously working towards the upliftment of weaker sections of society, and it stands against communal forces.

Electoral Performance

Though the party is mainly based in Uttar Pradesh, it tried its luck in other States too after its birth. In the Assembly election in Madhya Pradesh in 2003, the Samajwadi Party gained 7 seats, making it the third largest party in the State. When its candidate won the by-election of Lanji (Balaghat) in 2007, its total tally reached 8. In 2005, former Karnataka Chief Minister Bangarappa resigned from the BJP to join the Samajwadi Party and won his Lok Sabha seat from Shimoga on the Samajwadi Party ticket.

In the 2007, Uttar Pradesh Legislative Election, the SP won only 96 seats as compared to 146 in the previous election. As a result, Chief Minister Mulayam Singh Yadav had to resign, and the BSP under Mayawati, which won a majority of 207 seats, formed the Government. In the 2012 Legislative Assembly Elections of Uttar Pradesh, it registered a formidable victory with a clear majority in the House, thus enabling it to form the Government in the State. Akhilesh Yadav, son of Mulayam Singh Yadav became the Chief Minister of Uttar Pradesh. However, SP experienced a poll debacle in the 2017 UP Assembly elections. It could win only 47 seats, and its alliance partner, Congress, won only 7 seats. SP could secure only 5 seats in the Lok Sabha following the General Elections of 2019. In the UP Assembly Elections 2022, Samajwadi Party was able to win 111 seats only. It could secure only 37 seats in the Lok Sabha election of 2024 and is a part of the INDI gatbandhan.

All India Trinamool Congress (TMC)

The Trinamool Congress was born out of differences between Mamata Banerjee and the Congress over an alliance with the Communist Party. Founded in

1 January 1998, the party is led by the current Chief Minister Mamata Banerjee. After 34 years of Left rule in West Bengal, the Trinamool Congress led TMC-INC-SUCI(C) alliance in the 2011 Assembly elections won 227 seats, in the 294 seat Legislature. TMC is currently the second largest member of the ruling United Progressive Alliance (UPA) coalition.

In the 1998 Lok Sabha polls, TMC won 7 seats. In the next Lok Sabha election that was held in 1999, Trinamool Congress won 8 seats with BJP. In 2000, TMC won the Kolkata Municipal Corporation Elections as well. In the 2001, West Bengal Vidhan Sabha elections, TMC won 60 seats with Congress (I). In the 2004 Lok Sabha elections, TMC won 1 seat with Congress (I). In the 2006 Vidhan Sabha elections, TMC won 30 seats with Congress (I). In 2009 Lok Sabha election, Trinamool Congress and its allies won 26 seats in West Bengal. 19 seats were won by TMC, 6 were won by Congress and one by SUCI. TMC also has 5 MLAs in the Arunachal Pradesh Assembly, 7 MLAs in the Manipur Assembly, 1 MLA in Assam, and 1 MLA in Uttar Pradesh and 1 MP in Rajya Sabha from Jharkhand. In 2010, Trinamool Congress won the Kolkata Municipal Corporation polls and also the Bidhan Nagar (Salt Lake) Municipality elections. Its greatest victory, however, came in 2011 with the incredible victory in the West Bengal Assembly Elections defeating the Left Front. TMC won 22 seats in the Lok Sabha elections of 2019 and became the fifth largest party in the Lok Sabha.

Nandigram and Singur movements catapulted the TMC to a forthright position and ultimately to its major victory at the 2011 Assembly polls. Its vision is *Maa, Mati* and *Manush.*

The aim of the party as given in the Party Constitution is:

1. to make all round development of India in the political, economic, industrial, social, cultural, agricultural sectors and
2. to establish India as global power keeping in view the multi-lingual, multi-faceted, multi-ethnic, rich culture and heritage of India (Article I).

The objective of the party shall be:

1. To uphold and adhere, with true faith and allegiance, to the Constitution of India as by law established.
2. To uphold and work for the furtherance of the principles of Nationalism, Socialism, Secularism and Democracy.
3. To eradicate illiteracy, poverty and injustice and cause upliftment of the downtrodden by ensuring social equality, awakening of the masses by peaceful means, movement and participation in the lawful electoral process.
4. Allegiance to the Constitution of India.

The party also pledges to bear true faith and allegiance to the Constitution of India as by law established and to the principles of socialism, secularism and democracy and would uphold the sovereignty, unity and integrity of India.

The Manifesto of TMC for the 2011 Assembly elections had two parts—Part A vividly captures the sad story of the decline of the State with irrefutable and shocking evidence. The steady decay of West Bengal under the Left Rule is pathetic—the end result of the deliberate and incompetent policies over the last three and a half decades. Part B brings forth a blueprint of the regeneration and rejuvenation of Bengal that we, All India Trinamool Congress, visualize. It is too premature to assess the achievements or failure of the Government. It is time which will give us the evaluation of regime change in Bengal. The *Time* magazine named Ms. Mamata Banerjee as one of the "100 Most influential People in the World." Another high point of her one year old Government has been the visit by US Secretary of State, Hillary Clinton in May 2012. The Trinamool Congress had a landslide victory in 2016 State Legislative Assembly Elections, and Ms. Mamata Banerjee became the Chief Minister for the Second Term. Ms. Banerjee won the 2021 elections to the West Bengal Legislative Assembly with a thumping majority with 215 seats and became the Chief Minister for the Third term. It could secure 29 seats in the Lok Sabha election of 2024 and is a part of the INDI gatbandhan.

Aam Aadmi Party (AAP)

A party to emerge in the Indian political scenario on 26 November 2012, was the Aam Aadmi Party (AAP). It can be said to have its origin in the anti-corruption movement which demanded the introduction of Lok Pal and Lok Ayukta. It adopted the broom as its symbol. Currently, the founder leader of the party is Arvind Kejriwal.

AAP had its debut in the 2013 Delhi legislative Assembly elections. It won 28 seats and also formed a minority government with the support of the Congress party. It had a brief tenure and had to resign with Delhi coming under President's rule. Again in the 2015 Legislative Assembly elections, AAP had a sweeping victory with 67 seats out of 70. Arvind Kejriwal became the Chief Minister of Delhi. In the 16th Lok Sabha elections, AAP could manage to win 4 seats, and that too from Punjab. In the Feb 2020 Delhi Legislative Assembly elections AAP emerged as a major party winning 62 seats with the BJP winning 8 seats. Arvind Kejriwal beame the Chief Minister for another term.

In the 2017 Punjab Legislative Assembly election, AAP secured 20 seats. AAP won 92 seats in the 2022 Punjab Legislative Assembly election. Bhagwant Mann of AAP was sworn in as the Chief Minister of Punjab. It could secure only 3 seats in the Lok Sabha election of 2024 and is a part of the INDI gatbandhan. It has 10 setas in Rajya Sabha.

EXERCISES

I. Short Answer Questions: **(100 words)**

1. Briefly state the features of regional parties in India (any four).
2. Write a note on DMK.

3. Discuss briefly the presence of AIADMK as an important regional party.
4. Write a note on TDP.
5. Role of SAD in Punjab politics.
6. Write a note on AGP as a regional party.
7. Role of Shiv Sena as a regional Party.
8. Write a note on the success story of SP in Uttar Pradesh.

II. Long Answer Questions: (1200 words)

9. Examine the features of regional parties in India.
10. Discuss the position of DMK as a regional party in India.
11. State the role of AIADMK as a regional party.
12. Examine the role of TDP as a regional party.
13. Examine the role of SAD as a regional party in Punjab.
14. Discuss the role of AGP as a regional party.
15. Examine the role of Shiv Sena as in regional politics.
16. Discuss the emergence and gradual consolidation of position of SP.

REFERENCES

Awasthy, S.S., *Indian Government and Politics*, Har Anand Publications, New Delhi, 2006.

Béteille, André, *Caste, Class and Power: Changing Pattern of Stratification in a Tanjore Village*, Oxford University Press, New Delhi, 2012.

Brass, Paul R., *The Politics of India Since Independence*, Cambridge University Press, Delhi, 2004.

Fadia, Babulal, *State Politics in India*, Vol. 1, Radiant Publishers, New Delhi, 1984.

Ray Amitabha, "The State of Political Parties: Regional," in Chatterjee Rakhahari (Ed.), *Politics India: The State Society Interface*, South Asian Publishers, New Delhi, 2004.

Sharma, Aditi Dey, "The Party System: National," in Chatterjee Rakhahari (Ed.), *Politics India: the State Society Interface*, South Asian Publishers, New Delhi, 2004.

Sikri, S.L., *Indian Government and Politics*, Kalyani Publishers, New Delhi, 2004.

Singh, M.P. and Saxena, Rekha, *Indian Politics: Contemporary Issues and Concerns*, Prentice-Hall of India, Delhi, 2008.

Siwach, J.R., *Dynamics of Indian Government and Politics*, Sterling Publishers, Delhi, 1985.

18

Electoral Process in India

INTRODUCTION

The democratic process in India is ensured through elections of the people's representatives either to the Central Legislature or to the State Legislatures. Since 1952, the country has witnessed elections to the legislative bodies at both the National (17 Lok Sabha Elections) as well as State levels. To ensure free and fair elections in India, the Constitution provides for an Election Commission. The elections to the Parliament, President and Vice-President at the National level and elections to the State Legislatures are conducted by the Election Commission. Election Commission of India is a permanent and autonomous Constitutional body. The Election Commission was established in accordance with the Constitution on 25th January 1950. The Commission celebrated its Golden Jubilee in 2001 and Diamond Jubilee in 2011 and every year 25 January is celebrated as the National Voter's Day.

COMPOSITION, POWERS AND FUNCTIONS OF THE ELECTION COMMISSION

PART XV, Article 324 entrusts the superintendence, direction, and control of elections to the Election Commission of India. It states:

1. The superintendence, direction and control of the preparation of the electoral rolls for, and the conduct of, all elections to Parliament and to the Legislature of every State and of elections to the offices of

President and Vice-President held under this Constitution* shall be vested in a Commission (referred to in this Constitution as the Election Commission).

2. The Election Commission shall consist of the Chief Election Commissioner and such number of other Election Commissioners, if any, as the President may from time-to-time fix and the appointment of the Chief Election Commissioner and other Election Commissioners shall, subject to the provisions of any law made in that behalf by Parliament, will be appointed by the President.
3. When any other Election Commissioner is appointed the Chief Election Commissioner shall act as the Chairman of the Election Commission.
4. Before each general election to the House of the People and to the Legislative Assembly of each State, and before the first general election and thereafter before each biennial election to the Legislative Council of each State having such Council, the President may also appoint after consultation with the Election Commission such Regional Commissioners as he may consider necessary to assist the Election Commission in the performance of the functions conferred on the Commission by Clause (1).
5. Subject to the provisions of any law made by Parliament, the conditions of service and tenure of office of the Election Commissioners and the Regional Commissioners shall be such as the President may by rule determine:

   Provided that the Chief Election Commissioner shall not be removed from his office except in like manner and on the like grounds as a Judge of the Supreme Court and the conditions of service of the Chief Election Commissioner shall not be varied to his disadvantage after his appointment: Provided further that any other Election Commissioner or a Regional Commissioner shall not be removed from office except on the recommendation of the Chief Election Commissioner.
6. The President, or the Governor** of a State, shall, when so requested by the Election Commission, make available to the Election Commission or to a Regional Commissioner such staff as may be necessary for the discharge of the functions conferred on the Election Commission by Clause (1).

The Conduct of Election Rules, 1961 gives us a clear idea about the procedure of election in India. There are two major laws which further give

* The words "including the appointment of election tribunals for the decision of doubts and disputes arising out of or in connection with elections to parliament and to the Legislatures of States" omitted by the Constitution (Nineteenth Amendment) Act, 1996, Sec. 2.

**The words "or the Rajpramukh" omitted by the Constitution (Seventh Amendment) Act. 1956, Sec. 29 and Sch.

detailed procedure for conducting elections in India. The **Representation of the People Act, 1950**, which mainly deals with the preparation and revision of electoral rolls, allocation of seats and delimitation of constituencies and the **Representation of the People Act, 1951** which deals, in detail, with all aspects of conduct of elections, post election disputes and qualifications and disqualifications for membership in Parliament and State Legislatures. This 1951 Act also gives in details the provisions for qualification and disqualifications for membership to the Houses both at Centre and at the States, disqualifications for voting, registration of political parties, declaration of assets and liabilities, election expenses, corrupt practices and electoral offences. The Supreme Court of India has held that where the enacted laws are silent or make insufficient provision to deal with a given situation in the conduct of elections, the Election Commission has the residuary powers under the Constitution to act in an appropriate manner.

From the above two major laws and from the Articles 324–328 the powers and functions of the Election Commission can be summarized as:

1. Preparation of electoral rolls before every general elections and elections to State Legislatures and elections to local bodies
2. Registration of all eligible voters and updating the voter's lists from time-to-time
3. Supervision of the entire electoral machinery throughout the country for ensuring free and fair elections for all matters pertaining to the election of President, Vice-President, Parliament and State Legislatures
4. Delimitation of constituencies
5. Preparation of model code of conduct before every election
6. Notification of dates and schedules of election for filing nomination papers by aspiring party candidates followed by proper scrutiny before the actual election
7. Appointment of Election Officers for inquiring into disputes arising out of electoral arrangements
8. Requesting the President of India or the Governor of a State for requisitioning the staff necessary for conducting election
9. Rendering advice to the President or any Governors on the question of disqualification of any member of the Union or State Legislature
10. Cancellation of polls in the event of malpractice or irregularities
11. Recognition of political parties as All India or State level parties
12. Acting like a court for settling matters as giving recognition to a political party or allotting a symbol for electoral purposes
13. Preparation of broader for central broadcasts and telecasts and allocation of days and time to different political parties
14. To issue identity cards to the voters
15. Disqualification of candidate if he fails to submit election returns within prescribed time

From the foregoing discussion, it becomes quite evident that Election Commission enjoys vast array of power as far as superintendence, direction and control of all matters pertaining elections in India.

APPOINTMENT, REMOVAL AND TENURE OF ELECTION COMMISSIONERS

The Election Commission presently consists of a Chief Election Commissioner and two Election Commissioners who are appointed by the President. The tenure of the Commissioner is 6 years or up to 65 years of age, whichever is earlier. According to Article 324(5), the Chief Election Commissioner shall not be removed from his office except in the manner and on the like grounds as a judge of the Supreme Court. This means that the Chief Election Commissioner can be removed from office only through impeachment by Parliament, i.e., the Chief Election Commissioner may be removed from office by Parliament by moving a resolution to that effect, passed by absolute majority of the whole house as well as two-third majority present and voting charging him with 'proved misbehaviour' or 'incapacity'. The conditions of service of the Chief Election Commissioner shall not be varied to his disadvantage after his appointment. Other Election Commissioner or a Regional Commissioner shall not be removed from office except on the recommendation of the Chief Election Commissioner.

Until October 1989, there was just one Chief Election Commissioner. In 1989, The President of India, in a notification declared that beside the Chief Election Commissioner, the Commission should have two other Election Commissioners but this was revoked in January 1990. As a result of this, the two Election Commissioners lost their office and one of them challenged the revocation of the notification. The Supreme Court, however, rejected the petition and stated that the creation and abolition of posts was a prerogative of the Executive under Article 324(2). In 1991, however, the Parliament of India passed a law providing for the appointment of two Election Commissioners. This law was amended and renamed in 1993 as the **Chief Election Commissioner and other Election Commissioners (Conditions of Service) Amendment Act 1993.**

The Constitution does not prescribe any qualifications, academic or otherwise, for appointment to these offices. However, by convention, only senior civil servants, either serving or retired, of the rank of the cabinet secretary or secretary to the Government of India or of an equivalent rank have been appointed as the Chief Election Commissioner and Election Commissioners so far.

Since 15th May 2022, Sri Rajiv Kumar is the Chief Election Commissioner of India. He succeeded Sri Sushil Chandra. The two Election

Commissioners are Shri Gyanesh Kumar and Dr. Sukhbir Singh Sandhu. The Election Commission of India has completed 18 Lok Sabha elections till 2024.

As far as State Election Commissions are concerned the territorial work is distributed among separate units responsible for different zones into which the 35 constituent States and Union Territories of the India for election purposes. At the State level, the election work is supervised, subject to overall superintendence, direction and control of the Election Commission, by the Chief Electoral Officer of the State. He is appointed by the Commission from amongst senior civil servants whose name usually is proposed by the concerned State Government. He is helped by a team of supporting staff. At the district and constituency levels there are the District Election Officers, Electoral Registration Officers and Returning Officers and a host of persons acting as supporting functionaries and assisting them in discharging their electoral functions.

Regarding the independence of the Election Commission the Supreme Court, in *T.N. Seshan* v. *Union of India*, (1995) upheld that democracy being the basic feature of our constitutional set up, free and fair elections to our legislative bodies alone would ensure democracy in India. To guarantee a free and fair election process, therefore, election in the country should be entrusted to an independent body which would be insulated from political and/or executive interference. As this objective is achieved by the setting up of an Election Commission, a permanent body, under Article 324(1) of the Constitution, it must be respected. The Supreme Court also ruled that the Election Commissioners enjoyed co-equal status with the Chief Election Commissioner. As the Chief Election Commissioner, T.N. Seshan made all out effort to make the electoral system transparent, free and fair. He introduced innovative electoral reforms and tried to transform the Election Commission as a powerful body. In his endeavour to do so, he often came into confrontation with many politicians and sometimes his high-handedness or rigidity landed him into a number of Court cases. The Court was sometimes critical about the way the Chief Election Commissioner was functioning. In *T.N. Seshan* v. *Union of India,* the Supreme Court observed, "His (Seshan's) public utterances at times were so abrasive that this court had to caution him to exercise restraint on more occasions than one... This gave the impression that he was keen to project his own image. That he has very often been in newspapers and magazines and on television cannot be denied... The CEC has been seen in a commercial on television and in newspaper advertisement... The CEC is, it would appear, totally oblivious to sense of decorum and discretion that his high office requires even if the cause was laudable."

T.N. Seshan has been embroiled in controversy in his struggle to assert the independence of the Election Commission of India. In May 1993, Seshan threatened to cancel some of the by-elections due for May 19 and postpone indefinitely the Rajya Sabha (Upper House) elections due later that year. The ultimate result would have been a serious constitutional crisis. Meanwhile, he also cancelled or postponed elections or by-elections in areas where campaigning would obstruct drought relief work or where communal tensions were high. He cancelled the by-election for the Ranipet Assembly constituency in Tamil Nadu, objecting to the development programmes the State Government had announced, on the argument that they would influence the outcome of the poll. In October 1992, Seshan ordered the West Bengal Government to carry out a complete re-enumeration of the electoral rolls in 24 Assembly constituencies, in response to charges that large number of illegal immigrants from Bangladesh had been listed as voters. In Bihar, elections in no less than five constituencies were cancelled and the results in three others were countermanded, because of massive rigging and violence. The Election Commission also postponed elections in Punjab due for June 1991. In these actions, though Seshan's action can be said to be well within Constitutional limits as well as under the provisions of the Representation of the People Act, 1951 yet these sparked-off controversies and created tensions with politicians so much so that, at times, the politicians talked about his removal and initiation of impeachment proceedings against him. In 1996, M.S. Gill took charge as the Chief Election Commissioner and the Election Commission got back to its previous pace and worked as a multi-member body.

Later T.N. Seshan aspired for the post of President of India in 1997 (though he lost to K.R. Narayanan). Under overreaching Chief Election Commissioners such as T.N. Seshan (1990–96), the Election Commission of India did seek to extend its jurisdiction beyond constitutionally acceptable levels, but such attempts have been short-lived. After the Election Commission was made a three-member body, its functioning has become more institutionalized, and still it is functioning as an independent body and ensuring free, fair and less violent elections now-a-days.

ELECTORAL REFORMS

There has been a growing concern over the years in India about several aspects of our electoral system. The Election Commission has made changes in several areas to respond to some of the concerns. The Commission has taken several new initiatives to make the election procedure more strong and transparent. The Election Commission has introduced *inter alia*, certain schemes for use of State-owned electronic media for broadcast/telecast by political parties, time and again has taken initiatives to check criminalization of politics, has introduced also computerization of electoral rolls, has initiated the system of Voters Identity Cards and above all a Model Code of Conduct before every elections.

There have also been a number of Committees, which have examined the major issues pertaining to the reform of the existing electoral system and they have made a number of valuable recommendations. The important among them were:

1. Goswami Committee on Electoral Reforms (1990)
2. Vohra Committee Report (1993)
3. Indrajit Gupta Committee on State Funding of Elections (1998)
4. Law Commission Report on Reform of the Electoral Laws (1999)
5. National Commission to Review the Working of the Constitution (2001)
6. Election Commission of India–Proposed Electoral Reforms (2004)
7. The Second Administrative Reforms Commission (2008)

However, some critical issues pertaining to electoral reforms require legislative actions. Some laws have been passed in order to check criminalisation of politics, limiting the scope of defections and also creation of a poll fund yet a lot has to be done to ensure free and fair elections and check criminalization of politics.

The Representation of the People (Amendment) Act, 2002 was passed to amend the Representation of the People Act, 1951. It led to the amendment of Section 8 of Act of 1951.

This Act inserted provisions for disqualification as it stated that a person shall be disqualified, where the convicted person is sentenced to:

(i) only fine, for a period of six years from the date of such conviction;
(ii) imprisonment, from the date of such conviction and shall continue to be disqualified for a further period of six years since his release.

Currently, Rule 4A of the Conduct of Election Rules, 1961, prescribes that each candidate must file an affidavit (Form 26 appended to Conduct of Election Rules, 1961) regarding (i) cases, if any, in which the candidate has been accused of any offence punishable with imprisonment for two years or more in a pending case in which charges have been framed by the court, and (ii) cases of conviction for an offence other than any of the offences mentioned in Section 8 of Representation of the People Act, 1951, and sentenced to imprisonment for one year or more. In addition to this, pursuant to the order of the Supreme Court the Election Commission on 27 March 2003, has issued an order that candidates must file an additional affidavit stating information relating to all pending cases in which cognizance has been taken by a Court, assets and liabilities, and educational qualifications. The affidavit is given in a form prescribed by the Election Commission of India. Section 125A of the Representation of the People Act, 1951 prescribes penalties for withholding or providing incorrect information on Form 26, which amount to imprisonment of up to six months, or fine, or both.

Further, under the National Democratic Alliance (NDA) Government the **Constitution's Ninety-First Amendment Act, 2003 regarding Anti Defection Law and Restricting the Size of the Council of Minister** was introduced in 2003 by which the number of cabinet births was limited to just 15% of the total number of legislators to prevent horse trading during the course of regime change.

The 2003 Act provides:

1. In Article 164 of the Constitution, after Clause (1), the following clauses were inserted, namely:

    (1A) The total number of Ministers, including the Chief Minister, in the Council of Ministers in a State shall not exceed 15% of the total number of members of the Legislative Assembly of that State:

    Provided that the number of Ministers, including Chief Minister in a State shall not be less than twelve:

    Provided further that where the total number of Ministers including the Chief Minister in the Council of Ministers in any State at the commencement of the Constitution (Ninety-first Amendment) Act, 2003 exceeds the said 15% or the number specified in the first proviso, as the case may be, then, the total number of Ministers in that State shall be brought in conformity with the provisions of this clause within six months from such date as the President may by public notification appoint.

    (1B) A member of Legislative Assembly of a State or either House of the Legislature of a State having Legislative Council belonging to any political party who is disqualified for being a member of that House under paragraph 2 of the Tenth Schedule shall also be disqualified to be appointed as a Minister under Clause (1) for duration of the period commencing from the date of his disqualification till the date on which the term of his office as such member would expire or where he contests any election to the Legislative Assembly of a State or either House of the Legislature of a State having Legislative Council, as the case may be, before the expiry of such period, till the date on which he is declared elected, whichever is earlier."

2. After Article 361A of the Constitution, the following article shall be inserted, namely:

    361B. A member of a house belonging to any political party who is disqualified for being a member of the house under paragraph 2 of the Tenth Schedule shall also be disqualified to hold any remunerative political post for duration of the period commencing from the date of his disqualification till the date on which the term of his office as such member would expire or till the date on which he contests an election to a house and is declared elected, whichever is earlier. The "remunerative political post" means any office—

    (a) under the Central Government or the State Government where the salary or remuneration for such office is paid out of the public revenue of the Central Government or the State Government, as the case may be; or
    (b) under a body, whether incorporated or not, which is wholly or partially owned by the Central Government or the State Government

and the salary or remuneration for such office is paid by such body, except where such salary or remuneration paid is compensatory in nature.

3. Amendment of the Tenth Schedule of the Constitution led to the omission of paragraph 3 of the Tenth Schedule so as to bring split of political parties within the purview of disqualification based on defection.

Another reform that was brought about was regarding **open donation to political parties**. It was again under the NDA rule, companies, other than those owned by the government, became eligible to make donations to political parties under the proposed bill on state funding of elections. **The Elections and Other Related Laws (Amendment) Bill 2003** that was passed aimed at eliminating the influence of money power and pumping in of black money in elections to Parliament and State Assemblies. The Representation of the People Act of 1951 was suitably amended to allow companies, subject to the Companies' Act of 1956 and Income Tax Act of 1961, to make donations to political parties.

The **Law Commission of India Report on Reform of the Electoral Laws, 1999**, suggested that an amendment must be made to the Representation of the People Act, 1951, a new Section 4A after Section 4 must be inserted to make declaration of assets and criminal cases pending against the candidate part of the qualifications necessary for membership to the house of the People. The Commission kept Section 8 unchanged but suggested, however, the addition of a new section—Section 8B, which would provide a separate set of penalties for electoral offences and offences having a bearing upon the conduct of elections under Sections 153A and 505 IPC and serious offences punishable with death or life imprisonment. The proposed Section 8B would provide that framing of charges shall be a ground of disqualification, but this disqualification shall last only for a period of five years or till the acquittal of the person of those charges, whichever event happens earlier. If a candidate is found guilty they would automatically be disqualified under Section 8.

Constitutional Review Committee was constituted under the Chairmanship of Justice M.N. Venkatachaliah, former Chief Justice of India, in February 2000 to review the working of the Indian Constitution. Among some major proposals of the Venkatachaliah Commission, those related to reforms of the electoral process were—full proof method of electoral roll right at panchayat level constituency, introduction of Electronic Voting Machines (EVMs), empowering the Election Commission to take more stringent action against booth capturing, rigging and intimidation of voters, prohibition of using caste and communal hatred in election campaigns, checking criminalization, action against corrupt practices and speedy disposal of election petitions, setting limits to election cost, delimitation of constituencies, provisions for appointment of the Election Commission and the State Election Commissions, defining office of profit and other reform measures.

In **2004,** the **Election Commission** itself proposed some electoral reforms. The electoral reform proposals came in two parts. In the first part, the Commission had set out certain urgent proposals for electoral reforms in areas that have not been taken up in the past by the Commission and which have arisen due to implementation of certain laws enacted or based on certain directions given by the Supreme Court and the High Courts. In the second part, the Commission has reiterated some of the pending proposals that remain unresolved but need urgent action. Some of the important proposals were as follows:

Need to Increase the Security Deposit of Candidates

Under Section 34 of the Representation of the People Act, 1951, each candidate for election to the house of the People is required to deposit an amount of ₹10,000 as security deposit. For State Assembly elections and elections to the Council of States and Legislative Councils, the security deposit is ₹5,000. The amount of security deposit was last revised in 1996, raising the earlier amount of ₹500 for Lok Sabha elections and ₹250 for Assembly elections to the current levels. Prior to the 14th Lok Sabha Election, the Commission had made a proposal for increasing the security deposit to ₹20,000 in the case of election to the House of the People and ₹10,000 for Legislative Assembly election. For candidates belonging to Scheduled Castes and Scheduled Tribes, the deposit amount would be half the respective amounts. The Commission is also of the view that aforesaid Section 34 should be suitably amended so as to empower the Commission to prescribe the security deposit before every general election to the House of the People. Resorting to amendment of the Act will not be feasible before every general election.

Prevent Criminalization of Politics

The Commission proposed to debar a person, who is accused of serious criminal charges and where the Court is prima facie satisfied about his/her involvement in the crime, and consequently framed charges, from contesting elections in public interest. As a precautionary measure it also proposed that to prevent filing of any motivated cases by the ruling party, it may be provided that only those cases which were filed prior to six months before an election alone would lead to disqualification as proposed. It also suggested that persons found guilty by a Commission of Enquiry should also stand disqualified from contesting elections.

Restriction on the Number of Seats from which one may Contest

The Commission is of the view that the law should be amended to provide that a person cannot contest from more than one constituency at a time.

The Commission also suggested that if the present provision allowing a person to contest from two constituencies as existing at present is to be retained, then there should be an express provision in the law requiring a person who contests and wins election from two seats, resulting in a bye-election from one of the two constituencies, to deposit in the government account an appropriate amount of money being the expenditure for holding the bye-election. The amount could be ₹5,00,000 for State Assembly and Council election and ₹10,00,000 for election to the House of the People.

Restriction on Exit Polls and Opinion Polls

The Commission proposed some restrictions on publishing the results of opinion polls and exit polls to ensure free and fair elections. The Commission recommended that there should be a restriction on publishing the results of exit polls and surveys for a specified period during the election process.

Prohibition of Surrogate Advertisements in Print Media

The Commission was of the view that there should be clear provision to deal with cases of surrogate advertisements in print media. For this purpose, Section 127A of the Representation of the People Act, 1951 may be suitably amended, adding a new sub-section (2A) to the effect that in the case of any advertisements/election matter for or against any political party or candidate in print media, during the election period, the name and address of the publisher should be given along with the matter/advertisement. Sub-section (4) should also be suitably amended to include in its ambit the new proposed sub-section.

Provision for Negative/Neutral Voting

The Commission further, recommended that laws (22 and 49B of the Conduct of Election Rules, 1961) should be amended to specifically provide for negative/ neutral voting. The Commission suggested the addition of a provision in the ballot paper and the particulars on the ballot unit, in the column relating to names of candidates, after the entry relating to the last candidate, there shall be a column none of the above, to enable a voter to reject all the candidates, if he chooses so.

Appointment of Appellate Authority in Districts against Orders of Electoral Registration Officers

As per Section 24 of the Representation of the People Act, 1950, the Chief Electoral Officer of the State is the appellate authority. Access to the Chief Electoral Officer might be difficult for the intending appellants in many cases.

Therefore, the Commission recommended earlier and reiterated it again in this report that that Section 24 of the Representation of the People Act, 1950 should be amended to provide for an appeal against the order of the Electoral Registration Officer to the District Election Officer in the district itself.

Compulsory Maintenance of Accounts by Political Parties and Audit thereof by Agencies Specified by the Election Commission

The Commission recommended compulsory maintenance of accounts and proper auditing of the accounts of the political parties as per guidelines specified by the Election Commission.

Control on Government Sponsored Advertisements

The Commission proposed that where any general election is due on the expiration of the term of the House, advertisements of achievements of the governments, either Central or State, in any manner, should be prohibited for a period of six months prior to the date of expiry of the term of the House and in case of premature dissolution, the date of dissolution of the House. However, advertisements/dissemination of information on poverty alleviation and health related schemes could be exempted from the purview of such a ban.

Consideration for Political Advertisements on Television and Cable

The Commission was of the view that the Government may consider amending the relevant provisions of the Cable Television Network (Regulation) Rules, 1994 to provide for suitable advertisement code and monitoring mechanism.

Composition of Election Commission and Constitutional Protection of all Members of the Commission and Independent Secretariat for the Commission.

In order to ensure the independence of the Election Commission and to keep it insulated from external influences, the Commission recommended that Clause (5) of Article 324 of the Constitution, inter alia, provides the process of removal of the Chief Election Commissioner, but it does not provide similar protection to the Election Commissioners. It merely says that they cannot be removed from office except on the recommendation of the Chief Election Commissioner. The provision seemed to be inadequate and the Election Commission proposed an amendment to provide the same protection and safeguard in the matter of removability of Election Commissioners from office as is available to the Chief Election Commissioner.

Other Proposals of the Commission included anti-defection Law, use of common electoral rolls at elections conducted by the election commission and

The State Election Commissions, simplification of procedure for disqualification of a person found guilty of corrupt practice, making false declaration in connection with elections to be an offence and same number for all contesting candidates and amendment of Section 33 of the representation of the People Act, 1951.

In **2010 a background paper on Electoral reforms was prepared by the Legislative Department, Ministry of Law and Justice, Government of India,** co-sponsored by the Election Commission of India. This background paper addressed the earlier problems of criminalization of politics followed by proposals of disclosure of criminal antecedents of candidates, eligibility of candidates with criminal cases pending against them, negative and neutral voting, financing of elections especially official limits on election campaign expenses, disclosure audit of assets and liabilities of candidates, curbing the cost of campaigning, state funding of elections, proposals for conduct and better management of elections to curb irregularities in polling, Amendment of law to provide for filing of election petition even against defeated candidates on the grounds of corrupt practice, Restrictions on opinion polls, Prohibition of Campaign during the last 48 hours, misuse of religion for electoral gain by political parties and regulating political parties and auditing of their finances among other important proposals.

Elections to students' Union in the Universities and Colleges throughout India are conducted differently. The Supreme Court of India, in order to streamline the process of Students' Union Elections in Colleges and universities, ordered setting up of a Committee of experts to suggest guidelines of such elections. The Committee was mandated to make recommendations on aspects that are required to be observed to maintain academic atmosphere in the educational institutions with stress on indiscipline and divisions on the basis of political beliefs and other such avoidable considerations. The Committee was also mandated to express its views as to the eligibility of candidates, e.g., maximum age limit, standard of educational performance, maximum ceilings of expenses for the election, indication of the source of expenditure. The Committee was to examine as to whether it would be desirable to require the candidates to submit details of expenditure, furnishing of returns by the Union in respect of its transactions and scrutiny of the returns along with suggestion guidelines for forums for ventilating grievances in case a dispute arises as regards the fairness, eligibility of the candidate and/or the non-observance of norms while holding the elections. Thus, under the Chairmanship of Shri J.M. Lyngdoh (Former Chief Election Commissioner) the Committee was constituted to suggest guidelines for Student's Union elections in Universities and colleges. **The Report of the Committee constituted by Ministry of Human Resource Development, Government of India as per the direction of the Hon'ble Supreme Court of India to frame guidelines on Students' Union Elections in Colleges/Universities commonly known as the Lyngdoh Committee Report** was submitted to the Ministry of Human Resource Development Department of Secondary and Higher Education on 23 May 2006, recommending certain Guidelines for Students' Union Elections.

Certain new measure have been introduced by the Election Commission to ensure free and fair election in India like measure for tackling criminals from participating in the elections, computerization of electoral rolls, establishing a framework for using State-Owned Electronic Media for broadcast/telecast by political parties, and also chalking out measures for strict compliance to the Model Code of Conduct prepared by it before the elections. The Election Commission of India has the overall responsibility of superintendence direction, and control and conduct of free and fair elections. Before every election the Commission circulates a Model Code of Conduct and seeks to ensure strict compliance to it. The Commission circulated its First Code at the time of the fifth general elections, held in 1971. Since then, the code has been revised from time-to-time. The Code of Conduct lays down guidelines as to how political parties and candidates should conduct themselves during elections.

Certain recent steps that have been initiated by the National as well as State Election Commissions are programmes aimed at raising the level of consciousness among the youth about voting and the total election process as such. Celebration of National Voter's Day on 25 January of every year now is followed by series of programmes like debates, quiz, essay competition, Mock Parliament to elicit the opinions from the Youth about Parliamentary Democracy in India as well as encourage them to vote during elections. Advertisements in print as well as electronic media about the formalities regarding the mode of acquisition of application forms for entry of names in voter's list, securing a Voter's Identity Card, reporting about change of address, missing of names of valid voters and other issues pertaining to election processes are becoming useful for the public at large.

EXERCISES

I. Short Answer Questions: **(100 words)**

1. Write a note on Article 324 relating to the Election Commission of India.
2. Briefly state the functions of Election Commission of India.
3. State the procedure of appointment and removal of members of Election Commission of India.
4. Briefly state the main recommendations of the Law Commission of India Report on Reform of the Electoral Laws, 1999.
5. Write a note on the recommendations of Constitutional Review Committee.
6. Write a note on the Lyngdoh Committee Report, 2006.

II. Long Answer Questions: **(1200 words)**

7. Discuss the composition, powers and functions of Election Commission of India.
8. In the light of Constitutional provisions examine the role of Election Commission of India.
9. Elucidate on the various attempts of Electoral reform in India.
10. Do you think that the Election Commission can function as an independent body out of the clutches of political control? In the light of powers and position of the Election Commission argue your case citing examples.

REFERENCES

Bakshi, P.M., *The Constitution of India* (with selective comments), Universal Law Publishing, Delhi, 2000.

Basu, Durga Das, *Introduction to the Constitution of India*, Prentice-Hall of India, New Delhi, 1992.

Dhanoa v. *Union of India,* AIR 1991 SC 1745.

Dutta, Satyabrata, *Constitution Review: Venkatachaliah Commission,* Progressive Publishers, Calcutta, 2004.

Pylee, M.V., *India's Constitution*, S. Chand & Company, New Delhi, 1994.

T.N. Seshan v. *Union of India* (1995) 4 SCC 611.

The Representation of The People Act, 1950.

The Representation of The People Act, 1951.

The Representation of The People (Amendment) Act, 2002, Act no. 9 of 2003 [7th January 2003].

19

Role of Pressure Groups in Indian Politics

INTRODUCTION

Politics is all about "who gets what, when and how" and also about "authoritative allocation of values". It is the Government which has the authority to allocate resources among its people, and it is the people/groups who bargain with the Government to get maximum share of the resources. Whenever this interaction between the Government and groups is taken up for analysis, it is needless to say that the groups, which compete among themselves for a share of the limited resources, are either political parties or pressure groups. Political parties usually are interested in contesting the elections and becoming a part of the authority to do the allocation. Therefore, it is the pressure groups that are more or less interested in getting involved in political decision-making by either creating pressure on the government or else simply trying to influence the Government in power to formulate policies in their favour. Usually, a Pressure Group does not nurture political ambition, but in many cases they have political alignment.

A Pressure Group is an organized aggregate which seeks to influence the context of Governmental decisions without attempting to become a part of the government. They work for the protection or promotion of specific interests, which are deemed to be vital for the existence of the members of the group. However, between a political party and a pressure group there is interaction and interpenetration. When a political party controls a pressure group, it inhibits the capacity of the group to formulate pragmatic specific demands, but when groups control a political party, they inhibit the capacity of party to combine specific interests into the programmes for the masses. Further, a group may pursue its objectives with governmental agencies almost independently—autonomous of party control and enjoy privileged position. Another group may realize its goal in collaboration with a political party. A group may not be so powerful, and therefore, it may develop affiliations with political parties as per its own interests.

In India, there are also wide variety of pressure groups/interest groups which seek to influence the policies of the Government like, the Big business interest groups, trade unions, peasant organizations, Caste groups, religious groups, Teachers' and Student's associations, women's organizations, professional groups, tribal groups, MNCs, NRIs and so on. They all play an important role in the decision-making process of the Government, and powerful groups always have their demand met by the Government in the form of major policy decisions.

BIG BUSINESS INTEREST GROUPS

Asian Paints, Britannia Industries, Dr. Reddy Labs (DRL), HDFC Bank, ICICI Bank, Indo Gulf, Infosys Technologies, Mastek, Polaris Software, Rolta India, Satyam Computer, Visualsoft and Zee Telefilms, IT major Infosys Technologies, petrochemical giant Reliance Industries, and two-wheeler company Hero Honda Motors have been ranked as the top companies in India. Top business houses include the Reliance Group (Mukesh Ambani), Tata Group, Reliance Group (Anil Ambani), Bharti Group, Wipro, Sterlite Industries (India) Limited, DLF Group, Jindal Group, Adani Group, Aditya Birla Group and others. Mostly, these business houses deal with the Government on an individual basis. It is because of their command over the economy that they influence decision-making of the government. However, with objective of protecting their financial interests and to give a boost to their industrial policies, the bulk of business communities have powerful associations which emerge as the most powerful pressure/interest groups in India.

The most powerful lobby of the big business groups are Chambers of Commerce which is also known as a board of trade, and is a kind of business network. Its aim is to enhance the business interest of the members. Core interest areas of Chamber of Commerce are as follows:

1. Trade (National and International)
2. Industry (Domestic and International)
3. Professionals (e.g. CAs, lawyers, consultants)
4. Trade and Industry Associations and other Chambers of Commerce

In India the top Chambers of Commerce are:

- ASSOCHAM—organization representing Indian business in totality
- FICCI—Federation of Indian Chambers and Commerce and Industry
- Indian Merchants' Chamber—An apex body of trade, commerce and industry

- The Associated Chambers of Commerce and Industry—an organization representing all sectors of the Indian industry
- EU Chambers of Commerce—To facilitate greater business interaction between EU and India.
- Indian Chamber of Commerce—To accelerate agricultural growth in India
- Bombay Chamber of Commerce—Associated with the economic growth of Mumbai city
- Bengal Chamber of Commerce and Industry
- Bangalore Chamber of Industry and Commerce (BCIC)

The Associated Chambers of Commerce and Industry of India (ASSOCHAM)

The Associated Chambers of Commerce and Industry of India (ASSOCHAM) is an apex industry body which represents the interests of industry and trade. It interfaces with Government on policy issues and interacts with counterpart international organizations to promote bilateral economic issues. ASSOCHAM is represented on all national and local bodies, and is, thus, able to pro-actively convey industry viewpoints, as also communicate and debate issues relating to public-private partnerships for economic development. The members come from sectors like Trade (National and International), Industry (Domestic and International), Professionals (e.g. CAs, lawyers, and consultants), trade and industry associations and other Chambers of Commerce. The mission for ASSOCHAM is "our mission is to impact the policy and legislative environment so as to foster balanced economic, industrial and social development". Thus, ASSOCHAM influence formulation of policies/decisions for creating a healthy environment for trade and industry in India. For this, it ensures representation in most Government Advisory Committees, organizing Seminars, Workshops, Round Table meetings, Submit representations/memoranda and bring out publications, periodicals and discussion papers.

Federation of Indian Chambers and Commerce and Industry (FICCI)

FICCI was established in 1927, and is the largest and oldest apex business organization in India. Although FICCI is a non-government, not-for-profit organization, it is the voice of India's business and industry. FICCI draws its membership from the corporate sector, both private and public, including SMEs and MNCs. FICCI also has an indirect membership of over 2 lakh companies from various regional chambers of commerce. FICCI has several desks for catering to the needs of the organization. They are like Africa Desk, Arab Division, ASEAN Division, CIS DESK, East Asia, Europe Division, Latin America and Caribbean Division, SAARC Division and the US Division.

Indian Merchants' Chamber (IMC)

This is an old organization which was set up in the pre-independence era. In the wake of the Swadeshi Movement IMC was set up in 1907 to represent interests of Indian businesses. Currently, IMC is a premier Chamber of trade, commerce and industry in India. It has representation of more than 3000 members, comprising a cross section of the business community. The mode of operation of ICC is advocacy by organizing interactive meetings with ministers, senior bureaucrats and others to express as well as push forward its views. Its advocacy role focuses on matters affecting growth and development of businesses, on policy and implementation matters. Its headquarters is at Mumbai. Indian Merchants' Chamber includes Confederation of Indian Industry (CII).

Confederation of Indian Industry (CII)

Confederation of Indian Industry (CII) is a non-government, not-for-profit, industry led and industry managed organization which is India's premier business association, with a direct membership of over 7000 organizations from the private as well as public sectors, including SMEs and MNCs, and an indirect membership of over 90,000 companies from around 400 national and regional sectoral associations. CII works to create and sustain an environment conducive to the growth of industry in India, partnering industry and government alike through advisory and consultative processes. The sectors which are dealt by CII are agriculture, infrastructure, manufacturing, services and industrial competitiveness. CII's agenda has therefore, expanded to include inclusiveness and sustainability over and above its running theme of competitiveness. In its effort, it interacts with the Government to play a proactive role in the development of India's economy.

Indian Chamber of Commerce [ICC]

The Indian Chamber of Commerce (ICC) is also an important body of business and industry in Eastern and North-Eastern India. The membership of the Chamber comprises several of the large corporate groups in the country. Initially, set up by a group of pioneering industrialists led by Mr. G.D. Birla, the Indian Chamber was closely associated with the Indian Freedom Movement, as the first organized voice of indigenous Indian Industry. Several of the distinguished industry leaders in India, such as Mr. B.M. Birla, Sir Ardeshir Dalal, Sir Badridas Goenka, Mr. S.P. Jain, Lala Karamchand Thapar, Mr. Russi Mody, Mr. Ashok Jain, have acted as President of ICC. ICC has contributed to economic policy making and anticipates future needs, responds to these challenges and prepares the stakeholders of the economy to benefit from these changes and opportunities.

Other Chambers of Commerce which have a legacy and history of their own are the Bengal Chamber of Commerce and Industry which was set up in 1853, Delhi Chamber of Commerce, Bangalore Chamber of Industry and Commerce (BCIC) and others.

Undoubtedly, these organized business associations have a great impact on policy-making of the Government given the composition of each of these associations comprising of top industrialists of India. While ASSOCHAM pursues 'quiet' or 'latent' diplomacy, FICCI is more explicit and sometimes publicly critical about Government policies. The business pressure groups seek for fewer regulations and lower taxes, more foreign investment, liberalization, privatization, land acquisition, power and electricity, labour and licensing whatever is there for their own benefit. Vide their position they have easy access to the top politicians, cabinet members, Council of Ministers where they can lobby and get their objectives fulfilled.

WORKING CLASS AND TRADE UNION MOVEMENT

Early working class movements in India took place under the colonial masters when in 1877 the workers at the Empress Mills at Nagpur called a strike following a wage cut. Following this several other working class movements took place with a demand for regular payment of wages, a weekly holiday, and a mid-day recess among others. It is estimated that there were 25 strikes between 1882 and 1890. Due to lack of organization, these working class movements could not sustain themselves. The British Colonial Government to tackle such labour unrest adopted the first Factories Act in 1881. The Bombay Millhands' Association formed in 1890 under the leadership of Narayan Lokhande was the first workers' organization in India. Lokhande was the founder editor of the first labour journal *Dinabandhu*. Before the First World War attempts were made to form Trade Unions like in 1906 in the Postal Offices at Bombay and Calcutta. In 1908, mill workers in Bombay went on strike for a week to protest against the conviction of the nationalist leader Bal Gangadhar Tilak on charges of sedition.

After the First World War serious attempts were made to give trade union movements in India a concrete shape. The Madras Labour Union was founded in 1918. Although it was primarily an association of textile workers in the European owned Buckingham and Carnatic Mills, it also included workers in many other trades. The Mazdoor Mahajan-Textile Labour Association was formed in 1920. The year 1920 also marked the formation of the All India Trade Union Congress (AITUC). By 1924, there were 167 Trade Unions in India. In 1925, the Bombay Textile Labour Union (BTLU) was formed, and in 1926 another labour union was formed called the Girni Kamgar Mahamandal (GKM). The next important stage was the passage of Trade Unions Act of 1926. The Indian Trade Unions Act 1926 made it legal for any seven workers to combine in a Trade Union. It also removed the pursuit of legitimate trade union activity from the purview of civil and criminal proceedings. This is still the basic law governing trade unions in the country. In Bengal, a Workingmen's club was organized which also published a monthly journal titled *Bharat Sramajibi*. In 1928, All India Trade Union Federation (AITUF) was formed.

In the post-independence days by 1949 the prominent Trade Unions were:

1. The All India Trade Union Congress,
2. The Indian National Trade Union Congress,
3. The Hindu Mazdoor Sangh, and
4. The United Trade Union Congress

At present the most significant Trade Unions are:

1. All India Trade Union Congress (AITUC)
2. Bharatiya Mazdoor Sangh (BMS)
3. Centre of Indian Trade Unions (CITU)
4. Hind Mazdoor Kisan Panchayat (HMKP)
5. Hind Mazdoor Sabha (HMS)
6. Indian Federation of Free Trade Unions (IFFTU)
7. Indian National Trade Union Congress (INTUC)
8. National Front of Indian Trade Unions (NFITU)
9. National Labour Organization (NLO)
10. Trade Unions Co-ordination Centre (TUCC)
11. United Trade Union Congress (UTUC)
12. United Trade Union Congress— Lenin Sarani (UTUC - LS)

Besides these, there are also equally strong and well-organized bank employees union, State Government employees union, public employees, telecommunication employees, health services, financial sector employees and municipal employees and other professional groups. The important among them are:

All India Bank Officers Confederation (AIBOC) which is the premier organization of Bank Officers in India mostly organized purely on apolitical lines.

All India State Government Employees Federation (AISGF) is a trade union organization representing state employees and teachers of different states in India.

National Confederation of Officer's Association (NCOA) represents the managerial and supervisory staff of the Indian government owned public Enterprises.

Trade Union International (TUI) forms a part of the structure of World Federation of Trade Unions, representing the public employees, telecommunication employees, health services, financial sector employees and municipal employees of different countries of the world.

As pointed out earlier that these Trade Unions are most often linked to certain parties. However, the control of trade unions by political parties which may be ascribed as 'political unionism' is a much debated topic. In most of the cases, however, the Central Trade Unions to which various individual unions are affiliated, are closely associated with political parties. Table 19.1 will give an idea of major Trade Unions and their party affiliations.

With such a history of working class movement, it is needless to say that the Trade Unions are vital for the existence of the labour as it gives them a platform from where they can demand their dues from the Government. The important point is that most of the Trade Unions are affiliated to some political parties, either of leftist ideology or rightist ideology. However, with the present spree of globalization and the onslaught on the labours as a part of the Structural Adjustment Porgrammes (SAPs) and subsequent laying off of labours, privatization, closure, threats to pension, gratuity or other post-

Table 19.1 Trade Unions and their affiliations

Name of the Trade Unions	*Party Affiliations*
All India Central Council of Trade Unions	Communist Party of India (Marxist-Leninist) Liberation
All India Trade Union Congress	Communist Party of India
All India United Trade Union Centre	Socialist Unity Centre of India (Communist)
Bharatiya Mazdoor Sangh	Rashtriya Swayamsevak Sangh
Indian National Trade Union Congress	Indian National Congress
Indian National Trinamool Trade Union Congress	All India Trinamool Congress
Centre for Indian Trade Unions Communist Party of India (Marxist)	Communist Party of India (Marxist)
Hind Mazdoor Sabha	Socialists (mostly Forward Bloc and independent unionists)
Labour Progressive Federation	Dravida Munnetra Kazhagam
Trade Union Coordination Committee	All India Forward Bloc
United Trade Union Congress	Revolutionary Socialist Party

retirement benefits, the Trade Unions irrespective of their ideologies are fighting for their cause together. It must be noted at this juncture that these Trade Unions represents the workers of organized sectors. A huge labour force is engaged in informal sectors or unorganized sectors which are scattered and have no platforms to raise their voices. In the informal sector what is alarming is that there is presence of a huge women work force, who are left at the mercy of their employers and face discrimination with regard to wage, maternity benefits and have no post retirement benefits too. The trade union movement in India suffers from certain problems which adversely affect the efficacy of the Unions and their success in getting their demands fulfilled. These include fragmentation of unions, affiliation of the unions with political parties, lack of militancy by the established unions and a general apathy towards organizing workers employed in the unorganized sector of the economy. Despite such shortcoming Trade Unions do exert a great amount of influence in shaping of Government policies.

PEASANTS IN INDIAN POLITICS

Peasants and farmers though constitute a huge bulk are the most unorganized sector in India. However, if one looks back at the history of India, there are ample examples of peasant movements in India. The earlier peasant movements took place during the colonial rule against the oppression of the Britishers as well as against the *Zamindars* or landlord class like the Indigo uprising of 1860 and the Moplah uprising of 1921 in Malabar.

If one tries to find out the political maneuvering of the peasant struggles in the colonial days, then it would reveal that both the Congress and the Communist parties tried to mobilize the peasants. While the Congress was successful in drawing the support of a part of the rural community during its anti-imperialist agitations it was ambivalent as far as the idea of struggle against the landlords were concerned. A new chapter in peasant movement started with the formation of the All India Kisan Congress (AIKC) later renamed as the All India Kisan Sabha (AIKS), 1936, with the primary purpose of the Sabha was to mobilize the peasants, tenants-at-will, sharecroppers and landless agricultural labourers. The Tebhaga movement in Bengal (1946–47) and the Telangana movement (1946–51) in the former Hyderabad state were led by the AIKS. The point to be noted is that the Communist Party of India (CPI) was an integral part of the AIKS and prime mobilizer of the peasants.

The **Tebhaga movement** is one of the two great movements which took place in North Bengal and also in the districts of Dinajpur and Rangpur in East Bengal and Jalpaiguri and Malda in West Bengal. The movement aimed at the reduction in the share of the produce paid as rent, to the *Jotedars* who possessed rights on land. It was organized by the Kisan Sabha. It was only in 1946, when the Communist Party of India rallied behind the movement that it took a revolutionary turn. The main conflict arose during the time of the harvest season when the sharecroppers refused to provide the amount of paddy to the *Jotedars*. The Muslim League and the Congress supported the *Jotedars* and eventually were successful in suppressing the movement. The movement eventually collapsed and was officially called off in the summer of 1947. Though the movement failed, it had important implications for the entire history of peasant struggles in India.

The **Telangana peasant movement** started in mid-1946 and continued till the October of 1951. The movement engulfed the whole of the Telangana region of the Hyderabad state and the adjoining districts of the Andhra delta. It has been regarded as the most revolutionary of all the movements in India, in its character and political objectives. The CPI through its peasant wing, the Kisan Sabha, launched the movement against the oppressive system of exploitation in the entire region. The movement led by the Communists began in Nalgonda district in 1946, and then spread to the neighbouring Warangal and Bidar districts and finally engulfed the whole of the Telangana region. The objective of the movement was directed against the illegal and excessive extraction by the rural feudal aristocracy. The greatest demand was that all peasant debt should be written off. The movement became more virulent when in order to counter the oppression let loose by the aristocracy the peasantry launched the armed struggle.

The **Naxalbari peasant uprising** that occurred in the northern part of West Bengal is another of the major uprisings India has witnessed. It was led by a faction of the CPI (M) by two most prominent leaders Kanu Sanyal and Charu Mazumdar. It began in the foothills of the eastern Himalayas in West Bengal, in a place called Naxalbari within the subdivision of Siliguri in Darjeeling district. It is in Naxalbari, Kharibari and Phansidewa that the movement took a militant turn. Ten great tasks were specified which included *inter alia*, land which was not owned and tilled by peasant themselves was to be redistributed, peasants were to burn all legal deeds and documents, unequal agreements between the moneylenders and the peasants and they were to be declared null and void, hoarded rice were to be confiscated by the peasants and distributed among the peasants, all *jotedars* to be tried and sentenced to death, etc. Forcible occupations by the peasants took place and in many cases there were looting of rice and paddy and intimidation and assaults. The first pahse of Naxalbari movement came to a halt, when, under pressure from the Central Government, the stringent actions were taken by the West Bengal Police in the area although sporadic unrest continued for some time.

Both the mainstream Communist parties, the CPI and the CPI (M) have formed peasant organizations like the Kisan Sabhas and organization of agricultural labourers for mobilizing the concerned sections and have achieved limited success in Kerala, West Bengal, and Tripura and in some other states. Similarly the CPI (M-L) is active in Bihar and has formed its peasant front, the Bihar Pradesh Kisan Sabha (BPKS) which is active in many of the districts of Bihar including those districts which are now in the new state of Jharkhand, organizing the rural poor and also the middle peasants by taking up issues which affect them. Other organizations like the Bharatiya Kisan Union (BKU) in western Uttar Pradesh, Punjab and Haryana and the Shetkari Sangathan (SS) in Maharashtra and Gujarat can be ascribed as organizations comprised of rural rich. There are other organizations and movements in the country as well like the Karnataka Rajya Raitha Sangha movement and Vivasayigal Sangam movement in Tamil Nadu, the *Khedut* movement in south of Gujarat. They are very active and sometimes organizations like BKU and SS led campaigns of road and rail blockage and *gheraos* of State Legislatures. Yet, there are problems of ascribing the term nomenclature of peasants to these organizations as they comprise rich farmers. So more or less scholars prefer to call the movements led by them as farmer's movements.

Peasants have therefore been always a source of power in India, the power of the have-nots. They have struggled against oppression and exploitation of the landlords but given today their lack of organization mainstream peasant movements of the genre that we have discussed above are missing. Today, what India is experiencing is Maoist insurgencies or Naxalite movements spread across several States in India like Odisha, Jharkhand, Bihar, Andhra Pradesh, Chhattisgarh, Madhya Pradesh, Maharashtra, and West Bengal, which are serious threats to the integrity and security of India. These groups have been mobilizing the rural poor, in these states and using violence as a strategy to address the question of the rural poor but their activities are hurting the national integration of India. On its part the Government must also take some concrete steps to induce inclusive growth so that the rich and poor disparity in the economy and society is bridged and also try to bring the insurgents back to the mainstream social and political life of India. The AIKS mobilized the peasants in Maharashtra in March 2018 and February 2019 for restoration of farmer's rights and protest against the agrarian crisis and downplaying of the crisis along with complaints about the minimum effort on the part of the government to mitigate the sufferings of the peasantry. Farmers movement in India took an unprecedented turn in 2020 with the Parliament of India passing three farm laws which were deemed to be anti-farmers. Protests and sit-in demonstrations started from September 2020 and continued till December 2021 until the Government repealed the three farm laws. The farmers wanted a guarantee of MSP or minimum support price and also reminded the government of a return to protests if the bills were reintroduced in any form. A number of farmers' organization participated in the demontsrations like Samyukt Kisan Morcha, All India Kisan Sangharsh Coordination Committee, Bharatiya Kisan Union, All India Kisan Sabha and others.

MASS MEDIA AND SOCIAL MEDIA AND ITS IMPACT ON INDIAN POLITICS

The mass media has really become much powerful and in many ways they are influencing the Government. The most important mass media are Print media which include books, pamphlets, newspapers, magazines and others, Recordings (gramophone records, magnetic tapes, cassettes, CDs, DVDs), Cinema, Radio, Television, Internet, Mobile phones and now with Internet facilities.

But among all these, two have overwhelming followers and they comprise mainly of the vast array of English and vernacular print media and multiple 24/7 television channels. The main news agencies of Indian print media are the Press Trust of India and United News of India. *The Indian Express*, *The Hindustan Times*, *The Statesman*, and magazines like India Today, Outlook, and the Week, have a large readership in the entire country. They make people aware of the important national and international events. Sometimes, they become the tools of social change by igniting the minds of the people provided that the print media carries out is duty with full responsibility following the various acts and keeping in mind the Constitution and the security and national interests of India.

Globalization and massive technological revolution have changed the way news are presented today over the Television. The sense of seeing news, fast and live round the clock, 24×7 news broadcasts and updates has been able to put the Governments in difficult situations often. Whether it is the burden of coalition politics, or corruption issue, or bilateral issue, or nuclear issue, or even environmental issues and women's issues, the presentation of news has changed a lot from what it used to be in the past. Media has become a police, and every now and then, the Governments/individual Ministers/Public Servants are put to trial by media for their errors of omission and commission. However, sometimes media plays into the tune of the political parties, and become their mouthpieces and when this happens the news or information that is fed to the public is distorted.

Article 19 of the Indian Constitution upholds the freedom of Press, but this is subjected to certain reasonable restrictions imposed by the Constitution of India. Besides, the mass media has to abide by a number of laws in India like The Press and Registration of Books Act, 1867, The Press (Objectionable Matters) Act, 1951, The Newspaper (Prices and Pages) Act, 1956, Defence of India Act, 1962, Delivery of Books and Newspapers (Public Libraries) Act, 1954, The Working Journalists and other Newspaper Employees (Conditions of Service and Miscellaneous Provisions) Act, 1955, Civil Defence Act, 1968, Press Council Act, 1978 and others.

Before liberalization and explosion of hundreds of channels via Cable T.V., the mass media was wholly-controlled by the Government, which led the media project only what the government wanted the public to see and in a way in which it wanted the public to see it. However, with the onset of globalization and privatization, the situation has undergone a humongous change. The most viewed news channels are like NDTV, Star News, Times Now, Aaj Tak, CNN-IBN, BBC and so on. It is difficult for a democratic country like India to impose restrictions upon these channels as this is sure to invite public fury.

Broadcasting through Radio also has undergone revolutionary changes as the All India Radio is not the only radio station. Here also 24×7 there are several private channels going on air. As mobile phones have FM radio compatibility and people are also 24×7 hooked on to multiple radio FM channels if they do not have the access to television. So information has given power to the people to stay informed about society and polity.

With the whole new world of **Social Media** involving Internet which provides the basic structure and the backbone of communication, our lives can no longer be the same as they were even a decade ago. *Facebook, Twitter, Youtube, Linkedin,* to name a few have changed the way we look at the world, especially that of the youths. 'Physical Space' has greatly been consumed by 'Virtual Space'. Therefore, international relations and domestic politics cannot turn a blind eye to these developments. The happenings in North Africa or for that matter the crusade against corruption in India and the immense social networking across borders have made politicians think seriously about social media.

It is time now that the Government must acknowledge the fact that the people at large are informed about their functioning. The traditional media, electronic or print as well as the social media are feeding the people with the information. Moreover, the social media has given the people the power to connect with one another and share ideas and information. It has made it possible for the people to collaborate, coordinate and give voice to their concerns. The Arab Spring or Jasmine Revolution has shown how social media had become a very important factor when there was a near- total media blackout. This power of social media cannot be ignored by the Government. Therefore, one saw how the GOI came down heavily on the social media when the Telecom and Information Technology Minister declared the screening of contents before they are posted on social networking sites. This was mainly when the Anti-corruption movement was at its peak. One grave concern, which has arisen is that social media when used to spread hate campaigns or are misused by terrorists or by groups which do not act responsibly, whereby security of India is endangered, the government needs to take steps. The recent August 2012 happenings in the North-east of India and the incidents being presented with distortions in social media made the government ban and block some social media sites. Again the government must also ensure that it is not exceeding it limit and depriving the people of expressing opinions on these social media sites.

Empowering of people through news channel leave alone social media has shown how local people have organized themselves and have started protesting at the site of Koodankulam and Jaitapur Nuclear plants after the Fukushima disaster. Pressure from civil society, earlier had seen the adoption of Right to Information Act 2005. Now it is the civil society again which has forced the Government to review their version of Lokpal Bill. Therefore, situations have changed. Parliamentarians cannot ignore the public now.

EXERCISES

I. Short Answer Questions: **(100 words)**

1. Briefly write on the role of big business groups in Indian politics.
2. Write a note on working class activities in India with reference to Trade Union Movements.
3. Peasants in Indian Politics.
4. Write a note on the role of Media in Indian politics.
5. Emergence of social media and its impact upon politics.

II. Long Answer Questions: (1200 words)

6. Examine the role of Big Business interest groups in Indian politics.
7. Elucidate the role of trade unions in Indian politics.
8. Examine the role of peasants in Indian politics.
9. Examine the role of media in politics by bringing in the importance of both the traditional media and the social media.

REFERENCES

Awasthy, S.S., *Indian Government and Politics*, Har-Anand Publications, New Delhi, 2006.

Chatterjee Rakhahari, "Workers and their Trade Unions", in Chatterjee Rakhahari (Ed.), *Politics India: The State-Society Interface*, South Asian Publishers, New Delhi, 2004.

Gough Kathleen, *Indian Peasant Uprisings*, in Oomen, T.K. (Ed.), *Social Movements: Issues of Identity*, Vol. 1, Oxford University Press, New Delhi, 2011.

Sengupta Debjani, "Peasant Movements in India", in Chatterjee Rakhahari (Ed.), *Politics India: The State-Society Interface*, South Asian Publishers, New Delhi, 2004.

Shah, Ghanshyam, *Social Movements in India: A Review of Literature*, Sage Publications, New Delhi, 2007.

Singh, M.P. and Saxena, Rekha, *Indian Politics: Contemporary Issues and Concerns,* Prentice-Hall of India, New Delhi, 2008.

Sikri, S.L., *Indian Government and Politics*, Kalyani Publishers, New Delhi, 2004.

20

Challenges to the Indian Political System

INTRODUCTION

After more than 70 years of independence, the journey continues for Indian democracy. However, the journey has not been smooth for the Indian polity. There have arisen a number of challenges which have threatened the very basis of the polity. The challenges have come from different corners. Sometimes the caste factor has taken its toll on the functioning of the Indian political system, whereas at other times it is the religion which did not remain limited to the personal domain of one's faith, but transcended it only to engulf the entire political system. There have been pulls and pressures from regional fronts too. Exclusiveness had alienated the tribes and forceful integration brought out an opposite reaction from them. Tribes do pose a challenge to the existence of Indian State as sometimes their demand tantamount to autonomy or demand for separate statehood. At present, the criminalization and corruption of politics have placed the working of parliamentary democracy at peril. The administration being fraught with corruption has created dissatisfaction among the people and the rising challenge from civil society activism is questioning the efficacy of the Indian political system. This chapter has taken up a few challenges to Indian polity for discussion.

CASTE

The Report of the Indian Statutory Commission, 1930, observed that "Every Hindu necessarily belongs to the caste of his parents and in that caste he inevitably remains. No accumulation of wealth and no exercise of talents can alter his caste status; and marriage outside his caste is prohibited or severely discouraged." This in brief gives the essence of caste system in India. The system of caste has its roots in the *varna* system which originated after the invasion of the Aryans. *Varna* means colour of the skin and hair and *varna* system came to be realized as a distinction between two different races, the Aryan *varna* and the *Krsna varna.* Later this binary distinction evolved into a fourfold social structure based on varying ranks and functions of different groups. The *Purusasukta* contains the fourfold scheme of social stratification. The occupations of four ranks are related symbolically to the parts of the body of the *Purusa.* The reference in *Purusasukta* reads as:

> *The Brahmana was his mouth,*
> *The Rajanya was made of his two arms;*
> *His thighs became the Vaisya.*
> *From his feet was produced the Sudra.*

Thus, the Brahamanas were identified as the priests, the *Khatriyas* as warriors and protectors, the *Vis/Vaishya* with provider of services including trade and commerce and *Sudras* were the lowest in the ranking who were to serve the upper *Varnas.* With time, the functional distinctions got rigid as occupational specialization took place and the social mobility within the ranks of *Varna* became closed and particular services were identified with particular *varna.* Gradually, this *varna* system became localized and *jatis* emerged which was the local division of labour and stratification arising out of the occupational specialization of the society. This *jati-vyavastha* is what more or less corresponds to the present caste system in India. Generally, caste is regarded as a hereditary endogamous kinship group, ranked in terms of social and ritual status, linked by marriage and lineage and generally locally identifiable. Each caste has its own distinctive feature, customs, rituals, traditional occupation (diluted at present) and come to occupy a particular position in the local hierarchy of social status. André Béteille also upholds a similar kind of definition. He observes that caste may be defined as a small and named group of persons characterized by endogamy, hereditary membership, and a specific style of life which sometimes includes the pursuit by tradition of a particular occupation, and is usually associated with a more or less distinct ritual status in a hierarchical system. In India, there are innumerable castes, sub castes around which the whole system of social stratification revolves. What is important is that caste being a social feature has very much become part and parcel of politics. Hence, the need arises to study the role of caste in Indian politics. As Rajni Kothari truly observes that *casteism in politics* is thus no more and no less than *politicization of caste.*

Rajni Kothari, in his seminal work *Caste in Indian Politics,* rejects the prevailing dichotomy between traditional society and modern polity and examines the interaction between the two. The social system in India is organized around caste structures and caste identities. In dealing with the relationship between caste and politics, it would be wrong to put forth the question whether caste is disappearing or not. In reality, no social system disappears. One should ponder over the issue about what form of caste is taking under the impact of politics, and what form of id politics taking in a caste-oriented society. Those who complain of *casteism in politics* in India are really looking for a politics which has no basis in society. According to Kothari, these people probably lack a clear conception of either the nature of politics or the nature of the caste system. The process of politics is one of identifying and manipulating existing structures in order to mobilize support and consolidate positions. Since the caste structure provides one of the most important organizational clusters in India, politics must strive to organize itself through such a structure. The allege casteism in politics is nothing, but politicization of caste.

Kothari, states that there is a lot of give and take between caste and politics. By drawing the caste system into its web of organization, politics finds material for its articulation and moulds it into its own design. In making politics their sphere of activity, caste and kin groups gets a chance to assert their identity and to strive for positions drawing upon both the interacting structures are the real actors—new contestants for power. Politicians mobilize caste groupings and identities in order to organize their power. For them, caste is an extremely articulated and flexible basis for organization, something that is also available for political manipulation.

The advent of Britishers had led to a change in the nature of caste system in India by changing the land relationship. *Zamindars* or land-holders were created and these people usually belonged to the upper castes. The peasants and serfs came from the lower castes and also constituted the lower class in the society. Thus, class got intertwined with caste. With the introduction of western education the landed class got access to the education and the people were the first to fill up the ranks of colonial bureaucracy. Upper caste men mainly the *Brahamanas* became the haves and lower caste remained the have-nots. Gradually, the discontent of the non-*Brahaman* castes fuelled into caste–based movements in colonial India as the Non-*Brahaman* movement in Maharashtra led by Jyotirao Phule (1827–1990), in Tamil Nadu led by Periyar who also formed the Justice Party in 1920 after severing his connections with the Congress, no-rent campaigns in Bihar and Uttar Pradesh, Eka movement led by Baba Ramchandra in UP (1921) and the Kheda Satyagraha in Gujarat (between 1918–1919) to mention a few.

In post-independence era, the caste differences have got a new meaning when the various caste groups have assumed organizational forms like caste associations and caste-based political parties to mobilize their people and improve their social and economic conditions. The Constitution of India upholds the Right to equal protection of law and equality before law for all the citizens of India irrespective of caste, creed or other differences. The Constitution of India, further, has given several safeguards to protect the rights of the backward classes. The Constitution provides for certain types of reservations for the

Scheduled Castes and Scheduled Tribes like reservation of jobs in government services and in public sector, reservation in educational institutions, and reservations in legislative representations.

Article 15(4) deals with the reservation of seats in the educational institutions and it reads as:

"Nothing in Article 15 or Clause (2) of Article 29 shall prevent the state from making any special provision for the advancement of any socially and educationally backward classes of citizens or for the Scheduled Castes and Scheduled Tribes."

Articles 38 and 46 in the chapter of Directive Principles, confers upon the state the duty to strive for the welfare of the people in general and the backward classes in particular.

Article 38 states:

(1) the State shall strive to promote the welfare of the people by securing and promoting as effectively as it may a social order in which Justice—social, economic and political shall form all institutions of national life;
(2) the State shall in particular, strive to minimize the inequalities in income, and endeavour to eliminate the inequalities in status, facilities and opportunities not only amongst individuals, but also amongst group of people residing in different areas and engaged in different vocations.

Article 46 stipulates that "The state shall promote with special care the educational and the economic interest of the weaker sections of the people and in particular, of the Scheduled Castes and Tribes and shall protect them from injustices and all forms of exploitation."

Further, Article 340 of the Constitution provides for the appointment of a "**Commission to investigate the conditions of backward classes.**"

The Union Government in 1953 appointed the Kalelkar Commission under the provisions of Article 340 which submitted its report in 1956. However, the recommendations were in general not accepted by the Central Government. Again the Second Backward Classes Commission under Article 340 was appointed when the Janata Party came to power in 1978 led by B.P. Mandal. This Commission has come to be identified by as Mandal Commission and it submitted its report in 1980.

On the basis of the provisions of the Constitution of India, 15% of educational and government jobs were reserved for Scheduled Castes and 7.5% for Scheduled Tribes. Kalelkar Commission recommended reservation of 70% seats in technical and professional educational institutions for qualified students belonging to the backward classes. In 1963, the Supreme Court came out with its ruling that whatever may be the case, the reservations could not exceed 50%. In 1978, when the Second Backward Classes Commission was constituted under B.P. Mandal, the case of Other Backward Classes (OBCs) was considered. This Commission in its report, in 1980, recommended

27% reservation of seats in all scientific, technical and professional institutions run by the Central and State Governments for OBCs. It also stated that those States which already have implemented 27% of reservation for OBC would continue unaffected.

In 1990, the Central Government headed by V.P. Singh issued an Office memorandum extending the reservation of OBCs on the basis of recommendations of the Mandal Commission. This action of Government provoked agitation and wide range of protests and even self-immolation by students. Writ petitions were also filed in the Supreme Court against such policy of the Government. In 1992, the Supreme Court ruled that the Union Government can reserve 27% of the jobs for the OBCs, but the 'creamy layer' should be excluded from among the OBCs. Thereafter, the Government executed its order in 1993.

The reservation policy as it stands today is that 22.5% seats will be reserved for Scheduled Caste (15%) and Scheduled Tribes (7.5%) in all educational institutions maintained by public money. Added to this would be 27% reservations for OBCs. Therefore, total reservation will amount to 49.5%. Relaxations have been also provided in case of criteria for admission in educational institutions. In Lok Sabha and Rajya Sabha seats have been reserved for Scheduled Castes and Scheduled Tribes. The 73rd Constitutional Amendment Act, 1992 on Panchayati Raj system has also provided for reservations for seats in Panchayati Raj Institutions.

The introduction of universal adult franchise by the Constitution of India has led to the inclusion of huge section of the population into the fold of Indian politics especially in the arena of electoral politics. Now the political parties use the caste card to secure their votes. It is here that caste has come to play an important role in electoral politics. There has been a tendency on the part of every party to create caste-based vote banks. Thus, during elections the selection of candidates in particular cases where the motive is to woo specific voters belonging to a particular caste, there has been a tendency for encouraging caste-based selection of candidates and making appeals to the electorate along caste lines.

Many States have witnessed keen competition between two castes or caste clusters. In Rajasthan, the competition is between the *Jats* and *Rajputs*, in Gujarat between the *Patidars* and *Baniya-Brahmin*, in Karnataka tussle between *Vokkaligas* and *Lingayats*, in Andhra Pradesh between *Kammas* and *Reddis*, in Bihar between *Bhumidars*, *Kayasth* and *Rajput* and in Tamil Nadu and Maharashtra there were non-Brahmin movements. In Punjab, the backward castes were not very supportive of the demand for a separate State of Punjab by reorganizing the State on linguistic and communal lines as they feared that a reorganized Punjab would facilitate domination of *Jat* Sikhs. Caste conflicts are frequent in some States like Bihar where the Ranbir Sena, a militia of upper caste landlord get engaged in conflict with the Maoist Communist Centre (MCC) leading to a number of casualties.

What is noticeable at this juncture is the trend of politics revolving round the mobilization of the *Dalits* or the Backward Castes by playing or manipulating their interests. The 1990s have seen emergence of large number of caste-based political parties, garnering the support of Backward Castes and becoming an important factor in national and regional politics. There has emerged thus a trend which has been referred to as the 'mandalisation of politics'.

More or less, all parties play the caste-card whether during national elections or State elections. Instances can be found in Congress policy of providing 27% reservations in the 1970s under pressure from backward classes in Andhra Pradesh and also putting up many candidates from Backward Classes during 1970s elections only. Devraj Urs, the Chief Minister of Karantaka also reduced election tickets to upper castes aspirants from the Lingayat and Vokkaligas. In North India, in Uttar Pradesh caste seems to be an important determinant of politics. When Charan Singh became the Chief Minister of Uttar Pradesh in 1967–1968 by heading the United Front Government he also heavily banked upon caste appeal. He is said to have been popular among middle and backward castes. From 1990s after the 'mandalisation of politics' the *dalits* came to occupy the front seat of national and state politics. The backward castes became the target of the political parties who were keen in capturing the caste-based vote banks. Certain *dalit* parties came into existence like the Bahujan Samaj Party (BSP) in 1984. They became a factor in all elections. The Samajwadi Party (SP) was formed in 1992 which mainly tries to voice the demands of the OBCs. In the 1993 State elections, the BSP won as many as 67 seats. The Government was formed by Samajwadi Party in coalition with BSP and Mulayam Singh Yadav as the Chief Minister. The BSP withdrew its support in 1995, and the Government collapsed. It was BSP with BJP that formed another government with Mayawati as the first *dalit* woman Chief Minister in India. The BJP also has played caste cards as in Uttar Pradesh State election of 2012, Uma Bharti was inducted into BJP and she was given the mission to revive the position of BJP in Uttar Pradesh. This was done with the sole factor in mind that she could use her position as an OBC in attracting voters. Bangaru Laxman, a *dalit*, was also the BJP President from 2000–2001. Thus, more or less every political party time and again has played the caste-card. In Tamil Nadu too as pointed out earlier there is a non-Brahmin sentiment and likewise party politics also unfolds in the similar pattern with the allegation sometimes about oppression of the Brahmins or upper castes. DMK has been the mouthpiece of the non-Brahmin movement in Tamil Nadu. As André Béteille observed in his study of Sripuram, a village in Tanjore in Tamil Nadu, that with the introduction of Panchayati Raj Institutions there has been changes in the distribution of power. In Sripuram for instance, there has been a transfer of power from Brahmins to Non-Brahmins and this has become visible with the shift of the Panchayat office from the *agraharam* to the Non-Brahmin quarters associated with the replacement of a Brahmin President by a Non-Brahmin President.

However, the *dalit* political parties have failed to forge an alliance at national or even at regional level as they come together more or less on an ad hoc basis depending on their interests, calculations about power sharing and benefits of keeping out perceived adversaries. Thus BJP has worked out alliances in Uttar Pradesh between upper and lower/OBCs. The Bahujan Samaj Party and Samajwadi Party came together just for a short spell of time (after 1993 Assembly elections) and then the alliance broke apart.

What emerges is that caste and class typically overlap in the Indian case. Sudipta Kaviraj observes that "there has been a sort of class-effect of caste, without caste being whittled down." Caste has assumed certain political functions of class. Despite globalization, and expansion of labour market and economic mobility of people which have led to the horizontal integration of classes, caste still remains a dominant factor in Indian politics. While the Caste System is breaking down in social and cultural fields; conflicts between castes are intensified by party politics. A myth, that has been doing the rounds in Bihar after the Assembly elections of 2010, is that caste as a determining factor in politics has taken a back seat has been blasted. Nitish Kumar secured his first victory in 2005, because the Yadavs did not vote for Lalu as they were more concerned with good governance. Likewise in the Assembly elections of 2010, the Yadavs geared their support behind Nitish Kumar which secured him another term. This means the poll result was the positive effect of Nitish Kumar's five years in Government plus the caste factor. The 2011 Census of India was also based on caste which is a pointer that caste still remains an important factor in Indian politics. Even in the December 2017 Gujarat Assembly elections, caste became a core factor with the Patels/Patidars becoming a focal point of attention for political parties.

LANGUAGE

India is a land of diversity. In case of language too there is a multiplicity of languages in India. Therefore, there arise ethno-lingual problems in Indian politics. Individual mother tongues in India are numerous, and as per the 1961 census they are around 1,652. According to Census of India of 2001, there are 122 (22 Scheduled Languages + 100 non-Scheduled Languages) languages and 234 mother tongues.

Part XVII of the Constitution contains provisions relating to the Official language in India. Chapter I deals with the Language of the Union from Articles 343–344 and Chapter II under Articles 345–347 contains provisions dealing with regional languages. The Official Language Policy of India is stated under Article 343 which states that Hindi in Devanagari script is the official language of the Union. The form of numerals to be used for official purposes of the Union is the international form of Indian numerals [Article 343(1)]. In addition to Hindi language, English language may also be used for official purposes (Section 3 of the Official Languages Act). **Article 344** provides for the creation of Commission and Committee of Parliament on official language. **Article 345** states that as far as Official language or languages of a State is concerned, subject to the provisions of Articles 346 and 347, the Legislature of a State may, by law, adopt any one or more of the languages in use in the

State or Hindi as the Language or Languages to be used for all or any of the official purposes of that State. It also upholds that until the Legislature of the State otherwise provides by law, the English language shall continue to be used for those official purposes within the State for which it was being used immediately before the commencement of this Constitution.

Article 346 contains provisions for Official languages for Communication between one State and another or between a State and the Union. It states that the language for the time being authorized for use in the Union for official purposes shall be the official language for communication between one State and another State and between a State and the Union provided that if two or more States agree that the Hindi language should be the official language for communication between such States, that language may be used for such communication.

Article 347 deals with Special provision relating to language spoken by a section of the population of a State. On a demand being made in that behalf the President, if he is satisfied that a substantial proportion of the population of a State desire the use of any language spoken by them to be recognized by that State, direct that such language shall also be officially recognized throughout that State or any part thereof for such purpose as he may specify.

Chapter III, Articles 348–349 contains provisions for language of the Supreme Court, High Courts, etc., Chapter IV, Articles 350–351 on special directives for use of language.

Further, business in Parliament may be transacted in English or in Hindi. However, the Chairman of the Rajya Sabha or the Speaker of the Lok Sabha may permit any Member to address the House in his/her mother tongue under special circumstances **(Article 120). Article 210** is concerned about the language to be used in the Legislature which states that business in the Legislature of a State shall be transacted in the official language or languages of the State or in Hindi or in English provided that the Speaker of the Legislative Assembly or Chairman of the Legislative Council, or person acting as such, as the case may be, may permit any member who cannot adequately express himself in any of the languages aforesaid to address the House in his mother-tongue.

The **Official Language Act, 1963**, the **Official Language Rules, 1976** and various directives issued under them by the Department of Official Language, Ministry of Home Affairs prescribe the purposes of usage of Hindi and English. The official policy of the Government is that it adopts a posture of inducing progressive use of Hindi in the official work through persuasion, incentive and goodwill.

According to Article 344 of the Constitution, an Official Language Commission was appointed under the Chairmanship of B.G. Kher. The Commission submitted its report in 1956 which was made public in 1957. The main recommendation of the Commission was Hindi should be increasingly used for official purposes in place of English but also observed that it was neither necessary nor possible to pronounce at the time of the working of the commission whether a general changeover would be found practicable by 1965. Other recommendations were:

1. English should continue as an alternate medium for competitive examinations for All India Services and for the use in Supreme Court and High Courts.
2. Knowledge of Hindi should be made compulsory for recruitment to All India Services.
3. At the time of changeover entire Statue Book of the country should be in Hindi.
4. Regional Language may be retained for administrative and judicial purposes in the States, but when they were to communicate with other States or the Union Government, they were to communicate in Hindi.
5. The primary education should be imparted in the language of the region, but at the secondary stage instruction in Hindi should be made compulsory.
6. A National Academy of Languages should be established, preferably at Hyderabad, to develop 14 major languages of India, as specified in the Constitution.

Working on the provisions of the Constitution, and on the basis of the President's order, on 27th April 1960, a Committee was constituted in accordance with the provisions of Clause (4) of Article 344 of the Constitution to examine the recommendations of the first Official Language Commission and to report their opinion thereon to the President. The Committee submitted its report to the President on 8th February, 1959. The important points in the report indicating the Committee's general approach are as follows:

- The Constitution contains an integrated scheme of Official Language and its approach to the question is flexible and admits of appropriate adjustments being made within the framework of the scheme.
- Hindi terminology has to be evolved for scientific, administrative and legal purposes.
- English shall continue to be the principal official Language and Hindi the subsidiary Official Language till 1965. After 1965 Hindi was to become the principal Official Language of the Union and English as the subsidiary official language.
- An authorized translation of parliamentary legislation in English should be provided in Hindi.
- When the time comes for the changeover, the language of the Supreme Court shall be Hindi.
- In case of the language of the High Courts, when the time for the changeover comes, Hindi shall ordinarily be the language of judgements, decrees or orders in all regions.

Subsequently, the Official Language Act was enacted in 1963 and was again amended in 1967. The main provisions were:

1. English might continue to be used (even after 1965) in addition for all official purposes of the Union
2. A State which has adopted a language other than Hindi and English as official language of the State will have to publish both Hindi and English versions of the Acts of Legislature passed by it.
3. With the President's prior consent, the Governor of a State might authorize, after 1965, the use of Hindi or official language or the State for the purpose of issue of orders, judgements and decrees provided an English translation of the same was appended to that.

However, the adoption of an official language was not as easy task. Opposition to Hindi has always come from the Southern State before and after independence. Before independence, opposition arose to the imposition of teaching of Hindi language in secondary schools by C. Rajagopalachari in Tamil Nadu. Tamil Nadu had witnessed violent protests and agitation especially from the Self-Respect Movement led by Periyar and the Justice Party.

After independence efforts by the Indian Government to make Hindi the sole official language after 1965 were not acceptable to many non-Hindi Indian states, who wanted the continued use of English. The most virulent protests came from the Dravida Munnetra Kazhagam (DMK) which led the opposition to Hindi. The then Prime Minister Jawaharlal Nehru enacted the Official Languages Act in 1963 to ensure the continuing use of English beyond 1965. However, the text of the Act did not satisfy the DMK and they feared that his assurances might not be honoured by future administrations. Further, Gulzarilal Nanda's directive for promotion of use of Hindi after 1965 fuelled the ongoing agitations. Non-Hindi speaking States witnessed violent mass agitations like Tamil Nadu, Andhra Pradesh and West Bengal. The State Legislatures of Andhra and West Bengal had to come up with a policy of continuing English in the State. Facing such opposition the Congress Government led by Indira Gandhi carried out an amendment to the Official Language Act, 1963 to guarantee the indefinite use of Hindi and English as official languages.

Education Commission or the Kothari Commission was appointed in 1966 which tried to modify the three language formula provided in the Official Language Act, 1963. The Commission recommended:

1. Apart from the regional language, either Hindi or English or any other modern Indian or European language should be taught;
2. Regional languages should be adopted in the Universities within a period of ten years; and
3. All-India institutions may continue the use of English for the time being but in due course Hindi should be adopted in these institutions.

Despite such modifications resentment against the language policy still persisted. Whenever, the Government had shown its willingness to impose the use of Hindi on the non-Hindi-speaking people.

The linguistic reorganization of the States is also a pointer in that direction. The Dar Commission had observed that language can be one of the bases of reorganization of States. Initially, Congress also avoided the linguistic reorganization of States. However, things became turbulent as formation of States on basis of language became stronger. Andhra Pradesh was created in 1953 after there was a tremendous movement for the creation of this State was raised by the Telegu speaking people. There was further demand for linguistic reorganization of States, and thus in 1956, 14 States were formed. They were Andhra Pradesh, Assam, Bihar, Bombay, Jammu & Kashmir, Kerala, Madhya Pradesh, Madras, Mysore, Orissa, Punjab, Rajasthan, Uttar Pradesh and West Bengal. In 1960 Bombay was further bifurcated into Maharashtra and Gujarat following violent agitation. In 1966 Punjab was bifurcated in Punjab and Haryana and that also on the basis of language (see Chapter 6).

These linguistic basis of reorganization of States encouraged for further demand of statehood like that of Telangana which is still continuing with full vigour, Vidarbha in Maharashtra, Saurashtra in Gujarat, Jharkahnd areas in Bihar, Uttarakhand and Bundelkhand in Uttar Pradesh, Gorkhaland in West Bengal (is still being continued by Gorkha Jana Mukti Morcha), Chhattisgarh and Mahakosal in Madhya Pradesh to mention a few. Earlier Dravida Nadu was demanded by DMK and separate Punjabi *Suba* by Aakli Dal. Therefore, reorganization of States on linguistic basis had fuelled regionalism in Indian politics.

Currently, the Eighth Schedule to the Indian Constitution contains a list of 22 scheduled languages. At the time the Constitution was enacted, inclusion in this list meant that the language was entitled to representation on the Official Languages Commission, and that the language would be one of the bases that would be drawn upon to enrich Hindi, the Official Language of the Union. A candidate appearing in an examination conducted for public service at a higher level is entitled to use any of these languages as the medium of answering in All India Examinations. The 92nd Constitutional Amendment 2003 added 4 new languages—Bodo, Maithili, Dogri, and Santali—to the 8th Schedule of the Indian Constitution.

In the face of stiff opposition and protests, the Central Government decided to allow the State Governments to have their own official languages and also recognized constitutionally other languages of India. The Official policy of the Government has been that Hindi should be the official language of India while at the same time it has also acknowledged the official status of English in all States and the States also would have their own official language. The Eighth Schedule [Articles 344 (1) and 351] as it stands today include the following Languages:

1. Assamese	2. Bengali	3. Bodo	4. Dogri
5. Gujarati	6. Hindi	7. Kannada	8. Kashmiri
9. Konkani	10. Maithili	11. Malayalam	12. Manipuri
13. Marathi	14. Nepali	15. Oriya	16. Punjabi
17. Sanskrit	18. Santhali	19. Sindhi	20. Tamil
21. Telugu	22. Urdu		

Problem of linguistic minorities and status of minority language cannot be overlooked when one discusses the language problem in India. India being a land of diversity one cannot claim that other than the official language of the Union and the regional languages having the status of official languages in the States of India, the list of languages included under the Eighth Schedule cannot be an exhaustive one. There are a number of languages comprising the category of mother tongues which are totally unrecognized under the Eight Schedule. There had been language movements for recognition of Urdu as the second official language in Uttar Pradesh and U.P. There had been a demand for linguistic reorganization of the State of Punjab spearheaded by the Akali Dal movement for a Punjabi Suba for the Punjabi speaking people in the post-independence years. The linguistic reorganization of States in India shows how languages are important factors in politics of India. The Sarkaria Commission in its recommendation upheld the effective implementation of three language formula and also cautioned against politicization of language. Though, language movements of the earlier genre are not noticeable currently, but chances are always there for language to become a part of any identity movement in India.

RELIGION

India is a land of diversity. Its diversity is visible in terms of the multiple religions it has. The census 2011 reveals the religious composition in India which is shown in Table 20.1.

Table 20.1 Religious composition in India

Religious Composition	*Population*	*Percentage*
Hindus	827,578,868	80.5
Muslims	138,188,240	13.4
Christians	24,080,016	2.3
Sikhs	19,215,730	1.9
Buddhists	7,955,207	0.8
Jains	4,225,053	0.4
Other Religions and Persuasions	6,639,626	0.6
Religion not stated	727,588	0.1
Total*	1,028,610,328	100.0

*Census 2011, Ministry of Home Affairs

The Constitution of Indian in its Preamble declares India to be a Secular State (inserted by 42nd Constitutional Amendment Act, 1976) and not a theocratic one, possessing no official religion of its own. Further, the Constitution provides several provisions for religious freedoms in India. **Article 14** embodies: "The State shall not deny any person equality before the law or equal protection of the laws within the territory of India." **Article 15** ensures that (1) the State shall not discriminate against any citizen on grounds only of religion, race, caste, sex, place of birth or any of them. (2) No Citizen shall on grounds only of religion, race, caste, sex, place of birth or any of them be subject to any disability, liability, restriction or condition with regard to:

1. access to shops, public restaurants, hotels, places of public entertainment or
2. the use of wells, tanks, bathing ghats, roads and places of public resort maintained wholly or partly out of State funds or dedicated to the use of the general public.

Article 16 states that there shall be equality of opportunity for all citizens in matters relating to employment or appointment to any office under the State and no citizen shall, on grounds only of religion, race, caste, sex, descent, place of birth or any of them, be ineligible for any office under the State. **Article 25** enshrines the Freedom of Conscience and free Profession, practice and propagation of Religion. It states that "Subject to public order, morality and health and to the other provisions of this Part, all persons are equally entitled to freedom of conscience and the right freely to profess, practice and propagate religion. **Article 26** confers upon the religious groups the Freedom to Manage religious Affairs. It reads as—"Subject to public order, morality and health, every religious denomination or any section thereof shall have the right—

1. To establish and maintain institutions for religious and charitable purposes;
2. To manage its own affairs in matters of religion;
3. To own and acquire movable and immovable property; and
4. To administer such property in accordance with law."

Article 27 relates to the Freedom as to payment of taxes for promotion of any particular religion. **Article 28** provides that no religious instruction shall be provided in any educational institution wholly maintained out of State funds. **Article 29** gives the right to conserve the distinct language, script or culture and no citizen shall be denied admission into any educational institution maintained by the State or receiving aid out of State funds on grounds only of religion, race, caste, language or any of them. **Article 30** gives the rights to the minorities to establish and administer educational institutions and the State shall not, in granting aid to educational institutions, discriminate against any educational institutions on the ground that it is under the management of a minority, whether based on religion or language.

Despite such lofty provisions in the Constitution the reality is grim. As Ashis Nandy observes that "as India gets modernized, religious violence is increasing." He also hails the "traditional ways of life [which] have, over centuries, developed internal principles of tolerance." The challenge to India's secularism reached a crisis point with the demolition of Babri Masjid in Ayodhya on 6 December 1992.

In the pre-independence era, the Britishers had supplanted the seeds of communal disharmony by enacting several legislations which created a division between the two communities—the Hindus and the Muslims like the Government of India Act of 1909, 1919 and 1935 and ultimately the division of the country into two—India and Pakistan. Even before these legislations animosities between the two communities have taken place often. The first riot is thought to have taken place in Ahmedabad in 1730. Gyanendra Pandey, in his *The Construction of Communalism in Colonial North India*, had given a list of such riots which took place during the colonial era. The above acts only deepened the differences which ultimately found expression in the formation of Muslim League and in response to it, the Akhil Bharat Hindu Mahasabha was formed. The rift between the two communities was maneuvered by the British to weaken the Congress and history has shown how the Congress and the League had been at loggerheads on most occasions (See Chapter 1). In the 1946 elections, religion became a major issue while securing votes by all parties contesting the elections. The Muslim League boycotted the Government and continued their demand for a separate Pakistan which was finally granted in the Indian Independence Act, 1947. The partition has its own horrifying story of mass migration, refugee generation, clashes between the two communities, violence and deaths.

In the post-independence era, riots were witnessed in 1961 and then in 1963 (following the theft of holy relic of the Prophet from the Hazratbal Mosque in Kashmir). From late 1960s however, communal riots became more frequent. Rasheeduddin Khan in his *Bewildered India: Identity, Pluralism, Discord,* provides that over the period of forty years from 1950-1979 there had been 8175 riots giving an average of 204 riots per year. The causes for these riots have been different from those of pre-independence days. The causes of Muslim discontent were opposition to their demands for cultural and educational rights, official status for Urdu, preservation of Muslim personal law, job reservation and for a minority status for Aligarh Muslim University. The period following 1979–1988 a number of communal riots took place in India and one of the reasons was predominantly *Ramjanmabhumi*. In 1980s, there was much furore over the Shah Bano Case and Uniform Civil Code.

The point to be noted is that there grew a number of Muslim organizations which tried to protect Muslims interests like Jamait-Ul-Ulema, the Dini Talimi, Majlis-e-Musjawarat, the Iteahd-al-Musalmeen, the Anjuman-e-Taraqqi-Urdu. The All India Milli Council demanded reservation for Muslims in Parliament and State Legislatures. These organizations are alleged of fuelling communal sentiments. Simultaneously there has been also a rise of Hindu nationalism. Veer Savarkar, in his pamphlet, entitled *Hindutva: Who is a Hindu?* first gave an idea of Hindu nationalism which called for establishment of a *Hindu* nation to 'protect Hindus and revive the Hindu Culture.' Presently, the BJP has become the mouthpiece of Hindu Nationalism. The 1996 BJP Election Manifesto declared 'Hindutva or cultural nationalism shall be the rainbow which will bridge our present to our glorious past and pave the way for an equally glorious future.'

The noteworthy point is that religion is an integral part of Indian politics and almost all parties use religion to create their influence and consolidate their vote banks. The Congress has done so by cultivating the concept of *Ram Rajya* in the 1980s or propping up Bhinderwale to alienate the Akali Dal in Punjab to mention a few. The BJP catapulted itself to the forefront by playing the religious card in 1989 and 1991, and thereafter, in 1998 when it formed the BJP-led National Democratic Alliance (NDA) Government at the Centre which did not last for long but again it registered a massive victory in the 1999 Lok Sabha elections and the BJP-led NDA again formed the Government at the Centre which completed its five year term.

It must be pointed out that we have discussed the tension between two communities Hindu and the Muslims and the role of religion in the context of these two religions as far as Indian politics is concerned. This must not elude us from the fact that there are also tensions among Hindus-Sikhs (mostly after the assassination of Indira Gandhi in 1984), Hindu-Christians (mostly in Kerala and Orissa) and even Hindu-Buddhists (in Bihar particularly). In Orissa there have been violent attacks on the Christians especially in Kandhamal district in 2007. Another incident which has raised controversy and has seen the State of Gujarat witnessing communal violence has been the Godhra train fire incident in 2002. Therefore, religion poses challenges to the very stability of the political democracy in India.

TRIBE

The Constitution of India, Article 366 (25) defines Scheduled Tribes as "such tribes or tribal communities or part of or groups within such tribes or tribal communities as are deemed under Article 342 to the Scheduled Tribes (STs) for the purposes of this Constitution" which have been declared as such by the President through a public notification. The tribal people or *adivasis* of India according to 1991 Census they account for 67.76 million representing 8.08% of the country's population. According to the 2001 census, they constitute roughly 8.1% of the country's population.

Following the provisions of Article 342, the procedure to be followed for specification of a Scheduled Tribe is not prescribed. The Government for its official purpose uses a criterion that is based on attributes such as:

1. Geographical isolation
2. Backwardness
3. Distinctive culture, language and religion
4. Shyness of contact

The Scheduled Tribe groups who were identified as more isolated from the wider community and who maintain a distinctive cultural identity have been categorized as 'Particularly Vulnerable Tribal Groups' (PTGs) (previously known as Primitive Tribal Groups) by the Union Government. They are characterized by a low rate of growth of population, pre-agricultural level of technology and extremely low levels of literacy. So far 75 tribal communities have been identified as 'particularly vulnerable tribal groups' in different States of India.

Tribals are ethnic groups who have their own distinctive cultures, dialects, lifestyles, social structures, rituals, values and other traits unique to each tribe. During colonial rule there have been tribal movements and independent India has also witnessed frequent tribal unrest. Scholars have forwarded various typologies of tribal movements. Some classify the movements into ethnic, social and religious reformist, political autonomy movements and also sometimes secessionist movements. There also have been agrarian unrests. Recently, there have also been movements around issues of forest rights, environment and displacement of the tribals due to development projects. Another type of militant tribal force arrived in the Indian political scenario around the 1990s when scholars have pointed out that the tribals of Gujarat, Madhya Pradesh and Rajasthan had been mobilized by *Hindutva* forces against the Muslims and Christians, which thus, brought out a religious division among the tribals on the one hand and on the other, induced them to embrace militant activities.

During the colonial period, the tribal movement revolved around the gradual change of socio-economic structure affecting the livelihood and the very existence of the tribals. The merchant capital introduced by the British colonizers penetrated into the tribal economy affecting their relationship with the land and forest. Thus during the nationalist struggle against the British, the tribals also participated in nationalist and agrarian movements. The most prominent among the tribal movements are the Birsa Munda movement (in the nineteenth century) in Chhota Nagpur which aimed at the 'liquidation of the racial enemies, the *Dikus* (outsiders), European missionaries and officials and native Christians'. The Konda Dora of Salur in the Vishakhapatnam also launched movements against the British officers and caste-Hindus with religious fervor. The Santhal rebellions (1855) under the leadership of Sido and Kanhu are also well-known which was staged primarily against the British as well as the *Zamindars*. The Kol insurrection (1831–1832) was the result of the frustration and anger at the transformation of the agrarian system into feudal, *Zamindari* or individual tenures, influx of non-tribal settlers, new landlord-tenant relationship unknown to the tribals, all adding up to their despair and violence and unrest were the consequent reactions. The Kukis of Manipur revolted against the British policy of recruiting them into the army as coolies during World War I (1914–1918).

After independence, the tribals also agitated against land alienation, usury, forced labour, minimum wages, land grabbing. In Andhra Pradesh, the tribals fought against the landlords and forced labour with is identified as the Telangana movement (1946–1951). The Naxalbari movement (1967 onwards) in West Bengal was fought almost for similar reasons. The Saora of Andhra Pradesh revolted against forest department for the opposition to toddy tax which was as important issue in the Rampa rebellion in Andhra Pradesh (1879 and 1922–1924). The Kharwar of Palamau, Bihar before and also after independence had participated in forest *satyagraha* for restoration of their forest rights in 1930s and 1950s. The Tribals of Garhwal region waged movements against Forest Act and Forest Departments which deprived them of land and the right to collect forest product. *Adivasis* of Gujarat also agitated for minimum wages for forest work, the right to collect forest product and cultivate forest land. Tribal groups have also demanded more welfare schemes including reservation of jobs in government services. During 1960s and 1970s land grab movement and struggles for repudiation of debts, minimum wages, and exploitation were resorted to by the tribals against the landlords in Andhra Pradesh, Bihar, Maharashtra, Gujarat, and Madhya Pradesh. The *adivasi* mine workers also joined the non-*adivasi* mineworkers in Chhattisgarh to protest against exploitation of workers under Shankar Guha Niyogi who formed the Chhattisgarh Mukti Morcha in 1978.

However, the tribal protests assume a perilous proportion when demand for separate statehood or separate political entity arises. The tribals of Dang launched a struggle demanding a separate district within the former bilingual State of Bombay. There was also a demand for an autonomous tribal State in Gujarat. Though this movement failed but the *adivasi* identity or *adivasivad* persists. The tribals of Chhattisgarh demanded a separate State to protect themselves from the exploitation of *dikus* in 1930s, which continued till the present day. Today mega projects have led to massive tribal displacement. Movements have taken place wherever such displacement has resulted in loss of ancestral land and livelihood. The first such recorded movement was against the Munshi Project in Poona in 1921 which continued till 1924. Narmada Bachao Andolan is another such recent movement, where the civil society activists like Medha Patkar and others are fighting against the displacement of *adivasis* due to the construction of Sardar Sarovar Dam.

The North-east has witnessed unprecedented tribal unrest over a long period of time which were not only violent armed rebellion, but also demanded separate statehood and even secession. There were demand for autonomy from insurgent groups who even had launched armed rebellions like the Naga National Council (NNC), Nationalist Socialist Council of Nagaland (NSCN), Mizo National Front (MNF), People's Liberation Army (PLA) and People's Revolutionary Party of Kangleipak (PREPAK), All Tripura Tribal Force (ATTF), United Liberation Army of Assam (ULFA) and various others.

The policy that was followed by the Government towards the tribals after independence till 1960 can be regarded as the Nehru-Elwin model which comprised five principles and identified as *Panchsheel.* The principle can be summed up as:

1. Nothing should be imposed from above and traditional arts and culture must be encouraged.
2. Tribal rights to land and forest should be respected.
3. Training and creation of teams of tribals from amongst themselves to administer development activities. Not too much outsider must be involved.
4. Overbearing administration, by means of overwhelming imposition of multiplicity of schemes must be avoided. All work should be done keeping parity with the social and cultural institutions of the tribals.
5. Results must be judged not by statistics of the amount of money spent, but by the quality of human character that is evolved.

Currently, a separate Ministry of Tribal Affairs was carved out of Ministry of Social Justice and Empowerment which is the nodal agency for formulating police, planning and coordinating programmes and schemes for the development of Scheduled Tribes. This Ministry has prepared a draft of the National Tribal Policy with an integrated and holistic approach. This policy seeks to work for enhancement of human development index of Scheduled Tribes, improvement of infrastructure in Scheduled Tribes dominated areas, ensuring their control over the natural resources base, displacement from their habitat and resettlement, distribution of wealth and opportunities among tribals and empowerment. The Forest Act 2006 which is also known as The Scheduled Tribes and Other Traditional Forest Dwellers (Recognition of Forest Rights) Act, 2006 which is an important landmark in securing tribal rights as it contains provisions for ensuring forest-dwelling communities to land and resources so long denied to them because of outdated colonial laws.

More has to be done to lead to inclusion of tribals into the fold of mainstream political life of India so that they feel integrated, but not at the cost of losing their identity.

REGIONALISM

Regionalism as a concept is difficult to define especially in the Indian context. At the most it can be considered to be giving a priority to regional sentiments above the national which can be expressed in cultural, linguistic, economic, political and administrative terms. These sentiments may develop regional consciousness in such a way that there may be demand for autonomy, administrative decentralization, emergence of local patriotism and even secession from the mainland. The main element of regionalism is the shared sentiment of 'togetherness' among the people internalized from a wide variety of sources like common prosperity, common struggle, common legacy, common feeling of exploitation and the like which mark their 'separateness' from others. India being a land of diversity undoubtedly suffers from the pangs of regionalism.

Certain factors have led to the germination of regional feelings in different parts of India. First and foremost the political factors which sharpened the regional feelings must be highlighted. Immediately after independence till early 1970s, there was not much of regional upsurge as it was tempered by partition of the country barring a few movements in the South like the Dravidian movement. From 1970s till the 1980s over centralization efforts of Indira Gandhi followed by Rajiv Gandhi with the interjection of emergency rule in India in the 1970s, had fuelled the regional aspirations like in Assam and in Punjab. Both had to balance between the regional parties to keep the hold of the Congress over the country intact which sometimes involved in accommodating some regional political parties while distancing some and also signing of accords like the Punjab Accord (1985), Assam Accord (1985), Accord with Mizo National Front (1986) and the Tripura National Volunteers (1988).

From 1990s, there has been regionalization of national politics as in the Centre we have the presence of federal coalitions with regional parties as determining partners like the BJP-led NDA or the UPA-I and UPA-II. The Rashtriya Janata Dal (RJD) in Bihar, Samajwadi Party (SP) in Uttar Pradesh, Biju Janata Dal in Orissa, Janata Dal (Secular) in Karnataka, DMK, AIADMK, TDP and others are prominent non-Congress regional parties which now play decisive roles in national politics. Political issues now have become region-specific with voters opting for regional platform rather than All India political matters and thereby the base of political parties becoming region/state specific.

The other factors which spurted the feeling of regionalism were the feeling of being neglected by the Centre and too much of centralization. As the level of economic development was not on the same pedestal for all the States, the most backward regions often felt neglected. Fiscal policy of the Centre even with the integrating mechanisms like Planning Commission, National Development Council or even the inter-State Council could not bring about a balanced economic growth, an inclusive growth till today all over India. Thus, the differences in the level of economic development/backwardness snowballed into grievances against the Centre and a sense of guarding regional interests.

Further, certain actions of Central Government in the North-east had also fuelled regional sentiments like the Special Powers and the Disturbed Areas Act to contain violence and insurgency in the North-east. The Central Government also had launched 'Operation Bajrang' and 'Operation Rhino' to flush out the ULFA activities. Further, army reprisals as in Nagaland and in Mizoram in 1980, and the CRPF action in Manipur in 1984 had created discontent among the people at large. The Central Governments whosoever, in power, have always played the regional card by manipulating heterogeneity of the North-east. The North-eastern States also have a peripheral status in the Parliamentary system. They elect about 7% of Members of parliament and the reality is that no major decisions about the regional problems are taken in the region.

The sense of depravation, neglect armed with zeal to promote and protect regional interest by any means had led to the emergence of regional movements which threatened the unity and integrity of India. These movements have taken various forms like some were caste-based while others demanded secession, still others were communal, ethnic, tribal, economic, cultural, ethno-lingual to mention a few.

The most prominent movements which even demanded separate statehood were the demand for a Gorkha State previously by Gorkha National Liberation Front (GNLF) and later the demand resurfaced under the Gorkha Jana Mukti Morcha (GJMM) in West Bengal, Bodoland in Assam demanded by the Bodos and many others. The tribal areas of Jharkhand and areas of Uttar Pradesh have been under spells of violence. There have been secessionist movements in the North-east in the State like Nagaland, Manipur, Mizoram, Tripura, Meghalaya and others. Armed rebellion were spearheaded by Naga National Council (NNC), People's Liberation Army (PLA), Mizo National Front (MNF), People's revolutionary Party of Kanglei Pak (PREPAK), All Tripura Tribal Force (ATTF), United Liberation Front of Assam (ULFA) and may others. Earlier in Punjab there had been a demand for *Punjabi Suba* (see Chapter 17-discussion on Shiromani Akali Dal) and later the demand for *Khalistan* by Dal Khalsa activists and other Akali factions and down South the Dravidian movement demanding *Dravida Nadu*. There has been and still there are the ongoing terrorist activities in Kashmir as the demand for autonomy continues.

Regional demands have time and often seen reorganization of States and bifurcation and creation of new States. The latest being in 2000 when three new States were carved out of Uttar Pradesh, Bihar and Madhya Pradesh, namely, Uttarakhand, Jharkhand and Chhattisgarh. Not so much of tribal factor had been at the back of creation of these three States, but it was economic backwardness, social and educational backwardness and unfair allocation of revenues to these States for their development by the Centre which had triggered-off demand for separate statehood in these three otherwise mineral/forest resource rich States. The movement for a separate Telangana State carved out of Andhra Pradesh come to a boiling point with violent outbursts often taking place. Ultimately the Andhra Pradesh Reorganization Act, 2014 created a separate state of Telengana with Hyderabad as the common capital for a period of ten years and after that Andhra Pradesh will have a new capital.

CORRUPTION AND CRIMINALIZATION OF POLITICS

The Preamble to the Constitution of India gives us the very essence of the nature of Indian polity when it declares in clear terms that "WE, THE PEOPLE OF INDIA, having solemnly resolved to constitute India into a SOVEREIGN SOCIALIST SECULAR DEMOCRATIC REPUBLIC and to secure to all its citizens… IN OUR CONSTITUENT ASSEMBLY this twenty-sixth day of November, 1949, do HERE BY ADOPT, ENACT AND GIVE TO OURSELVES THIS CONSTITUTION." It acclaims the Republican character of the polity and sovereignty of the people. The democratic character as proclaimed in the Preamble is upheld by the constitutional provisions ensuring universal adult suffrage, democratically elected people's representation and responsibility of the Executive to the Legislature whether in the Centre or in the State.

The reality however, is not so smooth and *We the People of India* witness incidents bizarre and not in the spirit of Parliamentary democracy. For instance, the 2011 winter session of the Parliament saw a *logjam* over Foreign Direct Investment (FDI) issue and the Parliament could not function for 13 days. This results in hindering the public interest and wastage of public money. Further, there are allegations that some of the Parliamentarians have criminal records. The Election Commission has come up with certain guidelines often to debar persons with criminal records from contesting elections.

If these trends continue then there will be a mockery of Indian Parliamentary democracy soon. The loopholes in the functioning of both the Executive and the Legislature have frustrated the people of India and this frustration is now being utilized by the civil society to vent the discontent of the common people. In doing so the civil society has become *hyper-active* and in the face of Anti-corruption movement, the Indian parliamentary democracy stands challenged.

The urban-middle class of India has been swayed by the movement against corruption so much so that sometimes the MPs are facing the rage of the common man often. The cancer of corruption has made the very basis of Indian polity shaky. The year 2011 will be remembered in the history of Indian Government and Politics as the *Year of Scams.* India is now ranked 95th out of 178 countries according to the Transparency International's Index. Earlier India was ranked 88th out of 156 countries in the year of 2005. The Housing Scam, the Commonwealth Games Scam and the Telecom 2G Scam made headlines and definitely fuelled the civil society movement.

Despite the presence of Anti-Corruption laws in India like the Indian Penal Code, 1860, the Prevention of Corruption Act, 1988, the Benami Transactions (Prohibition) Act, 1988 and the Prevention of Money laundering Act, 2002, the number of scams is going up.

India is also a signatory to the UN Convention against Corruption since 2005 and it ratified the Convention in May 2011. The Convention covers a wide range of acts of corruption and also proposes certain preventive policies.

The whole debate about the Lokpal has frustrated the common man. Though the Right to Information Act was introduced in 2005, and currently it is perhaps the most effective tool of getting access to government information yet it is felt that a strong Lokpal is needed to check the corruption at all level of Governmental administration. If the Parliament functions well, the Government is not dogged with corruption and the public sentiment is respected, then the sanctity of Parliamentary democracy in India will be restored.

EXERCISES

I. Short Answer Questions: **(100 words)**

1. Write a note on politicization of Caste in India.
2. State the main features of the Official Language Act, 1963.
3. Briefly state the role of religion in Indian politics.
4. Write a note on Tribal politics in India.
5. Write a note on regionalism in Indian politics.

II. Long Answer Questions: **(1200 words)**

6. Examine Caste as an important factor in Indian politics.
7. Critically discuss the language problem in India.
8. Examine how religion has become a decisive factor in Indian politics.
9. Explain how tribes and their problems now challenge the politics of India.
10. What do you mean by regionalism? Explain how regionalism has come to play an important factor in Indian politics.
11. Do you agree that regionalization of politics hinders national integration. Argue your case.
12. Do you think that corruption and criminalization of politics in India has made the Indian polity weak and ineffective? Argue your case.

REFERENCES

Awasthy, S.S., *Indian Government and Politics*, Har-Anand Publications, New Delhi, Revised Edition, 2006.

Basu, Amrita, "The Dialectics of Hindu Nationalism," in Kohli Atul (Ed.), *The Success of India's Democracy*, Cambridge University Press, New Delhi, 2004.

Basu, Partha Pratim, "Religious Cleavage, Politics and communalism in India," in Chatterjee Rakhahari (Ed.), *Politics India: the State Society Interface*, South Asian Publishers, New Delhi, 2004.

Béteille, André, *Caste, Class and Power: Changing Pattern of Stratification in a Tanjore Village*, Oxford University Press, New Delhi, 2012.

Brass, Paul R., *The Politics of India Since Independence*, Cambridge University Press, Delhi, 2004.

Chatterjee, Partha (Ed.), *State and Politics in India*, Oxford University Press, New Delhi, 2007.

Chitkara, M.G. and Sharma, B.R., *Indian Republic: Issues and Perspective*, APH Publishing Corporation, New Delhi, 1997.

Das, Samir Kumar, "Tribal Politics in Contemporary India," in Chatterjee Rakhahari (Ed.), *Politics India: the State Society Interface*, South Asian Publishers, New Delhi, 2004.

Datta, Prabhat, *Regionalism in Indian Politics*, Sterling Publishers, New Delhi, 1993.

Dattagupta, Shobhanlal (Ed.), *India Politics and Society: Today and Tomorrow*, K.P. Baghchi & Company, Calcutta, 1998.

Fadia, Babulal, *State Politics in India*, Vol. 1, Radiant Publishers, New Delhi, 1984.

Gyanendra Pandey in his *The Construction of Communalism in Colonial North India*, Oxford University Press, Delhi, 1990.

Khan, Rasheeduddin, *Bewildered India: Identity, Pluralism, Discord*, Har-Anand Publications, New Delhi, New Delhi, 1994.

Kothari, Rajni (Ed.), *Caste in Indian Politics*, Orient Longman, New Delhi, 2004.

Mukhopadhyay, Jayati, "Language and Politics in India," in Chatterjee Rakhahari (Ed.), *Politics India: the State Society Interface*, South Asian Publishers, New Delhi, 2004.

Page, Charles H. and Maciver, R.M., *Society: An Introductory Analysis,* Macmillan India Limited, Madras, 1986.

Rath, Govinda Chandra (Ed.), *Tribal Development in India: The Contemporary Debate,* Sage Publications, New Delhi, 2006.

Sen, Amartya, "Secularism, Nationalism, and Modernity," in Bhargava Rajeev (Ed.), *Secularism and its Critics*, Oxford University Press, New Delhi, 1999.

Shah, Ghanshyam, *Social Movements in India: A Review of Literature*, Sage Publications, New Delhi, 2004.

Singh, M.P. and Saxena, Rekha, *Indian Politics: Contemporary Issues and Concerns*, Prentice-Hall of India, New Delhi, 2008.

Tambiah, Stanley J., "The Crisis of Secularism in India," in Bhargava Rajeev (Ed.), *Secularism and its Critics*, Oxford University Press, New Delhi, 1999.

http://www.tribal.nic.in/index.asp, an Official website of Government of India, Ministry of Tribal Affairs.

21

New Social Movements in India

INTRODUCTION

Social Movements are nothing new and they are taking place all around the globe, whether, they are based on certain issues or interests, under different institutional environments. In India also social movements have taken place around identity issues or interest-based activism. The movements may range from struggle emanating from the exploitation of the tribals, or the *dalits*, or movements based on language, religion or even caste. What is new about the 'new' social movements is the large scale participation of civil society mainly comprising the middle class and the youths who are more concerned about good governance and human rights, removal of corruption, protection of ecology and environment, gender equality, child rights, employment, rights of the most vulnerable and marginalized sections of the population and the like. The effect of globalization on the Indian society which has impacted on the different sections of the society in a variety of ways, have resulted in marginalization of the so called weaker section like women or the subaltern population which have increased the momentum of the new social movements. Mostly, Non Governmental Organizations (NGOs), various social action groups and sometimes political action groups identify their protest agenda and garner support and mobilize the movements targeting mostly State institutions as well as those that engage with the State, but in most cases, they identify the State as a dominant agent of oppression and oppressive policies.

ENVIRONMENTAL MOVEMENTS IN INDIA

Environmental movements have been fought in India mostly against large-scale industrialization and the ecological degradation resulting from such 'development' projects leading to the problem of survival of the victims of such development.

As has been pointed out by eminent scholars that development results in destruction of eco-friendly, labour intensive traditional means of production; pollution of the environment and depletion of bio mass; and as a result of the above two, deprivation of the ecosystem results in the loss of the sources of livelihood of the people. When India embarked on the policies of massive capital-intensive industrialization, the obvious fall out has been environmental damage and subsequent endangering of the lives of people. The most tragic industrial accident has been the poisoning caused by the leakage of Methyl Isocynate gas (MIC) in Bhopal. In the night of December 2–3, 1984 a catastrophe unfolded itself in the city of Bhopal, Madhya Pradesh when a deadly lethal gas floated over the city causing casualties to thousands of humans and animals and creating unbearable sufferings for those who survived as they developed genetic defects because of Methyl Isocynate gas (MIC) causing blindness, kidney and liver failure and a variety of chronic diseases. The people of Bhopal still continue to be a vulnerable population as 390 metric tonnes of poisonous waste lay around the factory area for 25 years awaiting court's decision. Justice has been denied to the victims of the tragedy as the main culprit Warren Anderson is absconding, and there are no chances of his extradition to India.

Other environmental hazards can be seen as being caused by heavy environmental pollution caused by thermal plants, the main effluent being flying ash, as in case of Kolaghat, West Bengal. Sewerage system, betel cultivation and floriculture have been worst hit by such fly ash disposal.

Other than these ozone depletion caused by the emission of carbon monoxide, methane, etc., from exhausts of automobiles and factories, biomass burning, and also by use of CFC (chlorofluorocarbon) used in manufacturing refrigerators, air conditioners, aerosols and others creating 'Green house effect' and 'Global Warming'. Several man-made factors also cause depletion of biomass like deforestation, filling up of tanks and ponds and converting agricultural lands into industrial estates, pollution of land, water and air, burning of fossil fuel, unlimited and unplanned use of agricultural and forest produce as raw materials for industries. Deforestation is also caused by the use of HYV (High Yielding Varieties), chemical fertilizers, pesticides and the like. Water scarcity is a problem that can be caused by consumption of huge amount of water by HYVs. Constructions of huge dams which are part of the modernization projects can also be the cause of environmental degradation and displacement of indigenous people and robbing them off from their age-old profession and attachment to the land.

Ecological movements have erupted wherever there have been threats to forests and agricultural lands by inundation, water logging, salinity resulting from the construction of large dams and massive irrigation projects like the Tehri Dam, Koel Karo, Sirsi and Inchampalli. Sometimes environmental movements may spring from the urge of the forest dwelling communities to save forest from destruction like the Chipko movement and similar movements in Western Ghats, the Aravallis and also the Vindhyas, and also in the tribal belts of India like in Singhbhum (Bihar) and in Bastar region (Madhya Pradesh). Ecological movements can also aim to save marine resources as well as indigenous fishing from mechanized fishing as in Kerala.

As Vandana Shiva points out that in India, ecological movements can be seen to have certain commonness although they may differ in their methods and their protest agenda. The commonness can be said to be in terms of:

1. Economic conflict between two types of economic activity—one aiming at securing survival for the people in a sustainable manner through a genuinely collective management and the other aiming at maximizing the growth rate even at the cost of bare survival of many.
2. Technological conflict arising out of the choice between two types of technologies, one indigenous which is labour-intensive and other western capital-intensive. The former causes lesser ecological hazards and the other annihilation of ecological pattern of a particular area.

Ecological movements therefore, focus their concern regarding the use of resource-hungry processes of modern technology and accompanying high ecological and social costs. These modern mega projects hit the survival of communities either directly or indirectly. For instance pulp production indirectly hits the need of water and land for agriculture of the communities, as these two factors are needed for their survival. Some prominent movements to save the environment have been discussed as follows:

Chipko Movement

Chipko Movement or hug-the-tree movement had its origin in the existential experience of the communities in the Garhwal Himalaya arising from the concern about the wrath of nature in the form of frequent floods and landslides caused by massive deforestation. The reformers realized that their survival is intricately linked with the existence of the forests in the Himalayas. The first Chipko movement started in March 1974 in Reni village in the Garhwal Himalayas, when a group of village women led by Gauri Devi hugged the trees and prevented the hired sawyers to cut them down for a sports goods company. The Chipko movement spread rapidly throughout the valley. There were some success stories like in February 1978 activists in Henwal valley saved the Advani forests. In December 1978, the forests of Badygard were saved and subsequently Chipko strategy was adopted by environment activists of Western Ghats to save forests and other ecologically vulnerable mountain systems of India. The most notable aspect of the Chipko movement was the use on non-violent Gandhian method of *satyagraha*, through the act of hugging trees to protect them from being cut. In Tehri district, Chipko activists went on to protest limestone mining in the Doon Valley (Dehradun) in the 1980s, and gradually the movement spread throughout the Dehradun district, which had earlier seen devastation of its forest cover leading to heavy loss of flora and fauna. The prominent people who made the movement popular and even internationally acclaimed, were Gauri Devi, Sudesha Devi, Bachni Devi, Chandi Prasad Bhatt, Sundarlal Bahuguna, Govind Singh Rawat, Dhoom Singh Negi, Shamsher Singh Bisht and Ghanasyam Raturi the Chipko poet, whose songs echo throughout the Himalayas. Chandi Prasad Bhatt was awarded the Ramon Magsaysay Award in 1982 and Sundarlal Bahuguna was awarded the Padma Vibhushan in 2009.

Narmada Bachao Andolan

The other major movement has been against the construction of Mega dams. India's planned economic development failed to take into consideration the displacement of huge number of people from the land where they have been living for generations. The most notable among such movements against the construction of such mega dams was the Narmada Bachao Andolan against the Sardar Sarovar Dam being built across the Narmada River in Gujarat—a movement which could reach out internationally and place the Government in an uncomfortable position. Other major ecological conflicts over dams were the Hirakud Dam in Sambalpur District of Orissa in 1946 and the Tehri Dam which is a multi-purpose rock and earth-fill embankment dam on the Bhagirathi River near Tehri in Uttarakhand. The Tehri dam has witnessed continuous questioning and protests by various people, including the noted environmentalist Sunderlal Bahuguna, who relentlessly fought for stopping the construction of the dam by his *dharna* at the dam site and by going on periodic fasts. The Tehri Bandh Virodhi Sangharsh Samiti has been a great mobilizer of this anti-dam movement. Chandi Prasad Bhatt, the Chipko movement leader, also spearheaded an anti-dam movement against the proposed construction of a dam at Vishnuprayag on the Alakananda River. Another popular resistance against the construction of dams was in Kerala over the Silent Valley Hydroelectric Project. There would have been loss of valuable Indian rain forests with the construction of the dam. The project was stalled and the Valley Project area is now a world heritage site for there are species recognized by UNESCO. Other notable anti-dams movements have been those against Koel Karo and Subaranarekha dams in Bihar, Bhopalpatnam-Inchampalli project on the Maharashtra-Madhya Pradesh border. The tribals are the worst affected and they have to fight continuously to stall construction of such dams which would displace them from their native lands.

Of all these the Narmada Bachao Andolan (NBA) has been the one to get most of the attention. The NBA is believed to get media visibility and catch international attention. Displacement of the oustees from the Narmada Dam area became the main issue as there was concern for their resettlement and rehabilitation and the quantum and quality of compensation. Moreover, the NBA brought to the fore the debate between the paradigm of development through the construction of mega projects like dams and culturocide (systematic dismantling of the lifestyle of people) and ecocide (the destruction of their ecology). Led by one of the prominent leaders, Medha Patkar, it has now assumed such a dimension that it has been successful in gaining support from NGOs all around the globe. Protestors showed their agitation through the mass media, hunger strikes, massive marches, rallies and the through the screening of several documentary films. Although they have been protesting peacefully, but they were harassed, arrested and beaten up by the police several times and the NBA is labeled as anti-developmental and ecologically fundamentalist. The Narmada Bachao Andolan has been pressurizing the World Bank to withdraw its loan from the project through media.

Narmada Bachao Andolan activists had filed a written petition with the Supreme Court of India, the nation's apex court, seeking stoppage of construction on the Sardar Sarovar dam. The court initially ruled the decision in the Andolan's favor thereby effecting an immediate stoppage of work at the dam and directing the concerned states to first complete the rehabilitation and replacement process, but in 2000 allowed the construction to proceed, allowing the height of the Narmada dam to be raised.

Narmada Bachao Andolan, with its leading spokespersons Medha Patkar, was the recipient of the Right Livelihood Award, 1991.

Other Movements

Another movement against the dam has started very recently when a massive public rally in Lakhimpur in February 2012 by the Brihottar Nadibandh Birudhi Nagarik Samiti (Greater Anti-Dam Citizens' Committee). They launched a two-day citizens' convention against the 2,000 MW Lower Subansiri hydel project. The first day of the convention was hosted by national anti-dam activist Himangshu Thakkar and environmentalists Rohan D'Souza and Neeraj Vaghlojkar, who opposed construction of the Mega dam in Lakhimpur district. In the recent Lakhimpur public rally, the anti-dam body, along with Narmada Bachao Andolan activist Medha Patkar, vowed to stop the dam's construction at any cost. Environmentalist urged the state government to focus on protecting the biodiversity of the region before construction of the Mega dam.

Reckless mining also creates environmental hazards. This results in the depletion, pollution and destruction of huge tracts of lands, forests and water bodies in the coalfield area. Mining in mountains is more hazardous as it affects the source of rivers and streams and disturbs the geographical structure of the area affecting the water cycle. There has been prolonged movement against mining like the movements to stall mining of limestone in the Doon valley in UP supported by the *Chipko* activists and the Save Gandhamardan Movement in Odisha against the Bharat Aluminum Company (BALCO).

Creation of Special Economic Zones (SEZs) are also fermenting protests against those being displaced. The Special Economic Zones Act, 2005, was passed by Parliament in May, 2005 which received Presidential assent on the 23 June 2005. The SEZ Act 2005 envisages key role for the State Governments in export promotion and creation of related infrastructure. In Odisha, tribals have been ousted from their native land because of massive industrial projects like land being acquired for Utkal Aluminia International Ltd. (UAIL) and Tata Steel Company. In most cases, the government has been repressive and have let loose violence against the protestors. Gradually, the protests against forced displacement have solidified and social activists forum like People's Forum to Oppose Displacement (PFOD) have become active. Another protest which has come to a boiling point is the $ 12 billion Pohang Iron and Steel Company (POSCO) project in Odisha which is the largest foreign investment project ever in India. Civil rights activists, academicians and eminent media persons in response to the grievances of the tribal leaders facing displacement as a consequent to the acquisition of their farming land for POSCO and Tata Steel in Odisha, have urged the governments to scrap the land allotment for mega projects. Activists say the project is in clear violation of environmental norms at the cost of the livelihood of thousands of farmers. Land to be given for Posco's Steel Plant has been classified as forest land. Under the Scheduled Tribes and Other Traditional Forest Dwellers (Recognition of Forest Rights) Act 2006, many of the people of the area are eligible for right over this land, especially the lands they are cultivating, as they have been living in the area for more than 75 years. Villagers are opposing government plans to lease fertile land to Posco for its three iron mining projects in Kandhahar, Kujanga and Paradip. In 2007, the West Bengal government decided to allow Indonesian-based Salim Group to set up a chemical hub at Nandigram under the Special Economic Zone policy. Soon controversy over the State Government plan to build a chemical hub in Nandigram led to opposition and wide scale protests and violence. Farmers refused to give their land and the protests snowballed under the banner of Bhoomi Raksha Committee followed by killings and bloodshed. This also left to the electoral debacle of the ruling CPM-led Left Front Government in West Bengal.

The Indian Constitution itself contains provisions for environmental protection. The Directive Principles of State Policy acknowledging the State's responsibility with regard to environmental protection has laid down under Article 48-A of our Constitution, that **"The State shall endeavour to protect and improve the environment and to safeguard the forests and wildlife of the country"**. Further, environmental protection is a fundamental duty of every citizen of this country and under Article 51A(g) of the Constitution embodies that **"It shall be the duty of every citizen of India to protect and improve the natural environment including forests, lakes, rivers and wildlife and to have compassion for living creatures."** Other than these certain Acts are also in place like The Indian Forest Act, 1927, The Electricity Act, 2003, the Forest Conservation Act, 1980, Environmental (Protection) Act,

1986, Air (Prevention and Control of Pollution) Act, 1981, Water (Prevention and Control), 1974, Wildlife Protection Act, 1972, The Biological Diversity Act, 2002, Hazardous Wastes (Management and Handling) Amendment Rules, 2003, Ozone Depleting Substances (Regulation and Control) Rules, 2000 and several others. The principal Environmental Regulatory Agency in India is the Ministry of Environment and Forests (MOEF). MOEF formulates environmental policies and accords environmental clearance for the projects. The State Pollution Control Board (SPCB) accords 'No Objection Certificate' (NOC) and 'Consent for Establishment and Operation' for the projects and a host of other Acts.

National Green Tribunal

The **National Green Tribunal** (NGT) has replaced an erstwhile institution the National Environment Appellate Authority (NEAA) which had been set up back in 1997, and where environmental approvals granted to industrial and infrastructure projects could be challenged by affected people and concerned citizens. On 4 July 2011, the National Green Tribunal (NGT) initiated its first set of hearings in New Delhi. One of the 26 cases that were transferred from the NEAA to the NGT was a challenge to the 1200 MW thermal power plant located in Jaigad, in Ratnagiri District of Maharashtra, planned by JSW Energy (Ratnagiri) Ltd. (JSWREL) which was given clearance. Another project on hold is Renuka Dam Project for which the Governments of Delhi and Himachal Pradesh had signed an agreement back in 1994 for the construction of this dam, which is to meet the ever-increasing demand for water for the National Capital Region (NCR). Some of the most controversial projects of recent years are also pending before the NGT like the case of the challenge to the environment clearance given to the 4 MTPA steel plant and captive port of the South Korean Pohang Steel Company (POSCO) in Jagatsinghpur of Odisha, which faces strong opposition from locals. Three cases have also been filed against the construction of the 300 MW thermal power project at inter-tidal area of Bhadreshwar coast in Kutch District of Gujarat, and another case has been filed against the grant of the Coastal Regulation Zone (CRZ) clearance for laying the water pipeline for the project. The affected fish-workers, salt pan owners and graziers are fighting for saving the remaining parts of inter-tidal areas crucial for all their survival. Other cases that have been filed in the NGT included also the 1750 MW Demwe Lower project on the Lohit River in Arunachal Pradesh.

The Role of Judiciary in Environmental Movements

The Judiciary in India also has played an important role in giving 'Green Verdict' for protecting the environment. On 16 April 1996, a division bench of the Supreme Court (SC) comprising Justices Kuldip Singh and S. Saghir Ahmed directed the Chief Justice of the Calcutta High Court to constitute a special division bench to hear environment-related petitions—and the nation's first green bench was born. The Supreme Court directed this bench to meet once a week.

The Constitution of the Calcutta bench was followed by another in Chennai. On 2 September 1996, while passing an interim order in the Madras Tanneries Case, a full bench of the Supreme Court, comprising Justices Kuldip Singh, Falzan-uddin and K. Venkataswami asked the Chief Justice of the Chennai High Court to constitute a special green bench to deal with environmental matters—including the tanneries case in that State.

Such benches have since then been set up in various other High Courts such as those of Madhya Pradesh, Calcutta and Punjab and Haryana. Further in the **Mangroves Case** the judgment delivered on 6 October 2007 the Bench of Chief Justice Dalveer Bhandari and Justice Dr. D.Y. Chandrachud proclaimed that "There shall be a total freeze on the destruction and cutting of mangroves in the entire state of Maharashtra.''

In the **Forest Land Case**, the Bombay High Court in March 2007 dismissed petitions filed by builders challenging the State Government's decision to notify land, including that near the Borivli National Park, on which their housing township projects were coming up as reserved forest area. The division bench of Chief Justice Swatanter Kumar and Justice S.C. Dharmadhikari said, "If the state desires not to allow any encroachments on the reserve forest land, we cannot in any manner prevent the state from doing so. In larger public interest to be subserved by protecting and safeguarding forest wealth, greenery and environment the petitions need to be dismissed.''

In another environment related case, the **Mill Land Case** the Supreme Court's verdict in 2008, has been a disappointment for civil society activists. The Supreme Court nullified the Bombay High Court order which directed the use of larger defunct mill lands for creation of parks, gardens and low-cost public housing. A bench comprising Justice S.B. Sinha and Justice P.P. Naolekar set aside a Bombay High Court judgment, and upheld that the sale of surplus lands by National Textile Corporation was legal. The housing activists have feared an urban chaos after the Supreme Court delivered its verdict.

India faces problems of environmental degradation and lack of governance on matters related to these. Therefore, most often, the States come into conflict with the public whenever certain projects get the signal for execution which affect the life and livelihood of many. Modernization is important, but there should be a balanced approach. Such projects must have a blueprint taking into consideration the displaced people, their livelihood, security, appropriate and adequate compensation if displaced and ensuring the preservation of their identity and culture and their traditional habitat. To minimize the environmental hazards and displacement, the approach should be, as suggested by some scholars as 'technological pluralism'. In other words, technology will be used for development, but then in such a manner that it would reduce displacement. Sustainable Development as proclaimed in the Rio Declaration (1992) should be the means of balancing environment and modernization, and these two should not be made contradictory, thereby inviting social movements.

WOMEN'S MOVEMENTS

Women in India, have always faced a dilemma between their social space—inside their home and outside society (the home and the world). According to the general perception the world is seen to be an external domain of the materialistic pursuit, and the home represent's one's spiritual self and true identity. The outside world therefore, is the arena for the male and the home is the right place for women. Thus, social roles according to gender has been ascribed to male and female in the society based on the classification of *ghar* (home) and *bahir* (world). Women are supposed to engage themselves with bearing, rearing and caring and should not dare to go out into the space allocated to male. Working women still have to struggle to get dignity and respect from the society.

Sex ratio is the most important population characteristics which highlights the social position of women in the society. There has been a continuous drop is sex ratio (Female/Male) in India during 1901–1991. The last decade has seen a reversal of the trend by fetching sex ratio to 933 in 2001 from 927 in 1991. The sex ratio was 932 in 2009. Though women are biologically stronger than men, they exhibit a higher mortality pattern in Asia because of prevailing gender based discrimination, infanticide and foeticide and relative neglect of females, especially in healthcare and medical attention. An interesting feature of declining Age Specific Mortality Rate (ASMR) has been observed for women since year 2000. In year 2000, ASMR for women was 8.9, and has come down to 6.8 in year 2008 which may seem to be a positive sign and may signal women's empowerment and access/consciousness about health facilities. The 2011 Census of India revealed the sex ratio for females per 1000 males is 940 females and child sex ratio for females is 914 per 1000 males. Below is given the Sex ratio at a glance derived from the 2011 Census:

State with Highest Female Sex Ratio, Kerala	1,058
State with Lowest Female Sex Ratio, Haryana	861
UT with Highest Female Sex Ratio, Pondicherry	1,001
UT with Lowest Female Sex Ratio, Daman & Diu	710
District with Highest Female Sex Ratio Mahe (Pondicherry)	1,147
District with Lowest Female Sex Ratio Daman (Daman & Diu)	591

[Census India 2011-http://www.censusindia.gov.in/Census_Data_2001/India_at_glance/fsex.aspx]

The Committee on the Status of Women in India (CSWI) 1971, submitted its report *Towards Equality* in May 1975. CSWI raised its concern over the continued invisibility of women in areas/sectors where they were largely involved. Therefore, the CSWI pleaded for a renewed concern that would reflect real life issues and aspirations of the majority of women. Decline in sex-ratio, increasing gender gaps in life expectancy, mortality and economic participation or the rising migration rate and the failure of the policies of the States to execute the pledges given in the Constitution had lead to a total neglect of women's problems and therefore their upliftment has become quite difficult. The CSWI highlighted the linkages between existing and growing social and economic disparities and women's status in education, the economy and society and the polity.

During the last three decades or more, the issues of rape, sexual harassment, domestic violence, infanticide, foeticide and other gender-based discrimination against women have come into fore and women's movements against such atrocious treatment towards the 'Second Sex'* have been condemned, coupled with demands for more secured position to be provided by the State. Cultural patterns of conduct often clash with the human rights norms and the maintenance of the status quo of patriarchal norms conflict with gender equality. Many of the practices defended in the name of culture impinge on human rights and are gender specific and the guardians of patriarchy tries to preserve all sorts of inequalities at the expense of women's rights. In the Indian context, predominantly in the villages or economically weaker societies and also in some cases in urban areas, a minor girl is often forced to marry as child brides. This often results in early widowhood, payment of dowry, deprivation of property as lopsided patriarchal inheritance systems under certain personal laws deprive women of a fair share of paternal property as well as the widows' right to property that varies under different customary laws, witch-hunting, restrictive dress codes, diet code and behaviour code that are direct violation of women's basic rights.

A large number of women's organizations have mushroomed especially from the 1990s when the crisis with regard to State, government and society has deepened. The All India Women's Conference is the oldest autonomous organization. Besides some of the government sponsored women's welfare organizations several groups/organization/activists have identified various issues relating to women as their agenda.

As far as women's organizations are concerned, the All India Women's Conference founded in 1927 is the oldest and has played significant role during the 1930s and 1940s in highlighting the subjugated position of women and also mobilized the middle-class women to fight for their rights. However, it has lost much of its momentum currently, and several other organizations have been formed to take up the women's issues like the National Federation of Indian Women (NFIW) which is a breakaway faction of AIWC and the All India Democratic Women's Association (AIDWA) formed by merging of a number of small and large organizations. One must point out at this juncture is that some of the major political parties have their women wings like the

* Second Sex is a book by the French existentialist Simone de Beauvoir written in 1949, where she highlighted status of women in society. This is a major contribution to feminist philosophy.

NFIW which is the women's wing of CPI , the AIDWA is the women's wing for CITU, the Rashtra Sevika Samiti of RSS, the Matri Mandal and Durga Vahini of VHP and the Mahila Morcha of BJP. The Mahila Dakshata Samiti (Women's Vigilance Committee) of the Janata Dal which have played an active role in the Anti-price rise movement of the 1970s. The women wings using their party affiliations act as important pressure groups in influencing Government decisions on gender related issues.

However, beside the party-based organizations, a large number of autonomous women's organizations have come into existence from 1970s onwards like Saheli in Delhi, Samata Manch, Stree Sangharsh Samiti, Stree Mukti Sangathan and the like. Three women's organizations which have set new directions in women's empowerment are the Self-Employed Women Association (SEWA) (Ahmedabad), Working Women's Forum (Madras) and Annapurna Mandal (Mumbai).

The groups/organizations working towards women's issues can be classified as:

1. Agitational, propaganda, consciousness-raising groups which may be termed as autonomous groups;
2. Grassroots or mass-based organizations like the trade unions, agricultural labourers' organization, democratic rights groups, tribal organizations and others which fight for women's issues;
3. Groups concentrating on providing services, shelter, homes to the needy women;
4. Professional women's organizations such as doctors, lawyers, scientists, researchers, journalists;
5. Women's wings or fronts of the political parties; and
6. Groups involved in research and documentation on women's issues.

Certain incidents, where the dignity of women has been violated, have given visibility to issues based on gender. From the 1970s, the contemporary women's movement tried to give visibility of the women's cause. The **Mathura rape case** spearheaded the women's movement in India. It was an incident in India wherein Mathura, a sixteen year old tribal girl, was allegedly raped by two policemen in the compound of Desai Ganj Police Station in Chandrapur district of Mahrashtra. The incident led to historical changes in Indian law. After violent protests, an FIR was lodged against the two guilty constables, Ganpat and Tukaram. The sessions court gave the judgment in the favour of accused, but the Nagpur Bench of Bombay High Court reversed the judgment and stated that passive submission due to fear induced by serious threats could not be construed as willing sexual intercourse. The Supreme Court however, acquitted the policemen. The judgment did not distinguish between consent and forcible submission. The case led to huge public outcry and was instrumental in bringing about wide-range of changes in rape laws in the country. However, even under the changed legal regime, hardly any substantive improvements seem to have taken place in the ground conditions. The Criminal Law Amendment Act, 1983 has made a statutory provision in the face of Section 114(A) of the Evidence Act, which states that if the victim says that she did not consent to the sexual intercourse, the Court shall presume that she did not consent. New laws were also enacted following the incident, the Section 376 (punishment for rape) of the Indian Penal Code underwent a change with the enactment and addition of Section 376(A), Section 376(B), Section 376(C), Section 376(D). The Mathura rape case was a landmark in women's movement in India.

The 1970s and the 1980s especially, witnessed anti-dowry agitation with slogans like 'Brides are not for Burning' and several other anti-dowry slogans. The Dahej Virodhi Chetna Manch formed in 1982 was most vocal against the atrocities and violence against brides for dowry. The popular agitation reached such a level that the Dowry Prohibition Act was amended in 1984 and 1986. Further, Section 498A was inserted into the Indian Penal Code in 1983 through an amendment. The practice of *Sati* caught the imagination of the public with the horrifying case of Roop Kanwar in Rajasthan (1987). Women activists groups like Janwadi Mahila Samity, Nari Chetna Manch, Rajasthan University Women's Association and Peoples Union for Civil Liberties condemned such heinous acts and demanded immediate Government action. Finally, the Commission of Sati Prevention Bill was passed in 1987.

The 1970s also witnessed movements against amniocentesis and sex selection and population policy. The Forum Against Sex-Determination and Sex-Pre Selection (FASDAP) fought against these issues. The governments were pressurized to follow up the findings by various groups and institutions like the All India Institute of Medical Sciences (AIIMS). The Government issued some circulars without much effect. It was only in the 1990s that some path-breaking legislations were adopted like the Pre-Natal Diagnostic Techniques (Regulation & Prevention of Misuse) Act, 1994, Pre-Natal Diagnostic Techniques (Regulation & Prevention of Misuse) Amendment Act, 2000 and Pre-Natal Diagnostic Techniques (Regulation & Prevention of Misuse) Amendment Act, 2002. However, sex-selection still continues in India while foeticide and infanticide are common and States like Haryana have the lowest female sex ratio.

The 1980s saw some tough fighting between the women's rights groups and the religious groups over issues like the separate personal law for Sikhs and the Muslim Women's Maintenance Act. After fiery debates and discussions and rage over the issues and ultimately with protests from the national women's organizations and several Sikh women organizations/groups, the Government of India refrained from passing the bill which would have deprived the Sikh women of their rights to a share in their father's property, or even right to divorce except through the dispensation of the religious heads, and would have legitimized polygamy. In 1986, after years of legal battles in the Supreme Court over the Shah Bano Case, the Government of India passed the Muslim

Women's (Protection of Rights of Divorce) Act 1986 which otherwise would have deprived divorced Muslim women of their right to seek maintenance under Section 125 of the Criminal Procedure Code, a secular law open to all communities.

Women have been parts of peasant movements and tribal movements like the Tebhaga, Telangana, Chipko movement and some agrarian, workers' and *adivasi* movements. Women also led anti-arrack (liquor) movement in Nallore district in Andhra Pradesh. *Dalit* women have been the worst sufferers and their cause has been taken up by several women's rights groups. The *Dalit* women bear the triple burden of caste, class and gender as a result of which they face torture, rape and murder often.

Struggle still continues and women truly have now become more empowered than their predecessors, but in India, there is no record of decline of violence against women or restricting the women to the arena of home and preventing her from coming out to the world. When atrocities are perpetuated by agents of States then also some women remain silent out of fear, whereas some like Chanu they fight. **Irom Sharmila Chanu**, of Manipur has been on a fast for over ten years demanding the revocation of the controversial Armed Forces (Special Powers) Act. Sharmila is currently under judicial custody, but has been lodged at the security ward of Jawaharlal Nehru Hospital in Imphal where she is being forced-fed through her nose. She launched her crusade against Armed Forces (Special Powers) Act, 1958 (AFSPA) after Assam Rifles personnel killed ten civilians at Malom village near Imphal airport on November 2000. Sharmila went on an indefinite fast three days later, demanding the repeal of the military act that gives unbridled powers to the armed forces and even to shoot people on mere suspicion. Her crusade shows the excesses that can be perpetrated by the agents of the States vide the wide range of powers being given to armed forces as in case of AFSPA in areas classified under the Act as disturbed areas in the States of Arunachal Pradesh, Assam, Manipur, Meghalaya, Mizoram, Nagaland and Tripura.

India became a signatory to the CEDAW in 1980 and ratified it in 1993. India submitted a declaration regarding Articles 5(a) and 16(1) that reiterates India's commitment to abide by the provisions "in conformity with its policy of non-interference in the personal affairs of any Community without its initiative and consent". India also registered a declaration regarding Article 16(2) on minimum marriage ages and compulsory registration; although India fully supports the principle, "it is not practical in a vast country like India with its variety of customs, religions and level of literacy" to implement it forcefully. In India, there are several laws relating to rights of women and girl child. The prominent among them are Commission of Sati (Prevention) Act, 1987, Dowry Prohibition Act, 1961, Indecent Representation of Women (Prohibition) Act, 1986, National Commission for Women Act, 1990, Protection of Women from Domestic Violence Act, 2005, Protection of Women against Sexual Harassment Bill, 2007 and Immoral Traffic (Prevention) Act, 1956.

There are also laws relating to marriage and divorce under personal law of different communities like the Hindu Marriage Act, 1955, Muslim Women (Protection of Rights on Divorce) Act, 1986, Parsi Marriage & Divorce Act, 1936, Special Marriages Act, 1954 and the like. There are also Laws relating to property, succession, inheritance, guardianship, adoption. Laws relating to abortion like Medical Termination of Pregnancy Act, 1971, Pre-Natal Diagnostic Techniques (Regulation & Prevention of Misuse) Act, 1994, Pre-Natal Diagnostic Techniques (Regulation & Prevention of Misuse) Amendment Act, 2000, and Pre-Natal Diagnostic Techniques (Regulation & Prevention of Misuse) Amendment Act, 2002. There are also laws relating to working women like the Equal Remuneration Act, 1976 and Maternity Benefit Act, 1961.

The Judiciary of India has also been active in upholding women's rights. The Supreme Court has issued what has come to be known as the **Vishakha guidelines**. Bhanwari Devi, a Saathin of a development programme run by the State Government of Rajasthan, fighting against child and multiple marriages in villages, tried to stop child marriage of Ramkaran Gujjar's infant daughter who was less than one year old. The marriage took place nevertheless, and the Gujjar family got infuriated by her interference, and on September 1992 five men including Ramkaran Gujjar, gang raped Bhanwari. Unable to get justice, women groups had filed a petition in the Supreme Court of India, under the name of, 'Vishakha', asking the Court to give certain directions regarding the sexual harassment that women face at the workplace. The result is the Supreme Court judgment on the 13 August 1997 which gave the Vishakha guidelines regarding prevention of sexual harassment at workplace. The objective of Vishakha guidelines is to arouse the consciousness about the concept of gender equality and to prevent sexual harassment of working women in all workplaces. Therefore, the Supreme Court judgment can be seen as an improvement on the existing laws and judicial pronouncements. The Sexual Harassment of Women At Work Place (Prevention, Prohibition and Redressal) Bill 2012 (now an Act) which was pending since December 2010 was passed by the Rajya Sabha on 28 February 2013. This was believed to be an improvement upon the Vishakha Guidelines issued by the Supreme Court in 1997. After the Delhi Rape Case of December 2012, the Criminal Law [Amendment] Bill, 2013 was passed by the Lok Sabha on 19 March 2013, and by the Rajya Sabha on 21 March 2013. The President of India has accorded his assent to the Bill on 2 April 2013, and it is now an Act. This Act has made acid attack, disrobing, voyeurism, subjection of woman to sexual offence resulting in her being reduced to the vegetative state (new Section, 326A) and human trafficking punishable offences.

The National Perspective Plan for Women (NPP) was prepared in 2000, without even consulting as women's rights activists/groups. The Women's organization vehemently criticized the report and pointed out that the proposed plan's recommendation to bring women 'into the mainstream of development' ignored the reality of women's marginalization being the result of such "mainstream" development.

They demanded among other things due recognition of national organizations of women at all levels of the planning and decision-making process. Women's movement have also pointed out that the post 1990 liberalization phase in India with its Structural Adjustment Programmes (SAPs) and the package of economic reform have made the position of women more vulnerable. Therefore, the contemporary women's movements have included the impact of new economic policies on women in organized sectors as well as unorganized sectors. They have upheld the necessity of recognizing the multi-dimensional roles of women as workers, peasants, producers, citizens, mothers, daughters and above all as women themselves, in order to get a complete picture of women in society and polity, and thereby fix their respective agenda.

The National Commission for Women (NCW) was set up as statutory body in January 1992 under the National Commission for Women Act, 1990 to:

1. review the Constitutional and Legal safeguards for women;
2. recommend remedial legislative measures;
3. facilitate redressal of grievances and
4. advise the Government on all policy matters affecting women.

The important issues addressed by the Commission include violence against women, sexual exploitation of women at work place, educational health and employment aspects, women in agriculture sector, women in Panchayati Raj, custodial justice, mental health institutions, etc. (See Chapter 22 for details)

Women Studies Centres and Schools

Women Studies Centres/Schools have been opened in several Colleges and Universities to provide academic research and study of women's issues as well as sensitize students about the rights of women and their social position. These Centres and Schools are not just restricted to their institutions, but they transcend the academic barrier and organize outreach programmes for women of slums or in backward districts regarding their reproductive health as well as legal rights.

These might seem to give us a ray of hope, whereas women get 33.3% reservation in Gram Panchayat (village assembly) and municipal elections the bill seeking 33.3% seat reservation to Parliament and Legislative Assemblies is still pending. In 2012 there were horrifying news of infanticide by their fathers in different parts of India like that of baby Afreen's case who died in a hospital in Bangalore. She was a baby of three months, and was battered and bruised by her father as she was unwanted. Afreen's story is the dehumanizing sequel to that of Baby Falak, the two-year-old, a victim of human trafficking, who died at AIIMS Trauma Centre in New Delhi, after battling brain damage and three cardiac arrests in 2012. Such incidents still happen and more gender sensitization is needed to overcome such gender inequality.

HUMAN RIGHTS MOVEMENTS

It is needless to say that 'Human Rights' pertain to human beings. Men are born with certain rights that are inalienable. Such is the conviction of Natural Rights Theory. But, such rights if not safeguarded and established on a legal edifice will seem 'fictitious' and 'rhetorical nonsense'. Therefore, a legal footage is always necessary. The oldest of the Human Rights documents is the English Magna Carta of 1215. However, a path-breaking achievement towards institutionalization of human rights, was made with the adoption of Universal Declaration of Human Rights (UDHR) in 1948 by the UNGA. Later, a host of other International Covenants/instruments on human rights were adopted, like the ICCPR, ICESR, CAT, CEDAW, CRC, CERD and others.

Human rights, as enshrined in these major international instruments are embodiments of basic rights of individuals, which he is entitled to enjoy as a human being. These are certain standards set to induce the States to respect the fundamental rights and freedoms of their citizens.

India, apart from being a party to several of these International Conventions, possesses a Constitution, which is a voluminous legal document for which it can really be proud of. Part-III of the Constitution on Fundamental Rights (enforceable) and Part-IV on Directive Principles (non-enforceable) incorporate most of the basic human rights principles as contained in these Conventions. A landmark development was made with the 86th Amendment, 2002, making Education a Fundamental Right under Article 21A.

Other human rights documents in India are:

1. Child Labour (Prohibition and Regulation) Act, 1986
2. The National Commission for Minorities Act, 1990
3. The National Commission for Women Act, 1990
4. The National Commission for Scheduled Castes and Scheduled Tribes (Constitution 65th Amendment Act, 1990)
5. Protection of Human Rights Act, 1993
6. The National Commission for Backward Classes Act, 1993
7. Persons with Disabilities (Equal Opportunities, Protection of Rights and Full Participation) Act, 1995

Some Acts relating to women are:

1. Dowry Prohibition Act, 1961
2. The Immoral Traffic (Prevention) Act, 1956
3. Indescent Representation of Women (Prohibition) Act, 1986
4. Madras Devadasi Prevention Act

Some intriguing human rights issue being faced today are like bonded labour, right to food, review of Child Marriage Restraint Act, Child labour, Trafficking of women and Children, problems of girl child, child abuse,

Sexual harassment of women at work place, domestic violence, sustainable development and environmental problems and an array of different kinds of human rights related problems despite several acts in place to prevent such abuses.

Human rights movement in India got a boost during the Emergency period, 1975–1977, and gained momentum during the post Emergency period. The mass arrests, by misusing MISA and NSA, of the leaders of the opposition, and the targeted apprehension of those who could present a challenge to an authoritarian State along with press censorship threatened the very basis of human rights in India. Different organizations like the People's Union for Civil Liberties (PUCL), the Peoples Union For Democratic Rights (PUDR), the Association for Protection of Democratic Rights, (APDR), Kolkata, Committee for Protection of Democratic Rights (CPDR), Mumbai, Andhra Pradesh Civil Liberties Committee (APCLC), Hyderabad, the Association for Democratic Rights (AFDR), Punjab and others voiced their concerns about the Human Rights violations during emergency, and are still fighting for protecting democratic rights of the people and protesting against violation of human and civil rights. Human rights movements have encompassed a number of issues including the tribal movement, peasant struggles, environmental movement, women's liberation movement, child rights movement, *dalit* movement and struggles of the differently-abled persons. Organizations have to work harder to address the human rights issues relating to issues like anti-terror laws, catch and kill policy towards the terrorists in Jammu & Kashmir, Assam militants and incidents like Mass cremation in Punjab case of 1984 (Nanabati Report), Anti-Sikh riots of 1984 as well as promote the causes of AIDS victim and fight against child abuse and host of other human rights issues. India too has to develop its policy regarding treatment of non-citizens, such as the refugees and the illegal migrants and give up ad hocism. The nature of human rights movement that emerged after Independence from British colonial rule during the emergency period has now changed. Human Rights violations arise out of implementation of State policy, may be through its law enforcement agencies such as the police and armed forces were they might get involved in serious human rights violations such as torture, false encounter killings and murders and so on.

The **National Human Rights Commission** (NHRC) was constituted on 12 October 1993. The Commission was established under the mandatory legislation of the Protection of Human Rights Act, 1993 to promote as well as protect the human rights of the citizens of India.

The NHRC is a statutory body and the Commission's purview covers the entire range of civil and political, as well as economic, social and cultural rights. Areas facing terrorism and insurgency, custodial death, rape and torture, reform of the police, prisons, and other institutions such as juvenile homes, mental hospitals and shelters for women have been given special attention. Other areas of concern for the Commission are the fundamental questions of equity and justice to the less privileged Scheduled Castes and Scheduled Tribes and the prevention of atrocities perpetrated against them. Rights of the disabled, access to public services, displacement of populations and especially of tribal by mega projects, food scarcity and allegation of death by starvation, rights of the child and rights of women subjected to violence, sexual harassment and discrimination among others. (See Chapter 22 for details)

The Governments of almost twenty States—like Andhra Pradesh, Assam, Bihar, Chhattisgarh, Gujarat, Jharkhand, Karnataka, Kerala, Maharashtra, Odisha, Sikkim, West Bengal, Himachal Pradesh, Jammu & Kashmir, Madhya Pradesh, Manipur, Punjab, Rajasthan, Tamil Nadu and others have already set up State Human Rights Commissions. The Government of West Bengal constituted West Bengal Human Rights Commission in 1995 under the Protection of Human Rights Act, 1993 with the objective of protection and promotion of human rights.

A number of human rights organizations have also emerged like the Association for Democratic Rights (AFDR, Punjab), Andhra Pradesh Civil Liberties Committee (APCLC, Andhra Pradesh), Association for Protection of Democratic Rights (APDR, West Bengal), Bandi Mukti Committee (West Bengal), Committee for Protection of Democratic Rights (CPDR, Nagpur), Coordination of Human Rights (COHR, Manipur), Campaign for Peace and Democracy in Manipur (CPDM, Delhi), Human Rights Forum (HRF, Andhra Pradesh), Lokshahi Hak Sangathana (LHS, Maharashtra), Manab Adhikar Sangram Samiti (MASS, Assam), Naga People's Movement for Human Rights (NPMHR), Organization for Protection of Democratic Rights (OPDR, Andhra Pradesh), People's Committee for Human Rights (PCHR, Jammu and Kashmir), People's Democratic Forum (PDF, Karnataka), People's Union for Civil Liberties (PUCL, National, Chhattisgarh, Jharkhand, Nagpur, Rajasthan, People's Union for Democratic Rights (PUDR, Delhi), People's Union for Human Rights (PUHR, Haryana) among others. They protested against the decision of the Government regarding the use of Section 39 of the Unlawful Activities Prevention Act (UAPA), issued by the Government in so-called 'public interest'.

Presently, there has been a new direction in creating a new regime of human rights by the adoption of Right to Information Act 2005 that has given the people of India much needed access to government information in response to citizen requests, and also by expanding the meaning of Fundamental Right to equality, life and personal liberty. In this process, the right to speedy trial, free legal aid, dignity, means and livelihood, education, housing, medical care, clean environment, right against torture, sexual harassment, solitary confinement, bondage and servitude, exploitation and so on emerge as human rights. These new reconceptualized rights provide legal resources to activate the Courts for their enforcement through Public Interest Litigation (PIL).

In the August 2019, the Unlawful Activities (Prevention) Amendment Act was passed which amended the UAPA, 1967. Under this Act individuals can be designated as terrorists and their properties can be seized. There can be investigation against such individuals by National Investigation Agency (NIA). Imposition of travel ban on such individuals can be done under this Act. The provisions of this Act have raised serious criticisms and opposition from human rights perspective. It has to be watched closely how this Act is implemented and whether it clashes with the basic human rights of individuals who may be designated as terrorist.

According to former Secretary General of the UN, Kofi Annan "We may have different, languages, different religions, may live in different parts of the world, but one thing that is common is that we all are human beings" and another thing that should be added is that human dignity should be respected to the fullest extent possible.

ANTI-CORRUPTION MOVEMENT

The year 2011 will be notoriously known in the history of Indian Government and Politics as the *Year of Scams.* A 2005 study conducted by Transparency International in 2011 ranked India as 95th out of 178 countries in Transparency International's Corruption Perceptions Index. The Housing Scam, the Commonwealth games Scam and the Scam of all scams—the Telecom 2G Scam, made headlines this year. It fuelled the civil society movement which took the people of India if not all, but still a considerable number into its fold because the disgust and discontent of the public with the way the Indian polity was functioning. The India Against Corruption group with key people like Anna Hazare, Arvind Kejriwal, Kiran Bedi, Shanti Bhushan, Prashant Bhushan and others have spear headed the anti-corruption movement in India by demanding a strong Jan Lokpal bill.

The problem arose when the Government showed its own version of Lokpal bill and Team Anna sticked to its own. The opposition parties also had their own version of Lokpal Bill, and so these were rounds of politicking in the Parliamentary sessions. Whether a Lokpal or no Lokpal, the reality is that the efficacy of the Parliament was then at crossroads. Healthy debate over any public policy or major reform bills are always welcome, but sometimes the stubbornness and rigidity of the Government in power, which might want the passage of a particular legislation at any cost, creates logjam which is harmful for functioning of any democracy. Major decisions remain pending, public money is wasted and patience of the public is put to test. Common man's frustration has been there for long, only the civil society had helped to voice the concern of the public and this public sentiment must be acknowledged by the Parliament. There are several Anti-corruption laws in India. They are:

1. Indian Penal Code, 1860
2. The Prevention of Corruption Act, 1988

3. The Benami Transactions (Prohibition) Act, 1988 to prohibit *benami* transactions
4. Prevention of Money Laundering Act, 2002

India is also a signatory to the UN Convention against Corruption since 2005 which was ratified in May 2011. Pressure from civil society, earlier had seen the adoption of Right to Information Act in 2005, and now it is the civil society again which has forced the Government to review the Government's version of Lokpal Bill. The Right to Information Act was introduced in 2005 which is a tool to bring information into public domain and that will keep a check on the functioning of the government at all levels whether at local level, or at a State level or at Central level. The Supreme Court has cancelled 122 telecommunications licenses awarded to companies in 2008. The team Anna-led movement though has drawn criticisms, yet it has highlighted the state of affairs in the country, and the people of India are looking up for a brighter future which will be nothing less than a corruption free India.

EXERCISES

1. Short Answer Questions: **(100 words)**

1. Write a note on ecological movements in India.
2. Write a note on the Narmada Bachao Andolan.
3. Write a note on the Chipko movement.
4. Briefly state the role of National Green Tribunal in India.
5. Briefly discuss the evolution of 'Green Justice' in India.
6. Write a note on Women's movements in India.
7. Write a note on Vishakha Case as an important landmark in tackling harassment of women at workplace.
8. Briefly state the role of National Human Rights Commission in India.
9. Write a note on Human Rights movements in India.
10. Write a note on the recent Anti-Corruption Movement in India.

II. Long Answer Questions: **(1200 words)**

11. Examine how ecology has come to play an important role in the emergence of new social movements based around environmental protection/preservation.
12. Discuss the gradual consolidation of environmental movements in India.
13. Examine the gradual growth of women's movements in India.
14. Give an account of women's movements in India.
15. Examine the state of Human Rights Movements in India.
16. Write a note on the Anti-Corruption Movements in India.

REFERENCES

Agnihotri, Indu, and Mazumdar, Vina, "Changing Terms of Political Discourse: Women's Movement in india, 1970s–1990s", in Oomen, T.K. (Ed.), *Social Movements: Issues of Identity*, Vol. 1, Oxford University Press, New Delhi, 2011.

Chattapadhyay, Tapan Kumar, *India and the Ecology Question: Confrontation and Reconstruction,* Ekushe, Calcutta, 1999.

Chatterjee, Bandana,, "Women and Politics in India", in Chatterjee Rakhahari (Ed.), *Politics India: The State-Society Interface*, South Asian Publishers, New Delhi, 2004.

Chatterjee, Partha, *The Nation and Its Fragments: Colonial and Postcolonial Histories*, Oxford University Press, New Delhi, 2001.

Kohli, Atul, *The Success of India's Democracy,* Cambridge University Press, New Delhi, 2004.

Oomen, T.K., "Protests Against Displacement by Development Projects" in Oomen, T.K. (Ed.), *Social Movements: Issues of Identity*, Vol. 1, Oxford University Press, New Delhi, 2011.

Shah, Ghanshyam, *Social Movements in India: A Review of Literature*, Sage Publications, New Delhi, 2007.

Shiva Vandana, "Ecology Movements in India", in Oomen, T.K. (Ed.), *Social Movements: Issues of Identity*, Vol. 1, Oxford University Press, New Delhi, 2011.

Singh, M.P. and Saxena, Rekha, *Indian Politics: Contemporary Issues and Concerns,* Prentice-Hall of India, New Delhi, 2008.

22

Commissions and Functionaries in India

INTRODUCTION

Administration is a multidimensional job. A huge and diverse country like India therefore needs a number of commissions and functionaries to smoothly run the administration on a regular basis. Some have been constituted from time to time by Acts and Statutes and others have been formed vide the provisions of the Constitution. This chapter will discuss some of the important commissions and functionaries in India.

THE PLANNING COMMISSION

The Planning Commission was set up by a Resolution of the Government of India on 15 March 1950. The Planning Commission has the prime responsibility of making assessment of all resources of the country, and formulating plans for striking an effective and balanced utilization of resources and augmenting all round development. It has been replaced by the NITI Aayog in 2015. [See Chapter 23 for updates]

THE NATIONAL DEVELOPMENT COUNCIL (NDC)

From the initial years of the drafting of the First Five Year Plan, a compelling need was felt to coordinate the execution of Plan and the development States of the Indian Union. The chief objective was promotion of common economic policies in important sectors and balanced and rapid development throughout the component units of the Indian Union. To give a positive direction to the

Planning in India and coordination of the policies and programmes of the five year plans, the National Development Council or Rashtriya Vikas Parishad was formed. The Rashtriya Vikas Parishad or the National Development Council (NDC) came into being on 6 August 1952.

Composition

In its original form it comprised of the Prime Minister as the Chairman, Chief Ministers of the State Governments and the members of the Planning Commission.

Currently, the organization of the Council comprises the Prime Minister, all the Union Cabinet Ministers, Chief Ministers of all States or their substitutes, representatives of the union territories and Members of the NITI Aayog. Ministers of State with independent charge are also invited to the deliberations of the Council. There have been occasions when the Reserve Bank Governor and other experts have been invited to address the meetings. The Prime Minister is the Chairman of the Council and the Secretary to the Commission acts as its Secretary and the Commission, who furnishes the Council with administrative and other assistance. The Council ordinarily meets twice a year. The council ordinarily passes no resolution formally. The large membership of the Council, which at one time rose to 50, reduced the utility of the Council. Thus in 1954, a Standing Committee was established with only nine Chief Ministers and a few Union Ministers as members. In addition, the Council has been appointing Committees from time-to-time for a detailed examination of certain problems. Prominent among them are Committee on population, Committee on micro-level planning, Committee on austerity, Committee on employment. Committee on literacy and Committee on medical education.

Functions of NDC

1. To review the working of the National Plan from time-to-time,
2. To consider important questions of social and economic policy affecting national development, and
3. To recommend measures for the achievement of the aims and the targets set out in the National Plan, including measures to secure the active participation and co-operation of the people, improve the efficiency of the administrative services, ensure the fullest development of the less advanced regions and sections of the community and, through sacrifice borne equally by all citizens, build up the resources for national development.

In October 1967, on the recommendations of the **Administrative Reforms Commission**, the Council was reconstituted. In the reconstituted Council, the Secretary of the Planning Commission acts as Secretary to the NDC and the Commission is expected to provide such administrative and other support as may be necessary. NDC now consists of the Prime Minister, all Union Cabinet Ministers, Chief Ministers of all States and Union Territories and the Members of the Planning Commission. The Lt. Governor and the Chief Executive Councilor of the remaining Union Territories and the respective Chief Ministers represent the Delhi Administration. It is also provided that other Union and States Ministers may be invited to participate in the deliberations of the NDC.

The functions were redefined to include:

1. Prescription of guidelines for the formulation of National Plan, including the assessment of resources for the Plan;
2. Consideration of National Plan as formulated by the Commission;
3. Considering important questions of social and economic policy affecting national development; and
4. The review of the working of the Plan from time-to-time and recommending such measures as are necessary for achieving the aims and targets to secure the active participation and cooperation of the people, improving the efficiency of the administrative services, ensuring the fullest development of the less advanced regions and sections of the community and, through sacrifice, borne equally, by all citizens, build up resources for national development.

The NDC has an important role to play in the coordination of the balanced economic growth of the country. However, there are several drawbacks in the functioning of the Council. The NDC meetings are irregular and are dogged with politics and partisanship. The NDC also does not engage in evaluation of the implementation of plans and it is far from being an effective body for coordinating the Centre-State planning relations. Yet it cannot be denied that the NDC helps in the coordination not only of policies and programmes of plans but also other matters of national importance. It provides a good forum for discussion and full and free exchange of views. NDC acts as a bridge between the Union Government, the Planning Commission and the State Governments.

With high hopes, the NDC was formed to advise and make its recommendations to the Central and State Governments. Since its inception, it has been functioning as a high power consultative body where the frame of the Five Year Plans, the important problems facing the Indian economy, and the policies, that have to be adopted for tiding over the urgent problems have been discussed and solutions arrived at. The success of this new planning organization could depend mainly on the tact and sagacity of the Prime Minister and Chief Minister.

THE INTER-STATE COUNCIL

The Constitution of India provides for a polity, which clearly defines spheres of authority between the Union and the States to be exercised in the fields assigned to them. Consistent with this, the Constitution has made an elaborate distribution of powers between the Union and the States in the areas of legislative, administrative and financial powers. The subject of Legislative Power has, accordingly, been classified into three Lists—Union List (List I), State List (List II) and the Concurrent List (List III) in the Seventh Schedule of the Constitution. Residuary powers of legislation have been vested in the Union Government. The Union Government has, from time-to-time, taken steps to look afresh at contentious issues between the Centre and States regarding the distribution of powers. One of the important recommendations of Sarkaria Commission was for establishing a permanent Inter-State Council as an independent national forum for consultation with a mandate well-defined in accordance with Article 263 of the Constitution of India. Pursuant to the recommendation. The Inter-State Council (ISC) was set up under Article 263 of the Constitution of India vide Presidential Order dated 28 May 1990.

Article 263 of the Constitution of India provides as under:

"If at any time it appears to the President that the public interest would be served by the establishment of a Council charged with the duty of—

- inquiring into and advising upon disputes which may have arisen between States;
- investigating and discussing subjects in which some or all of the States, or the Union and one or more of the States, have a common interest; or
- making recommendations upon any such subject and in particular, recommendations for the better co-ordination of policy and action with respect to that subject, it shall be lawful for the President by order to establish such a Council, and to define the nature of the duties to be performed by it and its organization and procedure."

The Inter-State Council Secretariat headed by the Secretary to the Government of India who looks into the affairs of the Inter-State Council and its Standing Committees. In addition, Inter-State Council Secretariat also is the Secretariat for Commission for Centre-State Relations. Secretary, Inter-State Council is the Member-Secretary of Inter-State Council and Commission for Centre-State Relations.

Composition

The Council was set up vide Presidential Order on 28 May 1990. Para 2 of the Presidential Order provides for the composition of the Council. According to this, the Council shall consist of Prime Minister as the Chairman and as members, Chief Ministers of all States, Chief Ministers of Union Territories having a Legislative Assembly and Administrators of Union Territories not having a Legislative Assembly and Governors of States under President's Rule (Governor's Rule in the case of J&K), Six Ministers of Cabinet rank in the and Union Council of Ministers to be nominated by the Prime Minister.

In October 2011, the Centre has reconstituted the Inter-State Council (ISC) and its Standing Committee, incorporating new members in these panels. The changes were made following the reshuffle in the Union Cabinet and states since the body was last reconstituted in 2009.

The ISC is empowered to discuss matters concerning one or more States and Union Territories. It is a recommendatory body with duties to investigate and discuss the subjects of common interest between the Union and State or States and also among the States, making recommendations particularly for better coordination of policy and action on these subjects and deliberating upon such other matters of general interest to the States which may be referred to it by its Chairman. The Council also deliberates upon such other matters of general interest to the States as may be referred by the Chairman to the Council.

A Standing Committee of the Inter-State Council has been constituted for continuous consultation and processing of matters for the consideration of the Council in 1996. The Standing Committee comprises Union Home Minister as Chairman and 5 Union Ministers of Cabinet Rank and 9 Chief Ministers of States as Members nominated by the Chairman of the Inter-State Council. The ISC is vested with the duty of the larger effort to consolidate federalism in India. Currently Prime Minister Narendra Modi is the Chairman of the ISC.

FINANCE COMMISSION

The Finance Commission of India was formed in the year 1951 under Article 280 of the Constitution of India with the passage of **The Finance Commission (Miscellaneous Provisions) Act, 1951**. The objective of forming the Finance Commission was to allocate resources of the revenue between the Union and the State Governments in India adequately. It is constituted by the President and all appointments to the commission are made by him as well.

Formation of Finance Commission of India

The detailed set up and of the Finance Commission has been provided in Article 280 of the Constitution of India. The Article states:

1. The President shall, within two years from the commencement of this Constitution and thereafter and at the expiration of every fifth year or at such time earlier time as the President considers necessary, by order constitute a Finance Commission which shall consist of a Chairman and four other members to be appointed by the President.

2. Parliament may by law determine the qualification which shall be requisite for appointment as members of the Commission and the manner in which they shall be selected.
3. It shall be the duty of the Commission to make recommendations to the President as to the distribution of the net proceeds of taxes which are to be, or may be divided between them under this chapter and the allocation between the States of the respective shares of such proceeds. It is also the duty of the Finance Commission to define the financial relations between the Union and the State and it also caters to the purpose of devolution of non-plan revenue resources.

Composition of Finance Commission of India

Article 280 empowers the Parliament to determine by law the qualifications of the members of the Commission and method of their selection. The Finance Commission of India has a Chairman along with four other members and a Secretary. The Chairman is the person who heads the Commission and presides over its activities. According to the **Finance Commission Act, 1951** the Chairman of the Finance Commission is selected among persons who have had the experience of public affairs, and four other members are selected among persons who are, or have been, or are qualified as judges of High Courts of India, or have knowledge of finance, or have vast experience in financial matters and are in administration, or have knowledge of economics. All the appointments are made by the President of India. A member can be disqualified on the following grounds, as provided by the Finance Commission Act, 1951, when a member is found to be of unsound mind or if he is found to be an undischarged insolvent or convicted of an offence of moral turpitude or his financial or other interests hamper his functioning as the member of the Commission.

The **tenure** of the office of the Member of the Finance Commission is specified by the President of India and they will be eligible for re-appointment. The salary of the members of the Finance Commission is according to the provisions laid down by the Constitution of India.

Functions of Finance Commission: Terms of Reference of the Finance Commission

Under the Constitution, the basis for sharing of divisible taxes by the Centre and the States and the principles governing grants-in-aid to the States have to be decided by the Finance Commission every five years. The President can refer to the Commission any other matter in the interest of sound finance.

It has become customary for the Presidential Order to mention certain considerations that a Commission shall have regard, among others, while making its recommendations. These considerations, by and large, reflected the emerging developments in Centre-State finances. The recommendations of the Commission together with an explanatory memorandum as to the action taken by the Government on them are laid before each house of Parliament. The Commission has to evaluate the increase in the Consolidated Fund of a State to affix the resources of the Panchayat in the State. It also has to evaluate the increase in the Consolidated Fund of a state to affix the resources of the Municipalities in the state. So far, thirteen Finance Commissions have given their reports.

As we have seen in Chapter 6 the Financial Relations between the Union and the States generally revolve round collection and distribution of taxes and duties between the Centre and the State. The distribution of revenues between the Centre and the State can be summarized as follows:

Distribution of Revenues between the Union and the States

1. Levy of duties by the Centre, but collected and retained by the States (Article 268)
2. Taxes and duties levied and collected by the Centre, but assigned in whole to the States (Article 269).
3. Sharing of the proceeds of all Union taxes between the Centre and the States under Article 270. (Effective from April 1, 1996, following the eightieth amendment to the Constitution replacing the earlier provisions relating to mandatory sharing of income tax under Article 270 and permissive sharing of Union excise duties under Article 272).
4. Statutory grants-in-aid of the revenues of States (Article 275)
5. Grants for any public purpose (Article 282).
6. Loans for any public purpose (Article 293).

From the above pattern of distribution of revenue and also provisions enabling transfer of resources from the Centre to the States, the Constitution provides for an institutional mechanism to facilitate such transfers. Differences in the developmental levels in Indian States necessitates the institution of the Finance Commission which has been formed under Article 280 of the Constitution to facilitate fiscal federalism in India.

Responsibilities of Finance Commission

Under the various provisions of the Constitution, the main responsibilities of a Finance Commission or the terms of reference are the following:

1. The distribution between the Union and the States of the net proceeds of taxes which are to be divided between them and the allocation between the States of the respective shares of such proceeds.
2. Determination of principles and quantum of grants-in-aid to States which are in need of such assistance.
3. Measures needed to augment the Consolidated Fund of a State to supplement the resources of the Panchayats and Municipalities in the State on the basis of the recommendations made by the Finance Commission of the State.
4. The continuance or modification of the terms of agreement entered into by the Government of India with the Government of any State; and
5. Any other matter referred to the Commission by the president in the interests of sound finance.

The third function was added following the 73rd and 74th amendments to the Constitution in 1992 conferring statutory status to the Panchayats and Municipalities.

Additional matters

The important additional matters referred to the Finance Commissions are:

1. Distribution of proceeds of additional excise duties in lieu of sales tax, distribution of grants to States in lieu of the tax under the repealed Railway Passenger Fares Act, 1957, modalities of financing relief expenditure, upgradation of standards of administration, special problems and the assessment of the debt position of the States.
2. A major debate regarding the recommendations of Finance Commissions relates to Finance Commissions restricting their assessment of State finances to non-Plan revenue account. There is no distinction between the expenditure on the Plan and non-Plan account in the Constitution. The budgetary classification of expenditure into Plan and non-Plan came into vogue with the introduction of centralized planning in India. On the whole, the Finance Commission refrained to deal with the Plan expenditure on the ground that the Planning Commission which had been specifically constituted should have unhampered authority in the domain of planning. The practical difficulties involved in making projections of Plan outlays by and large kept the subsequent Finance Commissions away from considering Plan revenue expenditure.

Powers of Finance Commission

Under the Finance Commission Act, 1951, the Commission has been given adequate powers in the exercise of its function and within its area of activity.

It has all the powers of the Civil Court as per the Code of Civil Procedure, 1908. It can call any witness, or can ask for the production of any public record or document from any court or office. It can ask any person to give information or document on matters as it may feel to be useful or relevant. It can function as a civil court in discharging its duties.

Undoubtedly, there has been considerable expansion in the role of the Commission from mainly being an arbitrator between the Centre and the States to being an architect of fiscal restructuring. Due to the changing fiscal environment there has been considerable expansion of the functions of the Finance Commission. It has the task of guiding the fiscal federalism in India so as to ensure smooth functioning of Centre-State fiscal relations.

THE COMPTROLLER AND AUDITOR-GENERAL OF INDIA (CAG)

The Constitution of India provides for a Comptroller and Auditor-General of India to be appointed by the President of India to keep an eye on the expenditure made by the Government. Chapter V, Articles 148–151 contains the provisions for the power and functions of the CAG.

Constitutional Provisions

Article 148 lays down that:

(1) There shall be a Comptroller and Auditor-General of India who shall be appointed by the President by warrant under his hand and seal and shall only be removed from office in like manner and on like grounds as a Judge of the Supreme Court.

(2) Every person appointed to be the Comptroller and Auditor-General of India shall, before he enters upon his office, make and subscribe before the President or some person appointed in that behalf by him, an oath or affirmation according to the form set out for the purpose in the Third Schedule.

(3) The salary and other conditions of service of the Comptroller and Auditor-General shall be such as may be determined by Parliament by law and, until they are so determined, shall be as specified in the Second Schedule:

Provided that neither the salary of a Comptroller and Auditor-General nor his rights in respect of leave of absence, pension or age of retirement shall be varied to his disadvantage after his appointment.

(4) The Comptroller and Auditor-General shall not be eligible for further office either under the Government of India or under the Government of any State after he has ceased to hold his office.

(5) Subject to the provisions of this Constitution and of any law made by parliament, the conditions of service of persons serving in the Indian Audit and Accounts Department and the administrative powers of the Comptroller and Auditor-General shall be such as may be prescribed by rules made by the President after consultation with the Comptroller and Auditor-General.

(6) The Administrative expenses of the office of the Comptroller and Auditor-General including all salaries, allowances and pensions payable to or in respect of persons serving in that office, shall be charged upon the Consolidated Fund of India.

Article 149 relates to the duties and powers of the Comptroller and Auditor-General. It reads as, "The Comptroller and Auditor-General shall perform such duties and exercise such powers in relation to the accounts of the Union and of the States and of any other authority or body as may be prescribed by or under any law made by Parliament and, until provision in that behalf is so made, shall perform such duties and exercise such powers in relation to the accounts of the Union and of the States as were conferred on or exercisable by the Auditor-General of India immediately before the commencement of this Constitution in relation to the accounts of the Dominion of India and of the provinces, respectively."

Article 150 deals with the form of accounts of the Union and of the States which shall be kept in such form as the President may, on the advice of the Comptroller and Auditor-General of India, prescribe.

Article 151 is related to the Audit report. It reads as:

1. The reports of the Comptroller and Auditor-General of India relating to the accounts of the Union shall be submitted to the president, who shall cause them to be laid before each House of Parliament.
2. The reports of the Comptroller and Auditor-General of India relating to the accounts of a State shall be submitted to the Governor of the State, who shall cause them to be laid before the Legislature of the State.

Oath or Affirmation

"I, <name>, having been appointed Comptroller and Auditor-General of India do swear in the name of God/solemnly affirm that I will bear true faith and allegiance to the Constitution of India as by law established, that I will uphold the sovereignty and integrity of India, that I will duly and faithfully and to the best of my ability, knowledge and judgment perform the duties of my office without fear or favour, affection or ill-will and that I will uphold the Constitution and the laws."

—*Constitution of India, Third Schedule, Part IV*

Term of Office

Under the CAG'S Duties, Power and Conditions of Service Act, 1971 the Comptroller and Auditor-General shall hold office for a term of six years from the date on which he assumes such office:

1. Provided that where he attains the age of sixty-five years before the expiry of the said term of six years, he shall vacate such office on the date on which he attains the said age.
2. Provided further that he may, at any time, by writing under his hand addressed to the President, resign his office.

Removal from Office

The CAG cannot be removed from office other than through a procedure of impeachment similar to what is applicable to a Judge of the Supreme Court of India. He can be removed from his office only on ground of proved misbehaviour or incapacity in a manner a judge of the Supreme Court is removed i.e., each House of the Parliament passing a resolution supported by two-thirds of the members present and voting and by a majority of the House.

Salaries and Allowances

The salary and allowances of Comptroller and Auditor General have been equated with the judges of the Supreme Court of India. The service conditions of those serving in the Audit and Accounts Department and the administrative powers of the Comptroller and Auditor General are to be laid down by the President by rules framed after consultation with the Comptroller and Auditor General. His salary and conditions of service cannot be changed to his disadvantage during his term of office except under a financial emergency. His salary and the administrative expenses of the office of the Comptroller and Auditor General are to be charged upon the Consolidated Fund of India, and are not subject to the vote of the Parliament.

Powers and Functions of CAG

The powers and functions of the CAG has been laid down in the **CAG's Duties, Power and Conditions of Service Act, 1971. Chapter III relates to the Duties and powers of the CAG**. They can be summed up as:

1. Comptroller and Auditor-General to compile accounts of Union and States.
   (a) The Comptroller and Auditor-General shall be responsible—
      (i) for compiling the accounts of the Union and of each State from the initial and subsidiary account rendered to the audit

and accounts offices under his control by treasuries, offices or departments responsible for the keeping of such accounts; and

(ii) for keeping such accounts in relation to any of the matters specified above as may be necessary.

2. The Comptroller and Auditor-General prepares the report.

   (a) The CAG shall from the accounts compiled by him or by the Government or any other person responsible in that behalf prepare in each year accounts (including, in the case of accounts compiled by him, appropriation accounts) showing under the respective heads the annual receipts and disbursements for the purpose of the Union, of each State and of each Union territory having a Legislative Assembly, and shall submit those accounts to the President or the Governor of a State or Administrator of the Union territory having a Legislative Assembly, as the case may be on or before such dates as he may, with the concurrence of the Government concerned.

3. Comptroller and Auditor-General to give information and render assistance to the Union and States.

   (a) The Comptroller and Auditor-General shall, in so far as the accounts, for the compilation or keeping of which he is responsible, enable him so to do, give to the Union government, to the State Governments or to the Governments of Union Territories having Legislative Assemblies, as the case may be, such information as they may, from time to time, require, and render such assistance in the preparation of their annual financial statements as they may reasonably ask for General Provisions Relating to Audit.

4. CAG shall audit all expenditure from the Consolidated Fund of India.

   (a) It shall be the duty of the Comptroller and Auditor-General:

      (i) to audit all expenditure from the Consolidated Fund of India and of each State and of each Union territory having a Legislative Assembly and to ascertain whether the moneys shown in the accounts as having been disbursed were legally available for and applicable to the service or purpose to which they have been applied or charged and whether the expenditure conforms to the authority which governs it;

      (ii) to audit all transactions of the Union and of the States relating to Contingency Funds and Public Accounts;

      (iii) to audit all trading, manufacturing, profit and loss accounts and balance-sheets and other subsidiary accounts kept in any department of the Union or of a State; and in each case to report on the expenditure, transactions or accounts so audited by him. Audit of receipts and expenditure of bodies or authorities substantially financed from Union or State Revenues

(b) Where any body or authority is substantially financed by grants or loans from the Consolidated Fund of India or of any State or of any Union territory having a Legislative Assembly, the Comptroller and Auditor-General shall, subject to the provisions of any law for the time being in, force applicable to the body or authority, as the case may be, audit all receipts and expenditure of that body or authority and to report on the receipts and expenditure audited by him.

(c) The Comptroller and Auditor-General may with the previous approval of the President or the Governor of a State or the Administrator of a Union territory having a Legislative Assembly, as the case may be, audit all receipts and expenditure of any body or authority where the grants or loans to such body or authority from the Consolidated Fund of India or of any State or of any Union territory having a Legislative Assembly, as the case may be in a financial year is not less than INR one crore.

(d) It shall be the duty of the Comptroller and Auditor-General to audit all receipts which are payable into the Consolidated Fund of India and of each State and of each Union territory having a Legislative Assembly, and to satisfy himself that the rules and procedures in that behalf are designed to secure an effective check on the assessment, collection and proper allocation of revenue and are being duly observed and to make for this purpose such examination of the accounts as he thinks fit and report thereon.

5. Audit of accounts of stores and stock.

(a) The Comptroller and Auditor-General shall have authority to audit and report on the accounts of stores and stock kept in any office or department of the Union or of a State.

(b) The Comptroller and Auditor-General shall in connection with the performance of his duties under the Act of 1971, have authority—

(i) to inspect any office of accounts under the control of the union or of a State, including treasuries, and such offices responsible for the keeping of initial or subsidiary accounts, as submit accounts to him;

(ii) to require that any accounts, books, papers and other documents which deal with or form the basis of or an otherwise relevant to the transactions to which his duties in respect of audit extend, shall be sent to such place as he may appoint for his inspection;

(iii) to put such questions or make such observations as he may consider necessary, to the person in charge of the office and to call for such information as he may require for the preparation of any account or report which it is his duty to prepare. The person who is in charge of any office or department, the accounts of which have to be inspected and audited by the

Comptroller and Auditor-General, shall afford all facilities for such inspection and comply with requests for information in as complete a form as possible and with all reasonable expedition.

6. Audit of Government companies and corporations.
   (a) The duties and powers of the Comptroller and Auditor-General in relation to the audit of the accounts of Government companies shall be performed and exercised by him in accordance with the provisions of the Companies Act, 1956 (1 of 1956) and audit of the accounts of corporations (not being companies) established by or under law made by Parliament shall be performed and exercised by him in accordance with the provisions of the respective legislations.
   (b) The Governor of a State or the Administrator of a Union territory having a Legislative Assembly may, where he is of opinion that it is necessary in the public interest so to do, request the Comptroller and Auditor-General to audit the accounts of a corporation established by law made by the Legislature of the State or of the Union territory, as the case may be, and where such request has been made, the Comptroller and Auditor-General shall audit the accounts of such corporation and shall have, for the purposes of such audit, right of access to the books and accounts of such corporation.
   (c) Laying of reports in relation to accounts of Government companies and corporation. The reports of the Comptroller and Auditor-General, in relation to audit of accounts of a Government company or a corporation referred to in Section 19, shall be submitted to the Government or Governments concerned. The Central Government shall cause every report received by it under sub-section to be laid, as soon as may be after it is received, before each House of Parliament. The State Government shall cause every report received by it under sub-section to be laid, as soon as may be after it is received, before the Legislature of the State.
7. The Comptroller and Auditor-General may propose to the President or the Governor of a State or the Administrator of a Union territory having a Legislative Assembly, as the case may be, that he may authorized to undertake the audit of accounts of any body or authority, the audit of the account of which has not been entrusted to him by law, if he is of opinion that such audit is necessary, because a substantial amount has been invested in, or advanced to, such body or authority by the Central or State Government or by the Government of a Union territory having a Legislative Assembly, and on such request being made, the President or the Governor or, the Administrator, as the case may be, may empower the Comptroller and Auditor-General to undertake the audit of the accounts of such body or authority.

Miscellaneous Powers and Duties

Chapter IV of the 1971 Act deals with the miscellaneous powers and duties of the CAG. They can be summed up as:

1. Delegation of Power of Comptroller and Auditor-General.
   Any power exercisable by the Comptroller and Auditor-General under the provisions of this Act, or any other law may be exercised by such officer of his department as may be authorized by him in this behalf by general or special order. Provided that except during the absence of the Comptroller and Auditor-General on leave or otherwise, no officer shall be authorized to submit on behalf of the Comptroller and Auditor-General any report which the Comptroller and Auditor-General is required by the Constitution or the Government of Union Territories Act, 1963 (20 of 1963) to submit to the President or the Governor of a State or the Administrator of a Union territory having a Legislative Assembly, as the case may be.
2. Power to Make Rules.
   (a) The Central Government may, after consultation with the Comptroller and Auditor-General, by notification in the official Gazette, make rules for carrying out the provisions of this Act in so far as they relate to the maintenance of accounts.
   (b) Such rules may provide for all or any of the following matters, namely:
      (i) the manner in which initial and subsidiary accounts shall be kept by the treasuries, offices and departments rendering accounts to audit and accounts offices;
      (ii) the manner in which the accounts of the Union or of a State or of any particular service or department or of any particular class or character, in respect of which the Comptroller and Auditor-General has been relieved from the responsibility of compiling or keeping the accounts, shall be compiled or kept;
      (iii) the manner in which the accounts of stores and stock shall be kept in any office or department of the Union or of a State, as the case may be;
      (iv) any other matter which is required to be or maybe, prescribed by rules
   (c) Every rule made under this section shall be laid, as soon as may be after it is made, before each House of Parliament, while it is in session, for a total period of thirty days which may be comprised in one Session or in two or more successive sessions, and if, before the expiry of the session immediately following the session or the successive sessions aforesaid both Houses agree in making any modification in the rule or both Houses agree that the rules should not be made, the rule shall thereafter have effect only in such

modified form or be of no effect, as the case may be; so, however, that any such modification or annulment shall be without prejudice to the validity of anything previously done under that rule.

3. Power to make regulations.
   (a) The Comptroller and Auditor-General is authorized to make regulations for carrying into effect the provisions of this Act in so far as they related to the scope and extent of audit, including laying down for the guidance of the Government Departments the general principles of Government accounting and the broad principles in regard to audit of receipts and expenditure.
4. Power to dispense with detailed audit.
   (a) The Comptroller and Auditor-General is authorized to dispense with, when circumstances so warrant, any part of detailed audit of any accounts or class of transactions and to apply such limited check in relation to such accounts or transactions as he may determine.

At the apex of the Indian Audit and Accounts Department is the office of the Comptroller and Auditor General which directs, monitors and controls all activities connected with audit, accounts and entitlement functions of the Department. There are separate divisions dealing with Accounts and Entitlements, Civil Audit, Railway Audit, Commercial Audit, Revenue Audit, Administration of Cadres, Training, Organization and Methods, Inspection of field offices, EDP and others. These divisions are headed by the Deputy/ Additional Deputy Comptroller and Auditor-General and Principal Directors.

Table 22.1 shows the list of Comptroller and Auditor-General of India.

Table 22.1 List of Comptroller and Auditor-Generals of India

Comptroller and Auditor General of India	*Tenure began from year*	*Tenure ended in year*
V. Narahari Rao	1948	1954
A.K. Chanda	1954	1960
Shilpa Jindal	1960	1966
S. Ranganathan	1966	1972
A. Bakshi	1972	1978
Gian Prakash	1978	1984
T.N. Chaturvedi	1984	1990
C.G. Somiah	1990	1996
V.K. Shunglu	1996	2002
V.N. Kaul	2002	2008
Vinod Rai	2008	2013
Shashi Kant Sharma	2013	2017
Rajiv Mehrishi	2017	2020
Girish Chandra Murmu	2020	present

There is also an International Relations Division which is the external affairs division of the CAG of India and is known as International Organization of Supreme Audit Institutions (INTOSAI). This division is the focal point for bilateral and multilateral interaction of the CAG with the Global audit fraternity. It deals with the following:

1. All matters related to International Organization of Supreme Audit Institutions (INTOSAI).
2. All matters related to Asian Organization of Supreme Audit Institutions (ASOSAI)
3. Matters related to the Global Working Group (GWG) and maintenance of the interactive website of the GWG.
4. External Audits of UN bodies and other International Organizations.
5. Bilateral Relations with other SAIs, including signing and follow up on MoUs
6. Interaction with other Supreme Audit Institutions and other Regional groups of INTOSAI.
7. Organizing seminars, meetings and workshops of international level.
8. Matters related to the Panel of External Auditors of the United Nations, its specilaized Agencies and International Atomic Energy Agency.

The Comptroller and Auditor General of India conducts different kinds of audit like Financial Audit, Compliance Audit, Performance Audit and EDP Audit. Further, the CAG undertakes Special Audit at the request of the Government. Thus, it can be seen how the CAG enhances the accountability of the Parliament and State Legislatures of India by carrying out audits in the public sector organizations. The CAG also has earned the honour of doing audit for the UN bodies and other international organizations. The CAG has been appointed as the external auditor of two major UN organizations—the International Atomic Energy Agency (IAEA), Vienna and World Intellectual Property Organization (WIPO), Geneva in 2011.

The unveiling of number of scams, the role of the CAG has come into focus. The CAG, in a number of cases like in the Adarsh Scam accused the state machinery of overlooking subversion of rules and regulations by the society and granting unreasonable concessions. In another case the CAG had pulled up the defence ministry for its imprudent decision to acquire forest land worth ₹73.26 crore in Faridabad to set up a centre for Defence Research and Development Organization (DRDO). The CAG also named large companies such as HCL Infosystems, state-owned Telco MTNL, US-based networking giant Cisco Systems, and digital media firm Hungama as colluding with the Organising Committee of the Commonwealth Games and causing a combined loss of ₹500 crore to exchequer in the Commonwealth Games Scam. The CAG has severely indicted former ISRO chief G. Madhavan Nair and senior officials of Indian Space Research Organisation (ISRO) and Antrix Corporation for their role in the S-band deal with Devas Multimedia. Thus, the CAG is like a watchdog which keeps a tab on the Government expenditure and exposes the irregularities wherever they occur.

THE ATTORNEY-GENERAL

The Attorney-General for India is the highest legal advisor of the Government of India, and its primary lawyer in the Supreme Court of India. The Attorney General has the right to participate in the proceedings of the Parliament, though not to vote. He does not have executive authority and is not a government minister and his functions are performed by the Law Minister of India. He has the right to speak and take part in the proceedings of either House and to be a member of any Parliamentary Committee, but is not entitled to vote. The Attorney-General is assisted by the Solicitor-General of India and several additional solicitors general and four Additional Solicitor-General. Table 22.2 lists Attorney-Generals of India from 1950 to the present.
Article 76 enumerates:

1. The President shall appoint a person who is qualified to be appointed a Judge of the Supreme Court to be Attorney-General of India.
2. It shall be the duty of the Attorney-General to give advice to the Government of India upon such legal matters, and to perform such other duties of a legal character, as may from time-to-time be referred or assigned to him by the President, and to discharge the functions conferred on him by or under this Constitution or any other law for the time being in force.
3. In the performance of his duties the Attorney-General shall have right of audience in all courts in the territory of India.
4. The Attorney-General shall hold office during the pleasure of the President, and shall receive such remuneration as the President may determine.

The Attorney-General of India, thus is appointed by the President of India under Article 76(1) of the Constitution of India, and holds office during the pleasure of the President. The President will appoint a person who is qualified to be appointed a judge of the Supreme Court as the Attorney-General of India. The duty of the Attorney-General is to advise the President on such legal matters and perform such other duties of legal character, as may from time-to-time be referred or assigned to him by the President. He has the right of audience in all courts in the territory of India. The Attorney-General is the highest legal officer of the Union Government who is appointed by the President, but unlike the practice in England where the Attorney-General is a member of the Cabinet, in India he is not.

The role of the Attorney-General can be summed up as:

1. giving advice to the Government of India upon such legal matters and to perform such other duties of legal character as may be referred or assigned to him/her by the President.
2. having the right of audience in all Courts in India as well as the right to participate in the proceedings of the Parliament, though not to vote.
3. appearing on behalf of Government of India in all cases (including suits, appeals and other proceedings) in the Supreme Court in which Government of India is concerned.
4. representing the Government of India in any reference made by the President to the Supreme Court under Article 143 of the Constitution.

The Attorney-General is to be consulted only in legal matters of real importance and only after the Ministry of Law has been consulted. All references to the Attorney-General are made by the Ministry of Law. The Attorney-General can accept briefs but cannot appear against the Government. The Attorney-General cannot defend an accused in the criminal proceedings and accept the directorship of a company without the permission of the Government.

The Attorney-General represents the government, but is allowed to take up private practice provided the other party is not the state. Because of this he is not paid salary, but a retainer to be determined by the President. The Attorney-General gets a retainer equivalent to the salary of a judge of a Supreme Court. However, there are allegations that the appointment of the Attorney-General is almost every time a political appointment dictated by the will of the ruling Government. The current Attorney-General is R. Venkataramani, who assumed the office from 01.10.2022.

Table 22.2 List of Attorney-Generals of India

Attorney-Generals	*Term*	*Incumbent Prime Minister*
M.C. Setalvad	28.01.1950–01.03.1963	Jawaharlal Nehru
C.K. Daphtary	02.03.1963–30.10.1968	Jawaharlal Nehru
Niren De	01.11.1968–31.03.1977	Indira Gandhi
S.V. Gupte	01.04.1977–08.08.1979	Morarji Desai
L.N. Sinha	09.08.1979–08.08.1983	Indira Gandhi
K. Parasaran	09.08.1983–08.12.1989	Indira Gandhi; Rajiv Gandhi
Soli Sorabjee	09.12.1989–02.12.1990	V.P. Singh; Chandra Shekhar G.
Ramaswamy	03.12.1990–23.11.1992	Chandra Shekhar G.; P.V. Narasimha Rao
Milon K. Banerji	21.11.1992–08.07.1996	P.V. Narasimha Rao
Ashok Desai	09.07.1996–06.04.1998	H.D. Deve Gowda; Inder Kumar Gujral
Soli Sorabjee	07.04.1998–04.06.2004	Atal Bihari Vajpayee
Milon K. Banerji	05.06.2004–07.06.2009	Manmohan Singh
Goolam Essaji Vahanvati	08.06.2009–11.06.2014	Manmohan Singh
Mukul Rohatgi	19.06.2014–18.06.2017	Narendra Modi
K.K. Venugopal	01.07.2017–30.09.2022	Narendra Modi
R. Venkataramani	01.10.2022–incumbent	Narendra Modi

THE CENTRAL VIGILANCE COMMISSION

On the recommendations of the Committee on Prevention of Corruption, headed by Shri K. Santhanam, to advise and guide Central Government agencies in the field of vigilance, the Central Vigilance Commission (CVC) was set up by the Government of India in February, 1964. With the promulgation of an Ordinance by the President, the Central Vigilance Commission has been made a multi-member Commission with **Statutory Status**, with effect from 25 August 1998. The CVC Bill was passed by both the Houses of Parliament in 2003 and the President gave his assent on 11 September 2003. Thus, the Central Vigilance Commission Act 2003 (No. 45 of 2003) came into effect from that date. Nittoor Srinivasa Rau became the first Chief Vigilance Commissioner of India.

CVC is conceived to be the apex vigilance institution, free of control from any executive authority, monitoring all vigilance activity under the Central Government, and advising various authorities in Central Government organizations in planning, executing, reviewing and reforming their vigilance work.

Composition of the Commission

The Commission shall consist of

- a Central Vigilance Commissioner—Chairperson; and
- not more than 2 Vigilance Commissioners—Members

The Central Vigilance Commission has its own Secretariat. The Secretariat consists of a Secretary of the rank of Additional Secretary to the GOI, one officer of the rank of Joint Secretary to the GOI, ten officers of the rank of Director/Deputy Secretary, 4 under Secretaries and office staff.

Chief Vigilance Officers assist in the discharge of the functions of the CVC. The Chief Vigilance Officers are considerably higher level officers who are appointed in each and every Department/Organization to assist the Head of the Department/Organization in all vigilance matters. The Chief Vigilance Officers constitute an important link between the organizations concerned and the Central Vigilance Commission, as also the CBI. **Chief Technical Examiners' Writing Wing (CTE)** constitutes the technical wing of the Central Vigilance Commission (India) and is manned by 2 Engineers of the rank of Chief Engineers (designated as Chief Technical Examiners) with supporting engineering staff. There is also a wing of **Commissioners for Department of Inquiries (CDI)**.

In the absence or death or resignation tendered by the Central Vigilance Commissioner, one of the Vigilance Commissioners shall act as the Central Vigilance Commissioner until the appointment of a new Vigilance Commissioner.

Powers and Functions of CVC

The Central Vigilance Commission is not an investigating agency. The only investigation conducted by the CVC is that of examining Civil Works of the Government which is carried on by the Chief Technical Officer. The CVC conducts its investigations through the CBI or through the Departmental Chief Vigilance Officers. The main purposes of this organization are–

1. Technical audit of construction works of Governmental organizations from a vigilance perspective;
2. Investigation of specific cases of complaints relating to construction works;
3. Extension of assistance to CBI in their investigations involving technical matters and for evaluation of properties in Delhi; and
4. Tendering of advice and assistance to the Commission and Chief Vigilance Officers in vigilance cases involving technical matters.

The CVC enjoys a wide array of powers which can be summed up as:

1. On the basis of the Government of India (GOI) Resolution on Public Interest Disclosure and Protection of Informer, dated April 2004, the Government of India has authorized the Central Vigilance Commission as the Designated Agency to receive written complaints for disclosure on any allegation of corruption or misuse of office and recommend appropriate action.
2. To exercise superintendence over the functioning of the Delhi Special Police Establishment (DSPE) with respect to investigation under the Prevention of Corruption Act, 1988; or offence under CRPC for certain categories of public servants and to give directions to the DSPE for purpose of discharging this responsibility;
   (a) To review the progress of investigations conducted by the DSPE into offences alleged to have been committed under the Prevention of Corruption Act;
   (b) To undertake an inquiry or cause an inquiry or investigation to be made into any transaction in which a public servant working in any organisation, to which the executive control of the Government of India extends, is suspected or alleged to have acted for an improper purpose or in a corrupt manner;
   (c) To tender independent and impartial advice to the disciplinary and other authorities in disciplinary cases, involving vigilance angle at different stages i.e. investigation, inquiry, appeal, review etc.;
   (d) To exercise a general check and supervision over vigilance and anti-corruption work in Ministries or Departments of the Government of India and other organizations to which the executive power of the Union extends; and

(e) To chair the Committee for selection of Director (CBI), Director (Enforcement Directorate) and officers of the level of SP and above in DSPE.

3. To undertake or cause an inquiry into complaints received under the Public Interest Disclosure and Protection of Informer and recommend appropriate action.

The Commission while conducting any inquiry has the power of a civil court and may (i) summon and enforce attendance of any person from any part of India and examine him on oath (ii) require the discovery and production of any document (iii) receive evidence on affidavits and (iv) require any public record or copy thereof from court or office.

Annual Report

The CVC submits annual report in which it gives an account of work done by it and also highlights the failures in the system under its jurisdiction like in various departments or organizations which resulted in corruption. It also prescribes preventive measures to control such irregularities.

Jurisdiction under CVC Act

1. Members of All India Services serving in connection with the affairs of the Union and Group A officers of the Central Government.
2. Board level appointees and other senior officers upto two grades below the Board level, in the Public Sector Undertakings of the Central Government;
3. Officers of the rank of Scale V and above in the Public Sector Banks;
4. Officers of the rank of Assistant Manager and above in the Insurance Sector (covered by LIC and GIC and four non-life insurance companies in the Public sector); and
5. Officers drawing basic pay of ₹8700 per month and above in autonomous bodies/local authorities or societies owned or controlled by the Central Government.

NATIONAL HUMAN RIGHTS COMMISSION (NHRC)

The two Covenants, namely, the International Convention on Economic, Social and Cultural Rights (ICESCR) and International Convention on Civil and Political Rights (ICCPR) in the year 1966, followed the Universal Declaration of Human Rights. The Universal Declaration of Human Rights was adopted by the General Assembly of India on 10 December 1948. These provide international standards for states to create their domestic human rights laws keeping in mind these standards. India a signatory to various human rights convention and itself has adopted a number of human rights laws/Acts. One such law is the Protection of Human Rights Act, 1993. Under this Act, India has constituted the National Human Rights Commission in 1993.

The **National Human Rights Commission** was constituted on 12 October 1993, under the mandatory legislation of the Protection of Human Rights Act, 1993. One of the chief objectives of the **National Human Rights Commission** in India, as outlined in the **Protection of Human Rights Act, 1993,** is to promote as well as protect the human rights of the citizens of India. National Human Rights Commission is an expression of India's concern for the protection and promotion of human rights.

Composition

As per Section 3 of the Act, the Commission shall consist of five members, three of whom should be from the judiciary and two "from amongst persons having knowledge of, or practical experience in, matters relating to human rights." The particular section reads as:

The Commission shall consist of:

1. a Chairperson who has been a Chief Justice of the Supreme Court;
2. one Member who is or has been, a Judge of the Supreme Court;
3. one Member who is, or has been the Chief Justice of a High Court;
4. two Members to be appointed from amongst persons having knowledge of, or practical experience in, matters relating to human rights.
5. The Chairperson of the National Commission for Minorities [the National Commission for the Scheduled Castes, the National Commission for the Scheduled Tribes] and the National Commission for Women shall be deemed to be Members of the Commission for the discharge of functions' specified in Section 12.

Section 4 of the Act provides the procedure for the appointment of the Chairperson. Selection of Chairperson of the Commission and members of the Commission is made on the recommendations of a committee consisting of the Prime Minister, Home Minister, Speaker and leader of the opposition in the House of the People and Deputy Chairman and leader of opposition in the Council of States.

No sitting Judge of the Supreme Court or sitting Chief Justice of a High Court shall be appointed except after consultation with the Chief Justice of India.

According to Section 11 of the Act, the Central Government shall make available to the Commission officers and other staff required for research, investigation, technical and administrative work.

Resignation and Removal of Chairperson and Members

Section 5 deals with the provisions regarding resignation and removal of the Chairperson and other members. The Chairperson or any member may, by notice in writing under his hand addressed to the President of India, resign his office. The Chairperson or any Member shall only be removed from his office by order of the President of India on the ground of proved misbehaviour or incapacity after the Supreme Court, on reference being made to it by the President, has, on Inquiry held in accordance with the procedure prescribed in that behalf by the Supreme Court, reported that the Chairperson or the Member, as the case may be, ought on any 'such' ground to be removed.

The President may, by order, remove from office the Chairperson or any Member if the Chairperson or such Member, as the case may be–

1. is adjudged an insolvent or
2. engages during his term of office in any paid employment outside the duties of his office;
3. or is unfit to continue in office by reason of infirmity of mind or body; or
4. is of unsound mind and stands so declared by a competent court;
5. or is convicted and sentenced to imprisonment for an offence which in the opinion of the President involves moral turpitude.

Tenure

According to Section 6 of the 1993 Act the term of office of Chairperson and the Members are:

1. A person appointed as Chairperson shall hold office for a term of five years from the date on which he enters upon his office or until he attains the age of seventy years, whichever is earlier.
2. A person appointed as a Member shall hold office for a term of five years from the date on which he enters upon his office and shall be eligible for re-appointment for another term of five years.

   Provided that no Member shall hold office after he has attained the age of seventy years.
3. On ceasing to hold office, a Chairperson or a Member shall be ineligible for further employment under the Government of India or under the Government of any State.

In the event of the occurrence of any vacancy in the office of the Chairperson by reason of his death, resignation or otherwise, the President may, by notification, authorize one of the Members to act as the Chairperson until the appointment of a new Chairperson to fill such vacancy. When the

Chairperson is unable to discharge his functions owing to absence on leave or otherwise, such one of the Members as the President may, by notification, authorize in this behalf, shall discharge the functions of the Chairperson until the date on which the Chairperson resumes his duties.

Independence and Resources

The autonomy of the Commission derives, inter alia, from the method of appointing its Chairperson and Members, their fixity of tenure, and statutory guarantees thereto, the status they have been accorded and the manner in which the staff responsible to the Commission—including its investigative agency—are appointed and conduct themselves. The financial autonomy of the Commission is spelt out in Section 32 of the Act. The Commission is supposed to be completely independent in its functioning, even though the Act does not say so. In fact, there are provisions in the Act which underscore the dependence of the Commission on the Government. As already stated, Section 11 of the Act makes it dependent on the government for its manpower requirements. According to Section 32 of the Act, the Central Government shall pay to the Commission by way of grants such sums of money as it may consider fit.

Investigation

The Act does not authorize the commission to enquire into complaints of violations of human rights committed by the members of the armed forces. "Armed Forces", as defined in Section 2(1)(a) of the Act, means not only the naval, military and air forces but also the central para-military forces. Since a very large number of complaints of human rights violations are directed against the members of the "armed forces", the Act obviously weakens the NHRC's effectiveness in providing redress to the public in such cases. The Commission, can under Section 19 of the Act do is to call for reports from the Central Government in such cases and then make recommendations to the Government or not "proceed with the complaint" at all. Under the Act, the Commission has no power to enforce its decisions. According to Section 18 of the Act, where the enquiry conducted by the Commission discloses violation of human rights, it can only advise the government to take action against guilty persons or grant relief to the victim. If any Government refuses to accept the advice, there is no provision in law which empowers the Commission to force the Government to implement its advice.

Functions of National Human Rights Commission

The Commission performs all or any of the following functions under the Human Rights Act, 1993. They are:

1. Inquire, on its initiative or on a petition presented to it by a victim or any person on his behalf, into complaint of—
   (a) Violation of human rights or abetment or
   (b) negligence in the prevention of such violation, by a public servant;
2. Intervene in any proceeding involving any allegation of violation of human rights pending before a court with the approval of such court;
3. Visit, under intimation to the State Government, any jail or any other institution under the control of the State Government, where persons are detained or lodged for purposes of treatment, reformation or protection to study the living condition of the inmates and make recommendations thereon.
4. Review the safeguards by or under the Constitution or any law for the time being in force for the protection of human rights and recommend measures for their effective implementation;
5. Review the factors, including acts of terrorism that inhibit the enjoyment of human rights and recommend appropriate remedial measures;
6. Study treaties and other international instruments on human rights and make recommendations for their effective implementation;
7. Undertake and promote research in the field of human rights;
8. Spread human rights literacy among various sections of society and promote awareness of the safeguards available for the protection of these rights through publications, the media, seminars and other available means;
9. encourage the efforts of non-Governmental organisations and institutions working in the field of human rights;
10. Such other functions as it may consider necessary for the promotion of human rights.

Powers Relating to Inquiries

Section 13 provides that while inquiring into complaints under the Act, the Commission shall have all the powers of a civil court trying a suit under the Code of Civil Procedure, 1908, and in particular the following, namely;

1. Summoning and enforcing the attendance of witnesses and examining them on oath;
2. Discovery and production of any document;
3. Receiving evidence on affidavits;
4. Requisitioning any public record or copy thereof from any court or office;
5. Issuing commissions for the examination of witnesses or documents;
6. Any other matter which may be prescribed.

Annual and Special Reports of the Commission

Under Section 20, the Commission shall submit an annual report to the Central Government and to the State Government concerned and may at any time submit special reports on any matter which, in its opinion, is of such urgency or importance that it should not be deferred till submission of the annual report. The Central Government and the State Government, as the case may be, shall cause the annual and special reports of the Commission to be laid before each House of Parliament or the State Legislature respectively, as the case maybe, along with a memorandum of action taken or proposed to be taken on the recommendations of the Commission and the reasons for non-acceptance of the recommendations, if any.

Assessment

The NHRC is a statutory body and the Commission's purview covers the entire range of civil and political, as well as economic, social and cultural rights. Custodial death, rape and torture, reform of the police, prisons, and other institutions such as juvenile homes, mental hospitals and shelters for women, child welfare, prevention of atrocities against Scheduled Castes and Scheduled Tribes, death by starvation, rights of the child, rights of women subjected to violence, sexual harassment and discrimination, and rights of minorities have been given special attention. The Commission works towards dissemination of information and awareness on human rights issues through it publication of priced and non-priced, on variety of subjects related to human rights like *Know Your Rights* and others.

There are some arguments against the way the NHRC is constituted. Usually appointment are made of persons belonging to judiciary with complete absence of representatives from civil society and the appointments are sometimes not free of political choices. Yet, it cannot be doubted that the NHRC has contributed to the protection and upliftment of human rights in India.

Seat of the Commission

The Commission is headquartered at Faridkot House, Copernicus Marg, New Delhi.

STATE HUMAN RIGHTS COMMISSION (SHRC)

Under the Protection of Human Rights Act, 1993, there are provisions relating to the constitution of a State Human Rights Commission in all States by the respective State Governments. Sections 21–29 deal elaborately with the composition, powers and functions of State Human Rights Commission.

Composition

The State Commission shall, with effect from the date as the State Government may by notification specify consist of five members. They are:

1. Chairperson who has been a Chief Justice of a High Court;
2. one Member who is, or has been, a Judge of a High Court or District Judge in the State with a minimum of seven years experience as District Judge;
3. two Members to be appointed from amongst persons having knowledge of, or practical experience in, matters relating to human rights.

Further, there shall be a Secretary who shall be the Chief Executive Officer of the State Commission and shall exercise such powers and discharge such functions of the State Commission as it may delegate to him.

Appointment of the Chairperson and Members of SHRC

The Chairperson and the other Members shall be appointed by the Governor by warrant under his hand and seal, provided that every appointment under this sub-section shall be made after obtaining the recommendation of a Committee consisting of the Chief Minister who should be the Chairperson, Speaker of the Legislative Assembly, Minister in-charge of the Department of Home, in that State, Leader of the Opposition in the Legislative Assembly. No sitting Judge of a High Court or a sitting District Judge shall be appointed except after consultation with the Chief Justice of the High Court of the concerned State.

Tenure

A person appointed as a Chairperson shall hold office for a term of five years from the date on which he enters upon his office or until he attains the age of seventy years, whichever is earlier. A person appointed as a Member shall hold office for a term of five years from the date on which he enters upon his office and shall be eligible for re-appointment for another term of five years provided that no Member shall hold office after he has attained the age of seventy years.

Removal and Resignation

The Chairperson or a Member of a State Commission may by notice in writing under his hand addressed to the Governor, resign his office. The Chairperson or any Member of the State Commission shall only be removed from his office by order of the President on the ground of proved misbehaviour or incapacity after the Supreme Court, on a reference being made to it by the President, has, on inquiry held in accordance with the procedure prescribed in that behalf by the Supreme Court, reported that the Chairperson or such Member, as the case maybe ought on any such ground to be removed.

The President may, by order remove from office, the Chairperson or any Member if the Chairperson or such Members, as the case maybe:

1. is adjudged an insolvent;
2. or engages during his term of office in any paid employment outside the duties of his office; or
3. is unfit to continue in office by reason of infirmity of mind or body; or
4. is of unsound mind and stand so declared by a competent court; or
5. is convicted and sentenced to imprisonment for an offence which in the opinion of the President involves moral turpitude.

Salaries and Terms of Service

The salaries and allowances payable to, and other terms and conditions of service of, the Chairperson and Members shall be such as may be prescribed by the State Government provided that neither the salary and allowances nor the other terms and conditions of service of the Chairperson or a Member shall be varied to his disadvantage after his appointment.

Staff of SHRC

The State Government shall make available to the Commission an officer not below the rank of a Secretary to the State Government who shall be the Secretary of the State Commission; and such police and investigative staff under an officer not below the rank of an Inspector General of Police, and such other officers and staff as may be necessary for the efficient performance of the functions of the State Commission.

Subject to such rules as may be made by the State Government in this behalf, the State Commission may appoint such other administrative, technical and scientific staff as it may consider necessary. The salaries, allowances and conditions of service of the officers and other staff appointed may be prescribed by the State Government.

Powers and Functions of State Human Rights Commission

A State Commission may inquire into violation of human rights only in respect of matters relatable to any of the entries enumerated in List II and List III in the Seventh Schedule to the Constitution.

Annual and Special Reports of the Commission

The State Commission shall submit an annual report to the State Government, and may at any time, submit special reports on any matter which, in its opinion, is of such urgency or importance that it should not be deferred till submission of the annual report.

The State Government shall cause the annual and special reports of the State Commission to be laid before each House of State Legislature where it consists of two Houses, or where such Legislature consists of one House, before that House along with a memorandum of action taken or proposed to be taken on the recommendations of the State Commission and the reasons for non-acceptance of the recommendations, if any.

Seat of the Commission

The headquarters of the State Commission shall be at such place as the State Government may, by notification, specify.

NATIONAL COMMISSION FOR WOMEN (NCW)

The National Commission for Women (NCW) was set up as statutory body in January 1992 under the National Commission for Women Act, 1990 (NCW Act No. 20 of 1990 of Government of India). The NCW was set up with the prime objective to:

1. review the Constitutional and Legal safeguards for women;
2. recommend remedial legislative measures;
3. facilitate redressal of grievances and
4. advise the Government on all policy matters affecting women.

The Committee on the Status of Women in India (CSWI) recommended nearly two decades ago, the setting up of a National Commission for women to fulfill the surveillance functions to facilitate redressal of grievances and to accelerate the socio-economic development of women. Since then, there have been several efforts in establishing a full-fledged body addressing the women's issues. Successive Committees/Commissions/Plans including the National Perspective Plan for Women (1988–2000) recommended the constitution of an apex body for women. During 1990, the Central Government held consultations with NGOs, social workers and experts, regarding the structure, functions, powers of the Commission proposed to be set up. Landmark was reached when in May 1990, the Bill was introduced in the Lok Sabha. In July 1990, the HRD Ministry organized a National Level Conference to elicit suggestions regarding the Bill. In August 1990, the government moved several amendments and introduced new provisions to vest the commission with the power of a civil court. The Bill was passed and received accent of the President on 30th August 1990.

The First Commission was constituted on 31st January 1992 with Mrs. Jayanti Patnaik as the Chairperson. The Second Commission was constituted in July 1995 with Dr. (Mrs.) Mohini Giri as the Chairperson. The Third Commission was constituted on January 1999 with Mrs. Vibha Parthasarathy as the Chairperson. The Fourth Commission was constituted in January 2002 and the government had nominated Dr. Poornima Advani as the Chairperson. The Fifth Commission has been constituted on February 2005 and the government nominated Dr. Girija Vyas as the Chairperson. After her, Smt. Mamta Sharma took over the charge as the Chairperson of the National Commission for Women from 2nd August 2011. She was succeeded by Smt. Lalitha Kumaramangalam who assumed office from 29 September, 2014. Currently Smt. Rekha Sharma is the Chairperson and she assumed office from 8 August, 2018. A monthly newsletter, titled *Rashtra Mahila*, is also published regularly in English and Hindi.

Composition

According to the National Commission for Women Act, 1990, the Commission shall consist of:

1. a Chairperson, committed to the cause of women, to be nominated by the Central Government.
2. five Members to be nominated by the Central Government from amongst persons of ability, integrity and standing who have had experience in law or legislation, trade unionism, management of an industry potential of women, women's voluntary organisations (including women activist), administration, economic development, health, education or social welfare; Provided that at least one Member each shall be from amongst the people belonging to the Scheduled Castes and Scheduled Tribes,
3. a Member-Secretary to be nominated by the Central Government who shall be:
   (a) an expert in the field of management, organisational structure or sociological movement, or
   (b) an officer who is a member of a civil service of the Union or of an all-India service or holds a civil post under the Union with appropriate experience

Mandate of the Commission

1. The commission shall perform all or any of the following functions, namely:

(a) Investigate and examine all matters relating to the safeguards provided for women under the Constitution and other laws;
(b) present to the Central Government, annually and at such other times as the Commission may deem fit, reports on the working of those safeguard;
(c) make in such reports recommendations for the effective implementation of those safeguards for the improving the conditions of women by the Union or any state;
(d) review, from time-to-time, the exiting provisions of the Constitution and other laws affecting women and recommend amendments thereto so as to suggest remedial legislative measures to meet any lacunae, inadequacies or shortcomings in such legislations;
(e) take up cases of violation of the provisions of the Constitution and of other laws relating to women with the appropriate authorities;
(f) look into complaints and take suo moto notice of matters relating to:
   (i) deprivation of women's rights;
   (ii) non-implementation of laws enacted to provide protection to women and also to achieve the objective of equality and development;
   (iii) non-compliance of policy decisions, guidelines or instructions aimed at mitigating hardships and ensuring welfare and providing relief to women, and take up the issues arising out of such matters with appropriate authorities;
(g) call for special studies or investigations into specific problems or situations arising out of discrimination and atrocities against women and identify the constraints so as to recommend strategies for their removal;
(h) undertake promotional and educational research so as to suggest ways of ensuring due representation of women in all spheres and identify factors responsible for impeding their advancement, such as, lack of access to housing and basic services, inadequate support services and technologies for reducing drudgery and occupational health hazards and for increasing their productivity;
(i) participate and advice on the planning process of socio-economic development of women;
(j) evaluate the progress of the development of women under the Union and any State;
(k) inspect or cause to inspected a jail, remand home, women's institution or other place of custody where women are kept as prisoners or otherwise and take up with the concerned authorities for remedial action, if found necessary;
(l) fund litigation involving issues affecting a large body of women;

(m) make periodical reports to the Government on any matter pertaining to women and in particular various difficulties under which women toil;

(n) any other matter which may be referred to it by Central Government.

The Reports of the Commission shall be laid before each House of Parliament by the Central Government along with memorandum explaining the action taken or proposed to be taken on the recommendations relating to the Union and the reasons for the non-acceptance, if any, of any such recommendations. If any such report or any part thereof relates to any matter with any State Government, then the Commission shall forward a copy of the report or part to such State Government. It shall be the duty of the State Government to ensure that the report is laid before the Legislature of the State along with a memorandum explaining the action taken or proposed to be taken on the recommendations relating to the State and the reasons for the non-acceptance, if any, of any such recommendations.

In keeping with its mandate, the Commission initiated various steps to improve the status of women and worked for their economic empowerment since its birth.

1. The Commission completed its visits to all the States/UTs except Lakshadweep, and prepared Gender Profiles to assess the status of women and their empowerment.
2. It received a large number of complaints and acted *suo moto* in several cases to provide speedy justice.
3. The Commission also took up the issue of child marriage, sponsored legal awareness programmes, Parivarik Mahila Lok Adalats.
4. The Commission reviewed laws such as Dowry Prohibition Act, 1961, PNDT Act 1994, Indian Penal Code 1860 and the National Commission for Women Act, 1990 to make them more stringent and effective.
5. It organized workshops/consultations, constituted expert committees on economic empowerment of women, conducted workshops/seminars for gender awareness and took up publicity campaign against female foeticide, violence against women, etc. in order to generate awareness in the society against these social evils.
6. The Commission also interacts with the media, social activists and academicians to suggest ways of ensuring due representation of women in all spheres.

Powers of the Commission

The Commission shall, while investigating any matter referred to it, shall have all the powers of a civil court trying a suit and, in particular in respect of summoning and enforcing the attendance of any person from any part of India and examining him on oath; requiring the discovery and production of any document; receiving evidence on affidavits; requisitioning any public record or copy thereof from any court or office; issuing commissions for the examination of witnesses and documents; and any other matter which may be prescribed.

In sexual harassment complaints, the concerned organizations are urged to expedite cases and the disposal is monitored. For serious crimes, the Commission constitutes an Inquiry Committee which makes spot enquiries, examines various witnesses, collects evidence and submits the report with recommendations. The complaints are also used as case studies for sensitization programmes for the Police, Judiciary, Prosecutors, Forensic Scientists, Defence Lawyers and other Administrative Functionaries.

The Commission works through various cells. They are:

1. Complaints and Counselling Cell
2. Legal Cell
3. Research and Studies Cell
4. Public Relations Cell
5. RTI Cell
6. NRI Cell

The most important cell is the **Complaints and Counselling Unit of National Commission for Women**. This cell processes the complaints received oral, written or *suo motu* under Section 10 of the NCW Act. The complaints received relate to domestic violence, harassment, dowry, torture, desertion, bigamy, rape, and refusal to register FIR, cruelty by husband, derivation, gender discrimination and sexual harassment at work place. The complaints are dealt with and tackled in various ways such as, Investigations by the police are expedited and monitored, disaggregated data are made available to various state authorities to facilitate action, family disputes are resolved or compromised through counselling.

Reports of the Commission

The Reports of the Commission shall be laid before each House of Parliament by the Central Government along with memorandum explaining the action taken or proposed to be taken on the recommendations relating to the Union and the reasons for the non-acceptance, if any, of any such recommendations. If any such report or any part thereof relates to any matter with which any State Government, then the Commission shall forward a copy of the report or part to such State Government. It shall be the duty of the State Government to ensure that the report is laid before the Legislature of the State along with a memorandum explaining the action taken or proposed to be taken on the recommendations relating to the State and the reasons for the non-acceptance, if any, of any such recommendations.

The important issues addressed by the Commission include violence against women, sexual exploitation of women at work place, educational health and employment aspects, women in agriculture sector, women in Panchayati Raj, custodial justice, mental health institutions, etc. As far as violence against women are concerned the NCW has adopted a Multi-Pronged strategy to tackle the problem of violence against women like generation of legal awareness among women, thus equipping them with the knowledge of their legal rights and with a capacity to use these rights, assisting women in redressal of their grievances through Pre-litigation services, facilitating speedy delivery of justice to women by organizing Parivarik Mahila Lok Adalats in different parts of the country, review of the existing provisions of the Constitution and other laws affecting women and recommending amendments thereto, any lacunae, inadequacies or shortcomings in such legislation's and various other significant steps to tackle the problem of violence against women as well as to sensitize the general public about the issues of women and their rights and work towards empowerment of women of India. The NCW holds public hearings on issues affecting large sections of women such as crime against women, women in unorganized labour sector, women in agriculture and women of minority groups. The deposition at these enquiries helps in appreciating and initiating remedial action.

THE UNION PUBLIC SERVICE COMMISSION

The Constitution provides for the creation of All India Services (AIS) common to the Union and the States. The All India Services Act, 1951 provides that the Central Government may make rules for regulating the recruitment and the conditions of service of persons appointed to the All India Services. Presently, only the IAS, the IPS and the IFS have been constituted as All India Services.

During the British rule in India, the Royal Commission on the Superior Civil Services (Lee Commission) urged the East India Company in its Report in 1924 to establish a public service commission in India. Before this, the Company had its own rules and regulations for the recruitment of personnel for manning their services. It was only in Government of India Act, 1919 that a provision was made for setting up a regular service commission for recruiting personnel for running the administration and services in the Government of India. The functions of the Commission were to be assigned by the Secretary of State in Council. It was only in 1926 that the first Central Service Commission was constituted. Further, The Government of India Act, 1935, also provided for setting up a Federal Public Service Commission. Article 315 of the present Constitution of India provides for the creation of Public Service Commissions both for the Union and the States and also for Joint State Public Service Commission. According to Article 316, the Chairman and other members of the Union Public Service Commission will be appointed by the President of India, who may by regulations, determine the number of members of the commission and their conditions of service and for the staff of the commission.

Constitutional Provisions

The Union Public Service Commission (UPSC) has been established under Article 315 of the Constitution of India. The Commission consists of a Chairman and ten Members.

Article 315 reads as:
Public Service Commissions for the Union and for the States:

1. Subject to the provisions of this article, there shall be a Public Service Commission for the Union and a Public Service Commission for each State.
2. Two or more States may agree that there shall be one Public Service Commission for that group of States, and if a resolution to that effect is passed by the House or, where there are two Houses, by each House of the Legislature of each of those States, Parliament may by law provide for the appointment of a Joint State Public Service Commission (referred to in this Chapter as Joint Commission) to serve the needs of those States.
3. Any such law as aforesaid may contain such incidental and consequential provisions as may be necessary or desirable for giving effect to the purposes of the law.
4. The Public Service Commission for the Union, if requested so to do by the Governor of a State, may, with the approval of the President, agree to serve all or any of the needs of the State.
5. References in this Constitution to the Union Public Service Commission or a State Public Service Commission shall, unless the context otherwise requires, be construed as references to the Commission serving the needs of the Union or, as the case may be, the State as respects the particular matter in question.

The Commission is serviced by a Secretariat headed by a Secretary with two Additional Secretaries, a number of Joint Secretaries, Deputy Secretaries and other supporting staff.

Composition of UPSC

The number of members and the conditions of services of the UPSC are determined by the President of India. The terms and conditions of service of Chairman and Members of the Commission are governed by the **Union Public Service Commission (Members) Regulations, 1969**. The number of members of the UPSC at present is ten members including the Chairman. Article 316 lays down that as nearly as may be one half of the members of every Public Service Commission shall be persons who at the dates of their respective appointments have held office at least for 10 years under the Government of

India. A member of the Union Public Service Commission will hold office for a term of 6 years or until he attains the age of 65. All the appointments and removals are made by the Indian President. The appointments to the UPSC are made on the recommendations of the Union cabinet. The dismissal/removal/suspension of a member of UPSC can be made under Article 317 only when a member has been charged with misbehaviour and such a charge, after investigation, has been established by the Supreme Court of India. He can also be removed from the service, if he has been declared of unsound mind, insolvent, a disqualified citizen or he got gainful employment outside his official responsibilities, without prior approval of the government. There are certain prohibitions as to holding of offices by members of the Commission on ceasing to hold their office under Article 319. On ceasing to hold office the Chairman of the UPSC shall be ineligible for further employment either under the Government of India or under the Government of a State. A member other than the Chairman of UPSC shall be eligible for appointment as the Chairman of the UPSC or as Chairman of SPSC, but not for any other employment either under the Government of India or under the Government of the State.

Expenses of UPSC

The expenses of the Union or a State Public Service Commission, including the salaries, allowances and pensions payable to or in respect of the members or staff of the Commission, shall be charged on the consolidated Fund of India or, as the case may be, the Consolidated Fund of the State (Article 322).

Powers and Functions of UPSC

Under Article 320, the Union Public Service Commission has been entrusted with the following duties and role under the Constitution:

1. Recruitment to services and posts under the Union through conduct of competitive examinations
2. Recruitment to services and posts under the Central Government by Selection through Interviews
3. Advising on the suitability of officers for appointment on promotion as well as transfer-on-deputation
4. Matters relating to methods of recruitment to civil services and civil posts
5. Principles to be followed in making promotions and transfers from one service to another
6. Advising the Government on all matters relating to methods of Recruitment to various services and posts
7. Disciplinary cases relating to different civil services and

8. Miscellaneous matters relating to grant of extraordinary pensions, reimbursement of legal expenses
9. Any other matter which the President may refer to the Commission

Of all the functions, the first two are mandatory functions and the rest are consultative or advisory functions of the UPSC. These functions are vital selection and recruitment of cadres to man the various Central Civil Services and Posts and the Services common to the Union and States (All-India Services).

Recruitment to Various Services and Posts

Under Article 320 of the Constitution of India, the Commission are, inter alia, required to be consulted on all matters relating to recruitment to civil services and posts. The UPSC is charged with the duty of recruiting cadres for Government service. Recruitment is usually done by direct recruitment; promotion; and transfer.

Among these three the most elaborate and large scale recruitment of new cadres is done through direct recruitment which is conducted either by conducting competitive examinations or by selection through interview or a combination of both.

The UPSC conducts competitive examinations for recruitment to services/ posts in various fields, such as Civil Services, Engineering, Medical and Forest Service and other public services. Along with these, competitive examinations are also held by the Commission under arrangements with the Ministry of Defence for entry to certain Defence Services, through the National Defence Academy, Indian Military Academy, Naval Academy, Air Force Academy and the Officers Training Academy.

Where the number of applicants is very large, the Commission, shortlist the candidates to be recruited on the basis of a written test followed by the interview. Two procedures are usually followed—either there is an objective-type written and/or practical test to evaluate the skill of the candidates followed by Interview, the final selection being decided by Interview, aided by the performance of the candidates in the written test or practical test or else an objective-type written and/or practical test to screen candidates to be called for interview, the final selection being decided by Interview only. The Commission can also shortlist the candidates to be called for the interview on the basis of certain pre-determined criteria related to the job where the candidates need not appear for written examination.

Recruitment also can take place through promotion in case of All India Services, all Central Government Services and other posts under the purview of the Central Government. These are usually departmental promotions, wherein consultation with the Commission, Chairman or a Member of the Commission presides over the Departmental Promotion Committee Meetings to consider promotions from one grade to another. When the recommendations of the

Departmental Promotion Committee are accepted by the Commission the selections are finalized.

The Recruitment Rules for a number of posts provide for appointment by Transfer on Deputation (including short-term contract) and Transfer for which prior consultation with the Commission is necessary for selection of an officer.

All India Services (AIS)

The All India Services Act, 1951 and Rules and Regulations that are framed under it, regulate the recruitment and conditions of service in respect of the All India Services concerning the three All India Services which include the Indian Administrative Service, the Indian Police Service and the Indian Forest Service.

The AIS Branch is primarily concerned with the promotions of the three All India Services viz. IAS, IPS, and IFS. The main functions are as follows:

1. Promotions of State Service officers to the IAS, IPS and IFS
2. Selection of Non-State Civil Service officers for appointment to the IAS under the IAS (Appointment by Selection) Regulations, 1997
3. Consequential Court Cases associated with the AIS promotions/ selection
4. Policy matters relating to All India Services and amendments in the Promotion Regulations.
5. The All India Services Cadre Rules provide for consultation with the Commission in the matter of appointment of non-Cadre State Service officers to the AIS Cadre posts if such appointment is made for a period exceeding six months.

Extension of Functions to Local Bodies

Article 321 also empowers the Parliament to extend the functions of the Public Service Commission to any local authority or other body corporate constituted by Law or by any public institutions.

Annual Reports

The Commission have a duty, under Article 323 of the Constitution to present annually to the President a Report on the work done by the Commission, and on receipt of such report, the President shall cause a copy, thereof together, with the Memorandum explaining, as respect the cases, if any, where the advice of the Commission was not accepted, the reasons for such non-acceptance to be laid before each House of the Parliament.

Impartiality of Union Public Service Commission

The following constitutional provisions are intended to make the Commission, both UPSC and SPSC, independent of any external influence:

1. Members are appointed for a fixed tenure of six years or until the attainment of sixty-five years of age in the case of UPSC, and sixty-two years in the case of SPSC.
2. The conditions of service of a member cannot be changed to his/her disadvantage during his tenure of office.
3. The removal of a member can take place by an order of the President on certain specific grounds in consultation of the Supreme Court.
4. The expenses of the commission are charged on the Consolidated Fund of India.

Thus, it can be said that to ensure the impartiality of the Union Public Service Commission, The Commission is responsible to the Parliament, through the Ministry for Home Affairs, for all its activities. The appointments in the commission are made by the President, and thus, both in the cases of appointment and dismissal the political government has no hand. Similarly, the members of the Service Commission will continue to hold office for a fixed tenure, and can be removed only on the ground. As a further measure towards securing impartiality, it has been provided that during the tenure of their office and after retirement, the members of the service commission shall not accept any gainful employment without the prior permission of the government.

THE STATE PUBLIC SERVICE COMMISSION (SPSC)

The Government of India Act 1935 provided for the establishment of a public service commission for each province. Article 315 of the present Constitution of India stipulates that there should be a State Public Service Commission for each State.

Though the Union Public Service Commission may, on a State government's request, take up work for that State with the President's consent, but Article 315 also provides that there shall be a State Public Service Commission for each State. There may be a Public Service Commission for two or more States. The Constitution provides—two or more States may agree that there shall be one Public Service Commission for that group of States, and if a resolution to that effect is passed by the House, or where there are two Houses, by each House of Legislature of each of those States, Parliament may by law provide for the appointment of a Joint State Public Service Commission to serve the needs of those States.

State Public Service Commission is entrusted with the conducting of various competitive examinations and recruitment of personnel at different levels. The Constitution of India provides for mandatory function of a Public

Service Commission for each state to conduct examinations for appointment to the various services of the state. Two or more states could share a single Public Service Commission.

Composition

There are no uniform rules governing the composition of the SPSC. Beside the Chairman, the number of other members can be seven or even two. The composition of the State Public Service Commission is more or less similar to that of the Union Public Service Commission. The members of the State Public Service Commission are appointed by the Governor on the recommendation of the Cabinet.

Article 316 provides the term and procedure of appointment of the members of SPSC. It states that half of the members of such Commission shall be in government service at least for ten years. The members shall hold office for six years or until he attains the age of sixty-two years. A member may by writing under his hand addressed to the Governor of the State resign from his office. The procedure of removal of the Chairman or the other members under Article 317 clearly states that the Chairman and the other members can be removed (a) by the order of the President on the ground of misbehaviour only after the Supreme Court has on enquiry recommended such removal (b) he/she can be removed by the President, if he/she has been proved to be an insolvent or is engaged during the term of his/her office in paid employment or is infirm of body or mind. There are certain prohibitions as to holding of offices by members of the Commission on ceasing to hold their office under Article 319. On ceasing to hold office the Chairman of the UPSC shall be ineligible for further employment either under the Government of India or under the Government of a State. A member other than the Chairman of UPSC shall be eligible for appointment as the Chairman of the UPSC or as Chairman of SPSC, but not for any other employment either under the Government of India or under the Government of the State.

Expenses of SPSC

The expenses of the State Public Service Commission including all salaries, allowances and pensions payable to or in respect of the members or staff of the Commission is charged on the Consolidated Fund of the State (Article 322).

Functions of State Public Service Commissions

The functions SPSC are quite similar to the UPSC and both their functions are laid down under Article 320 and Article 321. Only the jurisdiction of the Union Public Service Commission is far wider than that of the State Public Service Commission. The jurisdiction of the Union Public Service Commission extends across the entire length and breadth of the country, because it is related to the Civil Service of the Union Government. The Jurisdiction of the State Public Service Commission is limited within the State.

Under Article 320 there are mandatory and advisory or consultative functions of the SPSC. The State Public Service Commission shall discharge the following functions:

1. To conduct examinations for the appointment to the services of the State government;
2. To advise on all matters relating to methods of recruitment to State's civil service posts;
3. To advise on the principle to be followed in making appointments, promotions, transfers, etc.;
4. To advise on all disciplinary matters;
5. To advise on the settlement of claims, etc.;
6. Any other matter which the Governor may refer to the Commission.

The State Legislature, by an act, may provide for the exercise of additional functions for the State Public Service Commission (Article 321).

Recruitment to Various Services and Posts

The State Public Service Commission like the UPSC performs the crucial function of recruitment to various public services and posts in almost similar manner. A large number of examinations are held by the commissions annually which are notified in the leading local dailies of the state. Recruitments are either through examination followed by interview or just interview. Recruitment to various posts can also be filled up by promotion and transfers. The SPSC is also an advisory body and it has to be consulted by the Government on matters relating to recruitment, promotion, transfer, disciplinary cases and others.

Annual Reports

The Commission has a duty, under Article 323 of the Constitution to present annually to the Governor a Report as to the work done by the Commission and on receipt of such report, the Governor shall cause a copy thereof together with a memorandum explaining, as respect the cases, if any, where the advice of the Commission was not accepted, the reasons for such non-acceptance to be laid before each House/Houses of the Legislature of the State.

Impartiality of State Public Service Commission

To ensure the independence and impartiality of the SPSC, the Constitution provides that the Chairman and Members of SPSC cannot get re-appointment to the same office. Further employment of the Chairman in any Union and State Government and other members are also prohibited by the Constitutional provisions once they have been appointed as the Chairman or as other members of the SPSC under Article 319. The procedure of removal of the Chairman or the other members under Article 317 which clearly states that the Chairman and the other members can be removed (a) by the order of the President on the ground of misbehaviour only after the Supreme Court has on enquiry recommended such removal, (b) he/she can be removed by the President if he/she has been proved to be an insolvent or is engaged during the term of his/her office in paid employment or is infirm of body or mind, ensures the independence and impartiality of the Chairman and the other members of the SPSC.

PUBLIC ACCOUNTS COMMITTEE (PAC)

The Public Accounts Committee was first constituted in 1992, and since then, has continued to be an effective watchdog over Executive expenditure. The Committee on Public Accounts is constituted by Parliament each year for examination of accounts showing the appropriation of sums granted by Parliament for expenditure of Government of India, the Annual Finance Accounts of Government of India, and such other Accounts laid before Parliament as the Committee may deem fit such as accounts of autonomous and semi-autonomous bodies (except those of Public Undertakings and Government Companies which come under the purview of the Committee on Public Undertakings).

Composition of the Committee

The Committee consists of 22 members of which 15 members are elected by Lok Sabha every year from amongst its members according to the principle of proportional representation by means of single transferable vote and not more than 7 members of Rajya Sabha elected by that House in like manner. Chairman is appointed by the Speaker from amongst its members of Lok Sabha usually from among a member of the opposition. This was done for the first time for the period 1967–1968 and ever since then this has become a convention. No Minister is eligible to be elected as a member of the Committee, and if, at a time a particular member is elected to the Committee is appointed as a Minister, he then ceases to be a member of the Committee from the date of such appointment.

With the coming into force of the Constitution of India on 26th January 1950, the Committee became a Parliamentary Committee under the control of Speaker. Its Secretarial functions were transferred to the Parliament Secretariat (now Lok Sabha Secretariat).

Functions of the Committee

According to Article 308 of the Rules and Procedure and Conduct of the Business of the Lok Sabha the PAC has the primary duty to examine the accounts showing the appropriation of sums granted by the Parliament for the expenditure of the Government of India, the annual finance of the central Government and such other accounts as laid before the House as the PAC may think fit. For this the PAC relies on the reports of the Comptroller and Auditor-General of India thereon as also the Reports of the Comptroller and Auditor-General on Revenue Receipts mainly. In scrutinizing the Appropriation Accounts and the Reports of the Comptroller and Auditor-General thereon, it is the duty of the Committee to ensure that:

1. that the money shown in the accounts as having been disbursed were legally available for and, applicable to the service or purpose to which they have been applied or charged;
2. that the expenditure conforms to the authority which governs it; and
3. that every re-appropriation has been made in accordance with the provisions made in this behalf under rules framed by competent authority.

On the whole the PAC performs some crucial functions by keeping a strict vigil over public finance. It can be said to perform the functions of a watchdog of public finances by:

1. Ascertaining that money granted by Parliament has been spent by Government within the scope of the demand.
2. Considering the justification for spending more or less than the amount originally sanctioned. If any money has been spent on a service in excess of the amount granted by the House for the purpose, the Committee examines with reference to the facts of each case, the circumstances leading to such an excess and makes such recommendations as it may deem fit.
3. Examining cases involving losses, nugatory expenditure and financial irregularities.
4. Examining various aspects of Government's tax administration by scrutinizing the Reports of the Comptroller and Auditor-General on Revenue Receipts, the Committee.

Working of the Committee

The representatives of the Ministries appear before the Committee when examining the Accounts and Audit Reports relating to their Ministries. The Committee proceeds by way of interrogation of witnesses. The Comptroller and Auditor General attends the sittings of the Committee and assists it in its deliberations. The Committee may appoint one or more Sub-Committees/Sub-Groups to examine any particular matter. The Committee also appoints a few Working Groups/Sub-Committees to facilitate the examination of the various Accounts and Audit Reports and Sub-Committee to consider the action taken by the Government on the recommendations made by the Committee in its earlier Reports. All discussions held during tour by the Committee/Study Groups, with the representatives of the establishment, Ministries/Departments, non-official organizations, Labour Unions and others are treated as confidential and no one having access to the discussion, directly or indirectly is to communicate to the Press or any unauthorized person, any information about matters taken up during the discussions.

Reports of PAC

The main function of the PAC is to examine the report of the CAG submitted to the President who cause it to be laid before the Lok Sabha every year and which in turn refers to the PAC. Government takes action on the recommendations of the Committee, and submit Action Taken Notes to the Committee. The Committee then presents an Action Taken Report after considering the views of the Government. The Government further submits an "Action Taken Statement" on the action taken by the Government on the "Action Taken Report" of the Committee. The Action Taken Statement is generally laid before the House, without any further examination by the Committee.

In 2011, the Public Accounts Committee is probing into the 2G spectrum scam which has brought the committee to public attention. The Committee, on 4 April 2011, summoned Ratan Tata, Chairman of the Tata group, and Niira Radia, corporate lobbyist regarding the scam. PAC asked members of political parties to apologize to Comptroller and Auditor General of India for making allegations against it.

Thus, the PAC over the years have been successful in keeping a check on Government expenditure and wherever misappropriations take place, the PAC along with the CAG, who attends the meetings and intervenes to clarify the points or to assist the PAC, do not hesitate to point out the irregularities. The functioning of the PAC aims at creating a sense of responsibility while spending public money.

Estimates Committee

The composition and working of the Committee on Estimates are governed by the Rules of Procedure and Conduct of Business in Lok Sabha and Directions of the Speaker, Lok Sabha. The Estimates Committee is exclusively a Committee of the Lok Sabha. Rule 310 of the Rules of Procedure and Conduct of Business in Lok Sabha contains the provisions for the creation of Estimates Committee. It states that "There shall be a Committee on Estimates for the examination of such of the estimates as may seem fit to the Committee or are specifically referred to it by the House or the Speaker." The motion for election of the first Estimates Committee was adopted by the Provisional Parliament on 3rd April 1950 and the Committee was elected on 10th April 1950.

Composition of EC

The Committee consists of not more than 30 Members, although initially it had 25 members, from Lok Sabha who shall be elected by the House every year from amongst its members according to principle of promotional representation by means of single transferable vote. The Speaker is empowered to appoint the Chairman of the Committee from amongst its members. A Minister cannot be elected as a member of the Committee and if a member after his election to the Committee is appointed as a Minister, he ceases to be a member of the Committee from the date of such appointment.

Term of Office

The term of office of the Committee is one year. In April each year, a motion is moved in Lok Sabha by the Minister of Parliamentary Affairs, at the commencement of each Lok Sabha, and in subsequent years, by the Chairman of the Committee, calling upon members of the House to elect from amongst themselves 30 members to the Estimates Committee. The Committee is constituted every year in June and the work starts from July. The year plan is prepared by selecting such of the estimates as may seem fit to it. Then the office of the committee collects and collates the relevant materials.

Appointment of Chairman

The Chairman of the Committee is appointed by the Speaker from amongst the members elected in the Committee.

Functions

The most important function of the Committee is to suggest economies in expenditure. The Committee is strictly not concerned with the policy of the

Government. Its business is to ensure that within the framework of the policy, laid down by the government and the House, only the minimum expenditure needed for the purpose of fulfilling the objectives of the government would be incurred. The Committee continues the examination of the estimates from time-to-time throughout the financial year and may report to the House as its examination proceeds or on the conclusion of the examination. The functions of the Estimates Committee can be summed up as:

1. to report what economies, improvements in organization, efficiency or administrative reform, consistent with the policy underlying the estimates may be effected;
2. to suggest alternative policies in order to bring about efficiency and economy in administration;
3. to examine whether the money is well laid out within the limits of the policy implied in the estimates; and
4. to suggest the form in which the estimates shall be presented in the Parliament.
5. If the Committee finds that a particular policy laid down by Parliament is not leading to the expected or desired results or is leading to waste, it has a duty to bring it to the notice of the Lok Sabha that a change in policy is called for.

The Committee does not exercise its functions in relation to such Public Undertakings as this jurisdiction is allotted to the Committee on Public Undertakings by the Rules of Procedure of Lok Sabha or by the Speaker. The Committee also works towards finalization draft reports on the subjects on which evidence have been concluded by the previous Committee. The Committee also has no power as far as voting of grants in the Lok Sabha. It is to examine the entire estimates after they have been presented in the House. It can in no way influence the framing of estimates.

It may constitute sub-Committees, each having the powers of the undivided committee, to examine any matters that may be referred to it, and the reports of such sub-Committees are deemed to be the reports of the whole Committee, if they are approved at a sitting of the whole Committee.

The observations and recommendations of the Estimates Committee are contained in its report. A copy of the report is then submitted to the Lok Sabha. Conventionally, there is no formal debate on the reports of the Estimates Committee, but its reports are seen as guiding principles or directions to the Government.

The report contains three types of recommendations;

1. For improving the organization
2. For securing the economy
3. For providing guidance in the presentation of estimates.

The Estimates Committee is performing a useful role in the Indian administrative system. It keeps the machinery of administration under Parliamentary scrutiny. As it is a standing committee on administrative improvement, it can highlight the shortcomings and mistakes of public organizations in its reports, and thereby, try to secure efficiency and economy in administration.

EXERCISES

I. Short Answer Questions: **(100 words)**

1. State briefly the functions of Planning Commission in India.
2. State the role of National Development Council.
3. Briefly write on the importance of Inter-State Council.
4. Write a note on the Finance Commission of India.
5. Briefly state the Constitutional provisions relation to the CAG.
6. Briefly write on the position of Attorney-General of India.
7. Write a note on the NHRC.
8. Write a note of PAC.
9. Write a note on Estimates Committee.

II. Long Answer Questions: **(1200 words)**

10. Discuss the composition powers and functions of Planning Commission in India.
11. Discuss the composition powers and functions of National Development Council.
12. In the light of the provisions of the Indian Constitution examine the composition, powers and functions of Inter-State Council.
13. In the light of the Finance Commission Act, 1951, discuss the composition powers and functions of the Finance Commission of India.
14. In the light of the CAG'S Duties, Power and Conditions of Service Act, 1971, examine the powers, functions and position of CAG.
15. Write a note on the Attorney-General of India.
16. Examine the powers and functions of Central Vigilance Commission of India.
17. Discuss the importance of National Human Rights Commission of India by bringing out its powers and functions.
18. Discuss the powers and functions of the State Human Rights Commission.
19. As women's issues are receiving more attention in the present times do you think that the National Commission Women's has an

important role to play in this regard? Discuss by throwing light upon the powers and functions of National Commission for Women in India.

20. Discuss the Constitutional provisions and then examine the powers and functions of UPSC.
21. Discuss the powers and functions of State Public Service Commission.
22. Examine the importance of Public Accounts Committee.
23. Discuss the role of Estimates Committee.

REFERENCES

Bakshi, P.M., *The Constitution of India*, Universal Law Publishing, New Delhi, 2009.

CAG'S Duties, Power and Conditions of Service Act, 1971.

Government of India, *Constitution of India.*

Human Rights Act.

National Commission for Women Act, 1990.

Protection of Human Rights Act, 1993.

Sarkaria, Justice, Centre-State Relations, Government of India Report, 1990.

Sarkar Siuli, *Public Administration in India*, PHI Learning, New Delhi, 2010.

The Finance Commission (Miscellaneous Provisions) Act, 1951.

23

Development in Contemporary Administrative Structures and New Programmes/Policies

UNIQUE IDENTIFICATION AUTHORITY OF INDIA (UIDAI)

The Unique Identification Number (UID) of which AADHAR* is the brand name and logo was launched by the erstwhile Planning Commission. For the implementation of the UID project, the Government created the UIDAI as an attached to the then Planning Commission. On 25 June 2009, the Cabinet created and approved the position of the Chairperson of the UIDAI, and appointed Mr. Nandan Nilekani as the first Chairperson in the rank and status of a Cabinet Minister. Mr. Ram Sewak Sharma was appointed as the Director General.

It became a statutory body with the passage of Aadhaar (Targeted Delivery of Financial and Other Subsidies, Benefits and Services) Act, 2016 or the Aadhaar Act 2016 on 12 July, 2016.

UIDAI has been created with the objective to issue Unique Identification numbers (UID), known as AADHAAR to all residents of India in order to eliminate fake or duplicate identities and verify and authenticate identities in a cost-effective way. The important functions of UIDAI include enrolment, issuance, and authentication of AADHAAR. This also includes operation and management of AADHAAR lifecycle at all stages. UIDAI is also entrusted with the task to ensure the security of identity information and authentication records of individuals.

* **AADHAAR** number is a 12-digit random number issued by the UIDAI to the residents of India after satisfying the verification process laid down by the Authority. Only one **Aadhaar** is generated to the residents of India.

NITI AAYOG (NATIONAL INSTITUTION FOR TRANSFORMING INDIA)

On the basis of the report submitted by the Independent Evaluation Office to the Prime Minister Mr. Narendra Modi, in May 2014, the Planning Commission was scrapped. The report had recommended the dilution of the Planning Commission and its replacement by another body. Following the recommendation, the Planning Commission was diluted and replaced by National Development and Reform Commission (NDRC) in August 2014. Later on 1 January, 2015 by a Cabinet resolution the Planning Commission was replaced by the NITI Aayog or National Institution for Transforming India. The NITI Aayog held its first meeting on 8 February, 2015. The first meeting was chaired by the PM Mr. Narendra Modi.

Composition of NITI Aayog

The members constituting the body include:

- Chairperson—the Prime Minister of India
- Governing Council—Chief Ministers of all the States and Union Territories with Legislatures and Lieutenant Governors of other Union Territories.
- Regional Councils—Chief Ministers of States and Lieutenant Governors of Union territories in the region to address specific issues and contingencies impacting more than one state or a region.
- Full-time organizational framework—Vice-Chairperson, three full-time members, two part-time members (from leading Universities, research organizations and other relevant institutions in an ex-officio capacity), four ex-officio members of the Government of India) and a Secretariat.
- Experts and specialists from various fields.

Current Chairperson of NITI Aayog is Shri Narendra Modi, Prime Minister of India.

The NITI Aayog has been constituted with an aim to evolve a shared vision of national development priorities sectors. To devolve strategies with active involvement of states commensurate with national objectives is also another target of NITI Aayog. Fostering cooperative federalism is a goal that NITI Aayog aims to achieve.

National Skill Development Mission and NSDC

In pursuance of the decision of the Cabinet at its meeting held on 15.5.2008 on "Coordinated Action for Skill Development and setting up of the National

Skill Development Corporation", **Prime Minister's National Council on Skill Development** was constituted in July 2008.

The National Policy on Skill Development has been formulated by the Ministry of Labour and Employment, which has been approved by the Cabinet in its meeting held on 23rd February, 2009. The objective is to create a workforce empowered with improved skills, knowledge and internationally recognized qualifications to gain access to decent employment, and ensure India's competitiveness in the dynamic Global Labour market. It aims at increase in productivity of workforce both in the organized and the unorganized sectors, seeking increased participation of youth, women, disabled and other is advantaged sections, and to synergize efforts of various sectors and reform the present system.

The NSDC provides skill development funding either as loans or equity, and supports financial incentives to select private sector initiatives to improve financial viability through tax breaks and the like. NSDC's financing initiatives provide funding through loan, grants and equity.

The Finance Minister in his Budget Speech of 2013 proposed a scheme to encourage skill development for youth by providing monetary rewards for successful completion of approved training programs. Thus, the National Skill Certification and Monetary Reward Scheme was introduced.

NSDC at regular intervals submits data to the PM's National Council for Skill Development and subsequently to the National Skill Development Agency, as well as to the Ministry of Finance. Since the formation of Ministry of Skill Development and Entrepreneurship (MSDE), NSDC has been sharing regular information with the Ministries on a mutually agreed basis.

NATIONAL RAINFED AREA AUTHORITY (NRAA)

The mandate of NRAA include preparing a Perspective Plan for holistic and sustainable development of rainfed areas, coordinate and bring convergence within and among agriculture and watershed development programmes, promotion of farming systems, micro-enterprising, diversification, safety-nets, common property resource management, forest rehabilitation and internalization of social capital of landless and asset-less and monitoring of these activities at the Centre and State level by appropriate policies, programmes, professionalism, capacity building, monitoring and evaluation. For this the NRAA looks up to cooperation from NGOs, local communities and other like-minded organizations to foster sustainable development.

NRAA was previously attached to the Planning Commission but after the constitution of NITI Aayog, the PMO transferred NRAA from NITI Aayog to the Department of Agriculture, Cooperation and Farmer's Welfare (DAC&FW), Ministry of Agriculture and Farmers Welfare on 1 April, 2015.

NRAA is headed by CEO in the rank of Secretary to the Government of India and supported by five Technical Experts in the rank of Joint Secretary and five Directors and also by five Senior Technical Assistants.

INSURANCE REGULATORY AND DEVELOPMENT AUTHORITY OF INDIA (IRDA)

IRDA was established in 1999 under the *Insurance Regulatory and Development Authority Act*, 1999. This body is the primary regulatory body for insurance sector in India. This body comprise according to Section 4 of 1999 Act, a Chairman, 5 whole-time members and 4 part-time members. These members are appointed by the Government of India.

In 1972, with the passing of the General Insurance Business (Nationalization) Act, general insurance business was nationalized with effect from 1 January, 1973. In 1993, the Government set up a committee under the chairmanship of R.N. Malhotra, former Governor of RBI, to propose recommendations for reforms in the insurance sector. Following the recommendations of the Malhotra Committee Report, in 1999, the Insurance Regulatory and Development Authority (IRDA) was constituted as an autonomous body to regulate and develop the insurance industry. The IRDA was incorporated as a statutory body in April, 2000.

The mission of IRDAI is to protect the interests of the policy holders, to regulate, promote and ensure orderly growth of the insurance industry and matters connected with it. IRDAI is concerned with issuing, renewal, modification, withdrawal, suspension or cancellation of registrations of insurance companies. Along with it other important functions of IRDAI involve protection of the interests of the policy holders in matters concerning assigning of policy, nomination by policy holders, insurable interest, settlement of insurance claim, surrender value of policy and other terms and conditions of contracts of insurance, code of conduct and practical training for intermediary or insurance intermediaries and agents

TELECOM REGULATORY AUTHORITY OF INDIA (TRAI)

The Telecom Regulatory Authority of India (TRAI) is a statutory body which was created under the Telecom Regulatory Authority of India Act, 1997. The chief motive was to regulate telecom services, including fixation or revision of tariffs. It was established with a vision to work towards an emerging role of India in global information society.

Composition

According to the 1997 Act, the body shall comprise:

1. A Chairperson who is or has been a Judge of the Supreme Court or who is or has been Chief Justice of a High Court.
2. Members—not less than two but not more than six, who are to be appointed by the Central Government. A member shall be a person who has special knowledge of, any professional experience, in

telecommunication, industry, finance, accountancy, law, management and consumer affairs.

A person who is or has been in the service of Government shall not be appointed as a member unless such person has held the post of Secretary or Additional Secretary, or the post of Additional Secretary and Secretary to the Government of India or any equivalent post in the Central Government or the State Government for a period of three years.

One of the main objectives of TRAI is to provide a fair and transparent policy environment, which is conducive to fair competition. In pursuance of above objective TRAI has issued from time to time a large number of regulations, orders and directives to deal with issues coming before it and provided the required direction to the evolution of Indian telecom market from a Government owned monopoly to a multi operator multi service open competitive market. Functions related to Broadcasting and Cable Services Sector was also entrusted to TRAI from 2004.

The TRAI Act was amended by an ordinance, effective from 24 January 2000, establishing a Telecommunications Dispute Settlement and Appellate Tribunal **(TDSAT)** to take over the adjudicatory and disputes functions from TRAI in matters pertaining to disputes between licensor and licensee, service providers, service providers and consumers and even appeals against decisions or orders of TRAI.

SWACHH BHARAT MISSION (SBM)

Swachh Bharat Mission was launched by the present government under the leadership of the Prime Minister, Shri Narendra Modi on 2 October, 2014, the day when India celebrates Gandhi Jayanti. Swachh Bharat Mission is implemented by the Ministry of Urban Development and the Ministry of Drinking Water and Sanitation for urban and rural areas, respectively. It aims to provide every rural family with a toilet by 2019.

The objectives of SBM are:

1. Eliminate or reduce open defecation.
2. Construct latrines and work towards establishing an accountable mechanism of monitoring latrine use.
3. Create Public awareness about the drawbacks of open defecation and promotion of latrine use.
4. Eradication of manual scavenging.
5. Modern and Scientific solid and liquid waste management.

The Mission components include constructing individual, cluster and community toilets, public toilets, solid waste management, capacity building and Administrative training and expenses.

According to the Governments Report released in February 2016, out of 476 cities, a survey that was conducted shows Mysore to be the cleanest city in India.

BETI BACHAO BETI PADHAO

As has been discussed in earlier Chapter 21 about women's movements and rights in India, there is a declining Child Sex Ratio (CSR) which has been revealed in the 2011 Census.

The Census (2011) data showed a significant declining trend in the Child Sex Ratio (CSR), calculated as number of girls for every 1000 boys between age group of 0–6 years. The figure showed an all time low of number of girls at 918 in 2011 from 976 in 1961. The decline in CSR has been continued unabated since 1961.

"*Beti Bachao Beti Padhao*" (BBBP) Yojana (save daughter, educate daughter) or in other words 'Save the Girl Child' has been launched in October 2014 to save and empower the girl child in an effort to tackle the imbalance in CSR.

This is a joint initiative under the Ministry of Women and Child Development, Ministry of Health and Family Welfare and Ministry of Human Resource development.

The prime concerns of BBBP are:

- Prevention of gender biased sex selective elimination
- Ensuring survival and protection of the girl child
- Ensuring education and participation of the girl child.

500 AND 1000 RUPEES BANKNOTES SCRAPPED

The PM Mr. Narendra Modi in a televised speech announced that banknotes of value ₹500 and ₹1000 will be withdrawn from the midnight of 8 November, 2016 (expiry of 8 November, 2016). This demonetization of old ₹500 and ₹1000 notes was seen as a crack-down, while some say a surgical strike, on black money and counterfeit currencies. New banknotes of denomination ₹500 and ₹2000 have been introduced at their places. The World Bank in July, 2010 estimated the size of the shadow economy for India at 20.7% of the GDP in 1999, and rising to 23.2% in 2007, which adversely is affecting the poor and middle class and increasing the inflation. Thus, to curb the rising black money issue and fake currencies the Government of India came up with such a historic step.

From 10 November till 30 December, 2016, individuals were given the time to deposit old notes in their accounts or exchange the old notes at nearest bank or post office. Withdrawals from banks have been capped at ₹10,000 per day and ₹24,000 per week for the time being. Citizens must produce valid government identity cards like PAN, Aadhaar and Election Card at the time of exchange.

GST

Goods and Services Tax or GST is a uniform Indirect Tax which has replaced many Indirect Taxes imposed by Central government and State governments in India. Previously there were multiple taxes like Central Excise, Service tax, State VAT and others. On 29 March 2017 the Parliament of India passed the Goods and Services Tax Act which came into effect from 1 July 2017. There are multiple change-of-hands for an item goes through along its supply chain, for example from the stage of manufacturing to final sale to the consumer. Goods and Services Tax will be levied on each of these stages, which will make it a multi-stage tax.

The composition of a GST Council for making recommendations to the Union and the States was constituted as per Article 279A of the 101st Amendment. The GST Council is a joint forum of the Centre and the States. The composition of the GST Council is as follows:

- Union Finance Minister—the Chairperson.
- The Union Minister of State—in-charge of Revenue of finance as a Member.
- The Minister In-charge of finance or taxation or any other Minister nominated by each State Government as Members.

The 101st (One Hundred and First) Amendment Act, 2016 proclaimed that after Article 246 of the Constitution, Article 246A would be inserted. Article 246A contains the provisions that:

1. Notwithstanding anything contained in articles 246 and 254, Parliament, and, subject to clause (2), the Legislature of every State, have power to make laws with respect to goods and services tax imposed by the Union or by such State.
2. Parliament has exclusive power to make laws with respect to goods and services tax where the supply of goods, or of services, or both takes place in the course of Inter-State trade or commerce.

Subsequent changes were made to Articles 248, 249, 250, 268, 268A, 269, 269A (inserted), 270, 271, 279A (inserted), 286, 366, 368, Sixth Schedule and Seventh Schedule.

Categories of GST: IGST, CGST and SGST

CGST: This is Central Goods and Services Tax. Under GST, CGST is a tax levied on **Intra-State** supplies of both goods and services by the Central Government and will be governed by the CGST Act.

SGST: This is State Goods and Services Tax. Under GST, SGST is a tax levied on **Intra-State** supplies of both goods and services by the State Government and will be governed by the SGST Act.

IGST: IGST stands for Integrated Goods and Services Tax. IGST is applied in case of inter-State supply of goods or services where the location of the supplier and the place of supply are in different states. IGST is also applicable in cases of export or import of goods or services or when the supply of goods and services is made to or by a SEZ unit where the transaction is considered to be **Inter-State.** A seller has to collect IGST from the buyer in an Inter-State transaction.

In a Federal structure like India, there is concurrent jurisdiction for levy and collection of GST by the Centre (CGST) and the States (SGST). The Central government is supposed to collect IGST on supplies in the course of Inter-State trade or commerce including imports. Compensation on account of loss of revenue is to be given to States for five years. The tax structure with three types of taxes is hoped to help taxpayers take credit against each other which is believed to create a regime of 'One Nation, One Tax'.

There is a slab of four tiers of GST Tax Structure which are 5 per cent, 12 per cent, 18 per cent and 28 per cent with the lowest rates applicable to essential items and highest for luxury and demerit goods. These include items like SUVs, luxury cars and tobacco products.

GST on petroleum crude, high speed diesel, motor spirit or petrol, natural gas and aviation turbine fuel are to be levied later on recommendations of the GST Council.

Abrogation of Article 370

Article 370 was inserted as a temporary provision in 1949 (Part XXI of the Indian Constitution : Temporary, Transitional and Special Provisions). Under Article 370, the State of Jammu and Kashmir (J&K) enjoyed a special status. J&K made its own laws except finance, defence, foreign affairs and communications. There was a separate constitution and a separate flag. Property rights were denied to persons belonging to outside J&K. Article 370 had to be read along with Article 35A. This was introduced in 1954 by a Presidential order in order to continue the provisions made under Article 370 of the Indian Constitution. The provision of this Article also bars female residents of Jammu and Kashmir from property rights if they marry a person from outside the state. The provision also extends to the children of such women.

In his second term PM Modi's government abrogated the Article 370 which ended the special status of Jammu and Kashmir in August 2019. **The Jammu and Kashmir Reorganisation Act, 2019** reconstituted Jammu and Kashmir into two Indian-administered union territories, one to be called Jammu and Kashmir, and the other Ladakh, on 31 October 2019.

Citizenship Amendment Act (CAA) 2019

The passage of the Citizenship (Amendment) Act, 2019, in December 2019 amended the earlier Citizenship Act of 1955. It contains provisions for acquiring of citizenship by Hindu, Sikh, Buddhist, Jain, Parsi and Christian religious minorities who are fleeing persecution from three countries, namely, Pakistan, Bangladesh and Afghanistan. There is a wide-scale protest all over the country as CAA is being seen as divisive on the basis of religion. Future events have to closely watched as it has drawn international attention too.

The Bharatiya Nyaya Sanhita, 2023

On 23rd February, 2024 in the Gazette of India notified that in exercise of the powers conferred by sub-section (2) of section 1 of the Bharatiya Nyaya Sanhita, 2023 (45 of 2023), the Central Government hereby appoints the 1st day of July, 2024 as the date on which the provisions of the said Sanhita, except the provision of sub-section (2) of section 106, shall come into force. The Chapters of the Nyaya Sanhita are as follows:

CHAPTER I PRELIMARY (Short Title, Commencement, and Application)

CHAPTER II: OF PUNISHMENTS

CHAPTER III: GENERAL EXCEPTIONS

CHAPTER IV: OF ABETMENT, CRIMINAL CONSPIRACY AND ATTEMPT of Abetment

CHAPTER V: OF OFFENCES AGAINST WOMAN AND CHILDREN of Sexual offences

CHAPTER VI: OF OFFENCES AFFECTING THE HUMAN BODY of Offences Affecting Life

CHAPTER VII: OF OFFENCES AGAINST THE STATE

CHAPTER VIII: OF OFFENCES RELATING TO THE ARMY, NAVY AND AIR FORCE

CHAPTER IX: OF OFFENCES RELATING TO ELECTIONS

CHAPTER X: OF OFFENCES RELATING TO COIN, CURRENCY NOTES, BANK NOTES, AND GOVERNMENT STAMPS

CHAPTER XI: OF OFFENCES AGAINST THE PUBLIC TRANQUILLITY

CHAPTER XII: OF OFFENCES BY OR RELATING TO PUBLIC SERVANTS

CHAPTER XIII: OF CONTEMPTS OF THE LAWFUL AUTHORITY OF PUBLIC SERVANTS

CHAPTER XIV: OF FALSE EVIDENCE AND OFFENCES AGAINST PUBLIC JUSTICE

CHAPTER XV: OF OFFENCES AFFECTING THE PUBLIC HEALTH, SAFETY, CONVENIENCE, DECENCY AND MORALS

CHAPTER XVI: OF OFFENCES RELATING TO RELIGION

CHAPTER XVII: OF OFFENCES AGAINST PROPERTY

CHAPTER XVIII: OF OFFENCES RELATING TO DOCUMENTS AND TO PROPERTY MARKS

CHAPTER XVIII: OF OFFENCES RELATING TO DOCUMENTS AND TO PROPERTY MARKS

EXERCISES

I. Short Answer Questions: **(100 words)**

1. Write a note on AADHAR.
2. Briefly comment on demonetization policy of the BJP Government.
3. Write a note of **Beti Bachao Beti Padhao**.
4. Write on **Swachh Bharat Mission**.
5. Write notes on:
   (a) TRAI (b) IRDA
6. Briefly state the mission of NSDC.
7. Write a note on NITI AAYOG.
8. Write a note on National Rainfed Area Authority (NRAA)
9. Briefly write on GST.
10. Briefly write on the abrogation of Article 370.

II. Long Answer Questions: **(1200 words)**

1. Discuss the composition, powers and functions of NITI AAYOG.
2. State the functions of **Unique Identification Authority of India (UIDAI)**.
3. Examine the significance of the Mission—**Beti Bachao Beti Padhao**.
4. Comment on the **Swachh Bharat Mission**.
5. Analyze the policy of scrapping of old currencies (₹500 and ₹1000).
6. Write the functions of **TRAI**.
7. Comment on the functions of **IRDA**.
8. Elucidate on the significance of **NSDC**.
9. Discuss the significance of **NRAA**.
10. Examine the significance of GST as a uniform Indirect Tax.
11. Briefly discuss the features of **Bharatiya Nyaya Sanhita, 2023.**

Index